30106023731465

AF759254

HIGH DEMAND COLLECTION

Stamp indicates date for return

This item must be returned to the HDC

in the Edward Boyle Library

Do not return it to any other location

Fines will be charged for late returns

THE FORMATION OF THE CLASSICAL ISLAMIC WORLD

General Editor: Lawrence I. Conrad

Volume 27

The Formation of Islamic Law

THE FORMATION OF THE CLASSICAL ISLAMIC WORLD

General Editor: *Lawrence I. Conrad*

1	**Byzantium before the Rise of Islam**	*Averil Cameron*
2	**The Sasanian East before the Rise of Islam**	*Shaul Shaked*
3	**The Arabs and Arabia on the Eve of Islam**	*Frank E. Peters*
4	**The Life of Muḥammad**	*Uri Rubin*
5	**The Expansion of the Early Islamic State**	*Fred M. Donner*
6	**The Articulation of Islamic State Structures**	*Fred M. Donner*
7	**Problems of Political Cohesion in Early Islam**	*R. Stephen Humphreys*
8	**Arab–Byzantine Relations in Early Islamic Times**	*Michael Bonner*
9	**The Turks in the Early Islamic World**	*C.E. Bosworth*
10	**Patterns of Everyday Life**	*David Waines*
11	**Production and the Exploitation of Resources**	*Michael G. Morony*
12	**Manufacturing and Labour**	*Michael G. Morony*
13	**Trade and Exchange in Early Islam**	*A.L. Udovitch*
14	**Property and Consumption in Early Islamic Society**	*Baber Johansen*
15	**Cities in the Early Islamic World**	*Hugh Kennedy*
16	**Nomads and the Desert in the Early Islamic World**	*Hugh Kennedy*
17	**Society and the Individual in Early Islam**	to be announced
18	**Muslims and Others in Early Islamic Society**	*Robert E. Hoyland*
19	**The Christian Communities in the Early Islamic World**	*Sidney H. Griffith*
20	**The Jewish Communities of the Early Islamic World**	*David Wasserstein*
21	**Archaeology and Early Islam**	*Donald Whitcomb*
22	**Early Islamic Numismatics and Monetary History**	*Michael Bates*
23	**Early Islamic Art and Architecture**	*Jonathan Bloom*
24	**The Qur'ān: Style and Contents**	*Andrew Rippin*
25	**The Qur'ān: Formative Interpretation**	*Andrew Rippin*
26	**The Development of Islamic Ritual**	*G.R. Hawting*
27	**The Formation of Islamic Law**	*Wael B. Hallaq*
28	***Ḥadīth*: Origins and Development**	*Harald Motzki*
29	**Early Islamic Historiographical Traditions**	*Lawrence I. Conrad*
30	**Early Islamic Theology**	*Josef van Ess*
31	**Eschatology and Apocalyptic in Early Islam**	*Wilferd Madelung*
32	**Early Islamic Visions of Community**	*Wadād al-Qāḍī*
33	**Shī'ism: Origins and Early Development**	*Etan Kohlberg*
34	**Khārijite Movements in Early Islam**	*Ridwan al-Saiid*
35	**The Emergence of Islamic Mysticism**	*Bernd Radtke*
36	**The Islamic Philological Tradition**	*Ramzi Baalbaki*
37	**Early Arabic Poetry and Poetics**	*Suzanne Stetkevych*
38	**Early Arabic Prose Literature**	*Fedwa Malti-Douglas*
39	**The Rise of Islamic Philosophy**	*Everett Rowson*
40	**The Rise of Arab-Islamic Medicine**	*Lawrence I. Conrad*
41	**The Exact Sciences in Early Islam**	*Jamil Ragep*
42	**Magic and Divination in Early Islam**	*Emilie Savage-Smith*
43	**Education and Learning in the Early Islamic World**	*Claude Gilliot*
44	**The Early Islamic Manuscript Tradition**	*Jan Just Witkam*
45	**Early Islamic North Africa**	*Elizabeth Savage*
46	**The Formation of al-Andalus I**	*Manuela Marín*
47	**The Formation of al-Andalus II**	*M. Fierro/J. Samsó*
48	**The Modern Study of Early Islam**	*Lawrence I. Conrad*

THE FORMATION OF THE CLASSICAL ISLAMIC WORLD

General Editor: Lawrence I. Conrad

Volume 27

The Formation of Islamic Law

edited by
Wael B. Hallaq

ASHGATE
VARIORUM

This edition copyright © 2004 by Ashgate Publishing Limited, and Introduction by Wael B. Hallaq. For copyright of individual articles refer to the Acknowledgements.

Published in the series **The Formation of the Classical Islamic World** by

Ashgate Publishing Limited
Wey Court East
Union Road
Farnham
Surrey, GU9 7PT
England

Ashgate Publishing Company
Suite 420
101 Cherry Street
Burlington
VT 05401-4405
USA

British Library CIP Data
The Formation of Islamic Law. – (The Formation of the Classical Islamic World)
1. Islamic Law
I. Hallaq, Wael B., 1995–
340.5'9

US Library of Congress CIP Data
The Formation of Islamic/ edited by Wael B. Hallaq
p. cm. – (The Formation of the Classical Islamic World)
Includes bibliographical references and index.
1. Isamic Law – History I. Hallaq, Wael B., 1966 –
II. Series
LAW
340.5'9–dc21 2003043747

ISBN 978-0-86078-714-3

This volume is printed on acid-free paper.

MIX
Paper from responsible sources
FSC
www.fsc.org
FSC® C018575

Transfered to Digital Printing in 2011

Printed and bound in Great Britain by the MPG Books Group Ltd, UK

THE FORMATION OF THE CLASSICAL ISLAMIC WORLD- 27

CONTENTS

ACKNOWLEDGEMENTS

The chapters in this volume are taken from the sources listed below. The editor and publishers wish to thank the authors, original publishers or other copyright holders for permission to use their material as follows:

CHAPTER 1. I.M. Lapidus, "The Arab Conquests and the Formation of Islamic Society", in G.H.A. Juynboll, ed., *Studies on the First Century of Islamic Society* (Carbondale and Edwardsville, Illinois, 1982), pp. 49–72. Copyright © 1982 by the Board of Trustees, Southern Illinois University. Reprinted by permission of the publisher.

CHAPTER 2. Joseph Schacht, "Pre-Islamic Background and Early Development of Jurisprudence", in Majid Khadduri and Herbert Liebesney, eds., *Law in the Middle East*, Vol. 1 (Washington, D.C., 1955), pp. 28–56. Copyright © 1955 by the Middle East Institute.

CHAPTER 3. Joseph Schacht, "Foreign Elements in Ancient Islamic Law", *Journal of Comparative Legislation and International Law* 32 (Oxford, 1950), pp. 9–17. Copyright © 1950 by Oxford University Press. Reprinted by permission.

CHAPTER 4. S.D. Goitein, "The Birth-Hour of Muslim Law?: An Essay in Exegesis", *Muslim World* 50 (Hartford, CT, 1960), pp. 23–29.

CHAPTER 5. Patricia Crone, "Two Legal Problems Bearing on the Early History of the Qur'ān", *Jerusalem Studies in Arabic and Islam* 18 (Jerusalem, 1994), pp. 1–37.

CHAPTER 6. Ulrike Mitter, "Unconditional Manumission of Slaves in Early Islamic Law: A *Ḥadīth* Analysis", *Der Islam* 78 (Berlin, 2001), pp. 35–72. With kind permission of Walter de Gruyter GmbH & Co. KG.

CHAPTER 7. Harald Motzki, "The Role of Non-Arab Converts in the Development of Early Islamic Law", *Islamic Law and Society* 6 (Leiden, 1999), pp. 293–317. Copyright © 1999 Brill.

CHAPTER 8. Irit Abramski-Bligh, "The Judiciary (*Qāḍīs*) as a Governmental-Administrative Tool in Early Islam", *Journal of the Economic and Social History of the Orient* 35 (Leiden, 1992), pp. 40–71. Copyright © 1992 Brill.

CHAPTER 9. Zafar Ishaq Ansari, "Islamic Juristic Terminology before Šāfi'ī: A Semantic Analysis with Special Reference to Kūfa", *Arabica* 19 (Leiden, 1972), pp. 255–300. Copyright © 1972 Brill.

CHAPTER 10. Wael Hallaq, "Was al-Shafi'i the Master Architect of Islamic Jurisprudence?" *International Journal of Middle East Studies* 25 (Cambridge, 1993), pp. 587–605. Copyright © 1993 Cambridge University Press. Reprinted with permission.

CHAPTER 11. Devin Stewart, "Muḥammad b. Dā'ūd al-Ẓāhirī's Manual of Jurisprudence, *al-Wuṣūl ilā Maʿrifat al-Uṣūl*", in Bernard Weiss, ed., *Studies in Islamic Legal Theory* (Leiden, 2002), pp. 99–137. Copyright © 2002 Brill.

CHAPTER 12. Wael Hallaq, "Early *Ijtihād* and the Later Construction of Authority", in his *Authority, Continuity and Change in Islamic Law* (Cambridge, 2001), pp. 24–56. Copyright © 2001 Cambridge University Press. Reprinted with permission.

CHAPTER 13. Christopher Melchert, "The Formation of the Sunnī Schools of Law". First publication. Copyright © 2003 Christopher Melchert.

CHAPTER 14. Muhammad Qasim Zaman, "The Caliphs, the 'Ulamā', and the Law: Defining the Role and Function of the Caliph in the Early 'Abbāsid Period", *Islamic Law and Society* 4 (Leiden, 1997), pp. 1–36. Copyright © 1997 Brill.

Every effort has been made to trace all the copyright holders, but if any have been inadvertently overlooked the publishers will be pleased to make the necessary arrangement at the first opportunity.

PUBLISHER'S NOTE

The pagination of articles originally published in English has been maintained for this volume. In articles translated into English, the original pagination has been indicated in the text in bold-face type.

Erratum

The publisher regrets some pages of the Introduction have been transposed and to read the text correctly the pages should be read in the following order: xxiii, xxv, xxvi, xxiv, xxvii.

GENERAL EDITOR'S PREFACE

Since the days of Ignaz Goldziher (1850–1921), generally regarded as the founder of Islamic studies as a field of modern scholarship, the formative period in Islamic history has remained a prominent theme for research. In Goldziher's time it was possible for scholars to work with the whole of the field and practically all of its available sources, but more recently the increasing sophistication of scholarly methodologies, a broad diversification in research interests, and a phenomenal burgeoning of the catalogued and published source material available for study have combined to generate an increasing "compartmentalisation" of research into very specific areas, each with its own interests, priorities, agendas, methodologies, and controversies. While this has undoubtedly led to a deepening and broadening of our understanding in all of these areas, and hence is to be welcomed, it has also tended to isolate scholarship in one subject from research in other areas, and even more so from colleagues outside of Arab-Islamic studies, not to mention students and others seeking to familiarise themselves with a particular topic for the first time.

The Formation of the Classical Islamic World is a reference series that seeks to address this problem by making available a critical selection of the published research that has served to stimulate and define the way modern scholarship has come to understand the formative period of Islamic history, for these purposes taken to mean approximately AD 600–950. Each of the volumes in the series is edited by an expert on its subject, who has chosen a number of studies that taken together serve as a cogent introduction to the state of current knowledge on the topic, the issues and problems particular to it, and the range of scholarly opinion informing it. Articles originally published in languages other than English have been translated, and editors have provided critical introductions and select bibliographies for further reading.

A variety of criteria, varying by topic and in accordance with the judgements of the editors, have determined the contents of these volumes. In some cases an article has been included because it represents the best of current scholarship, the "cutting edge" work from which future research seems most likely to profit. Other articles—certainly no less valuable contributions—have been taken up for the skillful way in which they synthesise the state of scholarly knowledge. Yet others are older studies that—if in some ways now superseded—nevertheless merit attention for their illustration of thinking or conclusions that have long been important, or for the decisive stimulus they have provided to scholarly discussion. Some volumes cover themes that have emerged fairly recently, and here it has been necessary to include articles from outside the period covered by the series, as illustrations of paradigms and methodologies that may prove useful as research develops. Chapters from single author monographs have been considered only in very exceptional cases, and a certain emphasis has been encouraged on important studies that are less readily available than others.

In the present state of the field of early Arab-Islamic studies, in which it is routine for heated controversy to rage over what scholars a generation ago would have regarded as matters of simple fact, it is clearly essential for a series such as this to convey some sense of the richness and variety of the approaches and perspectives represented in the available literature. An effort has thus been made to gain broad international participation in editorial capacities, and to secure the collaboration of colleagues representing differing points of view. Throughout the series, however, the range of possible options for inclusion has been very large, and it is of course impossible to accommodate all of the outstanding research that has served to advance a particular subject. A representative selection of such work does, however, appear in the bibliography compiled by the editor of each volume at the end of the introduction.

The interests and priorities of the editors, and indeed, of the General Editor, will doubtless be evident throughout. Hopefully, however, the various volumes will be found to achieve well-rounded and representative syntheses useful not as the definitive word on their subjects—if, in fact, one can speak of such a thing in the present state of research—but as introductions comprising well-considered points of departure for more detailed inquiry.

A series pursued on this scale is only feasible with the good will and cooperation of colleagues in many areas of expertise. The General Editor would like to express his gratitude to the volume editors for the investment of their time and talents in an age when work of this kind is grossly undervalued, to the translators who have taken such care with the articles entrusted to them, and to Dr John Smedley and his staff at Ashgate for their support, assistance and guidance throughout.

Lawrence I. Conrad

INTRODUCTION
The Formation of Islamic Law

Wael B. Hallaq

OF THE FOURTEEN CENTURIES making up Islamic legal history, the first three have the dubious distinction of being severely vexed with various historiographical problems. As a rule, the earlier the century the more difficult and insoluble these problems become. Generally speaking, writing the history of the third/ninth century thus makes for an easier task than writing the history of the second/eighth century; and this latter, despite the grave historiographical difficulties associated with it, is far less problematic than the first.

The first obvious cause for these difficulties is the lack of sufficient historical evidence, be it literary, archival, archaeological or otherwise. This fact is particularly true of the first century, and more so of its beginning and middle than its end. The volume of literary evidence steadily increases over the span of the next two centuries, but the good fortune of documentary abundance is marred by serious problems of perceived inauthenticity and faulty attribution. Just when the literary sources begin to surface around the middle of the first century, leading many a modern scholar to think that the history of that period can now be reconstructed, a cloud of doubt is thrown on the historicity of these sources. The main case made against their usefulness for writing the history of the early period is that they cannot, as we now know them, be attributed to the time to which they are traditionally thought to belong. Rather, the argument goes, they represent at best a genuine core that had undergone a process of later redactions and accretions.[1]

Moreover, and as if the scarcity of source-material is not already a sufficiently serious problem, these three centuries also distinguish themselves as the most controversial in the field of Islamic (legal) studies in terms of interpretational approach, reflecting what might be termed an extreme case of hermeneutical perspectivism. As much as modern scholars are loath to admit it, this hermeneutical perspectivism is heavily entangled with cultural,

[1] On the controversy over dating of second/eighth and third/ninth century texts, see Bibliography, Section 7, below. It must be said, however, that the revisionist approach aiming to assign texts to later dates has been largely unsuccessful, for it has met with critical resistance from various quarters, and furthermore, has been left unheeded by historians working on the early period.

religious, political and other loyalties that have left us, roughly speaking, with two widely divergent camps of scholars. With few exceptions, the differences between the two camps are neither negligible nor reconcilable; if anything, they are nothing short of staggering. Whatever points the two camps may occasionally, if not rarely, agree upon, the rift between them is a methodological and hermeneutical divide of the first order, one that was created by the overarching fact that one camp derived its cultural, political and worldly suppositions from a reality of colonialist domination in which it both directly and obliquely participated, while the other emerged from a reality and history that it represented, nay, defended, as the final, gradually vanishing frontier of a subjugated, colonized religious culture. This frontier came to stand as the diametrical opposite of the colonizer's rationalism and scientism, as the only aspect of the present that is faithful to, if not a remnant of, the glorious religious past. To put it differently, the rift was prompted by a clash between the dominating modern and dominated traditionalism.

The traditionalist camp propounds a legal history whose anchors are religious, replicating the assumptions of the pious. What Western rationalism calls "historical truth" is not the concern of this brand of scholarship. "Historical truth", if it were to be recovered, would ultimately turn out to be nothing but the Truth as constructed by that particular conception of ideas, events and men who were *eventually made to be* the defining pillars of what was, and evolved into, Islamic culture, history, religion and law. In this conception and scheme of ideas, there is no room for mundane, worldly or materialistic considerations, and even less for so-called "Western causality". Historical motives and props must all be either noble or base, religious or irreligious, good or evil. Even as simple a factor as material self-interest, which may or may not have motivated a given historical act, is normatively viewed with the lens of piety or impiety that is transcendentally engendered rather than humanly inscribed. Nor is there a place for deconstructing the religious myths that all societies—including those of Judaism and Christianity—have needed and found essential for their ideological, even material, survival. For instance, the religious veneration that came to be associated with the founders of the legal schools was an essential ingredient of the authority that was constructed around their figures, an authority that was to replace the role of the state that other legal cultures so heavily depended upon as the foundation of their legal systems. But this authority-construction amounted in effect to a long historical process spanning a period of more than a century, before which time the figures of the founders were largely, if not entirely, devoid of this constructed authority.[2] The traditionalist camp's point of departure is the fully developed notion of "founders", already embellished with all the authority with which they came to be associated. Here, there can be no acknowledgement that the authoritative image enjoyed by the so-called founders must have emerged *post eventum*, and that it had little to do with the piety, accomplishments or degree of legal knowledge attained or not attained by these "founders". Whatever functions these posterior constructions came to play, they can hardly inform us who the historical founders "really" were, for if these constructions were necessary, they must already have been so for the period in which they came into existence, and even more so in subsequent periods. After all, if they came into being, they obviously did so for a purpose, and that purpose was legal in nature rather than historiographical. However, these constructions cannot be permitted to function as a genuine description of what went before except solely for the purpose of serving as ideological underpinnings to the goal that these constructions were meant to achieve in the first place.

The traditionalist camp is thus driven by hermeneutical imperatives organically connected with religious relevance, compounded by a defensive tenor typically adopted by the dominated. If history and historical narrative are to be sought after, it is for the purpose of constructing, enhancing and maintaining whatever is religious or anything that sustains religion. No historical event or narrative can be so revised as to displace or shake what religious history has traditionally come to represent, for such a displacement threatens to alter not only the logical sequence of the religious narrative that is inherently integral to faith, but also the moral and ethical content that this narrative is intended to represent. If Islam is to be at all justified as a religion, then it must possess substantive elements that distinguish it from competing religions, making it more than a mere replica of any of them. It must vie, as it did in this early period, for a position of uniqueness, in both ontology and purposiveness. Its claim was revisionist, namely, to lay down the true version of religious Truth that had been adulterated by Judaism and, later, by Christianity, and that was totally unknown to the lost souls of Arabia Deserta, the idolatrous Bedouins. This narrative stood since the early phases of Islam as the supreme explanatory cause behind the rise of the new religion, and as such could be displaced only at the risk of shak-

---

[2]See Wael Hallaq, *Authority, Continuity and Change in Islamic Law* (Cambridge, 2001), 24 ff. (Chapter 12, below).

ing the foundations of the entire faith. In fact, with the constancy of the faith's relevance to Muslims past and present, there could not have arisen a single reason that would prompt such a displacement, for no other narrative is as relevant and as indigenous to this history as that which represents revisionism and reformation.

If Islam came to reform, then it could not have come without commandments, or a law, or at least a legal blueprint. Nor could its law have been absent when its adherents conducted the most successful territorial conquest history has ever known, where an expansive militarized empire was soon thereafter erected and an entire imperial system came to function so effectively. In this narrative, the Muslim Arabs were masters who stood in need of no foreign law and, what is more, none could impose on them any such laws. This fact of perceived political and military superiority was consistent with the original impulse of propounding the law of God as revealed to Muslims, a law that had to be particular to the Muslims whose purpose was nothing less than correcting what had been adulterated by other monotheists. On this Muslim view, then, it would have been absurd to expect a community embarking on such a Mission to derive its reformist inspiration from the very entities that it was supposed to reform.

Outlined in the Qur'ān, the Mission was to be propounded and articulated by the Prophet, whose conduct was so consistent with God's will that his Sunna was sanctioned, *ab initio*, as an authoritative source of law. Despite its derivative nature, the Prophet's Sunna came to be constituted as a source equal in force to the Qu'ān, but offering a wealth of material barely matched by the concise, revealed text itself. Thus, Islamic law is said to have come into existence during the last years of the Prophet's life, but only to the extent that was needed by the Prophet to conduct the nascent *umma*'s affairs in Medina. The subsequent wave of the Rightly Guided caliphs, their Umayyad successors and the jurists of the time expanded the law as the need arose, and in accordance with the varied demands and hence different interpretations of each region. Out of this emerged centers of legal specialization and jurisprudential expertise in Medina, Mecca, Yemen, al-Kūfa, al-Baṣra, Syria, Egypt and Khurāsān.

An important element of this traditionalist narrative is the proposition that the Qur'ān and Prophetic Sunna came to be viewed by the faithful as sources of the law upon the death of the Apostle and that all legal solutions, therefore, must have and indeed were ultimately derived therefrom. The Rightly Guided caliphs continued on the path already paved by the Apostle, thereby partaking in the Prophetic role of mediating the discovery of God's law. As the immediate deputies of the late Prophet and his closest Companions (the *ṣaḥāba*), they knew not only what he did and said, but also how he thought and reacted (or would have reacted) to certain situations. They were also most familiar with the fundamental injunctions of the Qur'ān. This profound and extensive knowledge, the narrative continues, gave the caliphal jurisprudence in particular, and the Companions' legal scholarship in general, a certain authority which came to complement Qur'ānic and Sunnaic material as a source of law. The supplementary legal provisions of the early caliphs and the oldest Companions are said to have brought to closure the gate of revelation where, beyond this point, law could only be derived through interpretation of what had become fixed material sources. And this is precisely what the next generation, that of the Successors, accomplished. The class of legal specialists that emerged is said to have hailed from amongst these Successors (*tābiʿūn*), specialists whose main preoccupation was the study of all kinds of religious discourse that would lead to the elaboration of legal doctrine. Their scholarly activity included, among other things, the study of the Qur'ānic text, its exegesis, the principles of abrogation, legal language, Prophetic *ḥadīth*, Arabic grammar, and often arithmetic.

In spite of the legal accomplishments of the jurists and caliphs who lived and flourished during the first century and the two decades that followed, Islamic law as a methodologically structured system only emerged with the coming into being of the schools whose formations are associated with the careers of their eponyms: Abū Ḥanīfa (d. 150/767), Mālik (d. 179/795), al-Shāfiʿī (d. 204/820), and Ibn Ḥanbal (d. 241/855). All these school founders gained distinction in one way or another, but of them all it was al-Shāfiʿī who alone was recognized for juristic excellence, in that he was believed to have single-handedly elaborated a theory of jurisprudence and methodology of law (*uṣūl al-fiqh*). He is said to have been to law what Aristotle was to logic.[3]

What al-Shāfiʿī is said to have accomplished in this theory was to discover the general principles according to which the law had been constructed by the community of jurists and to delineate the hermeneutical and juristic methods through which law is—and should be—derived from its two primary sources, the Qur'ān and Prophetic Sunna, as well as through consensus and

[3]Some Ḥanafīs would beg to differ, arguing that the founding Ḥanafī masters contributed nearly as much to such jurisprudential developments. However, the overall weight of their discourse in the Muslim tradition remains secondary to that thrown behind al-Shāfiʿī's acclamation.

the inferential method of *qiyās*. Although this traditionalist narrative does not make clear the relationship of al-Shāfiʿī's methodology to the work of the other founding fathers and preceding jurists, it was clearly assumed that, while jurisprudence had been put *into practice* before al-Shāfiʿī, it was he who articulated in theoretical discourse what jurists had always done as a matter of juristic and judicial practice. By al-Shāfiʿī's death, or perhaps soon thereafter, positive law was deemed fully elaborated, the schools had taken a fairly developed form, and the theoretical foundations of the law had been sufficiently expounded in accordance to al-Shāfiʿī's *Risāla*.

The central problem associated with this narrative is its power to project backwards events and developments that could not have taken place during the periods assigned to them. The Qur'ān, for instance, could not have acquired the importance attributed to it as a comprehensive, canonical and foundational source of law immediately after the death of the Prophet. Even the early Muslim sources themselves do not attest to the Qur'ānic values, much less its legal content, as having the sort of dominance that would have rendered the Book an instantaneous and direct source of law. Nor is there evidence that the Sunna rose to equal prominence immediately after the Prophet's death, or that his Sunna was ever the only form of "model *dicta*" during the first century.[4] But such acknowledgements, which would entail a certain diminution in the weight of these legal sources, could not be made in the face of a profound veneration for the revealed Word and for the sanctity of the Prophet. The cumulative bulk of authority-constructed narrative that emerged in later periods had to be projected back to a time in which such constructive processes had just barely begun.

Perhaps there is no issue in the religious history of early Islam as controversial as that of the provenance of Prophetic material, and it is the second camp that has raised fundamental issues about this provenance.[5] The second camp's discursive repertoire can generally be defined as emanating from Orientalism, which has in part taken upon itself the mission of providing an indirect response to the tradionalist, Muslim narrative. Of the political and ideological tenor of Orientalism we shall say something later, but for now let

[4]On *sunan*, in contradistinction to Prophetic Sunna, see W.B. Hallaq, *The Origins and Early Evolution of Islamic Law and Jurisprudence* (Cambridge: Cambridge University Press, forthcoming), Chapters 2–3.

[5]It will be noted that this volume takes no more than a cursory interest in the controversy over Prophetic traditions and their authenticity, since such themes are the subject of another volume in this series, edited by Harald Motzki. For other writings, nonetheless, see Bibliography, Section 4, below.

it be noted that legal Orientalism has produced several, often considerably divergent, strands of thought. In this camp there are to be found published opinions ranging from those that are hostile to Muslim narrative (or even history) to others that confirm the narrative's contents. It is remarkable that the latter strand of Western scholarship is considered revisionist, having surfaced in this scholarship only recently. Its qualification as revisionist has been attributed to the fact that its findings stand against those developed by classical Western scholarship over the last century and a half. What is even more remarkable is that this revisionist scholarship emerged in spite of the fact that its critical scholarly apparatus is often nearly indistinguishable from (and at times more sophisticated than) that which has defined the *modus operandi* of classical Orientalism. Yet, this revisionism tends to confirm much of what the traditionalist narrative asserts.

Another revisionist strand within the Orientalist camp is one that has tended to discredit the traditionalist narrative altogether, confirming the general outlines of classical Orientalism and even going beyond these outlines, while adopting a highly skeptical approach to the Muslim sources.

The articles collected in this volume are intended to reflect the debates that have raged within the Western camp during the last half century. The topics with which these articles deal represent major issues that have defined the contours and substance of the legal history of the early Islamic period. A conscious attempt was made to include the widest spectrum of interpretation, from the mainstream voices to the revisionists on both sides of the center, i.e. those who tend to confirm much of the Muslim narrative and those who accept nearly nothing of it, arguing that even the mainstream version of Orientalism—already highly critical of the assumptions and accounts of this narrative—has been naïve in its outlook.

Another important consideration in the choice of subject matter has been to cover as much as possible of what constituted the formative period. Until recently, it has been thought that this period ended around the middle of the third century AH (ca. AD 850), when, following Joseph Schacht's findings, we thought that the legal schools, as personal juristic entities, came into existence and that, again after Schacht, Islamic law and legal theory reached their zenith or, at least, came of age. It has become clear now that Schacht's findings were largely incorrect[6] and that the point at which Islamic law came

[6]Elsewhere, I have argued that Schacht's great influence on the field is entirely unjustified, since much of his findings—certainly those associated with his chief contributions—are fundamentally flawed. There, I have also tried to explain why, despite the problematic nature of his work, Schacht became accepted as the dominant authority in the field. See

to contain all its major components must be dated to the middle of the fourth/tenth century, an entire century after we had thought.[7] Therefore, in this context, the definition of "formation" or "formative period" is that historical period which the legal system arose from rudimentary beginnings and then developed to a point where its constitutive features had acquired an identifiable shape.

"Identifiable" because all that is needed in the context of "formation" is the coming into existence of those attributes that distinguish and make unmistakably clear the constitutive features of that system. Insistence on more specific definitions would run the risk of locking historical systems into a rigid, even immutable, form, from which these systems were essentially free. In fact, there can be no universally accurate definition of any living organism, and legal systems no doubt are such organisms. In other words, there cannot be a true definition of a system that purports to cover various periods or epochs, for chronological change would necessarily alter a definition. "Formation", therefore, would have to be restricted to the evolution of the general features of the system, since the details—or what we might, philosophically speaking, call "accidental attributes"—endured constant movement and change and could never determine formative epochs. Thus, and to continue with our philosophical terminology, the search for formations must be defined in terms of "essential attributes" that make a thing what it is; or, conversely, the absence of any essential attribute would alter the very nature of the thing, rendering it qualitatively different from another in whom that attribute does exist. In the case of Islamic law, the essential attributes are mainly four:

1. the evolution of a complete judiciary, with full-fledged court systems and law of evidence and procedure;

2. the full elaboration of a positive legal doctrine;

3. the full emergence of a science of legal theory and legal methodology which, among other things, reflected a great deal of hermeneutical, intellectual and juristic self-consciousness;

Hallaq, "The Quest for Origins or Doctrine? Islamic Legal Studies as Colonialist Discourse", *UCLA Journal of Islamic and Near Eastern Law* 2.3 (2003, forthcoming).

[7]This assertion finds confirmation in the work of this writer and that of Christopher Melchert. See Hallaq, *Authority, Continuity and Change*, Chapters 2–3; *idem*, "Was al-Shafi'i the Master Architect of Islamic Jurisprudence?" (Chapter 10, below); Melchert, *The Formation of the Sunni Schools of Law* (Leiden, 1997), and his contribution here (Chapter 13, below).

4. the full emergence of the legal schools, a cardinal development that in turn presupposed the emergence of various doctrinal, educational and practice-based elements.

By the middle of the third/ninth century, the third and forth attributes did not yet exist in any complete form. By the middle of the fourth/tenth century, all of them did. And this is the cut-off point. All later developments, including change in legal doctrine or practice, are "accidental attributes" that—despite their importance for legal and social historians—do not affect the constitution of the phenomenon we call Islamic law. With or without this change, Islamic law, for our purposes here, will remain Islamic law. But without the legal schools or the science of legal theory, Islamic law cannot be deemed, in hindsight, complete.

Far more complex than plotting the end-point of the formative period is the determination of its beginning. It is no exaggeration to say that of all the major questions in Islamic legal history, the issues involved in studying these beginnings have proven the most challenging, if not elusive. The problems associated with "beginnings" have for long stemmed more from unproven assumptions than from any real historical evidence. It has been part of the classical Orientalist creed that the Arabia of the Prophet was a culturally impoverished region (and this remains the prevailing belief even today), and that when the Arabs built their sophisticated cities, empires and legal systems, they could not have drawn on their own vacuous cultural resources. Instead, in the course of their conquests and later expansion, they freely absorbed the cultural elements of the societies they conquered, including (but especially) the Byzantino-Roman, Sasanid, and Jewish civilizations. In this account, Syria and Iraq become the loci of legal transmission.

The problem with these assumptions has consistently been that they are unable to stand the test of scrutiny. Except in a few cases, attempts to demonstrate genetic links with these cultures have proven futile, if only because Arabia has provided an equally, if not more, convincing source for much of the law that Islam derived. Yet, while classical Orientalism seems to have been largely abandoned by many cultural and political historians engaged in the study of the first few decades of Islam—who have made considerable progress on the basis of literary and non-literary sources—the legal historian has not caught up with these developments. Instead, the latter is still operating under archaic assumptions that have been belabored, but never proven, by nineteenth-century scholars. In some cases, furthermore, there appears to be tremendous regress among some of these historians who are writing even nowadays.[8]

What can be accomplished by a fair-minded scholar is demonstrated in the first item in this collection (Chapter 1), which comes from a non-legal historian. In his article "The Arab Conquests and the Formation of Islamic Society", Ira Lapidus perceptively analyzes the conditions that prevailed in the Arabian peninsula immediately prior to the conquests and shows how these conditions "involved the development within Arabian society of the very same types of institutions and forms of culture which were already established in the empire societies".[9] Arabia was thus heavily influenced by these forms of culture, since no barrier whatsoever separated it from the empire regions. In fact, over the three or four centuries before the rise of Islam, the Arabian peoples had migrated slowly northwards, to the point where they had come to constitute much of the population of Iraq and, especially, Syria. When the conquests began, these Arab populations—who had already absorbed, and themselves participated in creating, the cultural forms of the North—joined their Southern Arab fellow tribesmen in building the new venture that became Islamic civilization. What is to be recalled here are the complex relationships that existed between these Southern Arabs and the societies of the North, be they Arab or non-Arab. South Arabia, it must be stressed, shared many of the northern cultural forms and institutions, and this must remain a fact of crucial importance in any analysis of the rise of an Islamic legal system. For it is this fact that explains the significant difficulties encountered when legal borrowings are assumed to emanate from the North, to the exclusion of Arabia itself. Lapidus' article, therefore, provides both the historical framework within which the Islamic conquests arose and the Peninsular backdrop against which the future Islamic institutions (including, by implication, law) began to develop largely on the basis of the legal culture that the conquering Arabs brought with them from their native land.

It will be readily obvious that in his "Pre-Islamic Background and Early Development of Jurisprudence" (Chapter 2), Joseph Schacht adopts a different approach, the underlying assumption of which is the postulate that Islamic law developed mostly on the basis of Iraqi and, to a lesser extent, Syrian traditions of law and legal practice. He maintains this position despite the fact that he could not overlook the "developed" nature of the law

---

[8]See Wael Hallaq, "The Use and Abuse of Evidence: the Question of Provincial and Roman Influences on Early Islamic Law", in W.B. Hallaq, *Law and Legal Theory in Classical and Medieval Islam* (Aldershot, 1995), IX; *idem*, "The Quest for Origins or Doctrine?"

[9]Lapidus, "Arab Conquests", 50 (Chapter 1, below).

that existed in the urbanized areas of the Peninsula, such as Medina and Mecca.[10] His admission that such a developed law existed in the homeland of the conquerors had no bearing whatsoever on his determination to champion Iraq as the real cradle of Islamic law. It was one of Schacht's cardinal conceptions—dictating much of his scholarship on the early formation of Islamic law—that Islamic law was not the natural evolutionary continuation of the Ḥijāzī legal forms supplemented by northern influences, but rather the result of administrative and popular Umayyad practices that were heavily colored by the legal traditions that had survived in the new lands ruled by the first Islamic dynasty. Islamic law thus began to be elaborated on the basis of these practices that were inspired by layers of ancient Near Eastern laws (this latter point constitutes Schacht's preoccupation in the next article "Foreign Elements in Islamic Law" [Chapter 3]). Of fundamental importance in this picture are the players in these developments, namely, the newly emerging groups of pious legal specialists who produced the first incarnation of an Islamic law around 100/718. Their successors, who were to continue their mission, succeeded in building a legal system, legal doctrine, schools of law, and a legal theory to boot.

Nor does Schacht find that the body of regulations contained in the Qur'ān have much to do with the evolution of a distinctively Islamic religious law from the outset. In fact, elsewhere, he argues that Qur'ānic legal norms, "apart from the most elementary rules... were introduced into Muhammadan law almost invariably at a secondary stage",[11] which he again assigns to the years immediately around 100/718. During the Prophet's lifetime, he argues, the Qur'ān never functioned as a legal authority, nor did Muhammad himself do so. The Prophet "wielded his almost absolute power not within but without the existing legal system; his authority was not legal, but for the believers, religious, and for the lukewarm, political".[12]

The clear implications of Schacht's argument—that neither the Prophet nor the Qur'ān constituted legal authority—are taken up by S.D. Goitein in his "The Birth-Hour of Muslim Law" (Chapter 4), where he protests that the Qur'ān cannot be seen as confined to a non-legal, religious role. He cites the critical event in the Prophet's career where his conflict with the Medinan Jews led him to an awareness of his role as a leader of a community that had gained the divine right of upholding a law, just as the Jews and Christians

[10]Schacht, *An Introduction to Islamic Law* (Oxford, 1964), 6–9.

[11]Schacht, *The Origins of Muhammadan Jurisprudence* (Oxford, 1950), 224.

[12]Schacht, "Pre-Islamic Background", 31 (Chapter 2, below).

from other legal systems",[19] they nonetheless "lend no support to the assumption that jurists of non-Arab descent brought solutions from their natal legal systems—Roman, Roman provincial and Jewish law—to early Islamic law".[20]

Motzki's article brings to a close the first part of this book, leaving the question of borrowings only marginally less elusive than it had been when European scholars embarked upon their investigation of the issue a century and a half ago. Thus far, it has not seriously occurred to modern Western scholars that the solution to the problem might lie in the Ḥijāz, where Islam began.[21] The current lack of interest in the Ḥijāz as a likely place of Islamic legal origins is prompted by the Orientalist assumption—expressed unequivocally by Crone[22]—that the entire Peninsula was culturally and institutionally arid, and thus incapable of producing the kind of elaborate and sophisticated law that became the Sharīʿa. Lapidus' article (Chapter 1), is merely a preliminary pronouncement against this archaic assumption, a pronouncement that is largely non-legal. Modern *legal* scholarship has thus far left the thesis of Ḥijāzī origins lamentably unexplored.[23]

The vacuum left by the thesis of foreign borrowings is merely one symptom of our staggering ignorance of what happened, in legal terms, during the few decades after the Prophet's death. However, we begin to see some features of the law at work in the careers of the legal administrators who flourished during the second half of the first century. In Chapter 8, Irit Bligh-Abramski sheds light on this class of administrators whose functions in the early period were so underdeveloped and substantially non-legal that we cannot call them anything more than proto-*qāḍīs*. Showing how they developed into a full-fledged judiciary, Bligh-Abramski sketches the main contours of this development from the middle of the first century to the end of the second and beyond, commenting among other things on the relationship between the judges and the political, ruling class. By virtue of

---

19 Motzki, "Role of Non-Arab Converts", 316 (Chapter 7, below).

20 *Ibid.*, 293.

21 Apart from the nearly forgotten essay of Gotthelf Bergsträsser, "Anfänge und Charakter des juristischen Denkens im Islam. Vorläufige Betrachtungen", *Der Islam* 14 (1925), 76–81, David Powers seems alone in stating, if only in passing, the possible influences of the Ḥijāz, although, to my knowledge, he nowhere pursues this line of thinking. See his "On Bequests in Early Islam", *Journal of Near Eastern Studies* 48 (1989), 185–200, at 199.

22 See Hallaq, "Use and Abuse of Evidence".

23 An initial attempt, providing the context for such an enquiry, is advanced in Hallaq, *The Origins and Early Evolution of Islamic Law*.

had upheld divine laws of their own. While Goitein does not make the argument that the Qur'ān functioned as an overarching source of law from the very beginning, he does make the important point—countering Schacht's claim—that the Qur'ān's authority and, by extension, that of the Prophet, could not have been devoid of legal content.

Intimately related to this theme is Patricia Crone's essay "Two Legal Problems Bearing on the Early History of the Quran" (Chapter 5), in which she attempts to show, basing herself on two exegetical examples, that "there is less continuity between Qur'ānic and Islamic law than one would expect" and that "Schacht underestimated the discontinuity to which he drew attention".[13] The two examples that Crone adduces come to bolster at least six other cases[14] that had earlier presented other scholars with exegetical problems and that in turn Crone takes to be illustrative of a disjunction between Qur'ānic legal doctrine and the Sharī'a. The fundamental problem as raised here is that shortly after the Prophet's death, his followers failed to remember what he—or the Qur'ān—meant by certain, mainly legal, expressions. The question for Crone then becomes: "how could the meaning of such terminology be forgotten if the rules it (i.e. the Qur'ān) formulated were explained and applied from the moment of their revelation?" However, one should not expect much in terms of an answer to this question, for Crone herself expressly admits her inability to provide a solution.[15]

The exegetical and other problems posed by Crone would indeed be serious and would thus require an explanation if we grant two interrelated assumptions, namely, that: 1) they are genuine problems; and 2) if they are, they constitute sufficient grounds to doubt the existence of continuity. For example, the two problems associated with *kalāla* and *kitāb* (or, for that matter, the stoning verse or the alleged problem that Sūrat al-Baqara 2, v. 282, is said to raise concerning written documents) may not turn out to be problems after all, a fact that reduces the importance of the remaining problems, relegating them to the status of marginal exceptions rather than serious issues pointing to a marked discontinuity. But even if the entire set of problems proved genuine, as Crone would clearly have it, the fact remains that aggregately, they can prove nothing beyond what the problems themselves present. In other words, they cannot and do not adjudge the entire relationship of (dis)continuity between the Qur'ān and the Sharī'a,

[13]Crone, "Two Legal Problems", 10 (Chapter 5, below).

[14]They are *jizya 'an yad*, *al-ṣamad*, *kalāla*, *īlāf*, the stoning penalty v. whipping, and written documents v. oral testimony.

[15]Crone, "Two Legal Problems", 21 (Chapter 5, below).

a relationship based upon hundreds of similar, even more important, legal cases.

Crone's assumption of discontinuity echoes the argument she presents in another of her works, entitled *Roman, Provincial and Islamic Law*.[16] In this work, the author argues—following in the footsteps of a long string of Orientalists (including Schacht)[17]—that Islamic law is substantially the product of foreign influence, in this case, of the provincial and Roman law that prevailed generally in the Fertile Crescent and, specifically, in Syria during the formation of Islamic society under the Umayyads. The case-study she brings to bear upon the question of borrowings is the institution of the patronate and the legal status of freedmen.

Crone's thesis, perhaps the most articulate in the field, has nevertheless been shown to suffer from fundamental methodological and substantive problems,[18] and as such it need not preoccupy us here. It did, however, render us a service in provoking serious research into the problem of manumission, an instance of which is Ulrike Mitter's article reproduced here (Chapter 6). Although Mitter addresses the limited issue of *tasyīb* (unconditional manumission of slaves), she brings a sophisticated method of *ḥadīth*-analysis to bear on the controversy over borrowing, in this case, from Roman and provincial law. Her findings positively favor the indigenous origins of the *ḥadīth*, convincingly showing the authenticity of these *ḥadīth*s and, at the same time, demonstrating that it was Arabian peninsular practices, not Roman or provincial law, that constituted the foundations of later juristic constructions of *tasyīb*.

For the argument in favor of foreign influences on early Islamic law to make sense, one must assume the existence of agents who supposedly mediated the transmission of foreign law into Islam. These agents are thought to have been the non-Arab converts who presumably knew and practiced the law of the conquered lands and who, by virtue of their conversion, brought it with them to the new religion. In his pioneering article (Chapter 7) reproduced here, Harald Motzki challenges this conventional wisdom on the basis of biographical data about the most important scholars who contributed to the formation of Islamic law. Motzki cautiously concludes that although his results do not preclude the possibility that "Islamic law borrowed resources

[16] (Cambridge, 1987).

[17] In spite of the fact that Crone does criticize him in certain details (but not on principle).

[18] In addition to Ulrike Mitter's article in this collection (Chapter 6), see Hallaq, "The Use and Abuse of Evidence".

their appointment and dismissal by this class, the judges and, with them, the judiciary as a whole, constituted the touchstone of the power dialectic between law and politics, an important theme that receives more attention in the final contribution to this volume (Chapter 14).

Developments in the judiciary were concurrent with other developments in the systemic and substantive doctrinal spheres of what was emerging as Islamic law. By the end of the first century (*ca.* AD 700–20), circles of legal specialists began to emerge, and with the scholarly activities that these circles involved, a body of legal doctrine also came into existence. The first half of the succeeding century witnessed both a refinement and expansion of this doctrine, which became, for the first time, an articulate positive law that formed the basis of all later juristic constructions. New technical legal concepts and new connotations of old ones began to surface in juristic writings, involving a long discursive process that was to endow legal concepts with relatively fixed connotations by the end of the third/ninth century. Zafar Ansari's contribution (Chapter 9) presents us with a survey of this terminological development, discussing, among other things, such key concepts as *ḥadīth*, *sunna*, consensus, and *qiyās* as had developed by the time the famous al-Shāfiʿī appeared on the scene.

In both modern Western and Islamic traditional scholarship, al-Shāfiʿī occupies an exceptionally distinguished status, virtually unrivaled by any other Muslim jurist. A major reason why this should be the case is the significant historical role that he has retrospectively been assigned as the "master architect" of Islamic jurisprudence. In effect, he has long been regarded as the designer of a structured theory of law whose constitutive hermeneutical and methodological components presuppose an organic relationship between and among the so-called "four sources": the Qur'ān, Prophetic Sunna, consensus and the inferential tool of *qiyās*.[24] Wael Hallaq's article "Was al-Shafiʿi the Master Architect of Islamic Jurisprudence?" (Chapter 10) questions this perception and argues that al-Shāfiʿī's *Risāla* falls well short of providing a theoretical scheme corresponding to the later works of legal theory (*uṣūl al-fiqh*). Perhaps more importantly, it shows that a full-fledged theory of these *uṣūl*, reflecting a highly structured theory of law, only emerged as late as a century after al-Shāfiʿī's death.[25] This finding is prompted not only by

[24]For a different analysis of the reasons behind the Western Islamicists' over-rated perception of al-Shāfiʿī, see Hallaq, "The Quest for Origins or Doctrine?"

[25]These findings were later confirmed, in their entirety, by Joseph Lowry, "Does Shāfiʿī have a Theory of Four Sources of Law?", in Bernard Weiss, ed., *Studies in Islamic Legal Theory* (Leiden, 2002), 23–50, and in part, by Christopher Melchert, *Formation of the*

the fact that such structured works cannot be documented in most of the third/ninth century, but also by the consideration that the subject matter of later *uṣūl al-fiqh* presupposed a synthesis of various jurisprudential and theological elements that had not yet been accomplished during the third/ninth century.

In Chapter 11, Devin Stewart acknowledges that neither al-Shāfiʿī's *Risāla* nor al-Shāfiʿī himself established the groundwork for later *uṣūl al-fiqh* developments, but argues, on the basis of reconstructed fragments, that works of *uṣūl* were nonetheless authored during the third/ninth century. Stewart, however, does not succeed in convincing the reader. The value of his article instead lies in showing that the issues raised in the third/ninth century *uṣūl* works are rudimentary, reflecting an earlier stage of development from which the structured *uṣūl* works of the next century partly emerged, and to which they formed, also partly, a discursive response. The provisional and partial, but not even synoptic, subject matter adduced by Stewart[26] confirms the emergence in that century of no more than a prototypical genre of *uṣūl*, one that is concerned with a limited number of polemical issues and still lagging behind in terms of structured legal methodology and hermeneutic.

The emergence of *uṣūl al-fiqh* as a structured methodology was not merely a reflection of a synthesis between rationalism and traditionalism, a synthesis that came to define Sunnism as a distinct legal, theological and political entity. *Uṣūl al-fiqh* was also a constitutive ingredient in the creation of *madhhab*s, the legal schools that, on the one hand, articulated once and for all the shape of legal doctrine and, on the other, contributed fundamentally to the phenomenon called Sunnism. It laid down the hermeneutics of the *madhhab as a doctrinal entity*,[27] the implication being that the final formation of the *madhhab*s as such entities could not have come into being without a structured theory by which legal authority and hermeneutics could be defined and finally articulated. It was on the basis of such a hermeneutic

Sunni Schools.

[26]Even if we grant that the fragments excerpted by Stewart are indeed those authored by Ibn Dāwūd, and even if we grant that these fragments may be compounded into a structured *uṣūl* theory (an assumption that can by no means be endorsed), Hallaq's dating of the emergence of *uṣūl* would be no more than three or four decades later than Stewart would like the date to be, since Ibn Dāwūd could not have written prior to 280/893, and indeed more likely did so closer to 290/902.

[27]There were other, earlier meanings of "*madhhab*", which are not intended here. For these meanings, see Hallaq, *Authority, Continuity and Change*, 155; *idem*, "From Regional to Personal Schools of Law? A Reevaluation", *Islamic Law and Society*, 8 (2001), 1–26, and Melchert, "Formation of the Sunni Schools" (Chapter 13, below).

(the result of a heightened degree of epistemic self-awareness) that the *madhhabs*, which had by definition to be attributed to a founder, came actually to construct the authority of that (supposed) founder.

Hallaq's second contribution in this volume (Chapter 12) follows up on the related themes of how the authority of al-Shāfiʿī and the other presumed founders of the legal schools was constructed, explaining not only the rise of these so-called founders to epistemic and hermeneutical prominence—a defining feature of legal authority—but also how the *madhhabs* as *doctrinal* entities came into being. The construction of school authority represented one of the most central processes that were involved in building the school structures, be they epistemological or doctrinal. At another level of analysis, the schools came into being also as a result of certain developments within the body of jurists who carried the burden of the entire province of law, developments having to do with the politics of the ruling class, the mounting pressures resulting from juridico-theological debates and, among other things, the rise of legal education as an institutionalized discipline. This latter development stands as the central theme in Christopher Melchert's piece (Chapter 13), which summarizes his research, based mainly on biographical dictionaries, into the role of education in building the schools through student loyalties. He also attempts to explain why the four schools survived, and even flourished, while others became extinct.

Why the four schools succeeded while the others failed is a question that, for many a modern scholar, is closely connected with the role played by the Islamic government in the legal system and the manner in which it influenced and used the legal profession.[28] On the other hand, it is precisely the overwhelming absence of the state from the province of Islamic law that may explain why the legal schools emerged at all, and why they turned out to be a distinctive Islamic phenomenon with no real parallel in other legal cultures. The construction of the school founders' authority as the axes of legal authority amounts to an act of compensation, substitution, replacement. Whereas in most other legal systems the body politic sanctions the law's authority, in Islam the state or government was as much subject to the law as the individual Muslim. The construction of the *madhhab* was therefore a process, an act, by which an equivalent form of authority is created to fill the gap the state had left behind. Although the process of

[28] On these and other explanations, see George Makdisi, "The Significance of the Schools of Law in Islamic Religious History", *International Journal of Middle East Studies* 10 (1979), 1–8, and references cited therein.

madhhab-construction began to manifest itself during the second half of the second/eighth century and took as long as another century and a half to be completed, its embryonic beginnings and the conditions that permitted its emergence can (and should) be traced back to the first decades of Islam when the chief participants in the creation of legal culture were private scholars rather than statesmen acting on behalf a body politic. Even when the latter happened to involve themselves in the making of this culture, their contributions were deemed individual, representing, in the long run, their personal opinions that had anything but the force of an edict. As M. Qasim Zaman shows in the last contribution to this volume (Chapter 14), the "caliph's participation in religious life was not in competition with, or over and above that of, the emergent Sunnī *'ulamā'*, but in conjunction with them".[29] And insofar as the principle of the rule of law was concerned, the caliphs also understood that they were just as much subject to the law as anyone else.

* * *

Enough has been said to indicate that the study of Islamic legal history during the formative period suffers from underdevelopment in a number of ways, and for a number of reasons. In the opening pages of this Introduction, enough was likewise said to show why Muslim scholars writing in the Muslim world have not been able to study this period with a view to discovering what indeed happened, to the extent, of course, that one can recover the past (a major problem that faces not only historians but the very craft of history as an attempt at reconstructing what is presumed to be knowable events of the past).[30] At the same time, one would expect, with all the critical, scientific apparatus at their disposal, that Western scholars would have attained a more accurate version of the truly historical than their Muslim counterparts. This, however, has not proven to be the case. The early legal history of Islam—not to mention other periods—remains in Western scholarship just as "fictive" (to use Hayden White's parlance) as the body of knowledge that Muslim scholars have thus far produced. One reason why this is the case is the intense concern, represented in the Western scholarly paradigm, to view Islamic origins as replicating the cultural patterns and institutions deemed

[29] Zaman, "The Caliphs, the 'Ulamā', and the Law", 4 (Chapter 14, below).

[30] On this and other related problems, see Hayden White, *The Content of the Form: Narrative Discourse and Histroical Representation* (Baltimore and London, 1987); also see L.B. Cebik, "Fiction and History: a Common Core?", *International Studies in Philosophy* 24 (1992), 47–63, although Cebik here disregards White's nuanced qualifications preventing the dismissal of history as a purely fiction.

to have been the sources of Western civilization. Hence the stubborn and persistent predilection for affirming fundamental dichotomies in the study of early legal developments: Arabia thus turns out to be culturally impoverished whereas the conquered lands of the North (mainly Syria and Iraq) are the abode of high civilization, a posited affirmation that compels the conclusion that the elaborate and sophisticated Sharīʿa could not have been the product of a desolate culture but must have rather taken over the northern legal forms under an Islamic veneer.

This cardinal tenet, which amounts to no more than an ideological doctrine,[31] in turn determined several other assumptions that have become highly operative not only in the choice of scholarly topics to be pursued (in itself an approach not without much prejudice) but also in the manner these topics are studied and treated. Thus, the possibility that the Ḥijāz was an integral part of the Near Eastern cultural *oikoumene* with institutional and legal forms akin to those of the north, has been *a priori* excluded. What is even more blatant is the complete dismissal of the very likely possibility that Roman and provincial law are themselves no more than the distillate of what Rome adopted of the Semitic cultural forms prevalent in the Fertile Crescent, mainly Syria (Bilād al-Shām). These Semitic forms, intrinsic to the Arabs of both the North and the South, constituted much of what later came to be Roman law, appropriated in typical fashion by the imperial state as its own.[32] This appropriation was happily, not to say conveniently, forgot-

[31] As I have shown in my "The Quest of Origins or Doctrine".

[32] See now Warwick Ball, *Rome in the East: the Transformation of an Empire* (London and New York, 2000), where a strong case is made in favor of the argument that the Near East had a far greater influence on Rome and Roman culture than the Roman Empire had on the Near East. Not only did the latter have a long history of urbanism and urban structures that predated both the Greeks and the Romans, but what came to be known as the Roman heritage of the Near East turns out, in many if not all respects, to be a heritage heavily indebted to the indigenous Semitic cultures of the ancient Near East, not to Greece or Rome. Although Ball's evidence is largely archaeological and architectural, he draws heavily on other types of material that inform political, military and even legal history. This work (perhaps together with Maurice Sartre's *L'Orient romain* [Paris, 1991], which in some respects anticipates Ball's work) easily allows for shifting the burden of proof onto the proponents of the thesis that the cultural and institutional forms existing in the pre-Islamic Near East were Roman, not Semitic. Also see Hallaq, "Use and Abuse", 30–31, and sources cited therein (n. 17).

On a more specific level, and in the larger context of his study, Ball comes rather close to arguing for Semitic origins of Roman law. When discussing, for instance, Beirut's Law School (said by many Orientalists to have influenced the early development of Islamic law), he makes the following observation: "At the beginning of the third century the [Phoenician, but Roman] Emperor Septimius Severus founded Beirut's most famous institution.

ten by Orientalists whose agenda is likewise one of appropriating the history of Islam, rendering it capable of being rewritten, even metamorphosed.[33] The Semitic and Romano-Semitic cultural forms of the Peninsular Arabs and of those Christian Arabs of the North were suppressed in favor of a dichotomy in which these Arabs stand, in their entirety, qualitatively distinct and separate from all other peoples in the region. With this scenario in place, it is easy to postulate Islam's heavy indebtedness to Europe's cultural predecessors. And *that* is the point.

The ramifications of these assumptions extend, as they are no doubt intended to do, far beyond questions of the pre-Islamic origins of Islamic law. Once the novelist writes her first chapter, she is bound by it, and everything that follows must fit. If Islam's legal tradition owes itself, in full or in good part, to foreign influences, then there can neither be a Qur'ānic legal substrate nor Prophetic legal dicta that could inspire, much less give rise to, an Islamic legal tradition. Any concession to such effects would deal a blow to the theory of foreign borrowing and would "unjustifiably" credit the "culturally impoverished" Arabs with legal and other achievements at the expense of the "genuine" culture-producing Greco-Romans and other "non-Arabs". The theory of foreign influence thus continues to serve its purpose in pushing the emergence of an Islamic law to the end of the first century AH, if not to the beginning of the second. This thesis comes in handy to explain the otherwise inexplicable, namely, that by the time of al-Shāfi'ī's death—a

---

This was the Law School, the first such institution in the Roman world, and it was enthusiastically supported by the [originally Near Eastern] Severan emperors. The Beirut Law School was to have a profound effect on Roman civilization. It represents the birth of Roman—hence European—jurisprudence, of which Justinian's monumental *Digest* was the first great achievement. It attracted many prominent legal minds, mostly drawn from the Phoenician population of the Levant itself. The most famous was Papinian, a native of Emesa, and his contemporary Ulpian, a native of Tyre. Both were patronised by the Severan dynasty... and both were acknowledged in Justinian's *Digest* as forming the basis of Roman Law. Beirut and its justly famous law school, and with it its profound legacy, is regarded as a 'Western' and Roman enclave in the Near East. But it was founded and promoted by emperors whose origins and destinies were intimately bound to Phoenician culture. Above all, it must be emphasised that... the environment of Beirut and its law school is the Near East, not Italy. Many of the great scholars who dominated it were natives of the Near East, however Romanised, notably Papinian and Ulpian. It drew upon literary traditions that stretched back to Sanchuniathon of Beirut in the seventh century BC and legal traditions that stretched back even further to the Judaic traditions of the early first millennium and the Mesopotamian law codes of the early second millennium. Ultimately, therefore, should we be viewing Beirut in the context of Rome or of Babylon?" (pp. 173–74).

[33]On this, see Hallaq, "Quest for Origins or Doctrine?"

century after the emergence of an Islamic law—the Sharīʿa had reached the zenith of development. Here too all the pieces of the puzzle fit or, should we say, are made to fit. If the Muslims did not borrow the constitutive elements of their legal tradition from others but had instead to create the tradition by their own effort and imagination, it would have been virtually impossible for them to construct such an imposing legal tradition by the time Shāfiʿī died. This is simply too short a period, and so, only borrowing can explain the swift upsurge of a highly developed law and legal system.

Al-Shāfiʿī therefore discharged a crucial function in the Orientalist scenario that had little to do with the quality and quantity of his contribution to juristic development. He was made not only a master architect of jurisprudence but also an unrivaled mind whose competence and mastery "had not been achieved before" and were "hardly equaled and never surpassed after him".[34] With al-Shāfiʿī, then, the pinnacle of Islamic law had been attained, lending at once justification and credence to the theory of foreign influences. But the theory that sketched the scenario of northern, foreign influence, of the emergence of *ḥadīth* and Islamic law at around AH 100, of the extraordinarily speedy development of this law, and of the unsurpassed influence and mental aptitude of al-Shāfiʿī, is the same theory that sentenced the post-Shāfiʿī era to a long-term scholarly imprisonment where a few, if any, developments could be expected to have taken place. The Muslim legal tradition after al-Shāfiʿī, Western paradigmatic scholarship has until recently told us, represented nothing more than a slavish heaping of commentary upon commentary, producing little more than Byzantine hair-splitting.[35] This complex and multi-layered theory—in effect no more than a doctrine—not only contributed to the stagnation of scholarship on the developmentally rich post-Shāfiʿī era, but operated to complete the doctrinal cycle that the theory was intended to accomplish in the first place: that in its origins, just as in the modern world (where the Sharīʿa has been virtually replaced by European codes), Islam needed the Western legal tradition to inject itself with life, in order to be able to cope properly with the stresses of imperial expansion fourteen centuries ago and with the challenges of modernity in the present day.[36]

But doctrine is no substitute for scholarship. Nor is religious narrative. Will there be a third, paradigmatic account?

[34] Schacht, *Origins*, 1.

[35] Although this attitude was summed up by N.J. Coulson in the early 1960s (*A History of Islamic Law* [Edinburgh, 1964]), 84, it continued to dominate the field until the 1980s.

[36] For a more detailed analysis of this theme, see Hallaq, "Quest for Origins or Doctrine?"

BIBLIOGRAPHY

General

Coulson, N.J. *A History of Islamic Law*. Edinburgh: Edinburgh University Press, 1964.

Hallaq, Wael. *The Origins and Early Evolution of Islamic Law and Jurisprudence*. Cambridge: Cambridge University Press, forthcoming.

________. "The Quest for Origins or Doctrine? Islamic Legal Studies as Colonialist Discourse", *UCLA Journal of Islamic and Near Eastern Law* 2 (2002–2003), 1–31.

Tyan, Emile. *Histoire de l'organisation judiciare en pays d'Islam*, 2nd ed. Leiden: E.J. Brill, 1960.

The Near East before Islam

Ball, Warwick. *Rome in the East: the Transformation of an Empire*. London and New York: Routledge, 2000.

Beeston, A.F.L. "Judaism and Christianity in Pre-Islamic Yemen", in *L'Arabie du sud*, I (Paris: Editions G.-P. Maisonneuve et Larose, 1984), 271–78.

________. "The Religions of Pre-Islamic Yemen", in *L'Arabie du sud*, I (Paris: Editions G.-P. Maisonneuve et Larose, 1984), 259–69.

Dussaud, René. *La Pénétration des arabes en Syrie avant l'Islam*. Paris: Paul Geuthner, 1955.

Hinds, Martin. "*Maghāzī* and *Sīra* in Early Islamic Scholarship", in his *Studies in Early Islamic History*, ed. Jere Bacharach, Lawrence I. Conrad and Patricia Crone (Princeton: Darwin Press, 1996), 188–98.

King, G.R.D. "Settlement in Western and Central Arabia and the Gulf in the Sixth–Eighth Centuries A.D.", in G.R.D. King and Averil Cameron, eds., *The Byzantine and Early Islamic Near East*, II: *Land Use and Settlement Patterns* (Princeton: Darwin Press, 1994), 181–212.

Kister, M.J. "Al-Ḥīra: Some Notes on its Relations with Arabia", *Arabica* 15 (1968), 143–69.

________. "On Strangers and Allies in Mecca", *Jerusalem Studies in Arabic and Islam* 13 (1990), 113–54.

Lecker, Michael. "On the Markets of Medina (Yathrib) in Pre-Islamic and Early Islamic Times", in Michael Lecker, *Jews and Arabs in Pre- and Early Islamic Arabia* (Aldershot: Ashgate, 1998).

Peters, F.E., ed. *The Arabs and Arabia on the Eve of Islam*, in Lawrence I. Conrad, ed., *The Formation of the Classical Islamic World*, III (Aldershot: Ashgate, 1999).

Piotrovsky, Mikhail B. "Late Ancient and Early Medieval Yemen: Settlement Traditions and Innovations", in G.R.D. King and Averil Cameron, eds., *The Byzantine and Early Islamic Near East*, II: *Land Use and Settlement Patterns* (Princeton: Darwin Press, 1994), 213–20.

Rubin, Uri. "Ḥanīfiyya and Ka'ba: an Inquiry into the Arabian Pre-Islamic Background of *dīn Ibrāhīm*", *Jerusalem Studies in Arabic and Islam* 13 (1990), 85–112.

Shahid, Irfan. *Byzantium and the Arabs in the Sixth Century*. Washington, D.C.: Dumbarton Oaks, 1995.

________. *Byzantium and the Semitic Orient before the Rise of Islam*. London: Variorum, 1988.

________. "The Islamic Pilgrimage", in *Akten des XII. Internationalen Kongresses für christliche Archäologie* (Münster: Aschendorffsche Verlagsbuchhandlung, 1995), 340–47.

________. "Pre-Islamic Arabia", in P.M. Holt and Bernard Lewis, eds., *The Cambridge History of Islam*, IA (Cambridge: Cambridge University Press, 1970), 3–29.

Watt, W. Montgomery. "The 'High God' in Pre-Islamic Mecca", *Ve Congrès International d'Arabisants et d'Islamisants* (Bruxelles: Centre pour l'étude des problèmes du monde musulman contemprain, 1970), 499–505.

Muḥammad and the Qur'ān

Hudgson, Marshall G.S. *The Venture of Islam*, I. Chicago: University of Chicago Press, 1974.

Kister, M.J. "The Market of the Prophet", *Journal of the Economic and Social History of the Orient* 8 (1965), 272–76.

Rubin, Uri. "Ḥanīfiyya and Ka'ba: an Inquiry into the Arabian Pre-Islamic Background of *dīn Ibrāhīm*", *Jerusalem Studies in Arabic and Islam* 13 (1990), 85–112.

________, ed. *The Life of Muhammad*, in Lawrence I. Conrad, ed., *The Formation of the Classical Islamic World*, IV (Aldershot: Ashgate, 1998).

Schoeler, Gregor. *Charakter und Authentie der muslimischen Überlieferung über das Leben Mohammeds*. Berlin: Walter de Gruyter, 1996.

Watt, W. Montgomery. "The Arabian Background of the Qur'ān", in *Studies in the History of Arabia*, I (Riyadh: University of Riyadh Press, 1399/1979), 3–13.

Controversy over Prophetic Ḥadīth

Abbott, Nabia. *Studies in Arabic Literary Papyri*, II. Chicago: University of Chicago Press, 1967.

Ansari, Zafar I. "The Authenticity of Traditions: a Critique of Joseph Schacht's Argument *e silentio*", *Hamdard Islamicus* 7 (1984), 51–61.

Azami, M.M. *On Schacht's Origins of Muhammadan Jurisprudence*. New York: John Wiley, 1985.

________. *Studies in Early* Ḥadīth *Literature*. Beirut: al-Maktab al-Islami, 1968.

Hallaq, Wael. "The Authenticity of Prophetic *Ḥadīth*: a Pseudo-Problem", *Studia Islamica* 89 (1999), 75–90.

Juynboll, G.H.A. *Muslim Tradition: Studies in Chronology, Provenance and Authorship of Early Ḥadīth*. Cambridge: Cambridge University Press, 1983.

Motzki, Harald. *Die Anfänge der islamischen Jurisprudenz: Ihr Entwicklung in Mekka bis zur Mitte des 2./8. Jahrhunderts*. Stuttgart: Franz Steiner, 1991; trans. Marion H. Katz, *The Origins of Islamic Jurisprudence: Meccan Fiqh before the Classical Schools*. Leiden: E.J. Brill, 2002.

________. "*Quo vadis Ḥadiṯ*-Forschung? Eine kritische Untersuchung von G.H.A. Juynboll: 'Nāfi', the *Mawlā* of Ibn 'Umar, and his Position in Muslim *Ḥadīth* Literature'", *Der Islam* 73 (1996), 40–80.

Law in the First Century of Islam

'Athamina, Khalil. "Al-Qaṣaṣ: Its Emergence, Religious Origin and its Socio-Political Impact on Early Muslim Society", *Studia Islamica* 76 (1992), 53–74.

Bravmann, M.M. *The Spiritual Background of Early Islam*. Leiden: E.J. Brill, 1972.

Crone, Patricia, and Martin Hinds. *God's Caliph: Religious Authority in the First Centuries of Islam*. Cambridge: Cambridge University Press, 1986.

Foster, Benjamin R. "Agoranomos and Muḥtasib", *Journal of the Economic and Social History of the Orient* 13 (1970), 128–44.

Goldfeld Y. "The Development of Theory on Qur'ānic Exegesis in Islamic Scholarship", *Studia Islamica* 67 (1988), 5–27.

Hallaq, Wael. "Use and Abuse of Evidence: the Question of Roman and Provincial Influences on Early Islamic Law", *Journal of the American Oriental Society* 110 (1989), 79–91; repr. in Wael Hallaq, *Law and Legal Theory in Classical and Medieval Islam* (Aldershot: Variorum, 1994), no. 9, 1–36.

Juynboll, G.H.A., ed. *Studies on the First Century of Islamic Society*. Carbondale and Edwardsville: Southern Illinois University Press, 1982.

Mitter, Ulrike. *Das Frühislamische Patronat*. Ph.D. dissertation: Katholieke Universiteit Nijmegen, 1999.

Powers, David S. *Studies in Qur'ān and Ḥadīth: the Formation of the Islamic Law of Inheritance*. Berkeley: University of California Press, 1986.

Schacht, Joseph. "Vom babylonischen zum islamischen Recht", *Orientalistische Literaturzeitung* (1927), 664–69.

________. "Le Droit musulman: solution de quelques problèmes relatifs à ses origins", *Revue algérienne, tunisienne et marocaine de législasion et de jurisprudence*, 1952, 1–13.

________. "Pre-Islamic Background and Early Development of Jurisprudence", in Majid Khadduri and H.J. Liebesny, eds., *Law in the Middle East* (Washington, D.C.: Middle East Institute, 1955), 28–56.

Siddiqi, M.A.S. *Early Development of Zakat Law and Ijtihad*. Karachi: Islamic Research Academy, 1983.

Islamic Law in the Second Century AH

Brunschvig, Robert. "Considérations sociologiques sur le droit musulman ancient", *Studia Islamica* 3 (1955), 61–73.

Calder, Norman. "*Ikhtilāf* and *Ijmāʿ* in Shāfiʿī's *Risāla*", *Studia Islamica* 58 (1983), 55–81.

Conrad, Gerhard. *Die Quḍāt Dimašq und der Maḏhab al-Auzāʿī*. Beirut: Franz Steiner, 1994.

Dutton, Yasin. *The Origins of Islamic Law: the Qur'an, the Muwaṭṭa' and Medinan ʿAmal*. Richmond: Curzon, 1999.

Frantz-Murphy, Gladys. "A Comparison of the Arabic and Earlier Egyptian Contract Formularies", *Journal of Near Eastern Studies* 40 (1981), 203–23; 44 (1985), 99–114; 47 (1988), 105–12, 269–80.

Hallaq, Wael. "From Regional to Personal Schools of Law? A Reevaluation", *Islamic Law and Society* 8 (2001), 1–26.

Hinds, Martin. "*Maghāzī* and *Sīra* in Early Islamic Scholarship", in his *Studies in Early Islamic History*, ed. Jere Bacharach, Lawrence I. Conrad and Patricia Crone (Princeton: Darwin Press, 1996), 188–98.

Lowry, Joseph. "Does Shāfiʿī have a Theory of Four Sources of Law?", in Bernard Weiss, ed., *Studies in Islamic Legal Theory* (Leiden: E.J. Brill, 2002), 23–50.

Motzki, Harald. *Die Anfänge der islamischen Jurisprudenz. Ihr Entwicklung in Mekka bis zur Mitte des 2./8. Jahrhunderts*. Stuttgart: Franz Steiner, 1991; trans. Marion H. Katz, *The Origins of Islamic Jurisprudence: Meccan Fiqh before the Classical Schools*. Leiden: E.J. Brill, 2002.

________. "Der Fiqh des Zuhrī: die Quellenproblematik", *Der Islam* 68 (1991), 1–44.

Nawas, John. "The Birth of an Elite: *Mawālī* and Arab Ulama", *Israel Oriental Studies*, forthcoming.

________. "The Emergence of *Fiqh* as a Distinct Discipline and the Ethnic Identity of the *Fuqahā'* in Early and Classical Islam", in Hilary Kilpatrick, Stefan Leder and B. Martel-Thoumin, eds., *Proceedings of the 19th Congress (1998) of the Union Européenne des Arabisants et Islamisants (UEAI)* (Leuven: Peeters, forthcoming).

Schacht, Joseph. *The Origins of Muhammadan Jurisprudence*. Oxford: Clarendon Press, 1950.

________. "Pre-Islamic Background and Early Development of Jurisprudence", in Majid Khadduri and H.J. Liebesny, eds., *Law in the Middle East* (Washington, D.C.: Middle East Institute, 1955), 28–56.

________. "The Schools of Law and Later Developments of Jurisprudence", in Majid Khadduri and H.J. Liebesny, eds., *Law in the Middle East* (Washington, D.C.: Middle East Institute, 1955), 57–84.

Shāfiʿī, Muḥammad ibn Idrīs. *Islamic Jurisprudence: Shafiʿi's Risala*, trans. Majid Khadduri. Baltimore: Johns Hopkins University Press, 1961.

Tsafrir, N. "The Spread of the Ḥanafī School in the Western Regions of the ʿAbbāsid Caliphate up to the end of the Third Century A.H." Ph.D. dissertation: Princeton University, 1993.

(Re)Dating Early Legal Texts

Calder, Norman. *Studies in Early Muslim Jurisprudence*. Oxford: Oxford University Press, 1993.

Dutton, Yasin. "*ʿAmal* v. *Ḥadīth* in Islamic Law: the Case of *Sadl al-Yadayn* (Holding One's Hands by One's Sides) When Doing Prayer", *Islamic Law and Society* 3 (1996), 13–40.

Hallaq, Wael. "On Dating Mālik's *Muwaṭṭa'*", *UCLA Journal of Islamic and Near Eastern Law* 1 (2002), 47–65.

Lowry, Joseph. "The Legal Hermeneutics of al-Shāfi'ī and Ibn Qutayba: a Reconsideration", *Islamic Law and Society*, forthcoming.

Motzki, Harald. "The Prophet and the Cat: On Dating Mālik's *Muwaṭṭa'* and Legal Traditions", *Jerusalem Studies in Arabic and Islam* 22 (1998), 18–83.

Muranyi, Miklos. "Die frühe Rechtsliteratur zwischen Quellenanalyse und Fiktion", *Islamic Law and Society* 4 (1997), 224–41.

Later Developments

Brockopp, Jonathan. *Early Maliki Law: Ibn 'Abd al-Ḥakam and his Major Compendium of Jurisprudence*. Leiden: E.J. Brill, 2000.

Conrad, Gerhard. *Die Quḍāt Dimašq und der Maḏhab al-Auzā'ī*. Beirut: Franz Steiner, 1994.

Frantz-Murphy, Gladys. "A Comparison of the Arabic and Earlier Egyptian Contract Formularies", *Journal of Near Eastern Studies* 40 (1981), 203–23; 44 (1985), 99–114; 47 (1988), 105–12, 269–80.

Goldziher, Ignaz. *The Ẓāhirīs: Their Doctrine and Their History*, trans. Wolfgang Behn. Leiden: E.J. Brill, 1971.

Halkin, A.S. "The Ḥashwiyya", *Journal of the American Oriental Society* 54 (1934), 1–28.

Hallaq, Wael B. *Authority, Continuity and Change in Islamic Law*. Cambridge: Cambridge University Press, 2001.

———. "From Regional to Personal Schools of Law? A Reevaluation", *Islamic Law and Society* 8 (2001), 1–26.

Hurvitz, N. "Aḥmad Ibn Ḥanbal and the Formation of Islamic Orthodoxy". Ph.D. dissertation: Princeton University, 1994.

Makdisi, George. "The Juridical Theology of Shāfi'ī: Origins and Significance of *Uṣūl al-Fiqh*", *Studia Islamica* 59 (1984), 5–47.

———. "The Significance of the Schools of Law in Islamic Religious History", *International Journal of Middle East Studies* 10 (1979), 1–8.

Melchert, Christopher. *The Formation of the Sunni Schools of Law*. Leiden: E.J. Brill, 1997.

———. "The Piety of the Hadith Folk", *International Journal of Middle East Studies* 34 (2002), 425–39.

Nawas, John. "The Birth of an Elite: *Mawālī* and Arab Ulama", *Israel Oriental Studies*, forthcoming.

________. "The Emergence of *Fiqh* as a Distinct Discipline and the Ethnic Identity of the *Fuqahā'* in Early and Classical Islam", in Hilary Kilpatrick, Stefan Leder and B. Martel-Thoumin, eds., *Proceedings of the 19th Congress (1998) of the Union Européenne des Arabisants et Islamisants (UEAI)* (Leuven: Peeters, forthcoming).

Talbi, Mohamed. "Law and Economy in Ifrīqiya (Tunisia) in the Third Islamic Century", in A.L. Udovitch, ed., *The Islamic Middle East 700–1900: Studies in Economic and Social History* (Princeton: Darwin Press, 1981), 209–49.

Tsafrir, N. "The Spread of the Ḥanafī School in the Western Regions of the 'Abbāsid Caliphate up to the end of the Third Century A.H." Ph.D. dissertation: Princeton University, 1993.

________. "The Beginnings of the Ḥanafī School in Iṣfahān", *Islamic Law and Society* 5 (1998), 1–21.

Weiss, Bernard, ed. *Studies in Islamic Legal Theory*. Leiden: E.J. Brill, 2002.

1

THE ARAB CONQUESTS AND THE FORMATION OF ISLAMIC SOCIETY

I.M. Lapidus

Preface

The Arab conquests were an epochal and cataclysmic event. Not only historians, but all peoples, of east and west, have been mystified by the sudden and mass migration and conquest by Arab nomadic peoples, and the defeat of refined and civilized societies by vigorous "barbarians." We are fascinated to see a new religion triumph over old faiths, corrupted empires be displaced by a new regime, and old civilizations die to serve the birth of a new. How are such sudden and extraordinary changes to be explained?

The facts are well known. Historians agree that a complete understanding of these events must include an account of Arabian history, the rise of Islam, the conquests, and the early history of Arab-Islamic civilization. Most historians emphasize one of several themes. Some stress the history and the institutions of pre-Islamic society so that we may better understand the subsequent contribution of Arab civilization to the development of the Middle East. Hence the emphasis is placed upon bedouin poetic and linguistic accomplishments, the structure of bedouin social life, the religions and monarchies of South Arabia, and Meccan commerce and religion. Other writers analyze the conjunction of social, political and religious conditions which make intelligible the rise of Islam. Still others deal with the mechanisms by which great tribal confederations are formed, how they were able to overwhelm the defenses of established empires, and why conquering peoples were assimilated into the polity and culture of the conquered peoples. Yet despite the impressive scholarship, the rise of Islam and the conquests still seem arbitrary developments in terms of Arabian and Middle Eastern history. Arabian history is portrayed as chaotic until the rise of Islam. In terms of the history of the Middle East, the Arab conquests are taken as an historic accident, a diversion from the true course of Middle Eastern developments.

I think that we can improve our perspective on these matters, and better comprehend the rise of Islam and the conquests, in their intrinsic relation to the development of Arabian society, and in their relation to the history of the conquests and the formation of a new civilization, by considering the conquests as an integral part of the relationship between Arabia and the Middle Eastern societies. For this we do not need new facts, but an interpretation of the historical process as a whole. This process was the joint and interrelated evolution of two types of societies--the empire type societies of the Middle East, Byzantine and Sasanian, and the "peripheral" society of Arabia. The genesis of the Arab conquests was profoundly influenced by the character of the environing civilization, just as the transformation of late Roman and Persian civilizations and the rise of Islamic civilization in the Middle East were influenced by the Arab conquests. The pre-conquest phase of this history involved the development within Arabian society of the very same types of institutions and forms of culture which were already established in the empire societies, a transformation which created the internal conditions for the rise of Islam and the Arab conquests. The post-conquest phase of this history entailed the integration of the conquering peoples and their home territories into a comprehensive new civilization. The conquest itself helped to complete the assimilation of the conquering peoples, begun in Arabia, into general Middle Eastern society, while the injection of new peoples and new values representing a variant but related form of Middle Eastern culture introduced an Arab and Islamic identity for Middle Eastern peoples.

This point of view turns our attention from the drama of the rise of Islam and the Arab conquests and brings to light the slow, lengthy, elaborate history by which Arabian and Middle Eastern empire societies were amalgamated. The epochal events associated with the rise of Islam and the Arab conquests are best understood, not as a purely Arabian development, nor as an imposition of an Arabian society upon the rest of the Middle East, but as an evolutionary process by which several Middle Eastern societies became more highly integrated and more highly developed.

Arabia and the Middle East

The key to this larger historical process lies in the long-term relationship between Arabia and the rest of Middle Eastern society. The two regions had developed in very different ways. In the empire Middle East the development of civilization was marked by several critical features. First was the development of an agricultural economy. Second was the emergence of complex forms of social organization superimposed on the small family or clientele groups which were the earliest forms of human society. The first complex societies in the Middle East were city societies, which were different from smaller groups in that they were characterized by non-familial forms of political leadership, social stratification, division of labor and new forms of cultural achievement including writing and monumental architecture. In ancient Mesopotamia, where the first cities took shape in the late fourth millenium B.C., the crucial development was the growing authority of priests and the increasing role of temple worship and temple structures in the life of agricultural communities. Temples absorbed numerous small clans into a new community. Priestly managers regulated the distribution of resources in the larger community, and, in the interests of the temple, favored the growth of specialized artisan, merchant, and farming activities outside the basic clan groups.

From the middle of the third millenium B.C. empires succeeded cities as the most extensive and complex form of social organization. Empires were regimes which dominated numerous smaller communities --families, tribes, cities, temples and regional states. They were commonly formed by conquerers who devised new means of military domination and administration to control their territories. Empires, however, must be understood not only as a type of political regime, but also as a form of society and culture. The formation of an empire had profound social consequences. Like the formation of the temple city, the formation of empires burst asunder the earlier forms of community. Empires detached individuals from the matrixes of clans and temples. To fight, to administer, to serve at court, to trade, to colonize distant lands, men were torn from their homes. Resources once committed to local communities were taxed or confiscated and redistributed in the interests of the state. Empires thus stimulated specialization of functions in society. Priests lost their administrative authority and became religious functionaries. Artisans and merchants were set free to work for the market. In turn, the increased scale of society, and the increased individualism implied by specialization and mobility, required new modes of cultural integration. Empires thus favored common languages, common laws, and common religions to forge bonds between ever more numerous and diverse individuals and communities over ever greater reaches of territory.

The empire type of society also fostered the development of new religious mentalities. In the ancient Middle East the archaic pantheon remained in force, but greater emphasis was placed upon the celestial gods and the supreme lord of the pantheon, for the gods of the wider heavens symbolized the larger and more impersonal order of the empire. At the same time, the breakdown of small communities allowed a sentiment of individuality to develop and to be expressed in the worship of personal gods with whom men stood in an intimate emotional relationship. The larger the empire, the greater the freedom of the individual; the wider the heavens, the more intimate the gods. Men assumed a personal relationship to the gods, and a personal responsibility for upholding the impersonal order of society and cosmos.

A late but crucial development in the religious mentality of the ancient Middle East was, of course, the birth of the monotheistic religions. Judaism, Zoroastrianism, Christianity, and later Islam represented a new conception of God, of man, and of human society. For these religions, the true reality was not within this world but transcended it utterly; man's destiny was not within the fabric of temple or empire but was, rather, his salvation beyond.

The new kind of religions not only represented a new mentality; they had profound social and political consequences. Archaic religion and early empire religions were cultic religions in the hands of specialists, closely identified with the political elite. The new religions, however, formed congregations, or churches, which assigned all believers an active religious role and united them as brothers in a common religious life regardless of other familial, tribal, communal, or political loyalties. In principle, the churches embraced mankind as a whole, though in fact they continued to represent the collective identity of particular peoples or regions. Thus, the formation of churches marked a differentiation of religious and political communities, of religious and political elites, and of secular and religious values.

By the seventh century, Middle Eastern empire societies, Roman and Sasanian, Christian and Zoroastrian, were characterized by agricultural and urban forms of economic production, citied societies, monotheistic religions and imperial regimes. Arabia was not part of these developments. For various reasons, primarily because of the prevailing climatic and ecological conditions, Arabia remained at a state of development which resembled the ancient rather than the evolved condition of the rest of the Middle East. In Arabia the primary communities--the bedouin clans --remained especially powerful, while urban, religous and royal institutions, though not absent, were relatively less developed. Whereas the empire world was predominantly agricultural, Arabia was primarily pastoral. While the empire world was citied, Arabia was the home of camps and oases. Whereas the empire peoples were committed to the monotheistic religions, Arabia was largely pagan. While the empire world was politically organized, Arabia was politically fragmented.

At the same time, Arabia was always in close contact with and strongly under the influence of the empire regions. There were no physical boundaries between Arabia and the Middle East proper. No rigid ethnic or demographic frontier isolated Arabia from the rest of the region; nor did great walls or political frontiers. Arabian peoples migrated slowly into the Middle East and themselves made up much of the population of the North Arabian desert and of Syria. Arabs in the fertile crescent region shared political forms, religious beliefs, economic connections, and physical space with the societies around them. Arabia was further connected to the rest of the region by itinerant preachers, who introduced monotheism into the largely pagan peninsula; by merchants who brought textiles, jewelry, and foodstuffs such as grain and wine into Arabia, and stimulated the taste for the good things of life; and by the political agents of the empire powers who intervened diplomatically and politically to extend their trading privileges, protect sympathetic religious populations, and advance their strategic interests. The Byzantines and the Sasanians disputed control of the Yemen, and both were active in creating spheres of influence in North Arabia. They also exported military technique to the Arabs. From both the Romans and the Persians the Arabs obtained new arms, and learned how to use mail coats of armor. They learned new tactics, and the importance of discipline. This seepage of military technique came through the Lakhmid and the Ghassanid states, sometimes through the enrollment of other Arabs as auxiliaries in the Roman or Persian armies, and sometimes through the unhappy experience of being repulsed by superior forces on the frontiers of the empires. This passing on of military ability was of great importance for the Arab conquests for it gradually equalized the quality of forces on either side of the frontier.

The civilization of the Middle Eastern empires was seeping into Arabia as happened everywhere where developed empires maintained frontiers with the politically and culturally less organized societies. Military expansion, trade, or missionary activities induced social change in still undeveloped societies. The need to mobilize the power and resources required to maintain political autonomy, or to carry on trade with empires, stimulated in less developed societies the same processes of stratification, specialization, and of community and identity formation by which the empires had themselves come into being. They generated in peripheral areas just those conditions which allowed for the eventual amalgamation of empire and outside areas into a single society.

The Basic Structures of Arabian Society

By the late sixth century, however, these inducements to evolutionary change had not gone so far as to absorb Arabia into the general civilization of the Middle East or to inspire in it the birth of a new civilization. The outbreak of the Arab movement and the subsequent mutual assimilation of Arabian and Middle Eastern empire societies seem to come suddenly in the early seventh century. How is this to be explained? The key to understanding this lies, I think, in a close study of the history within Arabian society of the relationship between the basic parochial small group bedouin society and the elements of urban, religious and royal institutions which represented the more evolved type of Middle Eastern society.

The nomadic pastoral clan was the most fundamental institution of Arabian society. It goes back at least to the beginning of camel domestication and the occupation of the Central Arabian desert in the thirteenth and twelfth centuries B.C. Bedouin peoples lived in tightly knit kinship groups, in patriarchal families formed of a father, his offspring and their families, living in a few tents. These families were further grouped into clans of about 100-300 tents which migrated together, owned their pasturage in common, and politically drew one line. Each clan was fundamentally an independent unit. All loyalties were absorbed by the group which acted as a collectivity to defend its individual members and to meet their responsibilities. If a member was harmed the clan would revenge him. If he did harm they would stand responsible with him for money, or indeed, for forfeiture of life. As a consequence of this <u>ʿaṣabiyya</u>, the bedouin clan regarded itself as a complete polity and recognized no authority outside of the group. The clans were led by a sheikh who was usually selected by the elders of the group from one of the aristocratic families, and always acted in accord with this council. He settled internal disputes according to the traditions of the group. His office was the embodiment of the clan tradition, and respect and willingness to follow his lead depended on the conviction of the tribesmen that the sheikh represented the true tradition, and that he epitomized the virtues of the clan. The sheikh had to be wealthy and generous to the needy and to his supporters, a man of tact and prudence, forebearing, resolute and practical, with the good judgment to avoid antagonizing the sensitive among his followers.

The mental universe of the bedouin was entirely defined by the clan. Poetry expressed his fundamental devotion to the prestige and security of the group; without the clan, the individual bedouin had no status, no place in the world, no life of his own. As Chelhod has pointed out, there is no way to express individuality or personality in the language of the bedouin. The term <u>wajh</u>, face, which applied to the chief, was a concept designating the <u>persona</u> of the group, rather than the individuality of the sheikh.

In certain conditions, these primary communities could be integrated into more inclusive, often stratified, bodies. At the points of contact between the fertile parts of Arabia and the desert, at oases, in Yemen, and in the northern margins where the Arabian desert touches the fertile crescent, the relationships between bedouin and sedentary peoples involved regular cooperation for the exchange of agricultural for pastoral products and for the organization of the caravan trade. Cooperation could lead to trade agreements and treaties among autonomous participants, and it could also lead to the formation of political confederations. Such confederations were formed by the domination of one tribe over others or through the recognition of an aristocratic family as leader of a confederation of clans. Though such groups did not show any of the ceremonial trappings or conceptions of political authority transcending the tribal or familial context which we usually associate with the development of full-fledged monarchies, their integrative functions were still important.

The integration of different groups could also occur on a religious basis. The formation of a ḥaram, a common sanctuary, allowed for worship of the same gods, economic exchange, sociable contact and political bargaining.

Only in the peripheral zones did monarchs and kingdoms, at times, prevail. In South Arabia, royal authority was first established about 1000 B.C. and lasted until Muslim times. In Yemen, the political elite was drawn from aristocratic tribes and controlled landed estates. Temples also had extensive holdings, while the common people were organized into clans which were obliged to provide agricultural and military services to the elites. Tributary and vassal tribes extended the power of the Yemeni kingdoms well into the interior of Arabia. In the north, kingdoms were less fully institutionalized. For example, the ancient Nabatean kingdom was ruled by a king who claimed a divinely given authority and had some centralized administration but really depended on the support of a coalition of clan and tribal chiefs.

Historical Tension and Change

The degree to which the individual bedouin clan was the predominant historical actor and the degree to which confederated or large scale societies were dominant was historically variable. The main factor regulating this balance was the degree to which sedentarized forms of economy and society imposed upon or were overwhelmed by pastoral forms. The history of Arabia was governed by the tension between the settled areas and the pastoral areas. From about 1000 B.C. until about A.D. 300 stable political organizations in the settled areas--Yemen, the Ḥijāz and on the northern periphery--successfully organized the interior of the peninsula and kept bedouin life subordinate to the agricultural and commercial economies of the settled kingdoms.

Settlement in Yemen dates back to the tenth century B.C. to the kingdoms of Saba', Ma'īn, Qitbān and Ḥaḍramawt, which were agricultural and trading societies active in the international spice and incense trade along the coasts of Arabia. By the fifth century B.C., Yemen was organized into kingdoms which had monarchical institutions, a stratified landed elite, a religious pantheon and organized temple worship of the gods, and encompassed agriculture, trading, and pastoral peoples. By 115 B.C., the Himyarites united the south. By A.D. 300 the union of southern kingdoms was still in force.

In the North Arabian desert, the first evidence of small kingdoms or confederations dates to the ninth and eighth centuries B.C. In the north, the influence of Middle Eastern empires and religions was important from earliest times. From the middle of the eighth to the middle of the seventh century B.C., Assyrian kings attempted to subdue the Arabs, secure the caravan routes, and extract tribute from the desert peoples, but permanent order was beyond their reach. By the early sixth century B.C., the Nabateans were in the course of forming a kingdom. Nabatean monarchical institutions and religious pantheon were derived from Syrian examples. By 587 B.C., they had replaced earlier peoples in North Arabia; by the end of the fourth century B.C., Petra was founded; and by the second century B.C. the Nabatean kingdom was fully established. By 85 B.C., the new kingdom had control of much of Jordan and Syria. Its business was the caravan trade with Yemen in the south and Egypt and Damascus and the coastal cities of Palestine. The kingdom lasted until A.D. 106 when it was destroyed by the Romans. Palmyra succeeded Petra, and extended monarchical control over the deserts and surrounding bordering areas. Urbanized capitals, elaborate temples, wide commercial networks, and strong Hellenistic culture marked Palmyran supremacy.

These kingdoms, northern and southern, maintained economic and political order in the peninsula as a whole, integrating the bedouins of the desert interiors into the political and cultural frameworks of the border states. The nomads functioned in peninsula-wide trade, linked settled places, and were absorbed in political coalitions sponsored by the northern and southern powers.

The phase of the border kingdoms did not last. The opening of sea routes for international trade in the first century B.C. proved to be a financial and political disaster for Yemen. Political power in the south weakened with the failure of overland routes; bedouin troops interfered in internal conflicts in South Arabia, pushed in against agricultural areas, and cut off Yemeni influence in the Ḥijāz and in central Arabia. In A.D. 328, Imru' al-Qays b. ʿAmr, king of the Arabs, took control of Najrān. In the north, Palmyra was destroyed in A.D. 271, the victim, as were the Nabateans, of Roman efforts to incorporate North Arabia directly into the empire. By the end of the third century, the grip of the old order was shattered.

However, the effort to re-establish the border kingdoms and to extend peripheral power throughout Arabia resumed. The period from early fourth century to the end of the sixth century represents a phase of efforts to re-establish the dominance of border kingdoms in the peninsula. From the beginning of the fourth century, the old kingdoms were being replaced by "middle period kingdoms" which tried to restore or to keep order in the desert and to protect trade and oasis cultivation. In Yemen, the Himyarite kingdom was restored, but not with effective powers of old. The lessened authority of kings, the increased power of "feudal" families and independent tribes, the decline of the economy, and the breakdown of the old cultural identity of the pagan archaic society under Jewish and Christian competition made it impossible fully to restore the old order. Still, in the fifth century, Yemeni influence extended over the bedouins of the Ḥijāz and central Arabia, mediated by the tribal confederation of Kinda. Kinda came into being in the fifth century and lasted about one hundred years. The authority of the Kinda family, however, was entirely personal and very limited. The confederation blossomed so long as the heirs to the chieftainship of Kinda were able men whom the bedouins of other tribes would respect, and the confederation managed to keep together on this uncertain basis for about four generations. No permanent state could be established without institutions of a more sophisticated and durable kind.

In the same period, the Yemen was severely disrupted by internal religious struggles and foreign invasion. In 512, Abyssinians invaded the country to restore Christian influence after the rise to power of a Jewish ruler, Dhū Nuwās. In 525 they succeeded in capturing control of the Yemen; in 535 they attacked central Arabia and in 570 penetrated the Ḥijāz. The South Arabian economy crumbled, and political unity was completely lost. In 572 the Sasanians took control of Yemen from the Abyssinians.

Similar efforts were made under Roman and Persian auspices to re-establish order on the northern borders of the Arabian desert. After the destruction of the kingdoms of Petra and Palmyra, Romans assimilated the old kingdoms as provinces of the empire and attempted to defend these provinces by recruiting Arab confederates to guard against other Arabs and against the Sasanians. The Banū Sāliḥ served as Roman auxiliaries throughout the fifth century and were replaced at the end of the century by the Ghassanids. The Ghassanids were an Arab Christian-Monophysite people. Their duty was to prevent the penetration of the bedouins from the desert into Syria and Palestine, to police and keep order on the frontiers between the Roman Empire and the desert, and to defend the Empire against the Persians and their clients. The Sasanian Empire also sustained a buffer state--the Kingdom of Lakhm--from A.D. 328 to A.D. 604. Along the border between Iraq and the desert the tribes of the area were organized into a new confederation under the leadership of the house of Lakhm whose capital was at Ḥīra, on the lower reaches of the Euphrates. Most of these peoples were Arameans and Nestorian Christians.

However, the new competitors were not so powerful as their predecessors. Kinda and Ghassan represented tribal confederations rather than kingdoms. While the Lakhmids at Ḥīra had an urban capital, a developed monarchy, differentiated from its tribal base of support, and were strongly supported by the Sasanians, they were severely hampered by Sasanian controls and Arab competition. In the north, by the end of the century, the Romans and the Persians both removed their vassals from power and attempted to absorb North Arabia into their respective empires. Ghassan was deprived of Roman backing in 584 and the Lakhmids were replaced by Sasanian governors in 602. The middle period confederations were destroyed by outside powers who could not replace even their ephemeral contributions to political and economic order.

In the sixth century, only Mecca stood out against the trend to political and social fragmentation. Mecca was a religious sanctuary, founded to serve the worship of the gods. From the fifth century, if not earlier, the shrine of Mecca, the Kaʿba, attracted pilgrims from all over Arabia. Mecca became the repository of the various idols and tribal gods of the peninsula, and the locus of an annual pilgrimage. The pilgrimage was also a period of truce which served not only for religious worship, but also for the arbitration of disputes, settlements of claims and debts, and of course, for trade. The Meccan fairs gave the Arabian tribes what sense they had of a common identity, and gave Mecca a kind of moral primacy in much of western and central Arabia.

These fairs were probably the origin of Mecca's commercial interests. The people called the Quraysh, who had taken control of Mecca in the fifth century, became a skilled retailing population, and in the sixth century international developments gave them a place in the spice trade as well. In the sixth century, difficulties with other routes diverted a good deal of traffic to the overland Arabian route. Byzantine sea power in the Red Sea and the Indian Ocean was on the decline. Piracy was endemic in the Red Sea. At the same time, the route from the Persian Gulf up the Tigris-Eurphrates rivers was harrassed by Sasanian exploitation, and was frequently disrupted by Lakhmid, Ghassanid, and Persian-Roman wars. By the middle of the sixth century, Mecca had become, as the heir to Petra and Palmyra, one of the important caravan cities of the Middle East. The Meccans carried from Yemen to Syria goods coming from Africa or the Far East--spices, aromatics, leather, drugs, cloth, and slaves--and imported into Arabia money, weapons, cereals and wine. The trade required treaties with Byzantine officials, and with the bedouins, to assure safe passage of the caravans, protection of water and pasture rights, and guides and scouts. Such arrangements eventually gave Mecca a sphere of political as well as commercial influence among the nomads and created a rough confederation of client tribes. With the decline of Abyssinia, Ghassan and Lakhm, a loose Meccan diplomatic hegemony in association with Tamim tribes was established. Mecca became crucial as the center of latter day efforts to maintain large scale economic and political organization in Arabia. Combining elements of tribal confederation with caravan city business organization and religious communal loyalties, Mecca attempted to maintain commercial and political order in the west and north of Arabia.

In most of Arabia, however, the failure of the border powers to restore effective control over the center of the peninsula resulted in progressive, but not uninterrupted, bedouinization. The discipline imposed by the settled peoples upon the desert weakened. Bedouin communities were set free of the political and commercial controls once exerted by the border Kingdoms. As early as the third century, bedouin groups made inroads upon the settled areas of South Arabia. By the fourth and fifth centuries and continuing into the sixth, large scale migrations of bedouin peoples in the North Arabian desert and to the margins of the fertile crescent were under way.

Within Arabia, violent conflict between clans and tribes became more frequent. Progressively, pastoral interests overcame agricultural interests. Bedouin migrations turned marginal regions in Yemen and on the borders of Iraq and Syria back to pasturage. The trade routes were increasingly harrassed by marauders, and the sedentary population drifted into pastoral activities as it became too difficult to sustain agricultural life and as commercial opportunities were lost. The "bedouinization of Arabia," of course, did not happen all at once. It was a gradual and cumulative process, shifting the ever-delicate balance between organized polities and clan society in favor of the latter. The predominant trend of the past centuries had been toward strengthening the bedouin clan, at the expense of economic prosperity and political security. Yet the tension between the interests of small groups and Mecca's political and religious confederacies remained high. The contrary trends would contribute explosively to the outbreak of the Arab conquests.

Bedouin Religion, Meccan Religion and Monotheism

The confrontation between strengthened small communities and trading and religious confederacy was reflected in the cultural as well as the political life of Arabia in the late sixth century. The religious culture of Arabia reflected the different levels of social organization of the bedouin tribe, the Meccan confederacy and the influence of the imperial powers. Just as the political realm was beset by the tension among different types of political and economic organization, cultural life was beset by incompatible visions of human life, human society, and conflicting concepts of the cosmos and the gods.

The poetic and religious culture of the clans remained a constant and fundamental element in bedouin life. By and large, the Arabian bedouin was a pagan, a polytheist, and an animist who believed that all natural objects and events were living spirits who could either be helpful or harmful to man. The universe of the Arabs was peopled with jinn--demons who had to be propitiated or controlled and defeated by the use of magic. By magical practices, the bedouin might determine his fate or coerce these forces, but he had no sympathetic relation with them. They were another tribe, not his own, though they invested his existence. The bedouins were also ancestor worshippers, worshippers of moon and star gods, and also of gods in the form of stones or trees placed in protective santuaries, or ḥarams. Otherwise the religiosity of the bedouin did not extend to the formation of a cult, nor to the cultivation of emotionally based spiritual capacities. Nor was his religion a philosophic or religious vision of the universe. Still, his religious beliefs were important in the bedouin's life. They expressed his sense of the sacred vested mysteriously in the plethora of forces which dominated the natural world and the being of man.

The religions of the politically more complex confederations and kingdoms were also pagan and polytheistic, but expressed a more differentiated concept of the divine, the natural and the human world. The tribal ḥarams or the temples of archaic kingdoms were devoted to regularized cultic worship. The Meccan Kaʿba, for example, the center of a pilgrimage, was the sanctuary of numerous gods arranged in a hierarchy. These gods were no longer simply identified with nature; they were considered to be distinct persons separate from the natural forces which, as willful beings, they controlled. Such gods had to be propitiated by sacrifices; one could communicate with them as persons, and the shrines in Mecca had a regular priesthood to assure their proper worship.

In an environment of shared sanctuaries, new conceptions of collective identity emerged. The annual trade and religious fairs at Mecca and other places of pilgrimage, which brought the numerous families and tribes of the peninsula together, focused the worship of tribal peoples upon common cults, allowed them to observe one another's mores, and standardized the language and customs by which they dealt with each other. Awareness of common religious beliefs and that the tradition of each clan was similar to the life ways of others, recognition of aristocratic tribes and families, agreed institutions regulating pasturage, warfare, and commerce, alliance and arbitration procedures, a poetic koine and poetic forms used by reciters throughout Arabia--marked the development of a collective identity transcending the individual clan. Von Grunebaum has argued that cultural integration in Arabia had proceeded so far as to create a single Arabian people, and Chelhod in Sociologie de l'Islam has argued the existence of an Arabian national culture, indeed an Arabian nation without a political state, before the time of Muḥammad.

In another sense there was a profound similarity

between the cultic confederation of Mecca and the fragmented life of the bedouin clans. The bedouin mentality and Meccan polytheism presented the same view of the person, society, and the universe. This view afforded no coherent conception of the human being as an entity. In ancient Arabic there is no single word corresponding to the soul. Qalb, rūḥ, nafs, wajh were the several terms in use; there was no conception of a self-conscious integrated personality. Also the plurality of the gods reflected and symbolized a fragmented view of the nature of society and of the forces which governed the cosmos. In the pagan view the self was without a center, society without wholeness, and the universe barren of overall meaning.

The monotheistic religions stood for something other. They were introduced into Arabia by foreign influences. Jewish and Christian settlements in Arabia, travelling preachers and merchants, the political pressure of the Byzantine empire and Abyssinia insinuated new ideas into the peninsula. By the sixth century, monotheism already had a certain vogue. Many non-believers understood the monotheistic religions; others, called ḥanīf in the Qur'ān, were believers in one God but not adherents of any particular faith. Others, in small oasis populations, had adopted Judaism or Christianity. Yemen and the border regions in the north, Lakhm and Ghassan, were officially Christian. Alongside of primary groups and pagan societies, Christianized societies reflecting larger Middle Eastern developments had formed. Their adherents were in the minority, and yet they were profoundly influential and, to many people, deeply appealing, both by the force of their teaching and by force of representing what was felt to be a more powerful, more sophisticated, and more profound civilization. The new religions taught that there was a single God who created the moral and spiritual order of the world; a God who made men individually responsible for their actions and faith; a God who made all men brethren, whatever their race or clan, and who made their salvation possible. Thus, they differed profoundly from the pagan in their sense of the unity of the universe and the meaningfulness of personalized experience. Whereas the one could only see a fragmented world composed of numerous, disorderly and arbitrary powers, the other saw a universe as a totality grounded in, and created and governed by a single being who was the source of both the material and spiritual order of the cosmos. Whereas the pagan world envisaged a society in which people were divided by clan and locality, each with its own community and its own gods, the monotheistic religions imagined a society in which common faith made men brothers in the quest for salvation. Whereas in the pagan view the human being was a concatenation of diverse forces without any moral or physical center a product of the fates, in the view of the monotheistic religions he was a moral, purposive creature whose ultimate object was redemption. In the view of the high religions, God, the universe, man, and society were part of a single and meaningful whole.

The monotheistic religions offered not only a new concept of the nature of man, God and the universe but also suggested new forms of communal and social organization. The possibilities were barely manifest, but in exceptional cases, such as the Christian community of Najrān, a new type of political organization in conjunction with new religious identifications was in evidence. Najrān was governed by three leading officials: a sayyid who acted as military commander and handled foreign relations; an ʿaqīb who dealt with internal affairs; and the bishop in charge of the church and the monastic communities. In Najrān, religion implied not only a different religious, but also a different political order, with recognition of the distinction between religious and secular authorities and communities. Similarly, Arabic speaking Nestorians of Ḥīra formed a congregation which coupled religious with tribal identity. Such communities were an image of developments which the higher religions inspired in Middle Eastern society at large and of the potentialities for further evolution within Arabian society itself.

Mecca was the center of diverse cultural tensions much as it was the focus of diverse political and social arrangements. Like the rest of Arabia, Mecca had its elements of conservative clan society, but it was also the focus of bedouin pilgrimage and of foreign religious influences. Mecca was therefore the most complex and heterogeneous place in Arabia. Here society had grown beyond the limitations of the clan and tribe and afforded some complexity of political and economic ties outside the confines of clan relationships. Mecca had a council of clans called a mala', which held a moral authority though it had no right to coerce any of the members or to enforce any council decisions without the co-operation of each individual clan. Mecca was also one of the few places to have a floating non-tribal population of individual exiles, refugees, outlaws, foreign merchants, and settlers. The very presence of different peoples, of different clans, of people who belonged to none of the clans, of foreigners, of people with diverse religious convictions, of people with differing views of life's purposes and values, moved Meccans away from the old tribal religions and moral conceptions. New conceptions of personal worth and social status, new social relationships were fostered by the development of a more complex society. On the positive side, the imperatives of commercial activity, and Arabian-wide contacts and identifications, set individual personalities free from the traditions of their clans, set free self-conscious, critical spirits, capable of experimenting with new values, who might conceive a universal God and ethical obligations. On the negative side, society suffered from economic competition, social conflict and moral confusion. Commercial activities brought social stratification on the basis of wealth, and morally unassimilable discrepancies between individual ambitions and the imperatives of clan loyalty. The Qur'ān condemned the displacement of tribal virtues by the ambition, greed, arrogance, and hedonism of the new rich.

Thus, as compared with the Middle East which had centuries earlier reached an equilibrium of cultural, religious and political institutions, Arabia was a transitional society. Elements of a regressive economy, strong parochial community life, and pagan religious mentality were balanced by tendencies toward political, cultural and religious unification and by the development of new forms of religious and political order. Widening mental horizons were coupled with resistance to new forms of sociocultural organization. Arabia was in ferment. A society in the midst of constructive political experiments was threatened by anarchy. Strong clan and tribal powers threatened to overwhelm the fragile forces of agricultural stability, commercial activity and political cohesion. Arabia was a society touched by imperial influences but without a central government, marked by the monotheistic religions but without embracing churches, transparent to the radiation of Middle Eastern ideas but not permeated by them. Arabia had yet to find its place in the Middle Eastern world.

The Conquests and the Assimilation of Arab Peoples into Empire Society

From this vantage, we can interpret the meaning of

the Arab conquests and their place in the evolution of Arabian society. They no longer appear as a sudden, unexpected, or accidental development, but as one which rose directly out of the conflict of different forms of religious, social and political organization in Arabia. In previous centuries the influence of the Middle East upon Arabia created conditions favorable to the development of elements of large-scale socio-political organization and for the development of monotheistic religious life in Arabia. Arabian society had reached a stage of development which brought intense political, social and moral conflict among alternative political and religious possibilities. With conflict came the potentiality for revolutionary change, a potentiality realized through the inspiration and leadership of the Prophet Muḥammad. Through the revelations of the Qur'ān, and his career as moral exemplar and politician, Muḥammad found the solution in principle to the conflicts within Arabian society. He could begin to integrate the otherwise anarchic small clans into a larger confederacy on the basis of religious loyalty, build a state structure through which political and economic order might eventually be achieved, and resolve the conflict of bedouin familial and Meccan commercial values in a new religious point of view. Muḥammad fused tribal society, the monotheistic religious mentality, with religious community, trading confederacy and political organization to create a new society built upon a "church"-like religious community and incipient imperial organization. Out of the manifold elements of the old order Muḥammad helped to generate a new dispensation for Arabia which gave it an institutional and cultural structure, parallel to, and on a par with, that of the larger Middle East. Under the aegis of Muḥammad, Arabia became a Middle Eastern type society in which parochial and tribal groups were integrated into a monotheistic community.

The Arab conquests were the result of the formation of the new community. They began as a result of the Muslim effort to build an Arabian-wide political and religious regime, and to impose its vision of the human and social order on Arabia. There is a good deal of uncertainty about how early and how clearly this objective was formulated. Muḥammad himself attempted to extend his religious and political influence throughout the Ḥijāz; Watt argues that his ambition extended to the Christian tribes on the borders of Syria; Shoufani in a recent book on the Riddah argues that from the time of the capitulation of Mecca, Muḥammad aspired to an Arabian and Syrian empire. In any case, within a year after Muḥammad's death, the leaders of the new community had decided to extend its boundaries beyond the tribes who had already submitted to Muḥammad's authority and to incorporate the whole of Arabia under the rule of Medina and Mecca. Whether the attacks on Syria and Iraq were decided in advance or whether they were a natural outgrowth of the fighting in Arabia--the result of splinter movements of tribes seeking to compensate themselves elsewhere for losses in Arabia --whether planned, or whether determined by events and responses to events, the construction of a new commercial, religious, and then political confederation in the Ḥijāz in disequilibrated and unsettled times, and in a vacuum of established powers, led to the conquest of much of the Middle East. The conquests began in reconnaissance and booty raids, but the early victories opened the way for a great flood of peoples to enter the fertile crescent, riding on the wave of initial successes. With the defeat of the Byzantine and the Sasanian Empires, a frontier between populations broke down; Arabian people moved into the lands of the Middle East.

Thus the conquests rose out of the process of religious and political consolidation in Arabia. In turn they set the stage for two crucial, interconnected developments. One was the completion of the historic process of transforming Arabian society and assimilating it into the larger society of the Middle East; the other was the reciprocal integration of Middle Eastern peoples into a new political and religious identity which marks the origin of a new Middle Eastern civilization in the wake of the nomadic conquests.

The first part of this double process--the integration of Arabian peoples into the general Middle Eastern society--was a function of the conquests and the migration of masses of Arabians into the fertile crescent and other parts of the empire Middle East. The migrations created two new arenas for the assimilation of Arabian peoples into the citied, religious and imperial institutions of the empire societies. In the courts of the Arab caliphs, Arabian and Middle Eastern political institutions and ideologies would be integrated, the Islamic religion bolstered and its repertoire of expression expanded by the assimilation of previous religious attainments of the Middle East, and a new cultural style, literary, artistic and scientific, elaborated on the basis of Middle Eastern precedents. The process by which a distinctive

Islamic cultural style, yet one which was based upon the past achievements of Middle Eastern civilizations, took shape has been frequently described and does not require further attention here. But there is another aspect of the integration of Arabian people into Middle Eastern society and culture which is less fully appreciated. In the great centers of Arab settlement, especially such garrison towns as Baṣra, Kūfa, and Fusṭāṭ, bedouin peoples were finally integrated into the general Middle Eastern society. They were citified, truly instructed in monotheistic religion and subjected to imperial regimes. In the villages and towns which the Arabs settled, the institutions of a new mass society were forged. In these settlements the pressures generated by sedentarization and urbanization, by the teachings of Islam, and by contact with other Middle Eastern peoples weakened the old tribal society, fostered new group and communal structures, intensified the stratification of society and the division of labor, and brought about the Islamic cultural developments which together amounted to a new stage in the history of Arab society.

Baṣra is the best known example of these developments. In Baṣra the traditional structure of the bedouin clan was disrupted. The exigencies of settlement and the requirements of military and fiscal administration led to the organization of the Arab settlers into new groups, which were clans and tribes in name only. To make uniform regiments and pay units, big clans were subdivided and smaller ones combined. The composition of these military units was also changeable. Newcomers had to be integrated into older units; with the settlement of Marw in 681, the remaining groups had to be reorganized. Clan solidarity was disrupted; new groups were created; only very small units of the older sort remained viable.

Another source of pressure on bedouin society was the breakdown of the barriers between the Arab and non-Arab populations of Iraq. Baṣra was flooded with non-Arabs. As the Arabs made use of defeated armies to recruit manpower for further advances, Iranian regiments were enlisted en masse. Arab governors brought back troops from the east to serve as police and bodyguards. Mercenaries came to the towns looking for work and wanting to throw in their lot with the conquerors. So did scribes, tax-collectors, clerks, estate managers, and even village chiefs and landowners. In addition, merchants in long distance trade and menial workers (including bath attendants, weavers, and spinners) also came to Baṣra; finally, itinerant construction and naval workers, fugitive peasants, migrant laborers, and slaves flooded the city. This non-Arab population was extremely diverse. Aside from Indians, Malays, Gypsies, Negroes, Turks, who came in small numbers from remote areas, the non-Arab population was mainly Iranian and Aramean, Nestorian Christian, with some Jews. Many kept their religions, but others converted to Islam. Some were taken into Arab clans as mawālī, others were not.

The absorption of this migrant population had important repercussions on the clans. As they absorbed mawālī, clans became less and less kinship groups and more and more political and economic groups built around a kinship core. In some cases, the mawālī even began to outnumber the Arabs. Not only was kinship weakened, but class distinctions came to be introduced. The mawālī themselves constituted an inferior class; furthermore, they affected the stratification of Arab clans. The gap between aristocratic and other clans widened as the influx of mawālī changed the relative power of the clans. For example, one tribe, the Tamīm, acquired former Persian cavalry units as its clients, while another, the Ḥanẓala, had slave laborers and weavers as its clients.

Within clans, the emergence of class distinctions was even more profound. We can see a growing differentiation on a class basis between the sheikh and the rest of the tribesmen. The sheikhs had always had higher status within the group, but in the city their administrative and military functions and other opportunities to prosper widened the gulf between the chiefs and their followers. Tribal chiefs became landowners, sometimes of lands granted to them by the caliphate, and formed a new aristocracy, taxed at favorable rates, whose interests diverged from the general interest of the city Arabs in a uniform revenue administration and in a steady supply of income for stipends. Lists of the residences or palaces of notables and tribal leaders, apart from the dwellings or quarters of their clans, and lists of agricultural estates owned privately by the chiefs and not as part of the collective pasture reserves of the clan, suggest that the notables were living apart and enjoying wealth, privileges, and a style of life not consistent with the ancient bedouin mores. Sedentarization broke up the social unity of the tribes. Class distinctions emerged in what once had been cohesive and integrated groups. Tribal society was breaking down in favor of a society stratified on the basis of class and power.

Under pressures of urbanization and contact with settled peoples, Arab society was also evolving into a more specialized, urbanized occupational structure. In Başra the Arabs had created a camp town, but settlement soon made it an important manufacturing and trading center. New international routes connected Başra with Iran and India. Başra was also a nodal point for trade with the Ḥijāz and Yemen. The city became a center for the importation and exportation of oriental luxuries, weapons, and money; also a city of regional importance in manufacturing, especially of cloth goods, and in banking, as a center for money changing. With the retirement of Arab townspeople from active military duty at the end of the seventh century, the working and commercial population must have been strengthened. Similarly, the new religion of Islam offered opportunities for social mobility through what we may call careers in religion--teaching, scholarship, and legal administration. While Arab clans remained the crucial unit of society, Islam, urbanization and interaction with non-Arab peoples converted a clan-based society into a more highly differentiated urban type of society.

These tendencies point to a post-conquest evolution of Arab society which repeated the process of social change by which previous Middle Eastern societies--stratified, specialized societies, culturally identified by allegiance to a monotheistic religion--had been established. The first century of Islam brought about just those changes which mark the emergence of an empire type society. In this period we see the formation of Arab-Islamic political institutions, the progressive differentiation of political and religious life, the birth of a new religious culture, and the spawning of a stratified, occupationally specialized mass society in an urban setting.

One further aspect of this evolution should be mentioned, though we cannot explore it--that is the reciprocal influence of Arab peoples upon the Middle East as a whole. The formation of an "Arab-empire type society" did not occur within Arabia itself, in isolation from the rest of the Middle East, but within the former empire provinces in conjunction with the reciprocal assimilation of Middle Eastern peoples into a shared Arabic and Islamic culture. The overall effect of the historic transformation of Arabian peoples under the influence of Middle Eastern society was not to generate a new and parallel civilization, but to merge the Arabian and Middle Eastern peoples into a single new civilization. Just as Arabian peoples were assimilated into the urbanized world of the Middle East, they in turn absorbed Middle Eastern peoples into the cultural identity of Islam and the political affiliation of the caliphate. In the formation of a new civilization the Arabs were absorbed into the economic and social structures of the Middle Eastern empire societies while lending to those societies a new cultural and political identity. From this point of view, the Arab conquests were not a "barbarian" invasion but a crucial moment in the process of interaction between peoples by which an "outside" people acquired the institutional and cultural forms--not the particular style--of empire peoples, and in the course of doing so forged, in conjunction with empire peoples, a new form of civilization.

Summary and Conclusion

What is the significance of the Arab conquests? What do they tell us about the relationship between outside and empire peoples? My argument has been that the case of Arabia and the Middle East is one in which outside peoples were in the process of an historic evolution which paralleled and recapitulated the historical sequences by which the empire civilizations themselves had come into being. In the course of this transformation, the influence of empire peoples upon outside peoples was a crucial factor. In Arabian history this influence manifested itself in the development of archaic political, commercial, and religious institutions and later in the diffusion of the higher religions through the peninsula. In Arabian history, however, the process of induced social change was never completed, but led rather to an historical crisis, the crisis of the sixth century in which the several unintegrated levels of Arabian society--bedouin groups, archaic religious and commercial communities, and monotheistic religious culture--were fused into a new and into the first Arabian-wide society. This new society conquered the empires and thereby moved the terrain of its own internal evolution into more intimate contact with the empire peoples. In the new Arab settlements, the process of social change, induced by Islamic religious identifications, and by contact with empire peoples, led to the integration of tribes into larger communities, the specialization and stratification of society, and the differentiation of religious and political institutions so that Arabian society at last acquired all of the institutional features of empire civilization. In the course of these developments a reciprocal Arab influence upon empire peoples led to changes which served to fuse Arabian and empire peoples into a single civilization.

At the same time, it is worth noting that no evolutionary development is ever complete. Each stage bears with it the marks of past levels of organization. In Arab-Islamic society, the power of the family and the clan remained potent both as a social institution and a cultural ideal. Other features of archaic society and culture remain embedded in the new order. The later history of Islamic societies, like the history of Arabia, may also be described in terms of the imminent tensions between successive levels of institutional and cultural development. In the maturation of a society, as in the growth of a person, the past is never lost, but lives on as an active force embedded in the present.

Bibliography

Adams, R.M., The Evolution of Urban Society (Chicago: 1966)

al-ʿAlī, Ṣāliḥ, al-Tanẓīmāt al-ijtimāʿiyya wa'l-iqtiṣādiyya fī'l Baṣra (Baghdad: 1965)

Altheim, F. and Stiehl, R., Die Araber in der alte Welt (Berlin: 1964-8)

Arberry, A.J., The Koran Interpreted (London: 1955)

al-Balādhurī, Futūḥ al-Buldān (Leiden: 1866), trans. P.K. Hitti and E.C. Murgotten, The Origins of the Islamic State (New York: 1916-1924)

Beeston, A.F.L., "Kingship in Ancient South Arabia," JESHO 15 (1972): 256-268

Bell, Richard, The Origin of Islam in its Christian Environment (London: 1926)

Bellah, R., "Religious Evolution," American Sociological Review 29 (1964): 358-374

Bousquet, G.H., "Observations sur la nature et les causes de la conquête arabe," Studia Islamica 6 (1956): 37-52
Caskel, W., Die Bedeutung der Beduinen in der Geschichte der Araber (Cologne: 1953)
——"The Bedouinization of Arabia," American Anthropologist, Memoirs 76 (1954): 36-46
Chelhod, J., Introduction à la Sociologie de l'Islam (Paris: 1958)
——Le Sacrifice chez les Arabes (Paris: 1955)
——Les Structures du Sacré chez les Arabes (Paris: 1964)
Dussaud, René, Les arabes en Syrie avant l'Islam (Paris: 1907)
Eikelman, Dale, "Musaylima," JESHO 10 (1967): 17-52
Eisenstadt, S.N., The Political Systems of Empires (New York: 1969)
Encyclopedia of Islam, new ed. articles: al-ʿArab, Badw, Djazīrat al-ʿArab
Fahd, T., La Divination arabe (Leiden: 1966)
——Le Panthéon de l'Arabie Centrale à la veille de l'Hégire (Paris: 1968)
Faris, N.A., The Arab Heritage (Princeton: 1944)
Gabrieli, F., ed. L'Antica Società Beduina (Rome: 1959)
Goldziher, Ignaz, Muhammedanische Studien, trans. S.M. Stern, Muslim Studies, vol. 1 (London: 1967)
von Grunebaum, G., "The Nature of Arab Unity before Islam," Arabica 10 (1963): 4-23
Kamerer, A., Pétra et la Nabatène (Paris: 1929)
Kawar, Irfan, "The Arabs in the Peace Treaty of A.D. 561," Arabica 3 (1956): 181-213
Kister, M.J., "Al-Ḥīra: some notes on its relations with Arabic," Arabica 11 (1968): 143-169
——"Mecca and Tamim," JESHO 8 (1965): 113-163
——"Some Reports Concerning Mecca from Jāhiliyya to Islam," JESHO 15 (1972): 61-93
Lammens, Henri, La Mecque à la veille de l'hégire (Beirut: 1924)
——L'Arabie occidentale avant l'hégire (Beirut: 1928)
——Le berceau de l'Islam (Rome: 1914)
Lattimore, Owen, Inner Asian Frontiers of China (New York: 1940)
Levi Della Vida, G., "Pre-Islamic Arabia," in Faris, N.A. (ed.), The Arab Heritage (Princeton: 1944), pp. 24-57
Massignon, L., "Explication du plan de Basra," Westostliche Abhandlungen R. Tschudi, 1954, pp. 157-174
——"Explication du plan de Kufa," Mélanges Maspéro 3 (1940): 337-360
Montagne, R., La Civilisation du Désert (Paris: 1947)

Nöldeke, T., Die ghassânischen Fürsten aus dem Hause Gafna (Berlin: 1887)
Obermann, J., "Islamic Origins: A Study in Background and Foundation," in N.A. Faris (ed.), The Arab Heritage (Princeton: 1944), pp. 58-120
Olinder, Gunnar, The Kings of Kinda of the Family of Ākil al-Murār (Lund: 1927)
Pellat, C., Le milieu Baṣrien et la formation de Ǧāḥiẓ (Paris: 1953)
Pigulevskaya, N., "Les Rapports Sociaux a Nedjrān," JESHO 4 (1961): 1-14
Rodinson, Maxime, "L'Arabie avant l'Islam," Encyclopédie de la Pléiade (Paris: L'Histoire Universelle, 1957)
——"The Life of Muhammad and the Sociological Problem of the Beginning of Islam," Diogenes 20 (1957): 28-51
Rothstein, Gustav, Die Dynastie der Laḥmiden in al-Ḥīra (Berlin: 1899)
Ryckmans, G., "Les religions préislamiques," L'Histoire générale des religions (Paris: 1960)
Ryckmans, J., L'Institution monarchique en Arabie méridionale avant l'Islam (Louvain: 1951)
Shahid, Irfan, "Pre-Islamic Arabia," Cambridge History of Islam, vol. 1 (Cambridge: 1970), pp. 3-29
Shoufani, Elias, Al-Riddah and the Muslim Conquest of Arabia (Toronto: 1972)
Torrey, Charles C., The Jewish Foundations of Islam (New York: 1933)
Watt, W.M., Muhammad at Mecca (Oxford: 1953)
——Muhammad at Medina (Oxford: 1956)
——"The Tribal Basis of the Islamic State," Dalla tribu allo state (Rome: 1962), pp. 154-160
Wellhausen, Julius, Reste arabischen Heidenthums (2nd edn., Berlin: 1897, 3rd edn., Berlin: 1961)
——Skizzen und Vorabeiten (6 vols.) (Berlin: 1884-99)
Wolf, E.R., "The Social Organization of Mecca and the Origins of Islam," Southwestern Journal of Anthropology 7 (1951): 329-356

2

PRE-ISLAMIC BACKGROUND AND EARLY DEVELOPMENT OF JURISPRUDENCE

Joseph Schacht

ISLAMIC LAW is the epitome of the Islamic spirit, the most typical manifestation of the Islamic way of life, the kernel of Islam itself. For the majority of Muslims, the law has always been and still is of much greater practical importance than the dogma. Even today the law remains a decisive element in the struggle which is being fought in Islam between traditionalism and modernism under the impact of Western ideas. It is impossible to understand the present legal development in the Islamic countries of the Middle East without a correct appreciation of the past history of legal theory, of positive law, and of legal practice in Islam.

Islamic law was created by Islam, but the raw material out of which it was formed was to a great extent non-Islamic.[1] This raw material, itself of varied provenance, was tested by religious and ethical standards, and gained a uniform character in the process. The operation of these standards, however, did not affect all fields of law equally; hardly noticeable in some cases, it led to the creation of novel institutions in others. Thus, in early Islam, legal institutions were only incompletely assimilated to the body of Islamic religious and ethical duties, and retained some of their own distinctive qualities.

Arabian law in the time of Muḥammad was not altogether rudimentary. Primitive indeed was the customary law of the Bedouin, some traces of which have survived in pre-Islamic and early Islamic poetry, and in tales of the tribes. The comparable conditions existing among the Bedouin in modern times, enable us to verify the information of these literary sources. Mecca, however, was a trading city in close commercial relations with South Arabia, Byzantine Syria, and Sassanian 'Iraq; and Medina was an oasis of palm-trees with a strong colony of Jews, mostly Arab converts. It is likely that both cities possessed a law or laws, probably

[1] For the whole of this chapter and the beginning of Chapter III, see J. Schacht, *The Origins of Muhammadan Jurisprudence* (Oxford, 1950); the same, *G. Bergsträsser's Grundzüge des islamischen Rechts* (Berlin and Leipzig, 1935), pp. 8 ff.

containing foreign elements, which was more highly developed than that of the Bedouin. We can form some idea of the character of commercial life in Mecca and of the kind of law which it presupposes. The customary commercial law of Mecca was enforced by the traders among themselves, in much the same way as was the Law Merchant in Western Europe. In the case of Medina and other settlements, it can be presumed that agricultural contracts and land law were of similar importance. The law of family relationships and of inheritance, and the whole of the penal law, however, both among the Bedouin and the sedentary population, was dominated by the ancient Arabian tribal system. This system implied the absence of legal protection for the individual outside his tribe, the absence of a developed concept of criminal justice and the subsumption of crimes under torts, the responsibility of the tribal group for the actions of its members, and therefore unlimited vengeance for homicide, mitigated by the institution of weregeld (blood money).

The absence of an organized political authority in Arab society, both Bedouin and sedentary, implied the absence of an organized judicial system.[2] This does not mean that private justice prevailed in settling litigation concerning property rights, succession, and torts other than homicide. In these cases, if protracted negotiation between the parties led to no result, recourse was normally had to an arbitrator (ḥakam). The arbitrator did not belong to a particular caste; the parties were free to appoint as ḥakam any person on whom they agreed, but he was hardly ever the chief of the tribe. A ḥakam was chosen for his personal qualities, his knowledge, his wisdom, his integrity, his reputation, and last but not least, his supernatural powers. As supernatural powers of divination were found most commonly among soothsayers (kāhin), they were most often resorted to as arbitrators. Certain families and tribes also gained the reputation of special competence in deciding lawsuits, and their members were often chosen as arbitrators. Besides choosing an arbitrator, the parties to a lawsuit had to agree on the cause in action, the question which they were to put before the ḥakam. In order to test his powers, the parties regularly made the ḥakam divine an agreed secret, for instance a hidden object and its hiding place. The ḥakam, on his part, was free to accept or to refuse to act in any particular litigation. If he agreed to act, each party had to give security, either property or hostages, as a guar-

[2] E. Tyan, *Histoire de l'organisation judiciaire en pays d'Islam* (Paris, 1938), Vol. I, pp. 30 ff.

antee that they would submit to his decision. The decision of the ḥakam, which was final, was not an enforceable judgment (the execution had indeed to be guaranteed by the security), but rather a statement of right on a disputed point. It therefore became easily an authoritative statement of what the law was, or ought to be; the function of the arbitrator merged into that of a lawmaker, an authoritative expounder of the normative legal custom or sunna. The arbitrators applied and at the same time developed the sunna; it was the sunna, with the force of public opinion behind it, which had in the first place insisted on the procedure of negotiation and arbitration. Though thoroughly changed by Islam, these conditions have left lasting traces in Islamic law.

Muḥammad emerged in Mecca as a religious reformer, and he protested strongly when his pagan countrymen regarded him as merely another soothsayer. Because of his personal authority, he was invited to Medina as an arbitrator in tribal disputes, and as the Prophet he became the ruler and the legal authority of the Muslim community. His rejection of the character of a kāhin brought with it the rejection of heathen arbitration, inasmuch as the arbitrators were often soothsayers.[3] Nevertheless, when he served as a judge in his community, the Prophet continued to act in the function of a ḥakam.[4] Whenever the Qur'ān speaks of the Prophet's judicial activity, the verb ḥakama and its derivatives are used whereas the verb *qaḍa'*, from which the term qāḍī was to be derived, refers in the Qur'ān regularly not to the judgment of a judge, but to a sovereign ordinance, either of Allah or of the Prophet. (It also occurs in connection with the Day of Judgment, but this is a judgment only in a figurative sense.) In a single verse, both verbs occur side by side;[5] here, the first refers to the arbitrating aspect of the Prophet's activity, whereas the second emphasizes the authoritative character of his decision. This isolated instance is the first indication of the emergence of a new, Islamic idea of the administration of justice. Thus, the Prophet attached great importance to being appointed by the believers as a ḥakam in their disputes, though the insistence of the Qur'ān on this point shows that the ancient freedom in the choice of a ḥakam still prevailed; the Prophet, too, reserved to himself the right of the ḥakam to refuse to act. His position as a Prophet, however, backed in the later stages of his career in Medina by a considerable political and

[3] Qur'ān IV, 60 (Egyptian ed.)
[4] Tyan, *op. cit.*, Vol. I, 85 ff.
[5] Qur'ān IV, 65.

military power, gave him a much greater authority than could be claimed by an arbitrator; he became a "Prophet-Lawgiver." However, he wielded his almost absolute power not within but without the existing legal system; his authority was not legal, but for the believers, religious, and for the lukewarm, political.

The legislation of the Prophet, too, was an innovation in the law of Arabia. Generally speaking, Muḥammad had little reason to change the prevailing customary law. His aim as a Prophet was not to create a new system of law; it was to teach men how to act, what to do and what to avoid, in order to pass the reckoning on the Day of Judgment and to enter Paradise. This is why Islam in general, and Islamic law in particular, is a system of duties, comprising ritual, legal, and moral obligations on the same footing, and bringing them all under the authority of the same religious command. Had religious and ethical standards been comprehensively applied to all aspects of human behavior, and had they been consistently followed in practice, there would have been no room and no need for a legal system in the narrow meaning of the term. This was in fact the original ideal of Muḥammad, and traces of it, such as the recurrent insistence on the merits of forgiveness and of deferring or renouncing one's claims, are found in the Qur'ān; but the Prophet finally had to resign himself to applying religious and ethical principles to the legal problems and relationships as he found them.

Thus we find in the Qur'ān injunctions to arbitrate with justice, not to offer bribes, to give true evidence, and to give full weight and measure. Contracts are safeguarded by the demand to put them in writing, to give earnest-money, and to call witnesses (all of these are pre-Islamic practices which the Qur'ān endorses); or, in short, by the command to fulfill them, a command which is typical of the ethical attitude of the Qur'ān toward legal matters. Even the prohibitions of gambling and of taking interest, though directly concerned with certain types of contracts, are not meant to lay down legal rules regulating the form and effects of these contracts, but to establish moral norms under which they are allowed or prohibited. The idea that such contracts, if they are concluded notwithstanding the prohibition, are invalid and do not create obligations, does not yet appear in the Qur'ān. The same attitude governs the Qur'ānic law of war and booty and the whole complex of family law. The law of war and booty is primarily concerned with determining the enemies who must be fought or may be fought, how the booty is to be distributed (within the general framework of the rules laid down by pre-Islamic custom), and how the conquered are to be treated. Family law and the law of inheritance are the only legal subjects that are fairly exhaustively treated in the Qur'ān, albeit in a number of scattered passages; here again the main emphasis is laid on the problem of how one should act towards women and children, orphans and relatives, dependents and slaves. The effects of a lawful action are not mentioned and are as a rule self-evident; but the effects of an unlawful action, for instance, the question of civil responsibility, are hardly envisaged either. Technical legal statements attaching legal consequences to certain sets of relevant facts or acts are lacking almost completely, as far as the law of obligations and family relations are concerned. They exist, and are indeed almost indispensable, in the field of penal law. It is easy to understand that the normative legislation of the Qur'ān incorporated sanctions for transgressions, but again they are essentially moral and only incidentally penal; the prohibition is the essential element, the provision concerning the punishment is a rule of action either for the organs of the newly created Islamic state, or for the victim and his next of kin who, according to ancient Arab ideas, had the right of retaliation. The Qur'ān is content to prohibit wine-drinking, gambling, and taking of interest without fixing a penalty (unless it be punishment in Hell). There are provisions concerning retaliation and weregeld, theft, unchastity, and slanderous allegation of unchastity, as well as procedure in the last two cases.

The reasons for Qur'ānic legislation on all these matters were, generally speaking, dissatisfaction with prevailing conditions, the tendency to improve the position of women and of the weak in general, and the desire to mitigate the practice of vengeance and retaliation; the prohibition of wine-drinking, gambling, and taking of interest, too, constitute a break with ancient Arabian standards of behavior. Besides, it had become necessary to deal with new problems which had arisen in family law, in the law of retaliation, and in the law of war because of the main political aim of the Prophet, the dissolution of the ancient tribal organization and the creation of a community of believers in its stead. It is possible that some actual disputes made the need obvious. Such disputes, it seems, were mainly responsible for legislation on matters of inheritance, a subject which is farthest removed from the action of moral principles and most closely connected with the granting of individual rights. In this case, too, Qur'ānic legislation lays down primarily not basic principles of law but rules of action regarding the estates of deceased persons; the ethical element appears in the urgent injunction to act justly in making wills, and generally in the tendency to allot shares in the inheritance to persons who had no claim to succession under the old customary law. This feature of Qur'ānic legislation was preserved in the system of Islamic law, and the purely legal attitude, which attaches legal consequences to relevant acts, is often superseded by the tendency to establish ethical standards for the believer.

The first three generations after the death of the Prophet, or in other words, the first century of Islam (seventh-eighth century A.D.) are in many respects the most important, though because of the scarcity of contemporary evidence, the most obscure period in the history of Islamic law. In this period, many distinctive features of Islamic law came into being and the nascent Islamic society created its own legal institutions. What little authentic evidence is available shows that the ancient Arab system of arbitration, and Arab customary law in general, continued under the first successors of the Prophet, the caliphs of Medina (seventh century A.D.) The caliphs, it is true, were the political leaders of the Islamic community after the death of the Prophet, but they do not seem to have acted as its supreme arbitrators, and there still remained room at a slightly later period for the exhortation to choose one's arbitrators from the tribe of the Prophet, the Quraysh. In their function as the supreme rulers and administrators, though of course devoid of the religious authority of the Prophet, the caliphs acted to a great extent as law-givers of the community; during the whole of this first century, the administrative and legislative activities of the Islamic government cannot be separated. This administrative legislation, however, was hardly, if at all, concerned with modifying the existing customary law;. its object was to provide for the need of organizing the newly conquered territories for the benefit of the Arabs. In the field of penal law, the first caliphs went beyond the penal sanctions enacted in the Qur'ān by punishing, for instance, the authors of satirical poems directed against rival tribes, a common form of poetic expression in ancient Arabia. The enforcement of the law of retaliation and weregeld continued to be the responsibility of the next of kin of the victim. That the first caliphs did not appoint qāḍīs and in general did not lay the foundations of what later became the Islamic system of administration of justice, is shown by the contradictions and inherent improbabilities of the stories which assert the contrary; the alleged instructions for judges given by the Caliph 'Umar, too, are a product of the third Islamic century.[6]

Towards the end of the period of the caliphs of Medina, about the middle of the first century of Islam, the Islamic community was rent by political schisms, and the two "sectarian" movements of the Khārijīs and of the Shī'a established themselves beside the "orthodox" or Sunnī majority. The doctrines of Islamic law as adopted by the Khārijīs and by the Shī'a do not vary greatly from those of the several orthodox schools of law. From this, it was once concluded that the essential features common to these several forms of Islamic law were worked out before the schism, i.e., earlier than the middle of the first Islamic century. But recent research has shown that the ancient sects of Islam, at the time they split from the orthodox community, could not have shared with the majority the essentials of a system of law which did not yet exist. Rather, they adopted the fully developed legal system of the orthodox community, making only superficial changes of their own, in the second half of the second century of Islam or even later.

At an early period, the ancient Arab idea of sunna, of precedent or tradition, reasserted itself in Islam.[7] The Arabs were, and are, bound by tradition and precedent. Whatever was customary was right and proper; whatever the forefathers had done deserved to be imitated. This was the golden rule of the Arabs whose existence on a narrow margin in an unpropitious environment did not leave them much room for experiments and innovations which might upset the balance of their lives. In this idea of precedent or sunna the whole conservatism of the Arabs found expression. They recognized, of course, that a sunna might have been laid down by an individual in the relatively recent past, but then that individual was considered the spokesman and representative of the whole group. The idea of sunna presented a formidable obstacle to every innovation, and in order to discredit anything it was, and still is, enough to call it an innovation. Islam, the greatest innovation that Arabia saw, had to overcome this opposition, and a hard fight it was. But once Islam had prevailed, even among one single group of Arabs, the old conservatism reasserted itself; what had shortly before been an innovation, now became the thing to do, a thing hallowed by precedent and tradi-

6 Tyan, *op. cit.*, Vol. I, 98 ff.

7 I. Goldziher, "The Principles of Law in Islam," in *The Historian's History of the World*, Vol. VIII (New York, 1904), pp. 294 ff.

tion, a sunna. This ancient Arab concept of sunna became one of the central concepts of Islamic law.

It would seem natural to suppose that the explicit precepts of the Qur'ān on legal matters were observed from the beginning, at least as far as turbulent Arab society in a time of revolutionary change was amenable to rules. There are, indeed, two early decisions concerning a problem of divorce, one of which is based on the authoritative version of the Qur'ān, and the other on a variant reading. As the variant readings were officially abolished during the reign of the Umayyad Caliph 'Abd al-Malik (A. H. 65-86), it can be concluded that the doctrine in question had been formulated not later than the middle of the first century of Islam. On the other hand, there are several cases in which the early doctrine of Islamic law diverged from the clear and explicit wording of the Qur'ān. One important example, which has remained typical of Islamic law, is the restriction of legal proof to the evidence of witnesses and the denial of validity to written documents. This contradicts an explicit ruling of the Qur'ān which endorsed the current practice of putting contracts into writing.[8] John of Damascus, who flourished between A.D. 700 and 750, mentions the insistence on witnesses as a characteristic custom of the Saracens, and this, too, was probably established about the middle of the first century of Islam. Nothing is known about its origin.

During the greater part of the first century, Islamic law in the technical meaning of the term did not yet exist. As had been the case in the time of the Prophet, law as such fell outside the sphere of religion, and as far as there were no religious or moral objections to specific transactions or modes of behavior, the technical aspects of law were a matter of indifference to the Muslims. This attitude of the early Muslims accounts for the widespread adoption of legal and administrative institutions of the conquered territories, drawing on Roman (including Roman provincial) law, Sassanian law, Talmudic law, and the canon law of the Eastern churches. Outstanding examples are the treatment of tolerated religions, the methods of taxation, and the institutions of emphyteusis and of pious endowments (waqf). The principle of the retention of pre-Islamic legal institutions under Islam was sometimes even explicitly acknowledged, as in the following passage by an author of the third Islamic century: "Abū Yūsuf held that if there exists in a country an ancient, non-Arab normative custom (sunna) which Islam has neither changed nor abolished,

[8] Q. II, 282.

and people complain to the caliph that it causes them hardship, he is not entitled to change it; but Mālik and al-Shāfi'ī held that he may change it even if it be ancient, because he ought to prohibit (in similar circumstances) every lawful normative custom which has been introduced by a Muslim, let alone those introduced by unbelievers."[9] Both opinions presuppose the retention of pre-Islamic legal practices as normal.

The influence exercised on early Islamic law by the legal systems of the conquered territories, however, was not restricted to legal customs and practices; it extended to the field of legal concepts and principles, and even to fundamental ideas of legal science, such as the methods of systematic reasoning, and the idea of the "consensus of the scholars." The legal concepts and maxims in question are of that general kind which would be familiar not only to lawyers but to all educated persons. We shall see later that Muhammadan jurisprudence started about the year A. H. 100. It follows not only that the whole first century of Islam was available for the adoption of foreign legal elements by nascent Islamic society, but that Islamic legal science began at a time when the door of Islamic civilization had been opened to potential transmitters of these legal concepts, the educated non-Arab converts to Islam. Some of the doctrines in question, such as the responsibility of the thief for twice the value of the object stolen, or the erection of adultery into a permanent impediment to marriage between the two guilty parties, did not succeed in gaining general acceptance, and only survived as unsuccessful or isolated opinions. This process of infiltration of foreign legal concepts and maxims into Islamic society through the medium of educated non-Arab converts extended over the greater part of the first century of Islam, but its results became apparent only early in the second century, when Islamic legal science came into being. That early Muḥammadan lawyers should have adopted consciously any principle of foreign law is out of the question.

We must now return to the middle of the first Islamic century, when the rule of the first caliphs of Medina was supplanted by that of the Umayyad caliphs of Damascus. The Umayyads were not the adversaries of Islam that they were often made out to be; on the contrary, it was they and their governors who were responsible for developing a number of the essential features of Islamic cult and ritual, of which they had found only rudimentary ele-

[9] Beladsori, *Liber expugnationis regionum*, ed. by de Goeje (Leiden, 1865), p. 448.

LEEDS UNIVERSITY LIBRARY

ments. Their main concern, it is true, was not with religion and religious law, but with political administration, and here they represented the organizing, centralizing and increasingly bureaucratic tendency of an orderly administration as against the Bedouin anarchy of the Arab way of life. Both Islamic religious ideal and Umayyad administration cooperated in creating a new framework for Arab Muslim society, which had been recruited indiscriminately from all Arab tribes and was spread thinly over the vast extent of the conquered territories. In many respects, Umayyad rule represents the consummation, after the turbulent interval of the Caliphate of Medina, of tendencies which were implied by the nature of the Islamic community under the Prophet. This is the background against which the emergence of Islamic law, of an Islamic administration of justice, and of Islamic jurisprudence must be viewed.

The administration of the Umayyads concentrated on waging war against the Byzantines and other external enemies, on collecting revenue from the subject population, and on paying subventions in money or in kind to the Arab beneficiaries; these were the essential functions of the Arab kingdom. We therefore find evidence of Umayyad regulations, or administrative law, particularly in the fields of the law of war and of fiscal law. The accountancy for payments of weregeld straddles the field of penal law, and whereas the Umayyads did not interfere with the working of retaliation as modified by the Qur'ān (all they did here was to try to prevent the recurrence of Arab tribal feuds which threatened the internal security of the state), they supervised the application of the purely Islamic penalties laid down in the Qur'ān and of similar punishments. They, or rather their governors, also took the important step of appointing Islamic judges or qāḍīs. The office of qāḍī was created in and for the new Islamic society which came into being, under the new conditions resulting from the Arab conquest, in the urban centers of the Arab kingdom. For this new society the arbitration of pre-Islamic Arabia and of the earliest period of Islam was no longer adequate.[10] The Arab ḥakam thus was supplanted by the Islamic qāḍī, who was a delegate of the governor. The governor, within the limits set for him by the caliph, had full authority over his province, administrative, legislative and judicial, without any conscious distinction of function, and he could, and in fact regularly did, delegate his judicial authority to his "legal secretary," the qāḍī. The governor retained,

[10] Tyan, *op. cit.* Vol. I. 114 ff.

however, the power of reserving for his own decision any lawsuit he wished, and, of course, the power of dismissing his qāḍī at will.

The jurisdiction of the qāḍī extended to Muslims only; the non-Muslim subject populations retained their own traditional legal institutions, including the ecclesiastical (and rabbinical) tribunals which in the last few centuries before the Muslim conquest had to a great extent duplicated the judicial organization of the Byzantine state. The Byzantine magistrates themselves, together with the other civil officers, had evacuated the lost provinces at the very beginning of the Muslim conquest; nevertheless, because of a fundamental similarity in general structure between late Byzantine and early Islamic organization of justice, it has been suggested that the latter was modeled on the former, a process which may have been part of the adoption by the Muslims of the administrative organization of their predecessors. One administrative office, of which the functions were partly judicial, was indeed taken over in this way: the office of the "inspector of the market" (*agoranomos*), who had a limited civil and criminal jurisdiction. But the early Muslims had not only the Byzantine example on which to model their earliest administration of justice: the "clerk of the court," whose services must have become indispensable at an early period, had the same function as the corresponding official in the Sassanian administration; this was well known to contemporary authors.

The earliest Islamic qāḍīs, officials of the Umayyad administration, by their decisions laid the basic foundations of what was to become Islamic law. We know their names, and there exists a considerable body of information on their lives and judgments, but it is difficult to separate the authentic from the fictitious. Legal doctrines that can be dated to the first century of the hijra are rare, but it is likely that some of the decisions which are attributed to those qāḍīs, and which are irregular by later standards, do indeed go back to that early period. In a slightly later period, we can actually see how the tendency to impose an oath on the plaintiff as a safeguard against the exclusive use of the evidence of witnesses grew out of the judicial practice at the beginning of the second century. The earliest Islamic qāḍīs gave judgment according to their own discretion, or "sound opinion" (ra'y) as it was called, basing themselves on customary practice, which in the nature of things incorporated administrative regulations, and took the letter and the spirit of the Qur'ānic legislation and of other recognized Islamic religious norms into account as much as they thought fit. The customary practice to which they referred was either that of the community under their jurisdiction or that of their own home district, and in this latter case conflicts were bound to arise. Though the legal subject matter had as yet not been Islamicized to any great extent beyond the stage reached in the Qur'ān, the office of qāḍī itself was an Islamic institution typical of the Umayyad period, in which administrative efficiency and the tendency to Islamicize went hand in hand. The Islamic character of the office of qāḍī is emphasized by a subsidiary appointment which was, during the Umayyad period, often combined with that of a qāḍī: the duty of qaṣaṣ, literally "story-telling," that is to say, the religious instruction and edification of the people. The scene was thus set for a more thorough process of Islamicizing the existing customary law.

The work of the qāḍīs inevitably became more and more specialized, and we may take it for granted that in the late Umayyad period (c. A. H. 100-130) appointments as a rule went to "specialists," by which are meant not technically trained professionals but persons sufficiently interested in the right administration of justice to have given the subject serious thought in their spare time, either individually or in discussion with like-minded friends. The main concern of these specialists, in the intellectual climate of the late Umayyad period, was naturally to know whether the customary law conformed to the Qur'ānic and generally Islamic norms; in other words: the specialists from whom the qāḍīs came increasingly to be recruited were found among those pious persons whose interest in religion caused them to elaborate, by individual reasoning, an Islamic way of life in all its aspects. These pious persons surveyed all fields of contemporary activities, including the field of law, not only administrative regulations but popular practice as well. In their theoretical contemplations they considered possible objections that could be made to recognized practices from the religious, and in particular, from the ritualistic or ethical point of view, and as a result endorsed, modified, or rejected them. They impregnated the sphere of law with religious and ethical ideas, subjected it to Islamic norms, and incorporated it into the body of duties incumbent on every Muslim. In doing this, they achieved on a much wider scale and in a vastly more detailed manner what the Prophet in the Qur'ān had tried to do for the early Islamic community of Medina. As a consequence, the popular and administrative practice of the late Umayyad period was transformed into Islamic law. The resulting theory still had to be translated into practice; this task was beyond the power of the pious specialists and had to be left to the interest and zeal of the caliphs, governors, qāḍīs, or individuals concerned. The origins of Islamic law then were such that it developed not in close connection with practice, but as the expression of a religious ideal in opposition to practice.

This process started from modest beginnings towards the end of the first century of the hijra; a specialist in religious law such as Ibrāhīm Nakha'ī of Kūfa (d. A. H. 95 or 96) did no more than give opinions on questions of ritual and perhaps on kindred problems of directly religious importance, cases of conscience concerning alms tax, marriage, divorce, and the like, but not on law proper. The pious specialists were private persons, or we might call them amateurs; they were animated by their personal interest in questions of right behavior, and they owed the respect, in which they were often and in an increasing measure held by the people and by some of the rulers, exclusively to their own single-minded concern with the ideals of a life according to the tenets of Islam. They often had occasion to criticize the actions and regulations of the government, just as they had to declare undesirable many popular practices, but they were not in political opposition to the Umayyads and to the established Islamic state; on the contrary, the whole of the Umayyad period, until the civil war which heralded the end of the dynasty, was sometimes reckoned as part of the "good old times," its practice was idealized and opposed to the realities of the actual administration.

As the groups of pious specialists grew in numbers and cohesion they developed, in the first few decades of the second century of the hijra, into what is known, for lack of a better name, as the "ancient schools of law." This term ought to imply neither any definite organization, nor a strict uniformity of doctrine within each school, nor any formal teaching, nor again any official status, nor even the existence of a body of law in our Western meaning of the term. The "scholars" or "lawyers," members of the ancient schools of law, continued to be private individuals, interested and therefore presumably knowledgeable in the Islamic ideals as they ought to prevail in all fields of life, including what we should call the field of law. These individuals were singled out from the great mass of the Muslims by the very fact of their special interest, the resultant reverence of the people, and the recognition as kindred spirits which they themselves accorded one another.

I have spoken of the ancient schools of law in the plural because, overlying the common Islamic background, there had developed in the several widely separated centers of the Islamic world during the first century of the hijra local practices, for example, those concerning details of ritual, or special transactions adapted to local conditions. Apart from these variations in subject-matter, the not inconsiderable difficulties of communication between their several centers made differences among the ancient schools of law unavoidable. These differences, however, were conditioned by geography rather than by any noticeable disagreement on principles or methods. The general attitude of all ancient schools of law towards Umayyad popular practice and Umayyad administrative regulations was essentially the same, whether they endorsed, modified, or rejected the practice which they found. Aside from this common basic attitude, however, there existed at the earliest stage of Islamic jurisprudence a considerable body of common doctrine which was subsequently reduced by increasing differentiation among the schools. This does not imply that Islamic jurisprudence in the earliest period was cultivated exclusively in one geographical center, but that one place nonetheless was the intellectual center of the first theoretizing and systematizing efforts which were to transform Umayyad popular and administrative practice into Islamic law. The ascendancy of a single center of Islamic jurisprudence must have been maintained over an appreciable period, because the common ancient element sometimes comprises several successive stages of doctrine. All indications go to prove that 'Iraq was this center. The ascendancy of 'Iraq in the development of religious law and jurisprudence in Islam continued during the whole of the second century.

The more important ancient schools of law of which we have knowledge are those of Kūfa and of Baṣra in 'Iraq, of Medina and of Mecca in Ḥijāz, and of Syria. Our information on the Kūfians and on the Medinese is incomparably more detailed than that concerning the Baṣrians and the Meccans, but the picture gained from the first two schools can be taken as typical. Egypt did not develop a school of law of its own, but fell under the influence of the other schools, particularly that of Medina.

An important aspect of the activity of the ancient schools of law was that they took the Qur'ānic norms seriously for the first time. Historically speaking, Islamic law did not derive directly from the Qur'ān; it developed out of a practice which often diverged from the Qur'ān's intentions and even from its explicit wording. It is true that a number of institutions, particularly in the law of family relations and of inheritance, not to mention cult and ritual, were based on the Qur'ān from the beginning. But apart from the most elementary rules, norms derived from the Qur'ān were introduced into Islamic law almost invariably at a secondary stage. In particular, at this stage, formal legal consequences were drawn from the essentially religious and ethical body of Qur'ānic maxims, and applied to those branches of law, such as contracts and torts, which were not covered in detail by the Qur'ānic legislation. The zenith of this introduction of Qur'ānic norms into early Islamic law coincides with the rise of the ancient schools at the beginning of the second century of the hijra.

The ancient schools of law shared not only a common attitude towards Umayyad practice and a considerable body of positive religious law, but the essentials of legal theory, not all of which were systematically self-evident. The central idea of this theory was that of the "living tradition of the school," as represented by the constant doctrine of its authoritative representatives. This idea dominated the development of legal doctrine in the ancient schools during the whole of the second century of the hijra. It presents itself under two aspects: retrospective and contemporaneous. Retrospectively, it appears as sunna or "practice" ('amal), or as "well-established precedent" (sunna maḍiya) or "ancient practice" (amr qadīm). This "practice" partly reflects the actual custom of the local community, but it also contains a theoretical or ideal element, so that it comes to mean normative sunna—the usage as it ought to be. This ideal practice, which was presumed constant though it in fact developed as Islamic ideas were imposed on the legal subject-matter, was found in the unanimous doctrine of the representative religious scholars of each center, in the teaching of those whom the people of every region recognized as their leading specialists in religious law, whose opinion they accepted and to whose decision they submitted. It is only the opinion of the majority that counts; small minorities of scholars are disregarded. The consensus of the scholars, representing the common denominator of doctrine achieved in each generation, expresses the contemporaneous aspect of the living tradition of each school. How this consensus works is described by an ancient scholar of Baṣra in the following terms: "Whenever I find a generation of scholars at a seat of knowledge, in their majority, holding the same opinion, I call this 'consensus,' whether their predecessors agreed or disagreed with it, because the majority would not agree on anything in ignorance of the doctrine of their predecessors, and would abandon the previous doctrine only on account of a repeal (for instance in the Qur'ān, which their predecessors had overlooked) or because they knew of some better argument, even if they did not mention it." In the result, the decision on what constitutes normative practice is left to the last generation of the representatives of each school of law.

The consensus of the scholars is different from the consensus of all Muslims on essentials. This last, in the nature of things, covers the whole of the Islamic world but is vague and general, whereas the consensus of the scholars is geographically limited to the seat of the school in question, is concrete and detailed, but also tolerant and not exclusive, recognizing as it does the existence of other doctrines in other centers. Both kinds of consensus count as final arguments in the ancient schools of law, though the consensus of the scholars is of much greater practical importance and is the real basis of their teaching. It is only natural that the consensus of all Muslims should be considered infallible; that the consensus of the scholars should be regarded as infallible, too, is not equally obvious and the whole highly organized concept seems to have been influenced from abroad.

Originally, the consensus of the scholars was anonymous, that is to say, it was the average opinion of the representatives of a school, and not the individual doctrines of the most prominent scholars. The living tradition of the ancient schools maintained its essentially anonymous character well into the second half of the second century of the hijra. Nevertheless, the idea of continuity inherent in the concept of sunna or idealized practice, together with the need of creating some kind of theoretical justification for what so far had been an instinctive reliance on the opinions of the majority led, from the first decades of the second century onwards, to the living tradition being projected backwards and to its being ascribed to some of the great figures of the past. The Kūfians were the first in attributing the doctrine of their school to the ancient Kūfian authority Ibrāhīm Nakha'ī, mentioned above, although this body of elementary legal doctrine had very little to do with the few authentic opinions of the historical Ibrāhīm. It rather represents the stage of legal teaching achieved in the time of Ḥammād ibn Abī Sulaymān (d. A. H. 120), the first Kūfian lawyer whose doctrine we can regard as fully historical. By a literary convention, which found particular favor in 'Iraq, it was customary for a scholar or author to put his own doctrine or work under the aegis of an ancient authority. The Medinese followed suit and projected their own teaching back to a number of ancient authorities who had died in the last years of the first or in the very first years of the second century of the hijra. At a later period, seven amongst them were chosen as representative; they are the so-called "Seven Lawyers of Medina," the most prominent of whom is Sa'īd ibn Musayyib. Hardly any of the doctrines ascribed to these ancient authorities can be considered authentic. The transmission of legal doctrine in Medina becomes historically ascertainable only at about the same time as in 'Iraq, with Zuhrī (d. A. H. 124) and with his younger contemporary Rabī'a ibn Abī 'Abd al-Raḥmān.

The process of going backwards for a theoretical foundation of Islamic religious law as it was being taught in the ancient schools did not stop with the choosing of these relatively late authorities. At the same time at which the doctrine of the school of Kūfa was retrospectively attributed to Ibrahīm Nakha'ī, and perhaps even slightly earlier, that doctrine and the local practice which in the last resort was its basis were directly connected with the very beginnings of Islam in Kūfa, beginnings associated with Ibn Mas'ūd, a Companion of the Prophet. It was, however, not to Ibn Mas'ūd himself that reference was made in the first place, but to an informal group of "Companions of Ibn Mas'ūd" who were, in some general way, taken to guarantee the authentic and uninterrupted transmission of the correct practice and doctrine in Kūfa. At a secondary stage, the general reference to the Companions of Ibn Mas'ūd gave rise to a formal and explicit reference to Ibn Mas'ūd himself, and a considerable body of early Kūfian doctrine was attributed to him. Though this body of doctrine differed in a number of details from the general teaching of the Kūfian school which went under the name of Ibrāhīm Nakha'ī, Ibrāhīm appears as the main transmitter from Ibn Mas'ūd, and many opinions were projected back from Ibrāhīm still farther to Ibn Mas'ūd. The historical Ibrāhīm had not had personal contact with the historical Ibn Mas'ūd, but some members of the originally anonymous Companions of Ibn Mas'ūd were later identified as older relatives of Ibrāhīm, and these formed a family link between the two authorities. Ibn Mas'ūd thus became the eponymy of the doctrine of the school of Kūfa. The corresponding eponymy of the Meccans was Ibn 'Abbās, another Companion of the Prophet, and references to him, too, alternate with references to the Companions of Ibn 'Abbās. The two main authorities of the Medinese among the Companions of the Prophet were the Caliph 'Umar and his son

Ibn 'Umar. Each ancient school of law, having projected its doctrine back to its own eponymy, who was invariably a local Companion of the Prophet, claimed his authority as the basis of its teaching. This association with Companions of the Prophet was called taqlīd.

Nor did the search for a solid theoretical foundation of the doctrine of the ancient schools of law stop at the Companions of the Prophet: there remained a further step. This step was taken in 'Iraq, perhaps in Baṣra, where not later than in the very first *years of the second century of the hijra, the sunna, the practice of* the local community and the doctrine of its scholars, were called "sunna of the Prophet." This term put the ideal practice of each community of Muslims directly under the authority of the Prophet. It expressed an axiom, but did not yet imply the existence of positive information in the form of "traditions" which became prevalent later, that the Prophet by his words or actions had in fact originated or approved that practice. This originally 'Iraqi concept of the sunna of the Prophet was taken over by the Syrians; their idea of living tradition was the uninterrupted practice of the Muslims, beginning with the Prophet, maintained by the first caliphs and by the later rulers, and verified by the scholars. The Medinese, on the other hand, hardly used this concept.

It was not long before various movements arose in opposition to the opinions held by the majorities in the ancient schools of law. In Kūfa, for instance, where the name of Ibn Mas'ūd had become attached to the main stream of legal doctrine, any opinions which were put forward in opposition to the traditional doctrine of the majority had to invoke an equally high, or possibly an even higher, authority, and for this purpose the name of the Caliph 'Alī, who had made Kūfa his headquarters, presented itself easily. The doctrines which in Kūfa go under the name of 'Alī do not embody the coherent teaching of any individual group; all we can say is that, generally speaking, they represent opinions advanced in opposition to the living tradition, that is, to the contemporary average teaching, of the school of Kūfa. One group of doctrines attributed to 'Alī represents crude and primitive analogies, early unsuccessful efforts to systematize; they reflect the opinions of groups or individuals who were ahead of the majority of their contemporaries in Kūfa in systematic legal thought. Another group of unsuccessful opinions ascribed to 'Alī shows a rigorous and meticulous tendency, and goes farther than the average doctrine of the Kūfians in taking religious and ethical considerations into account. Unsuccessful 'Iraqi opinions of this type, attributed to 'Alī, correspond almost regularly to doctrines attested in Medina, where most of them represent the common opinion. It is in keeping with the relatively later development of the Medinese school that a body of doctrines which remained unsuccessful in Kūfa, where it could not overcome the already established tradition of a school of law, succeeded to a considerable degree to gain recognition in Medina.

In contrast to the opposition in Kūfa, the opposition in Medina reflected the activity of the Traditionists. The movement of the Traditionists, the most important single event in the history of Islamic law in the second century of the hijra, was the natural outcome and continuation of a movement of religiously and ethically inspired opposition to the ancient schools of law. The schools of law themselves represented an Islamic opposition to popular and administrative practice under the later Umayyads, and the opposition group which developed into the Traditionist movement emphasized this tendency. The main thesis of the Traditionists, as opposed to the ancient schools of law, was that formal "traditions" deriving from the Prophet superseded the living tradition of the school. It was not enough for the ancient schools to claim that their doctrines as a whole were based on the teachings of Companions of the Prophet who were likely to know the intentions of their master best, or even that their living tradition represented the sunna of the Prophet. The Traditionists produced detailed statements or "traditions" which claimed to be the reports of ear or eyewitnesses on the words or actions of the Prophet, handed down orally by an uninterrupted chain of trustworthy persons. Hardly any of these traditions, as far as rules of law are concerned, can be considered authentic; they were put into circulation, no doubt from the loftiest of motives, by the Traditionists themselves from the first half of the second century onwards. Occasionally, the Traditionists acknowledged this activity more or less openly, as in the traditions which report the Prophet as having said: "Sayings attributed to me which agree with the Qur'ān go back to me, whether I actually said them or not,' and "Whatever good sayings there are, I said them."

The Traditionists were not confined to Medina, but existed in other centers of Islam where they formed groups in opposition to, but nevertheless in contact with, the local schools of law. Their standards of reasoning were inferior to those of the ancient schools, and even Shāfi'ī, who at the end of the second century was to succeed in making their main thesis prevail in Islamic law, complained repeatedly that their superficial and uncritical adherence to traditions led them into error, and that their failure to reason systematically put them at a disadvantage. The Traditionists' own feeling of inferiority expressed itself in the following saying ascribed to the Prophet: "Luck to the man who hears my words, remembers them, guards them, and hands them on; many a transmitter of legal knowledge is no lawyer himself, and many a one transmits legal knowledge to persons who are more learned in it than he is."

The Traditionists disliked all human reasoning and personal opinion which had become an integral part of the living tradition of the ancient schools and which had, indeed, been a constituent element of Islamic legal thought from its very beginnings. They put into circulation a number of traditions in which they disparaged human reasoning in law. They were also presumably responsible for some of the traditions directed against Umayyad popular and administrative practice, although it is not always possible to determine whether a particular doctrine originated in Traditionist circles or within the ancient schools of law. The introduction of Islamic norms into all aspects of life, including the sphere of law, was by no means a distinctive interest of the Traditionists; they were preceded in this by the ancient schools of law themselves. The general tendency of the Traditionists was the same as that of the other opponents of the dominant schools in 'Iraq and in Medina: a certain inclination towards strictness and rigidity which was not, however, without exceptions. They were occasionally interested in purely legal issues, for reasons which now escape us, but their main concern was with subordinating the legal subject-matter to moral principles. There are, for instance, two traditions put into circulation by the Traditionists in Medina, according to which the Prophet had prohibited underbidding and overbidding, and certain practices which might create an artificial rise or fall in prices. Their aim was to make these practices illegal in the same way as, say, the taking of interest was illegal, so that contracts concluded in defiance of the prohibition would be invalid. These particular traditions did not prevail with the Medinese, who, in common with the 'Iraqis, minimized them by interpretation, and the effort of the Traditionists to change the doctrine of the ancient schools of law remained unsuccessful in this case.

Initially the ancient schools of law, Medinese as well as 'Iraqi, offered strong resistance to the disturbing element represented by the traditions from the Prophet. It has often been presumed that it was the most natural thing, from the first generation after the Prophet onwards, to refer in all cases to his real or alleged rulings. This was not the case. Traditions from the Prophet had to overcome strong opposition, and the arguments against them and in their favor extended over most of the second century of the hijra. At the same time it is obvious that once the authority of the Prophet, the highest in Islam, had been invoked, the thesis of the Traditionists, consciously formulated, was certain of success, and the ancient schools had no real defense against the rising tide of traditions from the Prophet. The best they could do was to minimize them by interpretation and to embody their own attitude and doctrines in other alleged traditions from the Prophet, but this meant that the Traditionists had gained their point. Though the ancient schools of law were brought to pay lip-service to the principle of the Traditionists, they did not, however, necessarily change their positive legal doctrine to the full extent desired by the latter group. The Traditionists were sometimes successful in bringing about a change of doctrine, and when this happened, the doctrine of the minority in opposition became indistinguishable from that of the majority of the school; but they often failed, and we find whole groups of "unsuccessful" Medinese and 'Iraqi doctrines expressed in traditions from the Prophet. It goes without saying that the interaction of legal doctrines and traditions must be regarded as a unitary process, the several aspects and phases of which can be separated only for the sake of analysis. All this introduced inconsistencies into the teachings of the ancient schools of law and these schools accepted traditions from the Prophet only as far as they agreed with their own living tradition or idealized "practice"—that is to say, the practice as it ought to be. The next step was to be taken by Shāfi'ī at the end of the second century of the hijra.

The discussion so far has been concerned mainly with the tendency of the early specialists to Islamicize, that is, to introduce Islamic norms into the sphere of the law. This endeavor was, however, accompanied by the parallel and complementary tendency to reason and to systematize. Reasoning was inherent in Islamic law from its very beginnings. It started with the exercise of personal opinion and of individual judgment on the part of the earliest specialists and qāḍīs. It would be a gratuitous assumption to regard the independent decision of the specialist or of the magistrate as anterior to rudimentary analogy and the striving after consistency. Both elements are found intimately connected in the earliest period which the sources allow us to discern. Nevertheless, this individual reasoning, whether completely independent and personal or inspired by an effort for consistency, started from vague beginnings, without direction or method, and moved towards an increasingly strict discipline.

The oldest stage of legal reasoning is represented by 'Iraqi traditions which show crude and primitive conclusions reached by analogy. An old conclusion of this kind, which prevailed in the 'Iraqi doctrine, was to demand a fourfold confession of the culprit before he incurred the punishment for unchastity, by analogy with the four witnesses prescribed for this case by the Qur'ān. This was originally merely the result of systematic reasoning. The 'Iraqi opposition groups exaggerated the underlying tendency towards caution, and put into circulation a tradition relating that 'Alī once turned away an offending woman four times and punished her only after her fifth confession; this opinion did not achieve recognition. The original 'Iraqi doctrine requiring four confessions spread into Ḥijāz, and was there incorporated in a group of traditions under the authority of the Prophet, the final result of which was a tradition concerning a man called Ma'iz who committed unchastity and confessed, but was turned away three times by the Prophet and punished only after his fourth confession. Although ultimately expressed in traditions from the Prophet, the doctrine did not prevail in the school of Medina and remained confined to 'Iraq. The underlying conclusion by analogy provoked another comparable opinion which held that the Qur'ānic punishment of mutilation for theft could be applied only after a twofold confession by the culprit, by analogy with the two witnesses demanded in this case. This doctrine was again expressed in a tradition from 'Alī, but was only partly successful in 'Iraq.

The minimum value of stolen goods, for the Qur'ānic punishment for theft to be applicable, was fixed by some 'Iraqis by a crude analogy with the five fingers, at five dirhams. The generally accepted doctrine in 'Iraq, however, fixed it arbitrarily at ten dirhams, and as a justification of this discretionary decision traditions from Ibn Mas'ūd, 'Alī, and even the Prophet were cited. This doctrine has to be regarded as the original opinion, and the analogical reasoning as a refinement which was finally unsuccessful. The minimum value of stolen goods provided the starting point for fixing, by a crude analogy, the minimum amount of the ṣadāq, the contractual payment made by the bridegroom to the bride which was an essential element of the contract of marriage. Here, too, the original 'Iraqi decision was arbitrary: "We think it shocking," they said, "that intercourse should become lawful for a trifling amount," and therefore Ibrāhīm Nakha'ī disapproved of a ṣadāq of less than forty, and once he said of less than ten dirhams." This discretionary decision was later modified, not for the better, by a crude analogy, according to which the use of a part of the body of the wife by the husband ought not to be made lawful for an amount less than that set for the loss of a limb through the punishment for theft, and the minimum amount of ṣadāq was fixed at ten dirhams. This reasoning was expressed in a tradition from 'Alī. The Medinese recognized originally no minimum amount of ṣadāq; only Mālik, followed by his personal disciples, adopted the 'Iraqi analogical reasoning, and starting from his own doctrine that the punishment of mutilation could be applied only in cases where the minimum value of the stolen goods was three dirhams, fixed the minimum ṣadāq at the same amount. At the same time, the 'Iraqis had found this crude analogy unsatisfactory, and fell back on the authority of traditions which had appeared in the meantime.

The results of this early systematic reasoning were not infrequently expressed in the form of legal "puzzles," or in the form of legal maxims or slogans, which were sometimes rhyming or alliterative. Some typical slogans are: "there is no divorce and no manumission under duress"; "the child belongs to the marriage bed"; "profit goes with responsibility"; "the security takes the place of that for which it is given" ('Iraqi); and, in favor of the opposite doctrine, "the security is not forfeited" (Medinese). These maxims became a favorite mode of expressing legal doctrines in 'Iraq and in Ḥijāz in the first half of the second century of the hijra, and reflect a stage when legal doctrines were not yet automatically expressed in traditions, though most of them gradually acquired the form of traditions. The element of personal discretion and individual opinion in Islamic law was prior to the growth of traditions, particularly of traditions from the Prophet, and it was due only to the essential success of the Traditionists that most of these originally independent decisions of scholars were put into the form of traditions.

The literary period in Islamic law begins about the year A. H. 150, and from then onwards the development of technical legal thought can be followed step by step from scholar to scholar. It tended, first, to become more and more perfected until it reached the zenith of its development at the end of the second century. There is secondly an increasing dependence on traditions, as a greater number of authoritative traditions came into being. Thirdly, considerations of a religious and ethical kind, which represented one aspect of the process of Islamicizing the legal subject-matter, tended to permeate systematic reasoning, and both tendencies became inextricably mixed in the result. All three tendencies culminated in the teachings of Shāfi'ī as will become evident from a short survey of the thought of some of the main representatives of Islamic law in the second century of Islam.

The opinions of the Syrian Awzā'ī (d. A. H. 157), for instance, represent the oldest solutions adopted by Islamic jurisprudence, whether he maintained the current practice, or regulated it, or Islamicized it as was usual with him, or gave a seemingly simple and natural decision as yet untouched by systematic refinements. The archaic character of Awzā'ī's doctrine makes it likely that he conserved the teaching of his predecessors in the generation before him. When the doctrine which goes under his name was formulated, the Islamicizing and systematizing tendencies of earliest Muḥammadan jurisprudence had, it is true, already started to operate, but they were still far from having penetrated the whole of the raw material offered by the practice. The doctrine as given by Awzā'ī therefore often appears inconsistent. His systematic reasoning, though appreciable in extent, is generally rudimentary, and his legal thought shows as a rule a rigid formalism.

The reasoning of the Medinese Mālik (d. A. H. 179), on the whole, is comparable to that of Awzā'ī, particularly in the dependence of both on the practice, the living tradition, the consensus of the scholars, rather than on systematic thought. The accepted doctrine of the Medinese school, which Mālik aimed to set forth, was itself to a great extent founded on the individual reasoning of the school's representatives. In combining extensive use of reasoning with dependence on the living tradition, Mālik seems typical of the Medinese. In the majority of cases, we find Mālik's reasoning inspired by material considerations, by practical expediency, and by the tendency to Islamicize. There are a fair number of cases where his technical legal thought shows itself to be sound and consistent.

In 'Iraq, the discussion of technical legal problems must have started slightly earlier than the time of Ibn Abī Layla, a qāḍī of Kūfa (d. A. H. 148). His doctrine, taken as a whole, shows a considerable amount of technical legal thought, but it is generally of a primitive kind, somewhat clumsy, shortsighted, and often unfortunate in its results. His loose and imperfect method is not incompatible with formalism and the stubborn drawing of consequences. A rigid formalism is perhaps the most persistent single typical feature of his legal thought. Nevertheless, his technical reasoning is far from rudimentary; the striving for systematic consistency, the action of general trends and principles pervade his whole doctrine. In a great number of cases, Ibn Abī Layla's doctrine represents seemingly natural and practical common sense, and rough-and-ready decisions. This practical, common sense reasoning of his often takes practical, and particularly Islamic-ethical considerations into account. Connected with these considerations is Ibn Abī Layla's regard for actual practice, a tendency reinforced by his being a qāḍī. There are numerous traces of his activity as a qāḍī in his doctrine, last but not least his conservatism, so that he represents an earlier stage in the development of Islamic jurisprudence than his contemporary Abū Ḥanīfa.

With respect to 'Iraqi legal reasoning as represented by Ibn Abī Layla, Abū Ḥanīfa (d. A. H. 150) seems to have played the part of a theoretical systematizer who achieved considerable progress in technical legal thought. Not being a qāḍī, Abū Ḥanīfa was less restricted than Ibn Abī Layla by considerations of practice. At the same time, he was less firmly guided by the needs of the administration of justice, and whereas Ibn Abī Layla's doctrine is often primitive but practical, Abū Ḥanīfa's, though more highly developed, is often tentative and, as it proved to be, unsatisfactory. In Abū Ḥanīfa's doctrine, systematic consistency has become normal. The emphasis shifts from the practical aspects of legal reasoning—Islamicizing, common-sense decisions, and other considerations which were still prevalent in Ibn Abī Layla's doctrine—to the technical and formal qualities of legal thought. Traces of primitive reasoning and systematic inconsistencies remain, but they are relatively few in number. More significant than these features are those numerous cases which show Abū Ḥanīfa's legal thought to be not only more broadly based and more thoroughly applied than that of his predecessors, but technically more highly developed, more circumspect, and more refined. Abū Ḥanīfa's legal thought was, however, not final, and his companions and disciples rejected an appreciable part of it as defective.

Of Abū Ḥanīfa's disciple Abū Yūsuf (d. A. H. 182) it need only be said that he was more dependent on traditions than his master, because there were a greater number of authoritative traditions in existence in his time, and that compared with his increasing dependence on traditions, other kinds of practical considerations are less prominent in his doctrine. Sometimes the contemporary sources state directly, and in other cases it is probable, that Abū Yūsuf's experience as a qāḍī caused him to change his opinions on matters of law. But these frequent changes of opinion also betray some uncertainty and immaturity, and his legal thought is on the whole of a lower standard than that of Abū Ḥanīfa. It is also less original and thoroughly dependent on that of his master. Abū Yūsuf represents the beginning of the process by which the ancient 'Iraqi school of Kūfa was replaced by that of the followers of Abū Ḥanīfa.

Shaybānī (d. A. H. 189), the great disciple both of Abū Ḥanīfa and of Abū Yūsuf, depends even more on traditions than Abū Yūsuf does. This shows itself not only in changes of doctrine under the influence of traditions, but in his habit of duplicating his systematic reasoning by arguments taken from traditions, and in the habitual formula "We follow this" by which he almost invariably rounds off his references to traditions from the Prophet and from other authorities, even when he does not, in fact, follow them. Shaybānī used independent personal opinion to the extent common in the ancient schools of law, but most of his reasoning that appears in the guise of personal opinion is in fact strict analogy or systematic reasoning. To this extent; Shaybānī prepared the way for Shāfi'ī's rejection, on principle, of discretionary decisions and insistence on strict analogical reasoning. Systematic reasoning is the feature most typical of Shaybānī's technical legal thought. It is by far superior to that of his predecessors in general and to that of Abū Yūsuf in particular; it is the most perfect of its kind to be achieved before Shāfi'ī. Shaybānī was the great systematizer of the Kūfian doctrine. He was also a prolific writer, and his voluminous works, which he put under the authority of his master, Abū Ḥanīfa, became the rallying point of the Ḥanafī school which emerged from the ancient school of Kūfa.

In Shāfi'ī (d. A. H. 204), who considered himself a member of the school of Medina though he made the essential thesis of the Traditionists prevail in Islamic law, legal reasoning reached its zenith; it hardly ever again approached and never surpassed the standard he set. When Shāfi'ī wrote, the process of Islamicizing the law, of impregnating it with religious and ethical ideas, had in the main been completed. We therefore find him hardly ever influenced in his conscious legal thought by practical considerations of a religious and ethical kind, such as played an important part in the doctrines of his predecessors. We also find him more consistent than the earlier jurists in separating the moral and the legal aspects, whenever both arise with regard to the same problem. In this respect, Shāfi'ī did not carry out the program of the Traditionists who had tried to identify the categories "forbidden" and "invalid." The sphere of law retained a technical character of its own, and legal relationships were not completely reduced to or expressed in terms of religious and ethical duties. On the other hand, Shāfi'ī's fundamental dependence on formal traditions from the Prophet, in which he followed the Traditionists, implied a different, formal way of Islamicizing the legal doctrine. In theory, Shāfi'ī distinguished sharply between the argument taken from traditions and the result of systematic thought. In his actual reasoning, however, both aspects are closely interwoven; he shows himself tradition bound and systematic at the same time, and this new synthesis may be considered typical of his legal thought. Shāfi'ī's systematic reasoning has its limitations. It breaks down occasionally over irrational traditions or institutions which defy rationalizing. More serious are those faults which come from his polemical attitude towards the ancient schools of law, an attitude which in the case of the Medinese is mitigated by a sentimental attachment, but which in the case of the 'Iraqis is allowed full scope. His dependence upon traditions from the Prophet, too, by making it impossible for him to reject straightforwardly any traditions except on the authority of another, contrary, tradition from the Prophet, is responsible for inconclusive arguments and arbitrary interpretations. But the limitations and faults of Shāfi'ī's reasoning cannot detract from the unprecedentedly high quality of his technical legal thought, which stands out beyond doubt as the greatest individual achievement in Islamic jurisprudence.

Shāfi'ī recognized in principle only strict analogical and systematic reasoning, to the exclusion of arbitrary opinions and discretionary decisions such as had been customary amongst his predecessors. This is one of the important innovations by which his legal theory became utterly different from that of the ancient schools. His legal theory is much more logical and formally consistent than that of his predecessors, whom he blames continually for what appears to him as a mass of inconsistencies. It is based, as previously stated, on the thesis of the Traditionists that nothing can override the authority of a formal tradition from the Prophet. In accepting this, Shāfi'ī cut himself off from the natural and continuous development of doctrine in the ancient schools of law. For him, the sunna is no longer the approved practice as recognized by the representative scholars, it is identical with the content of formal traditions from the Prophet, even though such a tradition be transmitted by only one person in each generation. According to Shāfi'ī, one must not conclude that the Companions of the Prophet knew the intentions of their master best and would therefore not have held opinions incompatible with them. The opinions held and practices inaugurated by persons other than Companions of the Prophet were, of course, in Shāfi'ī's eyes, of no authority whatsoever. This new idea of the sunna as embodied in formal traditions from the Prophet disposed of the concept of living tradition of the ancient schools, even when the living tradition was loosely called "*sunna* of the Prophet." Traditions from the Prophet could not even be invalidated by reference to the Qur'ān. Shāfi'ī took it for granted that the Qur'ān did not contradict the traditions from the Prophet, and that the traditions explained the Qur'ān; the Qur'ān had therefore to be interpreted in the light of the traditions, and not vice versa. The consensus of the scholars, which expressed the living tradition of each ancient school, also became irrelevant for Shāfi'ī; he even denied its existence, and fell back on the general consensus of all Muslims on essentials. The thesis that "everything of which the Muslims approve or disapprove is good or bad in the sight of Allah" had been formulated shortly before Shāfi'ī. Shāfi'ī developed it further, but the principle, as he formulated it, that the community of Muslims would never agree on an error, was put into the form of a tradition from the Prophet only towards the middle of the third century of the hijra. This general consensus was sufficiently vague for it to allow Shāfi'ī to follow the traditions from the Prophet concerning all details. If detailed traditions from the Prophet were to have overriding authority, there was no room left for the exercise of personal opinion, and human reasoning had to be restricted to making correct inferences and drawing systematic conclusions from the traditions. Shāfi'ī was so serious in his main contention that he declared himself prepared to abandon any doctrine of his by which he might unwittingly have contradicted a tradition from the Prophet.

These, in short, were the principles of Shāfi'ī's legal theory. It was a ruthless innovation, and took him some time to elaborate, so that his writings contain numerous traces of the development of his ideas and some unsolved inconsistencies. But notwithstanding all this, Shāfi'ī's legal theory was a magnificently coherent system and superior by far to the theory of the ancient schools. It was the achievement of a powerful mind, and at the same time the logical outcome of a process which started when traditions from the Prophet were first adduced as arguments in law. The development of legal theory in the second century of Islam was dominated by the struggle between two concepts: that of the common doctrine of the community, and that of the authority of traditions from the Prophet. The doctrine of the ancient schools of law represented an uneasy compromise; Shāfi'ī vindicated the thesis of the Traditionists, and the later schools had no choice but to adopt the essentials of his legal theory.

3

FOREIGN ELEMENTS IN ANCIENT ISLAMIC LAW[1]

Joseph Schacht

FOREIGN ELEMENTS IN ANCIENT ISLAMIC LAW [1]

[*Contributed by* JOSEPH SCHACHT, ESQ.]

So much has been written on the problem of foreign elements in ancient Muhammadan law, and with so little result, that to discuss the subject afresh can be justified only if the author adduces new relevant facts or brings new light to bear

[1] A French version of this paper, slightly shortened, was read to Section I(D) of the Third International Congress of Comparative Law, London, August, 1950.

on the elements of the case.[2] At first sight it might seem surprising that one should look for foreign influences in a legal system that unmistakably bears the stamp of uniqueness.[3] But the fact that many prominent features of Islamic civilization, notwithstanding a deceptive Arab appearance, turn out to be borrowings from the Hellenistic and the Iranian world, to mention only these two, poses the question, though without prejudice as to its answer, of similar conditions in the field of law.[4] Furthermore, the riddle of the origins of Muhammadan jurisprudence, once the obviously artificial theory of the Muhammadan lawyers was disregarded, seemed to postulate the unknown quantity of foreign influences as the easiest explanation. The difficulties inherent in both problems, the problem of origins and the problem of foreign elements, have lately been reviewed by Professor Bousquet in a paper which he aptly speaks of the mystery surrounding the genesis of Muhammadan legal science.[5] A solution of this mystery, such as I have attempted in my forthcoming book on *The Origins of Muhammadan Jurisprudence*,[6] will, I hope, enable us to approach the problem of foreign elements in ancient Islamic law from a new angle.

There are four legal systems whose influence on nascent Muhammadan law and jurisprudence is at least possible: Persian Sassanian law, Roman Byzantine (including Roman provincial) law, the canon law of the Eastern churches, and Talmudic law. Outside the sphere of law proper, the far-reaching influence of Judaism and Christianity on Islamic cult and ritual, and that of Roman Byzantine and Persian Sassanian administration on Islamic political and fiscal institutions are matters of common knowledge. It is important for our purpose to realize that these foreign elements have been so thoroughly assimilated and Islamicized that, taken in their ordinary Islamic setting, they hardly seem to reveal a trace of their foreign origin. What was possible here, was possible also in the sphere of law proper, and the difference between the spirit of Islamic law and the spirit of Roman law, for instance, which is indeed striking, does not in itself preclude the possibility of more or less extensive influences.

Of the four legal systems mentioned, very little is known of Persian Sassanian law, so that the question of its influence on ancient Muhammadan law has remained purely hypothetical. The question of a possible influence on the part of the canon law of the Eastern churches has hardly been studied by specialists so far. Influences of Talmudic on ancient Islamic law, on the contrary, have often been pointed out and are easy to account for;[7] the spirit of both systems, too, is similar. As regards the relations between Roman and Islamic law, a number of parallels have been established which are too numerous and too striking to be coincidences.[8] Most of these parallels concern individual rules and whole institutions of positive law, and these can be explained as the natural result of the continuation of legal and commercial practice in the territories conquered by the Saracens, just as ancient Arab legal and commercial practices survived into Islamic law. The principle of the continuation of pre-Islamic legal institutions under Islam is explicitly stated in a passage in Baladhuri which reads:[9] "Abu

[2] For bibliographies, see F. Köprülü, art. *Fikih*, in *Islâm Ansiklopedisi*, part 36, Istanbul, 1947; G.-H. Bousquet, in *Bulletin des Etudes Arabes*, viii, No. 36, Algiers, 1948.

[3] See J. Schacht, *G. Bergsträsser's Grundzüge des islamischen Rechts*, Berlin and Leipzig, 1935, p. 2.

[4] On the non-Arab character of Islamic civilization, see C. H. Becker, *Islamstudien*, i, Leipzig, 1924, pp. 14 ff., 28 ff.

[5] *Le mystère de la formation et des origines du fiqh*, in *Revue Algérienne, Tunisienne et Marocaine de Législation et de Jurisprudence*, lxiii, part 1, Algiers, 1947, pp. 66–80.

[6] Clarendon Press, 1950.

[7] Cf. Bousquet, *Le mystère* ... , p. 76 f.; Bergsträsser, in *Der Islam*, xiv, 81.

[8] We are not concerned here with assessing the extent of the borrowings which Islamic law may have made from Talmudic and from Roman law, but with investigating the problem of whether such borrowings, as far as legal science is concerned, may possibly have taken place.

[9] *Liber expugnationis regionum*, ed. de Goeje, Leiden, 1865, p. 448. Baladhuri died in A.H. 279.

The evidence available to us now shows that Muhammadan legal science started in Iraq about A.H. 100. The development of doctrine in Medina was invariably secondary to and dependent upon that in Iraq. The early lawyers of Islam at the beginning of the second century of the Hegira took the popular and administrative practice of their time as their raw material and endorsed, modified, or rejected it, thereby creating Muhammadan law. "Traditions" purporting to relate legal decisions and relevant actions of the Prophet are considerably later, and as a rule do not originally express the doctrine of the ancient schools of law in Islam, but opinions proposed in opposition to them. The first specialists in religious law at the end of the first century A.H. concentrated their attention on questions of ritual and perhaps on kindred problems of directly religious interest, such as questions of conscience relating to alms tax, marriage and divorce. Legal problems, in the sense in which we use the word, began to be worked out not earlier than in the second century A.H. The legal opinions ascribed to authorities of the first century turn out, on closer investigation, to be spurious. This applies specifically to the information concerning Sa'id b. Musaiyib which led Bergsträsser to the dilemma that I mentioned before. The ancient sects of Islam, when they split from the "orthodox" community about the middle of the first century A.H., did not share with the majority the essentials of a law which did not yet exist, but they adopted the fully developed legal system of the "orthodox" community, making only superficial changes of their own, in the second half of the second century. These results which, much to my own surprise, the weight of the evidence forced upon me, put of course a new complexion on the whole problem of foreign elements in ancient Muhammadan law. What is important is not so much that the whole first century of the Hegira had been available for their adoption, if adoption of foreign elements there was, but that Muhammadan jurisprudence began only at a time when the door of Islamic civilization became widely open to the potential transmitters who were the educated non-Arab converts to Islam, and that its centre was not Medina but Iraq.[17]

I do not suggest that Iraq was ever a country of Roman law, but at the period in question it was deeply imbued with the spirit of Hellenistic civilization and at the same time contained great centres of Talmudic learning.[18] These are all the data we need in order to account for the existence of concepts and maxims of Roman jurisprudence in early Islamic legal science, and the regular occurrence of parallels in Talmudic law. If we survey those legal concepts and maxims whose common occurrence in Roman and Islamic jurisprudence seems to call for admitting an influence of the former on the latter, we find them mostly of that general kind which would be familiar not only to lawyers but to rhetors and generally to those who had received an Hellenistic education. Now Professor D. Daube has shown that Rabbinic methods of legal interpretation, which present reasonings familiar to earlier Roman legal classics, are deeply influenced not by those classics themselves but by Hellenistic rhetoric which was taught all over the Hellenistic world.[19] The same explanation is sufficient, and indeed necessary, in order to account for the presence in ancient Islamic legal science of Greek logic, as exemplified by conclusions *a maiore ad minus* and negatively *a minore ad maius*, the argument of the *sorites*, the concepts of genus and species, the *regressus ad infinitum*, and a whole technique of disputation. On the borderline between logic and legal science stands the principle of *istishab*, that is the presumption

[17] We know little about the Syrian school of law in early Islam, but we do know that the Syrians were influenced by Iraqian reasoning.

[18] See, e.g., A. Christensen, *L'Iran sous les Sassanides*, 2nd ed., Copenhagen, 1944, index s.v. *hellénisme*; M. Rostovtzeff, *The Social and Economic History of the Hellenistic World*, iii, Oxford, 194[illegible], index s.v. *Mesopotamia*. M. Meyerhof, *Von Alexandrien nach Bagdad*, Berlin, 1930, p. 14 f (= *Sitzungsber. Preuss. Akad. Wiss. Phil.-hist. Kl.*, xxiii, 400 f.).

[19] In *Law Quarterly Review*, lii, 265 f.; in *Tulane Law Review*, xviii, 365 f.; and in *Hebrew Union College Annual*, xxii, Cincinnati, 1949.

that a legal status, once established, continues until the contrary is proved.[20] To legal science belongs the principle of *istislah*, or *utilitatis ratio*.[21] *Qiyas*, which is the technical term for analogy, systematic reasoning, must for linguistic reasons have been borrowed from Rabbinic *heqqesh*, itself presumably a translation of the Greek term συμβάλλειν.[22]

The central idea of the ancient schools of law in Islam, the idea of consensus itself, seems to have been taken over from Roman law via the schools of rhetoric. I am not speaking of the general consensus of the community at large on the essential duties of the Muslim, a definition to which Shafi'i towards the end of the second century of the Hegira tried to reduce the concept. This idea and its workings before and after Shafi'i are so natural that the question of foreign influence does not arise. The ancient schools of law, however, had a highly organized concept of the "consensus of the scholars" which consisted in the considered opinion of their majority and expressed the "living tradition" of the school. This concept corresponds to the *opinio prudentium* of Roman law, the authority of which was stated by the Emperor Severus in the following terms: "In ambiguitatibus quae ex legibus proficiscuntur, consuetudinem aut rerum perpetuo similiter iudicatarum auctoritatem vim legis obtinere debere."[23] This is again a general maxim which would be familiar not only to lawyers but to all who had studied rhetoric, and it is this fact which makes an influence, first suggested by Goldziher, feasible and, in view of other similar instances, likely.[24]

There is a maxim in Islamic law that "the child belongs to the [marriage] bed." This maxim, which was intended to decide disputes about paternity, has been regarded, on insufficient evidence, as an authentic rule of pre-Islamic Arab practice, but Goldziher has shown that it had not yet prevailed in the middle Umaiyad period, say about A.H. 75. In the middle of the second century, it had been put into the mouth of the Prophet, but it is, strictly speaking, incompatible with the Koranic rulings regarding paternity, and in Islamic law as it exists the maxim, though often quoted, is never taken at its face value.[25] In order to decide cases of disputed paternity, Muhammadan law falls back not on the maxim but on the old Arab procedure of calling in professional physiognomists. It is likely that the maxim, which agrees neither with old Arab custom nor with the Koran, but has its parallel in the Roman legal maxim "pater est quem nuptiae demonstrant," penetrated from outside into Islamic discussions, though it did not succeed in modifying positive law. Again it is a norm which would be familiar to all persons trained in Greco-Roman rhetoric.[26]

There was no punishment for theft in pre-Islamic Arabia, and the mutilation of the culprit by cutting off his hand was introduced by the Koran.[27] The idea of pecuniary penalties is, and has been from the beginning, foreign to Muhammadan law. The earliest doctrine, which was maintained by the Iraqians, even made the Koranic punishment for theft incompatible with the responsibility of the thief for damages; according to the mitigated and therefore inconsistent doctrine of the Medinese, the claim for monetary compensation lapsed if the thief

[20] For Roman and Talmudic parallels, see D. Santillana, *Istituzioni di diritto musulmano malichita*, 2nd ed., i, 327; Goldziher, in *Vienna Oriental Journal*, i, 231 ff.

[21] For parallels, see Santillana, *ibid.*, 71; Goldziher, *ibid.*, 229. The oldest document, in which this consideration is expressed, is an Iraqian "tradition," on which see my *Origins*, p. 111.

[22] See Margoliouth, in *J.R.A.S.*, 1910, p. 320; and my *Origins*, p. 99 f.

[23] Both on the Roman and on the Islamic side, custom and practice are reduced to the considered opinion of the lawyers.

[24] Cf. *Origins*, p. 83.

[25] Zurqani's commentary on Malik's *Muwatta'*, xxxvi, 20, explains the systematic difficulties inherent in the "tradition" from the Prophet.

[26] Cf. *Origins*, p. 181 f.

[27] Mutilation as a punishment of coin-clippers and counterfeiters is advocated by spurious "traditions" quoted in Baladhuri, *ibid.*, 470. R. S. Lopez, in *Byzantion*, xvi, 445 ff., has suggested a Byzantine origin. If this is correct, it would be a case of proposed adoption of a judicial practice which existed in the conquered territories.

was subject to the Koranic punishment and insolvent; if the stolen object still existed in the possession of the thief, it was of course returned to its owner.[28] In any case, any damage culpably inflicted gives rise to a claim for simple compensation only. If we therefore find some legal "traditions" unsuccessfully advocating as part of the punishment of a thief to whom the Koranic penalty cannot be applied, that he should be responsible for double the value of the object stolen,[29] we must look outside for the source of this idea which can have its origin neither in pre-Islamic Arab customary law nor in the Koran, and which contradicts a consistently applied principle of Muhammadan law.[30] The Roman law of *furtum* offers itself instantly as the most likely source.

By an extension of the idea of theft which, too, went against an acknowledged principle of Islamic law, the effort was made in a related type of legal "tradition" to make a person who was guilty of stealing by finding and concealing a stray camel, responsible for twice its value, or for returning it and another camel of equal value.[31] This was not to apply to all cases of stealing by finding, but only to the special case concerning stray camels, and it was destined to remain as little successful as the suggested pecuniary penalty for theft from which it was derived.

Under the traditional approach to the early history of Islamic law and jurisprudence it would have been difficult, if not impossible, to admit the influence of a Roman legal idea on legal "traditions" which were uncritically regarded as more or less genuine reflexions if not of the actual rulings of Muhammad, at least of the customary law of Medina. Now we know that this kind of legal "tradition" purporting to go back to the Prophet was put into circulation when the second century of the Hegira was well under way, in order to change the established doctrine of the ancient schools of law.[32]

In this instance of the penalty for theft it is out of the question either that parts of the practical administration of penal law in conquered Byzantine territory should have been continued by the Muslims amongst themselves, or that early Muhammadan lawyers should have adopted consciously any principle of Roman law—if only for the simple reason that the Islamic (unsuccessful) legal doctrines differ in many important respects from the teachings of Roman law on *furtum*—but we must conclude that the general idea of holding the thief responsible, under certain conditions, for double the amount he had stolen became familiar to some Muslims through Christian converts and was taken over by them. This idea is one that every educated person among the original inhabitants of Iraq and Syria would know. By the process which I am trying to elucidate, the Muslims appropriated, as it were, worn-off coins of ideas, transmitted to them after a long usage and after many of their distinctive features had been effaced. In this respect, the adoption of Roman legal ideas and maxims by the Muslims through the intermediary of the schools of rhetoric and through persons with an Hellenistic education resembles the contemporaneous introduction of Greek philosophical ideas and problems into Islamic theology.

In pre-Islamic Arab usage, the term *rahn*, "security," meant a kind of earnest money which was given as a guarantee and material proof of a contract, particu-

[28] The two doctrines mentioned survived in the Hanafi and the Malaki school respectively (cf. Schacht, *G. Bergsträsser's Grundzüge*, p. 101; Santillana, ibid., ii, 455). Only Shafi'i, at the end of the second century, and his school accepted the unrestricted responsibility of the thief for simple damages.

[29] See Ibn Hanbal, ii, 180, 207; Abu Dawud, x, xxxvii, 13; Nasa'i, xlvi, 12; Baihaqi, viii, 278; *Kanz al'Ummal* iii, 1513, 1529, 1544. A derived form occurs in Malik's *Muwatta'*, xxxvi, 38 (ed. Cairo, 1310, iii, 211), and in Baihaqi, loc. cit.

[30] The followers of "traditions," and therefore the Hanbali school, naturally adopt this doctrine in respect to the cases directly mentioned in them, though it breaks the system (cf. Ibn Quadama, *Mughni*, x, 262 ff.). The irregularity of the derived form of the "tradition" (see the preceding note) from the point of view of Muhammadan law is pointed out by Shafi'i, *Treatise III*, 69 (*Umm*, vii, 215).

[31] See Abu Dawud, x; Baihaqi, vi, 191; *Kanz al-'Ummal*, vii, 3808, 3841. A fine of one-third of the value is imposed in a parallel version in *Kanz al-'Ummal*, vii, 3826, 3827.

[32] Cf. *Origins*, pp. 66, 178.

larly when there was no scribe available to put it into writing. The word occurs in this meaning in the Koran.[33] Used of persons, it meant a kind of hostages who were produced by each party to a lawsuit as a guarantee that the parties would submit to the decision of the arbitrator.[34] But the ancient schools of law recognized neither the institution of earnest money nor that of hostages, and knew *rahn* only in the new meaning of a security for the payment of a debt. The foreign origin of this doctrine which neglects old Arab usage and an explicit passage in the Koran is probable, and Roman law presents us with an obvious model in the institution of *pignus*.[34a] The Muslims found this institution in the conquered Byzantine provinces, and their early lawyers approved of a corresponding elementary definition of *rahn*. When they came to work out the details of their doctrine, it evolved through essentially the same sequence of stages as it had done, many centuries earlier, in Roman law.

The oldest known opinion states that "the security takes the place of that for which it is given," for instance, if the security perishes whilst it is in the possession of the creditor. This opinion was held in Iraq; it was also known in Medina and in Mecca. Somewhat later, however, the Iraqian school mitigated this extreme doctrine. The old Iraqian maxim was countered in Medina by the opposite maxim "the security is not forfeited," for instance, if the debtor fails to pay the debt within the stipulated time. This is a late, polemical counter-statement and does not adequately express the Medinese doctrine which is considerably influenced by the mitigated doctrine of the Iraqian school. The doctrines of the Iraqian and of the Medinese school survive in the Hanafi and in the Maliki school respectively, and represent two successive stages in abandoning the oldest opinion. Shafi'i completed this process and was the first consistently to apply to securities the concept of a deposit on trust.[35] A technical influence of Roman on nascent Muhammadan jurisprudence is out of the question in any of these stages.

To mention at least one similar case of contact between the canon law of the Eastern churches and ancient Muhammadan law: the law of Islam, it is well known, is very severe against adultery and fornication, but it has never erected them into impediments to marriage.[36] Muhammadan law knows prohibited degrees, but they are all based either on consanguinity or on affinity or on fosterage. All other impediments to marriage can be remedied by appropriate action, for instance, a man who is married to four wives can marry again if he repudiates one of them, or the Muslim who wants to marry a polytheist woman can do so if she adopts Islam; the only permanent impediment to marriage, outside the prohibited degrees, is created between a former husband and wife who have undergone the formal procedure of mutual imprecation known as *li'an*.[37] Now it is very surprising to find in Maliki law (and, with differences of detail, in the law of the so-called "Twelver" Shiites) a permanent impediment to marriage between a man and a woman who have gone through a form of marriage during the waiting period (*'idda*) following the termination of a previous marriage of the woman to another husband,[38] and have had intercourse. This impediment arises even from a bona fide marriage, it arises even if the intercourse itself has taken place after the end of the waiting period in question, but it does not arise if they have gone through a form of marriage during the existence of a previous marriage of the woman, or have had intercourse during it. The systematic basis for this

[33] Sura ii, 283.

[34] Cf. E. Tyan, *Histoire de l'Organisation Judiciaire en Pays d'Islam*, i, Paris, 1938, p. 73 f.

[34a] The Sassanian *graßth*, on the other hand, denotes the *antichresis* rather than the *pignus* proper; cf. A. Pagliaro, *L'anticresi nel diritto sasanidico*, in *Rivista degli Studi Orientali*, xv, 275 ff.

[35] Cf. *Origins*, p. 186 f.

[36] Except for one particular doctrine, on which see below.

[37] See *Encyclopædia of Islam*, ii, s.v.

[38] During the *'idda*, the woman is barred from remarrying.

doctrine in the Maliki school is a Medinese "tradition" concerning a decision of the Caliph 'Umar, interpreted literally and restrictively; the doctrine is the minimum consistent with its wording. That this was not the original purport of the tradition is evident. What its import was becomes clear from a group of earlier Iraqian "traditions" of a kind which regularly corresponds to that type of Medinese tradition, save that they were not successful in influencing the doctrine of the Iraqian school. Now these ancient Iraqian "traditions" aim at erecting adultery or fornication into a permanent impediment to marriage.[39] This doctrine, which prevailed only in the law of the Ibadi sect and is otherwise unprecedented in Muhammadan law, is a well-known feature of canon law. Again it was not canon law itself that influenced Muhammadan jurisprudence, but the Christian converts to Islam brought their ideas of adultery as an impediment to marriage with them into their new religion, and this concept found expression in the "traditions" in question.[40]

I will take my last example from Persian Sassanian law, of which I said before that we know very little. But we do know that Ibn Muqaffa', a Persian secretary of state who served under the last Umaiyads and the first "Abbasids and died about A.H. 140, in a memorandum or treatise which he wrote in the last few years of his life,[41] suggested that the Caliph should review the doctrines of the ancient schools of law, and codify and enact his own decisions. These considerations lie quite outside the compass of the ancient lawyers of Islam, and are obviously influenced by Sassanian administrative tradition.[42] This Persian idea and its rejection by the specialists in Muhammadan law was transferred into an Islamic setting and expressed in an anecdote according to which one of the early 'Abbasid Caliphs, either Mansur, or Mahdi, or Harun al-Rashid, intended to endow Malik's *Muwatta'* with the character of an official code, and desisted only on the entreaties of Malik himself.[43] This shows how thoroughly foreign elements were incorporated into an Islamic background.

I trust I have shown that legal concepts and principles, including even fundamental ideas of legal science, entered Muhammadan law from outside, in particular from Roman law, and have further shown how their adoption took place. Whether these influences amount to little or much is irrelevant; the important fact is that they did happen. The examples which I have given are restricted to cases I had occasion to investigate myself when working out, without any reference to the question of possible influences from outside, the new approach to the early history of Muhammadan law and jurisprudence of which I spoke before. This new approach not only frees us from the apparent impossibility of accounting for parallels which cannot be coincidences,[44] it enables us to establish the early history of Islamic law and jurisprudence, a task that must precede any reference to outside parallels. My aim in presenting these remarks is not to give any final solutions, it is merely to re-establish the subject, in Goldziher's words, as "one of the most attractive problems of this branch of Islamic studies."

[39] The Medinese "tradition," in other words, treats a marriage during the '*idda* as if it were adultery.

[40] I intend to treat of this problem in detail in a separate paper.

[41] *Risala fil-Sahaba*.

[42] Cf. *Origins*, p. 95.

[43] *See Encyclopædia of Islam*, iii, s.v. *Malik b. Anas*. For other anecdotes of similar tendency, see *Origins*, p. 96 and n.1.

[44] I have taken particular care to show the irregular or unprecedented character of doctrines which must be derived from other than purely Arab and Islamic sources.

4

THE BIRTH-HOUR OF MUSLIM LAW? AN ESSAY IN EXEGESIS

S.D. Goitein

Islamic religion is characterized by the prominence of legal conceptions in its system: The Sharīᶜah, or holy law, is its very essence, and Fiqh, or religious jurisprudence, is its science (*ᶜilm*) par excellence. The minute observation of many commandments is its most conspicuous practical aspect; the free fellowship of religious scholars, who do not need authorization by any government to interpret, develop, and apply its law, is its most representative body, and even the purely legal sections of the Fiqh are studied reverently as an act of worship.

All these features are so familiar to the student of Islam that they seem to be natural and need no explanation of their provenance. In fact, however, their origin and early formation are far from being fully known and may partly elude our knowledge forever. There is, of course, a striking resemblance between early Islam and Judaism in all the aspects mentioned above. However, as many of these seem to originate from parallel developments rather than from borrowing, the similarity between the two religions poses problems rather than solves them.

During the last few years there has been a considerable amount of discussion on this question of the origin and early development of Muslim law. At the third international congress of Comparative Law, held in London in August 1950, Professor Joseph Schacht surveyed the problem in a paper entitled "Foreign Elements in Ancient Islamic Law" (*Journal of Comparative Legislation,* 1950), which stressed in particular the parallels between Islamic and Roman Law. Shortly afterwards, Professor S. Vesey Fitzgerald of London published an article in the *Law Quarterly Journal,* January 1951, pp. 81-102, the very name of which ("The A l l e g e d Debt of Islamic to Roman Law") betrays the author's opinion that Islamic jurisprudence was not influenced by Roman legal science. It is not surprising, therefore, that one scholar, Professor Bousquet of Algiers, speaks about the m y s t e r y surrounding the genesis of Muḥammadan legal science (in his article "Le Mystère de la Formation et des Origines du Fiqh" in *Revue Algérienne ... de Législation et de Jurisprudence, Algiers,* 1947, pp. 66-80).

The present paper is not concerned with the origin of Fiqh, the science of Muslim Jurisprudence, but with that of Muslim law itself, i.e. the legal parts of the Sharīᶜah. As everyone knows, the Sharīᶜah does not differentiate between purely legal matters, such as contracts or the laws of inheritance, and religious duties, such as prayers and fasting; all alike are part of the Holy Law. Through detailed interpretation of a significant passage in the Qur'ān, this paper tries to answer the question whether this particular character of the Sharīᶜah goes back to the founder of Islam himself, and if so, at what juncture of his activities did a tendency towards it become evident.

It has often been stressed that the Qurʾān contains comparatively little legal matter and that the little it contains is entirely unsystematic and haphazard; or as an article on the subject put it: "It is evident that Muḥammad himself made no attempt to work out any comprehensive legal system, a task for which he seems to have been singularly ill-suited; instead, he contented himself with what went little beyond 'ad hoc' amendments to the existing customary law" (J. N. D. Anderson, *The Muslim World,* Vol. xl. 1950, p. 245). A number of modern authors on Muslim Law have repeated a statement, obviously going back to Count Ostorog's book *The Angora Reform,* p. 19, that of the 6236 verses of the Qurʾān, no more than about five hundred, less than one-twelfth, could be considered as having legal import.

However, these statements need some qualification. The average length of a verse in the Qurʾān varies from one to three lines (in the Egyptian edition), while those of legal content usually comprise three to six, and some are considerably longer, e.g. verse 282 of the second Surah, which stretches over fifteen lines. Thus, from the purely arithmetical point of view, legal matters occupy a far larger part of the Qurʾān than assumed by the aforesaid estimate. And there is another very important point to be considered. As is well known, the Qurʾān teems with repetitions; the same thing seems to be said over and again, often in the same words; in legal matters, however, repetitions are rare, and when they occur, they usually contain some progress in legislation. According to the view of the Muslim theologians, expressed for instance by Al-Ghazālī in his *Jawāhir al-Qurʾān,* strictly speaking, no repetitions occur in the holy book of Islam. In any case, if one condenses its subject matter to its mere content, under the five main headings of preaching, polemics, stories, allusions to the Prophet's life, and legislation, one will reach the conclusion that proportionately the Qurʾān does not contain less legal material than the Pentateuch, the Torah, which is known in world literature as "The Law."

The accepted view of Muḥammad's career as a law-giver seems to be that while in Mecca he acted solely as preacher and prophet, whereas in Medina the requirements of an ever-growing community forced him to give legal decisions from time to time. This view is based on the fact that Muḥammad sincerely and most vehemently believed that the Last Judgment and the end of the known physical world was imminent. What purpose was there, then, in expounding an elaborate legal system, when all human beings were to come to an end soon? It is true that even the earliest parts of the Qurʾān are not devoid of legal matters; for instance, when Muḥammad enjoins the true believers to keep to their pledges and contracts, to stand by their testimony (Surah lxx. 32-33) and to be just in measure and weight (Surah lxxxiii. 1-3), or when he objected from the outset to usury, i.e. the taking of interest (Surah

xxx. 39). However, these prescriptions are religious and moral commandments rather than pieces of formal legislation.

On the other hand, Tor Andrae has rightly shown (in his book *Muhammad, The Man and his Faith,* Chapter 6) that even in Mecca Muḥammad conceived the religious community as a social and even political unit, *ummah* — a conception which no doubt has to account for the astonishing fact that soon after his arrival at Medina, he was able to organize the whole population of the town, Muslims and non-Muslims, as one body politic, called *ummah* [1]. Muḥammad's biographer, Ibn Isḥāq, has preserved the document constituting this *ummah,* and even the most critical minds do not cast doubt on its authenticity. This document, which contains forty seven paragraphs, betrays a highly legalistic and even formalistic mind — a fact which is not surprising in a son of a flourishing city of merchants. The same holds true of the many treaties contracted by him with Arab tribes, discussed in special studies by Wellhausen (Skizzen IV, 1889) and Jacob Sperber (Die Sendschreiben M's), and in the well-known books of Muḥammad Ḥamīdullāh.

In contrast with this, one has to concede that many Medinan Surahs, which are contemporary with the deeds just referred to, contain little or no legal material, while it is abundantly clear from the testimony of *Ḥadīth, Sīrah* and *Tafsīr,* as well as from inner evidence, that many legal questions must have been brought before Muḥammad and decided by him at that time. For according to the Arab as well as the old Israelite conception, law is not a fixed order imposed and exercised by the power of an organized community and need not be created by a king or a legal assembly. Law is a truth, which exists forever and which has only to be discovered by a wise man; the judge in pre-Islamic Arabia was called *al-ḥakam,* cf. Hebrew *ḥākhām,* the wise man who is inspired by the spirit of God. The vast literature on Arab tribal custom shows that in many cases the judges were not the chiefs of the tribes or other persons of authority, but wise men, often from some distant locale, who were famous for their inspiration and experience.

To this may be added the astonishing fact that during a prolonged study of the language and life of the Jews in Yemen, the writer came across quite a number of cases where, in out-of-the-way areas, the Jewish ᶜāqil, i.e. the headman of the local community, was approached by Arab tribesmen to settle minor disputes of theirs. Similarly, Kaᶜb ibn al-Ashraf, one of the prominent Jews of Medina, used to serve as a judge to non-Jews. However, Muḥammad was the outstanding spiritual authority in the town, and according to Arabic conceptions, it was only natural that he should act as a *ḥakam* not only for Muslims, but also,

[1] W. Montgomery Watt, *Muhammad at Medina,* Oxford 1956, p. 227, assumes that "the Constitution" — as he calls the document under discussion — was promulgated after year 5 of the Hijrah. For many reasons, which cannot be discussed here, this surmise is unacceptable.

as we shall see, for unbelievers, including Jews, although these had, as the Qur'ān reports, their own *rabbāniyyūn* and *aḥbār* (in Hebrew, *rabbānīm* and *ḥavērīm*), rabbis and scholars, who guided them in legal matters.

Why, then, were so few of these legal decisions incorporated in the many Surahs of the early Medinan period? To my mind, the answer to this question can only be that it occurred to Muḥammad only at a relatively late period that even strictly legal matters were not religiously irrelevant, but were part and parcel of the divine revelation and were included in the heavenly book, which was the source of all religions. I believe that we have an exact account of this most fateful development in the Prophet's career in a lengthy Quranic passage namely Surah v. 42-51, to the discussion of which the rest of this paper will be devoted.

In verses 42-43, Muḥammad expresses his astonishment that the Jews of Medina applied to him as judge, although they were in the possession of a divinely revealed law. God says to Muḥammad: "When they come to you, you may act as a judge between them or you may turn away from them; ... (43) But why should they make you their judge, seeing that in their hand is the Torah, containing the judgment of God? ... (44) Verily, we have sent down the Torah containing guidance and light, by it the prophets ... gave judgment for the Jews, as likewise did the rabbis and the scholars by such portion of the Book of God, as they were entrusted with; ... [2] (45) Therein We have prescribed for them: A life (verbally soul) for a life, an eye for an eye, etc.; ... [3] (46) In their footsteps we caused Jesus, son of Mary, to follow, confirming the Torah which was before him, and we gave him the Gospel, wherein is guidance and light; ... (47) Let the people of the Gospel judge by that which God has sent down therein. Who so do not judge by what God has sent down, such are evil doers. (48) And unto you we have sent down the Book with the Truth, confirming whatever Book was before, and as a watcher over it; so judge between them by what God has sent down and do not follow their inclinations away from the truth which has come to you, for each one we have made a fixed way and an open road." After this there follows again an admonishment to judge only according to the divine law, and the passage concludes with the exclamation (50) "Do they then desire the (mode of) judgment of the Time of Ignorance? But who is better than God in judgment to a people who have certainty in their belief?"

The import of these lines seems evident. Some members of the Jewish community of Medina had applied to Muḥammad's court, but there arose difficulties; perhaps one party refused to accept his decision. As may be learned from the end of the passage, and from other verses

[2] By that time, Muḥammad was well aware of the fact that in addition to the *Taurāt* or Bible, the Jewish scholars used other books which they believed to contain God's commandments.

[3] An illusion to the well-known passage of the Pentateuch.

of the Qur'ān, in particular from the eighth Surah, and from various stories reported by the *Ḥadīth,* among the Muslims, too, there were some who had *ahwā'*, inclinations, i.e. took a critical attitude towards the Prophet's judgments. Owing to the close connection between spiritual leadership and the role of a judge, such an attitude was dangerous. Hitherto, according to our hypothesis, Muḥammad had not regarded his judicial activities as part of his prophetic office. This was now to change. From that time onward, *ḥukm al-Jāhiliyyah,* the mode of judgment of the Time of Ignorance, had to be given up. The decision of legal questions was now a matter of one's religion, exactly as the beliefs about God or resurrection or Muḥammad's prophetic mission. That is why this passage is followed by another one, in which the true believers are enjoined not to take Jews or Christians as their patrons (*awliyā'*), as had frequently been the case before, because each community was to be regarded as a completely separate entity in itself. Religion had become totalitarian, comprising all departments of life, including the hitherto neutral aspect of law. Muḥammad regrets this fact; "If God had wished," he says, "he would have made all mankind one community" (Surah v. 4a). But, for the time being, such was God's will, and humanity was bound to comply with it.

It would, of course, be extremely useful if we knew exactly when these verses were first promulgated. As usual, the Muslim commentators and other authors dealing with the *asbāb al-nuzūl,* the occasions of the promulgation of parts of the Qur'ān, differ widely on this point. Some make the whole fifth Surah the last of the Prophet's utterings, and in this they are followed, e.g., by Professor Blachère in his new, chronologically arranged, French translation, Vol. III, p. 1110 (1951), though he states, that the various parts of this Surah seem to belong to considerably different times. Another widely diffused traditional view connects our passage with a contest of nobility between two Jewish tribes, which would entail a very early date. My own opinion is that the repeated references to the Jewish rabbis and scholars can only fit a time when there still remained a considerable number of Jews in Medina, i.e. before the end of the fifth year of the Hijrah, while the complete confessional segregation of Christians, Jews, and Muslims, here advocated, points to a rather developed stage of Muḥammad's activities. The most suitable date for this passage would therefore be the fifth year of the Hijrah, five years before Muḥammad's death, a date suggested, for other reasons of course, by such eminent Muslim authors as Al-Zuhrī, Al-Wāqidī, and Al-Ṭabarī (cf. Noeldeke, *Geschichte des Qur'āns,* I, p. 231, note 1).

It would hardly be an exaggeration to say that this passage indicates the birth-hour of Muslim law. As has been shown here, more legal material is contained in later parts of the Qur'ān than is usually believed. But this is not the decisive point. What matters, as Professor H. A. R. Gibb has emphasized in his *Muhammedanism,* is the attitude which regards everything, including, seemingly, religiously irrelevant legal matters, as emanating from God through His true prophet. This attitude, as we believe, was first clearly conceived and expressed in the passage just discussed, approximately halfway through the ten years which Muḥammad passed in Medina.

There remains the question whether this conception of the heavenly origin of law came to Muḥammad from outside or was developed by him independently. Here the historian may meet the theologian halfway. According to the tenets of the predominant Muslim theology, the Qurʾān, like God himself, is eternally pre-existent. The historian may find that ideas which at a certain date found expression in the Qurʾān were pre-existent in Muḥammad's original preaching, as is to be found in the early chapters of the Qurʾān. This is indeed the case with the idea of the Sharīʿah. It is contained in Muḥammad's original view of the religious *ummah* as a social and even political entity, in his early idea of the prophets as lawgivers and in his own first attempts at the codification of basic socio-religious duties, contained in Surahs xvii, 23-38 and vi. 151-152, which Al-Thaʿālibi in his *Kitāb al Ārāʾis* already recognized as a replica of the Biblical ten commandments. [4] However, it is a far cry from these early beginnings to the conception of Islam as a separate denomination exacting all-embracing duties, as expressed in the passage from Surah v discussed above. For this elaborate address clearly indicates a complete change of attitude, a turning point, in the thinking of the Prophet on the relation between law and religion. As was usual with Muḥammad, a thorough pragmatist, the change came about in the wake of some practical problem which he had to solve. Some Jews had come to litigate before him and something went wrong with the case. God then gives His prophet the permission to refuse to act as a judge for non-Muslims, if he chose to do so. This particular incident, however, served as an occasion for a far wider ruling: the Muslims and the adherers of other religions had to have different laws altogether, for law was a part of the prophetic message, with the consequence that the followers of different prophets could be properly judged only by those who believed in their respective revelations. In pagan times, people did not care what religion their judges had, as long as they were competent and inspired men. With Islam — according to the new conception — law, even civil law, had become part of the message which was contained in one heavenly Book, but was sent in different forms to different peoples.

The emphatic and detailed exposition of the new idea in the passage under discussion; the repeated references in Surah v to the Jewish rabbis and scholars who gave judgments according to the Law revealed by God; the quotation from the Pentateuch, which deals not with

---

[4] H. Hirschfeld, *New Researches,* p. 81. H. Grimme, *Mohammad,* II, pp. 115-118.

theological matters, but with questions of criminal law; and, finally the very occasion which gave rise to the promulgation of Surah v. 41-52, suggest that Muḥammad, at a certain stage of his prophetical and political career in Medina, suddenly became aware of the fact that the scriptures revealed before him contained not only religious and moral injunctions, but also detailed laws concerning matters which were religiously irrelevant. This new knowledge, together with some difficulties incurred in practice, created in him the belief — which was well in line with his original idea of religion as a constitution for a body politic — that he, too, had to recognize the details of civil law as inseparable constituents of God's message. In other words, the idea of the Sharīᶜah was not the result of post-Quranic developments, but was formulated by Muḥammad himself.

The results obtained here seem to be at variance with the conclusions of Joseph Schacht's penetrating study *The Origins of Muhammedan Jurisprudence,* Oxford, 1950. Schacht assumes that during the first century of the Hijrah, law still fell outside the sphere of religion and was brought into its orbit only during the 2nd century, when Muslim jurisprudence, properly speaking, came into being.

There is, however, no basic contradiction between the two views. As Goldziher in the first chapter of his *Muhammedan Studies,* called *Dīn* and *Muruwwa,* has shown, it took generations, until the Muslim spirit of "religion" replaced the pagan conception of "virtue" as the essential quality of a man. In the same way, it is only natural that *ḥukm al-Jāhiliyyah,* judgment according to arbitrary opinion or established local practice, did not disappear immediately and altogether after Muḥammad denounced it, but was replaced only gradually — and, as is well-known, never completely — by a legal system worked out on religious lines. However, it seems to emerge clearly, from our analysis of the lengthy passage in Surah v, that it was Muḥammad himself who envisaged law as part of divine revelation.

5

TWO LEGAL PROBLEMS BEARING ON THE EARLY HISTORY OF THE QUR'ĀN[1]

Patricia Crone

The Qur'ān is generally supposed to have originated in a social, cultural and linguistic environment familiar to the early commentators, whose activities began shortly after Muḥammad's death and many of whom were natives of the two cities in which he had been active; yet they not infrequently seem to have forgotten the original meaning of the text.[2] It is clear, for example, that they did not remember what Muḥammad had meant by the expressions *jizya ʿan yad,*[3] *al-ṣamad,*[4] *kalāla*[5] or *īlāf*; indeed, the whole of Sūra

---

1 I should like to thank David Powers, Frank Stewart and Fritz Zimmermann, as well as Etan Kohlberg, Sarah Stroumsa and other participants in the fourth Jāhiliyya colloquium, for commenting on earlier drafts of this paper; I am particularly indebted to Frank Stewart, whose reaction to the first draft accounts for most of such clarity as the present version possesses.

2 Rippin would like Islamicists to forget about the original meaning of the Qur'ān (A. Rippin [ed.], *Approaches to the History and Interpretation of the Qur'ān*, Oxford 1988, pp. 2ff.). But though the study of *tafsīr* certainly should not focus on it alone, a historian of the rise of Islam cannot do without it. Rippin objects that "the scholar will never become a seventh-century Arabian townsperson but will remain forever a twentieth-century historian or philologian"; but we will never become tenth-century Iraqis, nineteenth-century Egyptians or anyone else in our own or other people's past either, nor will we ever become anything other than ourselves in the present. Should we then abandon altogether the attempt to understand what other people are trying to say?

3 F. Rosenthal, 'Some Minor Problems in the Qur'ān', *The Joshua Starr Memorial Volume*, New York 1953, pp. 68ff.; cf. C. Cahen, 'Coran IX-29', *Arabica* 9, 1962; M.M. Bravmann, 'A propos de Qur'ān IX-29', *Arabica* 10, 1963; id., 'The Ancient Arab Background of the Qur'ānic Concept *al-Gizyatu ʿan Yadin*', in his *The Spiritual Background of Early Islam*, Leiden 1972 (reprinted from *Arabica* 13, 1966, and 14, 1967); M.J. Kister, '"ʿAn Yadin" (*Qur'ān*, IX/29)', *Arabica* 11, 1964; and now also U. Rubin, 'Qur'ān and *Tafsīr*. The case of "ʿan Yadin"', *Der Islam* 70, 1993.

106 (*Quraysh*), in which the word *īlāf* occurs, was as opaque to them as it is to us;[6] and the same is true of the so-called 'mysterious letters'.[7] *Kalāla* is a rather unusual case in that several traditions (attributed to ʿUmar) openly admit that the meaning of this word was unknown;[8] more commonly, the exegetes hide their ignorance behind a profusion of interpretations so contradictory that they can only be guesswork. "It might", as Rosenthal observes, "seem an all too obvious and unconvincing argument to point to the constant differences of the interpreters and conclude from their disagreement that none of them is right. However, there is something to such an argument".[9] There is indeed. Given that the entire exegetical tradition is characterized by a proliferation of diverse interpretations, it is legitimate to wonder whether guesswork did not play as great a role in its creation as did recollection;[10] but the tradition is not necessarily right even when it is unanimous. In this paper I shall first adduce an example of a Qurʾānic passage misunderstood by the exegetes without there being any disagreement whatsoever about the interpretation, and next discuss the exegetical memory loss with reference to the discontinuity between Qurʾānic legislation and Islamic law, of which I shall adduce another example.

---

4 Rosenthal, 'Some Minor Problems', pp. 72ff. According to U. Rubin, '*Al-Ṣamad* and the High God: An Interpretation of *sūra* CXII', *Der Islam* 61, 1984, the exegetical tradition does preserve the meaning of this word (cf. below, note 25).

5 D.S. Powers, 'The Islamic Law of Inheritance Reconsidered: A New Reading of Q. 4:12B', *Studia Islamica* 55, 1982; cf. also id., 'The Will of Saʿd b. Abî Waqqâṣ: A Reassessment', *Studia Islamica* 58, 1983; id., 'On the Abrogation of the Bequest Verses', *Arabica* 29, 1983; id., *Studies in Qurʾān and Ḥadīth*, Berkeley, Los Angeles and London 1986.

6 M. Cook, *Muhammad*, Oxford 1983, pp. 71f.; P. Crone, *Meccan Trade and the Rise of Islam*, Princeton and Oxford 1987, pp. 205ff. For a recent attempt to pinpoint the original meaning of *īlāf*, see U. Rubin, 'The *Īlāf* of Quraysh', *Arabica* 31, 1984.

7 Cf. A.T. Welch, *EI*[2], s.v. 'al-Ḳurʾān', col. 412.

8 Powers, 'Islamic Law of Inheritance Reconsidered', pp. 74f.

9 Rosenthal, 'Some Minor Problems', p. 68.

10 Cf. I. Goldziher, *Die Richtungen der Islamischen Koranauslegung*, Leiden 1920, pp. 83f.

Legal problems bearing on the date of the Qur'ān 3

I. *Kitāb* in 24:33

The first thirty-four verses of Sūra 24 (*al-Nūr*) are concerned with sexual morality. The Sūra starts by laying down the penalty for fornicators and proceeds to accusations of unchastity, laying down the penalty for *qadhf*, specifying the procedure of *li'ān*, and engaging in a long diatribe against *ifk*; next it regulates entry into other people's houses, sets out rules regarding modest demeanour, encourages marriage, and concludes with a statement that "now we have sent down to you signs making all clear..." Thereafter the subject matter changes; verse 35 starts the celebrated 'mystic' passage of the Qur'ān after which the Sūra is named.

Sūrat al-Nūr 1-34 is thus a treatise on chastity (with the exception of verse 22, which has no apparent bearing on the subject). Verses 32-33 go as follows:

٣٢ وَأَنْكِحُوا
ٱلْأَيَامَى مِنْكُمْ وَٱلصَّالِحِينَ مِنْ عِبَادِكُمْ وَإِمَائِكُمْ إِنْ يَكُونُوا فُقَرَاءَ يُغْنِهِمُ ٱللَّهُ مِنْ فَضْلِهِ
وَٱللَّهُ وَاسِعٌ عَلِيمٌ ٣٣ وَلْيَسْتَعْفِفِ ٱلَّذِينَ لَا يَجِدُونَ نِكَاحًا حَتَّى يُغْنِيَهُمُ ٱللَّهُ مِنْ فَضْلِهِ
وَٱلَّذِينَ يَبْتَغُونَ ٱلْكِتَابَ مِمَّا مَلَكَتْ أَيْمَانُكُمْ فَكَاتِبُوهُمْ إِنْ عَلِمْتُمْ فِيهِمْ خَيْرًا وَآتُوهُمْ مِنْ
مَالِ ٱللَّهِ ٱلَّذِي آتَاكُمْ وَلَا تُكْرِهُوا فَتَيَاتِكُمْ عَلَى ٱلْبِغَاءِ إِنْ أَرَدْنَ تَحَصُّنًا لِتَبْتَغُوا عَرَضَ
ٱلْحَيَوٰةِ ٱلدُّنْيَا وَمَنْ يُكْرِهْهُنَّ فَإِنَّ ٱللَّهَ مِنْ بَعْدِ إِكْرَاهِهِنَّ غَفُورٌ رَحِيمٌ/

32. a. "Marry off the spouseless among you, and your slaves and slavegirls that are righteous;
    b. if they are poor, God will enrich them of His bounty.
    c. God is all-embracing, all-knowing.

33. a. And let those who do not find a match be abstinent till God enriches them of His bounty.
    b. And for those in your possesion who desire a *kitāb*, write them a *kitāb* if you know some good in them.
    c. And give them of the wealth of God that He has given you.
    d. And do not compel your slavegirls to prostitution, if they desire to live in chastity, in order that you may pursue the goods of the present life.
    e. If anyone compels them, then after the compulsion laid upon them, God will be all-forgiving, all-compassionate".

It should be clear that verse 33b-e is a loose paraphrase of verses 32a-33a.

32a: "Marry off the spouseless among you, and your slaves and slavegirls that are righteous" = 33b: "And for those in your possession who desire a *kitāb*, write them a *kitāb* if you know some good in them".
32b: "if they are poor, God will enrich them" = 33c: "and give them of the wealth of God that He has given you".
33a: "And let those who do not find a match be abstinent till God enriches them of His bounty" = 33d: "And do not compel your slavegirls to prostitution, if they desire to live in chastity, in order that you may pursue the goods of the present life".
32c: "God is all-embracing, all-knowing" = 33e: "If anyone compels them, then after the compulsion laid upon them, God will be all-forgiving, all-compassionate".

It should also be clear that 32c has been misplaced (it ought to have followed rather than preceded 33a), and that this is why the verse division has gone wrong. Our concern is not with verse division, however, but rather with the meaning of *kitāb*. There can be no doubt that the word means a marriage contract here (cf. Hebrew *ketubah*).[11] The passage is about marrying off the spouseless in general and slaves and slavegirls in particular: if they are too poor to afford the dower, God will provide/you should provide out of the money God gives you; if they must wait, let them be abstinent/do not force them into prostitution. This is in keeping with the fact that, as mentioned already, the general subject is sexual morality.

Yet *all* Muslim commentators understand *kitāb* as a manumission document, more precisely as a contract of manumission in return

11 Marriage contract is also one of the meanings of *kitāb* in modern Arabic (cf. H. Wehr, *A Dictionary of Modern Written Arabic*, ed. J.M. Cowan, Wiesbaden 1966; M. Hinds and S. Badawī, *A Dictionary of Egyptian Arabic*, Beirut 1986, s.v.), and it is attested in medieval Arabic too (R. Dozy, *Supplément aux dictionnaires arabes*, Leiden 1881, s.v.; drawn to my attention by E. Kohlberg); but the dictionaries of classical Arabic fail to record it (cf. E.W. Lane, *An Arabic-English Lexicon*, London 1863-93; *Wörterbuch der klassischen arabischen Sprache*, Wiesbaden 1970— , s.v.). Though it does of course mean a written contract in general, a foreign usage may be reflected here.

for payment of a specified sum in instalments over a specified period (usually known as ***kitāba*** or ***mukātaba***). This understanding is faithfully reflected in both Bell's and Arberry's translations:
Bell: "And for those in your possession who desire the writing (of manumission) write it if ye know any good in them".
Arberry: "Those your right hands own who seek emancipation, contract with them accordingly, if you know some good in them".

Though manumission is plainly out of context here, there seems to be no trace of disagreement over the meaning of the word, be it in Sunnī,[12] Shī'ī,[13] Khārijī,[14] or for that matter Islamicist literature.[15] The commentators argued about the the phrase "if you know some good in them", the issue being whether it was a reference to moral probity or to financial ability. They also disagreed on whether the Qur'ānic verse made it obligatory or merely recommended for the owner of a slave to contract a slave in ***kitāba*** if

12 'Abd al-Razzāq b. Hammām al-Ṣan'ānī, *al-Muṣannaf*, ed. H.-R. al-A'ẓamī, Beirut 1970-72, vol. 8, nos. 15570-95; 'Abdallāh b. Muḥammad Ibn Abī Shayba, *Kitāb al-muṣannaf fī 'l-aḥādīth wa 'l-āthār*, ed. M.A. al-Nadwī, Bombay 1979-83, vol. 7, nos. 2886-95; Muqātil b. Sulaymān, *Kitāb tafsīr al-khams mi'at āya min al-Qur'ān*, ed. I. Goldfeld, Ramat Gan 1980, pp. 234f.; Muḥammad b. Jarīr al-Ṭabarī, *Jāmi' al-bayān fī tafsīr al-Qur'ān*, Cairo 1321-28, vol. 18, pp. 88ff.; 'Abdallāh b. 'Umar al-Bayḍāwī, *Anwār al-tanzīl wa-asrār al-ta'wīl*, Istanbul n.d., vol. 2, p. 140; Fakhr al-Dīn al-Rāzī, *al-Tafsīr al-kabīr*, Cairo n.d., vol. 23, pp. 215ff.; Abū Bakr Muḥammad b. 'Abdallāh Ibn al-'Arabī, *Aḥkām al-Qur'ān*, ed. 'A.M. Bajāwī, vol. 3 [Cairo] 1957, pp. 1369ff.; Muḥammad b. Aḥmad al-Qurṭubī, *al-Jāmi' li-aḥkām al-Qur'ān*, Cairo 1933-50, vol. 12, pp. 244ff.; Ismā'īl b. 'Umar Ibn Kathīr, *Tafsīr al-Qur'ān al-'aẓīm*, Cairo n.d., vol. 3, pp. 287f.

13 Abū 'l-Ḥasan b. 'Alī b. Ibrāhīm al-Qummī, *Tafsīr*, ed. T. al-Mūsawī al-Jazā'irī, Najaf 1387, vol. 2, p. 102; Muḥammad b. al-Ḥasan al-Ṭūsī, *Tafsīr al-tibyān*, ed. A.H.Q. al-'Āmilī, vol. 7, Najaf 1962, pp. 433f.; Sa'īd b. Hibat Allāh al-Rāwandī, *Fiqh al-Qur'ān*, ed. A. al-Ḥusaynī and M. al-Mar'ashī, Qumm 1397-99, vol. 2, pp. 215f.

14 Abū Ghānim Bishr b. Ghānim al-Khurāsānī, *Kitāb al-mudawwana al-kubrā*, ed. M. Aṭfayyish, [Beirut 1974], vol. 2, pp. 177f.; Abu 'l-Hawārī al-'Umānī al-Ibāḍī, *al-Dirāya wa-kanz al-ghināya fī tafsīr khams mi'at āya*, n.p. 1974, p. 216.

15 In addition to translations of the Qu'rān, see R. Roberts, *The Social Laws of the Qoran*, London 1925, pp. 59f.; J. Schacht, *The Origins of Muhammadan Jurisprudence*, Oxford 1950, p. 279.

the slave so desired. And they took the injunction "give them of the wealth of God that He has given you" to mean that the manumitter ought charitably to forgo the last instalments. The one thing they never considered was the possibility that *kitāb* here meant marriage contract rather than manumission document. The institution of *kitāba* has its roots in provincial law, and it does not owe a single feature to the Qur'ān, not even the practice of charitably forgoing the last instalments: the charitable practice was read into the book rather than derived from it.[16] The Qur'ān does not in fact refer to the institution at all. Why then did the Muslims come to see *kitāba* here? Even if the exegetes had forgotten the original meaning of *kitāb* in this verse, they could easily have deduced it from the context, yet they never tried.[17] But why *did* they forget the original meaning? It seems unlikely that they should have displaced or suppressed it because they needed to find a Qur'ānic sanction for *kitāba*, for numerous institutions of Islamic law are validated by Ḥadīth alone, and *kitāba* was not an especially controversial procedure in need of a Qur'ānic peg. Given the continuous nature of the tradition, moreover, the original meaning ought to have been difficult to displace.

Rosenthal suggests that the gaps in the exegetical recollection should be explained with reference to the disparity between Muḥammad's personal knowledge and that of his followers on the one hand, and the discontinuity between Muḥammad's environment and that of the exegetes on the other: Muḥammad may have been familiar with foreign words and topics that were unknown to his audience; and since a number of traditions assert that he disliked being questioned about religious matters, he may have refused to explain himself when he was not understood; at the same time the pagan environment

---

16 Cf. P. Crone, *Roman, Provincial and Islamic Law*, Cambrige 1987, ch. 5, esp. pp. 72f., 145[100].

17 They were not even worried by the use of *kitāb* for *kitāba*, though the only other attestations of *kitāb* in that sense seem to reflect the usage of the Qur'ān itself ('Abd al-Razzāq, *Muṣannaf*, vol. 8, no. 15578; Muḥammad Ibn Sa'd, *al-Ṭabaqāt al-kubrā*, Beirut 1957-60, vol. 5, pp. 85, 86; Aḥmad b. Abī Ṭayfūr, *Kitāb Baghdād*, vol. 6, ed. H. Keller, Leipzig 1908, p. 164). It did however worry Schacht (*Origins*, p. 279 and the note thereto).

was shrinking and idioms were changing.[18] In short, though the early commentators were familiar with the environment in which the Qur'ān originated, the continuity should not be envisaged as total.

This is a reasonable explanation which copes well enough with examples such as *al-ṣamad* and *al-rajīm* in the expression *al-shayṭān al-rajīm* (an Ethiopian loan-word which the commentators wrongly took to be an Arabic word meaning 'stoned'; it is however an uncertain example of exegetical failure to remember, in that Muḥammad may have understood it the same way).[19] It could perhaps account for the fate of the mysterious letters, too (on the assumption, for example, that Muḥammad refused to divulge their meaning so as to heighten their impact). But it hardly suffices to explain how the meaning of an entire (if short and fragmentary) sūra could be lost, and it cannot cope at all with the fact that the meaning of *legal* terms was forgotten. It may well be that *kalāla* was a foreign word known to Muḥammad and not to his audience, but we can hardly suppose that he kept his knowledge to himself in this case; for without knowledge of the meaning of *kalāla*, one is left without a key to Qur'ānic rules of succession. If Muḥammad intended these rules to be applied, he must have explained what *kalāla* meant; and once the rules were applied, his understanding of the term must have been embedded in practice, where it ought to have survived even though the pagan environment receded and other terminology changed, and where indeed it ought to have been retrievable even if Muḥammad's explanations were forgotten. *Jizya 'an yad* and the *kitāb* of 24:33 are likewise legal terms which Muḥammad must have been at pains to ensure that his followers understood correctly and which thus ought to have remained unproblematic whether he used them in an idiosyncratic sense or not. But in all three cases the terms owe their classical meaning to exegetical reasoning rather than to simple recollection; in all three cases, then, we must assume that Muḥammad's explanations were forgotten *and* that practice based thereon came to an end. There seems to have been discontinuity of a more drastic kind than Rosenthal's argument allows for.

18 Rosenthal, 'Some Minor Problems', p. 68.

19 Rosenthal, 'Some Minor Problems', pp. 83f. (Ethiopian *ragama* means 'to curse'.)

8 *Patricia Crone*

Powers, to whom Islamicists owe their awareness of the *kalāla* problem, rightly offers a theory of a more radical nature: in his view the original meaning of Qur'ānic *kalāla* was suppressed for political reasons in the decades after Muḥammad's death, along with the original import of the Qur'ānic rules of succession.[20] But this theory does not seem to work. For one thing, Powers can scarcely be said to have proved that Muḥammad's followers were once familiar with what he takes to be the original meaning of *kalāla* (female in-law)[21] or the original meaning of Qur'ānic inheritance law in general;[22] nor is the reader persuaded that there were political reasons to suppress them.[23] What one does infer from his work is rather that the meaning of *kalāla* and attendant inheritance law had never

---

20 Powers, *Studies*, ch. 4.

21 He argues that the traditions in which ʿUmar agonizes about the meaning of *kalāla* are carefully coded anecdotes put into circulation by people who knew the real meaning of the *kalāla* verses, but who were debarred from saying so directly because the issue was too controversial (*Studies*, pp. 32ff.). But one needs more sensitivity to innuendo than I possess to be persuaded of a secret message in these traditions.

22 No exegete ever read *yūrith* for *yūrath* in Qur. 4:12b/15, or discerned a distinction between testate and intestate succession in the book (with the exception of al-Qurṭubī, cf. Powers, *Studies*, p. 186), or between primary and secondary heirs; everyone in Powers' opinion wrongly took the Qur'ān to rule that males are entitled to twice the shares of females, and so on.

23 According to Powers, Qur. 4:12b/15 originally referred to the possibility of designating a testamentary heir, which was embarrassing to those who claimed that Muḥammad had died without designating a successor (*Studies*, pp. 113ff.). But a verse enabling a man to bequeath his property to a female in-law or wife (as it does in Powers' reconstruction) has no obvious bearing on political succession; and if it did have political implications, its meaning ought to have been preserved by those who claimed that Muḥammad *had* designated a successor; but there is no trace of it among the Shīʿites. By what mechanisms, moreover, could the early caliphs suppress the original meaning of a verse which (*ex hypothesi*) many other Companions had heard and understood correctly while the Prophet was still alive? "Islamic society... was not the sort of monolithic totalitarian culture in which a few ideologues could impose their views... on a community which knew them to be untrue", as Kennedy points out with reference to Crone and Cook in the mistaken belief that the authors of *Hagarism* proposed a conspiracy theory (H. Kennedy, *The Prophet and the Age of the Caliphates*, London and New York 1986, p. 357).

been known: there was nothing to remember, nothing to suppress; all one sees are frantic attempts to make sense of a recalcitrant text.[24] For another thing, *kalāla* is only one among several examples of exegetical memory loss and Powers' conspiracy theory cannot easily be extended to cover the parallel cases. It seems unlikely that the original meaning of terms as diverse as *al-ṣamad, jizya ʿan yad, īlāf, kalāla* and *kitāb*, not to mention *Sūrat Quraysh* and the mysterious letters, should have been suppressed for political reasons, though suppression (for theological rather than political reasons) is also postulated by Rubin in his discussion of *al-ṣamad*: early Islamic history is getting more and more Machiavellian.[25] It might reasonably be objected that there could be a number of factors behind the exegetical failure to remember, deliberate suppression being involved in the case of *kalāla* (and, if one accepts Rubin's argument, *al-ṣamad*), other factors being at work in other cases. But the number of cases is now sufficiently large for separate explanations to have a makeshift appearance; a single theory accounting for all the known examples, and indeed for all those likely to turn up in future, would be more convincing. At the very least, we need a single theory for all the

24 The fact that the Muslims seem never to have known the original meaning does not of course imply that Powers has failed to discover it. Whether he has or not is a separate question without bearing on the problem at hand.

25 Powers' suppression theory does at least have the merit of acknowledging that something has been genuinely lost. By contrast, what Rubin takes to be the original meaning of *al-ṣamad* (*al-maṣmūd ilayhi*) is an interpretation common in the exegetical tradition from Abū ʿUbayda to modern times: in what sense was it suppressed? Al-Ṭabarī may not cite any traditions in its favour, but he knew the interpretation nonetheless (and in fact opted for it himself); and the actual traditions reappear in works composed after his death (Rubin, '*Al-Ṣamad*', pp. 203, 211). Presumably, then, Rubin simply means that the (in his view) original interpretation of the word went out of favour and thus came to coexist with alternative explanations, though it remained perfectly well known until today. But nothing suggests that it started as the *only* interpretation: alternative explanations are present in the earliest material (e.g., Muqātil in Rubin, ibid., p. 214n). The meaning of *al-ṣamad* was thus controversial as far back as the tradition will take us. Sound philological scholarship may have enabled the exegetes to *discover* the original meaning of this word (cf. ibid., p. 211), but they did not *remember* what it was supposed to mean.

examples involving law. For law is the most exoteric of subjects, and the oblivion affecting the legal terminology of the Qurʾān poses the same intractable problem whatever the specific terms involved: how could the meaning of such terminology be forgotten if the rules it formulated were explained and applied from the moment of their revelation?

This takes us to another well-known problem, namely that there is less continuity between Qurʾānic and Islamic law than one would expect. Schacht, to whom most Islamicists owe their awareness of this problem, held that certain rules were based on the Qurʾān from the start, "particularly in family law and law of inheritance, not to mention cult and ritual";[26] but even so, he argued, "anything which goes beyond the most perfunctory attention given to the Koranic norms and the most elementary conclusions drawn from them belongs almost invariably to a secondary stage in the development of doctrine";[27] and he noted that "there are several cases in which the early doctrine of Islamic law diverged from the clear and explicit wording of the Koran", giving the rejection of the validity of written documents (contrary to 2:282) as his main example.[28] Burton's work on the stoning penalty for *zinā* and other conflicts between Qurʾān and Sharīʿa,[29] Powers' work on inheritance, and Hawting's work on the rights of the divorced woman during her waiting period[30] all suggest that Schacht understimated the discontinuity to which he drew attention:[31] of rules based on the

---

26 Schacht, *Origins*, p. 224; id., *An Introduction to Islamic Law*, Oxford 1964, p. 18.

27 Schacht, *Origins*, p. 227; id., *Introduction*, p. 18.

28 Schacht, *Introduction*, pp. 18f.; id., *Origins*, pp. 188, 226.

29 J. Burton, *The Collection of the Qurʾān*, Cambridge 1977, pp. 55 (inheritance law), 61 (widows' rights), 72ff. (stoning penalty).

30 G.R. Hawting, 'The Role of Qurʾān and *Ḥadīth* in the Legal Controversy about the Rights of a Divorced Woman during Her "Waiting Period" ('Idda)', *Bulletin of the School of Oriental and African Studies* 52, 1989.

31 Powers' contribution is the most significant in that it postulates drastic discontinuity in the very core of Islamic law, yet it is meant as a refutation of Schacht's thesis. Powers takes Schacht to claim that the development of Islamic law only began about a hundred years after the Prophet's death and tries to prove that it began before (see *Studies*, pp. 1-8, 209); but what Schacht

Qur'ān from the start we no longer possess a single clear-cut example. But how is it to be explained? Schacht argued that "Muhammadan law did not derive directly from the Koran but developed... out of popular and administrative practice under the Umayyads, and this practice often diverged from the intentions and even the explicit wording of the Koran".[32] But this merely restates the question: why did the popular and administrative practice of the Umayyad period diverge from the explicit wording of the Qur'ān? Some might invoke the supposed secular-mindedness of the Umayyads, but this is a stereotype which Schacht rightly rejected and which moreover fails to help in that it contrasts the popular (pious) and official (impious) practice of the Umayyad period instead of linking them.[33] Others might argue that Qur'ānic legislation is likely to have been swamped by Jāhilī practice when the mass of Arab tribesmen joined the *umma*, and by non-Arab practice when they conquered the Middle East; but there does not seem to be any resurgence of either Jāhilī or Middle Eastern practice behind the adoption of the stoning penalty or the rejection of written evidence,[34] nor does the discontinuity between Qur'ānic and Islamic inheritance law discovered by Powers seem to be explicable in such terms. One would in any case have expected Qur'ānic law to survive the inundation. There is nothing problematic about the proposition that a mass of extra-Qur'ānic law, sometimes un-Qur'ānic in spirit, was *added* to the Qur'ānic core, but how did Qur'ānic law come to be *undone*? If

actually claimed is that the *evidence* only takes us back to about 100 A.H. not that nothing happened in the preceding century (Schacht, *Origins*, p. 5). Schacht did claim that the law as we know it from the second century onwards is surprisingly un-Qur'ānic, but that is precisely what Powers himself concludes.

32 Schacht, *Origins*, p. 224.

33 Schacht, *Introduction*, p. 23; cf. also P. Crone and M. Hinds, *God's Caliph: Religious Authority in the First Centuries of Islam*, Cambridge 1986, p. 23.

34 The stoning penalty reflects Pentateuchal doctrine, not Middle Eastern practice. The rejection of written evidence went against *both* Qur'ānic law *and* Jāhilī practice according to Schacht, who notes that 'nothing definite is known about the origin of this feature' (*Origins*, p. 188; cf. *Introduction*, pp. 18f., but without documentation of the alleged Jāhilī practice).

flogging had been the official penalty for *zinā* since the revelation of the flogging verses, and if the Muslims had regularly recited these verses thereafter, how did the discontinuity set in?

Coulson's key objection to Schacht's work was precisely that it postulates an impossible discontinuity, and his argument is relevant even though it is focused on Ḥadīth rather than the Qur'ān. He points out that Qur'ānic legislation was revealed in response to practical problems (this being how the tradition presents it), but that it cannot have been implemented without further clarification; for it tends to leave fundamental questions unanswered, and its precise implications are often unclear. It follows that Qur'ānic legislation must have been supplemented with rulings of other kinds from the start, first by the Prophet, later by his Companions, and thereafter by the lawyers: why then does Schacht systematically deny the authenticity of rulings if they are credited to the Prophet and his Companions rather than to lawyers? In Coulsons's opinion, Schacht postulates a void where there must have been continuous development: the community cannot have left its legal problems unsolved, and the lawyers cannot totally have forgotten how the law was applied before their own time.[35]

This is an eminently reasonable argument. If Qur'ānic legislation was implemented, the development of Qur'ānic into Islamic law ought indeed to have been continuous, and the Prophet's understanding of the law ought indeed to have been preserved, be it in words or practice or both (unless deliberate suppression was involved, which I shall henceforth assume was not the case). But the void postulated by Schacht is real: how would Coulson account for the adoption of the stoning penalty, the rejection of written evidence, the uncertainty regarding the meaning of *kalāla*, or the misunderstanding of the word *kitāb*? The Prophet must, *ex hypothesi*, have explained and implemented the law in each of these cases, and he is indeed said to have done so in Ḥadīth; but what Ḥadīth presents him as implementing is Islamic law, complete with its divergence from Qur'ānic legislation: Ḥadīth does not refute the void, but on the contrary illustrates it. *If* Qur'ānic law was implemented, there cannot have

35 N.J. Coulson, *A History of Islamic Law*, Edinburgh 1964, part 1, esp. chs. 1 and 5.

been a void; but *if* there is a void, it would follow that Qur'ānic law cannot have been implemented.

That Qur'ānic law should have remained a dead letter until a secondary stage of legal development is a fairly startling proposition, but Burton seems to take it for granted. According to him, the discontinuity between the two arises from the fact that Qur'ānic legislation did not reach the lawyers directly: what they took up was not the book itself, let alone practice based on it, but rather exegetical versions of its contents. *Tafsīr* generated *sunna* for the lawyers: thus 5:42-49 generated stories about Muḥammad applying the stoning penalty in cases of adultery, and this *sunna* won legal recognition, its incompatibility with 24:2 (which specifies flogging) notwithstanding.[36] The lawyers did not in Burton's view pay any serious attention to the text itself until about 800, when they were confronted with Qur'ānic fundamentalists.[37]

Now this theory could certainly account for the misunderstanding of *kitāb* in 24:33, provided that we take Burton's exegetes to have been story-tellers (which is in fact how he seems to envisage them himself).[38] The *quṣṣāṣ*, whose contribution to the exegetical tradition is well attested, were not fussy about the accuracy of their interpretations, and the stories they told in explanation of 24:33 are typical of their approach. Although the verse forms part of a larger unit which must have been composed or, as they saw it, revealed, together they happily assigned different occasions of revelation to the component parts of the verse (not to mention the unit). Thus 33b ("and for those in your possession who desire a *kitāb*...") was allegedly revealed about a slave of Ḥuwayṭib b. ʿAbd al-ʿUzzā or Ḥāṭib b. Abī Baltaʿa who wanted a *kitāba* but

36 Burton, *Collection*, ch. 4. The argument is restated in his 'Law and Exegesis: The Penalty for Adultery in Islam', in G.R. Hawting and A.-K. A. Shareef (eds.), *Approaches to the Qur'ān*, London and New York 1993.

37 Burton, *Collection*, pp. 19ff., 161, 177, et passim. Al-Shāfiʿī (d. 822) is presented as the leading opponent of the 'Qur'ān party' and the person to whom the *sunna* owed its rescue (pp. 24ff., 92).

38 Ibid., pp. 70, 185. The *qāṣṣ* is explicitly mentioned in his 'Law and Exegesis', p 270.

whose owner refused to give him one;[39] but 33d ("and constrain not your slavegirls to prostitution...") was supposedly triggered by a slavegirl or slavegirls of ʿAbdallāh b. Ubayy, who had one, two or six, whose names were such-and-such and whom he prostituted, though she/they were unwilling; so she/they went to the Prophet, whereupon this statement was revealed.[40] Both claims must be pure fiction. But given this approach, it is not particularly strange that *kitāb* should have been understood as *kitāba*: the sheer fact that the word was mentioned in the context of slaves probably sufficed to suggest a manumission document to the *quṣṣāṣ*, generating instant stories based on this understanding of the word. The stories they told, or some of them, survive in exegetical works of the most reputable kind, and the lawyers never doubted that 24:33 was concerned with manumission: they misunderstood *kitāb* just as they ignored the flogging penalty (which is prescribed in the same 'treatise on chastity'), and it could well be that they took their cue from story-telling exegetes in both cases.

But why should the interpretation of Qurʾānic law have been left to *quṣṣāṣ*? Burton's answer that the lawyers did not regard the scripture as a source of law until about 800 begs the question how they could have had a scripture containing legislation *without* regarding it as a source of law? Are we to take it that even the Prophet did not see it as such (implying that he made no attempt to put its legislation into practice), or that his concept of the Qurʾān as a source of law was forgotten by later generations (who forgot his contribution to practice, too)? Neither hypothesis is very persuasive. If the Prophet enacted legislation that was rapidly incorporated into a scripture recited by everyone thereafter, it is hard to see how anyone could have failed to endow it with supreme authority over and above all

39 ʿAlī b. Aḥmad al-Wāḥidī, *Asbāb al-nuzūl*, Beirut 1316, p. 245; al-Qurṭubī, *Aḥkām*, vol. 12, p. 244.

40 al-Wāḥidī, *Asbāb*, pp. 245ff., with numerous versions; al-Rāzī, *Tafsīr*, vol. 23, p. 220; al-Qurṭubī, *Aḥkām*, vol. 12, p. 254; Ibn Kathīr, *Tafsīr*, vol. 3, pp. 288f., with other versions; Ibn al-ʿArabī, *Aḥkām*, vol. 3, p. 1374; al-Ṭūsī, *Ṭibyān*, vol. 7, p. 434; Ibn Ḥajar, *al-Iṣāba fī tamyīz al-ṣaḥāba*, Cairo 1328, vol. 4, pp. 408f. (s.v. 'Muʿāda').

other forms of law, that of the Pentateuch included. Even if the conquests disrupted practice and the story-tellers muddled things with their stories thereafter, the flogging verse is quite unambiguous; and the caliphs would have been in a position to ensure that practice was restored to what they took to be its original form. The scholars might in due course have disputed the validity of the caliphal understanding of right practice and quarreled among themselves over the reconciliation of Qur. 4:15, which prescribes lifelong incarceration for women guilty of gross moral turpitude, and Qur. 24:2, which prescribes flogging for both men and women guilty of unlawful intercourse; but why should they have quarreled over *stoning*?

Burton compounds the problem by arguing that Muḥammad collected his own revelations.[41] A prophet who fixes his own message in writing is presumably motivated by a desire to be correctly understood long after he has died, meaning that he will do his best to endow his contemporaries, too, with a correct understanding of his message, which in this particular case must have meant explaining (if not implementing) its legal passages on a par with the rest. Yet the lawyers suffered from amnesia after his death and took their clues from the story-tellers. It does not make sense.

What is more, the amnesia was not confined to the lawyers. The significance of non-legal terms and passages such as *al-ṣamad, īlāf, Sūrat Quraysh* in general and the mysterious letters was also forgotten, while at the same time the story-tellers took it upon themselves to supply not just *sunna* to the lawyers but also *tafsīr* in general and Prophetic biography in particular to scholarly exegetes and historians.[42] This goes well enough with Burton's view of exegesis as a universal bottleneck through which every verse of the Qur'ān, and indeed every item of historical recollection, had to pass in order to reach the believers;[43] but a universal bottleneck

41 Burton, *Collection*, pp. 239f.

42 Cf. H. Birkeland, *The Legend of the Opening of Muhammad's Breast*, Oslo 1955; and/or id., *The Lord Guideth*, Oslo 1956, pp. 38-55 (on Sūra 94); Crone, *Meccan Trade*, ch. 9 (on Sūra 106).

43 My summary of Burton's views here rests less on his *Collection* than on his written and oral contributions to the colloquia on Ḥadīth held at Oxford 1982, Cambridge 1985 and Oxford 1988.

cannot be explained with reference to the attitude of lawyers. What Burton conjures up is not a situation in which the lawyers paid scant attention to the scripture, but rather one in which the story-tellers had sole access to it: according to him, the Qur'ān existed for purposes of generating wild *tafsīr* but not for purposes of sober checking, with the paradoxical result that it generated divergence from itself. But if the scripture had been available since the time of the Prophet, how can the story-tellers have had a monopoly on it? Everyone would have been in a position to check their stories against the text, and the existence of a canonical scripture must rapidly have engendered scholarly exegetes, who were rivals of the *quṣṣās* rather than their allies.[44] How then could the story-tellers reign supreme for long enough actually to shape the classical understanding of the book? Burton's theory cries out for some sort of modification.

We are thus left with Wansbrough. Wansbrough would reject all the arguments reviewed so far as based on a faulty premise inasmuch as they all assume the Qur'ān to be a collection of Muḥammad's revelations collected in Medina before the centre of the Muslim community had been transferred to the non-Arab Middle East. According to Wansbrough, the Qur'ān did not originate in Arabia, nor indeed did Islam: the Arabs had not established a new religious community of their own by the time they left Arabia; rather, they chanced upon a new sectarian development in the Middle East (Iraq?) after the conquests and proceeded to adopt it as their own, rewriting its history and giving it an Arab imprint in the process. The Qur'ān emerged out of a diversity of sources as part of this process, in which the story-tellers played a crucial role: the popular sermon was the instrument of both transmission and explication of the Prophetic *logia*, which had originated in a sectarian environment and from which the Qur'ānic canon was eventually separated; but its text crystallized so slowly that one cannot speak of a *ne varietur* version

---

44 Cf. J. Pedersen, 'The Islamic Preacher', in *Ignace Goldziher Memorial Volume*, vol. 1, Budapest 1948; id., 'The Criticism of the Islamic Preacher', *Die Welt des Islams* 2, 1953.

until about 800 A.D.[45] (that is about the time that Burton would have his lawyers begin to pay attention to its text).[46]

As it stands, this theory can only be saved on the assumption that all evidence purporting to date from before 800, be it Muslim or non-Muslim, literary or documentary, is by definition inauthentic, or in other words that evidence incompatible with the theory is *ipso facto* wrong.[47] The contention that the *ne varietur* Qur'ān only emerged about 800 could moreover be said to fall between two stools: on the one hand, a scripture undoubtedly existed before 800,[48] so the date proposed is too late; but on the other hand, it was only in the tenth century that seven *ne varietur* versions of

---

45 J. Wansbrough, *Qur'anic Studies*, Oxford 1977; id., *The Sectarian Milieu*, Oxford 1978.

46 Both authors would seem to imply that ʿUthmān only came to be credited with the creation of the *textus receptus* about 800 A.D.; for Wansbrough would hardly go so far as to argue that there were stories about the canonization of the Qur'ān before it had actually been canonized, while Burton holds all the stories of the collection and canonization of the Qur'ān to be engendered by theories of *naskh*, which were evolved when Qur'ānic fundamentalists forced the jurists to confront the discrepancies between the Qur'ān and *fiqh* (*Collection*, pp. 161f.), that is, not long before al-Shāfiʿī. Yet the story of ʿUthmān's canonization of the Qur'ān is deeply entrenched in the tradition when it emerges into full light about 800.

47 Leaving aside the early non-Muslim sources, whose testimony Wansbrough naturally rejects (cf. *Doctrina Iacobi*, pseudo-Sebeos, and other accounts in P. Crone and M. Cook, *Hagarism: The Making of the Islamic World*, Cambridge 1977; Wansbrough, *Sectarian Milieu*, pp. 117f.), there are monotheist coins and inscriptions from the time of Muʿāwiya onwards which can hardly be dismissed as so many literary stereotypes (and which are not discussed), while the first coin to identify Muḥammad as *rasūl Allāh* dates from 66/685f (Crone and Hinds, *God's Caliph*, pp. 24f.). Where should one fit in "the establishment of a *modus vivendi* between the new authority and the indigenous communities, and the distillation of a doctrinal precipitate (a common denominator) acceptable initially to an academic élite, eventually an emblem of submission (*islām*) to political authority" (Wansbrough, *Sectarian Milieu*, p. 127)?

48 Specimens of Qur'ānic material such as the Dome of the Rock inscription or the legend on the reformed coinage do not prove that the materials had stabilized as a scripture, partly because they are snippets and partly because they mix up what are now verses in different sūras. But the sheer fact that the sixteen mangled lines of the Khirbet el-Mird fragment are recognizable as

this scripture were canonized,[49] so the date proposed is also too early. More precisely, the contention is unclear: Wansbrough does not explain what he means by *ne varietur* in a context in which uniformity was never achieved.

His suggestion that we should abandon the premise of all existing arguments is nonetheless very helpful in the present context; for if the Qur'ān was only put together some time *after* the conquests, we have the 'void' we need in order for things to get out of kilter. For a start, we could accommodate the evidence that the Muslims once accepted the Pentateuch as their scripture, or as

Qur. 3:102f does suggest that there was a stable text by the late Umayyad period (cf. M.J. Kister, 'On an Early Fragment of the Qur'ān', *Studies... Presented to L. Nemoy*, Ramat-Gan 1982; see A. Grohmann, *Arabic Papyri from Ḫirbet el-Mird*, Louvain 1963, p. xi, on the date of the site); and a Nubian papyrus datable to 741/758 contains two Qur'ānic quotations preceded by *wa-'llāh tabāraka wa-ta'ālā yaqūlu fī kitābihi* (M. Hinds and H. Sakkout, 'A Letter from the Governor of Egypt to the King of Nubia Concerning Egyptian-Nubian Relations in 141/758', in W. al-Qāḍī (ed.), *Studia Arabica et Islamica, Festschrift for Iḥsān 'Abbās*, Beirut 1981, p. 218, lines 7-11), so it can no longer be claimed that "those sources which may with some assurance be dated before the end of the second/eighth century (and thus before Ibn Isḥāq) contain no reference to Muslim scripture" (Wansbrough, *Sectarian Milieu*, p. 58). Moreover, one would expect a scripture, in the sense of a stable text regarded as supremely authoritative, to announce its presence by deeply colouring all diction and thought; and the supposedly mid-Umayyad, possibly late Umayyad, possibly even early 'Abbāsid, but at any rate not *ninth-century* theological epistles are indeed permeated by the Qur'ān in this way (cf. M. Cook, *Early Muslim Dogma*, Cambridge 1981, p. 16 *et passim*). To Wansbrough this simply means that they must be too late to count (cf. *Qur'anic Studies*, pp. 160-63, on the letter ascribed to al-Ḥasan al-Baṣrī). The letter of the late Umayyad caliph al-Walīd II regarding his successors is similarly replete with Qur'ānic citations and allusions, but to a follower of Wansbrough there can be no question of accepting it as authentic (cf. N. Calder's reaction in his review of Crone and Hinds, *God's Caliph*, in *Journal of Semitic Studies* 32, 1987, pp. 376f.). Followers of Wansbrough will now have to explain away the letters of 'Abd al-Ḥamīd b. Yaḥyā too (cf. W. al-Qāḍī, 'The Impact of the Qur'ān on Arabic Literature during the Late Umayyad Period: The Case of 'Abd al-Ḥamīd's Epistolography', in G.R. Hawting and A.-K.A. Shareef (eds.), *Approaches to the Qur'ān*, London and New York 1993.

49 Cf. Welch in *Encyclopaedia of Islam*[2], s.v. 'al-Ḳur'ān', cols. 408f.

one of them, which would allow us to explain why the lawyers took stories in which Muḥammad inflicts a Pentateuchal penalty on Jews to establish a *sunna* for Muslims: it is not otherwise clear why this 'gossip' (as Burton calls it) should have been endowed with legal significance,[50] or why the lawyers assumed the Prophet also to have adopted other Pentateuchal law that happens not to contradict the Qur'ān.[51] If, further, the Qur'ān was codified and canonized after the conquests, it ceases to be problematic that the reception of its legislation belongs to a secondary stage. And finally, a belated canonization of the book would give us a period in between, in which a variety of religious works, including proto-Qur'ānic materials, were in circulation without having coalesced as an Arab scripture, that is, without there being a single work endowed with overriding authority, general availability and a presumption of internal coherence. In the absence of a book available to all in written and oral transmission, the welter of Arab and non-Arab books endowed with ill-defined degrees of authoritativeness would have been directly accessible only to those who could actually read them, except insofar as parts of them were recited in prayer and other cultic contexts. Where, then, would one turn for information on the prophets' messages, and for explanation of the passages recited, if not to story-tellers and other self-appointed experts who professed to have read such books, or to have had them read to them, or to have heard from those who had? Long after the Qur'ān had been canonized, experts of this kind continued to supply information on the sayings and doings of Muḥammad's predecessors.[52] In the absence of a supremely authoritative book canonized in the Ḥijāz,

50 Cf. Burton, *Collection*, pp. 70, 185. The question is raised in his 'Law and Exegesis', pp. 273f., but I cannot see that it is answered.

51 Cf. P. Crone, 'Jāhilī and Jewish Law: The *Qasāma*', *Jerusalem Studies in Arabic and Islam* 4, 1984, pp. 166-82. N. Calder, *Studies in Early Muslim Jurisprudence*, Oxford 1993, p. 212, charges me with creating "an ingenious link between Deut. 21:1-9 and the Ḥanafī law of *qasāma*". But since the Muslims themselves assert that the *qasāma* is a Biblical institution and offer a loose translation of Deut. 21:1-9 in support of this claim, it takes more ingenuity to deny the link than to affirm it.

52 Cf. *Encyclopaedia of Islam*², s.v. 'Isrā'īliyyāt'.

moreover, there cannot have been a tradition of scholarly exegesis rooted in the Ḥijāz. The scholars must have arrived at a later stage, breaking the monopoly of the story-tellers, but taking over rather than rejecting their interpretations: they had no independent recollection of their own. There must of course have been people who remembered what Muḥammad said and did in historical fact, but such people will have been few and far between once the vast majority of Arabs had joined the *umma* and settled in the conquered lands; and one would assume them to have put their knowledge to story-telling use so as not to be outdone by those who drew crowds even though their credentials were inferior, meaning that genuine recollection will soon have entered the general pool of story-telling material, where it will have been lost. In short, we would have a situation in which story-telling exegetes did indeed enjoy a monopoly on revelation, be it that of the prophets or that of the Prophet, and in which all revelation and historical knowledge passed through Burton's exegetical bottleneck, to be denuded of original meaning in the process.

So far, so good. But if we envisage the story-tellers as both transmitters and explicators of the materials from which the Qur'ān was to emerge, how do we explain the fact that they were utterly uninhibited when it came to interpretation, yet remarkably disciplined when it came to the text? They did not substitute *kitāba* for *kitāb*, replace *īlāf* with a more familiar word or otherwise improve on what they did not understand, as one would have expected them to do. *Pace* Wansbrough, the text seems to have been endowed with immutability, or something close to it, from an early date.[53] This is something of a problem. It goes well enough with Burton's view that the Qur'ān existed as a document long before it existed as a source, but the objection to this view remains

53 According to Burton, "the very unhelpfulness of the Qur'ān document when called upon to behave as the Qur'ān source, and the frequent embarrassment it caused the Muslim scholars, speak very strongly for its authenticity as a document, in the sense that it does not have any of the appearance of having been concocted after the evolution of the legal doctrine with the aim of supplying its documentation" (*Collection*, p. 187). This is certainly true, but then nobody suspects the lawyers of having concocted it. The fact that it was not really intelligible to the story-tellers either does however point to a loose end in Wansbrough's theory.

as before: how can the Muslims have possessed a book which they regarded as supremely authoritative for purposes of recitation, but not for purposes of law? *Pace* Burton, the assumption of nonscriptural form does seem to be indispensable when we turn to the fate of Qurʾānic legislation. It is thanks to their diametrically opposed views on the stability of the text in the dark centuries before c. 800 that Wansbrough and Burton offer contrasting theories rather than identical ones, their views being highly compatible in other respects; and since neither theory is acceptable as it stands, the solution must lie somewhere in between. But how it should be envisaged I do not know. I must accordingly confine myself to the observation that a theory of belated codification and canonization works very well in the present context, not only in that it would allow us to explain all the examples so far known of exegetical ignorance of, and juristic lack of attention to, the import of Qurʾānic passages, but also in that it could be assumed to work for future examples as well. It certainly works for the three examples that have turned up since Wansbrough wrote, the first being Powers' inheritance laws and the second the *kitāb* that I have already discussed; the third is the rule to which I shall now proceed.

II. The DAEP Rule

The DAEP rule relates to succession, more precisely to the devolution of the property of freedmen and freedwomen. The example is more complex than that of *kitāb*, so the reader will have to put up with a few preliminary remarks.

For purposes of presentation we may divide an individual's relatives into two broad categories, male agnates (males related to the individual through male links) and all the rest, whom we may call cognates. The first of these categories is actually found in classical Sunnī law (male agnates being known as *ʿaṣaba*), but the second is not: classical Sunnī law divides the relatives here called cognates into two distinct classes, with quite different rules of inheritance applying to each class. The first comprises all the cognates who have been awarded a fixed share of the estate in the Qurʾān; they are known as *aṣḥāb* or *dhawūʾ l-farāʾiḍ/ashām* and are generally referred to in English as Qurʾānic heirs. The second class is made up of all the remaining cognates, who are known as *dhawū ʾl-arḥām* and referred to in English as uterine or distant heirs, or outer family; I shall call them non-Qur'ānic cognates in this article.

Classical Sunnī law regulates the relationship between the three classes of heirs as follows. Qur'ānic heirs cannot be excluded by representatives of the other classes, but nor do they exclude male agnates: if the *de cujus* leaves Qur'ānic heirs and male agnatic relatives, one allots the former their Qur'ānic share and awards the residue (if any) to the latter. But male agnates and Qur'ānic heirs alike exlude non-Qur'ānic cognates, who are only called to succession in the absence of heirs of other types (with the exception of the spouse relict) and who are not recognized as heirs at all by the Mālikīs.[54]

The manumitter (whether male or female) counts as a male agnate for purposes of succession to his or her freedman or freedwoman. If the latter leaves genuine male agnatic relatives (e.g. a son), the manumitter is excluded by the rules governing priority within the agnatic class (the nearer in degree excludes the more remote); but if no genuine male agnatic relatives are present, the manumitter will inherit together with Qur'ānic heirs and exclude non-Qur'ānic cognates.[55]

Now in pre-classical law, the manumitter was treated quite differently. He was excluded by Qur'ānic heirs instead of inheriting along with them; and he was excluded by non-Qur'ānic cognates, too, instead of excluding them. In other words, *all* cognates excluded the manumitter. I have discussed this rule elsewhere from the point of view of the history of *walā'*,[56] but in the present context its significance is this: most of the traditions which support this rule show no awareness of the fact that cognates comprise two wholly different classes of heirs; the traditions do not divide them into a Qur'ānic and a non-Qur'ānic variety, but rather treat them all as members of a single category, which they call *dhawū 'l-arḥām*.

For lack of a more graceful term, I have dubbed the pre-classical doctrine the DAEP rule (*dhawū 'l-arḥām* exclude patrons). The

---

54 On all of this, see N.J. Coulson, *Succession in the Muslim Family*, Cambridge 1971.

55 Crone, *Roman, Provincial and Islamic law*, pp. 36f.

56 Ibid., pp. 79f.

acronym refers to patrons rather than manumitters because the latter were only one out of two types of patron acknowledged in early law, which treated them almost identically, and the traditions do not always specify which type of patron they have in mind. It is invariably the manumitter rather than the contractual patron who is mentioned in the traditions that do specify, and this is as might be expected: freedmen are far more prominent than contractual patrons in the early sources (legal or non-legal), and most schools eventually rejected the contractual patronate altogether.[57] But the DAEP rule must be presumed to have applied to patrons of both kinds.

We may now turn to the material, which can be divided into three groups.

1. Numerous early authorities, especially Kūfan ones, are said to have awarded the entire estate to a *dhū raḥim* at the expense of a patron. This was the correct solution according to ʿUmar,[58] ʿAlī,[59] and ʿUmar II[60] among the caliphs. It was also the correct solution in the eyes of

---

57 Ibid., pp. 38, 91.

58 *Kāna ʿUmar wa-ʾbn Masʿūd yuwarrithāni [dhawī] ʾl-arḥām dūna ʾl-mawālī. Qāla, fa-qultu: fa-ʿAlī b. Abī Ṭālib? Qāla: kāna ashaddahum fī dhālika*, as a much cited tradition has it (ʿAbd al-Razzāq, *Muṣannaf*, vol. 9, no. 16197; H.-P. Raddatz, 'Frühislamisches Erbrecht nach dem *Kitāb al-farāʾiḍ* des Sufyān aṯ-Ṯaurī', *Die Welt des Islams* 13, 1971, p. 40 [omits the statement on ʿAlī]; Ibn Abī Shayba, *Muṣannaf*, vol. 11, no. 11205 [omits *dūna ʾl-mawālī*]; al-Shāfiʿī, *Kitāb al-umm*, Būlāq 1321-25, vol. 7, p. 166; Aḥmad b. al-Ḥusayn al-Bayhaqī, *al-Sunan al-kubrā*, Hyderabad 1344-55, vol. 6, p. 242, top. Cf. also Muḥammad b. Yūsuf Aṭfayyish, *Sharḥ al-nīl wa-shifāʾ al-ʿalīl*, vol. 8, Cairo 1343, p. 394). For other traditions on ʿUmar, see ʿAbd al-Razzāq, *Muṣannaf*, vol. 9, nos. 16196, 16203.

59 Cf. the preceding note; Ibn Abī Shayba, *Muṣannaf*, vol. 11, no. 11208; Bayhaqī, *Sunan*, vol. 6, pp. 241f.; al-Muḥammad b. Yaʿqūb al-Kulaynī, *al-Uṣūl min al-kāfī*, ed. ʿA.A. al-Ghaffārī, Tehran 1377-81, vol. 7, pp. 135f.; Muḥammad b. ʿAlī Ibn Bābūya, *Man lā yaḥḍuruhu ʾl-faqīh*, ed. H.M. al-Kharsān, Tehran 1390, vol. 4, p. 223, nos. 709-10; Muḥammad b. al-Ḥasan al-Ṭūsī, *Tahdhīb al-aḥkām*, ed. H.M. al-Kharsān, vol. 9, Tehran 1382, pp. 328ff.; N.B.E. Baillie, *A Digest of Moohummudan Law*², vol. 2, London 1887, p. 346.

60 ʿAbdallāh b. Aḥmad Ibn Qudāma, *al-Mughnī*, ed. T.M. al-Zaynī et al., Cairo 1968-70, vol. 6, p. 323, no. 4830.

Shurayḥ,[61] Masrūq,[62] Ibn Mas'ūd,[63] Ibn Mas'ūd's son, grandson[64] and nephew,[65] al-Sha'bī,[66] al-Aswad, 'Alqama,[67] 'Abīda[68] and Ibrāhīm al-Nakha'ī in Kūfa;[69] Jābir b. Zayd in Baṣra;[70] Mu'ādh b. Jabal,[71] Abū 'l-Dardā'[72] and Maymūn b. Mihrān in Syria;[73] Ibn 'Abbās, Mujāhid and 'Aṭā' in Mecca;[74] Jābir al-Anṣārī,[75] Muḥammad al-Bāqir[76] and Ja'far al-Ṣādiq in Medina;[77] as well as Ṭāwūs in the Yemen.[78] This

---

61 Abū 'Ubayd al-Qāsim b. Sallām, *Kitāb al-amwāl*, ed. M.Kh. Harās, Cairo 1968, p. 309, no. 529; cf. also Aṭfayyish, *Nīl*, vol. 8, p. 394.

62 'Abd al-Razzāq, *Muṣannaf*, vol. 9, no. 16203; Ibn Qudāma, *Mughnī*, vol. 6, p. 323, no. 4830; Aṭfayyish, *Nīl*, vol. 8, p. 394.

63 Cf. above, note 58; also 'Abd al-Razzāq, *Muṣannaf*, vol. 9, nos. 16196, 16203; Ibn Abī Shayba, *Muṣannaf*, vol. 11, no. 11218 (fails to specify that the competitor was a patron; appears in the chapter on *radd*); Bayhaqī, *Sunan*, pp. 241f.; Ibn Qudāma, *Mughnī* , vol. 6, p. 323, no. 4830; Aṭfayyish, *Nīl*, vol. 8, p. 394.

64 I.e., Abū 'Ubayda b. 'Abdallāh b. Mas'ūd and al-Qāsim b. 'Abd al-Raḥmān b. 'Abdallah b. Mas'ūd ('Abd al-Razzāq, *Muṣannaf*, vol. 9, nos. 16204-5; Ibn Abī Shayba, *Muṣannaf*, vol. 11, no. 11218 [fails to specify that the competitor was a patron]; Ibn Qudāma, *Mughnī*, vol. 6, p. 323, no. 4830).

65 I.e., 'Abdallāh b. 'Utba b. Mas'ūd (Ibn Qudāma, *Mughnī*, vol. 6, p. 323, no. 4830). He is counted as a Medinese by some (Ibn Ḥajar, *Tahdhīb al-tahdhīb*, Hyderabad 1325-27, vol. 5, p. 311).

66 'Abd al-Razzāq, *Muṣannaf*, vol. 9, no. 16203; Ibn Qudāma, *Mughnī*, vol. 6, p. 323, no. 4830; Aṭfayyish, *Nīl*, vol. 8, p. 394.

67 'Abd al-Razzāq, *Muṣannaf*, vol. 9, no. 16196 ('Alqama); Raddatz, 'Erbrecht', p. 40 ('Alqama); Ibn Qudāma, *Mughnī*, vol. 6, p. 323, no. 4830; Aṭfayyish, *Nīl*, vol. 8, p. 394 (both).

68 Ibn Qudāma, *Mughnī*, vol. 6, p. 323, no. 4830.

69 'Abd al-Razzāq, *Muṣannaf*, vol. 9, nos. 16196, 16203; Ibn Qudāma, *Mughnī*, vol. 6, p. 323, no. 4830; Aṭfayyish, *Nīl*, vol. 8, p. 394.

70 Ibn Qudāma, *Mughnī*, vol. 6, p. 323, no. 4830; Aṭfayyish, *Nīl*, p. 394.

71 Aṭfayyish, *Nīl*, vol. 8, p. 394.

72 Ibid.; cf. Ibn Abī Shayba, *Muṣannaf*, vol. 11, no. 11207, on Abū 'l-Dardā' (who awards the entire estate to a maternal half-brother in the absence of other heirs, no mention being made of a patron).

73 Ibn Qudāma, *Mughnī*, vol. 6, p. 323, no. 4830.

74 Aṭfayyish, *Nīl*, vol. 8, p. 394.

75 Baillie, *Digest*, vol. 2, p. 346.

76 Ibn Bābūya, *Man lā yaḥḍuruhu al-faqīh*, vol. 4, p. 223, no. 708; Baillie, *Digest*, vol. 2, p. 346.

77 al-Kulaynī, *Kāfī*, vol. 7, pp. 135f.

78 Aṭfayyish, *Nīl*, vol. 8, p. 394.

material gives us the pre-classical rule, or rather half of it, and establishes that it was widely accepted. It only gives us half of the rule because nothing indicates that *dhū raḥim* means other than non-Qur'ānic cognate here. But what types of heirs did the above-mentioned authorities have in mind?

2. Some traditions answer this question by adducing case law.

(a) A freedwoman of ʿAlqama's died leaving a maternal half-sister's son or daughter, or a maternal half-brother's daughter,[79] plus ʿAlqama, her patron. ʿAlqama awarded the entire estate to the surviving relative with the comment that it was hers by right.[80] ʿAlī awarded the entire estate to a maternal aunt and a paternal grandmother in competition with patrons.[81]

The heirs in question are non-Qur'ānic cognates, that is *dhawū ʿl-arḥām* in the classical sense of the word.[82]

(b) Ibn Masʿūd's grandson similarly awarded the entire estate of a freedwoman to her mother rather than to her patrons.[83] ʿAlī gave the entire estate to a sister at the expense of the patrons,[84] and both Ibn Masʿūd and his son used to do the same.[85] ʿAlī also gave the entire estate to a daughter,[86] and when

79 ʿAbd al-Razzāq, *Muṣannaf*, vol. 9, no. 16196; Ibn Abī Shayba, *Muṣannaf*, vol. 11, no. 11212; Raddatz, 'Erbrecht', p. 40.

80 Thus the first two sources referred to in the previous note (the third is exceedingly concise). Compare Ibn Abī Shayba, *Muṣannaf*, vol. 11, no. 11210, where ʿAlqama's client gratuitously bequeaths a third of his estate to his patron's family, leaving the rest to his maternal sister's son (who would thus have been the sole heir if the freedwoman had died intestate).

81 al-Kulaynī, *Kāfī*, vol. 7, p. 135, no. 2; al-Ṭūsī, *Tahdhīb*, vol. 9, p. 329, no. 1183; Baillie, *Digest*, vol. 2, p. 346 (maternal aunt); Ibn Abī Shayba, *Muṣannaf*, vol. 11, no. 11211 (paternal grandmother).

82 Though grandmothers are treated differently from the bulk of non-Qur'ānic cognates in classical law (cf. Coulson, *Succession*, pp. 60f.).

83 ʿAbd al-Razzāq , *Muṣannaf*, vol. 9, no. 16205.

84 al-Ṭūsī, *Tahdhīb*, vol. 9, p. 330, no. 1189.

85 ʿAbd al-Razzāq, *Muṣannaf*, vol. 9, no. 16204. This tradition makes no explicit mention of a patron, and it is later cited in illustration of *radd* (vol. 10, no. 19130). But ʿAbd al-Razzāq presumably took it to be a case of sister versus patron when he put it in his *bāb mīrāth dhī ʿl-qarāba* (compare the similar case above, note 63).

86 al-Ṭūsī, *Tahdhīb*, vol. 9, p. 330, nos. 1186f. (where the daughters are slaves whose manumission is purchased, presumably out of the estate); pp. 331f., nos. 1192f. (where the widow gets her eighth); cf. also no. 1195.

> Ibrāhīm al-Nakhaʿī was reminded that the Prophet had given only half the estate to the daughter in the classical case of Ibnat Ḥamza, awarding the remaining half to the patroness, he tried to explain it away, implying that he himself would have given the entire estate to the daughter.[87]

In this material the cognates are Qurʾānic heirs, not *dhawū ʾl-arḥām* in the classical sense; yet they are adduced in illustration of the same rule as their non-Qurʾānic counterparts.

3. Finally, ʿAbd al-Karīm b. Abī ʾl-Mukhāriq (d. 126/743f) sets out the doctrine as follows:[88]

> When a man died leaving patrons who had freed him, but no *dhū raḥim* other than [for instance] a mother or maternal aunt, they would award the estate to her and not call the patron to succession together with her; for they do not call patrons to succession together with a *dhū raḥim.*

Here a Qurʾānic cognate (mother) and a non-Qurʾānic one (maternal aunt) are explicitly enumerated as heirs of the same type, covered by the same rule.

There is no doubt that the terminology at least is odd in these traditions, but the fact that the propounders of the DAEP rule speak of both types of cognates as *dhawū ʾl- arḥām* does not necessarily mean that they were ignorant of the distinction between them. It is possible that the pre-Islamic Arabs operated with the two broad categories of relatives outlined above, that is male agnates and cognates in the sense of the rest (who may or may not have been heirs); if this is correct, and if the cognates were known as *dhawū ʾl-arḥām*, one would expect the term occasionally to have been used in its undifferentiated sense even after the Qurʾān had divided the cognatic category into two. But is it correct? The hypothetical Jāhilī usage is not reflected in the Qurʾān, in which no terms for

---

87 Raddatz, 'Erbrecht', p. 39 (where *innahā* should be emended to *innamā*); ʿAbd al-Razzāq, *Muṣannaf*, vol. 9, no. 16212; Ibn Abī Shayba, *Muṣannaf*, vol. 11, no. 11209; al-Bayhaqī, *Sunan*, vol. 6, pp. 242: *innamā aṭʿamahā rasūl Allāh ṣalʿam ṭuʿmatan* (to which the response in ʿAbd al-Razzāq is that if he did so, then we will too).

88 ʿAbd al-Razzāq, *Muṣannaf*, vol. 9, no. 16203: *inna ʾl-rajul idhā māta wa-taraka mawāliyahu ʾlladhīna aʿtaqūhu wa-lam yadaʿ dhā raḥim illā umman aw khālatan dafaʿū mīrāthahu ilayhā wa-lam yuwarrithū mawāliyahu maʿahā, wa-innahum lā yuwarrithūna mawāliyahu maʿa dhī raḥim.*

either agnates or cognates are used at all.[89] (The cognates in receipt of shares are referred to in specific terms as mother, daughter, sister and the like.) It could with equal plausibility be argued that the cognatic category encountered in these traditions was created and named by the early lawyers; and if this is correct, we must note that the category was un-Qurʾānic, not only in the sense that *dhawū ʾl-arḥām* was employed to mean cognates rather than relatives in general, but more particularly in that cognates were assigned to a single category even though the Qurʾān had awarded shares to some of them and failed to mention the rest.

However this may be, it is not only the terminology that is odd in our traditions. The material could admittedly be harmonized with classical law on the assumption that the Qurʾānic and non-Qurʾānic cognates were treated differently even though they were covered by the same term and the result was the same too: the so-called *dhawū ʾl-arḥām* of 2(b), who were in fact Qurʾānic heirs, were first awarded their Qurʾānic shares and next given the rest of the estate by *radd*,[90] whereas the genuine *dhawū ʾl-arḥām* of 2(a) were first awarded Qurʾānic shares by recourse to the mechanisms of *qarāba* or *tanzīl*[91] and next given the residue by *radd* again. There are in fact a few traditions in respect of which this assumption is valid: one mentions both Qurʾānic shares and *radd*,[92] while another explicitly distinguishes between Qurʾānic and non-Qurʾānic heirs.[93] And the

89 *Wa-ūlū ʾl-arḥām baʿḍuhum awlā bi-baʿḍin* (Qur. 8:76; 33:6). As Mundy notes, the term is not suggestive of priority of agnates over cognates and affines (M. Mundy, 'The Family, Inheritance, and Islam: A Re-examination of the Sociology of Farā iḍ Law', in A. al-Azmeh (ed.), *Islamic Law: Social and Historical Contexts*, London 1988, p. 32, where the absence of a term for agnatic relatives as such is also noted); it obviously does not suggest a purely cognatic category either.

90 Cf. Coulson, *Succession*, pp. 49ff.

91 Ibid., ch. 7.

92 Ibn Abī Shayba, *Muṣannaf*, vol. 11, no. 11208; Ibn Bābūya, *Man lā yaḥḍuruhu al-faqīh*, vol. 4, p. 224, no. 712, where the client leaves a daughter and a wife: ʿAlī gave the wife an eighth and the daughter a half, awarding the residue to the daughter by *radd* and excluding the patrons.

93 ʿAlī would exclude the patron from succession in the presence of a *dhū qarāba* even if the latter was not a recipient of *al-mīrāth al-mafrūḍ* (al-Kulaynī, *Kāfī*, vol. 7, p. 136, no. 7).

transmitters, fully aware that adherents of the DAEP rule figure in traditions on *radd* and *tanzīl* as well,[94] undoubtedly subscribed to the assumption with respect to the entirety of the material.[95] They would hardly have transmitted it if they did not.

But if we disregard the exceptional traditions,[96] the assumption becomes gratuitous. In what is both the earliest and the fullest account of the DAEP rule, that of ʿAbd al-Razzāq b. Hammām, the traditions give no indication of a differentiation between the heirs of 2(a) and 2(b); indeed, ʿAbd al-Karīm's account of the rule explicitly conflates them. The *prima facie* reading of ʿAbd al-Razzāq's material is that all the heirs involved are treated identically: all are awarded the entire estate, not through a combination of Qurʾānic shares, *qarāba, tanzīl* or *radd*, but simply because awarding the entire estate to the only heir is the obvious solution for anyone who is not constrained to think in terms of fixed shares. When Ibrāhīm al-Nakhaʿī tried to explain away the case of Ibnat Ḥamza, in which the Prophet gives the daughter her Qurʾānic maximum of half the estate and hands the rest to the manumitter, al-Shaʿbī is supposed to have objected that "you do not know whether this took place before

94 ʿAbd al-Razzāq's *bāb mīrāth al-qarāba* includes material on *radd*, and one of his traditions on non-Qurʾānic cognates versus patrons recurs in his chapter on *radd* (cf. above, note 85). Ibn Abī Shayba's chapter on *man kāna yuwarrithu dhawī ʾl-arḥām dūna ʾl-mawālī* is followed by one on *radd*, again with some overlap between the two (cf. above notes 63, 92).

95 Cf. ʿAbd al-Razzāq, *Muṣannaf*, vol. 10, nos. 19112-17; Ibn Abī Shayba, *Muṣannaf*, vol. 11, nos. 11213ff.; Raddatz, 'Erbrecht', p. 40; Ibn Qudāma, *Mughnī*, vol. 6, p. 319, no. 4826. In fact there is a strong tendency in Ibn Abī Shayba for the traditions on non-Qurʾānic cognates versus patrons to become traditions about non-Qurʾānic cognates *tout court*. Note also how Shurayḥ appears as an adherent of the DAEP rule in Abū ʿUbayd (above, note 61), but as a supporter of the rights of non-Qurʾānic cognates in general in Muḥammad b. Khalaf Wakīʿ, *Akhbār al-quḍāt*, ed. ʿA.M. al-Marāghī, Cairo 1947-50, vol. 2, p. 321.

96 The first (above, note 92) is exceptional also in that it involves two heirs on the client's side, i.e. it does not confine its attention to the relative priority of two classes of heirs, but seeks to apportion rights within these classes too. The second (note 93) formulates the DAEP rule in the language of a tenth-century author.

or after [the revelation of] the *farāʾiḍ*", meaning that Ibrāhīm's supposition that the daughter had a right to the entire estate only made sense on the assumption that the Qur'ānic laws of inheritance had not been revealed at the time.[97] This is my understanding too.

To clinch the case is difficult. If there was a pre-Qur'ānic stage of Islamic law, the chances are that most of the evidence relating thereto will have disappeared, not because there was a Machiavellian conspiracy to suppress it, but rather because the Muslims devoted immense energy to ironing out inconsistencies within the tradition and none at all to transmitting material that had become unintelligible or plain wrong to them. Only ambiguous evidence (such as the DAEP rule itself) is likely to have slipped through the net. One tradition does come close to clinching the case, but as might be expected, the cost of its survival was corruption. It goes as follows:[98]

أَخبرنا عبد الرزاق قال: أَخبرني سليمان الأَحول عن أَبي حبيب العراقي أَن امرأة كان لها ابن، فتوُفِّيَ وله خمسون دينارًا، ليس له وارث إلا أمه، ومواليه بعيد منه، فقال له أَبو الشعثاءِ: ويحك خذيها ولا تعطيها شيئاً.

ʿAbd al-Razzāq — Ibn Jurayj — Sulaymān al-Aḥwal — Abū Ḥabīb al-ʿIrāqī: a woman had a son who died leaving fifty dinars. He had no heirs apart from his mother and his patrons, [who] was/were distant (masc. sg.) from him. So Abū ʾl-Shaʿthāʾ said to him (*sic*): 'Poor you, take (fem. sg.) them and do not (fem. sg.) give her (*sic*) anything'.

---

97 Raddatz, 'Erbrecht', pp. 39f. This was presumably meant as a crushing reply to Ibrāhīm (compare the response in ʿAbd al-Razzāq, above, note 87). But al-Shaʿbī elsewhere figures as a supporter of the DAEP rule (above, note 66), and the Imāmīs and Nāṣirī Zaydīs took al-Shaʿbī to be coming to Ibrāhīm's rescue: he was suggesting that the case of Ibnat Ḥamza *was* enacted before the revelation of the inheritance laws, and thus abrogated by it (cf. below, note 110). Sufyān al-Thawrī also seems to have read it in this vein (below, note 119).

98 ʿAbd al-Razzāq, *Muṣannaf*, vol. 9, no. 16206. As regards the *isnād*, Ibn Jurayj and Sulaymān al-Aḥwal are well-known Meccans, but who was Abū Ḥabīb al-ʿIrāqī? Ibn Ḥajar lists one man of that *kunya* (*Tahdhīb*, vol. 12, p. 68), and al-Dūlābī lists seven (*Kitāb al-kunā wa-ʾl-asmāʾ*, Hyderabad 1322, vol. 1, p. 143); but none of them seems to fit.

There are several ways in which this garbled text could be emended. For a start, how many patrons were there? The number of patrons does not affect the rules, but it does affect the sense of this tradition; for if there was only one (reading *wa-mawlāhu ba'īd minhu*), the patron could be the "him" addressed, and Abū 'l-Sha'thā''s statement could in that case be emended to "take them [reading *khudhhā* for *khudhīhā*] and do not give her [reading *lā tu'ṭihā* for *lā tu'ṭīhā*] anything": the tradition would disinherit the mother. But it is quite possible that the plural *mawālih* and the singular *ba'īd* should be left unemended, since there are other early passages in which *ba'īd* is treated as invariable when used as a predicate of persons;[99] if so, there were several patrons and someone else was addressed. If Abū 'l-Sha'thā' was talking to the mother (reading *lahā* for *lahu*), his statement could be emended to "take them, and do not give him [reading *tu'ṭīhi* for *tu'ṭīhā*] anything": the tradition disinherits the patron. This would certainly make more sense if Abū 'l-Sha'thā' is Jābir b. Zayd, a well known propounder of the DAEP rule.[100] Both of these readings rest on the assumption that the text describes a case taken to Abū 'l-Sha'thā', who is acting as judge; but one could also construe it as a tradition of the question-answer type: "...Abū Ḥabīb al-'Irāqī [who asked Abū 'l-Sha'thā' about the case of] a woman who...so Abū Sha'thā' said to him,..." This reading fits the fact that Jābir does not seem to have held office as judge, nor does Sulaym b. Aswad al-Muḥāribī, a Kūfan Abū 'l-Sha'thā' who died in 83/702 and whose views on the DAEP rule are not recorded.[101] The question-answer hypothesis also goes well with the *wayḥaki* of the answer ('Poor you, don't you know?'); but it does not exactly make it easier to emend the rest of Abū 'l-Sha'thā''s statement.

---

99 T. Nöldeke, *Zur Grammatik des klassischen Arabisch*, Vienna 1897 (revised A. Spitaler, Darmstadt 1963), p. 22n. I owe both the point and the reference to Dr. L. Conrad.

100 See the reference given above, note 70.

101 Jābir b. Zayd and Sulaym b. al-Aswad al-Muḥāribī are the only two men with the *kunya* Abū 'l-Sha'thā' listed by Ibn Ḥajar (*Tahdhīb*, vol. 12, p. 127). Al-Dūlābī adds others, but none is relevant (*Kitāb al-kunā*, vol. 2, pp. 5f.).

However we emend it, he is saying that somebody is to be given nothing, so who is the somebody? The tradition should be read in conjunction with another in which al-Qāsim b. ʿAbd al-Raḥmān, the grandson of Ibn Masʿūd, excludes a patron from succession in the presence of a mother, awarding the entire estate to the latter on the grounds that it was she who had born and bred the deceased, that is, on moral grounds.[102] In Abū ʾl-Shaʿthāʾ's tradition, too, the mother has a better right in moral terms than the patrons, for we are told that the latter were distant, meaning that their legal connection with the client was remote:[103] some benefactor (*mawlā munʿim*) in the past had freed his slave or guided an infidel to Islam, but these people had merely inherited the patronate. Unlike the mother, then, they had no claim to gratitude from the deceased. Now information of this kind is never irrelevant, so the question is whether the tradition endorses the mother's moral right or mentions it in order to demonstrate its irrelevance. If we take it to endorse her right, it is saying that the patrons had no right to succession because they were distant, thereby implying that they would or might have been called to succession if they had been closer. This is an implausible and otherwise unattested legal doctrine. On the other hand, if the tradition is saying that patrons take the estate *even though* they are distant, it establishes that the moral considerations invoked by al-Qāsim are irrelevant: the law is the law however unjust it may seem at times. This too would yield an otherwise unattested doctrine (patrons exclude mothers), but there is nothing implausible about it: the client owes his legal personality to his manumitter/guide to Islam, not to his mother, and the patron is the person "closest to him in life and death", as a tradition puts it.[104] One frequently feels

---

102 ʿAbd al-Razzāq, *Muṣannaf*, vol. 9, no. 16205: *ḥamaltihi fī baṭniki wa-arḍaʿtihi bi-thadyiki, laki ʾl-māl kulluhu.*

103 Compare Abū ʾl-Faraj al-Iṣbahānī, *Kitāb al-aghānī*, Cairo 1927-74, vol. 4, p. 26 (*min baʿīd al-walāʾ*). The terms *qarīb* and *baʿīd* are commonplace in connection with genealogical relationships too.

104 *Man aslama ʿalā yadayhi fa-huwa mawlāhu/huwa awlā ʾl-nās bi-maḥyāhu wa-mamātihi*, see for example Shāfiʿī, *Umm*, vol. 6, p. 186; al-Tirmidhī, *al-Ṣaḥīḥ*, Cairo 1931-34, vol. 8, p. 265; al-Bukhārī, *Le recueil des traditions mahométanes*, ed. L. Krehl and T.W. Juynboll, Leiden 1862-1908, vol. 4, p. 289; Abū Dāwūd, *Ṣaḥīḥ*

that this expression must once have been rather more seriously meant than the rights of the patron in recorded law would suggest.

If the mother was excluded, we have clinched the case: Qur'ānic shares were unknown, or at any rate ignored. But what if this reading is wrong? Yet another mother excluding yet another patron does not clinch anything unless the tradition is polemical against those who would do the reverse. But it could of course simply be polemical against those who would have her share with the patron. In al-Qāsim's tradition the mother is awarded *al-māl kulluh*, suggesting that the alternative was to restrict her to her Qur'ānic share, not to exclude her: the issue was her right to *radd*. Abū 'l-Sha'thā''s tradition could be similarly understood, since we are explicitly told that somebody (the mother?) takes *all* the property and gives the other party *nothing*. This would make good classical sense of the tradition as far as the mother is concerned, but it gets us into trouble with the patrons again, for the tradition would now be implying that they did not get the residue because they were distant whereas they would or might have got it if they had been close, which still does not make any sense at all. The assumption that the issue was all or nothing to either patron or mother works much better. But the text is too ambivalent for this reading to be proved.

All is not lost, however, for the case can still be corroborated by indirect means. As mentioned already, classical Sunnī law does not accept the DAEP rule: the patron inherits along with Qur'ānic cognates and excludes non-Qur'ānic ones, instead of being excluded by both. But the rule did not disappear without a trace: all schools of Kūfan origin[105] preserve it to a greater or lesser extent. Thus

---

sunan al-muṣṭafā, Cairo 1348, vol. 2, p. 20; Ibn al-Athīr, *al-Nihāya fī gharīb al-ḥadīth*, ed. T.A. al-Zāwī and M.M. al-Ṭannāḥī, Cairo 1963-65, vol. 5, p. 229; Ibn Ḥajar, *Tahdhīb*, vol. 6, p. 47 (s.v. "'Abdallāh b. Mawhab").

105 The Imāmīs are usually classified as a Medinese school, rather than a Kūfan one, but cf. Crone, *Roman, Provincial and Islamic Law*, p. 21 (and note the alignment between Ḥanafīs, Zaydīs and Imāmīs on contractual clientage on p. 38; between Zaydīs and Imāmīs on *kitāba* on p. 76; and between Ḥanafīs, Zaydīs, Imāmīs and Ibāḍīs, i.e. all the Iraqis, on p. 95, section iii, on bequests). It should be obvious from what follows that the Imāmī position on respective rights of patron and *dhawū 'l-arḥām* is anything but Medinese even though it is ascribed to imams who resided in Medina and occasionally to other Medinese authorities too (such as Jābir al-Anṣārī, above, note 75).

the Ḥanafīs and Qāsimī Zaydīs continued to apply the DAEP rule to the *contractual* patron: whereas the manumitter counts as an agnate, the contractual patron only inherits in the absence of all relatives, be they male agnates or cognates of the Qur'ānic *or* non-Qur'ānic variety.[106] The contractual patron is absent from the Kufan work ascribed to Zayd b. ʿAlī, and here the manumitter excludes non-Qur'ānic cognates precisely as he does in Sunnī law; but the DAEP rule still applies when the manumitter is in competition with *Qur'ānic* cognates: they exclude him instead of sharing with him.[107] The Nāṣirī Zaydīs also dropped the contractual patron, but they preserved the DAEP rule unchanged in respect of the manumitter: both Qur'ānic *and* non-Qur'ānic cognates exclude him.[108] And the Imāmīs preserved the rule intact: the manumitter *and* the contractual patron inherit only in the absence of all relatives, be they agnates, Qur'ānic cognates *or* non-Qur'ānic cognates.[109] The Nāṣirīs and Imāmīs disliked the case of Ibnat Ḥamza as heartily as did Ibrāhīm al-Nakhaʿī.[110]

What the Kūfan schools show us is clearly fractured parts of what must once have been a single doctrine, as in fact it still is in the case of the Imāmīs. The fracture has occurred along the divide between manumitter and contractual patron and has split the applicability of the doctrine in half; but the result is wonderfully symmetrical in that the schools have preserved the rule for *different* halves of the whole: the Nāṣirīs and pseudo-Zayd

---

106 Crone, *Roman, Provincial and Islamic Law*, pp. 38f. and note 49 thereto.

107 Zayd b. ʿAlī (attrib.), *Majmūʿ al-fiqh*, ed. E. Griffini, Milan 1919, p. 255, 849f.

108 Crone, *Roman, Provincial and Islamic Law*, p. 37.

109 Ibid., pp. 37, 38f.

110 The Imāmīs dismiss it as a tradition related by the *mukhālifūn* which is *muwāfiq li-madhāhib al-ʿāmma*, due to *taqiyya*, contradicted by another version, *munqaṭiʿ*, enacted before the revelation of the *farā'iḍ* and abrogated by it, disliked by Ibrāhīm al-Nakhaʿī, and at all events superfluous as the truth is clear from the Qur'ān regardless of Ḥadīth! (Ibn Bābūya, *Man lā yaḥḍuruhu al-faqīh*, vol. 4, pp. 223f., no. 711; al-Ṭūsī, *Tahdhīb*, vol. 9, nos. 1190-92). The Nāṣirī Zaydīs likewise regarded it as contrary to the book of God, weak and disapproved of by al-Shaʿbī and other traditionists (Muḥammad b. Yaʿqūb al-Hawsamī, *Kitāb sharḥ al-ibāna*, MS Ambrosiana, D. 224, fols. 101a, 123a). Compare above, note 97.

retain it when the cognates are in competition with a manumitter, the Ḥanafīs and Qāsimis when they are in competition with a contractual patron. In pseudo-Zayd there is an additional fracture along the divide between Qur'ānic and non-Qur'ānic cognates, the old rule being preserved only for Qur'ānic cognates in competition with a manumitter; and the result is asymmetrical in that no school retains it only for non-Qur'ānic cognates in competition with him. But then nobody would, for the obvious reason that non-Qur'ānic cognates could not be placed in a better position than their Qur'ānic counterparts (by continuing to exclude manumitters even when Qur'ānic heirs had come to share with them); and it is in any case its preservation in connection with the *Qur'ānic* half of the former *dhawū 'l-arḥām* that is significant. Besides, the Imāmīs make up for the missing piece by preserving the rule intact. The DAEP rule must indeed have been to the effect that all cognates were heirs of the same type; all excluded manumitters and contractual patrons, who were heirs of the same type too.

Presumably the adherents of the DAEP rule held cognates of any kind to exclude patrons for the simple reason that they were blood relations whereas patrons were not: heirs by *nasab* exclude heirs by *sabab* (the spouse relict excepted), as the Imāmīs were later to put it.[111] The distinction between Qur'ānic and non-Qur'ānic blood relations is intrusive to this line of thought; indeed, it must have been this very distinction (in combination with a new stress on agnatic ties) that caused the fracture.[112] The Imāmīs managed to *accommodate* the distinction, but their laws of inheritance can hardly be said to be based on it: "[Imami] Shi'i jurisprudence majestically sweeps aside all those troublesome distinctions and divisions, between Qur'ānic and other heirs, and between agnatic and non-agnatic relatives, in which the generality of Muslim jurists were enmeshed", as Coulson

---

111 Crone, *Roman, Provincial and Islamic Law*, p. 148, note 27.

112 Classical Sunnī inheritance law may be characterized as agnatic succession modified by Qur'ānic legislation (Coulson, *Succession*, p. 33); but the view that the agnatic rules were a straight carry-over from tribal Arabia is undoubtedly mistaken (cf. Mundy, 'The Family, Inheritance, and Islam', pp. 30, 47; Powers, *Studies*, ch. 3; Crone, *Roman, Provincial and Islamic Law*, p. 80).

puts it.[113] The Imāmīs swept them aside, it would appear, because they were committed to an archaic doctrine formulated before the distinctions in question had made their appearance. Their inheritance laws may thus be a counterpart to their conception of the imamate, both being elaborations of doctrines once common to the Muslim world at large.[114] Archaisms are also well attested in other types of Imāmī law.[115]

When then did the fracture of the DAEP rule outside Imāmī circles occur? The unfractured rule is ascribed to Companions, Successors and later authorities, but not to the Prophet; apparently, it did not live to be defended in terms of the classical rules of the game. It was however widely adhered to, we are told, by authorities who died in the 730s, such as ʿAṭāʾ (d. 114/732), Muḥammad al-Bāqir (d. 114 or 119/733 or 737), al-Qāsim b. ʿAbd al-Raḥmān (d. 120/738f) and Maymūn b. Mihrān (d. 118 or 126/736 or 743f),[116] so it must have been current in the 730s and, given that some of these ascriptions are likely to be spurious, presumably in the generation thereafter too. But in that generation it was on the way out. Though still supported by Jaʿfar al-Ṣādiq (d. 148/765)[117] and, apparently, Ibn Abī Laylā (d. 148/765)[118] and Sufyān al-Thawrī (d. 116/778),[119] it

113 Coulson, *Succession*, p. 110.

114 Cf. Crone and Hinds, *God's Caliph*.

115 Crone, *Roman, Provincial and Islamic Law*, index, s.v. 'Imāmī law', for six examples relating to the law of slavery and *walāʾ*.

116 Cf. above, notes 64, 73, 74, 76.

117 al-Kulaynī, *Kāfī*, vol. 7, pp. 135f.

118 S. al-Maḥmaṣānī, *al-Awzāʿī wa-taʿālīmuhu ʾl-insāniyya wa-ʾl-qānūniyya*, Beirut 1978, p. 229, claims that he disinherited all non-Qurʾānic cognates. This is not implausible, given his Medinese inclination; but no references are given, and the claim is contradicted by al-Ḥusayn b. Aḥmad al-Siyāghī, *Kitāb al-rawḍ al-naḍīr*, completed by ʿAbbās b. Aḥmad al-Ḥasanī, Cairo 1347-49, vol. 5, p. 64; cf. also Ibn Qudāma, *Mughnī*, vol. 6, p. 319, no. 4826. (The question is not broached in Abū Yūsuf, *Ikhtilāf Abī Ḥanīfa wa-ʾbn Abī Laylā*, ed. A.-W. al-Afghānī, Hyderabad 1358, or Wakīʿ, *Quḍāt*, vol. 3, pp. 129ff.)

119 Sufyān al-Thawrī starts his *bāb fī ʾl-mawālī*, with the Ibnat Ḥamza tradition, complete with Ibrāhīm al-Nakhaʿī's attempt to explain it away and al-Shaʿbī's reply; but he proceeds to cite another tradition in which a *dhū raḥim* excludes a patron, suggesting that he too construed al-Shaʿbī's reply as a dismissal of Ibnat

appears in its fractured form in the doctrine attributed to Abū Ḥanīfa (d. 150/767)[120] and the Kūfan work ascribed to Zayd b. ʿAlī,[121] and it was wholly abandoned by al-Awzāʿī (d. 157/774),[122] Mālik (d. 179/795)[123] and later school founders.[124] The DAEP rule thus seems to have lost out at the hands of men who flourished about 120-50/740-70. But these men can hardly have been the first to be confronted with the problem that made the rule inviable. Assuming that the problem made its appearance at least a generation before it was solved, the jurists' discovery of the Qurʾānic cognates must be dated to 90-120/710-40 at the latest. An earlier date would be preferable, but there are limits to how much earlier we can make it

Ḥamza's case (Raddatz, 'Erbrecht', pp. 39f.; cf. above, notes 97, 110). That he was a supporter of the DAEP rule is in fact stated by both Ibn Qudāma (*Mughnī*, vol. 6, p. 310, no. 4826) and al-Siyāghī, or rather his continuator (*Rawḍ*, vol. 5, p. 64). The claim to the contrary is thus unlikely to be correct (Sarakhsī, *Mabsūṭ*, vol. 30, p. 3).

120 See for example Muḥammad b. al-Ḥasan al-Shaybānī, *Kitāb al-aṣl*, ed. A.-W. al-Afghānī, vol. 4 (1), Hyderabad 1973, p. 166, from al-Shaʿbī: Ibn Masʿūd used only to call the manumitter to succession in the absence of *dhū qarāba*, but Abū Ḥanīfa held the patron to have a better right with reference to the tradition about Ibnat Ḥamza.

121 Cf. above, note 107. (On the date of this work, see W. Madelung, *Der Imam al-Qāsim b. Ibrāhīm und die Glaubenslehre der Zaiditen*, Berlin 1965, pp. 54ff.) Note that ʿAlī, reputedly the most vigorous supporter of the DAEP rule (above, notes 58f.), is here made to endorse the priority of manumitters over non-Qurʾānic cognates.

122 Maḥmaṣānī, *al-Awzāʿī*, p. 229, where al-Awzāʿī espouses the Mālikī disinheritance of all non-Qurʾānic cognates. No reference is given, but compare Ibn Qudāma, *Mughnī*, vol. 6, p. 319, no. 4826; al-Siyāghī, *Rawḍ*, vol. 5, p. 64.

123 Cf. Mālik, *Muwaṭṭa*ʾ, Cairo n.d., vol. 1, pp. 338f. (*Kitāb al-farāʾiḍ, bāb man lā mīrāth lahu*).

124 Al-Shāfiʿī disinherited the non-Qurʾānic cognates altogether after the fashion of the Medinese (cf. his *Umm*, vol. 6, p. 166; Sarakhsī, *Mabsūṭ*, vol. 30, p. 3; Ibn Qudāma, *Mughnī*, vol. 6, p. 319, no. 4826), though his followers abandoned this position. Abū Thawr, Dāwūd al-Ẓāhirī and al-Ṭabarī also disinherited them (Ibn Qudāma, *loc. cit.*), as did al-Qāsim b. Ibrāhīm, though the Zaydīs at large did not (Siyāghī, *Rawḍ*, vol. 5, p. 64; Madelung, *al-Qāsim*, pp. 134f.).

if the DAEP rule was still commonly accepted in the 730s. Simplistic calculations based on a single example have their limits too, of course; but for what it is worth, the evidence of the DAEP rule suggests a mid-Umayyad date for the arrival of the canonical scripture.[125]

We may now summarize. Three legal terms of the Qur'ān (*kalāla, jizya ʿan yad, kitāb* in 24:33) were unintelligible to the early commentators, as were several non-legal phrases and passages (*al-ṣamad*, possibly *al-rajīm*, the mysterious letters and *Sūrat Quraysh*). At the same time Qur'ānic legislation seems to have been partly ignored and partly misunderstood by the lawyers, two of whose rules (stoning penalty, rejection of written evidence) contradict the book, while a third (DAEP rule) fails to take account of it; and a whole cluster of rules (Powers' inheritance laws) seems to misrepresent its intentions. This is a fairly impressive score, and it cries out for a unitary explanation; but it is not easy to see how such an explanation can be provided without abandoning the conventional account of how the Qur'ān was born.

125 Compare the conjectural date in Crone and Cook, *Hagarism*, p. 18.

6

UNCONDITIONAL MANUMISSION OF SLAVES IN EARLY ISLAMIC LAW: A *ḤADĪTH* ANALYSIS[1]

Ulrike Mitter

1. Introduction

In studying the origins and the development of Islamic law in the first and second Islamic century, the question arises whether there is a genetic link between Islamic law and previous, non-Arabic legal systems or not. The answers given to this question have always been and still are very divergent.[2]

Now, it is well known that the Arab conquerors of Byzantine and Sassanian provinces retained a substantial part of the administrative customs of these former empires together with the Greek and the Persian languages and indigenous administrators and secretaries. That is mainly why it seems quite inevitable to many Western orientalists that Islamic law must have been influenced to a great degree by the legal systems of the conquered countries – especially when they take into account the quick development of Islamic law.[3] As a matter of fact, a great number of parallels between Islamic law and other legal systems have been issued forth to lend support to the theory of adoptions from previous legal systems. But it is not sufficient to point out such similarities. There are good reasons, as will be seen, to assume that some of the Islamic institutions which allegedly are borrowings from foreign legal systems had actually

---

1) This article is a revised version of a chapter of my doctoral thesis *Das frühislamische Patronat*. It was first presented as a paper at the *International Medieval Congress* in Leeds in 1997. I wish to thank David Sargeant for proof-reading the present article.

2) One just has to have a look at the discussion in *Der Islam* (number 77/1) between HARALD MOTZKI and IRENE SCHNEIDER to get an impression of the different opinions. See also the next paragraph on the role of foreign elements.

3) Important features of Islamic law were elaborated already in the work of Abū Yūsuf (d. 182 A.H.) and al-Shāfiʿī (d. 204 A.H.).

been developed by early Muslims themselves during their legal discussions.

In this article, I will approach the problem of borrowings in Islamic law not by way of a comparison of legal systems but by way of a detailed analysis of the legal traditions *(aḥādīth)*. Such an analysis allows us to date the *aḥādīth* and, thereby, to come to know something about the development of a legal institution.

The institution which will be analyzed here is the Islamic patronate *(walā')*. For the detailed analysis I have chosen one aspect of the whole complex of *walā'*: the unconditional manumission of slaves *(tasyīb)*. The development of *walā'* was discussed at length by PATRICIA CRONE in her book *Roman, provincial and Islamic law.* She proposed the theory that the origins of *walā'* are to be found in the late-Roman law. Her book represents one of the very few attempts to really prove foreign adoptions in Islamic law and not simply to assert them. But, as will be shown, some reservations are called for against her study. It is my intention to go into discussion with Crone's interpretation and dating of the relevant *aḥādīth*. Before going into details, I would like to summarize very briefly the main theories which were developed by Western scholars concerning the origins of Islamic law and the role of foreign influences.

2. The role of foreign elements in the origins of Islamic law

At the end of the 19th century IGNAZ GOLDZIHER spoke about a genetic link between Roman and Islamic law.[4]) Other studies followed which tried to show that borrowings from foreign legal systems played a mayor role in the origins of Islamic law.[5]) The underlying assumption was that the Muslims in the first Islamic century were not interested in legal issues and Islamic law was poorly developed – in opposition to what the *aḥādīth*

---

4) GOLDZIHER, *Muhammedanische Studien*, II, 1890, 76–76. Preceeding to GOLDZIHER, some scholars discussed the significance of parallels between Roman and Islamic law. For example ALFRED VON KREMER, *Culturgeschichte*, 1875–77. According to CRONE, *Roman law,* 1, the first study comparing Islamic law to Roman law seems to have been the one of ADRIAAN RELAND, *Dissertationes*, 1707–08.

5) For example CARL H. BECKER, "'Ušr", 1904; FRANZ F. SCHMIDT, "Occupatio", 1910; MARCEL MORAND, *Etudes,* 1910; WILLI HEFFENING, *Fremdenrecht* 1925. For a summary of the stand of field concerning foreign influences in Islamic law see CRONE, *Roman law,* 1–17.

would have us believe. *Aḥādīth* reporting events and legal opinions from this period are said to be spurious. They are said to reflect the opinions and methods of later jurists who, in order to strengthen their own doctrines, ascribed them first to early lawyers, then to the Successors *(tābiʿūn)*, then to the Companions of Muḥammad *(ṣaḥāba)* and finally to the Prophet himself. In this view, as a rule of thumb, the traditions of the Prophet are considered to be the youngest ones, not the oldest. This chronology was elaborated by JOSEPH SCHACHT in 1950[6]) who based himself on the theories of GOLDZIHER. It has been accepted since then by most Western orientalists.[7])

As a consequence of the supposedly non-existence of traditions and the few legal rules in the Qurʾān, the Muslims are said to have orientated themselfs on the legal systems which they found in the conquered countries.[8]) For SCHACHT, it was the rhetorically educated non-Arab converts in *Iraq* who transmitted some maxims of classical Roman law into Islamic law.[9]) CRONE maintains that the Umayyad caliphs in Syria, counseled by Byzantine administrators, are responsible for introducing elements of late-Roman and provincial law.[10]) According to CARL HEINRICH BECKER, it was the Islamic governors and administrators of Egypt who copied the Roman institution of the *emphyteusis*.[11]) Recently, IRENE SCHNEIDER developed a modified version of this argumentation.[12]) According to her, the Muslims in the first century did have a jurisprudence, but this jurisprudence is supposed to be rooted in non-Arabic legal systems – at least in the area of debt slavery.[13])

---

6) SCHACHT, *Origins*, 4–5 and 15ff. cf. also Motzki, Anfänge, 30 and 46.

7) For example by CRONE, *Roman law*, 80.

8) Presupposing sometimes that the "Barbarian" Arabs could not have thought about legal solutions themselves. SCHMIDT, *Occupatio*, 319, asserts that Abū Yūsuf tried to explain Roman regulations which he did not fully understand. GOLDZIHER, "Fiqh", 132, tells us that the Arabs were *"völlig ungeschult"* and originated *"aus armseligen sozialen Verhältnissen"*. SEYMOUR V. FITZGERALD, "Alleged Debt", 81, quotes a "rash writer" by saying: "the Arabs added nothing to Roman law but a few mistakes".

9) SCHACHT, "Foreign Elements", 13–14; id., "Droit byzantin", 201–202; id., *Introduction*, 20.

10) CRONE, *Roman law*, 90–91; cf. CRONE/HINDS, *God's Caliph*.

11) BECKER, "ʿUšr", 224 and 228.

12) SCHNEIDER, *Schuldknechtschaft*.

13) SCHNEIDER does not want to generalize this conclusion ("Narrativität", 115).

In many of the cases where borrowings are assumed, above all in the older studies, there is no other evidence than rather rough parallels between Islamic law and the other legal system in question. But the existence of a parallel is by no means sufficient proof of borrowing. A parallel could, for example, also have arisen from an identical juridical question which generated similar solutions. Even if more than just a parallel can be adduced in favor of the theory of borrowing, the argumentation often is not convincing.[14])

Another group of Western scholars propose that Islamic law may have developed more continuously out of the old-Arabic customary law of Medina and Mekka. GOTTHELF BERGSTRÄSSER, who accepted the *aḥādīth* as authentic without analyzing them,[15]) stated (in 1925) that the old-Arabic law could have contained Roman and other elements which had reached the Arabian peninsula through commercial contact.[16]) Since SCHACHT, and rightly so, it is no longer possible to be too uncritical towards *aḥādīth*. Nevertheless, modern researchers such as DAVID POWERS and HARALD MOTZKI came in part to similar conclusions as BERGSTRÄSSER.[17]) This is the line of the article in hand, too. It will be argued on the basis of a thorough analysis and dating of *aḥādīth* that *tasyīb* and *walāʾ* were developed by Muslim lawyers without borrowings from Roman law in Islamic time.

3. The Islamic patronate

When a slave is freed by his master, the freedman and his descendants are bound forever to the manumitter in a relationship of patronage or clientage *(walāʾ)*.[18]) This is the rule in classical Islamic law. Both, patron

[14]) Examples for supposed borrowings from non-Arabic legal systems in private and public Islamic law are compiled and shortly discussed in MITTER, *Patronat*, 19–84. For a discussion of the problems one has to cope with while researching parallels and borrowings in Islamic law, see ibid., 85–91 and MITTER, "Problemen".

[15]) BERGSTRÄSSER, "Anfänge", 81.

[16]) Ibid., 80. The "constant state of flux between North and South" in pre-Islamic times is stressed by HALLAQ, "Use and Abuse", 5–6.

[17]) POWERS, "Bequests", 199, maintains that "Near Eastern provincial law [...] was operating in the Hijaz during the lifetime of the Prophet and possibly for some time before that". MOTZKI, *Anfänge*, 119, note 227, states after the dating of a tradition that *"die Herkunft der Maxime aus anderen Rechtstraditionen allenfalls gerettet werden [könnte], wenn man die Übernahme in die vorislamische Zeit verlegt"*.

[18]) The patronate by manumission is called *walāʾ al-ʿitq*. There is also a contractual form of patronate *(walāʾ al-muwālāt)* which will not be treated here.

and client are called *mawlā* (pl. *mawālī*).[19] *Walā'* is regarded as a sort of kinship tie between the patron and his client. The patron has a title to the freedman's estate in the absence of certain heirs, and he is obliged to pay blood-money on behalf of his client.[20]

What are the roots of this Islamic patronate? According to CRONE, there was no individual patronate in pre-Islamic Arabia, but the patronate was collective.[21] If there were contracts between manumitter and freedman, these were no contracts of clientage, but labour contracts.[22] The patron never had a title to the estate of his client in return for paying bloodmoney on his client's behalf.[23] Since, therefore, in her opinion pre-Islamic Arabia cannot be the source of the Islamic *walā'*,[24] CRONE looks for another source.

According to her, an individual tie between patron and client together with the patron's right of succession did not exist in other legal systems of the region either,[25] but it did exist in Roman law.[26] Roman law, therefore, has to be regarded as the source of the Islamic patronate. CRONE asserts that "if the Arab conquests had not included Roman provinces, there would not have been an Islamic patronate of the type we know".[27] She points out coincidences between the late-Roman and the early Islamic patronate and concludes that both were influenced by Hellenistic provincial practice where the patronate was regarded as a reward for the manumitter.[28] CRONE suggests that it could have been the first Umayyad caliph Muʿāwiya (d. 60)[29] who introduced this late-Roman patronate, because Muʿāwiya, resided in Syria, was surrounded by a Byzantine staff and had to handle the problem of integrating converts and newcomers to Islamic society, the biggest share of them being freedmen.

---

19) For the diverse meanings of *walā'* and *mawlā* see HEND GILLI-ELEWY, "Aspekte", 126–130.

20) For an introduction to the patronate see ROBERT BRUNSCHVIG, "ʿAbd", 30–31; CRONE, "Mawlā"; id., *Roman law*, 34–42.

21) Ibid., 43–44.

22) Ibid., 58.

23) Ibid., 62.

24) CRONE's arguments to this respect, though, are not convincing. See HALLAQ, "Use and Abuse", 9–17.

25) CRONE, *Roman law*, 64.

26) Ibid., 77–78 and literature quoted there.

27) Ibid., 78.

28) Ibid., 78 and 84–86.

29) The year of death of Muslim scholars and caliphs will always be given according to the Islamic calendar.

CRONE suggests that it may have been for this purpose that Muʿāwiya introduced the Roman patronate.[30]

To be sure, the supposedly late-Roman features of *walāʾ* were already gone in classical Islamic law, but still traceable in what CRONE calls "pre-classical" law.[31] As mentioned already, in classical law *walāʾ* is considered to be a kinship tie which implies that the patron is supposed to inherit as the last agnate *(ʿaṣaba)* of his client. The patronate cannot be bought, sold or given away. It cannot be inherited like a normal piece of property and it is not possible to renounce it.[32] CRONE detects a very different situation in "pre-classical" law and describes it as follows: *Walāʾ* was not regarded as a kinship tie but simply as a residue of ownership. It could be alienated, inherited like property and renounced. Normally, the patron was not regarded as an agnatic heir. He was excluded from succession by every relative of the client, however remote.[33] At the end of the first century, the lawyers started reshaping the institution of *walāʾ* because the relationship of dependence was now considered to be an insult to converts and freedmen. Contractual patronate over free converts became mostly forbidden. It was due to this reshaping that *walāʾ* retained once again the tribal look of a ficticious kinship tie, something it did not have in the beginning.[34] So far CRONE's theory, the consistency of which will be tested now on the basis of the example of *tasyīb*.

---

30) CRONE, *Roman law*, 90–91. According to HALLAQ "Use and Abuse", 7 and 9, however, the function of *walāʾ* had not been integrating converts and newcomers into Islamic society. He emphazises that the patronate upon freed slaves *(walāʾ al-ʿitq)* has nothing to do with regulating the status of non-Arab outsiders because slaves already were members of Islamic society. As to the very different contractual patronate *(walāʾ al-muwālāt)*, this institution "may, but does not necessarily, involve converts". As will be seen in the end of this article, Muʿāwiya could not have been be responsible for introducing the patronate, anyway.

31) In CRONE's opinion, "pre-classical" Islamic law is preserved in the law of the Iraqi schools and in "early *ḥadīth*" (*Roman law*, 23 and 26–27).

32) Cf. ibid., 36–40.

33) Ibid., 79–84.

34) Ibid., 91. CRONE developed the theory that many features of Islamic law which have a tribal appearance had actually been reshaped by lawyers who were hostile to the Umayyad dynasty and to their introduction of foreign elements into Islamic law. The seemingly tribal elements are, therefore, held to be later than the Umayyad practice and no indication for continuity between tribal and Islamic law. Cf. CRONE, "Jahili and Jewish Law", 154–155.

4. Tasyīb: *Crone's view*

A slave who is freed unconditionally is called *sā'iba* (pl. *sawā'ib*). He is released without restraints and free to go wherever he wants. His manumitter renounces the patronate and the freedman can choose another patron if he wants to.[35] Most of the later Muslim lawyers disapprove of the practice of *tasyīb*.[36]

According to CRONE, rejection of *tasyīb* represents a later stage in the development of Islamic law. In the beginning, things were different and it had been possible for the manumitter to renounce the patronate.[37] This she attributes to the influence of late-Roman practices upon early Islamic law. CRONE reconstructs the history of unconditional manumission in Roman and Islamic law as follows:

Freeing a slave without claiming his patronate was not allowed in classical Roman law. But it became possible in late-Roman law under the influence of the Greek *paramonē* (which means: remain by). In the Hellenistic world, *paramonē* was the usual relationship between freedman and manumitter. The slave – who was adopted by his master – had to serve the master and gained full freedom on his death. In time, adoption became unusual and the institution transformed into a sort of conditional manumission whereby the freedman had to serve his former master for several years. If he wanted to, the manumitter could renounce these paramonar obligations. After the Romans had conquered the Greek provinces, *paramonē* and Roman patronate got mixed up. On a par with the renunciation of paramonar obligations, people started to renounce the patronate. Under Justinian (527–65 A. D.), this provincial practice gained the status of Roman law. Then the Arabs conquered the Roman provinces, became acquainted with the provincial practice and introduced it into their legal

---

35) The definition of *tasyīb in lisān al-ʿarab* (I, 478) goes: *wa-kāna ar-rağulu idhā aʿtaqa ʿabdan wa-qāla: huwa sā'ibun, fa-qad ʿataqa, wa-lā yakūnu walā'uhu li-muʿtiqihi, wa-yadaʿu mālahu ḥaythu shā'a, wa-huwa lladhī warada an-nahī ʿanhu* (If a man frees his slave and says: "Your are a *sā'iba*", than he is free without his *walā'* belonging to his manumitter, and he can put his estate where he pleases [i. e. he is free to choose a new patron and bequeth his estate to him]. This is what has been forbidden).

36) See, for example, AL-SHĀFIʿĪ, *al-Umm*, VI, 185–186 and AL-MARGHĪNĀNĪ, *Hidāya*, III, 271. Al-Marghīnānī quotes Abū Ḥanīfa by saying that *tasyīb* is not allowed and *walā'* belongs to the manumitter. Then he and adds himself that renunciation of *walā'* contradicts the text of the Qur'ān.

37) CRONE, *Roman law*, 81 and 91.

system. That is why in pre-classical Islamic law, renunciation of the patronate had been possible until the modification of the institution by Islamic scholars.[38])

Now, it seems that in pre-Islamic Arabia, *tasyīb* of slaves was not unknown.[39]) Why, then, could the institution known to the Islamic lawyers not be the continuation of this pre-Islamic institution? In the view of Crone, the reason is that in pre-Islamic Arabia *tasyīb* meant something different, that is, freeing a slave "without stipulations of further service".[40]) Freeing him without claiming his patronate and his inheritance (as it is the case in Islamic law) was, in her words, "something new reminiscent of the Roman patronate" which had been introduced by Muʿāwiya.[41]) Her argument for interpreting the pre-Islamic institution in the way she does is that animals, too, were freed by exempting them from further services, "and *tasyīb* of slaves must surely once have been the same".[42])

According to Crone, there was thus an old-Arabic phase (*tasyīb* as renunciation of paramonar service) which passed with Muʿāwiya into the "pre-classical" phase (*tasyīb* as renunciation of patronate) and from the second century onwards into the "classical" phase (*tasyīb* forbidden). Whether this view is tenable or not, we will see after the analysis of the traditions.

In order to support her theory of late-Roman influence on the early Islamic *walāʾ*, Crone makes a sharp distinction between an early "pre-classical" doctrine and a later "classical" doctrine. To both doctrines she attaches the proper *aḥādīth* deciding, thereby, from the content of a tradition whether it is older or younger. Following Schacht's above men-

[38]) Ibid., 64–67 (*paramonē* in the classical world) and 84–85 (parallels between late-Roman and pre-classical Islamic law).

[39]) The sources for *tasyīb* of slaves in pre-Islamic Arabia are scarce, but we have some indications for its existence. As a concrete example for *tasyīb* in pre-Islamic times, the sources mention the case of Sālim. Since the Sālim tradition existed in the middle of the first century (see below, 53 ff.), it is probable that the *tasyīb* of Sālim actually happend. Islamic lawyers did not doubt that in the *"jāhilīya"* slaves were freed *sāʾibatan*. This is made clear by the Ibn Masʿūd tradition where *tasyīb* is called a pre-Islamic practice (cf. below, 60). See also al-Ṭabarī, *Tafsīr*, XI, 116–132 and al-Zurqānī, *Sharḥ*, IV, 125. Cf. Juda, *Mawālī*, 24. In addition, my analysis of the traditions enable conclusions to be drawn regarding *tasyīb* before Islam (see below, 68).

[40]) Crone, *Roman law*, 67.

[41]) Ibid., 85.

[42]) Ibid., 68.

tioned "rule of thumb", she assumes that traditions of the Prophet, the *ṣaḥāba* and mainly of the *tābiʿūn* are spurious anyway. In addition, she holds that traditions which admit *tasyīb* purport the "preclassical" doctrine. So, they must be the older ones. Traditions which disapprove of *tasyīb* are to be the "classical" ones and thus generally younger.[43]) This is not a very safe method of dating traditions because it takes a relative chronology which is based on the *matn* as the starting point for judging the authenticity of *aḥādīth*.

Dating *aḥādīth* mainly by their content is so very problematic because the meaning of a tradition is not always clear. If the interpretation of a tradition happens to be wrong, also its dating, based on this interpretation, will be incorrect.[44]) In many cases, for example, it is hardly possible to decide whether a *ḥadīth* is pro or contra *tasyīb*. This is, to my mind, due to the fact that many early Muslims were more interested in the practical need of distributing the estate of a deceased *sāʾiba* than in deciding whether or not this kind of manumission should be allowed. I will come back to this point later.

If we try to interpret the traditions regarding permission or prohibition of *tasyīb*, we find three main possibilites.[45]) First, the manumitter renounces the *walāʾ* and the *sāʾiba* chooses a patron of his own, which means that *tasyīb* is fully recognised (Crone's "pre-classical" doctrine). Secondly, the patronate belongs to the manumitter in all circumstances, which means that *tasyīb* is not admitted at all (the core "classical" doctrine). Thirdly, the manumitter renounces the patronate, but the *sāʾiba* is not allowed to choose a patron and his patronate passes to the Muslims at large, which means that *tasyīb* is only allowed on the part of the manumitter (the weak "classical" doctrine).[46])

Things got more complicated when a *sāʾiba* who was allowed to choose a new patron – *tasyīb* accepted – died without having done so. To whom belongs his inheritance? The options given in the traditions are either to the Muslims at large[47]) or to the manumitter.[48]) If it is the manumitter

---

[43]) See ibid., 81, and the notes given there. See also ibid., 91.

[44]) Cf. Motzki's critical remarks with regard to Schacht's usage of such *matn*-based chronologies. Motzki, "Fiqh", 3.

[45]) For the three groups see Ibn Rushd/Nyazee, *Bidāyat*, II, 439.

[46]) Cf. Crone, *Roman law*, 81 (references for the first group are given in note 43, for the second group in note 44, and for the third group in note 45).

[47]) See for example ʿAbd al-Razzāq, *Muṣannaf*, IX, nos. 16228 and 16235 (both al-Zuhrī).

[48]) Ibid., no. 16236 (ʿAṭāʾ).

who gets the inheritance, what does that mean? Receiving the inheritance (together with the responsibility for the blood-money) means, getting the patronate. It is true that the manumitter is allowed to buy and rescue slaves with that money if he wishes to do so, but the inheritance was given to him in the first place. Would this imply a subsequent refusal of *tasyīb* when it was allowed initially?

This confusing situation probably is the reason why CRONE quotes traditions in a quite arbitrary manner as evidence respectively for her "classical" doctrine (refusal of *tasyīb*) and her "pre-classical" doctrine (acceptance of *tasyīb*). In two cases, CRONE adduces one and the same tradition for both doctrines, the "classical" and the "pre-classical" one.

One of these traditions deals with a certain Ṭāriq b. al-Muraqqaʿ who freed a slave *sāʾibitan*. The *sāʾiba* died, whereupon ʿUmar b. al-Khaṭṭāb (d. 23) gave his inheritance to his manumitter Ṭāriq. He refused to accept it, and ʿUmar decreed that slaves should be bought and released with that money.[49]) On the one hand, CRONE uses this tradition as evidence for the "pre-classical" doctrine: *Tasyīb* is allowed. No patronate arises after manumission because the manumitter Ṭāriq declared his slave to be *sāʾiba*. Only because the *sāʾiba* died without patron, the inheritance passes to Ṭāriq despite his renunciation of the patronate. On the other hand, CRONE uses the tradition as evidence for the core "classical" doctrine: *Tasyīb* is forbidden. The renunciation of the patronate by Ṭāriq is void because he gets the inheritance. If he renounces it, slaves could be bought and released with that money.[50])

One thing is for sure: In this tradition, the inheritance is awarded to the manumitter. When applying the tradition to the "pre-classical" doctrine, CRONE, obviously, stresses the fact that *tasyīb* happened. Applying the tradition to the "classical" doctrine, she must have paid attention only to the fact that it is the manumitter who gets the inheritance. This confusion is a first indication of the fact that a clear differentiation between the two doctrines is missing and that the tradition should be interpreted differently.[51])

---

[49]) Ibid., no. 16226. For the whole text and a detailed analysis of the Ṭāriq *ḥadīth* see below, 46 ff. In some variants, it is not a *"sāʾiba"*, but *"sawāʾib"* who were freed.

[50]) CRONE, *Roman law*, 81 and notes 43 ("pre-classical" doctrine) and 44 ("classical" doctrine).

[51]) As will be argued below, 51.

In the second tradition which Crone adduces as evidence for both of the two doctrines, the Medinense lawyer al-Zuhrī (d. 124) expresses his opinion about a slave who is freed *sā'ibatan*. According to al-Zuhrī, the inheritance of the *sā'iba* and the obligation of paying blood-money on his behalf should be assigned to the Muslims at large and the manumitter should not get anything.[52] Crone, first, holds this tradition to express the "pre-classical" doctrine because no patronate arises between manumitter and freedman.[53] Then, she holds it to express the weak "classical" doctrine presuming that the *sā'iba* is not allowed to choose a patron of his own.[54]

Because of the "incompleteness" of this tradition, one could indeed get the impression that al-Zuhrī was of the same opinion as his pupil Mālik who did not allow the *sā'iba* to choose a new patron though he did concede to the manumitter the right to renounce the patronate. Both scholars assigned the patronate to the Muslims at large, that is, to the state. If we take a close look to all traditions of al-Zuhrī, however, we find out that al-Zuhrī *does* allow the *sā'iba* to choose a new patron. He, therefore, endorses *tasyīb* totally, and only if the *sā'iba* died without a new patron, he assigns the patronate to the Muslims at large. This is stated explicitely by Mālik himself.[55] If at all, al-Zuhrī advocates the "pre-classical" doctrine.[56]

In my opinion, it is impossible to make any conclusive statements on the age of a *ḥadīth* by classifiying the traditions as "classical" and "pre-classical" ones and claiming that the "pre-classical" ones are the older *aḥādīth*. The development of a doctrine should be reconstructed not by constructing a relative chronology based only on the textes of a tradition but by applying a *combined* analysis of the *asānīd* and the *mutūn*: the *isnād-cum-matn* analysis.

---

52) 'Abd al-Razzāq, *Muṣannaf*, IX, no. 16228.

53) Crone, *Roman law*, 81, note 43.

54) Ibid., 81, note 45. According to Crone, this tradition is "ascribed to Zuhrī, whereas, in my opinion, it is an authentic tradition. Cf. also below, note 119.

55) Next to the tradition mentioned above in note 52, see also 'Abd al-Razzāq, *Muṣannaf*, IX, no. 16235 and X, no. 18426; Mālik b. Anas, *Muwaṭṭa'*, chapt. 38, no. 25; al-Zurqānī, *Sharḥ*, IV, 125.

56) Also later Muslim scholars thought that al-Zuhrī withheld the right of choosing a new patron from the *sā'iba*. Cf. below, 65, note 128.

5. Tasyīb: *Results of the isnād-cum-matn analysis*

How does the *isnād-cum-matn* analysis work? First, all available versions of a tradition are to be collected,[57]) and second, the *asānīd* of the versions are to be presented schematically in an *isnād* bundle. The bundle will reveal common transmitters – the so called "common links" (cls) – in the different generations. By comparing the *mutūn* of the versions and by enlisting meticulously their differences and common features, it will be possible to find out if the texts are really going back to the cls which appear in the *isnād* bundle or if one text or another is ascribed falsely to the authority.[58])

What are the results of such an *isnād-cum-matn* analysis if applied to the traditions concerning *tasyīb*? In what follows, I will analyze some traditions by detail, starting with two traditions ascribed to ʿUmar b. al-Khaṭṭāb.

ʿUmar b. al-Khaṭṭāb

The Ṭāriq tradition (see diagram 1) has just been mentioned in connection with CRONE's working method. It can be found in the pre-canonical works of ʿABD AL-RAZZĀQ,[59]) IBN ABĪ SHAYBA,[60]) SAʿĪD B. MANṢŪR[61]) and AL-SHĀFIʿĪ,[62]) and in the later works of IBN QUDĀMA[63]) and AL-BAYHAQĪ.[64]) An analysis of the *asānīd* of this tradition shows that the oldest cl is the early Meccan scholar ʿAṭāʾ b. Abī Rabāḥ (d. 114).

Can we be sure that the tradition is really going back to ʿAṭāʾ? There are six transmitters of ʿAṭāʾ's text: Ibn Jurayj (Mecca, d. 150), Abū Bishr [Ǧaʿfar b. Īyās] (Baṣra, d. between 123 and 131), Bisṭām b. Muslim

---

57) Above all, if there are only few versions. If there are dozens, the important thing is not absolute completeness but the collection of versions with different *asānīd*. Once the independence of a version is obvious, it is not necessary to collect further texts which would prove the same thing.

58) This combined analysis of *asānīd* and *mutūn* allows further-reaching results than a pure *isnād* analysis. For the *isnād* analysis see GAUTIER H. A. JUYNBOLL, "Society" and "Nāfiʿ". For the *isnād-cum-matn* analysis see MOTZKI, "Quo vadis" and "Prophet" and GREGOR SCHOELER, *Charakter*.

59) ʿABD AL-RAZZĀQ, *Muṣannaf*. IX, no. 16226.

60) IBN ABĪ SHAYBA, *Muṣannaf*, XI, no. 11481.

61) SAʿĪD B. MANṢŪR, *Sunan*, III, no. 223.

62) AL-SHĀFTIʿĪ, *Shifā*, II, no. 683 and 684.

63) IBN QUDĀMA, *al-Mughnī*, VI, no. 4938, ll. 17–19.

64) AL-BAYHAQĪ, *Sunan*, X, 300–301.

Diagram 1

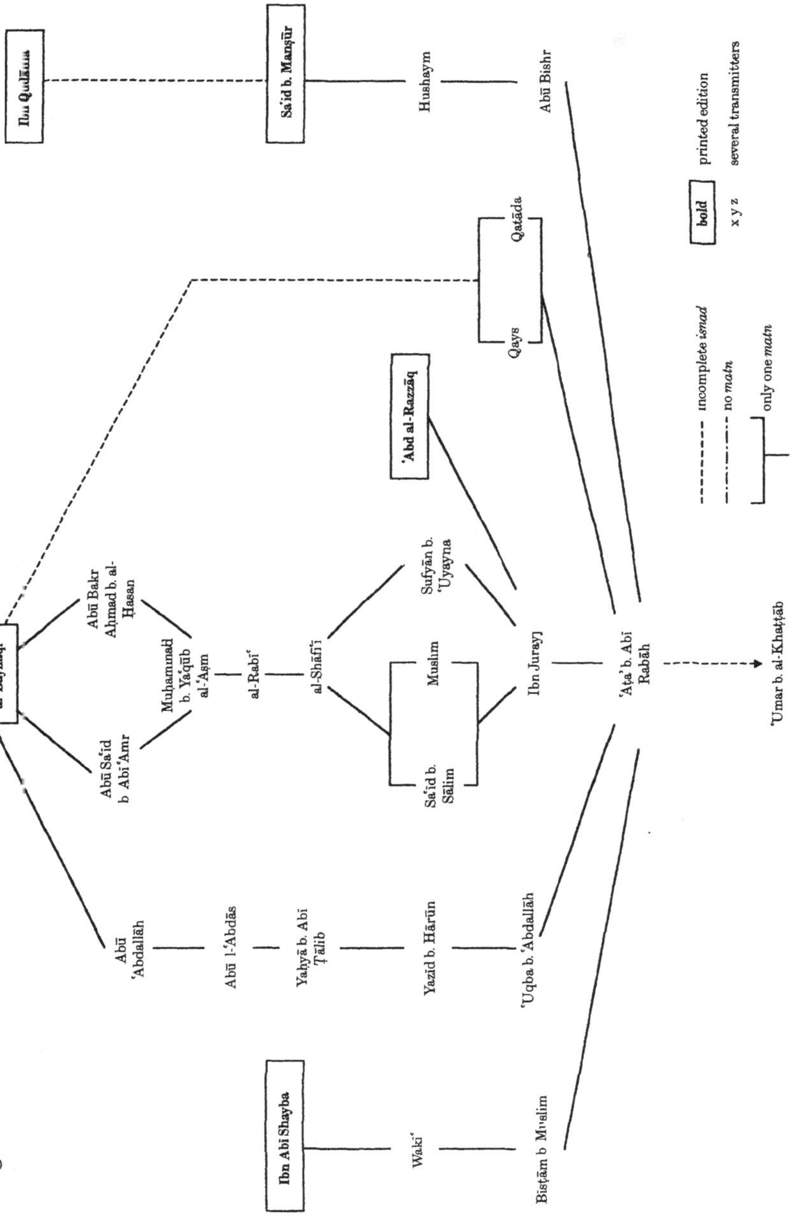
Saʿīd b. Manṣūr
Hushaym
Abū Bishr
Qatāda
Qays
ʿAbd al-Razzāq
al-Bayhaqī
Abū Bakr Aḥmad b. al-Ḥasan
Abū Saʿīd b Abī ʿAmr
Muḥammad b. Yaʿqūb al-ʿAṣm
al-Rabīʿ
al-Shāfiʿī
Sufyān b. ʿUyayna
Muslim
Saʿīd b. Sālim
Ibn Jurayj
ʿAṭāʾ b. Abī Rabāḥ
ʿUmar b. al-Khaṭṭāb
Abū ʿAbdallāh
Abū l-ʿAbdās
Yaḥyā b. Abī Ṭālib
Yazīd b. Hārūn
ʿUqba b. ʿAbdallāh
Ibn Abī Shayba
Wakīʿ
Bisṭām b Muslim
incomplete isnad
no matn
only one matn
bold printed edition
x y z several transmitters

(Baṣra), ʿUqba b. ʿAbdallāh (Baṣra),[65]) and – with only one *matn* – Qays b. Saʿd (Mecca, d. 119) and Ibn Qatāda [b. Diʿāma] (Baṣra, d. 117). Only one of them is a partial common link (pcl),[66]) namely Ibn Jurayj. His text is transmitted by ʿAbd al-Razzāq, Sufyān b. ʿUyayna and – with one *matn* – by Saʿīd b. Sālim and Muslim. The other scholars are mentioned in single strands.

According to Gautier H. A. Juynboll, a single strand cannot be regarded as historical path of transmission of a *ḥadīth* because it could easily be falsified by later scholars. Therefore, a cl who does not have several pcls among his pupils is not to be regarded as a real cl, but as a "seeming cl".[67]) Applied to the Ṭāriq tradition, this would mean that not ʿAṭāʾ, as a seeming cl, would be responsible for the tradition but his pupil Ibn Jurayj – who, by the way, according to this definition is a seeming cl too. But it is wrong to take single strands *a priori* to be spurious.[68]) As will be seen, the analysis of the *mutūn* corroborates the fact that ʿAṭāʾ is a real cl.

As an example, I will give the translation of Ibn Jurayj's text which is transmitted by ʿAbd al-Razzāq:

> Ibn Jurayj told us and said: ʿAṭāʾ told me: "Ṭāriq, the *mawlā* of Ibn Abī ʿAlqama, bought and released the [slave] family of a family which was moving to Syria. They went back to the Yemen." I [Ibn Jurayj] asked: "Did he release them unconditionally or did he release them in the normal way *(sayyabahum au aʿtaqahum iʿtāqan)*?" He [ʿAṭā] said: He released them unconditionally". He said: "Then they died and left sixteen or seventeen thousand dirhem. Ṭāriq was written to [but] he refused to take their inheritance. Yaʿlā[69]) wrote on this to ʿUmar. ʿUmar wrote to Yaʿlā that it [the inheritance] should be given to Ṭāriq. If he refused to take it, then you, [Yaʿlā], should buy and release slaves with [the money]."

Each text has elements which do not apperar in the other texts. For example, all three versions of Ibn Jurayj's text – and only they – have a

---

[65]) Bistām and ʿUqba are mentioned by Ibn Ḥajar, *Iṣāba*, I, no. 808 and V, no. 440, respectively, without year of death. They must have been died between 120 and 150, approximately.

[66]) Pupils of cls who have several pupils themselves are "partial common links", according to the terminology of Juynboll, "Nāfiʿ", 211, which will be applied here.

[67]) Ibid., 211 and 214.

[68]) On this point cf. Motzki, "Quo vadis", 48–54.

[69]) On the person of Yaʿlā see below note 73.

whole "family of slaves" which is released.[70]) In the versions of Abū Bishr and Bisṭām b. Muslim a "slave"[71]) is freed and in the version of ʿUqba b. ʿAbdallāh it is simply a "man". Only in the version of Qays and Qatāta, ʿUmar writes that Ṭāriq is most entitled to inherit from the *sā'iba*. There are also some details which appear in two or more different texts. The *kunya* of Ṭāriq – Ibn al-Muraqqaʿ – is mentioned in the version of Ibn Jurayj,[72]) Abū Bishr and Bisṭām b. Muslim. A prolongated ending of the story – containing the numer of the bought and released slaves – appears in the versions of Abū Bishr and ʿUqba b. ʿAbdallāh. A person who is writing to ʿUmar is mentioned in all variants exept in the one of Bisṭām b. Muslim.[73])

Apart from these differences, the story in each version in the same. Such a pattern of differences and common features is very unlikely to have been falsified. We can imagine falsifiers inventing new *asānīd* for an existing text, what would lead to identical texts with different *asānīd*.[74])

---

70) The three versions are not identical. To give an example: ʿAbd al-Razzāq has the family of slaves returning to the Yemen; according to Muslim and Saʿīd b. Sālim the family of slaves originated in the Yemen; in the version of Sufyān b. ʿUyaina the Yemenitic motive is missing altogether. In two versions (of Ibn ʿUyaina and Muslim/Saʿīd) it is said that the inheritance goes to the heirs of Ṭāriq. The differences show that the versions are transmitted independently from Ibn Jurayj and that Ibn Jurayj is a real pcl although his pupils are no pcls themselves.

71) In the text of Abū Bishr as found in Ibn Qudāma, though, (see above, note 63), Ṭāriq freed *"sawā'ib"*. Ibn Qudāma cites this text (without the upper part of the *isnād*) from Saʿīd b. Mansūr – Hushaim – Abū Bishr. Normally, his quotations from Saʿīd are identical with the text in Saʿīd's *Sunan*, but here, we have many differences down to the name of Abū Bishr himself who in Ibn Qudāma appears as "Bishr".

72) At least in two variants of Ibn Jurayj's text, namely the one of Ibn ʿUyaina and the one of Muslim and Saʿīd b. Sālim. ʿAbd al-Razzāq does not mention it.

73) In the version of ʿUqba b. ʿAbdallāh, the writer is the governeur of Mekka. In other versions he is the governeur of the Yemen. He is called either Yaʿlā (in ʿAbd al-Razzāq's version of Ibn Jurayj) or Yaʿlā b. Umayya (in the version of Abū Bishr) or Yaʿlā b. Munīya (probably a mistake of copying, in the version of Qays and Qatāda).

74) This is nothing strange from the second half of the second century onwards. Pupils of Mālik b. Anas, for example, often cite Mālik's text almost identically. But in the first century, the versions normally differ considerably from each other. If (nearly) identical versions are ascribed to different authorities, we can conclude that one version is the copy of the other. In such a case, the attribution to one of the two authorities would be falsified or at least defective. The *isnād-cum-matn* analysis thus can be used as a method to detect spurious traditions. For an

But it is not conceivable that, in addition, the falsifiers should have constructed a special *matn* for each new transmitter. In the case of cls, these skilled falsifiers would as well have followed the unwritten rule that all versions of a cl have to have some elements in common which are not turning up in the versions of other transmitters. The pattern is no speciality of the versions of the Ṭāriq tradition but it is inherent in almost every tradition. This shows definitely that the pattern did not come about by falsification. It has to be regarded as a structure which took shape during the transmission process.

Because of the differences of the five versions of ʿAṭāʾs text, we can conclude that the versions are independent. Their joint features are, therefore, due to their origin from a common source. What can this source be other than ʿAṭāʾ? He is responsible for passing on at least the basic elements of the story which are shared by *all* versions. Namely: A letter is written to ʿUmar asking for an advice on the inheritance of a *sāʾiba* freed by Ṭāriq. In his answer, ʿUmar writes that the inheritance should be given to Ṭāriq.

ʿAṭāʾ does not name any authority for the Ṭāriq tradition. Schacht and Juynboll hold the cl to be the person who is responsible for the *matn* and the older part of the *isnād*.[75]) Looking at ʿAṭāʾs tradition, it might seem that in this case their assumption could be correct. In the material I went through, ʿAṭāʾ is the only transmitter of this *ḥadīth*. Therefore, we cannot check out if ʿAṭāʾ transmitted an older circulating tradition or if he invented the text. At least, we cannot check this out by way of a comparison of texts. But taking into account the findings of Motzki concerning ʿAṭāʾ, there is no reason to assume *a priori* that ʿAṭāʾ invented the whole story. ʿAṭāʾ can be regarded as a reliable scholar who makes much effort to be accurate in transmitting.[76]) It ist not at all likely that such a scholar made up a whole tradition about ʿUmar. More probably, ʿAṭāʾ transmitted an ʿUmar tradition which was circulating around the turn of the century.

---

example of such a defective tradition see Mitter, *Patronat*, 135–136. It concerns a version of the Barīra tradition which is the basis of the institution of *walāʾ*. Cf below, note 132.

[75]) Schacht, *Origins*, chapt. 4, especially 172; Juynboll, "Nāfiʿ", 210. For Juynboll, it has to be a real cl who is regarded as responsible.

[76]) At least in the material provided by Ibn Jurayj in the *Muṣannaf* of ʿAbd al-Razzāq. For example, ʿAṭāʾ sometimes confesses frankly that he does not remember well who told him a *ḥadīth* (Motzki, *Anfänge*, 84), and sometimes he transmits indirectly from ʿĀʾisha although in other cases he asserts transmitting directly from her (ibid., 136). Frequently, ʿAṭāʾ mentions his sources only after an explicit question of his pupils (Ibid., 97 ff. and 105-6). Obviously, it was not necessary for him to mention them always because in his time, the *ra'y* of a scholar was authoritative.

Turning now to the content of the Ṭāriq *ḥadīth*, we can safely presume that the deceased *sā'iba* left no agnatic relatives. Otherwise, they would inherit in the first place, according to the Islamic law of inheritance.[77]) Presumably, there was no new patron either, because Ṭāriq who was reluctant to accept the inheritance of his freedman did not mention any. Would we not expect him to have done so if there were any? Presuming that the *sā'iba* left no new patron, resolves also the otherwise existing inconsistency that, first, *tasyīb* obviously had been accepted and that it subsequently must have been declared invalid by ʿUmar who, passing over the new patron, awarded Ṭāriq the inheritance. More probably, the situation was as follows: There was no patron who cold have taken the inheritance and, so, someone else had to be found who would receive it. The problem was resolved by declaring the manumitter to be the one in charge. ʿUmar did not want to decide about the question whether *tasyīb* was or was not be allowed. He had to resolve a practical problem, which he did. Implicitly, he accepted the *tasyīb* performed by Ṭāriq.[78]) It was only because the *sā'iba* died without any heirs that the manumitter was asked to take the inheritance.

Most probably, ʿAṭā' took the tradition as a pro-*tasyīb* tradition, according to his own opinion that a *sā'iba* may choose a new patron and that his inheritance only passes to his manumitter if he dies without a new patron.[79]) Later jurists, however, seem to interpret this tradition rather in the sense of rejecting *tasyīb*.[80])

The second *ḥadīth* of ʿUmar which I would like to analyze in some detail is the one concerning Sālim b. Maʿqil (see diagram 2). Sālim had been the slave of a woman of the *anṣār* who freed him in pre-Islamic times as a *sā'iba* whereupon he took Abū Ḥudhayfa as his patron.[81]) When Sālim

[77]) The inheritance is distributed as follows: If there are Qur'ānic heirs like a mother or a daughter, they inherit their shares of the estate. The rest (or the whole estate, if there are no Qur'ānic heirs) goes to the agnates of the deceased *mawlā*. If there are no agnates, the patron is intitled to inherit (the whole estate or the rest of it after deduction of the shares). At least, if he is regarded as an agnatic heir, at all. If he is regarded as the last heir of his *mawlā*, he would be excluded even by the remotest relative. This doctrine did not gain acceptance in classical Islamic law. For the two doctrines – patron as agnatic heir or last heir – cf. MITTER, *Patronat*, 145ff.

[78]) This is corroborated by the fact that later lawyers as ʿUmar's son ʿAbdallāh and as ʿAtā' did accept *tasyīb* too. Cf. below, 58 and 62.

[79]) See ʿABD AL-RAZZĀQ, *Muṣannaf*, IX, no. 16151.

[80]) Cf. below, 57.

[81]) Abū Ḥudhayfa seems to have been the husband of this *anṣārī* woman. See IBN ḤAJAR, *Iṣāba*, II, 56 and IBN SAʿD, *Ṭabqāt*, III, 86.

Diagram 2

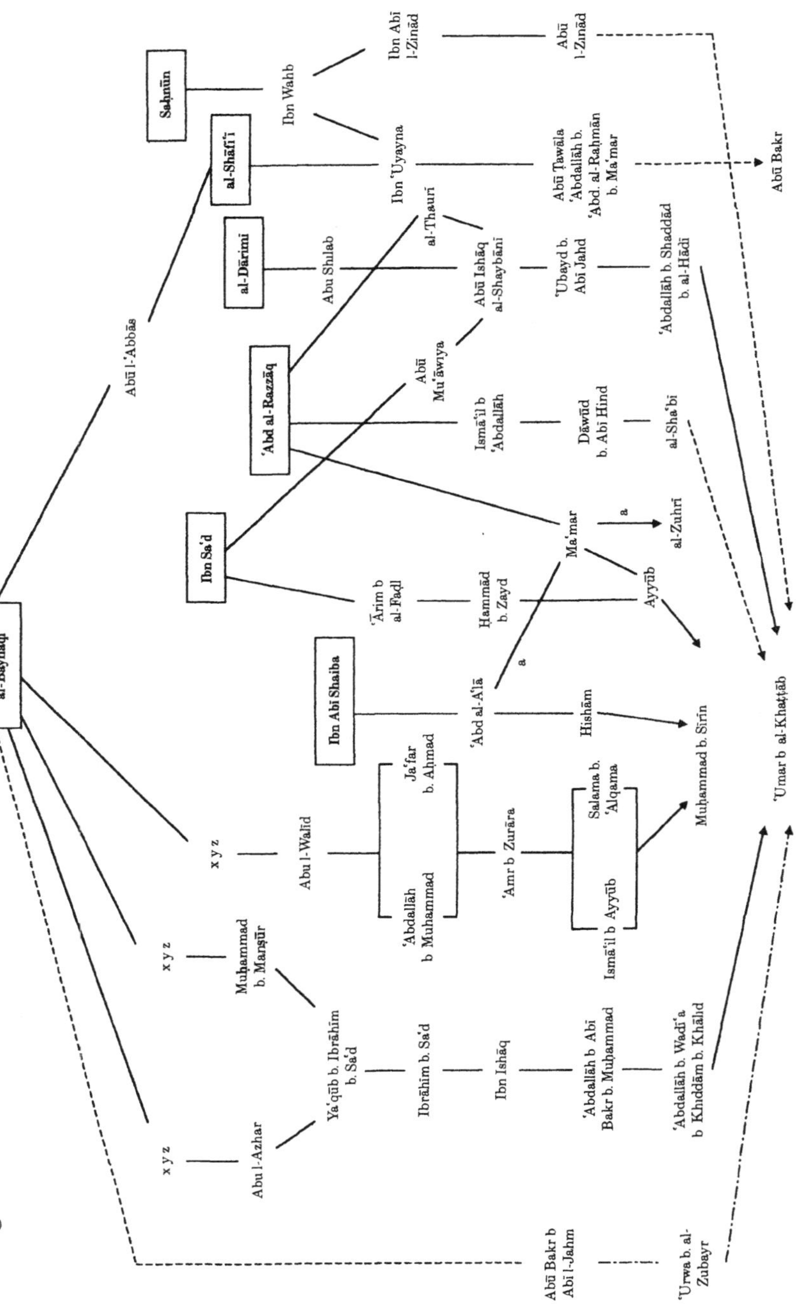
Saḥnūn
al-Shāfiʿī
al-Dārimī
ʿAbd al-Razzāq
Ibn Saʿd
Ibn Abī Shaiba
al-Bayhaqī
Abū l-ʿAbbās
Ibn Wahb
Ibn Abī l-Zinād
Abū l-Zinād
Ibn ʿUyayna
Abū Ṭawāla ʿAbdallāh b. ʿAbd. al-Raḥmān b. Maʿmar
Abū Bakr
al-Thaurī
Abu Shihab
Abū Isḥāq al-Shaybānī
ʿUbayd b. Abī Jahd
ʿAbdallāh b. Shaddād b. al-Hādī
Abū Muʿāwiya
Ismāʿīl b ʿAbdallāh
Dāwūd b. Abī Hind
al-Shaʿbī
Maʿmar
a
al-Zuhrī
Ayyūb
ʿĀrim b al-Faḍl
Ḥammād b. Zayd
ʿAbd al-Aʿlā
a
Hishām
Muḥammad b. Sīrīn
ʿUmar b al-Khaṭṭāb
Jaʿfar b. Aḥmad
ʿAbdallāh b Muḥammad
x y z
Abu l-Walīd
ʿAmr b Zurāra
Salama b. ʿAlqama
Ismāʿīl b Ayyūb
x y z
Muḥammad b. Manṣūr
Yaʿqūb b. Ibrāhīm b. Saʿd
Ibrāhīm b. Saʿd
Ibn Isḥāq
ʿAbdallāh b Abī Bakr b. Muḥammad
ʿAbdallāh b. Wadīʿa b Khiddām b. Khālid
x y z
Abu l-Azhar
Abū Bakr b Abī l-Jahm
ʿUrwa b. al-Zubayr

died in the battle of Yamāma (in the year 12), according to most authorities, his estate was given by ʿUmar b. al-Khaṭṭāb to the *anṣārī* woman or to her descendants with the provision that, if they were not willing to keep it, it should pass to the public treasury.

The Sālim *ḥadīth* is mentioned by ʿABD AL-RAZZĀQ,[82] IBN ABĪ SHAYBA,[83] SAḤNŪN,[84] AL-DĀRIMĪ,[85] IBN SAʿD,[86] AL-SHĀFIʿĪ,[87] AL-BAYHAQĪ[88] and IBN QUDĀMA.[89] It is going back to five authorities who lived at the end of the first century. These authorities are Muḥammad b. Sīrīn (Baṣra, d. 110) – who is the only cl in the first generation of transmitters – ʿĀmir al-Shaʿbī (Kūfa, d. 103), ʿAbdallāh b. Shaddād b. al-Hādī (Kūfa, d. 81 or 82), ʿAbdallāh b. Wadīʿa b. Khidām (Medina, d. 63)[90] and ʿUrwa b. al-Zubayr[91] (Medina, d. 94 or 99). Furthermore, there are three Medinense transmitters of the first decades of the second century: al-Zuhrī (d. 124), Abū l-Zinād (d. between 130 and 132) and Abū Ṭawāla ʿAbdallāh b. ʿAbd al-Raḥmān b. Maʿmar (d. 134).

Here is the text of the longest version of the Sālim tradition, the one of ʿAbdallāh b. Wadīʿa b. Khidām which is transmitted by al-Bayhaqī:

> Sālim, the *mawlā* of Abū Ḥudhayfa, had been the *mawlā* of a woman of us whose name was Salmā bint Yuʿār.[92] She released him in the *jāhilīya* as a *sāʾiba*. When he was wounded [and killed] in [the battle of] Yamāma, [the question of] his inheritance was presented to ʿUmar b. al-Khaṭṭāb. He sent for Wadīʿa b. Khidām and said: "This is the inherit-

---

82) ʿABD AL-RAZZĀQ, *Muṣnnaf*, IX, nos. 16232, 16233 and 16237.

83) IBN ABĪ SHAYBA, *Muṣannaf*, XI, nos. 11482 and 11559.

84) SAḤNŪN, *Mudawwana*, II, 558–599.

85) AL-DĀRIMĪ, *Sunan*, II, no. 2983.

86) IBN SAʿD, *Ṭabaqāt*, III, 86 and 88.

87) AL-SHĀFIʿĪ, *Umm*, IV, 133, l. 6ff.

88) AL-BAYHAQĪ, *Sunan*, X, 300, ll. 14–19.

89) IBN QUDĀMA, *Mughnī*, VI, no. 4938, l. 23ff. His version has no *isnād* and, therefore, does not serve for dating the Sālim *ḥadīth*.

90) According to al-Wāqidī (IBN ḤAJAR, *Tahdhīb*, VI, no. 132), ʿAbdallāh b. Wadīʿa died at the day of al-Ḥarra. This battle took place in the year 63 (WELLHAUSEN, *Reich*, 97–98).

91) ʿUrwa b. al-Zubayr is mentioned by al-Bayhaqī without any *matn* as transmitter of this *ḥadīth*.

92) Different names of the *anṣārī* woman are current. In the version of ʿAbdallāh b. Shaddād, the woman is called ʿAmra. In the version of ʿAbdallāh b. ʿAbd al-Raḥman b. Maʿmar she is called ʿAmra bint Yuʿār. In the version given by Ibn Qudāma without an *isnād*, the woman has the name Lubnā bint Yuʿār. More versions of the name are given in IBN ḤAJAR, *Iṣāba*, II, 56, ll. 15–18.

> ance of your *mawlā* and you are most entitled to it." He [Wadīʿa] said: "Commander of the Faithful, God already gave us enough for him [that is, in form of a reward in the hereafter]. Our companion did release him as a *sāʾiba* and we do not want to take something from him" – or he said: "steal". And so, ʿUmar gave it [the inheritance] to the public treasury.

The versions of all authorities have their own typical characteristics. For example, only in the above translated version of ʿAbdallāh b. Wadīʿa, Wadīʿa b. Khiddām – father of ʿAbdallāh and heir of the *anṣārī* woman – is speaking with ʿUmar, and only in this version is it said that the slave had been freed in pre-Islamic times.[93] In the text of ʿAbdallāh b. Shaddād, not only the order of the elements is different, but the story has a very different ending: after the rejection of the inheritance by the heirs of the *anṣārīya*, it is not the public treasury who gets the money but the mother of Sālim. The cl Muḥammad b. Sīrīn has a short version and even does not name ʿUmar.[94] Also al-Shaʿbī has a short version with an unusual formulation of ʿUmar's decision.

The three younger versions, too, have special characteristics. Al-Zuhrī's short version mentions that Sālim was adopted by Abū Ḥudhayfa. According to Abū Ṭawāla (who has a long, but problematic, version), it was not ʿUmar but Abū Bakr who decided about the inheritance.[95] Abū l-Zinād has a very short version but, nevertheless, the wording is different from the wording of the other versions.

Such differences are an indication of the independence of each version. We can conclude, therefore, that the versions go back to the authority given in the *asānīd*. But here again, the essence of the story in each

[93]) Such details normally appear in traditions which are transmitted in the family of a person who has been involved in the story. In SCHACHT's opinion, a "family *isnād*" has to be regarded as spurious (see *Origins*, 170). But in cases when we have a tradition transmitted by both, the family of an acting person and scholars not belonging to that family, the analysis of the *mutūn* often shows that the version with the family *isnād* is even old and reliable as are the other versions. Cf. MITTER, *Patronat*, 153.

[94]) There are three versions of the text of Muḥammad b. Sīrīn. They are transmitted by Ayyūb (ʿABD AL-RAZZĀQ, *Muṣannaf*, IX, no. 16232 and IBN SAʿD, *Ṭabaqāt*, III, 86), Hishām (IBN ABĪ SHAYBA, *Muṣannaf*, XI, no. 11482) and Salama b. ʿAlqama and Ismāʿīl b. Ayyūb with one *matn* (AL-BAYHAQĪ, *Sunan*, X, 300, ll. 11–13). The three versions are very similar but their common elements are formulated quite differently. This means that the versions are independent from each other but have a common source, namely Ibn Sīrīn.

[95]) This is likely to be a transmitting error, possibly caused by the fact that the battle of Yamāma, in which Sālim died, took place under the reign of Abū Bakr.

version is the same and there are common elements shared by different versions. This points to the fact that there has to be one source common to all versions. What is this source?

In contrast to the tradition of Ṭāriq which (by means of a comparison of the *mutūn*) cannot be traced back further than to the *tābiʿ* ʿAṭāʾ, here we have a tradition which is transmitted by six scholars of the generation of the *tābiʿūn*: ʿAbdallāh b. Wadīʿa and ʿAbdallāh b. Shaddād who died before the year 100 and Muḥammad b. Sīrīn, al-Shaʿbī, al-Zuhrī and Abū l-Zinād who died afterwards.[96]) We can rule out the possibility that the common source of all versions might be the short version of the cl Ibn Sīrīn The comparison of the *mutūn* could prove the textual independence of the older versions of Ibn Wadʿīa and Ibn Shaddād, although they are single strands. We cannot exclude, however, the possibility that the younger versions may be based in one way or another on the two older texts of Ibn Wadīʿa and Ibn Shaddād. Their wording speaks against a direct copying, but it is probable that different versions of the older texts were current in Medina and in Iraq and were adopted subsequently by younger scholars who did not name their sources.

In view of the fact that so many different versions of this ʿUmar tradition were current at the end – and two of them even in the middle – of the first century, it is probable that they are reflecting a historical event.[97]) The tradition, and with it the legal problem, would then go back to a much earlier time than Crone suggests for the "classical" (and even for the "pre-classical") doctrine.

---

[96]) The other two transmitters have to be left out. Of ʿUrwa b. al-Zubayr, I have no text, and Abū Ṭawāla is no *tābiʿ*. His text is not likely to be independent, anyway. Cf. Mitter, *Patronat*, 235–236.

[97]) The source of the detailed tradition of ʿAbdallāh b. Wadīʿa surely is his father, Wadīʿa b. Khaddām, who is not mentioned in the *isnād* but in the *matn*. He is an eyewitness to the ruling of ʿUmar. The source of the tradition of ʿAbdallāh b. Shaddād is not that obvious. According to Ibn Ḥajar, *Tahdhīb*, V, 251, Ibn Shaddād transmitted directly from ʿUmar who died in the year 23. If it is correct that Ibn Shaddād died in the year 81 at the day of the battle of Dujayl (ibid., 252), and if he was about 15 years old when ʿUmar died, he would have been past 70 on Dujayl day. This would probably be too old for fighting. But even if Ibn Shaddād heard about the ruling of ʿUmar from somebody else, this other person is not likely to be ʿAbdallāh b. Wadīʿa or his father. There are too many differences between the traditions of Ibn Shaddād and Ibn Wadīʿa. Probably, the informant of Ibn Shaddād came from the family of Sālim, because it is mentionend in Ibn Shaddād's tradition that ʿUmar gives the inheritance to the mother of Sālim after the rejection of the inheritance by the family of Wadīʿa.

At first sight, this tradition seems to reject *tasyīb*. That is why, according to CRONE, it is a late tradition which expresses the "classical" doctrine: "the manumission is valid, but the renunciation [of the patronate] is void".[98]) Apparently, the new patron of Sālim, Abū Ḥudhayfa, has no right to inherit although he presumably had been responsible for Sālim. He even adopted Sālim as his son and married him to a woman of social standing.[99]) Nevertheless, ʿUmar gave the inheritance of Sālim to (the heirs of) the *anṣārī* woman who manumitted him. Seen this way, it would mean that ʿUmar did not accept *tasyīb*.

Things change, however, when we consider the fact that Abū Ḥudhayfa himself died on Yamāma day.[100]) So there was no new patron. We cannot be totally sure, however, whether or not there were agnatic relatives of Abū Ḥudhayfa who would as his heirs have taken the inheritence of the freedman[101]) – always presuming that there were no agnatic relatives of Sālim himself who would inherit in the first place.[102]) But we can ask the same question as in the case of Ṭāriq: Could the heirs of the *anṣārīya* not be expected to mention agnates of the new patron Abū Ḥudhayfa if there were any, because after all they themselves did not want to take the inheritance? Very probably, Abū Ḥudhayfa did not have a son, because otherwise he may not have adopted Sālim.

If Abū Ḥudhayfa had left agnates and ʿUmar notwithstanding gave the inheritance to the family of the manumitter this indeed would amount to a refusal of the legal consequences of *tasyīb*. But if there were no agnates, the situation would be the same as in the tradition of Ṭāriq. That is: A *sāʾiba* died without relatives and without a new patron (or family of his), and somebody had to be found who would take his inheritance. *Tasyīb*, then, would be regarded valid as long as no problems appear because of missing heirs. Either way, we may take it for granted that

[98]) CRONE, *Roman law*, 81 and note 44.

[99]) IBN SAʿD, *Ṭabaqāt*, III, 86.

[100]) Ibid., 85; IBN ḤAJAR, *Iṣāba*, II, 57, l. 24.

[101]) A woman, as a rule, cannot inherit the estate of a deceased *mawlā* if it is not her own *maulā*. After the death of a patron, the *walāʾ* and the right to inherit always passes to the so called *"kubr"* which is the next male agnate of the patron. Cf. CRONE, *Roman law*, 82–83 and MITTER, *Patronat*, 292–293.

[102]) The fact that Sālim left no agnates is indirectly confirmed by the tradition of Ibn Shaddād in which it is stated that Sālim's mother got the whole estate. If Sālim had have left agnates, his mother only would have inherited the Qurʾānic third and not the whole estate. Ibn Shaddād is the only scholar who has this element. Therefore, we have no possibilty to prove the authenticity of it.

ʿUmar had an inclination to assign the resonsibility for the *sāʾiba* to his manumitter – be it always or just in case of the absence of a new patron. What we have, therefore, is a tradition of ʿUmar in which a clear link is made between the manumitter and the inheritance of the *sāʾiba*.

In the works of later scholars, the traditions of Sālim and Ṭāriq normally appear in the context of traditions which reject *tasyīb* and assign the patronate to the manumitter. IBN QUDĀMA[103]) (d. 620), for example, cites both traditions after having mentioned various traditions to the effect that the patronate always belongs to the manumitter, and one tradition of Ibn Masʿūd who proclaims that Muslims should not free slaves as *sawāʾib*.[104]) IBN QUDĀMA adds a tradition of Manṣūr b. al-Muʿtamir (d. 133) who says that, according to ʿUmar and Ibn Masʿūd, the inheritance of a *sāʾiba* belongs to his manumitter. Most probably, by naming ʿUmar, Manṣūr b. al-Muʿtamir had the traditions of Sālim and Ṭāriq in his mind.

AL-BAYHAQĪ[105]) (d. 428) mentions the traditions of Sālim and Ṭāriq in the same context. He starts the chapter on *tasyīb* with the Barīra tradition which says that the Prophet assigned the patronate to the manumitter,[106]) afterwards listing several versions of the traditions of Sālim and Ṭāriq without touching on the problem of whether or not there was a new patron, suggesting thereby that the patronate in all circumstances belongs to the manumitter and *tasyīb* is not allowed. In the following chapter, AL-BAIHAQĪ collects traditions of ʿUmar and his son on the religious merit of refusing the inheritance of a *sāʾiba* if *tasyīb* was allowed.[107])

The fact that in later works *tasyīb* was forbidden[108]) does not necessarily mean that in an earlier period, *tasyīb* was forbidden too, and that the

[103]) IBN QUDĀMĀ, *Mughnī*, VI, no. 4938.

[104]) For analysis and interpretation of Ibn Masʿūd's tradition see below, 60f.

[105]) AL-BAYHAQĪ, *Sunan*, X, 299–302.

[106]) On the Barīra tradition cf. below, 65.

[107]) For the tradition of Ibn ʿUmar, see below, 58f. The tradition of ʿUmar b. al-Khaṭṭāb is mentioned in ʿAbd al-RazzĀQ, *Muṣannaf*, IX, nos. 16229 and 16574–75; IBN ABĪ SHAYBA, XI, no. 11475; AL-DĀRIMĪ, *Sunan*, II, no. 3119; AL-BAYHAQĪ, *Sunan*, X, 301; IBN QUDĀMA, *Mughnī*, VI, no. 4938. In this tradition, ʿUmar is said to have declared that "*ṣadaqa* (alms) and *sāʾiba* are for their day (of resurrection)" – meaning that one should not profit from them in the present world. The cl of that tradition is Abū ʿUthmān al-Nahdī (d. 75, 95 or 100; cf. IBN ḤAJAR, *Tahdhīb*, V, no. 546). This tradition is discussed more detailed in MITTER, *Patronat*, 242–243.

[108]) See also AL-MARGHĪNĀNĪ, *al-Hidāya*, III, 271, citing Abū Ḥanīfa.

traditions of Sālim and Ṭāriq should be interpreted as prohibiting *tasyīb*. To the contrary, I think that *tasyīb* in the beginning was practised and only later became forbidden. So far, I agree with CRONE. But, as the dating of the traditions has shown, the right (or duty) of the manumitter to inherit the estate of his *sā'iba* – for CRONE an indication for the rejection of *tasyīb* – gained acceptance much earlier than she assumes.

To my mind, however, it is wrong to approach the traditions by asking whether or not according to them *tasyīb* is allowed. If we do, we will get a distorted impression of the legal situation because this, obviously, was not the question early lawyers and caliphs primarily dealt with. They were confronted with a situation in which *tasyīb* was practised, and their main concern was to find someone responsible for paying the blood-money[109]) and, first of all, for taking the inheritance of the freedman. If we look at the traditions this way, many of the seeming inconsistencies disappear, as has been shown with the traditions of Ṭāriq and Sālim.

Now, the juridical content of two traditions of the *ṣaḥāba* ʿAbdallāh b. ʿUmar (d. 74) and ʿAbdallāh b. Masʿūd (d. 32) will be analyzed,[110]) starting with the tradition of Ibn ʿUmar.

ʿAbdallāh b. ʿUmar and ʿAbdallāh b. Masʿūd

ʿAbdallāh b. ʿUmar b. al-Khaṭṭāb (d. 74) is said to have practised *tasyīb*. When he inherited the estate of his deceased *sā'iba*, he did not want to keep it and spent it for freeing slaves.[111]) If we try to interpret

[109]) An early example for a tradition dealing with the problem of the blood-money on behalf of a *sā'iba* is an ʿUmar tradition which I call the "*arqam*-tradition". In this tradition we are told that a *sā'iba* injured somebody and ʿUmar held no one responsible for paying the blood-money because there was no new patron and the manumitter was not known. ʿUmar said further that if the *sā'iba* would have been the injured one, blood-money should have been paid for him. The injured party, not being happy with ʿUmars decision, compares the *sā'iba* with an *arqam*-snake. This tradition surely existed in the time of Sulaymān b. Yasār (d. 104 or 107) and perhaps is going back to a historical event. See MITTER, *Patronat*, 238–242.

[110]) Probably, the two traditions are authentic. For a short *isnād-cum-matn*-analysis see notes 111 and 113.

[111]) I have three versions of this tradition – a long one and two short ones. In the long version it is Ibn ʿUmars father, ʿUmar b. al-Khaṭṭāb, who has manumitted the *sā'iba*. The inheritences of the *sā'iba* is given to Ibn ʿUmar who rejects it, but his brother ʿĀṣim is willing to take it, and Ibn ʿUmar agreed. In the two short ver-

this tradition as to whether *tasyīb* is allowed or forbidden we have to face a contradiction. On one hand, *tasyīb* was practised by Ibn ʿUmar which means that he renounced the patronate and with it the right to inherit. That is, why CRONE classifies the Ibn ʿUmar tradition as "pre-classical". On the other hand, Ibn ʿUmar received the inheritance after the death of his *sāʾiba*. Getting the inheritance normally means being the patron. Does this imply that Ibn ʿUmar's *tasyīb* and his renunciation of the patronate was declared void afterwards? (For the same reason CRONE classifies the Ṭāriq and the Sālim tradition as classical). I do not think so.

If we read the tradition in another way, we find it more consistent. The important thing was finding a person who would be responsible for the freedman and his estate. Ibn ʿUmar released a *sāʾiba* who presumably died without leaving relatives or a new patron. So, who should take his inheritance (and pay the blood-money if there were still a pending claim)? The only responsible person one could think of was Ibn ʿUmar. It could have been the government too, but as far as I see, the early Muslims tended to hold the manumitter responsible.[112]) Ibn ʿUmar, therefore, got the inheritance which does not mean that his *tasyīb* was declared void (his rejection of the inheritance was even held up as an example) but which simply means that there was nobody else who could be responsible for the freedman. This implies, however, that there was a certain tie between the

---

sions, the elements of the father and the brother of Ibn ʿUmar are missing. Compared to each other, also the short versions have quite different a wording and order of elements. There is no textual dependence between the three texts. But despite all differences, the essence of the story (as given above in the text) is the same in all three versions. This means that the textually independent versions have to have a common source. This result fits the evidence of the *isnād* bundle which shows independent *asānīd* comming together in the cl Ibn ʿUmar. The long version is transmitted by Ibn Hubayra from Ziyād b. Nuʿaym (d. 95) from Ibn ʿUmar (AL-BAYHAQĪ, *Sunan*, X, 302, ll. 6–11). One of the short versions is transmitted by Sulaymān al-Taymī from Bakr b. ʿAbdallāh al-Muzanī (d. 106) from Ibn ʿUmar (ʿABD AL-RAZZĀQ, *Muṣannaf*, IX, no. 16231; IBN ABĪ SHAYBA, *Muṣannaf*, XI, 11476; AL-BAYHAQĪ, *Sunan*, X, 302), the other one by ʿAlī b. Zayd b. Judʿān from ʿAmmār (d. about 100, probably) from Ibn ʿUmar (ʿABD AL-RAZZĀQ, *Muṣannaf*, IX, no. 16230). Ziyād b. Nuʿaym claims to be an eyewitness to the event described by him in the long version. Perhaps, the transmitters of the short versions are refering to the same event, but the differences of their texts show that their source is not Ziyād's tradition. They might have heard the story from Ibn ʿUmar afterwards.

112) In contrast to lawyers from the end of the first century onwards. Cf. below, 63.

freedman and his former master which could not be broken up so easily even if the slave was freed as a *sā'iba*.

The tradition of Ibn Masʿūd (d. 32), too, can be interpreted in this sense. Ibn Masʿūd is said to have given the inheritance of a *sā'iba* to the manumitter, adding in some versions that Muslims should not practice *tasyīb*.[113]) We have to assume that the freedman died without leaving relatives and in all probability without having a new patron.[114]) It is true that Ibn Masʿūd in some versions of this tradition rejected *tasyīb* by saying that *tasyīb* was practised in pre-Islamic times and should not be practised by Muslims. But even if this statement was part of the original text, which is not sure,[115]) we do not have to conclude that the performed *tasyīb*

113) For this tradition, I know of seven transmitters of the first century originating from different geographical regions: Ibrāhīm al-Nakhaʿī (Kūfa, d. 96), al-Shaʿbī (Kūfa, d. 103), Huzayl b. Shuraḥbīl (Kūfa, d. after 83), ʿAlqama b. Qays (Kūfa, d. 62), Qatāda (Baṣra, d. 117), ʿAṭā' (Mecca, d. 114), and al-Qāsim b. Muḥammad (Medina d. 106). (See ʿAbd al-Razzāq, *Muṣannaf*, IX, nos. 16222 and 16223; Saʿīd b. Manṣūr, *Sunan*, III, no. 225; Ibn Abī Shayba, *Muṣannaf*, XI, nos. 11473 and 11474; al-Dārimī, *Sunan*, II, no. 3125; al-Bayhaqī, *Sunan*, X, 300; Ibn Qudāma, *Mughnī*, VI, 413, ll. 14–17). Their versions show the well-known pattern: On the one hand, there are a lot of elements which some versions or others have in common, and on the other hand, the version of each transmitter has its own characteristic elements. We can conclude that they are independent versions which originate in a common source. There is no other cl than Ibn Masʿūd himself (exept for the late pcl Sufyān al-Thaurī (d. 161), whose text, though, cannot be the source of the six other texts because all texts are quite different). Is Ibn Masʿūd the common source? Most of the *tābiʿūn* do not transmit directly from him exept for, perhaps, ʿAlqama or Huzayl. But these scholars, too, are not likely to be the source of all the other texts because this would require half a dozen of scholars omitting the name of ʿAlqama or Huzayl and modifiying the text. More probably, it was common knowledge at the end of the first century that Ibn Masʿūd gave the inheritance of a *sā'iba* to the manumitter. If so many lawyers of the *tābiʿūn* generation are reporting independently on a decision of Ibn Masʿūd, their traditions possibly are going back to a historical event.

114) In one version of the text of Huzayl b. Shurḥbīl (Ibn Qudāma, *Mughnī*, VI, no. 4938, l. 19), it is explicitely stated that the *sā'iba* died without leaving any heirs.

115) The clear rejection of *tasyīb* by Ibn Masʿūd appears only in the three versions of the Kūfan Huzayl b. Shuraḥbīl and the version of the Meccan ʿAṭā'. It does not fit in the context of decisions of early Muslims who generally accept *tasyīb*, but it does correspondent perfectly to the opinion of later lawyers. Therefore, the question arises if, perhaps, it was not an original statement of Ibn Masʿūd but was introduced later. Let us have a look at the *matn*. The texts of Huzayl and ʿAṭā' seem

is declared void by Ibn Masʿūd. More probably, Ibn Masʿūd gave the inheritance to the manumitter because there was nobody else who could take it, and he may have used this opportunity to express his opinion that *tasyīb* is no Islamic practice. Even stronger than ʿUmar, he may have had the feeling that the relationship between manumitter and freedman should not be dissolved. Such an unwillingness of accepting *tasyīb* can be attributed to the need of avoiding cases of *sawāʾib* hanging around without any relatives and patrons who, if necessary, could be responsible for paying blood-money and taking the inheritance.

Summing up, we can propound the working hypothesis that in the analyzed traditions, the *sāʾiba* died without relatives and without a new patron – presuming that if there were any heirs, it would have been mentioned. Because there are not, the authorities and scholars had to think about somebody else who could be responsible for the *sāʾiba*. They, obviously, did not had the intention to abolish *tasyīb* altogether. To the

---

to be textually independent, which, if true, would mean that the common elements are going back to a common source. The anti-*tasyīb* statement would than go back to Ibn Masʿūd, whom Huzayl and ʿAṭāʾ are mentioning as their source. But in this case, such a far reaching conclusion is not advisable because the anti-*tasyīb* statement is identical in both texts. More precisely, the wording of the version of ʿAṭāʾ is identical with one of the three slightly different wordings of the version of Huzayl which are all transmitted by the cl Sufyān al-Thaurī. This identical wording is suspicious. The statement is too long to be a maxime which can be used identically by many lawyers (as e.g. the maxime *al-walāʾ lil-kubr* [meaning, the patronatical rights belong after the death of the manumitter to his next agnate]; cf. MITTER, *Patronat*, 293 ff.). Therefore, the statement in one of the two texts is likely to be a copy of the other one. Although there is no ultimate proof, it seems to me that the statement originally belongs to the version of Huzayl. The reason is that there are several versions of Huzayl's text in four different *ḥadīth* collections and only one version of ʿAṭāʾ's text in one *ḥadīth* collection. In addition, we have at least the security that al-Thaurī (d. 161) transmitted the Huzayl tradition together with the statement. Very probably, he transmitted it from Abū Qays (d. 120), because one of the *asānīd* is ʿAbd al-Razzāq – al-Thaurī – Abū Qays, and, in general, the informations of the former two in the *Muṣannaf* of ʿAbd al-Razzāq are reliable. (Al-Thaurī has so much *raʾy* – cf. Motzki, *Anfänge*, 57 – that he obviously did not need to ascribe his opinion to older authorities). If the statement belongs to Huzayl's version, it does not belong to the tradition of ʿAṭāʾ. This does not necessarily mean that the whole tradition of ʿAṭāʾ was falsified by a later scholar. It is just as possible that an authentic ʿAṭāʾ-tradition was "completed" by introducing the anti-*tasyīb* statement. What we have, therefore, is a statement which does not fit in the early context and which only belongs to one of the seven versions of the Ibn Masʿūd tradition. In all probability, the statement is not going back to Ibn Masʿūd.

contrary, *tasyīb* was perfectly admitted as long as there were no problems because of missing heirs. We can assume that the traditions are not about prohibition or admission of *tasyīb* but about responsibility. This assumption seems to work better than an *a priori* classification of the traditions into early ones which allow *tasyīb* and later ones which reject it. All analyzed traditions are early, also the seemingly "classical" ones, and they, too, are not anti-*tasyīb* traditions.[116]

Lawyers of the tābiʿūn generation

In some hitherto not mentioned traditions, however, the lawyers decided in principle about *tasyīb*. They reflected in a systematical manner about the question whether *tasyīb* should be allowed or not; and if it is allowed, whether the manumitter or the Muslims at large should get the patronate in case the freedman died without a new patron; and if it is not allowed, who should get the patronate, and so forth. In these traditions, for the first time the questions of inheritance and blood-money were combined.

This kind of tradition can be characterized as juridical argumentation on the basis of ficticious cases. In contrast, the traditions analyzed above are "anecdotes" describing historical cases and including dialogues and names of persons. Whereas the anecdotes are ascribed to very early authorities of the first century as ʿUmar and his son, the traditions containing juridical statements allegedly go back to *tābiʿūn* living in the end of the first century and later. In many cases, the *isnād-cum-matn* analysis can show the authenticity of the *tābiʿūn* traditions.[117]

Some of the lawyers approve of *tasyīb*, others disapprove of it. ʿAṭāʾ and al-Zuhrī belong to the group of jurists who approve of *tasyīb*. But whereas the Meccan ʿAṭāʾ (d. 114) gave the inheritance of a *sāʾiba* who died

---

116) In favour of our hypothesis, we can adduce the classification of early jurists dealing with *tasyīb* which is carried out by IBN RUSHD. His criterion is the assignation of the patronate and not the prohibition or permission of *tasyīb*. For him it is important to whom the patronate (which implies the responsibility for the *sāʾiba*) is given. Of course, assigning the patronate to the manumitter in all circumstances, whether or not there is a new patron, amounts to the prohibition of *tasyīb*. Nevertheless, it is a different approach to the problem. Cf. IBN RUSHD/NYAZEE, *Bidāya*, II, 439.

117) For a detailed analysis of these traditions which cannot be carried out here, see MITTER, *Patronat*, 252–261.

without a patron to the manumitter,[118]) according to the Medinese al-Zuhrī (d. 124), the patronate belongs to the treasury and by no means to the manumitter of the *sā'iba*. The sultan is the heir of the *sā'iba* and pays the blood-money on his behalf.[119]) In contrast to most of the early authorities, he obviously did not think that there has to be a tie whatsoever between the manumitter and the *sā'iba*. He, therefore, is one of the few *tābiʿūn* who accepts *tasyīb* with all it's consequences.

The early Kūfan scholar ʿĀmir al-Shaʿbī (d. 103) probably was an opponent of *tasyīb*. There are three traditions which have him express his opinion in different wording. 1. The *sā'iba* does not have the right to put his estate where he pleases (meaning that he cannot choose a new patron who will have the right to be his heir).[120]) 2. The patronate of the *sā'iba* belongs to the manumitter.[121]) 3. The manumitter gets the inheritance and has the obligation of paying blood-money on behalf of the *sā'iba*.[122]) Exept for the first tradition, for which I have no variants, it is not totally clear, however, if al-Shaʿbī *always* gave the patronate to the manumitter or only if there was no new patron (as al-Zuhrī does). We have to be very cautious with conclusions here because rejection of *tasyīb* was an exception at the end of the first and beginning of the second century. But also the wording of the second and third tradition gives the impression that what al-Shaʿbī had in mind was indeed a general rejection of *tasyīb*.[123])

---

118) ʿAbd al-Razzāq, *Muṣannaf*, IX, no. 16152; Saʿīd b. Manṣūr, *Sunan*, III, no. 227; Ibn Qudāma, *Mughnī*, VI, no. 4938, ll. 8–9. The ʿAṭā' tradition is transmitted by Ibn Jurayj, a pupil of ʿAṭā', and can be regarded as authentic. Ibn Jurayj adds that another teacher of his, ʿAmr b Dīnār (d. 126), is of the same opinion.

119) For al-Zuhrī's opinion there are three independent versions, transmitted by Mālik, Maʿmar and Ibn Jurayj. For the sources see above notes 52 and 55.

120) ʿAbd al-Razzāq, *Muṣannaf*, IX, no. 16234.

121) Ibn Abī Shayba, *Muṣannaf*, XI, no. 11477; al-Dārimī, *Sunan*, II, no. 3120.

122) ʿAbd al-Razzāq, *Muṣannaf*, IX, no. 16225 and X, no. 18427. The *matn* of tradition no. 16225 is defective. It reads as follows: *al-sā'ibatu yarithuhu mawlāhu lladhī aʿtaqahu wa-yarithuhu ʿanhu*. We have to substitute the second *yarithuhu* by *yaʿqilu*.

123) In one *matn*, not only the "inheritance" of the *sā'iba* is given to the manumitter – as in traditions of other scholars – but explicitely the *"walā'"*. Another *matn* reads: "For every *sā'iba*-freedman his patron has to pay the blood-money and his patron is his heir". Both sounds as if al-Shaʿbī gave the full responsibility for the *sā'iba* to the manumitter, notwithstandig his renunciation of *walā'*. In addition, there is no tradition which has al-Shaʿbī allowing *tasyīb* (as happens with al-Zuhrī) but one tradition which has him prohibiting it.

It is obvious, that the lawyers at the turn of the century had very diverse opinions about whether or not *tasyīb* was allowed and who has to be responsible for the *sā'iba*.

6. Conclusions

After the analysis and dating of the traditions we can state that, on the whole, the traditions have existed in the time of the oldest authority mentioned in the *isnād* and many of them can be regarded as authentic.[124]) On this basis, we can give now the outlines of the development of *tasyīb*.

The traditions of ʿUmar and his companions show that until the turn of the century, *tasyīb* was usual practice and not rejected by the scholars (with, perhaps, the exeption of Ibn Masʿūd). But, and this is important, at the same time there was a clear inclination to hold the manumitter to be entitled to the inheritance (despite his renunciation) if there was no new patron. Assigning the inheritance to the manumitter, however, did not amount to a rejection of *tasyīb*.

At the beginning of the second century, the lawyers in general still did accept *tasyīb* but they started to approach the problem in a more systematic and theoretical way and decided if the manumitter or the state has to be regarded responsible for a *sā'iba* without a new patron. There are also traditions of *tābiʿūn* rejecting *tasyīb* altogether, but they are exeptions.[125])

From the middle of the second century onwards, *tasyīb* became forbidden. Whereas Abū Ḥanīfa (d. 150) and al-Shāfiʿī (d. 204) declared it void altogether,[126]) Mālik (d. 179) still accepted some of the legal implications of *tasyīb*. He characterized it as "manumission for God" and conceded the renunciation of *walā'* by the manumitter, but deprived the

[124]) There are also traditions concerning *tasyīb* which can not be dated because of missing variants. For example the traditions of the Medinense ʿAbd al-Raḥmān al-Ḥārith (Mitter, *Patronat*, 254) and the Baṣrien al-Ḥasan (ibid., 258–259).

[125]) Next to the tradition of al-Shaʿbī which was discussed above, there is a tradition of two Syrian scholars, Rashīd b. Saʿd and Ḍamra b. Ḥabīb (Saʿīd b. Manṣūr, *Sunan*, III/1, no. 228 and al-Dārimī, *Sunan*, II, no. 123). This tradition, though, could be a falsification. Cf. Mitter, *Patronat*, 260.

[126]) For Abū Ḥanīfa see al-Marghīnānī, *Hidāya*, III, 271. For al-Shāfiʿī see *Umm*, IV, 127.

sā'iba from his right to choose a new patron. Instead, he assigned his *walā'* to the Muslims at large.[127]) After the rejection of *tasyīb*, the traditions of ʿUmar and al-Zuhrī were re-interpreted by Muslim scholars. Although al-Zuhrī explicitely accepted *tasyīb* and ʿUmar, too, did not reject it but looked for a responsible person, later lawyers took these traditions for examples of rejection of *tasyīb*.[128])

The question is, why *tasyīb* became forbidden when renouncing the patronate even had been regarded as a religious merit.[129]) Later lawyers, if they provide an explanation for their disapproval at all, mention the Qur'ānic prohibition of freeing camels without restraints[130]) and the Barīra tradition, according to which the patronate belongs to the manumitter.[131]) But early lawyers such as ʿAṭā' had have no problems with accepting *tasyīb* despite these Qur'ānic and Prophetic evidences which they surely knew.[132]) According to CRONE, *tasyīb* became forbidden when *walā'* was no longer regarded as a residue of ownership but as a kinship tie *(nasab)*. Then, she argues, it was no longer possible to renounce the pa-

[127]) MĀLIK, *Muwaṭṭa'*, chapt. 38, no. 25; AL-ZURQĀNĪ, *Sharḥ*, IV, 125.

[128]) See also IBN QUDĀMA, *Mughnī*, VI, no. 4938, He mentions Mālik together with al-Zuhrī and ʿUmar b. ʿAbdalʿazīz although the last two accept *tasyīb*.

[129]) Cf. above, note 107.

[130]) In the Qur'ān (5:103), only *tasyīb* of a camel is forbidden but the scholars interpreted this as forbidding *tasyīb* of slaves, too. The verse reads (in the translation of RICHARD BELL): "And Allāh hath not appointed any baḥīra or sā'iba nor waṣīla or ḥāmī; those who have disbelieved devise falsehood against Allāh, the most of them not having intelligence." A *sā'iba* is a "she-camel that was set at liberty to pasture where it would" and that is not ridden nor "laden with a burden" anymore (LANE, IV, 1481). For the meaning of this verse, which is not totally clear cf. RUDI PARET, *Kommentar*, 130–131.

[131]) In this tradition, ʿĀ'isha wants to buy the slave-girl Barīra, to release her and to gain the patronate upon her. The former owners of Barīra are willing to sell her, but they want to keep the patronate for themselves. Muḥammad advises ʿĀ'isha just to do what she wants, because the patronate belongs to the manumitter anyway *(al-walā' li-man aʿtaqa)*, no matter what condition the owners are stipulating. The muslim scholars took this tradition to mean that a manumitter cannot renounce the patronate because it always belongs to him. For one example of this important and widespread tradition see AL-BUKHĀRĪ, *Ṣaḥīḥ, buyūʿ* (34) no. 73. The tradition is discussed in detail in MITTER, *Patronat*, 101–144.

[132]) The Barīra tradition goes back to ʿĀ'isha (d. 58) and perhaps contains an authentic statement of the Prophet Muḥammad. It was known throughout the Ḥijāz and the Iraq at a very early date (ibid., 142) and ʿAṭā' must have known it, too The fact that ʿAṭā' repeatedly used Qur'ānic verses for his juridical argumentation is shown by MOTZKI, *Anfänge*, 98 ff.

tronate.[133]) But this argument must be rejected because the idea of *walāʾ* as a kinship tie existed from the very beginning of Islam,[134]) and *tasyīb*, nevertheless, continued to be possible. As the opinion of Mālik shows, even in a time when the classical *walāʾ* had been fully developed it was still possible to permit the patron to renounce *walāʾ*. Obviously, the kinship doctrine has never been a reason to prohibit *tasyīb*.

In my opinion, the change of mind could have been initiated by the beginning of systematic reasoning of the *tābiʿūn*. When thinking thoroughly on the consequences of allowing *tasyīb*, inconsistencies – as described above – must have become more and more obvious.[135]) Another, sheer practical reason for abolishing *tasyīb* could also have been the intention of many patrons to release their slaves as *sawāʾib* because in this way, they could evade the duty of paying blood-money for their *mawālī*.[136]) If a *sāʾiba* did not take a new patron, there could arise the unpleasant situation that an injury inflicted by the *sāʾiba* may not be payed for by anybody.[137]) The scholars may have wished to prevent such problems by abolishing *tasyīb*.

We can conclude that the pros and cons of *tasyīb* were discussed controversially until the middle of the second century. As early as in the time of ʿUmar, the inheritance of a deceased *sāʾiba* was given to the manumitter against his will when there was no new patron. This would suggest on the one hand that the entitlement to the inheritance was regarded as a strong right of the manumitter and on the other hand that *tasyīb* meant renunciation of this right (although the authorities could not always show consideration for this renunciation).

---

133) CRONE, *Roman law*, 81.

134) This is the result of my analysis of the *walāʾ*. See MITTER, *Patronat*, 346.

135) See above, 43–44. That is, why MĀLIK had to assign the inheritance of a *sāʾiba* (whom he does not allow to take a new patron) to the Muslims at large. If the manumitter got the inheritance despite his legal renunciation, his *tasyīb* would have been annulated afterwards. By assigning the inheritance to the Muslims, the validity of *tasyīb* is guaranteed and the problem of responsibility is solved.

136) Certainly, by practising *tasyīb* the manumitter is loosing his claim to succesion, too, but then surely not all *sawāʾib* were leaving big estates, anyway. Furthermore, the relatives of a *sāʾiba* are entitled to inherit in the first place. The manumitter thus may often have ended up with nothing. For the opinion of ʿAṭāʾ and Sufyān al-Thaurī on patrons who refuse to pay the blood-money see ʿABD AL-RAZZĀQ, *Muṣannaf*, IX, nos. 17852 and 17855. More examples in CRONE, *Roman law*, 62 note 183.

137) Cf. above, note 109, what is said in connection with the *arqam*-tradition.

The theory of Crone regarding the development of *tasyīb* – first it was accepted and from the second century onwards rejected – in part could be proven right by means of the *isnād-cum-matn* analysis. Yes, the majority of scholars in the first century did indeed accept *tasyīb* and later scholars did reject it. But with regard to this consent we have to bring out two important reservations, the second resulting from the first. First, the traditions in general are much older than Crone assumes. Secondly, *tasyīb* already in pre-Umayyad time meant manumission of slaves without claiming one's right to inherit, thus without patronate.[138]) The Muslims did *not* just become acquainted with this kind of *tasyīb* in Umayyad time but knew it already in the time of ʿUmar b. al-Khaṭṭāb and his contemporarians. This became clear from the fact that traditions with a so-called "classical" content (the inheritance is given to the manumitter despite his renunciation) existed in ʿUmar's time. This is even earlier than Crone's "pre-classical" doctrine which only started with Muʿāwiya. But these traditions have to be interpreted differently, more in the sense of the "pre-classical" doctrine. In contrast to what Crone assumes, in my opinion assigning the inheritance to the manumitter did not mean rejecting *tasyīb*. *Tasyīb* was accepted, but the situation required a decision which ran counter to this acceptance.

Apart from *tasyīb*, also other aspects of *walāʾ* – like sale of *walāʾ*, the right of succesion by the patron and the transition of *walāʾ* to the heirs of the patron after his death – show time and again that features of the „classical" doctrine can be found early in the first century.[139]) This means that the dividing-line between Crone's "pre-classical" and "classical" doctrine is blurred. The doctrines often represent different solutions for the same juridical problem and are not two successive stages of development. As a consequence, the early Islamic patronate seems to have had a

---

[138]) According to Crone (*Roman law*, 68), *tasyīb* in pre-Islamic Arabia and early Islam meant freeing a slave without making it a condition that the freedman remains with his former master and serves him. Pre-Umayyad *tasyīb* was in her opinion the same as the Greek renunciation of *paramonar* services. (Cf. also above 41.) It is not impossible altogether that some early Muslim manumitters did understand by *tasyīb* renunciation of further service. There are examples for the stipulated condition of remaining and serving after the manumission (see Crone 68 ff.). This means that the renunciation of such conditions could also have been known and that this renunciation was named *tasyīb*, too. The important thing is, however, that *tasyīb* as renunciation of *walāʾ* was definitely known, too.

[139]) A detailed analysis of many traditions on different aspects of *walāʾ* is given in Mitter, *Patronat*, passim.

more classical appearance and the similarity of the late-Roman patronate with the early *walāʾ* diminishes.

What does all this mean for the theory that the Umayyad caliph Muʿāwiya adopted the concept of an individual patronate from Byzantine legal practices in Syria and, once adopted, the institution was developed and modified? Since the individual patronate (which confers to the manumitter a title to his freedman's estate and imposes on him the obligation of paying blood-money on his freedman's behalf) was a well-known institution since the first decades of Islam, this theory looses any plausibility. If someone as early as ʿUmar b. al-Khaṭṭāb can be connected with this kind of patronate, we can rule out entirely the possibility that it was introduced in Umayyad times.

Could the individual *walāʾ* have been adopted in the time of ʿUmar?[140]) The answer is: Theoretically yes, but practically no. Theoretically, the contact of the early Muslims with Byzantine institutiond is imaginable. But, to me, it is rather unlikely that ʿUmar could have been interested in and acquainted with the legal system of the just subdued people. In that time, the Arabs lived in camps and did not mix with the inhabitants of the conquered countries.[141]) In my opinion, it is far more probable that ʿUmar decided according to pre-Islamic Arabic law than according to Byzantine law.[142]) By this, possibility of Roman or provincial influence upon the development of *tasyīb* and *walāʾ* is not precluded, but it must (if at all) have taken place in *pre*-Islamic times as suggested by BERGSTRÄSSER.

Walāʾ is only *one* of the numerous institutions and regulations which according to Western scholars had been borrowed by Muslim lawyers from Byzantine law or other legal systems. It would certainly mean overemphasizing the evidence and jumping to conclusions if we would conclude now that Islamic law developed largely out of pre-Islamic customary law without borrowings worth mentioning in the time of the Umayyads and ʿAbbāsids. Borrowings are likely to have happened, per-

---

140) With regard to *tasyīb* of slaves, I did not come across any *aḥādīṯ* of the Prophet. I only know of two Prophetic traditions on *tasyīb* of *camels*. One of them, which condems this practice, can be dated back to the cl al-Zuhrī (see e. g. AL-BUKHĀRĪ, *Ṣaḥīḥ*, II, *manāqib* (61) no. 13 and IBN ḤANBAL, *Musnad*, II, no. 8808). The other tradition, which is about not paying blood-money for an injury inflicted by a *sāʾiba*-camel, cannot be dated at all (see ibid., III, no. 14822).

141) CAHEN, *Islam*, 27.

142) That pre-Islamic Arabic law could well be the source ot the Islamic *walāʾ* is suggested also by HALLAQ. See above, note 24.

haps more likely in the field of public law and theory of law than in the field of private law. What the evidence concerning *walāʾ* shows, is that we have to analyze and date the *aḥādīth* very carefully before claiming the borrowing of an institution in Islámic time.[143]) Arabia in pre-Islamic times surely was not a region without legal regulations. We know that the Arabs had many rules regarding interpersonal relations,[144]) and as has been shown now, rules concerning the individual *walāʾ* between manumitter and freedman were part of them.

Bibliography of the cited literature

ʿABD AL-RAZZĀQ AL-ṢANʿĀNĪ, *al-Muṣannaf*, ed. by ḤABĪB AL-RAḤMĀN AL-AʿẒAMĪ, 11 vols., Beirut 1430/1983. First edition 1391/1972.

AL-BAYHAQĪ, ABŪ BAKR AḤMAD B. AL-ḤUSAYN, *al-Sunan al-kubrā*, 10 vol., Haydarabad 1344–1355.

BECKER, CARL HEINRICH, "Die Entstehung von ʿUšr und Ḫarāğland", *Islamstudien*, Leipzig 1924, vol. 1, 218–233. First printed in *Zeitschrift für Assyriologie* 18 (1904), 103 pp.

BERGSTRÄSSER, GOTTHELF, "Anfänge und Charakter des juristischen Denkens im Islam. Vorläufige Betrachtungen", *Der Islam*, 14 (1925), 76–81.

BRUNSCHVIG, ROBERT, "ʿAbd", *The Encyclopaedia of Islam. New Edition*, ed. by H. A. R. GIBB et al., vol. 1, Leiden/London 1960, 24–40.

BUKHĀRĪ, ABŪ ʿABDALLĀH MUḤAMMAD B. ISMĀʿĪL AL-, *al-Djāmiʿ al-Ṣaḥīḥ*, Leiden 1862–1908.

CAHEN, CLAUDE, *Der Islam I. Vom Ursprung bis zu den Anfängen des Osmanenreiches*, Frankfurt 1982[7] (1968[1]).

CRONE, PATRICIA, "Mawlā", *The Encyclopaedia of Islam. New Edition*, ed. by H. A. R. GIBB et al., vol. 6, Leiden 1991, 874–882.

CRONE, PATRICIA, "Jahili and Jewish Law: The Qasāma", *Jerusalem Studies in Arabic and Islam* 4 (1984), 153–201.

CRONE, PATRICIA, *Roman, provincial and Islamic law. The origins of the Islamic patronate*, Cambridge 1987.

CRONE, PATRICIA and HINDS, MARTIN, *God's Caliph. Religious Authority in the First Centuries of Islam*, Cambridge 1987.

FITZGERALD, SEYMOUR VESEY, "The Alleged Debt of Islamic to Roman Law", *The Law Quarterly Review* 67 (1951), 81–102.

143) If there are *aḥādīth*, at least. If there are not, the method of *isnād-cum-matn* analysis cannot be applied, of course, and other methods have to be developed.

144) Cf. REINERT, *Recht* and MOTZKI, "Entstehung", 152–153.

GILLI-ELEWY, HEND, "Soziale Aspekte frühislamischer Sklaverei", *Der Islam*, 77/1 (2000).

GOLDZIHER, IGNAZ, "Fiqh", *Enzyklopädie des Islam*, ed. by Th. HOUTSMA et al., vol. 2., Leiden/Leipzig 1927, 106–111.

GOLDZIHER, IGNAZ, *Muhammedanische Studien*, 2 vols., Halle 1889–1890.

HALLAQ, WAEL B., "The Use an Abuse of Evidence: The Question of Provincial and Roman Influence on Early Islamic Law", *Journal of American Oriental Society* 110: 79–91, New York 1989, 1–36. Reprinted in id.: *Law and Legal Theory in Classical and Medieval Islam*, Aldershot (Hampshire) and Brookfield (Vermont) 1995, article IX.

HEFFENING, WILLI, *Das islamische Fremdenrecht bis zu den islamisch-fränkischen Staatsverträgen. Eine rechtshistorische Studie zum Fiqh*, Hannover 1925.

IBN ABĪ SHAYBA, *al-Muṣannaf*, ed. by MUḤAMMAD AḤMAD AL-NADWĪ, 15 vols., Bombay 1973–83.

IBN ḤAJAR AL-ʿASQALĀNĪ, ABŪ L-FAḌL AḤMAD B. ʿALĪ, *al-Iṣāba fī tamyīz al-ṣaḥāba*, 8 vols. in 4, Beirut n. d.

IBN ḤAJAR AL-ʿASQALĀNĪ, ABŪ L-FAḌL AḤMAD B. ʿALĪ, *Tahdhīb al-tahdhīb al-kamāl fī maʿrifat al-rijāl*, 12 vols., Haydarabad 1325/1907. Reprinted Beirut 1968.

IBN MANṢŪR, MUḤAMMAD B. MUKARRAM, *Lisān al-ʿarab*, 15 vols., Beirut n. d.

IBN QUDĀMA, ʿABDALLĀH B. AḤMAD, *al-Mughnī*, 10 vols., Cairo 1968–69.

IBN RUSHD: see NYAZEE

IBN SAʿD, ABŪ, ʿABDALLĀH MUḤAMMAD, *al-Ṭabaqāt al-kubrā*, 8 vols., Beirut 1376/1957–1380/1960.

JUDA, JAMAL, *Die sozialen und wirtschaftlichen Aspekte der Mawālī in frühislamischer Zeit*, Tübingen 1983.

JUYNBOLL, GAUTIER H. A., "Nāfiʿ, the *mawlā* of Ibn ʿUmar, and his position in Muslim *ḥadīth* Literature", *Der Islam* 70 (1993), 207–244.

KREMER, ALFRED VON, *Culturgeschichte des Orients unter den Chalifen*, 2 vols., Wien 1875–77.

LANE, EDWARD WILLIAM, *Arabic-English Lexicon*, 8 vols., New York 1863–93. Reprinted 1956.

Lisān al-ʿarab, see IBN MANṢŪR

MĀLIK B. ANAS, *al-Muwaṭṭaʾ, riwāyāt* Yaḥyā b. Yaḥyā al-Masmūdī, ed. by MUḤAMMAD FUʾĀD ʿABD AL-BAQĪ, Cairo 19--.

MĀLIK B. ANAS, *al-Muwaṭṭaʾ, riwāyāt* Muḥammad al-Shaybānī, ed. by ʿABD AL-WAHHĀB ʿABD AL-LAṬĪF, Cairo 1967.

AL-MARGHĪNĀNĪ, ʿALĪ B. ABĪ BAKR, *al-Hidāya*, 4 vols., Cairo 1980.

MITTER, ULRIKE, *Das frühislamische Patronat. Eine Untersuchung zur Rolle von fremden Elementen bei der Entwicklung des islamischen Rechts*, Univ. Diss., Nijmegen 1999.

MITTER, ULRIKE, "Problemen van het onderzoek naar ontleningen aan niet-Arabische rechtsstelsels in het ontstaan en de ontwikkeling van het islamitisch recht", *Sharqiyyāt*, 9/2 (1997), 107–123.

MORAND, MARCEL, *Etudes de droit musulman algérien*, Algier 1910.

MOTZKI, HARALD, *Die Anfänge der islamischen Jurisprudenz. Ihre Entwicklung in Mekka bis zur Mitte des 2./8. Jahrhunderts*, Wiesbaden 1991.

MOTZKI, HARALD, "Die Entstehung des Rechts", in: ALBRECHT NOTH/JÜRGEN PAUL (ed.): *Der islamische Orient. Grundzüge seiner Geschichte*, Würzburg 1998, 151–172.

MOTZKI, HARALD, "Der Fiqh des -Zuhrī: die Quellenproblematik", *Der Islam* 68 (1991), 1–44.

MOTZKI, HARALD, "Der Prophet und die Schuldner. Eine *Ḥadīṯ*-Untersuchung auf dem Prüfstand", *Der Islam*, 77/1 (2000), 1–83.

MOTZKI, HARALD, "*Quo vadis, ḥadīṯ*-Forschung? Eine kritische Untersuchung von G. H. A. Juynboll: 'Nāfiʿ', the *maulā* of Ibn ʿUmar, and his position in Muslim *ḥadīṯ* Literature'", *Der Islam* 73 (1996), 40–80 and 192–231 (second part).

NYAZEE, IMRAN AHSAN KHAN (translation): *Ibn Rushd. The distinguished jurist's primer. Bidāyat al-muǧtahid*, 2 vols., Reading/UK 1996.

PARET, RUDI, *Der Koran. Kommentar und Konkordanz*, Stuttgart/Berlin/Köln/Mainz 1972. Reprinted 1980.

POWERS, DAVID S., "On Bequests in Early Islam", *Journal of Near Eastern Studies*, 48/3 (1989), 185–200.

REINERT, W., *Das Recht in der altarabischen Poesie*, Phil. Diss., Köln 1963.

RELAND, ADRIAAN, *Dissertationes Miscellanea*, trajecti ad Rhenum 1707–8.

SAḤNŪN, ʿABD AL-SALĀM B. SAʿĪD AL-TANŪKHĪ, *al-Mudawwana al-kubrā*, 5 vols., Beirut 1410/1994.

SAʿĪD B. MANṢŪR, *al-Sunan*, ed. by ḤABĪB AL-RAḤMĀN AL-AʿẒAMĪ, vol. 3/1,2 (in 1), Bombay 1982/1403.

SARAKHSĪ, SHAMS AL-AʾIMMA AL-, *al-Mabsūṭ*, 30 parts in 15 vols., Cairo 1324–31/1906–13.

SCHACHT, JOSEPH, "Droit byzantin et droit musulman", *Academia Nazionale dei Lincei, Fondazione Allesandro Volta, Atti dei Convegni*, 12 (1957), 197–230.

SCHACHT, JOSEPH, "Foreign Elements in Ancient Islamic Law", *Journal of Comparative Legislation and International Law*, 32 (1950), 9–17.

SCHACHT, JOSEPH, *An Introduction to Islamic Law*, Oxford 1964.

SCHACHT, JOSEPH, *The Origins of Muhammadan Jurisprudence*, Oxford 1950.

SCHMIDT, FRANZ FREDERIK, "Die occupatio im islamischen Recht", *Der Islam* 1 (1910), 300–353.

SCHNEIDER, IRENE, *Kinderverkauf und Schuldknechtschaft. Untersuchungen zur vorliterarischen Phase des islamischen Rechts*, Stuttgart 1999.

SCHNEIDER, IRENE, "Narrativität und Authentizität: Die Geschichte vom weisen Propheten, dem dreisten Dieb und dem koranfesten Gläubiger", *Der Islam*, 77/1 (2000), 84–115.

SCHOELER, GREGOR, *Charakter und Authentie der muslimischen Überlieferung über das Leben Mohammeds*, Berlin/New York 1996.

AL-SHĀFIʿĪ, MUḤAMMAD B. IDRĪS, *al-Umm*, 8 vols. in 4, Beirut n. d.

AL-SHĀFIʿĪ, MUḤAMMAD B, IDRĪS, *Shifāʾ al-ʿiyy bi-takhrīj wa-taḥqīq musnad al-Shāfiʿī bi-tartīb al-ʿalāma al-Sindī*, 2 vol., Cairo 1416/1996.

AL-ṬABARĪ, MUḤAMMAD B. JARĪR, *Tafsīr*, ed. by MAḤMŪD MUḤAMMAD SHĀKIR, 15 vols., Cairo 1955.

WATT, W. MONTGOMERY, *Muḥammad at Medina*, Oxford 1956.

WELLHAUSEN, JULIUS, *Das arabische Reich und sein Sturz*, Berlin 1902.

AL-ZURQĀNĪ, MUḤAMMAD B. ʿABD AL-BĀQĪ, *Sharḥ al-Zurqānī ʿalā Muwaṭṭaʾ al-Imām Mālik*, 4 vols., Beirut 1411/1990.

7

THE ROLE OF NON-ARAB CONVERTS IN THE DEVELOPMENT OF EARLY ISLAMIC LAW*

Harald Motzki

Abstract

Western scholarship has attached considerable importance to the role played by scholars of non-Arab descent in the formative period of Islamic law and jurisprudence. This view can be challenged. In a sample taken from a biographical collection of important legal scholars compiled in the fifth/eleventh century, "true" Arabs constituted the majority; three quarters of the non-Arab scholars had an eastern background and came from the regions of the former Sassanian empire; and only a few scholars had clearly Christian or Jewish roots. This result lends no support to the assumption that jurists of non-Arab descent brought solutions from their natal legal systems—Roman, Roman provincial and Jewish law—to early Islamic law.

Introduction

ONE FINDS THE FOLLOWING TRADITION in Abū Isḥāq al-Shīrāzī's *Ṭabaqāt al-fuqahā'*, a prosopography of Muslim jurists written in the fifth century of the Islamic era/eleventh century CE: "When the ʿAbādila had died—ʿAbd Allāh b. ʿAbbās, ʿAbd Allāh b. al-Zubayr, ʿAbd Allāh b. ʿUmar and ʿAbd Allāh b. ʿAmr b. al-ʿĀṣ—legal knowledge in all countries passed to the *mawālī* [i.e. clients of non-Arab origin]. The lawyer of Mecca was ʿAṭā', that of Yemen Ṭāwūs, that of the Yamāma Yaḥyā b. Abī Kathīr, that of Baṣra al-Ḥasan [al-Baṣrī], that of Kūfa Ibrāhīm al-Nakhaʿī, that of Syria Makḥūl, that of Khurāsān ʿAṭā' al-Khurāsānī. The only exception is Medina; God gave to this city a man from [the tribe of] Quraysh, an undisputed lawyer [named] Saʿīd b. al-Musayyab."[1]

---

* I would like to thank John Nawas for making me think about the issue of non-Arab converts to Islam and inviting me to present the results of my thinking to the International Medieval Congress held at the University of Leeds in July 1997. I am grateful to the editors of *ILS* and the outside readers for their helpful comments on the first draft of the article.

1 Abū Isḥāq al-Shīrāzī, *Ṭabaqāt al-fuqahā'* (Beirut 1401/1981), 58, quoting ʿAbd al-Raḥmān b. Zayd b. Aslam (d. 182/798-99), who was a *mawlā*. Shīrāzī mentions this tradition in the lemma of Ibn al-Musayyab without further comment. It is unlikely that he agreed with ʿAbd al-Raḥmān's opinion regarding the role of

This statement suggests that in the first generation after the Prophet Muḥammad, legal knowledge (*fiqh*) was held mostly by Arabs, but that already in the second generation, that is to say, in the second half of the first Islamic/seventh century CE, legal knowledge had passed to converts of non-Arab origin in nearly all parts of the Islamic realm.

If this statement is true, it raises several questions. What were the reasons for this change? Was the dominance of *mawālī* in this branch of knowledge only a short interval or did this phenomenon continue? Where did the non-Arab clients come from? What culture did they bring with them? What impact did they have on Islamic *fiqh*?

Western scholarship has tackled these issues since the second half of the nineteenth century. Writing in 1866, Paul de Lagarde observed that there was *no* Semite among the Muslims who was brilliant in scholarship.[2] Alfred von Kremer was a little more cautious: "Fast scheint es dass diese wissenschaftlichen Studien (Koranlesung, Exegese, Traditionskunde und Rechtswissenschaft) in den ersten zwei Jahrhunderten *vorwiegend* von Clienten betrieben werden".[3] This judgment was shared by Goldziher, who admitted that some Arabs engaged in scholarship, but thought that only a *tiny minority* were successful.[4] Convinced of the numerical superiority of the non-Arabs in Muslim scholarship, Goldziher predicted that a statistical study of this issue would prove the point.[5]

A statistical study such as that proposed by Goldziher has not been undertaken until the present time. Perhaps the authority of the

the *mawālī* scholars since his collection of *fuqahā'* contradicts it. A similar statement purportedly was made by al-Zuhrī in a dialogue between himself and the caliph ʿAbd al-Malik, but here two other names are added—Yazīd b. Abī Ḥabīb (Egypt) and Maymūn b. Mihrān (al-Jazīra); Saʿīd b. al-Musayyab and Yaḥyā b. Kathīr are missing; and al-Ḍaḥḥāk b. al-Muzāḥim replaces ʿAṭā' as the leading scholar of Khurāsān. Cf. I. Goldziher, *Muhammedanische Studien* (Halle 1889), I, 114-15. Another version of this dialogue is found in Ibn Manẓūr, *Mukhtaṣar Tārīkh Dimashq li-Ibn ʿAsākir* (Damascus 1984-88), XVII, 70-71. Here Ibrāhīm al-Nakhaʿī is classified as an Arab.

2 P. de Lagarde, *Gesammelte Abhandlungen* (n. p., 1866 [Osnabrück, 1966]), 8, n. 4 (emphasis mine). See also Goldziher, *Studien*, I, 109.

3 A. von Kremer, *Culturgeschichtliche Streifzüge auf dem Gebiete des Islams* (Leipzig, 1873), 16 (emphasis mine). See also Goldziher, *Studien*, I, 109.

4 Goldziher, *Studien*, I, 112: "Damit will nicht gesagt sein, dass die Araber sich der Pflege der Wissenschaft völlig verschlossen. Die Gelehrtengeschichte des Islam weist manchen echten Araber auf...". 113: "Dies gelang nur einer *kleinen Minorität*, welche auf geistigem Gebiete von den neuerworbenen Fremdlingen, die ihren mitgeborenen Bildungstrieb nur auf die durch die Eroberung erzeugten Verhältnisse anzuwenden hatten, leicht überflügelt wurde." (emphasis mine).

5 Ibid. 114: "Eine statistische Behandlung dieser Verhältnisse schlösse für alle Fälle sehr zu Ungunsten der Araber".

influential and highly respected Islamicist prevented it. In any case, similar opinions are current today.[6] The general view of recent Western scholarship, as expressed by Patricia Crone, may be summarized as follows: Following the Arab-Muslim conquest of the Middle East, there began a process of integration of non-Arabs into Arab-Muslim society. Although non-Arabs initially were exposed to ethnic prejudices, "their education, skills and sheer number was such that they rapidly achieved positions of influence", "came to dominate the world of scholarship" and "played a crucial role in the formation of the Islamic faith".[7] The underlying idea is that the former local élites of the conquered territories were rapidly assimilated into Muslim society, putting their superior skills and culture to the service of their new masters, the Arabs. The idea seems plausible and until recently I concurred with it. After reading extensively in the biographical literature, however, I have been persuaded that the number of Arab scholars was not as low as I thought. In an effort to substantiate this impression, I decided to undertake a statistical investigation of the issue.

The view that non-Arabs dominated Islamic scholarship is not intended simply as a statement of fact. It is often linked—sometimes implicitly—with the idea that the high level of Islamic culture cannot be the product of people living at the fringe of the advanced civilizations of the ancient world. Thus, non-Arab scholars, with their higher education and culture, must have been responsible for this achievement, as von Kremer and Goldziher believed.[8]

Additionally, the "crucial role" of non-Arab scholars would explain the many instances of borrowing from Roman, Roman provincial, and, to a minor extent, Persian civilization, and from Christianity and Judaism, which Western scholars have detected in Islamic civilization during its formative period. Two advocates of this view were Goldziher and Joseph Schacht.[9] Schacht dated the beginning of Iranian and

---

6 M.J. Kister concludes a recent article with the statement: "The transmission of *ḥadīths*, edifying stories, stories of the prophets and saints, was widely disseminated by the new generations of scholars [i.e. from the beginning of the second century onwards, H.M.], among whom the *mawālī probably* formed the majority." (emphasis mine). See M.J. Kister, "*...Lā taqra'ū l-qur'āna ʿalā l-muṣḥafiyyīn wa-lā taḥmilū l-ʿilma ʿani l-ṣaḥafiyyīn...* Some Notes on the Transmission of *Ḥadīth*", in *Jerusalem Studies in Arabic and Islam* 22 (1998), 127-62, esp. 162.

7 P. Crone, "*Mawlā*", in *EI*[2], VI, 874-82, esp. 877.

8 Goldziher regarded Islamic scholarship as "fremde Bildung", cf. *Studien* I, 112 and II, 53.

9 See Goldziher, Studien, II, 75-76 ("Das *Fikh* ist ebensowenig Produkt des arabischen Geistes, wie es die Grammatik (*nahu*) und die dogmatische Dialektik (*kalām*) sind. Und die Muhammedaner älterer Zeiten hatten ein klares Bewusstsein

Hellenistic influences on Arab-Islamic civilization to the second half of the first century of Islam (c. 670-720) and he saw this process reaching its zenith in the second century. Its first fruits became recognizable in the field of law.[10] How did the influence take place? According to Schacht, Islamic jurisprudence "started in Iraq about AH 100", "at a time when the door of Islamic civilization became widely open to the potential transmitters who were educated non-Arab converts to Islam".[11] Christian converts to Islam, for example, were supposedly responsible for parallels between Islamic law and canon law of the Christian Eastern churches.[12] To explain the influence of Roman law in a region such as Iraq, which never was a Roman or Byzantine province, Schacht refers to "persons with an [sic] Hellenistic education".[13] He does not assume that the first Muslim jurists consciously adopted principles of foreign laws by consulting lawbooks, but that the converts among them were inspired by their traditional education which contained elements of jurisprudence.[14]

I propose to challenge the idea that Islamic jurisprudence is mainly the product of non-Arab scholars who were responsible for the alleged borrowings from, or influences on, pre-Islamic laws from outside the Arabian peninsula. I do not intend to replace this idea with a new one, but only to show that we cannot be sure about it and that the issue requires the further attention of Islamicists. My arguments are based on a statistical analysis of biographical data available about the most important jurists of the first and second centuries AH (excluding the generation of the Prophet's companions). I shall concentrate on the following issues: What is the ratio of jurists of Arab to those of non-Arab descent? Is there really a domination of non-Arabs? Is the ratio the same in the different centers of jurisprudence? What are the origins

von diesem importierten Charakter des *Fikh*"). For a summary of Goldziher's opinion cf. P. Crone, *Roman, provincial and Islamic law. The origins of the Islamic patronate* (Cambridge, 1987), 102-06.

[10] *The Legacy of Islam*, ed. J. Schacht/C.E. Bosworth (Oxford, 1974), 6. A convenient summary of the history of the issue of influences and borrowings from pre-Islamic law systems is given in Crone, *Roman*, ch. 1.

[11] J. Schacht, "Foreign Elements in Ancient Islamic Law", in *Journal of Comparative Legislation* (1950), 9-17, esp. 13.

[12] Ibid. 17.

[13] Ibid. 15.

[14] J. Schacht, "Droit byzantin et droit musulman", in *Convegno di scienze morali storiche e filologiche, 1956* (Rome 1957) (Accademia nazionale dei Lincei. Fondazione Alessandro Volta. Atti dei convegni, 12), 97-218, esp. 201-03. Schacht's identification of Hellenistic rhetorical education as possible source of borrowings has been rejected by Crone. Cf. her *Roman*, 9-10.

of the non-Arabs scholars? What is their degree of integration into Arab-Muslim society?

To identify "important legal scholars", I have used al-Shīrāzī's aforementioned *Ṭabaqāt al-fuqahāʾ*. The book provides a selection of those *fuqahāʾ* whom al-Shīrāzī (d. 476 AH/1083 CE) regarded as most important. His selection has two advantages. First, it is available—whereas it will be some time before we have a large and readily accessible database of Muslim *fuqahāʾ* who flourished during the first two centuries. Second, it is of a limited size, which makes it well suited for a pilot study such as the present one. Al-Shīrāzī's sample appears to have certain shortcomings, but these shortcomings, in my view, are not fatal, as I shall explain: (1) Some may argue that the limited size of the sample affects the reliability of the results. This is true but it does not render the results insignificant. They are provisional, of course, and need to be checked on the basis of a larger sample.[15] (2) Al-Shīrāzī's selection may be biased in favor of Shāfiʿī scholars. This objection is unwarranted, as there is no indication that al-Shīrāzī had a preference for one or more early regional centers of jurisprudence at the expense of others. Even the most important scholars of the rival schools are represented.[16] (3) Schacht has argued that Islamic jurisprudence did not *exist* in the first century AH; if this were true, Islamic traditions concerning the *fuqahāʾ* of the first century would not be trustworthy. But as I have shown elsewhere Islamic jurisprudence started already one-half or three quarters of a century earlier than Schacht posited.[17]

[15] A step in this direction is the sample of 1,049 Muslim scholars of the first four centuries of Islam that has been compiled by Monique Bernards and John Nawas within the framework of the Netherlands Ulama Project (NUP). The project, which was initiated by the universities of Nijmegen, Utrecht and Leiden and is funded by the Netherlands Organization for Scientific Research (NWO), contains other databases as well. For a general description of the NUP see J. Nawas and M. Bernards, "A preliminary report of the Netherlands Ulama Project (NUP): The evolution of the class of *ʿulamāʾ* in Islam with special emphasis on the non-Arab converts (*mawālī*) from the first through fourth century AH", in *Law, Christianity and Modernism in Islamic Society. Proceedings of the Eighteenth Congress of the Union Européenne des Arabisants et Islamisants held at the Katholieke Universiteit Leuven (September 3 - September 9, 1996)*, ed. U. Vermeulen and J. M. F. van Reeth (Leuven 1998), 97-107.

[16] As we shall see below, this is corroborated by a comparison of the results of the present study with the main database of the NUP.

[17] Cf. H. Motzki, *Die Anfänge der islamischen Jurisprudenz. Ihre Entwicklung in Mekka bis zur Mitte des 2./8. Jahrhunderts*, (Stuttgart, 1991); idem, "The *Muṣannaf* of ʿAbd al-Razzāq al-Ṣanʿānī as a source of authentic *aḥādīth* of the first Islamic century", in *Journal of Near Eastern Studies* 50 (1991), 1-21; idem, "Der *Fiqh* des -Zuhrī: die Quellenproblematik", in *Der Islam* 68 (1991), 1-44; idem, "*Quo vadis Ḥadīṯ*-Forschung? - Eine kritische Untersuchung von G.H.A. Juynboll: "Nāfiʿ the *mawlā* of Ibn ʿUmar, and his position in Muslim *ḥadīth* Literature", in

I used al-Shīrāzī's selection of *fuqahā'* only as basis to form a sample. I added a few scholars who are not mentioned by al-Shīrāzī, but who I consider important, and a few others who are mentioned by al-Shīrāzī in the framework of the classical schools of jurisprudence, but who belong to the second century. I left out a few individuals mentioned in his collection because they belong to the third century. The final sample consists of 115 individuals, 108 taken from al-Shīrāzī and seven added by myself. Because al-Shīrāzī's information concerning the scholars is mostly very concise and limited, I generally took the information on them not from him but from Ibn Ḥajar's (d. 852 AH/1449 CE) *Tahdhīb al-tahdhīb*. In addition, al-Shīrāzī's information has been used, and other biographical compilations have been consulted as well.[18]

The easiest method to identify scholars of non-Arab descent is to determine whether an individual is explicitly referred to as a *mawlā* in the sources. If there is no such qualification, the individual can been taken to be an Arab. This is the method followed in my investigation. It is in accordance with Crone's opinion that the term *mawlā*, "applied to the inferior party in an Islamic context, ...almost always means a client of the type recognized in early Islamic law..." and that this type of client "was a non-Arab freedman, convert or other newcomer in Muslim society".[19] This assumption is corroborated by my own experience using the late biographical literature, where the term *mawlā* indicates non-Arab descent.

This clear-cut distinction conceals several problems, however. The concept of *walā'* and the term *mawlā* referred originally to a social status, not an ethnic origin. In pre-Islamic times there were several forms of *walā'*, the most important being *walā' al-ḥilf* (confederacy), *walā' al-jiwār* (neighborhood) and *walā' al-ʿitāqa* (relationship between a patron and his former slave after the slave has been freed and become a client).[20] All three types of *mawālī* could be Arabs or non-

---

Der Islam 73 (1996), 40-80; 193-231; idem, "Die Entstehung des islamischen Rechts", in *Der islamische Orient—Grundzüge seiner Geschichte*, ed. A. Noth/J. Paul (Würzburg, 1998), 151-73; idem, "The Prophet and the Cat: on dating Mālik's *Muwaṭṭa'* and legal traditions", in *Jerusalem Studies in Arabic and Islam* 22 (1998), 18-83.

18 Ibn Ḥajar's *Tahdhīb al-tahdhīb* is especially well suited for my purpose because the author (based on a critical evaluation of earlier sources) consistently mentions whether a scholar must be considered as a *mawlā*.

19 Crone, "*Mawlā*", 874.

20 Cf. Goldziher, *Studien*, I, 105-06 and J. Juda, *Die sozialen und wirtschaftlichen Aspekte der Mawālī in frühislamischer Zeit*, Ph.D. thesis, Fakultät für Kulturwissenschaften (Tübingen 1983), ch. 1.

Arabs; they could be integrated into an Arab tribe and thereby receive or claim this tribe's genealogy. Besides, non-Arabs (and Arabs of course) could be adopted by Arabs and in this way receive an Arab genealogy. Consequently, an individual with an Arab genealogy was not necessarily always a "true" Arab, and a *mawlā* was not always a non-Arab. This confusing situation and terminology changed gradually during the first Islamic century as a result of social and conceptual changes brought about by the development of the Islamic community as a new type of society in Arabia (e.g. the prohibition of adoption, *ḥilf* and the enslavement of Arabs) and by the expansion of the new community into areas inhabited by non-Arabs. These changes resulted in an enormous influx of non-Arabs, slaves and free people, so that the category of *mawālī* was filled nearly exclusively by non-Arabs and the term was restricted to them. In general, the terminology seems to have been inspired by the later concept, but there are a few instances in which the judgment of biographers and genealogists that an individual is an Arab is contradicted by other information. I call such individuals Arab *mawālī*.

The contradictory information concerning the Arab *mawālī* can be explained by several assumptions: (1) The individual in question had a non-Arab descent but tried to disguise it with a fabricated Arab genealogy. His deception was detected, however, by some people. (2) The ancestors of a scholar were non-Arabs who were integrated into an Arab tribe by *ḥilf* or other form of *walā'* already in pre-Islamic times, so that the descendants came to be considered as Arabs although their true origin was not forgotten completely. (3) The scholar in question was of Arab descent but one of his ancestors had been a slave or *ḥalīf* and, as such, was integrated into an Arab tribe to which he did not originally belong. (4) The contradiction results from a misunderstanding of reports concerning the scholar in question.[21] With regard to assumptions (2) and (3), continuity of the earlier and broader concept of *walā'* in the period of transition from pre-Islamic times to the second century AH may have contributed to the confusion.

Numbers

According to al-Shīrāzī there were nine centers of Islamic jurisprudence in the period of the "*fuqahā' al-tābiʿīn*" (the Successor jurists):[22]

---

[21] For a possible example see below note 36.

[22] By this term he means the independent jurists who do not belong to the classical *sunnī* schools of jurisprudence.

Medina, Mecca, Yemen, Syria and al-Jazīra (the northern part of Mesopotamia), Egypt, Kūfa, Baṣra, Baghdad and Khurāsān. The scholars belonging to this class were active roughly between 50 AH/670 CE and 300 AH/912 CE. Since my study is limited to the first two centuries, I have disregarded all Baghdādī scholars mentioned by al-Shīrāzī because they belong to the third century AH/ninth century CE. I will now go over the groups center by center in the order presented by al-Shīrāzī:[23]

Fuqahā' of Medina

- Sa'īd b. al-Musayyab (A),[24] 'Urwa b. al-Zubayr (A), al-Qāsim b. Muḥammad b. Abī Bakr (A), Abū Bakr b. 'Abd al-Raḥmān (A), 'Ubayd Allāh b. 'Abd Allāh b. 'Utba b. Mas'ūd (A), Khārija b. Zayd b. Thābit (A), Sulaymān b. Yasār (n), Abū Salama b. 'Abd al-Raḥmān b. 'Awf (A), Sālim b. 'Abd Allāh b. 'Umar (A), Muḥammad b. 'Alī b. Abī Ṭālib (A), Qabīṣa b. Dhu'ayb (A), 'Abd al-Malik b. Marwān (A)
- 'Alī b. al-Ḥusayn b. 'Alī (A), al-Ḥasan b. Muḥammad b. al-Ḥanafiyya (A), [Nāfi', *mawlā* of 'Abd Allāh b. 'Umar] (n), Muḥammad b. Muslim b. 'Ubayd Allāh b. Shihāb al-Zuhrī (A), 'Umar b. 'Abd al-'Azīz b. Marwān (A), Muḥammad b. 'Alī b. al-Ḥusayn b. 'Alī (A), 'Abd al-Raḥmān b. al-Qāsim b. Muḥammad (A), Rabī'a b. Abī 'Abd al-Raḥmān Farrūkh (n), Abū Zinād 'Abd Allāh b. Dhakwān (n), 'Abd Allāh b. Yazīd b. Hurmuz (n), Yaḥyā b. Sa'īd b. Qays al-Anṣārī (A)
- Muḥammad b. 'Abd al-Raḥmān b. al-Mughīra b. Abī Dhi'b (A), 'Abd al-'Azīz b. 'Abd Allāh b. Abī Salama [Dīnār or Maymūn] al-Mājishūn (n), 'Abd Allāh b. Muḥammad b. Abī Sabra (A), Kathīr b. Farqad (A), Mālik b. Anas (A)

Our sample contains twenty-eight names[25] divided into three generations (*ṭabaqāt*). It begins with Sa'īd b. al-Musayyab (d. around 94 AH/714 CE) and closes with Mālik b. Anas (d. 179 AH/796 CE).[26] The first generation includes twelve persons of whom only one is a

[23] The names of Arabs mentioned by Shīrāzī have sometimes been shortened; the genealogies of non-Arab scholars, on the contrary, have been completed [in brackets] with elements taken from other sources.
[24] (A) means "of Arab descent", (n) "of non-Arab descent".
[25] Twenty-seven from Shīrāzī and one (Nāfi') added by myself.
[26] Shīrāzī, *Ṭabaqāt*, 57-68.

non-Arab *mawlā*. The others were mostly members of Quraysh, the tribe of the Prophet. Many of them were sons or nephews of his Companions who played a leading role after his death. The second generation includes eleven scholars, of whom four were *mawālī*, while the others were mostly grandsons of leading Companions. The third generation includes five persons, of whom two were from Quraysh, two were from Medinese tribes and one was of non-Arab origin. In total, then, there were twenty-two Arabs and only six scholars of non-Arab origin at Medina (ratio 8:2).

Fuqahā' of Mecca

- 'Aṭā' b. Abī Rabāḥ [Aslam](n), Mujāhid b. Jabr (n), 'Abd Allāh b. 'Ubayd Allāh b. Abī Mulayka (A), 'Amr b. Dīnār (n), 'Ikrima, *mawlā* of 'Abd Allāh b. 'Abbās, (n), [Abū l-Zubayr Muḥammad b. Muslim b. Tadrus] (n)
- 'Abd Allāh b. Abī Najīḥ [Yasār] (n), 'Abd al-Malik b. 'Abd al-'Azīz b. Jurayj (n)
- Muslim b. Khālid [b. Farwa or Qarqara of Jarja] al-Zanjī (n)
- Muḥammad b. Idrīs [al-Shāfi'ī] (A)

For Mekka we have ten names.[27] The first is 'Aṭā' b. Abī Rabāḥ (d. 114 AH/733 CE), the last is al-Shāfi'ī (d. 204 AH/820 CE). In the first generation we find five *mawālī* and one Arab, in the second generation two scholars, both non-Arabs, in the third one *mawlā*, and in the fourth generation one Arab scholar. Altogether there were two Arabs and eight non-Arabs (ratio 2:8), almost the opposite of the situation in Medina.

Fuqahā' of Yemen

- Ṭāwūs b. Kaysān (n), 'Aṭā' b. Markabūdh (n),[28] Sharāḥīl b. Shuraḥbīl (n), Ḥanash b. 'Abd Allāh (n), Wahb b. Munabbih (n)
- [Ma'mar b. Rāshid] (n)
- ['Abd al-Razzāq b. Hammām b. Nāfi'] (n)

---

27 Nine given by Shīrāzī, *Ṭabaqāt*, 73 and one (Abū l-Zubayr) added by myself.

28 Cf. Ibn Sa'd, *al-Ṭabaqāt al-kubrā* (Beirut, n.d.), V, 533, 544.

Yemenite legal scholarship is represented by seven persons,[29] all of non-Arab origin. The first is Ṭāwūs b. Kaysān (d. 106 AH/725 CE), the last ʿAbd al-Razzāq (d. 211 AH/827 CE). Three of the Yemenite jurists (Ṭawūs, Maʿmar and ʿAbd al-Razzāq) are *mawālī*, the other four are from the *abnāʾ al-furs* (or *al-fāris*), the descendants born in Yemen of members of the Persian colony which was established by the Sassanian kings in the last decades of the sixth century CE and who administered the country until the time of Muḥammad's prophetic activity.[30]

Fuqahāʾ of Syria and the Jazīra

- Abū Idrīs ʿĀʾidh Allāh b. ʿAbd Allāh al-Khawlānī (A), Shahr b. Ḥawshab al-Ashʿarī (A)
- ʿAbd Allāh b. [Abī] Zakariyyāʾ (A), Hāniʾ b. Kulthūm (A), Rajāʾ b. Ḥaywa al-Kindī (A), Makḥūl b. ʿAbd Allāh [Suhrāb] (n), Abū Ayyūb Sulaymān b. Mūsā al-Ashdaq (n), (al-Jazīra) Maymūn b. Mihrān (n)
- ʿAbd al-Raḥmān b. ʿAmr b. [Abī ʿAmr] Yaḥmid al-Awzāʿī (n), Yazīd b. Yazīd b. Jābir (A), ʿAbd al-Raḥmān b. Yazīd b. Jābir (A), Yaḥyā b. Yaḥyā al-Ghassānī (A), Muḥammad b. al-Walīd b. Ghāmir al-Zabīdī (A), Saʿīd b. ʿAbd al-ʿAzīz al-Tanūkhī (A)

As the most important lawyers of Syria and the Jazīra, Shīrāzī gives fourteen names. The list is headed by Abū Idrīs al-Khawlānī (d. 80 AH/689 CE) and closes with Saʿīd b. ʿAbd al-ʿAzīz al-Tanūkhī (d. 166 AH/783 CE).[31] The first generation includes two scholars, both Arabs, but one of them a *mawlā*.[32] The second generation comprises six persons, three Arabs and three non-Arabs, the third generation includes

---

29 Five from Shīrāzī, *Ṭabaqāt*, 73-74 and two (Maʿmar b. Rāshid, ʿAbd al-Razzāq) added by myself.

30 Cf. K.V. Zettersteen, "*al-Abnāʾ* (II)", in *EI*², I, 102.

31 Shīrāzī, *Ṭabaqāt*, 74-77. I have arranged individuals at the end of his list in the proper chronological order.

32 Shahr b. Ḥawshab al-Ashʿarī. According to Ibn Ḥajar al-ʿAsqalānī, *Tahdhīb al-tahdhīb* (Hyderabad, 1325-27/1907-09), IV, 369 Shahr b. Ḥawshab al-Ashʿarī was a *mawlā* of Asmāʾ bint Yazīd b. al-Sakan, who belonged to the Aws. In W. Caskel, *Ǧamharat an-nasab. Das genealogische Werk des Hišām ibn Muḥammad al-Kalbī* (Leiden, 1966), I, 273 a Shahr b. Khawshab (*sic*) is mentioned among the Banū Ashʿar. The difference in the father's name seems to be due to a scribal error or misreading (both Ibn Saʿd, *Ṭabaqāt,* VII, 449 and Shīrāzī give the name of the father as Ḥawshab) and in both cases the same person seems to be meant. Here we have a case of an Arab *mawlā*.

six scholars of whom only one is a *mawlā* of non-Arab descent. Altogether, only four of the Syrians could be identified as non-Arabs by descent. One of the Arab scholars was probably descended from an Arab family which had been formerly Christian.[33] In terms of proportion, 30 percent were non-Arab scholars while 70 percent were Arabs. In Syria as in Medina, the Arabs obviously outnumbered the non-Arab scholars.

Fuqahā' of Egypt

- ʿAbd al-Raḥmān b. ʿUsayla al-Ṣunābḥī (A), ʿAbd Allāh b. Mālik al-Jīshānī (A), Marthad b. ʿAbd Allāh al-Yazanī (A)
- [Yazīd b. Abī Ḥabīb] (n), Bukayr b. ʿAbd Allāh b. al-Ashajj (n), Abū Umayya ʿAmr b. al-Ḥārith b. Yaʿqūb (n)
- al-Layth b. Saʿd b. ʿAbd al-Raḥmān (n), [ʿAbd Allāh b. Lahīʿa] (A)

For Egypt, our sample contains only eight scholars. The first is Ibn ʿUsayla al-Ṣunābḥī (d. between 70 and 80 AH/690-700 CE), the last ʿAbd Allāh b. Lahīʿa (d. 174 AH/791 CE).[34] The first generation consists of three Arabs, the second generation of three *mawālī*. The third generation consists of one Arab and one non-Arab scholar. For Egypt, the number of Arab jurists (4) and the number of *mawālī* (4) is equal.

Fuqahā' of Kūfa

- ʿAlqama b. Qays al-Nakhaʿī (A), al-Aswad b. Yazīd al-Nakhaʿī (A), Masrūq b. al-Ajdaʿ al-Ḥamdānī (A), ʿUbayd b. ʿAmr al-Hamdānī (A), Shurayḥ b. al-Ḥārith (A), al-Ḥārith [b. ʿAbd Allāh] al-Aʿwar [al-Ḥamdānī] (A)
- ʿĀmir b. Sharāḥīl al-Shaʿbī [al-Ḥimyarī] (A), Saʿīd b. Jubayr b. Hishām (n), Ibrāhīm b. Yazīd b. al-Aswad al-Nakhaʿī (A)
- al-Ḥakam b. ʿUtayba al-Kindī (n), Ḥammād b. Abī Sulaymān [Muslim] (n), Ḥabīb b. Abī Thābit [Qays b. Dīnār] (n), al-Ḥārith b. Yazīd al-ʿUqlī (A), al-Mughīra b. Miqsam al-Ḍabbī (n), Ziyād b. Kulayb [al-Tamīmī] (A), al-Qaʿqāʿ b. Yazīd (A), [Sulaymān b.

[33] Yaḥyā b. Yaḥyā al-Ghassānī, a conclusion based on his and his father's name and his descent from the Ghassān, a tribal group which accepted Christianity before the advent of Islam. Cf. I. Shahīd, "Ghassān", in *EI*^{2}, II, 1020-21.

[34] Added to Shīrāzī's list (see *Ṭabaqāt*, 77-78) by myself. In addition, I added Yazīd b. Abī Ḥabīb in the second generation. Shīrāzī mentions him as pupil of Marthad b. ʿAbd Allāh al-Yazanī but not among the important *fuqahā'*.

Mihrān] al-Aʿmash (n), Manṣūr b. Muʿtamir (A), ʿAbd Allāh b. Shubruma [al-Ḍabbī] (A), Muḥammad b. ʿAbd al-Raḥmān b. Abī Laylā [Yasār] (A), Sufyān b. Saʿīd b. Masrūq al-Thawrī (A), al-Ḥasan b. Ṣāliḥ b. Ḥayy al-Ḥamdānī (A), Sharīk b. ʿAbd Allāh b. Abī Sharīk al-Nakhaʿī (A), Abū Ḥanīfa al-Nuʿmān b. Thābit b. Zūṭā b. Māh (n)

- [Abū Yūsuf Yaʿqūb b. Ibrāhīm] (A), [Muḥammad b. al-Ḥasan b. Farqad al-Shaybānī] (n)

With twenty-six names, Kūfa is second only to Medina in terms of the number of scholars.[35] The first is ʿAlqama b. Qays (d. 62 AH/682 CE), the last Muḥammad al-Shaybānī (d. 189 AH/805 CE). The first generation consists of six persons, collectively designated as "the students of ʿAbd Allāh b. Masʿūd". All of them are of Arab origin.[36] In the second generation, we find two Arabs[37] and one *mawlā*.[38] In the

35 Shīrāzī, *Ṭabaqāt*, 79-86 lists among the "successors" only twenty-three scholars. Since his list of important Kūfan scholars stops at the middle of the second century, I added two scholars of the second half of the century (Abū Yūsuf and al-Shaybānī) who are not included in his list of *tābiʿūn* scholars because he classified them as members of the Ḥanafī school.

36 Shurayḥ b. al-Ḥārith, the famous judge of Kūfa, is generally regarded as an Arab of the tribe of Kinda (see Ibn Ḥajar, *Tahdhīb*, IV, 326, Ibn Saʿd, *Ṭabaqāt*, VI, 131, and Caskel, *Ǧamharat*, I, 233, II, 533), but according to some he was *min awlād al-furs*, i.e. a descendant of the Persians who remained in Yemen after the Sassanian occupation (cf. Ibn Ḥajar, *Tahdhīb*, IV, 326 and Ibn Manẓūr, *Mukhtaṣar*, X, 294-302). In some traditions he says of himself that he is a Yemenite registered in the *dīwān* of Kinda (*ʿidādī fī Kinda, diwānī fī Kinda*); in one instance this is taken to mean that he was a *mawlā* in the sense of being of non-Arab descent (cf. Ibn Saʿd, *Ṭabaqāt*, VI, 132), but this interpretation is not necessarily correct. The tradition seems to have the hidden objective of playing down the difference between Arabs and *mawālī*. Possibly, the opinion that he was *min awlād al-furs* derives from the failure to grasp the bias of such traditions.

37 Ibrāhīm al-Nakhaʿī is considered by most authors as an Arab (cf. Ibn Saʿd, *Ṭabaqāt*, VI, 270; Caskel, *Ǧamharat*, I, 264, II, 352; Ibn Ḥibbān, *al-Thiqāt* (Hydarabad 1398/1978), IV, 8; Shīrāzī, *Ṭabaqāt*, 82, Dhahabī, *Tadhkira*, I, 73; Ibn Ḥajar, *Tahdhīb*, I, 177). A few traditions indicate that he was a *mawlā*: ʿAbd al-Raḥmān b. Zayd b. Aslam took him for one in the tradition quoted at the beginning of this article (see also note 1), and in Balādhurī, *Ansāb al-ashrāf* (Beirut 1398/1978), III, 95 it is reported that he was registered as *mawlā* in the *dīwān* (*al-jund*) of al-Nakhaʿ (on this and other cases of *mawālī* registered in the *dīwān* cf. Juda, *Mawālī*, 120-31, esp. 127). These traditions are contradicted, however, by the information that his mother was an Arab woman (Mulayka bint Qays b. ʿAbd Allāh b. Mālik b. ʿAlqama b. al-Nakhaʿ; cf. Caskel, *Ǧamharat*, I, 264, II, 352), the sister of ʿAlqama b. Qays al-Nakhaʿī (cf. Ibn Ḥibbān, *al-Thiqāt*, IV, 8); the marriage between a non-Arab *mawlā* and an Arab woman was disapproved in the first Islamic century and such marriages were rare (cf. Juda, *Mawālī*, 178-81). This is another case of an Arab *mawlā*.

38 According Ibn Ḥajar, *Tahdhīb*, IV, 11 and Shīrāzī, *Ṭabaqāt*, 82, Saʿīd b. Jubayr was a *mawlā* of the Wāliba b. al-Ḥārith, a division of Banū Asad, and

third generation the ratio between Arabs and non-Arabs becomes more balanced, nine Arabs versus six non-Arabs.[39] In the fourth generation we have one Arab and one *mawlā*. Altogether the Arab scholars of Kūfa (18) outnumber the *mawālī* (8) in a ratio of 7:3.

Fuqahā' of Baṣra

- al-Ḥasan b. Abī l-Ḥasan [Yasār] al-Baṣrī (n), Jābir b. Zayd al-Azdī (A), Muḥammad b. Sīrīn (n), Abū l-ʿĀliya Rufayʿ b. Mihrān (n), Ḥumayd b. ʿAbd al-Raḥmān al-Ḥimyarī (A), Muslim b. Yasār (n), Abū Qilāba ʿAbd Allāh b. Zayd al-Azdī (A)
- Qatāda b. Diʿāma al-Sadūsī (A), Ayyūb b. Abī Tamīma [Kaysān] al-Sakhtiyānī (n), Yūnus b. ʿUbayd [b. Dīnār] (n), ʿAbd Allāh b. ʿAwn b. Arṭabān (n), Ashʿath b. ʿAbd al-Malik al-Ḥumrānī (n), Ibrāhīm b. Muslim al-Makkī (A), Hishām [b. Abī ʿAbd Allāh Sanbar] (n) Dāwūd b. Abī Hind [Dīnār b. ʿUdhāfir or Ṭahmān al-Qushayrī] (n), Ḥumayd b. Abī Ḥumayd [Tayraw, Tayrawayh, Zādhawayh, Dāwaraw, Ṭarkhān, Mihrān, ʿAbd al-Raḥmān or Makhlad] al-Ṭawīl (n), ʿUthmān b. Sulaymān [or Muslim b. Jarmūz or Hurmuz] al-Battī (n),
- ʿUbayd Allāh b. al-Ḥasan b. al-Ḥaṣan al-ʿAnbarī (A), Abd al-Raḥmān b. Mahdī b. Ḥassān (n)

The legal scholarship of Baṣra is represented by nineteen names.[40] The list opens with al-Ḥasan al-Baṣrī (d. 110 AH/729 CE) and closes with ʿAbd al-Raḥmān b. Mahdī (d. 198 AH/814 CE). In the first generation there is already a slight majority of four *mawālī* scholars

according to Ibn Qutayba, *al-Maʿārif* (Beirut, 1407/1987), 253 he was black.

[39] My conclusions concerning the descent of a few scholars in this group calls for a comment: al-Ḥakam b. ʿUtayba was the *mawlā* of Kinda and must not confused with al-Ḥakam b. ʿUtayba b. al-Nahhās (see Ibn Ḥajar, *Tahdhīb*, II, 432; on the latter cf. Caskel, *Ǧamhara*, I, 157). He is therefore counted as non-Arab. Manṣūr b. Muʿtamir al-Sulamī is an Arab according to Ibn Ḥajar, *Tahdhīb*, X, 312 and Caskel, *Ǧamhara*, I, 124, but according to Ibn Qutayba, *Maʿārif*, 268, some said "that he was an Ethiopian" (*min al-Ḥabasha*). He is, however, not explicitly termed a *mawlā*. Therefore, I classified him among the Arabs. Perhaps he was an Arab whose black ancestors had been integrated into Arab tribes for many years. Muḥammad b. ʿAbd al-Raḥmān b. Abī Laylā is generally considered an Arab (cf. Ibn Ḥajar, *Tahdhīb*, IX, 303-03; Caskel, *Ǧamhara*, I, 177) and so he is counted here. His grandfather, however, is said to have been a *mawlā* of the Anṣār or, more specifically, of Banū ʿAmr b. ʿAwf (cf. Caskel, *Ǧamhara*, II, 591-92; Ibn Ḥajar, *al-Iṣāba fī tamyīz al-ṣaḥāba* (Beirut, n.d.), VI, 369, no. 9465). This would make him an Arab *mawlā*.

[40] I removed one individual (Suwār b. ʿAbd Allāh) mentioned in Shīrāzī, *Ṭabaqāt*, 87-91, because he belongs mostly to the third/ninth century.

against three Arabs. In the second generation, only two of ten persons are Arabs, the others being *mawālī* of non-Arab descent. In the third generation we find one Arab and one *mawlā*. Altogether, at Baṣra, thirteen of the nineteen scholars were of non-Arab descent (ratio: 7:3).

Fuqahāʾ of Khurāsān

- ʿAṭā b. Abī Muslim [ʿAbd Allāh or Maysara] al-Khurāsānī (n), al-Ḍaḥḥāk b. Muzāhim al-Hilālī (A), ʿAbd Allāh b. al-Mubārak al-Marwazī (n)

With regard to Khurāsān, Shīrāzī mentions only three scholars, of whom two are *mawālī*.[41]

* * *

Altogether, the Arab scholars in our sample clearly outnumber the non-Arabs: sixty-three Arabs against fifty-two *mawālī* whose non-Arab origin is either certain or very likely (ratio 55:45). The conventional wisdom in Islamic scholarship that the non-Arab *mawālī* by "sheer number came to dominate the world of scholarship" cannot, therefore, be substantiated, at least as far as the élite of Islamic jurisprudence before the establishment of the classical schools of jurisprudence is concerned.[42]

It is striking that some places or regions had high percentages of non-Arab *fuqahāʾ* (Yemen 100 percent, Mekka 80 percent, Baṣra 70 percent), while other centers display the opposite pattern (Medina 20

41 Shīrāzī, *Ṭabaqāt*, 93-94. I left out Ibn Rāhwayh who flourished in the third century AH.

42 The data contained in the NUP database (see notes 15 and 16) corroborate—on the whole—the results of the present study, even if the difference between both categories of scholars is smaller than in my sample. For the period between 81 and 240 AH the percentage of Arab *fuqahāʾ* is 49 (count: 58), that of scholars of non-Arab descent is 51 (count: 60). Even if the sample is enlarged by including scholars who are not *fuqahāʾ* (count 314), the ratio between Arabs and *mawālī* remains almost the same (deviation 0.45 percent). Source: J. Nawas, "The evolution of *fiqh* and the ethnicity of its practitioners over the first four centuries of Islam", paper presented at the International Medieval Congress, University of Leeds, 19-17 July 1997. A more elaborate version of this essay will be published as "The emergence of *fiqh* as a distinct discipline and the ethnic identity of the *fuqahāʾ* in early and classical Islam", in *Proceedings of the 19th Congress (1998) of the Union Européenne des Arabisants et Islamisants (UEAI)*, ed. H. Kilpatrick, S. Leder, and B. Martel-Thoumian (Halle, in press).

percent, Syria 30 percent, Kufa 30 percent). And contrary to what one might have expected,[43] the number of important non-Arab scholars is as a rule not higher in the centers of jurisprudence situated *outside* the Arabian peninsula. Non-Arab scholars formed merely a minority in certain centers outside Arabia, while dominating certain centers inside Arabia.

If one calculates the proportion of Arab and non-Arab scholars per generation of scholars, in the first generation there were 63 percent Arabs versus 37 percent non-Arabs. In the second generation we find 40 percent Arabs and 60 percent non-Arabs, almost the opposite. In the third generation the proportion again reverses itself and the Arabs enjoy a numerical superiority, with 63 percent. In the fourth generation, which includes only a few scholars, the ratio is equal but too small to be significant. These results contradict the opinion expressed in the Muslim tradition quoted at the beginning of this article, namely, that after the generation of the Companions legal knowledge passed to the *mawālī* in nearly all regions of the Islamic kingdom.

How can we explain the difference between the impression of Muslim and Western scholars on the role of non-Arab scholars and the results of the statistical investigation? As far as the Muslim view is concerned, it seems likely that opinions such as that of ʿAbd al-Raḥmān b. Zayd b. Aslam or of traditions such as those about al-Zuhrī and the caliph ʿAbd al-Malik have their origin in the conflict between the Arabs and the *mawālī* which was a major issue from the end of the first until the beginning of the third Islamic century.[44] The Arabs, who considered themselves the superior race, feared and opposed the growing influence of non-Arabs in the kingdom. Such Arab anxiety is articulated in the traditions reporting the dialogue between al-Zuhrī and ʿAbd al-Malik. The *mawālī*, on the other hand, gave expression to their growing self-assurance by pointing to their achievements and to the services they were supplying to Islam. This seems to be reflected in the statement of ʿAbd al-Raḥmān b. Zayd, himself a *mawlā*.

Western scholarship seems to have been impressed by Muslim traditions which highlight the leading role played by *mawālī* scholars and by the fact that some outstanding jurists and scholars, e.g. al-Ḥasan al-Baṣrī, Abū Ḥanīfa and Muḥammad al-Shaybānī, were

43 See G.H.A. Juynboll, *Muslim Tradition. Studies in chronology, provenance and authorship of early hadith* (Cambridge, 1983), 132-33.

44 Goldziher's chapter "ʿArab und ʿAğam" remains a useful summary of the conflict between Arabs and *mawālī*. Cf. his *Studien*, I, 101-46.

mawālī. The error is a result of generalization. But why were the many important Arab scholars overlooked? One reason may be that Western scholars tended to think very little of Arab civilization and of the cultural capacities of Arabs at the time of the rise of Islam, and could not imagine that the flowering of Islamic culture could be the work of Arabs. It had to have been the members of the pre-Islamic advanced civilizations, above all the Hellenistic, i.e. "Western", one, who were responsible for the achievements of Islamic culture and civilization.[45]

The Cultural Background of the Legal Scholars of Non-Arab Descent

We come now to the second set of questions posed in the introduction: Where did the non-Arab scholars come from? To what extent were they integrated into Arab-Muslim society? Information on the cultural background of non-Arab legal scholars is scarce. Only on occasion do the sources explicitly state where a person of non-Arab descent or his ancestors came from. Mostly, the sources indicate merely that someone was the *mawlā* of a tribe, clan or individual. In such cases, his name, or the names of his ancestors, can provide a clue as to the probable region of origin. Names of early Muslim scholars have only seldom been studied for such a purpose.[46] The following conclusions should therefore be taken as provisional; they need to be verified on the basis of a larger database.

When comparing the names belonging to scholars of Arab and non-Arab descent living in the first two centuries AH, several peculiarities are noticeable: (1) names of the non-Arabs are mostly shorter, i.e. they lack the extensive genealogy borne by many Arabs mentioned in the sources. Sometimes even a father's name is lacking. (2) The use of the *kunya* in the genealogy is more characteristic for the names of *mawālī* than of Arabs. The *kunya* contained in the genealogy of a *mawlā* often replaces a foreign name, and we can assume that the ancestor who bore the *kunya* had converted to Islam. (3) In the genealogies of *mawālī* scholars certain names occur which are not used by Arabs; if the origin of these names could be identified, the cultural origin of the scholar in question would be determined. (4) Some names, although seemingly Arabic, are typical for *mawālī* and are rarely used by "true Arabs". These observations can be helpful in cases in which it is uncertain

[45] Several examples of disparaging remarks on the abilities of the Arabs are found in Goldziher, *Studien*, I, 108, 109, 112.

[46] An exception is R.W. Bulliet, *Conversion to Islam in the Medieval Period. An Essay in Quantitative History* (Cambridge and London, 1979).

whether an individual should be classified as being of Arab or non-Arab descent. In the following, I present some examples of *mawālī* names taken from my sample.

Names which can be identified as Iranian: Farrūkh, Hurmuz, Mihrān, Markabūdh, Zūṭā, Māh, Arṭabān, ʿUdhāfir, Tayrawayh,[47] Kaysān, Suhrāb, Sīrīn, Sanbar,[48] Jarmūz,[49] or al-Mājashūn (or Mājishūn), which is a nickname.[50] Names like Jurayj and Tadrus are obviously of Greek origin (Georgós, Theōdoros); a name like Yaḥmad may be Indian;[51] Ṭarkhān is Turkish.[52] The name Qarqara or Jarja (two different spellings of the same name) is not Arabic;[53] I could not determine, however, to which language it belongs.

Many *mawālī*, however, had Arabic or seemingly Arabic names which they adopted or received either when they were integrated into an Arab family or upon conversion. This makes it difficult to determine their origin. But even in such cases names can be informative. As mentioned, among the *mawālī* certain names occur with a higher frequency than among Arabs and seem to be typical, even if these names are Arabic and were also used by Arabs, e.g. Yasār, Maysara, Maymūn, Dīnār, Nāfiʿ and Muslim. Yasār (happiness, prosperity)

---

47 Cf. Ph. Gignoux, *Iranisches Personennamenbuch, Band II: Mitteliranische Personennamen, Faszikel 2: Noms propres sassanides en moyen-perse épigraphique* (Wien 1986), no. 352: Farrox, no. 448: Hormizd, no. 630: Mihrān, no. 575: Mardbūd, no. 589: Mardaybūd, no. 1088: Zōtiy, no. 510: Māh, no. 125: Ardavān, no. 990: Vēh-Šābuhr, no. 306: Dārāy-veh. I am indebted to R.E. Emmerick (Hamburg) for his advice concerning the names which I suspected to be of Persian origin.

48 Cf. F. Justi, *Iranisches Namenbuch* (Marburg 1895 [Hildesheim 1963]), 152 a: Kaitān/Kaidān, 312b-313a: Suhrāb (also Gignoux, *Iranisches Namenbuch II*, no. 868: Šahrāb), 302b-303a: Šīrīn, 281b, 282a: Σαμβαρης / Σαναβαρης.

49 Probably a misreading of Hurmuz or Hurmuzd, also given as an alternative in the sources, cf. Ibn Ḥajar, *Tahdhīb*, VII, 153-54; al-Bukhārī, *al-Taʾrīkh al-kabīr* (Beirut, n.d.), III/2, 244 (no. 2287).

50 According to Ibn Mardawayh in his *Taʾrīkh Iṣbahān*, the first bearer of this nickname, Abū Salama Dīnār or Maymūn al-Mājashūn, the grandfather of ʿAbd al-ʿAzīz b. ʿAbd Allāh, originated from Iṣbahān. See al-Samʿānī, *al-Ansāb* (Hyderabad, 1962ff.), V, 107; Ibn Manẓūr, *Mukhtaṣar*, XXVIII, 43-44; and al-Mizzī, *Tahdhīb al-kamāl fī asmāʾ al-rijāl* (Beirut, 1992), XVIII, 155.

51 The name of the grandfather of al-Awzāʿī. According to some traditions he was descended from captives of Sind. Cf. Ibn Ḥajar, *Tahdhīb*, VI, 239; Ibn Manẓūr, *Mukhtaṣar*, XIV, 313 ff.

52 Cf. J. Th. Zenker, *Türkisch-Arabisch-Persisches Handwörterbuch* (Leipzig, 1866 [Hildesheim, 1979], I-II, 277, 597; G. Doerfer, *Türkische und mongolische Elemente im Neupersischen*, vol. 2 (Wiesbaden, 1965), 495 ff.

53 This is the name of the grandfather of the Meccan scholar Muslim b. Khālid, whose epithet, "al-Zanjī", indicates that he may have been of African origin; the sources differ, however, as to why he had this *laqab*. Cf. Mizzī, *Tahdhīb*, XVII, 508-09, 512.

seems to be—at least in some cases—the Arabic translation of the Persian name Pērōz (happy, successful).[54] This may also be the case with Maysara and Maymūn, which have a similar meaning. Other names, like Farrūkh, have a meaning in Arabic,[55] but were not names used by Arabs and were homonyms of foreign names.[56] Dīnār (from the Roman *denarius*) and Nāfiʿ (useful) seem to have been popular as names for slaves even if they were borne also by some Arabs. Patrons may also have given the name Muslim to a converted slave, and newly converted fathers obviously favored this name for one of their male children. [57]

My investigation into the origin of the scholars of non-Arab descent, based on their genealogies and on explicit information in the sources concerning their origin, has produced the following results: All of the six *mawālī* active in Medina had a Persian background. Among the eight Meccan *mawālī* there was one of Nubian or Ethiopian origin (ʿAṭāʾ)[58] and one Berber (ʿIkrima). The other six are more difficult to identify: two of them had an ancestor with a Greek-Christian name and could have come from Syria or Egypt (Abū Zubayr, Ibn Jurayj), one may have had a Persian father (Ibn Abī Najīḥ), another an Ethiopian background (Mujāhid),[59] a third came from the Yemen and could have had Persian, Ethiopian or other roots (ʿAmr b. Dīnār), and the origin of the last (Muslim b. Khālid) may be African.[60] Of the seven Yemenite

54 See the case of al-Ḥasan al-Baṣrī's father (H. Ritter, "Ḥasan al-Baṣrī", in *EI*², III, 247) and the father of Sulaymān (Ibn Manẓūr, *Mukhtaṣar*, X, 193).

55 The meaning is: "Ears of wheat of which the final condition had become apparent and of which the grain has become organized and compact". E.W. Lane, *Arabic-English Lexicon* (London, 1877), II, 2363. The Arabic word may be of Persian origin.

56 In our sample the name Farrūkh is borne by individuals who seem to have had a Persian background (see Ibn Qutayba, *Maʿārif*, 274). On the Persian name "Farrox" see note 47. The use of homonym names was noted already by Goldziher, *Studien*, I, 133.

57 This does not mean that the bearers of these names had always been non-Arabs, non-Muslims or slaves by descent.

58 According to Abū Dāwūd al-Sijistānī in Ibn Ḥajar, *Tahdhīb*, VII, 200 he was a *nūbī*; according to Ibn Manẓūr, *Mukhtaṣar*, XXII, 219 he was a *ḥabashī*. For a detailed biography of ʿAṭāʾ with a discussion of the reliability of the information on him, see Motzki, *Anfänge*, 219-33.

59 His father's name, Jabr, is common among Arabs, but it may be a homonym of the Ethiopian name Gäbr (servant). My colleagues, Dr. Veronika Six (Hamburg) and Prof. Dr. Manfred Kropp (Mainz), confirmed my assumption that the name could be Ethiopian. There is also an old Jewish name Geber (cf. L. Koehler/W. Baumgartner, *Lexicon in veteris testamenti libros* (Leiden, 1958), 168; 1 Kings 4: 13, 19), but I could not determine whether the name continued to be used. See also below note 75.

60 See note 53.

scholars, four or five are regarded as *abnāʾ al-furs*, descendents of the Sassanian occupation forces who stayed in Yemen during the last decades of the sixth and the first decades of the seventh century CE; the others were *mawālī* (Ṭāwūs, Maʿmar, ʿAbd al-Razzāq) of probably Persian origin.[61] Among the four non-Arab scholars of Syria we find one with a Persian ancestry (Maymūn),[62] another whose grandfather originated from the Indus valley (al-Awzāʿī),[63] a third with a Persian or Indian background (Makḥūl),[64] while the last came perhaps from a Jewish family of uncertain geographical origin (Sulaymān b. Mūsā).[65] Of the four Egyptians one can be identified as Persian (al-Layth),[66] another as Nubian (Yazīd b. Abī Ḥabīb).[67] I could not determine the descent of the other two. It is striking that among the important Muslim jurists of Syria and Egypt during the first two centuries none were obviously of Syrian, Greek or Coptic Christian origin. The ethnic background of the eight *mawālī* of Kufa is difficult to determine. Two of them were of Persian descent,[68] and one was black.[69] The origin of the other five remains obscure, although I imagine that most of them came from Mesopotamia and the eastern regions of the former Sassanid empire which had been conquered by tribes who had settled at Kufa. Amongst the thirteen *mawālī* scholars of Baṣra, nine clearly had Persian roots,[70] and three others may have had the same back-

---

61 Ṭāwūs b. Kaysān was a *mawlā* of the *abnāʾ al-furs* or of the Banū Ḥamdān (see Ibn Ḥajar, *Tahdhīb*, V, 8; Ibn Qutayba, *Maʿārif*, 258. Goldziher's statement that he originated from the *abnāʾ* themselves [*Studien*, I, 113, note 3] is not substantiated by the sources which I have consulted). Maʿmar b. Rāshid, *mawlā* of the Azd, probably had Persian roots because he originated from Baṣra. ʿAbd al-Razzāq is considered by most sources as a *mawlā* of the Banū Ḥimyar, but in Ibn Manẓūr, *Mukhtaṣar*, XV, 98 he is identified as a descendant of the *abnāʾ*. Both can be true. There are other cases of *abnāʾ* who had been *mawālī*, e.g. Mūsā b. Bādhān, the son of the governor of the Sassanids in Yemen, is said to have been a *mawlā* of the Banū Jumaḥ or Makhzūm or Madhhij (see Mizzī, *Tahdhīb*, XXII, 5; Ibn Ḥajar, *Tahdhīb*, III, 216-18).

62 According to al-Shīrāzī, *Ṭabaqāt*, 77 and Ibn Manẓūr, *Mukhtaṣar*, XXVI, 60-68 his father was among the captives of Iṣṭakhr.

63 According to Shīrāzī, *Ṭabaqāt*, 76 he belonged to the captives of the Yemenites and according to Abū Zurʿa al-Dimashqī he belonged to the captives of Sind (Ibn Ḥajar, *Tahdhīb*, VI, 239).

64 The information on Makḥūl is contradictory: Sind (cf. al-Shīrāzī, *Ṭabaqāt*, 75; Ibn Qutayba, *Maʿārif*, 257), Persia (Ibn Ḥajar, *Tahdhīb*, X, 291).

65 This conclusion is based solely on the names Sulaymān and Mūsā.

66 "*Naḥnu min al-furs min Iṣbahān*", Ibn Ḥajar, *Tahdhīb*, VIII, 459.

67 Cf. Dhahabī, *Tadhkirat al-ḥuffāẓ* (Beirut, n.d.), I, 129.

68 Sulaymān b. Mihrān (Ibn Ḥajar, *Tahdhīb*, IV, 222-26) and Abū Ḥanīfa (Ibn Ḥajar, *Tahdhīb*, X, 449-52; J. Schacht, "Abū Ḥanīfa al-Nuʿmān", in *EI*[2], I, 123).

69 Saʿīd b. Jubayr (Ibn Qutayba, *Maʿārif*, 253).

70 Al-Ḥasan al-Baṣrī, Muḥammad b. Sīrīn, Abū l-ʿĀliya Rufayʿ, Ayyūb b. Abī Tamīma, ʿAbd Allāh b. ʿAwn, Hishām b. ʿAbd Allāh, Dāwūd b. Abī Hind,

ground.[71] The origin of the remaining one (Muslim b. Yasār) is obscure. Of the two *mawālī* scholars of Khurāsān, one is of Persian, the other of Turkish descent.[72]

Most of the scholars of non-Arab descent have an Iranian background. This is certain for 50 percent (26 individuals) and probable for 21 percent (eleven individuals). This gives a total of 71 percent. If we add the scholars of Indian and Turkish origin, the proportion rises to nearly 77 percent. Just under 10 percent came from Ethiopia, Nubia and Northern Africa to the west of Egypt (five individuals). Less than 10 percent (five individuals) had, or can be presumed to have had, a Syrian or Egyptian Christian (two scholars) or a Jewish background (three individuals). The ethnic, cultural or religious origin of 12 percent of the non-Arab scholars remains completely obscure. [73]

How close were these scholars to their origins? Answering this question may give us an impression as to the degree of their integration into Arab-Muslim society. The question can be answered without hesitation in cases in which concrete information on an individual, his ancestors and the circumstances of their entrance into Muslim society is available. This is, however, often not the case. In the absence of such information, conclusions can be drawn from the genealogy, if it contains names that are foreign or typical of slaves and *mawālī*, and from the dates of a scholar's life. Here, however, a problem arises: Did an individual give up his name upon conversion and adopt an Islamic name instead, as usually happens in modern times, or did he keep his original name and give Islamic names only to his children born after conversion?

The fact that in several genealogies of *mawālī* the Islamic names end with a *kunya*, the bearer of which has a foreign or typical *mawālī* name, speaks in favor of the assumption that in principal there was no change of names upon conversion. The new convert adopted only an Islamic or Arabic *kunya* and often (not always) his descendants used

Ḥumayd al-Ṭawīl, ʿUthmān b. Sulaymān.

[71] Yūnus b. ʿUbayd, Ashʿath b. ʿAbd al-Malik, Ismāʿīl b. Muslim. Their descent is not mentioned in the biographical literature, and also their genealogies give no clue as to their origin. We can, however, assume that they originated from the Eastern provinces, because they were *mawālī* of Arab tribes garrisoned in Mesopotamia and active in the conquests of the East.

[72] Of Persian descent: ʿAṭā" b. Abī Muslim originated from Balkh; the name of his father was (according to some) Maysara, cf. Ibn Ḥajar, *Tahdhīb*, VII, 212. Of Turkish origin: ʿAbd Allāh b. al-Mubārak (his father was *turkī*, his mother *khwarizmiyya*), Ibn Ḥajar, *Tahdhīb*, V, 384.

[73] This is more than 100 percent because the Christian and Jewish scholars are included in the categories of geographical origin.

only this *kunya*. Examples are: Rabīʿa b. Abī ʿAbd al-Raḥmān [Farrūkh], ʿAbd al-ʿAzīz b. ʿAbd Allāh b. Abī Salama [Dīnār/ Maymūn], ʿAṭāʾ b. Abī Rabāḥ [Aslam], ʿAbd Allāh b. Abī Najiḥ [Yasār], al-Ḥasan b. Abī l-Ḥasan [Yasār] al-Baṣrī, Ayyūb b. Abī Tamīma [Kaysān], Hishām b. Abī ʿAbd Allāh [Sanbar], Dāwūd b. Abī Hind [Dīnār], Ḥumayd b. Abī Ḥumayd [Tayrawayh/ Ṭarkhān].

In cases in which no *kunya* is used, we can adopt the rule that the individual who comes after the last bearer of an Arab name converted to Islam. For example, the genealogy of the famous jurist Abū Ḥanīfa is as follows: Abū Ḥanīfa al-Nuʿmān b. Thābit b. Zūṭā b. Māh. He and his father Thābit have Arabic names, whereas his grandfather and great-grandfather have Persian names. According to my rule, his grandfather entered Arab-Islamic society and gave his son an Arabic name. This is corroborated by reports in the sources that his grandfather originated from Kābul, became a slave of the Arabian tribe Taym-Allāh b. Thaʿlaba, converted to Islam and was set free.[74]

As for names used by Arabs but more typical of *mawalī*, like Yasār, Maysara, Maymūn, Nāfiʿ, Dīnār and an Islamic name like Muslim, we can assume that the bearer of the name entered Arab society as a slave and received his Arabic or Islamic name from his owner in place of his original foreign name; or, alternatively, that one of his descendants changed the foreign name into an Arabic one.[75]

The following examples illustrate three cases of scholars who represent different types of integration into Arab-Islamic society: converts of the first, second and third generation.

Nāfiʿ, the mawlā of Ibn ʿUmar. His father's name is unknown. According to the earliest and probably most reliable information, Nāfiʿ became a slave of Ibn ʿUmar during the conquest of the Iranian town of Naysābūr and the surrounding regions in the year 30 AH/651 CE, a

---

74 Al-Khaṭīb al-Baghdādī, *Taʾrīkh Baghdād* (Beirut n.d.), XIII, 324-25 (according to a grandson of Abū Ḥanīfa). Cf. also Schacht, "Abū Ḥanīfa", 123. For the rule, see also Bulliet, *Conversion*, 19.

75 For an example of a descendant who changed a foreign name into an Arabic one, cf. Goldziher, *Studien*, I, 133, note 2. The name Yasār may—in some cases at least—also be a homonym of a foreign name; possibly there was an Aramaic equivalent of the Hebrew *yashar* (just, upright, pious, cf. Koehler/Baumgartner, *Lexicon*, 414). That this name (and e.g. the name Jabr, too, see above note 59) was considered as foreign when the bearer of it was a slave or *mawlā* is illustrated by the traditions on the Jewish and Christian "informants" of Muḥammad. On these traditions cf. Cl. Gilliot, "Les 'informateurs' juifs et chrétiens de Muḥammad. Reprise d'un problème traité par Aloys Sprenger et Theodor Nöldeke", in *Jerusalem Studies in Arabic and Islam* 22 (1998), 84-126. A slave could, of course, also receive a typical Arabic name.

campaign in which Ibn ʿUmar participated. Since Nāfiʿ died in 117 AH/735 CE he must have been a small child, perhaps an infant, at the time he became the property of Ibn ʿUmar.[76] He surely got his Arabic name from his patron, in whose home at Medina he must have grown up. Consequently, he could not have brought with him much knowledge of his culture of origin. This is one of the few examples of a scholar who entered Muslim society himself.

Al-Ḥasan al-Baṣrī. The father of this famous scholar was taken prisoner during the conquest of Iraq. He was brought to Medina, received an Arabic name in place of his Persian one, and was later liberated by his owner, an Arab-Muslim woman, surely only after his conversion to Islam. Al-Ḥasan was born of his father's marriage at Medina to a slave woman who was later liberated, and he grew up in Wādī al-Qurā, north of Medina. In this and most other cases in which the father of a scholar became a member of Arab-Muslim society, the scholar himself received his education in an Arab-Muslim environment, which makes it highly unlikely that he retained much of the culture of his ancestors.

ʿAbd al-Malik b. ʿAbd al-ʿAzīz b. Jurayj. His grandfather's name was Greek, Jurayj, i.e. Georg(os). The fact that he gave his son a Muslim name—ʿAbd al-ʿAzīz—suggests that the grandfather himself had joined Arab-Muslim society and become a Muslim. This conclusion, based on ʿAbd al-Malik's genealogy, is corroborated by the information of the sources that his grandfather had been a Byzantine slave owned by Umm Ḥabīb bint Jubayr, the wife of ʿAbd al-ʿAzīz b. ʿAbd Allāh b. Khālid b. Asīd who belonged to the Banū Umayya.[77] Since the descendants of Jurayj are known as *mawālī* of the clan of Khālid b. Asīd, we can assume that Jurayj was freed after he had converted to Islam. Thus, this Meccan scholar represents an individual whose integration into Muslim society began already with his grandfather. ʿAbd al-Malik's father, ʿAbd al-ʿAzīz, was already regarded as a Muslim scholar and traditionist.[78]

If one classifies the scholars according to their date of entrance into Arab-Muslim society, it appears that only a few were first generation converts. Our sample includes no more than five such individuals.[79] Most scholars belong to the second generation, which means that entry

---

[76] See Motzki, "*Quo vadis*", 55-57.
[77] See for his biography Motzki, *Anfänge*, 239-54.
[78] See Ibn Ḥajar, *Tahdhīb*, VI, 333.
[79] Nāfiʿ, *mawlā* of Ibn ʿUmar, ʿIkrima, *mawlā* of Ibn ʿAbbās, Makḥūl, Maymūn b. Mihrān and Rafīʿ b. Mihrān.

into Arab-Muslim society had already been made by their fathers. This is certain in the case of twenty scholars. Thirteen others, finally, belong to the third generation of *mawālī*. For the rest the information is too scant to allow a classification. I could not find any indication that an important early legal scholar received his education, not to mention a legal education, in his culture of origin and afterwards became a Muslim jurist. This may be due to the scarcity of information provided by the sources. I imagine that in towns in which the Arabs and their clients lived in close proximity to a non-Muslim majority, as in Fusṭāṭ, converts continued to have contacts with their former co-religionists, and there are indeed some examples of this;[80] on the other hand I also imagine that converts were expelled from their former religious communities, that contact with them was avoided, and that converts tried to demonstrate the sincerity of their conversions by breaking their relations with their former co-religionists and avoiding anything that could be interpreted as sympathy for their former belief. In any case, among the scholars included in my sample, there are only a few who may have grown up in a mainly non-Muslim milieu.

Conclusion

Western scholars have attached great importance to the role played, quantitatively and qualitatively, by scholars of non-Arab descent in the formative period of Islamic scholarship in general and jurisprudence in particular. A statistical investigation based on a sample of important Muslim jurists of the first two Islamic centuries, however, lends no support to this assumption. "True Arabs" constitute the majority among the selected group. Equally unfounded is the tacit assumption that the number of scholars of non-Arab descent was higher in the centers situated in the regions of ancient high cultures outside the Arabian peninsula—regarded as crucial in the formative period of Islamic jurisprudence—than it was in Arabia. Although my sample is small, I predict that the result will not be substantially different if a much larger

[80] For example, ʿAbd Allāh b. Wahb, who is considered a Mālikī scholar by Shīrāzī (*Ṭabaqāt*, 150) and is not contained in my sample. According to a tradition only rarely encountered in the sources, he learned writing and reading from a Christian (cf. Miklos Muranyi, *ʿAbd Allāh b. Wahb (125/743-197/812) Leben und Werk. Al-Muwaṭṭaʾ, Kitāb al-muḥāraba herausgegeben und kommentiert* (Wiesbaden 1992), 18). I wonder, however, whether the learning of reading and writing—or even attendance at a Christian primary school—is likely to have imparted the legal knowledge which Islamic jurisprudence is assumed to have borrowed from Christianity, Roman or Roman provincial law.

database is analyzed (even if the *ḥadīth* scholars are included).[81] This has to be checked by further investigations. It is desirable to study the question of the number and impact of *mawālī* scholars in other fields of Islamic scholarship, such as *tafsīr, ḥadīth* and grammar.

According to several Islamicists, Islamic law inherited many solutions from Roman, Roman provincial, Christian or Jewish law.[82] Some of these scholars considered the early Muslim jurists of non-Arab origin as responsible for the purported borrowings. The investigation of the ethnic origin of the non-Arab scholars contained in my sample shows, however, that three quarters of them had an eastern background and came from the regions of the former Sassanian empire. They can hardly have been responsible for Islamic borrowings from Roman and Roman provincial law.[83] Scholars with clearly Christian or Jewish roots are very few in number. Additionally, most of these scholars are Muslims of the second and third generation, whereas most first-generation scholars entered Arab-Muslim society as children and thus grew up in an Arab-Muslim environment cut off from their ethnic roots. These findings lend no support to the assumption that scholars of non-Arab origins brought the purported borrowings with them from their native legal systems.

On the basis of the quantitative analysis presented here I cannot claim that there was no case of borrowing by a non-Arab scholar from the law in which he or his ancestors grew up. The results of this study suggest only that we can no longer take for granted the idea that scholars of non-Arab descent were the most natural vehicles of borrowings from pre-Islamic non-Arab legal systems. It is certainly possible that there were scholars who received their education in their culture of origin, then converted and introduced legal solutions of their former law systems into Islamic jurisprudence. Such cases must, however, be demonstrated. I do not know of such a case from the first two centuries AH.

In principle, the results of this study do not affect the theory that Islamic law borrowed resources from other legal systems. The results do suggest that we should give greater attention to the exact manner in which a proposed borrowing took place. If it is claimed, for example,

---

81 See note 42.
82 See note 10.
83 Schacht's assumption that this sort of borrowing came into Islamic jurisprudence via the Hellenistic rhetorical education can be dismissed since it "never imparted much legal knowledge", cf. Crone, *Roman*, 9.

that the maxim "*al-walad li-l-firāsh*" was borrowed from the Roman legal maxim "*pater est quem iustae nuptiae demonstrant*",[84] it should be shown that the first Muslim jurists who circulated the maxim were non-Arabs who originated from the former Byzantine territory.

[84] The Roman origin of the Islamic maxim has been proposed by Goldziher (*Studien*, I, 188) and Schacht (*Origins*, 181-82). Crone (*Roman*, 10-11, 105-06) rejected it, but her argument that there is also a Jewish parallel does not necessarily exclude a Roman origin. On this maxim see also Motzki, *Anfänge*, 76, 83, esp. 115-20 and U. Rubin, "'*Al-walad li-l-firāsh*'. On the Islamic Campaign against '*zinā*'", in *Studia Islamica* 78 (1993), 5-26.

8

THE JUDICIARY (*QĀḌĪS*) AS A GOVERNMENTAL-ADMINISTRATIVE TOOL IN EARLY ISLAM

Irit Abramski-Bligh

According to Islamic theory, the *sharīʿa* (holy law) is independent of any political control. Even the caliph, the head of the Islamic community, is accountable to the *sharīʿa* and must obey and protect it. Theoretically, this belief confers a special role on the *ʿulamāʾ*, the scholarly guardians and interpreters of the *sharīʿa*. From the earliest days of the Islamic polity, the *ʿulamāʾ* have enjoyed de jure autonomy and independence in religious questions from the arbitrary will of the caliph.[1]

In practice, the status and authority of the scholars as an organized group was not formalized until the Ottoman period, when they were forced into a bureaucratic governmental framework.[2] But even under the Rāshidūn, the Umayyads, and the ʿAbbāsids, various official religious positions were created and staffed, including *qāḍī* (judge), *muḥtasib* (supervisor of morals and the market-place), *muʿallim* or *mukattib* (schoolteacher) and *mudarris al-fiqh* (lecturer in legal science). Some who filled these posts, however, may not really

---

1) See, for example, Abū Yūsuf, *Kitāb al-kharāj* in A. Ben Shemesh, *Taxation in Islam* (London, 1969) III, p. 35; Cl. Cahen, "The Body Politic" in G. von Grunebaum (ed.) *Unity and Variety in Muslim Civilization* (Chicago Univ. Press, 1975) pp. 137, 143; I. Lapidus, "The Separation of State and Religion in the Development of Early Islamic Society," *International Journal of Middle East Studies* VI (1975).

2) H. A. R. Gibb and H. Bowen, *Islamic Society and the West*, vol. 1, pt. 2 (Oxford Univ. Press, London, 1957) pp. 79-138; N. Itzkowitz, "Eighteenth Century Ottoman Realities," *Studia Islamica* 16 (1962) pp. 73-94.

have been *ʿulamāʾ*; furthermore, the offices frequently involved nonreligious work as well. In addition, there were *ʿulamāʾ* in completely nonreligious offices.

In this paper, we aim to trace the entry of the *ʿulamāʾ* into the governmental-administrative system of early Islam (up to 320/932), using the example of the *qāḍī*, the first religious functionary to appear.

In the Umayyad and early ʿAbbāsid periods, the office of *qāḍī* had not yet been rationalized as a clearly religious-judical post. *Qāḍīs* were frequently assigned a variety of nonjudicial functions, and *ʿulamāʾ* would often receive dual or multiple appointments to administrative as well as judicial or religious positions. Furthermore, not every *qāḍī* was a genuine *ʿālim*.

In any case, most *ʿulamāʾ* in the early Islamic era remained outside the government hierarchy as uninstitutionalized men of learning, supporting themselves through trade, crafts and other secular occupations. Some refused governmental offices on principle, even under threat of punishment.[3]) One cannot speak about the *ʿulamāʾ* as a distinct interest group or organized social elite in early Islamic times. Lapidus calls them "an administrative and social, as well as a religious elite," but admits that they "were not a distinct class, but a category of persons overlapping other classes and social divisions permeating the whole society,"[4]) even in the later Middle Ages.

The independence and rising status of the *qāḍī* gained formal sanction in the bureaucratic centralization and rationalization under Hārūn al-Rashiīd. Then, under the Muʿtazilite caliphs (198/813-233/847), the political role of the *qāḍī* became even more crucial. Respected *ʿulamāʾ* had often been used to buttress the legitimacy of

3) ʿAlī b. Khalīl al-Ṭarābulusī, *Muʿīn al-ḥukkām* (Egypt, 1973) p. 8; Muḥammad b. Khalaf al-Wakīʿ, *Akhbār al-Q7ḍāt* (Cairo, 1950) I, pp. 7-13, 22. For an analysis of this type of tradition see: N. J. Coulson, "Doctrine and Practice in Islamic Law," *Bulletin of the School of Oriental and African Studies* XVIII (1956) pt. 2, pp. 211-226; also: idem, *Conflicts and Tensions in Islamic Jurisprudence* (Chicago, 1969) pp. 58-76.

4) Ira Lapidus, *Muslim Cities in the Later Middle Ages* (Cambridge, 1967) p. 108.

both Umayyad and ʿAbbāsid rule, but the novel attempt to impose religious-ideological uniformity throughout the Islamic realm, and the Muʿtazilite emphasis on the primacy of reason, made the *qāḍī* indispensible.

After the caliphs failed in their attempt to impose Muʿtazilite doctrines, the position of the *qāḍī* was made equal to that of other influential officials in the governmental administration.

The crystalization of the administrative institutions in general and of the *qāḍī* in particular, however, was accompanied by an undercurrent of rivalry within the ruling elite for influence upon the caliph and decision-making power in the empire. The most bitter rivalry developed between the head of the bureaucracy, the vizier, and the head of the *ʿulamāʾ*, the chief *qāḍī*, who was incorporated in the governmental machinery (see the detailed description of the office below).

The military, which constituted the most essential part of the ruling elite, stood above this competition since they possessed real power. On the other hand, both the *kuttāb* (clerks) and the *ʿulamāʾ* represented the learned, professionally trained intellectuals. The *kuttāb* were influenced by pre-Islamic, mostly Iranian culture, whereas the *ʿulamāʾ* were trained basically in Islamic religious studies. These two groups competed for recognition of their capacity to establish rules for effective government. Through this competition both institutions (the vizierate and the chief judiciary) were strengthened and crystalized. In the period under consideration (41/661-320/932), which also coincided with the formation of classical Islamic institutions, there were certain stages in which one of the two rivals held the edge. This was due to the combination of historical circumstances. In the Muʿtazilite period (198/813-233/847) the *qāḍī* was caliph's most indispensible official for religious purposes; in the period from al-Muʿtaḍid to al-Muqtadir (279/892-320-932), during the attempt to recover the caliphal treasury, the vizier, who was deliberately picked from the ranks of financial administration, became the most vital governmental aide to the caliph. In this article we devote our attention to only one of the two rival forces, the judiciary, and attempt to review the development of the institution from its inception to its crystalization. Emphasized here are the specific characteristics of the office which, though held by an *ʿālim* (who represented the *sharīʿa* and stood above any temporal authority), still became a governmental tool.

Nonjudicial Functions of Umayyad and Early ʿAbbāsid Qāḍīs

Government under Islam did not recognize any separation of powers and worked according to the principle of *tafwīḍ*, delegation of powers from a single supreme authority, the caliph. Any official could be entrusted with various types of functions simultaneously. The *qāḍī*, as *nāʾib* (delegate) of the caliph, was entrusted with nonjudicial as well as judicial duties, especially in the period prior to the reform of Hārūn al-Rashīd. There were *qāḍīs* in posts ranging from *amīr* (governor of a province) to *ʿarīf* (tribal administrator).

To what extent did the Arabic term *qāḍī* denote general administrative as well as judicial responsibilities? On the basis of the *Qurʾān* the word *qāḍāʾ* can be understood as God's eternal *decision* or *decree* concerning all beings (later interpreted as "predestination").[5]) But the root *q ḍ y* literally implies "to consumate" or "to carry out one's duty" as well as "to determine" and "to decide."[6]) Thus the term *qāḍī* provided a much more inclusive and suitable description of the general representative of the authority than the restricted, older term *ḥakam* (literally "arbitrator", later "judge" as well). Since the judgment of a *qāḍī* once uttered could never be withdrawn, the

---

5) For example: Qurʾān, II, 117: "*fa-idhā qaḍā amr (an) fa-innamā yaqūlu lahu: kun! fa-yakūnu*—When He decreeth a thing, He saith unto it only: Be! and it is." Marmaduke Pickthall, *The Meaning of the Glorious Koran* (London, 1930), cf. also: II, 47, XIX, 35, XL, 68; XIX, 71. For other examples see entry "qaḍāʾ" in: Muḥammad Fuʾād ʿAbd al-Bāqī, *Al-muʿjam al-mufahras li-alfāẓ al-Qurʾān al-karīm* (Cairo, 1364 [1944]).

6) Ibn Manẓūr, *Lisān al-ʿArab* (Beirut, 1956); E. W. Lane, *An Arabic-English Lexicon* (London 1863-93), Suppl. Additional connotations of *qaḍā* which might be helpful are: "completed," "accomplished," "fully performed."

Qurʾānic term *qāḍāʾ* expressed his judicial functions very well; the additional connotations of "consummation" and "carrying out" (*qāḍāʾ bi-maʿnā al-ʿamal*) applied to his nonjudicial functions.[7]

ʿĀMIL (TAX COLLECTOR) AND AMĪR (GOVERNOR). The clearest example of the amalgamation of executive and judicial powers was the frequent appointment of *qāḍīs* as governors and tax collectors. This practice was especially prevalent in the pre-Umayyad and early Umayyad periods, before the classification of powers became more specialized, but there are examples from the ʿAbbāsid period as well, especially before the judicial system was centralized by Hārūn al-Rashīd. In the period of al-Manṣūr and al-Mahdī, the combined post of *imāra* (governorship) and *qāḍāʾ* was still mentioned.[8] This is not surprising, because even the division of responsibilities between *amīr* and *ʿāmil* was not yet clear-cut. Judicial functions were merely an added responsibility given to the delegate of the authority.

An *amīr* was more essential for good administration than a *qāḍī*, because an *amīr* could often manage without a *qāḍī*. Indeed, provinces sometimes lacked a *qāḍī* for several years,[9] but there are no similar cases of vacant *amīr* before the reform of Hārūn al-Rashīd. The *amīr* was usually appointed first, and he in turn chose the *ʿāmil* and the *qāḍī*.

The *amīr* was first and foremost a military commander. By assuming the office, the *qāḍī* became a member of the military elite with supreme authority in the province. Indeed, we know of *qāḍīs* who did actually serve as military commanders. For example, in Muʿāwiyaʾs reign, Faḍāla b. ʿUbayd al-Anṣārī was in charge of both *ghazw*

7) Cf., D. G. Dannhauer, *Untersuchungen zur frühen Geschichte des Qāḍī-amtes* (Bonn, 1975) p. 44; E. Tyan, "Ḳāḍī," *EI²*; Margoliouth, "Omar's instructions to the Ḳāḍī," *Journal of the Royal Asiatic Society* XXXIV (1910) pp. 312-313.

8) Wakīʿ, II, 60, 80, 122; III, 277 (the latter example is in Muʿtaṣim's period).

9) See, for example, Kindī, *Kitāb al-wulāt waʾl-quḍāt* (Leiden & London, 1912) pp. 441, 518; Ibn Ṭūlūn, *Quḍāt Dimashq* ed. S. D. al-Munajjid (Damascus, 1956) p. 22.

(military raiding) and *qāḍā'* (jurisdiction). Another example was ᶜAbd al-Raḥmān b. al-Ḥasḥās al-ᶜUdhrī, *qāḍī* of Damascus for ᶜUmar II and Yazīd II. According to Crone, he was also known as ᶜUbayd b. al-Ḥasḥās al-Ūdhrī, the governor of Damascus.[10])

However, the title of *qāḍī al-jund* used in the Umayyad period did not imply a "*qāḍī* of the army," as it appears not only in reference to Syria, which was indeed known for its organization in *junūd* (military administrative districts), but also in reference to Egypt. Since the office existed only in relatively early periods (the latest citation is for Hishām's reign, 106/724-126/743), *qāḍī al-jund* is probably equivalent to a regular *qāḍī* whose authority in that period was over the population of Muslim warriors still organized in military units in *amṣār* (town camps).[11])

In some cases the *qāḍī* was entrusted with only part of the responsibilities of an *amīr*, most commonly leadership in prayer (*ṣalāt*) and supervision of the treasury (*bayt al-māl*) and the land tax (*kharāj*).[12]) In other words, he was concerned more with the administrative rather than military responsibilities of the governor.

ṢĀḤIB AL-SHURṬA (CHIEF OF POLICE). Ibn Khaldụn notes the double function of this official. He was not only an executive-military authority charged with pursuing and punishing criminals, but also a judiciary official who examined the facts and judged the offenders.[13]) The position was first established during the caliphate of ᶜAlī and

---

10) Ibn Ṭūlūn, *Quḍāt Dimashq*, pp. 2-3; Wakīᶜ, III, 203, 201: *Fragmenta Historicorum Arabicorum* ed. M. J. de Goeje (Leiden, 1871), p. 81; Khalīfa b. Khayyāṭ, *Ta'rīkh* (Najaf, 1967) p. 330; P. Crone, *Slaves on Horses* (Cambridge, 1980) p. 127.

11) Kindī, *Quḍāt Miṣr* (Leiden) p. 341; cf. Abū Zurᶜa *Ta'rīkh* in Ibn Ṭūlūn, *Quḍāt Dimashq*, p. 416. Here there is a clear explanation that *jund* means "administrative district."

12) Wakīᶜ, 60, 80, 122, 182; III, 202, 216; Ibn ᶜAsākir *Ta'rīkh madīnat Dimashq*, ed. Fayṣal (Damascus, 1977) pp. 386-7; Kindī, *Quḍāt Miṣr*, ed. J. H. Gottheil (Paris, 1908) pp. 9, 11-12, 14, 28.

13) Ibn Khaldūn, *Muqaddima*, tr. F. Rosenthal, I, 457.

continued to develop in the period of Umayyad rule. Its original function was to maintain and command a force of troops to be used anywhere at the caliph's command. In this aspect, the post was in fact a broadening of the office of the *ṣāḥib al-ḥaras* (chief of the caliph's personal guard). The term *shurṭa* (from the Latin *cohort*) apparently at first denoted a general's or governor's guard. [14])

As early as the Umayyad period, the sources also allude to the judiciary function of the post. The Umayyad caliphs often delegated the functions of *shurṭa* and *qāḍāʾ* to a single official. Thus, for reasons of expediency, the combined office could be in charge of both criminal and religious law. This combination occurred most often in Egypt, where six out of fifteen Umayyad *qāḍī*s cited in Kindi were also in charge of the *shurṭa*. [15]) Perhaps the reason for this phenomenon is the relative homogeneity of the population in this province, which enabled the governor to entrust two offices to one man. The phenomenon was less prevalent elsewhere. [16])

The judicial authority of the chief of police, however, differed in principle from the authority of the *qāḍī*. By law the *qāḍī* was not entitled to initiate a trial. He could judge only those cases brought before him, as had been the case with the pre-Islamic *ḥakam* (arbitrator). [17]) On the contrary, the chief of police, as the official in charge of public order, could force alleged transgressors to stand trial.

ʿAbbāsid sources refer to a new office sometimes entrusted to a *qāḍī*—the supervision of the local urban militia (*aḥdāth*), especially under al-Manṣūr and al-Mahdī. In contrast to the police (*shurṭa*) and the caliph's personal guard (*ḥaras*), the *aḥdāth* (literally "young men")

---

14) Ṭabarī, *Taʾrīkh al-rusul waʾl-mulūk* (Leiden, 1967) II, p. 7; J. Schacht, *An Introduction to Islamic Law* (Oxford, 1964), p. 50.

15) Kindī, *Quḍāt Miṣr* (Paris), 11-12, 14, 19, 22, 23, 41.

16) In Baṣra: Wakīʿ, II, 57-58, 60, 80, 81, 84, 95; in Kūfa: Wakīʿ, III, 118; in Medina: Wakīʿ, I, 118, 254.

17) Cf., the story in Balādhurī, *Ansāb al-ashrāf* ed. M. Schloessinger and M. J. Kister (Jerusalem, 1971), IV a, 111.

did not constitute a professional force; they were usually recruited from the lower classes.[18])

QĀṢṢ (PREACHER). Literally, a *qāṣṣ* is a "storyteller"; in practice, he served some of the same functions as the *khaṭīb* (preacher in the mosque).[19])Because of its political character in Islam, the sermon (*khuṭba*) was usually delivered by the governor of the province, at least during the Friday prayer, but the *quṣṣāṣ* occasionally gave the same sermon at other times.

Qaṣāṣ (the practice of telling religious stories) took place at two distinct levels: as a spontaneous activity without official sanction, and as an official activity performed by *quṣṣāṣ* appointed by the caliph or the governor. The authorities used the *quṣṣāṣ* to propagandize on behalf of the ruling dynasty,[20]) yet some of them served religious ends as well, interpreting the *Qurʾān* and *Ḥadīth* in the language of the crowd.

The profession later deteriorated as more and more unqualified people joined its ranks, aiming only to please the crowd by inventing false traditions.[21]) But in the earlier period, when most of the *quṣṣāṣ* were pious and conscientious, they were occasionally appointed *qāḍīs*. One such appointee was ʿĀʾidh Allāh b. ʿAbd Allāh Abū Idrīs al-Khawlānī who served in Damascus under ʿAbd al-Malik; there were many other such cases in Egypt.[22]) One may assume that the *qāṣṣ* was a predecessor to the *wāʿidh* (preacher) of later periods.

---

18) Wakīʿ, II, 80. In al-Manṣūr's period a certain Siwār b. ʿAbd Allāh was appointed over *qaḍāʾ*, *ṣalāt* and *aḥdāth* in Baṣra; in al-Mahdī's period there was separate appointment for *qaḍāʾ* and *aḥdāth* (Wakīʿ II, 122); cf. Cl. Cahen, "Aḥdāth" *EI²*.

19) Ibn Ḥanbal, *Musnad* (Bulaq, 1895), IV, 105; Ibn al-Jawzī, *Kitāb al-quṣṣāṣ waʾl-mudhakkirīn*, ed. and tr. Merlin L. Swartz (Beirut, 1971) pp. 21, 144 (§ 30, § 334).

20) Ṭabarī, II, 112; I. Goldziher, *Muslim Studies* (London, 1971) II, pp. 44, 150-156.

21) Jāḥiẓ, *Kitāb al-bayān waʾl-tabyīn* (Egypt, 1968) II, pp. 9-11; Ibn al-Jawzī, *Quṣṣāṣ*, 98-121; Ṭabarī, III, 2131, 2165.

22) Ibn Ṭūlūn, *Quḍāt Dimashq*, 5; Ibn ʿAsākir (ed. Faysal), 522; Wakīʿ, III, 221, 225, 229, 239.

ᶜARĪF (OFFICIAL IN MATTERS OF CUSTOMARY LAW—ᶜURF). The precise function of this office is not clear in the sources. The title *ᶜarīf* was given to various financial and military officials without denoting a specific established institution. It is plausible that the term had different meanings in various periods.

The sources tell of at least three *qāḍī*s who were also *ᶜarīf*s. ᶜAbīda b. Qays al-Salmānī was both the *qāḍī* of Kūfa and the *ᶜarīf* of his tribe in the early Umayyad period (before ᶜAbd al-Malik).[23] According to Ibn Saᶜd, his responsibility as *ᶜarīf* was to distribute the stipend (*ᶜaṭā*ʾ) due to the warriors among the members of the tribe. In this function the office of the *ᶜarīf* was probably part of the military bureaucracy of the pre-Umayyad and Umayyad empire. The source report that the armies of Kūfa were divided into numerous units (*ᶜirāfa*), each headed by an *ᶜarīf*, who would distribute the stipend, and probably collect blood money as well.[24]

A *qāḍī* of Egypt, ᶜAbd al-Raḥmān b. Muᶜāwiya, also held the title of *ᶜarīf*. In this case, *ᶜarīf* was an official specially appointed in each tribe and responsible for guarding the interests of orphans. ᶜAbd al-Raḥmān is mentioned as the first *qāḍī* to fill this post. Later, legal theory considered this responsibility to be among the standard duties of a *qāḍī*.[25]

A third example of a *qāḍī-ᶜarīf* in the early Umayyad period was Shurayḥ, the legendary judge of Kūfa. Here the term *ᶜarīf* seems to mean an assistant to the controller of markets, the *muḥtasib* of later periods. Wakīᶜ alludes to *ᶜarīf*s at several markets, whose responsibilities were combined and entrusted to Shurayḥ. In this case, the *ᶜarīf* was not strictly a tribal official, and the term may be a throwback to an earlier period.[26]

---

23) Wakīʾ, II, 399-402.
24) Ṭabarī, I, 2496; Ibn Saᶜd, *Kitāb al-ṭabaqāt al-kubrā* (Beirut, 1958-60) VI, 62-63.
25) About ᶜAbd al-Raḥmān b. Muᶜāwiya see: Kindī, *Quḍāt Miṣr*, (Leiden) 22, 325; for other examples see: Māwardī, *al-Aḥkām al-sulṭānīyah* (Cairo, n.d.), 67.
26) Wakīᶜ, II, 347; cf., Abū al-Faraj al-Iṣfahānī, *Kitāb al-aghānī* (Bulaq, 1868) II, 186; Ṣāliḥ El-ᶜAlī, "ᶜArīf" *EI*².

In sum, three types of extra-judicial offices were at times conferred on a *qāḍī*, involving: (1) matters of public order (*ṣāḥib al-shurṭa*, chief of the *aḥdāth*, and *ʿarīf*); (2) tax collection and the distribution of stipends (*ʿāmil* and *ʿarīf*); and (3) preaching and leading the community in prayer, (*qāṣṣ* and amīr).

But the appointment to *qāḍāʾ* did not automatically confer non-judicial administrative roles; the sources specify each particular case where extra-judicial duties were granted. For example, on caliph al-Manṣūr's appointment of Sawwār b. ʿAbd Allāh b. Qudāma as *qāḍī* of Baṣra it is said: "*kataba Abū Jaʿfar ilā Sawwār an yuwallīhi ṣalāt Baṣra wa-shurṭatahā maʿa al-qaḍāʾ*" ("Abū Jaʿfar wrote to Sawwār that he appointed him to lead the prayer of Baṣra and its police together with the qāḍāʾ").[27] Other examples can be found: "*māta amīr(an) wa-qāḍī(yan)*" ("he died as amīr and *qāḍī*"), or: "*lā aqūlu ḥattā tuʾammirūnī kaʾannahu yarā anna lil-amīr fī hadhā mā laysa lil-qaḍī*" ("I won't deliver my judgment until you make me *amīr*, as if he believed that the *amīr* had in this matter [authority] which the *qāḍī* [himself] did not possess").[28]

The latter citation clearly shows the relative position of the *qāḍī* within the administrative hierarchy in the Umayyad period. The *amīr*, as governor-general, was the supreme authority in the province, and the *qāḍī* was directly dependent on his goodwill. According to the sources, the Umayyads gave the governors authority to appoint and dismiss the *qāḍī*s: "*wa-kānat wulāt al-buldān ilayhim al-qaḍāʾ yuwallūna man arādū*" ("the governors of the provinces were in charge of the *qāḍāʾ*; they appointed to it whom they wished").[29]

This practice continued in the early ʿAbbāsid period, but the new trend was towards centralization, with provincial *qāḍī*s directly appointed by caliphs.[30]

---

27) Wakīʿ, II, 60.
28) Ibn Saʿd, VI, 63; Wakīʿ, II, 81.
29) Wakīʿ, I, 141; cf., Wakīʿ, I, 113; III, 239,235; Kindī, *Quḍāt Miṣr* (Leiden) pp. 363, 377, 385, 393.
30) Kindī, *Quḍāt Miṣr* (Leiden) 363, Yaʿqūbī, *Taʾrīkh* (Beirut, 197-), II, p. 401.

Differences Between Provinces in Nonjudicial Appointments

The Umayyad and early ʿAbbāsid practice of multiple appointments was not uniformly observed. Notable differences between the provinces can be attested.

EGYPT. Such multiple appointments were most common in Egypt, although we have no evidence of even a single case in which *imāra* and *qaḍāʾ* were conferred on the same individual there. Of the fifteen Umayyad *qāḍīs* of Egypt mentioned in Kindī, eight received official appointments to either *shurṭa*, *gaṣaṣ*, or *bayt al-māl*. In fact, these cover the three main functions of any governor: maintaining public order, presiding over and leading prayer, and administering taxes. Since the population of Egypt was relatively homogeneous and obedient, the *amīr* did not fear to delegate power and responsibilities to his assistant, the *qāḍī*.[31])

MECCA AND MEDINA. In these two holy cities nonjudicial appointments for *qāḍīs* were extremely rare. Only three cases of combined nomination appear in the detailed lists of Wakīʾ, which include dozens of *qāḍīs*; all three involved appointment as both *amīr* and *qāḍī*. In this period Medina was the fortress of Islamic tradition, and its leading *ʿulamāʾ* were not interested in politics—or so one might gather from the stereotyped, pious biographies of the *qāḍīs*. But there was an additional, more practical reason for the paucity of *qāḍīs* with broad governmental responsibilities. The office of governor was far less stable in Medina than in Egypt, as the caliphs deliberately changed incumbents frequently. The position usually served as a springboard to far more prestigious posts such as the governorship of Iraq or Egypt. Some governors of Medina even became caliphs.[32]) One may

31) Kindī, *Quḍāt Miṣr* (Paris), pp. 11-12, 14, 19, 22, 23, 41.

32) The prominent viceroys of Iraq, Ḥajjāj b. Yūsuf and Khālid al-Qasrī, began their careers as governors in the Ḥijāz (Khalīfa b. Khayyāṭ, 294, 323); two Umayyad Caliphs, Marwān b. al-Ḥakam and ʿUmar b. ʿAbd al-ʿAzīz, were kept for a time at a distance from the captial as governors of Medina (ibid., 189, 315).

suppose that the *amīr* of Medina was usually not secure enough in his province to delegate too much power to one aide.

BAṢRA. All the recorded cases of *qāḍīs* with nonjudicial functions in Baṣra were actually *amīrs*. The list of Wakīᶜ mentions six such cases. It seems that in Baṣra, as in Kūfa, the combined appointments were due to specific historical circumstances and the personal qualities of the *qāḍīs*. For example, ᶜUbayd Allāh. b. Abī Bakra was appointed to this dual position in Baṣra by ᶜAbd al-Malik, who needed a strong hand there once the revolt of the Zubayrids had been suppressed.[33]) Similarly, in the period of consolidation of Ābbāsid rule, al-Manṣūr named Sawwār b. ᶜAbd Allāh b. Qudāma as both *qāḍī* and *amīr* in Baṣra after he had ably handled the revolt of the Zanj.[34]) Sawwār was a strong and knowledgeable *qāḍī* who exercised considerable influence on al-Manṣūr. A similar case involved al-Manṣūr's appointment of ᶜUbayd Allāh b. al-Ḥasan al-ᶜAnbarī to the *ṣalāt* as well as the *qāḍāʾ*; Al-Mahdī later dismissed him from both the *ṣalāt* and the *qāḍāʾ*, and entrusted him with the reorganization of the treasury at Baṣra. Al-ᶜAnbarī was a very learned *ᶜālim* who was interested in politics as well. He composed an essay for al-Mahdī on proper statesmanship according to the *sharīᶜa*.[35])

KŪFA. Shurayḥ b. Ḥārith al-Kindī, a half-legendary figure, was said to have been given enormous powers on the strength of his prestige as an *ᶜālim*.[36]) According to the sources he was both *qāḍī* and chief of police. A variety of other administrative appointments were granted to *qāḍīs* in Kūfa. Abū Burda b. Abī Mūsa al-Ashᶜarī was given charge of the treasury by al-Ḥajāj, after solving several difficult

---

33) Wakīᶜ, I, 302. It was before the appointment of Ḥajjāj as all powerful viceroy of Iraq.

34) Wakīᶜ, II, 57-58, 60, 80.

35) Wakīᶜ, II, 91, 95, 122, 97-105.

36) Wakīᶜ, II, 320, 330, 397; Ibn Saᶜd, VI, 90-100; cf. J. Schacht, *The Origins of Muhammadan Jurisprudence* (Oxford, 1964), pp. 228 f.

problems concerning the property of those who had migrated from farmland to town.[37] The governor of al-Saffāḥ, ʿĪsā b. Mūsā, tried to force ʿAbd Allāh b. Shibrima to accept both *qāḍāʾ* and *shurṭa* in Kūfa, but Ibn Shibrima refused. ʿĪsā b. Mūsā was in need of a loyal assistant in Kūfā to help back his claim to succeed al-Manṣūr on the throne.[38]

In Kūfa, in contrast to Baṣra, the nonjudicial duties given to *qāḍīs* did not include governorship (*imāra*) but, as in Egypt, they did include positions related to public order and the treasury.

SYRIA. The Umayyad *qāḍīs* of Syria were entrusted with a range of prestigious nonjudicial appointments from subgovernor of a city to preacher (*qāṣṣ*), but they were never given administrative and financial offices such as the *shurṭa* or *bayt al-māl*. However, they were given one office not filled by *qāḍīs* in any other province—substitute to the caliph (*khalīfat al-khalīfa*). For example, Bilāl b. Abī Dardāʾ al-Khazrajī replaced ʿAbd al-Malik when needed: "*wa-kāna khalīfat(an) li-ʿAbd al- Malik ʿalā Dimahq, yuṣallī bihim wa-yaqḍī baynahum.*" ("He acted as a substitute for ʿAbd al-Malik over Damascus, led them in prayer, and judged among them"). *Qadis* performed similar functions in Muʿāwiya's time.[39]

Since the caliph himself administered Umayyad Syria without the aid of any provincial governor, he also appointed the *qāḍīs*,[40] who were in charge of religious life rather than public order or administration. In a relatively old source, Abū Zurʿa (d. 281/394) portrays the *qāḍīs* of Shām as counterparts of "aṣḥāb Rasūl Allāh" (Muḥammad's companions) perceiving both groups as disseminators of Islamic tradition, in the stereotyped manner of the biographical sources. In

37) Wakīʿ, II, 409-410.
38) Wakīʿ, III, 118; see also: J. Lassner, *The Shaping of ʿAbbāsid Rule* (Princeton, 1980) pp. 36-37.
39) Wakīʿ, III, 202, cf., Wakīʿ, III, 216, 199-200; Ibn Ṭūlūn, *Quḍāt Damashq*, 2.
40) E. K. M. Zambauer, *Manuel de genealogie et de chronologie pour l'histoire de l'Islam* (Hanovre, 1927), p. 28, note 3.

this respect, the position of the Syrian *qāḍīs* was similar to that of the Medinese.[41])

Even considering the partiality of the sources, it is plausible that most of the *qāḍīs*, although they probably lacked formal training, pursued religious studies and were considered learned men. In Syria, there were several examples of *qāḍīs* appointed to teach law and Qur᾽ān readings, the monopoly of the *ᶜulamā᾽* in all periods of history.[42]) However, the sources do not specify how intensive the religious training of the *qāḍīs* was.

The fact that many *qāḍīs* made their living by engaging in trade and handicrafts, or combined judicial functions with administrative careers, does not necessarily prove that they lacked religious education. Some *qāḍīs* engaged in commerce because the salary of a judge was not sufficient. Others refused payment on principle and preferred to support themselves by some other means.[43]) But those *qāḍī-amīrs* cited in the sources primarily in their capacity as military commanders and administrators had probably received the training of the military elite, rather than the systematic religious education of an *ᶜālim*.[44]) In other words, while some *qāḍīs* were *ᶜulamā᾽*, not all of them were. Until the period of Hārūn al-Rashīd, the office did not possess a definite religious coloration; it was a position of authority which needed religious sanction.[45])

---

41) Abū Zurᶜa, *Ta᾽rīkh*, in Ibn Ṭūlūn, 416.

42) Ibn ᶜAsākir, *al-Ta᾽rīkh al-kabīr* (Tahdhīb) ed. A. Q. Badrān (Damascus, 1911) 203; Ibn ᶜAsākir (ed. Faysal), 522.

43) Ibn Ḥajar al-ᶜAsqalānī, *Tahdhīb al-tahdhīb* (Beirut, 1907) IV, 327; Kindī, *Quḍāt Miṣr* (Leiden) 348-52, 435; al-Khaṭīb al-Baghdādī, *Ta᾽rīkh Baghdād*, ed. M. Amīn Khānijī (Cairo, 1931), VII, 342. For an extensive study on the subject see: Haim J. Cohen, *The Economic Background and the Secular Occupation of Muslim Jurisprudents and Traditionalists in the Classical Period of Islam* (in Hebrew). Ph.D. thesis (Jerusalem, 1962), esp. pp. 12, 69.

44) See: Ibn Ṭūlūn, *Quḍāt Dimashq*, 2 (Faḍāla b. ᶜUbayd al-Anṣārī); Wakīᶜ, III, 203, 201; *Fragmenta*, p. 81; Khalīfa b. Khayyāṭ, p. 330; Crone, p. 127 (ᶜUthmān b. Saᶜīd alᶜUdhrī).

45) Similarly, in the pre-Islamic period, *al-ḥakam*, the tribal arbitrator was looking for a quasi-religious source to sanction his position. Cf., R. Serjeant, "Ḥaram and Ḥawṭa," *Melanges Ṭāha Ḥusain* (Cairo, 1962), pp. 41-52.

Social Origins of the Qāḍī

Umayyad and early ᶜAbbāsid *qāḍīs* were Arabs. Any *mawālī* (non-Arab Muslims) are pointed out in the source as exceptional. For example, Wakīᶜ comments on the appointment by governor Khālid al-Qasrī of ᶜAbd allāh b. Ziyād b. Samᶜān as *qāḍī* of Medina: "no *mawlā* except him was *qāḍī* there in Medina."[46]) The Persian *mawlā* Ḥasan al-Baṣrī served as a *qāḍī* in the reign of ᶜUmar II, but only briefly. His career pattern was quite exceptional. He began as a secretary, devoting himself to religious studies.[47])

In fact, a high percentage of the early *qāḍīs* belonged to Yamanite tribes of the so-called "southern" faction. It is difficult to determine whether this trend was accidental or deliberate. One possible explanation for the appointment of Yamanites to *qāḍā*ʾ is that the tribes of Medina, the *anṣār* (Muḥammad's helpers), are considered Yamanite by origin. To belong to those tribes or to be related to Medina added to a *qāḍī*'s prestige.

The Prophet Muḥammad himself had administered justice in Medina thus becoming the first *ḥakam* of the young Islamic community. Later on, when the empire expanded and absorbed new civilizations, Medina remained the fortress of the *sunna*. It made sense ideologically for both the first Umayyads and the first ᶜAbbāsids to choose *qāḍīs* from the circles which had the reputation of being the most ardent disciples of Muḥammad's tradition. The sources even cite a tradition from the Prophet saying: "the *qāḍā*ʾ office is established in *anṣār*."[48])

There was a certain hereditary tendency among the holders of the *qāḍā*ʾ office from its very inception. Many *qāḍīs* trained their sons in the profession, and later they too were appointed *qāḍīs*. The families

46) Wakīᶜ, I, 222; cf., Wakīᶜ, III, 129, 204-206 for a reflection on this subject.

47) Balādhurī, *Futūḥ al-buldān*, ed. M. Y. de Goeje (Leiden, 1866), p. 394; Wakīᶜ II, 307.

48) Wakīᶜ, III, 243, cf., Wakīᶜ III, 129, 241, 199-202; Ibn Ṭūlūn, *Quḍāt Dimashq*, 1-4; Wakīᶜ, II, 153, 406.

of Abū al-Dardāʾ al-Anṣārī and Abū Zurʿa al-Thaqafī in Damascus, ʿAbd al-Raḥmān b. Abī Laylā al-Anṣārī in Kūfa, and Abū Mūsā al-Ashʿarī and Sawwār b. ʿAbd Allāh b. Qudāma al-ʿAnbarī in Baṣra are but a few examples. Of course, the *qāḍī*s were not mere technocrats passing down professional secrets from father to son. In the main, they were scholars who gained ideological power through their learning; however, some tried to train their sons in order to preserve the prestige of the post within the family.

To a certain extent, the ʿAbbāsids retained the Umayyad administrative framework as well as personnel for reasons of expediency—similar to the way that pre-Islamic bureaucratic personnel was integrated into Umayyad governmental machinery.[49]) The continuity of personnel between the Umayyad and ʿAbbāsid periods is less obvious in the *qaḍāʾ* than in other branches of the administration, but there were far more examples than one might expect. The first *qāḍī* of the first ʿAbbāsid caliph Abū al-ʿAbbās (and later the first *qāḍī* of Baghdād under al-Manṣūr) was yaḥyā b. Saʿīd al-Anṣārī, who had served in the Umayyad period as *qāḍī* of Medina under Walīd b. ʿAbd al-Malik. Yaḥyā's scholarship and his *anṣārī* descent won the respect of the new rulers, despite his service with their rival predecessors.[50])

One of the most powerful *qāḍī*s of the Muʿtazilite period, the chief *qāḍī* of al-Maʾmūn, Yaḥyā b. Aktham al-Tamīmī, traced his descent even beyond the Umayyad era, to Aktham Ibn al-Saifī, "Judge of the Arabs", a chief of the Tamīm tribe in pre-Islamic time renowned for his wisdom as *ḥakam*. His family also included other learned men, among them scribes and poets.[51])

Aḥmad b. Abī Duʾād b. Jarīr al-Iyādī, chief *qāḍī* of al-Maʾmūn, an ardent supporter of Muʿtazilite and pro-ʿAbbāsid doctrines, came

49) I. Bligh-Abramski: "Evolution Versus Revolution: Umayyad Elements in the ʿAbbāsid Regime," *Der Islam*, vol. 65 (1988).

50) Wakīʿ, III, 241, 243-44.

51) Ibn Khallikān, *Wafayāt al-aʿyān*, tr. G. DeSlane (Paris, 1843), IV, 33; Ibn Ḥazm, *Jamharat Ansāb al-ʿArab* (Cairo, 1948), p. 200.

from a Syrian family which had been close to the Umayyads. He confessed that his own grandfather had provided shelter for ᶜAbd al-Raḥmān b. Muᶜāwiya b. Hishām, the founder of the Umayyad dynasty in Spain, when he was fleeing from the ᶜAbbāsids.[52]) The Banū Abī al-Shawārib family, which supplied eight chief *qāḍī*s between 250/868 and 417/1026, was actually related to the Umayyad caliphs themselves.[53])

The later ᶜAbbāsid period saw an even stronger hereditary tendency in the *qāḍā*ᵓ office. The reorganization of the judiciary and the new requirements of formal religious training strengthened this trend.

The Judiciary Reform

Gradual changes in the status and functions of the *qāḍī* were institutionalized in the judicial reform under Hārūn al-Rashīd (170/786-193/809), which formed an important component of the new administrative centralization and rationalization. The jurisdictional bounds of the office were much more narrowly prescribed, but its incumbents gained more practical autonomy and prestige—especially the chief *qāḍī* in Baghdād. At the same time, with the growing despotism of the temporal power, the *qāḍī*s were subject to dismissal at the whim of the central government, and could not coherently put their legal theory into practice.[54]) The creation of the office of the chief *qāḍī* was the first step in the hierarchical organization of the ᶜ*ulamā*ᵓ. It is hard to establish why the reform took place under Hārūn—the project was not planned by the caliph. Hārūn was preoccupied with military campaigns against Byzantium and tended to delegate his authority to high officials: governmental matters to the vizier Yaḥyā b. Khālid al-Barmakī (d. 190/805) and judicial ones to

52) Ibn Khallikān, *Wafayāt*, I, 61-66; Ibn Ḥazm, *Jamhara*, 308.
53) Ṭabarī, III, 1428, 1533, 1684; Ibn Ḥazm, *Jamhara* 104-5.
54) Schacht, *Introduction*, 48-50; Kindī, *Quḍāt Miṣr* (Leiden), 332-333, 368; Wakīᶜ, III, 235, 239, 254, 256.

Abū Yūsuf al-Kūfī (d. 182/798). Both major Islamic institutions, the vizirate and the office of *Qāḍī al-quḍāh*, were fully developed and crystalized only after Hārūn. Abū Yūsuf was merely the first to receive the title of chief judge, with specific powers to appoint *qāḍīs* in the whole empire.

Until the period of Hārūn al-Rashīd, the *qāḍīs*, even those without specific nonjudicial appointments, were part of the general administrative system. They handled criminal as well as other cases, probably using both *sharīʿa* (Islamic law) and *ʿurf* (local practice). The new administrative principles narrowed their judicial functions, limiting them to matters of *sharīʿa* law. [55])

Furthermore, after the reform of Hārūn al-Rashīd, extrajudicial appointments became infrequent and rare. However, some inclusion of financial-administrative duties in the responsibilities of a *qāḍī* who received a general (*ʿāmm*) appointment became regular. This most often involved the administration of charitable foundations (*awqāf*) and the care of certain sections of the treasury, especially the funds for orphans. Even in later periods (tenth and eleventh centuries), the collection of certain taxes was routinely assigned to the *qāḍī*: the *ṣadaqa* (alms tax, prescribed for Muslims) and the *jizya* (poll tax of non-Muslims). [56])

But within this more restricted jurisdiction, the provincial *qāḍī* now exercised greater autonomy. [57]) He was gradually removed from the authority of the governor, who no longer controlled judicial appointments—the provincial posts were now generally filled either by the caliph directly, or by the chief qadi or the vizier with the caliph's confirmation. Al-Manṣūr was the first caliph to assign judges

55) On this subject see: A. Mez, *The Renaissance of Islam* (Patna, 1937), pp. 230-231; Crone, p. 86 and note 682.

56) See: M. Gil: "Taxation in Palestine During the First Period of Muslim Occupation" (in Hebrew), *Zion, Quarterly for Research in Jewish History* XLV, no. 4 (Jerusalem, 1980), pp. 271-72.

57) Ibn Ṭūlūn, *Quḍāt Dimashq*, 19-20; Ibn al-ʿAdīm, *Zubdat al-ḥalab min taʾrīkh Ḥalab*, ed. S. Dahān (Damascus, 1951), 70; Tanūkhī, *Nishwār al-muḥāḍarah* (Beirut, 1971-2), I, 116-117.

to provincial capitals; his descendants followed his example. The Umayyads had also tried to centralize the appointment of *qāḍīs*, but not on a systematic basis. The independence of the *qāḍī* from the governor created a potential source of friction between the two branches of provincial administration, but it also strengthened the caliph's control.[58])

Of course, the *amīr* continued to exercise some influence. For example, Abū Zurʿa, the famous *qāḍī* of Egypt, collaborated in the revolt of the governor, Ibn Ṭūlūn against the ʿAbbāsids.[59]) In another example, a governor of Egypt, Kāfūr, prevented a *qāḍī* from giving an independent judgment.[60]) Judicial independence still depended on the personal honesty and courage of the individual *qāḍī*. The sources cite examples from the Umayyad and ʿAbbāsid periods of pliable *qāḍīs*,[61]) as well as others brave enough to pass judgment against the will of the secular authorities.[62])

With their professional autonomy more secure, the provincial *qāḍīs* now tried to win a concomitant degree of prestige and respect within the Islamic community. In this spirit, Wakīʿ reports the case of an individual imprisoned in the reign of al-Maʾmūn for being rude to a *qāḍī* of Wāsiṭ, Sayf b. Jābir. When asked about the severe punishment, the *qāḍī* answered:

> If he had insulted, or even cursed me when I was not a *qāḍī* I would not have said a word to him. But I imprisoned him for the sake of the Muslims, for if a *qāḍī* is humiliated, the Muslims are affected.[63])

The *qāḍīs* became more daring in taking advantage of their formal powers, and not only in matters of prestige. For example, since the

58) Kindī, *Quḍāt Miṣr* (Leiden) 368; Yaʿqūbī, II, 401; Nez, 217-18. For Umayyad centralizing tendencies concerning the *qaḍāʾ* see: Kindī, *Quḍāt Miṣr* (Leiden), pp. 332-33.

59) Ibn Ṭūlūn, *Quḍāt Dimashq* 23; cf., Ibn al-ʿAdīm, *Zubda* 86; the Ṭūlūnid governors of Syria appointed its *qāḍīs*.

60) Kindī, *Quḍāt Miṣr* (Leiden), 583-4.

61) Tanūkhī, *Nishwār*, I, 130.

62) Wakīʿ, I, 167-8; Ibn Ṭūlūn, *Quḍāt Dimsahq*, 21-22.

63) Wakīʿ, III, 313.

property of orphans and heirless people was kept in the public treasury of each province, the *qāḍī* as guardian and administrator of this property had access to the *bayt al-māl*; in several cases, he became *de facto* administrator of the treasury.[64])

Hārūn al-Rashid created the honorific title of *qāḍī al-quḍāt*, or chief *qāḍī*, as mentioned above, for Abū Yūsuf, *qāḍī* of Baghdād. Schacht has pointed out that the title was originally no more than a gesture of respect for the *qāḍī* of the capital, whom the caliphs would normally consult on the administration of justice. It seems, however, that Abū Yūsuf, and even more so his successors, counseled the caliphs on judicial appointments and dismissals throughout the empire. Their full title was *qāḍī quḍāt al-dunyā*, "the *qāḍī* of the *qāḍī*s of the world", as they were "appointed deputy (*yastanību*) of the caliph in all the provinces in matters of justice".[65])

Thus the ᶜAbbāsids created a judicial hierarchy under the authority of the caliph. The chief *qāḍī* generally nominated the main provincial judges, who in turn delegated their powers to various representatives on the local level. Each *qāḍī* would be assigned jurisdiction over a geographically limited district. For this purpose, al-Hādī had already divided Baghdād into two districts—east and west— with a *qāḍī* over each.

It has been suggested that the office of *qāḍī al-quḍāt* is of Persian origin, deriving from the Zoroastrian *mōbedhān mōbedh* (priest of priests). As supreme head of the ecclesiastical hierarchy, the priest of priests also served as chief judge, whose decisions could not be disputed.[66]) But even if the title looks like a free translation influenced by the Persian office, the institution itself seems to be inherently Islamic.

---

64) Kindī, *Quḍāt Miṣr* (Leiden), 405, 451, 470.

65) Schacht, *Introduction*, 50-51; cf., Ibn Kathīr, *Al-Bidāya waʾl-nihāya* (Cairo, 1932-9), X, p. 180.

66) Khwārizmī, *Kitāb mafātīḥ al-ᶜulūm*, ed. G. Van Vloten (Leiden, 1895), p. 116. Masᶜūdī, *Tanbīh waʾl-ishrāf* (Cairo, 1937), p. 103; M. Guidi, "Mōbedh," *EI*[1].

Golden Age of the Chief Qāḍī

Not long after Hārūn's reign, the position of chief *qāḍī* in the governmental hierarchy reached its apogee; its incumbents were in some respects second in power only to the caliph. Under the Muᶜtazilite rulers—al-Maʾmūn, al-Muᶜtaṣim and al-Wāthiq (198/813-233/847)—the chief *qāḍī* and the *ᶜulamāʾ* were particularly indispensable as legal and religious experts.

For the first time in Islamic history the caliphs were trying to impose an ideological **religious** uniformity in order to strengthen ᶜAbbāsid claims to legitimacy, using the *miḥna* (inquisition) to root out opposition. Until then both the Umayyads and the early ᶜAbbāsids had fostered secular **dynastic** ideology, each claiming to be the worthiest to gain power. In the Muᶜtazilite era, for the first and last time an attempt was made to interfere with religious dogmas which until then had been the sphere of the *ᶜulamāʾ* alone. The caliphs sided with the Muᶜtaziliate *ᶜulamāʾ* against the traditionalists. Thus, al-Maʾmūn (198/813-218/833) made a special visit to Damascus to examine the judges there and enforce his decree that only judges who held Muᶜtazilite views could hold office.[67]) Such policies had been suggested to the caliph al-Manṣūr half a century earlier by Ibn al-Muqaffāᶜ (d. 139/756) in his *Risālat al-ṣaḥāba.* Ibn al-Muqaffāᶜ had suggested that the caliph could strengthen his legitimacy and effective rule by undertaking a codification of laws and juridicial decrees, unifying under his own authority the different opinions of the legal scholars.[68]) Al-Manṣūr had rejected this notion of caliphal authority over ideology, but it was not totally abandoned as some scholars claim.[69]) Al-Maʾmūn and his two successors did largely succeed in imposing their authority on religious dogma, enforcing Muᶜtazilite ideas.

---

67) Yaᶜqūbī, *Taʾrīkh* (Beirut, 197–), II, pp. 467-8.
68) Ibn al-Muqaffāᶜ, "Risāla fī ṣaḥāba" in M. Kurd ᶜAlī (ed.) *Rasāʾil al-bulaghāʾ* (Cairo, 1946), pp. 136-7.
69) S. D. Goitein, "A Turning Point in the History of the Islamic State," in *Studies in Islamic History and Institutions* (Leiden, 1968), pp. 164-66.

A caliph trying to impose ideological uniformity would naturally choose an ʿ*ālim* rather than a *kātib* (secretary, or vizier) for his second in command and chief counselor. Ibn Khallikān mentions quite explicitly that the chief *qāḍī* was more powerful than the vizier in this period:

> The viziers charged with the direction of public affairs took no decision without submitting it to the chief *qāḍī* Yaḥyā (b. Aktham) for approval. We know of no persons having ever obtained such complete influence over the mind of his sovereign *except* Yaḥyā b. Aktham and Aḥmad Ibn Abī Duwād. [70])

Yaḥyā accompanied al-Maʾmūn on his expeditions to Syria and Egypt in 215/830, and on the campaigns against the Byzantines in 216/831. This behavior seems more suited to a personal secretary than a *qāḍī*, but in al-Maʾmūn's turbulent times a readily available ideologist was quite indispensible. On his deathbed, al-Maʾmūn advised his brother and heir al-Muʿtaṣim:

> As for Abū ʿAbd Allāh Aḥmad b. Abī Duwād the chief *qāḍī*, let him never cease to be the associate of your councils on every subject, for he is most worthy of having such confidence placed in him, and I recommended you not to take a vizier when I die. [71])

With the termination of the Muʿtazilite era the caliphs no longer tried to control dogma and religious doctrines, since the inquisition failed to produce any tangible results. The caliphs usually sought reconciliation with the orthodoxy, some of them through détente with the Shīʿites. But pro-Shīʿite or anti-Shīʿite gestures did not involve official interference in the religious issues. [72]) Hence, the chief *qāḍī* lost his high position as a second in command after the caliph, for the latter stopped pressing religious uniformity. The office of the chief *qāḍī*, however, was by then deeply rooted in the governmental Islamic administration.

---

70) Ibn Khallikān, *Wafayāt*, I, p. 65.

71) Ibn Khallikān, *Wafayāt*, V, 211; cf. Ṭabarī, III, 1104, 1143; D. Sourdel, *Le Vizirat ʿAbbaside de 749 a 936* (Damascus, 1959-60), 307.

72) On the pro-Shīʿite gestures made by the caliphs, see: D. Sourdel, "La politique religieuse de successeurs d'al-Mutawakkil", *Studia Islamica* XIII (1960).

Political-Ideological Role of the Qāḍī

The chief *qāḍī*'s greatest source of power was always his ideological role. Both Umayyads and ʿAbbāsids used the *ʿulamāʾ*, and notably the *qāḍīs*, to promote certain ideas and enhance the popularity of their regimes. In turn, the *qāḍīs* used their position as advisers to promote social and political theories that enhanced the role of the *ʿulamāʾ* in the Islamic realm.

Although few pro-Umayyad traditions have been preserved, we know that the Umayyads tried to influence public opinion in their favor and silence the voices of religious opposition with the help of religious circles themselves, although the latter were not always cooperative.

The careers of three prominent *ʿulamāʾ* illustrate this policy. The most famous was Muḥammad b. ʿUbayd Allāh, Ibn Shihāb al-Zuhrī (d. 124/741), a celebrated traditionist from Ḥijāz. Despite his piety, he did not shun the Umayyad court, and he was part of the caliph's entourage. Yazīd II (101/719-105/723) made him a judge, and Hishām employed him as a tutor for his sons. One story tells of the Umayyad prince Ibrāhīm b. al-Walīd, who came to al-Zuhrī with a notebook he had written and asked his permission to represent its contents as *ḥadīths* (traditions) communicated by the scholar himself. Al-Zuhrī agreed, saying: "Who else could have told you the *ḥadīths*?"[73])

Thus the Umayyads were able to circulate pro-Umayyad traditions under the name of al-Zuhrī. Since al-Zuhrī was generally esteemed by the Muslim community as one of the preservers of Islamic tradition, his cooperation was very useful to the ruling dynasty. Goldziher interprets al-Zuhrī's collaboration as evidence of his inability to withstand pressure from governing circles[74]) but the image of the Umayyads as wicked princes "who forced people to write *ḥadīths*"

73) Ibn ʿAsākir, *Tahdhīb*, II, 303; Ibn Saʿd, VII, 6, 157; Ṭabarī, II, 1635, 1811; Ibn Qutayba, *Kitāb al-maʿārif*, ed. Wüstenfeld (Göttingen, 1850), 239.

74) I. Goldziher, *Muslim Studies*, II, p. 47.

was in fact a fabrication by ᶜAbbāsid sources[75]). Ibn Qutayba writes of al-Zuhrī's devote service to ᶜAbd al-Malik and Hishām, and mentions an estate he owned in Palestine. He was totally assimilated into the Umayyad governmental system. Nevertheless, whenever al-Zuhrī found fault with an Umayyad prince, he did not hesitate to criticize him, as in the case of Walid II's indulgence in wine. [76])

Al-Ḥasan b. Abī al-Ḥasan, Yasār al-Baṣrī (d. 110/728) is another example of a devout preacher who eventually became part of the administrative religious establishment. He began his public career as secretary to a governor of Sijistān, before deciding to devote his life to learning. The sources are not clear on his subsequent career. [77]) One account has Ḥasan al-Baṣrī as a *qāḍī* in the camp of the rebel Ibn al-Ashᶜath (100/699-101/700). This is hardly plausible, however, as others quote his response to an offer to join the rebels: "the violent actions of tyrants were a punishment sent by God which could not be opposed by the sword, but had to be endured with patience." [78]) It is more likely that he served as *qāḍī* of Baṣra for a short period in the reign of the pious ᶜUmar b. ᶜAbd al-ᶜAzīz (Umar II), as reported by the other two versions in Wakīᶜ. [79])

Ḥasan al-Baṣrī did not hesitate to criticize unjust actions by secular rulers. But his sincere and upright religious personality did not make him a partisan of any organized anti-Umayyad faction. [80]) His participation in public life was more moral than political. For example, he spoke to the caliph ᶜUmar II on behalf of the governor of Baṣra, ᶜAdī b. ᶜArṭaʾa al-Fazārī, about the problems of water supply in that city; he considered the welfare of the people of Baṣra to be the respon-

---

75) Al-Khaṭīb al-Baghdādī, *Taqyīd al-ᶜilm* (Damascus, 1949), 107.

76) Ibn Qutayba, *Maᶜārif*, 239; Ṭabarī, II, 1811.

77) Balādhurī, *Futūḥ*, 394; Wakīᶜ, II, 307, cf., H. Schaeder, "Ḥasan al-Baṣrī, Studien zur Frühgeschichte des Islam," *Der Islam*, IV (1925), 49-50.

78) Ibn Saᶜd, VII, 119; Schaeder, 56-57; H. Ritter, "Studien zur Geschichte der islamischen Frommigkeit," *Der Islam*, XXI (1933), 51.

79) Wakīᶜ, II, 307.

80) It seems, however, that he sympathized with the Shīᶜites because of his quasi-Muᶜtazilite ideas. Various religious parties considered him as one of them: Muᶜtazilites, Ṣūfis, Futuwwa—see H. Ritter, "Ḥasan al-Baṣrī," *EI*[2].

sibility of religious leaders.[81]) But his greatest political impact was as ideological guide to caliphs such as ʿAbd al-Malik and ʿUmar II.

When ʿAbd al-Malik heard that al-Ḥasan had discussed predestination (*qadar*) in a manner which the ruler found objectionable, the caliph deemed it necessary to send him a short personal letter demanding that he explain and justify his views. The Umayyad rulers were interested in fostering the belief in predestination as a justification for their acts—"Everything is from God" (*Qurʾān* IV, 78/80)—including some injustice of the Umayyad rulers. Ḥasan's long reply challenging traditional views on predestination was an implied criticism of the Umayyads, especially of the viceroy of Iraq, al-Ḥajjāj. He denied that evil human actions proceed from God; the responsibility for sin and wrongdoing falls on the shoulders of the doer himself. By insisting that the terms "decree" (*qāḍāʾ*) and "predestination" (*qadar*) refer simply to God's commandments to His believers, Ḥasan neutralized many verses in the *Qurʾān* which apparently advocate predestination.[82])

The sources do not report ʿAbd al-Malik's reaction, but the incident did preserve Ḥasan's moral authority in the eyes of his contemporaries and his political status through the period of ʿUmar II and up to Yazīd II's time.

Before ascending the throne, ʿUmar II wrote to the two men considered the most pious of the age, Ḥasan al-Baṣrī and Muṭarrif b. ʿAbd Allāh b. al-Shikhkhir, asking them to prey for him and give him guidance. Both scholars gave vague replies; they emphasized the temporary character of this world and said the piety of ʿUmar II should be a soothing remedy for its wounds.[83]) Significant is the caliph's request for the approval of the *ʿulamāʾ* in accepting political office.

The third example of involvement by an *ʿālim* in the Umayyad

---

81) Balādhurī, *Futūḥ*, 369-370; Ibn al-Athīr *al-Kāmil fī al-taʾrīkh*, ed. C. J. Tomberg (Leiden, 1851-76), V, 51, 53; Ṭabarī, II, 1979; cf. Schaeder, 64-66.

82) Ritter, "Islamische Frommigkeit," 69, 70; on this topic see an extensive study by M. Schwartz, "The letter of Ḥasan al-Baṣrī," *Oriens*, XX (1967), p. 20.

83) Ibn ʿAbd al-Ḥakam, *Sīrat ʿUmar b. ʿAbd al-ʿAzīz*, (Cairo, 1928) 149-150.

political system is that of ᶜAmir b. Shurāḥil al-Shaᶜbī al-Kūfī (d. 103/721), a famous *faqīh* (religious lawyer) and collector of religious and historical traditions. He competes with Ibn Isḥāq as an authority on historical events, and is often cited by Ṭabarī in his annals. Much like Ḥasan al-Baṣrī, he served as a *qāḍī* in the period of ᶜUmar b. ᶜAbd al-ᶜAzīz. His ideas, however, were opposed to those of al-Ḥasan. Al-Shaᶜbī preferred to rely on *ḥadīth* rather than on reason (*raʾy*), thus rejecting Muᶜtazilite principles. His attitude toward the earlier caliphs foreshadowed that of the Ḥanbalites: he approved of both ᶜUthmān and ᶜAlī, displaying no preference.[84]) Consequently, he did not criticize the Umayyads, and chose neutrality among the various parties. The following statement is typical:

> Love the family of your Prophet (*ahl al-bayt*) without being Shīᶜite... and believe that what is good derives from God and what is evil is of your own making without being Qadarī, and obey the Imām even if he is a black slave without being a Kharijite, and commit what is beyond your understanding to God without being a Murjiʾte.[85])

Al-Shaᶜbī was sent by al-Ḥajjāj to the court of ᶜAbd al-Malik to serve as a tutor to his sons. He also served as the *imām* (prayer leader) and *ᶜarīf* of this tribe, and as the caliph's envoy to the Byzantines.[86]) These were all clearly political functions; they demonstrate the high esteem his religious and historical knowledge won him in the Umayyad court.

Al-Shaᶜbī's diplomatic mission was undertaken at a time when Umayyad-Byzantine relations were at their lowest ebb. The Islamic rulers were trying to prove their superiority in all possible ways; they wanted to display economic independence, administrative unification and achievements in architecture and learning. Al-Shaᶜbī's wide knowledge and expertise in Islamic customs and history impressed

84) Ibn ᶜAsākir (ed. Fayṣal), 152, 164-65.
85) Ibid, 182; cf., Ibn Saᶜd, VI, 173.
86) Ibn ᶜAsākir (ed. Fayṣal), 199-202; cf., al-Khaṭīb al-Baghdādī, *Taʾrīkh Baghdād*, XII, 231. About his appointments as *imām* and *ᶜarīf* see: Ibn Saᶜd, VI, 173.

the Byzantine ruler. Muslim sources have preserved an embarassing anecdote which attests to the authenticity of the story: When asked who was considered worthier in the Islamic community, the fathers or the sons, al-Shaᶜbī dutifully answered: "The fathers." "And who is worthier, the sons or the grandsons?" "The sons of course," answered al-Shaᶜbī. Then the Byzantine ruler said, "Praise be God that he sent you to me! Due to the fact that each of your descendants will acquire more and more evil, the generations which follow will eventually be apes and pigs."[87])

Even more than the Umayyads, the ᶜAbbāsids used the religious knowledge of the *ᶜulamā*ᵓ and their authority in the community to promote ideas favorable to themselves. Their special relationship with the *qāḍīs* goes back to al-Manṣūr's appointment of ᶜUbayd Allāh b. al-Ḥasan al-ᶜAnbarī al-Tamīmī (d. 168/784) as *qāḍī* of Baṣra. In his letter of investiture, al-Manṣūr called the *qāḍī* "a screen (*ḥujāb*) between God and the ruler," and "a deposition of trust (*amāna*) from the caliph to his subjects."[88])

Al-ᶜAnbarī's letter to Manṣūr's successor, al-Mahdī, with its theoretical guidelines to the caliph on practical matters of administration, can be viewed as an expression of continued loyalty.[89])

The epistle covers four areas: the importance of continuing the tradition of the *thughūr* (border land); the systematic appointment of judges (*ḥukkām*); the balanced collection of the land tax (*fay*ᵓ and *kharāj*); and the imposition of proportional taxation on trade (*ṣadaqāt*). Al-ᶜAnbarī states that each caliph must be familiar with established practices. With regard to the judges, he emphasizes that many regulations do not derive from the *Qur*ᵓ*ān* or the *sunna* but rather from the *qāḍī*'s independent judgment (*ijtihād*),[90]) thus the importance of appointing a man with piety, shrewdness and religious knowledge

87) Ibn ᶜAsākir (ed. Faysal), 202.
88) Wakīᶜ, II, 91; see his biography in Ibn Ḥajar al-ᶜAsqalānī, *Tandhīb al-tandhīb*.
89) Wakīᶜ, II, 100-105.
90) Ibid., II, 101.

(ᶜ*ilm*), in that order of importance. Naturally, he attributes to the *qāḍī* control (*haymana*) over all other branches of government; he himself had been appointed to both *qāḍāʾ* and *ṣalāt*, and was occasionally entrusted with financial matters as well. [91])

Abū Yūsuf, Yaᶜqūb b. Ibrāhīm al-Anṣārī, al-Kūfī (d. 182/798), chief *qāḍī* of Hārūn al-Rashīd and one of the founders of the Ḥanafī school of law, wrote his *Kitāb al-kharāj*, a treatise on public finance, taxation, criminal justice and other practical administrative questions, at the request of the caliph. This was not a short letter like that of al-ᶜAnbarī but a serious legal study.

In the introductory chapter, Abū Yūsuf compares the responsibility of the caliph before God to that of the shepherd before the owner of the flock. Like Ḥasan al-Baṣrī, he regards a wicked ruler as a punishment by God of his community:

> Rulers are a scourge through whom God punishes those He decides to punish. So do not meet God's scourge with hot temper and anger but with humility and submission. [92])

In other words, obedience to the ruler is mandatory, even if he is evil. Nevertheless, Abū Yūsuf does not aggrandize; the ruler is merely a shield (*junna*) behind which one fights and on whom one relies. He is obliged to obey the *Qurʾān* and the *sunna*. He may change administrative orders, but he stands below the *sharīᶜa*. According to Abū Yūsuf,

> "a building cannot last if it is not based on the fear of Allāh. Otherwise, Allāh will smite the foundation of the building and crumble it on top of he who built it." [93])

Abū Yūsuf bolsters the status of the ᶜ*ulamāʾ* and the chief *qāḍī*. He was conscious of his own power; the caliph consulted him—the

---

91) Ibid., II, 95, 122.

92) A. Ben Shemesh's translation of Abū Yūsuf, *Kitāb al-Kharāj* in *Taxation in Islam* (London, 1969), III, 43; cf., the same attitude towards tyrants (*ṭaghiya*) of Ḥasan al-Baṣrī-Ibn Saᶜd, VII, 119.

93) Abū Yūsuf, *Kitāb al-kharāj*, tr. Ben Shemesh, In *Taxation*, III, 35.

ʿālim—and not the vizier, on administrative matters, which should have been the natural sphere of the viziers and their secretaries.

Abū Yūsuf had good reason to feel confident about his position. The very fact that he was asked to write a book on administrative matters symbolizes the triumph of the *ʿulamāʾ* over the secretaries in questions of doctrine. The first scholar to write a study bearing the same title—*Kitāo al-kharāj*—had been the vizier of al-Mahdī, Abū ʿUbayd Allāh, Muʿāwiya b. Yasār, who had rationalized the taxation system in the empire, and transferred the levy system in southern Iraq from the *misāḥa* (a fixed land tax) to the *muqāsama* (a proportionate tribute in kind). Abū Yūsuf did not even mention the earlier work composed hardly a generation before, though he had probably read it or at least heard about it.[94])

Abū ʿUbayd Allāh's career had a shameful end, which may help explain why Hārūn al-Rashīd turned to an *ʿalim* rather than a secretary—he wished to avoid the mistake his father al-Mahdī had made. One of the vizier's many enemies (Rabīʿ b. Yūnus *mawlā* al-Manṣūr, future vizier to al-Mahdī), jealous of Abū ʿUbayd Allāh's prestige and his standing with the caliph, accused him of neglecting the religious education of his own son. After the son was found guilty of heresy (*zandaqa*), the father lost his position as chief of Dīwān al-Rasāʾil (chancery) and vizier.[95])

The episode cast a shadow of *zandaqa* on Abū ʿUbayd Allāh himself and rendered his book unworthy from a religious point of view. Hārūn al-Rashīd needed a new book by a Muslim religious scholar to provide a proper foundation for a just administration. For this purpose, he could not have found a more suitable scholar than his chief

---

94) About personal data of Abū ʿUbayd Allāh's career see: Ibn al-Ṭiqṭiqā, *al-Fakhrī* (Beirut, 1966), p. 182, which mentions ʿAbū ʿUbayd Allāh's *Kitāb al-kharāj*. Reference to this study (*risāla*) is also in Qudāma b. Jaʿfar, *Kitāb al-kharāj*, MS 5907, Bibliotheque Nationale (Paris), fl. 101a-b; cf., Ben shemesh, *Taxation*, III, pp. 9-12.

95) Jahshiyārī, *Kitāb al-wuzarāʾ waʾl-kuttāb* (Cairo, 1937), 156, 151-154, 167; Ṭabarī, III, 487-490; Ibn al-Ṭiqṭiqā, 182-183.

judge, one of the founders of the Ḥanafite school, whose authority and advice could not be challenged.

Decline of the Chief Qāḍī

The offices of chief *qāḍī* and vizier first appeared at approximately the same time, in the reign of Hārūn al-Rashīd. The vizierate took much more time to crystallize as an institution, but eventually it became as rooted as the chief qāḍīship in the Islamic administration.

Even under the Muʿtazilite caliphs, when the chief *qāḍī* was the caliph's second in command, the vizier's superiority in terms of protocol and social standing was acknowledged. Chief *qāḍī* Ibn Abī Duwād, principle counselor to al-Muʿtaṣim in matters of state policy and ideology, was ordered to stand up in the presence of the vizier Muḥammad b. Ābd al-Malik al-Zayyāt.[96)]

After the Muʿtazilite period, the office of chief *qāḍī* slowly declined in comparison to the vizier. By the time of al-Muwaffaq and especially al-Muʿtaḍid (269/883-289/902), who initiated an overall financial recovery of the empire and looked for an expert in finances, the vizier had clearly supplanted him as second to the caliph. The vizier even came to appoint the chief *qāḍī*, and occasionally the provincial *qāḍīs* as well, in consultation with the chief *qāḍī*.[97)]

The rivalry between the *ʿulamāʾ* and the secretaries on access to the caliph was resolved through the crystallization of two separate spheres of influence. The doctrinal-ideological sphere was left to the *ʿulamāʾ* (in this respect they were victorious), while political power and ceremonial supremacy was conferred upon the vizier, especially if he had financial training.

In pure judicial matters, the *qāḍī*'s decisions became more and more bound to Islamic law. Given the rigidity of the formal rules of evidence (*shahāda*), it became impossible for him to undertake

---

96) Ibn Khallikān, *Wafayāt*, I, 62.

97) Wakīʿ, III, 254, 256; for the authority of the vizier in appointing *qāḍīs* see: Tanūkhī, *Nishwār*, I, 117, 130.

criminal investigations, and the political authorities transferred control over most criminal justice responsibilities to the police (*shurṭa*) and the military governors. Administrative transgressions were referred to the court of investigation of complaints (*maẓālim*).

Conclusions

In sum, although the *ʿulamāʾ* in the early Islamic period did not constitute an organized social elite, some representative figures—notably the *qāḍī*s—actively participated in shaping the Islamic governmental machine, both technically and ideologically. Technically, they served in various administrative offices. Ideologically, they provided the community with religious legitimacy.

Serving as *quṣṣāṣ*, *imams*, or chief *qāḍī*s, these *ʿulamāʾ* helped the caliphs promote certain ideas that enhanced the popularity of the regime. Some of these ideas, in the form of works like the *Kitāb al-kharāj* of Abū Yūsuf, helped mold the administrative system of the Islamic empire as a whole. In other cases, *ʿulamāʾ* served as caliphal delegates to the outside world, bringing knowledge of Islamic universalism to foreign rulers, and spreading the glory of the caliphs. Thus, despite the stereotyped descriptions in the sources of *ʿulamāʾ* and *qāḍī*s preoccupied with learning, many had careers that were at least partly non-religious.

Although the *ʿulamāʾ* functionaries depended on the arbitrary will of the ruler for their appointment and continued service, they did possess a certain autonomy of judgment, and would in fact often remind the caliph of his duty to obey the *sharīʿa*. When the *qāḍī* al-ʿAnbarī wrote to al-Manṣūr that many Islamic regulations derived solely from the *qāḍī*'s independent judgment (*ijtihād*), by implication he was excluding any judgment by someone who was not an *ʿālim*. True, the *ʿulamāʾ* were not independent in political matters, but they were the only ones who could grant legitimation to political acts.

The practical establishment of this ideological authority was a slow and gradual process, accompanied by a bitter rivalry at the highest government ranks with the viziers, who were influenced by pre-Islamic models of secretarial culture. The formal, hierarchical supremacy of the viziers was never in question, but the actual balance of governmental power and influence tilted back and forth.

Hārūn al-Rashīd's judicial reform clarified the division of labor between the two factors. The *ᶜulamāʾ* won unchallenged ideological supremacy. When Harthama b. Aᶜyun was invested as governor of Khurāsān, al-Rashīd recommended: "In all things he should take the book of God as his model of conduct, but in doubtful cases he must hold his hands and ask the authorities on law, religion and knowledge of the book of God."[98]) Then, when the *Kitāb al-kharāj* of the *ᶜālim*, Abū Yūsuf, was preferred to the *Kitāb al-Kharāj* of the vizier, Abū ᶜUbayd Allāh, as a model of administrative theory, the victory of the *ᶜulamāʾ* in the ideological field was complete.

From then on, the *ᶜulamā*'s opinion had to be heard on important political decisions, if only for the sake of form. When caliphs were deposed, or successors chosen, leading *ᶜulamāʾ*, such as *qāḍī*s and *ᶜudūl* (professional witnesses) are often mentioned as mandatory witnesses.[99]) Even military officers understood this rule, and used the services of the *ᶜulamāʾ* to legalize their actions, sometimes even to fight the caliph himself.[100]) Even in the later Middle Ages, which are outside of the period examined here, it was the chief *qāḍī*, and not the vizier, who defined the ideological norms of the Islamic polity. In these definitions, he served as both obedient tool of the administration and an independent ideological power—the only lawful representative of the *Sharīᶜa*.

---

98) *Fragmenta*, 314, Ṭabarī, III, 717; cf. Goldziher *Muslim Studies*, II, p. 75.

99) *Fragmenta*, 561; Miskawayh, *Tajārib al-umam*, ed. H. F. Amedroz (London, 1920), II, pp. 1, 67.

100) Miskawayh, II, 188.

9

ISLAMIC JURISTIC TERMINOLOGY BEFORE ŠĀFI'Ī: A SEMANTIC ANALYSIS WITH SPECIAL REFERENCE TO KŪFA

Zafar Ishaq Ansari

THE development of Islamic jurisprudence, particularly its early, formative phase has increasingly attracted the attention of scholars. The present paper does not aim at discussing the early development of Islamic jurisprudence as such. Its purpose is merely to study the terminology employed in the early period of Islam, especially in the writings of the second century authors, to subject some of the important terms used in *fiqh* to semantic analysis, to consider the character and significance of this terminology and explore its possible bearing on the issues which confront the students of the early history of Islamic jurisprudence.

What strikes one at the very outset of this investigation, as will be substantiated in the following pages, is the comparative lack of fixity in the technical connotation of the terms in use. It also shows that a number of concepts—some of them of quite fundamental importance in law—had been in existence and had influenced the thinking of people for quite some time. Nevertheless, they had as yet not acquired a standard, technical mould for their expression. Hence, these concepts were expressed in a variety of ways and through a variety of interchangeable terms and expressions. The simultaneous use of the same terms in technical as well as non-technical sense presents a baffling problem for the student of the early period of Islamic *fiqh*. The difficulty that presents itself is not merely that many terms have gradually changed their connotation over the course of centuries. No less serious is the difficulty which arises owing to the use of these terms in a multiplicity of meanings by one and the same author and often in the same work. Despite this fluid and confusing state of affairs, the process of the terms acquiring an increasingly technical connotation is clearly noticeable and around the middle of the second century it did not seem very far from its point of culmination.

Let us now turn to a semantic survey and analysis of some of the important terms in use during the period under study.

I. *Ḥadīṯ*

In the early Islamic literature, the terms *ḥadīṯ*, *aṯar*, *riwāya* and *ḫabar* were used more or less interchangeably. As yet *ḥadīṯ* did not exclusively mean [a report about] "the utterance, the action, the tacit approval and the *ṣifa* of the Prophet" [1]. Nor was *aṯar* generally used in the technical sense in which it was used in the classical times, in the sense of a tradition from some Companion [2] (as distinguished from a tradition from the Prophet).

Coming to *ḥadīṯ*, it would be instructive to examine carefully its use, for instance, in an important work of the second century *viz.* Abū Yūsuf's *K. al-Radd ʿalā Siyar al-Awzāʿī* [3], insofar as the conclusions thus arrived at are corroborated, in our view, by the study of the use of this term in other works of the second century, particularly those of Abū Yūsuf and Šaybānī, the representatives of the Kūfian school of *fiqh*.

In this work the term *ḥadīṯ* occurs twenty five times. Out of these it is only on three occasions that it either does not refer to the Prophet, or refers to others besides him as well [4]. Except for

---

1. ʿABD AL-NABĪ B. ʿABD AL-RASŪL, *Dustūr al- ʿUlamāʾ*, 4 vols., (Hyderabad, 1329), see vol. II, p. 15. (Cited hereafter as *Dustūr al- ʿUlamāʾ*). For distinction between *ḫabar* and *ḥadīṯ*, even during the first two centuries of Islām see Nabia ABBOTT, *Studies in Arabic Literary Papyri*, (Chicago, 1957), vol. I, p. 7.

2. *Dustūr al-ʿUlamāʾ*, vol. I, p. 37; AL-ZABĪDĪ, *Tāǧ al-ʿArūs*, 10 vols., (Būlāq, 1285-1307), vol. III, p. 4. It is significant that Šāfiʿī, generally reserved the term *aṯar* for traditions from the Companions. (See J. SCHACHT, *The Origins of Muhammadan Jurisprudence*, II impression, Oxford, 1959), p. 16. (Cited hereafter as *Origins*).

3. Whenever page numbers of this book (cited hereafter as *Tr.* IX), have been cited in this paper, they refer to the edition of this treatise published under the editorship of Abū l-Wafāʾ al-Afġānī from Cairo in 1357 A.H. In general we have referred to sections and paragraphs and in this we have followed the division made by Schacht in *Origins*, p. 335.

4. The instances of this kind of use are the following:
(i) For a tradition regarding the distribution of booty during the caliphate of ʿUmar and of ʿUṯmān. (*Tr.* IX, I, p. 5.).
(ii) For a tradition from ʿUmar and ʿAlī (*Ibid.*, 15, p. 52).
(iii) Another use: "We have received none except one *ḥadīṯ* from the Prophet or his Companions." (*Ibid.*, 9, p. 41. Emphasis is our own).
To these should be added the following examples of the use of the term with reference to traditions from the Companions in other works of Abū Yūsuf and Šaybānī. See ABŪ YŪSUF, *K. al-Ḫarāǧ*, (cited hereafter as *Ḫarāǧ*), (Cairo, 1352 A.H.), p. 19, (in connection with ʿUmar's approval of a certain principle in the distribution of booty); p. 65, (referring to several traditions with the same content, attributed to the Prophet and to ʿUmar); p. 70 (a

the three above-mentioned instances, all the rest of the uses of *ḥadīṯ* have reference to the Prophet. The following is an account of the use of the term with reference to the Prophet:

(1) *Ḥadīṯ rasūl Allāh.* (*Tr.* IX, 2, p. 14; 20, p. 63; 50, p. 135)
(2) *Ḥadīṯ ʿan rasūl Allāh.* (*Ibid.*, 5, p. 29 and p. 30, ll. 6 and 8, and p. 31, l. 2; 20, p. 64, l. 5 f.; 22, p. 69; 43, p. 121)
(3) *Ḥadīṯ rafaʿahu ilā rasūl Allāh.* (*Ibid.*, 1, p. 11)
(4) *Wa-qad balaġanā ʿan rasūl Allāh ʿan al-ṯiqāt ḥadīṯ musnad ʿan al-riǧāl al-maʿrūfīn bi-l-fiqh al-maʾmūnīn ʿalayhim.* (*Ibid.*, 2, pp. 15 f.)

(This expresses the growing formalism of the traditions from the Prophet, the higher value of the traditions which had *isnād* and the transmitters of which were well known for their moral and mental qualities).

(5) *Iyyāka wa-šāḏḏ al-ḥadīṯ.* (*Ibid.*, 5, p. 31. With slight modification, *ibid.*, 5, pp. 34 f., and 38, p. 105)

(This is a warning made after mentioning ʿUmar's practice of not accepting "tradition from the Prophet" without the testimony of two witnesses).

(6) *Al-ḥadīṯ fī hāḏā kaṯīr wa-l-sunna fī hāḏā maʿrūfa.* (*Ibid.*, 7, p. 38. With slight alteration *ibid.*, 8, p. 40). (On both the occasions the statement is preceded by the mention of traditions from the Prophet).
(7) *Fa-ʿalayka min al-ḥadīṯ fīmā taʿrifuhu l-ʿāmma.* (*Ibid.*, 5, p. 24. Repeated with slight modification *ibid.*, 5, p. 31).

This last statement (i.e. on p. 24) has been made by Abū Yūsuf while refuting the authenticity of an alleged tradition from the Prophet cited by Awzāʿī relating to the Prophet's apportioning of share in booty to those who had been killed. Abū Yūsuf says: "We do not know that the Prophet apportioned the share of any of those killed on the day of Badr, or Ḥunayn . . . although a number of well-known people were killed and we do not know that he apportioned the share [in the booty] to any of them . . .". (After this he adds the expression quoted above, which is followed by a tradition from the Prophet).

---

tradition from ʿUmar with which Ibn ʿAbbās agreed); Muḥammad b. al-Ḥasan AL-ŠAYBĀNĪ, *al-Muwaṭṭaʾ*, (Lucknow, 1306 A.H.), (cited hereafter as *Muw. Š.*), p. 323, (a tradition from ʿAlī); *ibid.*, p. 97, (a *ḥadīṯ* from ʿUmar). See also AL-ŠAYBĀNĪ, *K. al-Ḥuǧaǧ*, (Lucknow, 1888), (cited hereafter as *Ḥuǧaǧ*), p. 164, etc.

(8) *Inna l-ḥadīṯ sa-yafšū ʿannī.* (*Ibid.*, 5, p. 25).
(The person to whom the saying is attributed is the Prophet himself).
(9) *Mā ǧāʾa fī hāḏā min al-aḥādīṯ kaṯīr.* (*Ibid.*, 7, p. 38).
(The sentence is preceded by the words: "We do not know that the Prophet apportioned the share of women in the booty . . .").

This shows that even though *ḥadīṯ* had not acquired its exclusivist technical connotation, *viz.* that of traditions about "the utterance, action, the tacit approval, or the *ṣifa* of the Prophet . . ." [1], which it did acquire in the following centuries in Islamic religious literature particularly in the works of *ḥadīṯ* and *fiqh*. Nevertheless, it was heading in that direction and was fairly close to that point. This is evident from the fact that the term *ḥadīṯ* has been used in an overwhelming majority of cases with reference to traditions from the Prophet [2] and refers much less to traditions from the Companions. As for its use in the sense of "tradition" or "report" as such, this usage is quite rare [3].

The above analysis also throws light on the process of the formation of technical terms. It shows how the increasing use of a term in a particular context made that context an almost essential part of the meaning of the term, at least in the scientific usage. To take up the instance of *ḥadīṯ*, it originally meant "communication" [4] (besides meaning, when used as an adjective, 'new'). In the pre-Islamic times it was used with reference to the narration of historical episodes of the distant past. It referred to the glorious deeds of

1. See above p. [2], n. 1. For the examples of its use in the sense of 'tradition' as such, without any reference to the Prophet and/or the Companions, see *Ḫarāǧ*, p. 6, where Abū Yūsuf mentions to the Caliph that he has written for him "good *aḥādīṯ*". See also *ibid.*, p. 39 where a *šayḫ* of al-Ḥīra (according to another manuscript, al-Ǧazīra), from whom Abū Yūsuf had inquired about the agreements concluded between the conquering Muslims and the local populace, etc., writes to Abū Yūsuf the information available to him, making it clear that it was not derived from the *fuqahāʾ*, but consisted of *aḥādīṯ* of the specialists in these matters (*man yuʾṣaf bi-ʿilm ḏālik*).

2. For a few instances of the use of the term *ḥadīṯ* in the sense of traditions from the Prophet, see *Ḫarāǧ*, p. 89 (*aḥādīṯ* from the Messenger of Allāh); p. 121 (*ḥadīṯ* from the Messenger of Allāh); p. 18 (reference to *aḥādīṯ* and *āṯār* followed by citation of two traditions from the Prophet); *Muw. Š.*, pp. 261 and 389; *Ḥuǧaǧ*, pp. 2, 3, 15, 51, 57, 189 (*al-ḥadīṯ al-mustafīḍ* from Ibn ʿAbbās that the Messenger of Allāh . . .); p. 201, ll. 3 and 5; p. 230, and often.

3. For the use of the term *ḥadīṯ* in the sense of 'tradition' as such, see n. 1 above.

4. Fīrūzābādī, *Qāmūs*, II edition, 4 vols., (Cairo, 1952 A.D.), vol. I, p. 170.

the tribes, the *ayyām* [1]. It was from this background that the word gradually developed its technical Islamic connotation. And now since the Prophet (and his Companions) were looked upon as the heroes of the new society, the heralds of the new age, "communications" generally centered around them. Later, the context of the use of the term, even when explicit reference to the Prophet was not made, signified "communication" about or from the Prophet. In short, it was partly frequency of using a term in a certain context, combined with the strong consciousness of the paramount importance of the Prophet, which ultimately fixed its technical connotation.

II. *Sunna*

Another key-word in the *fiqh* literature of the early as well as of the subsequent period is *sunna*. The difficulty with regard to *sunna* arises because it seems to be used in different meanings, and at times it is not quite clear whether the *sunna* in question refers to the *sunna* of the Prophet, or of the Companions, or to the principle derived from the *sunna* of the Prophet and/or the Companions which has been reinforced by consensus.

Looking at the word etymologically, the root *SNN* from which the word *sunna* is derived seems to have referred originally to the "flow and continuity of a thing with ease and smoothness" [2]. Hence, if a person poured water on another person's face in such a manner that the water easily flowed away, the standard form of expressing this action was to say: "*sanantu l-mā' ʿalā waǧhih*" [3]. It was because of this that *sunna* began to be used in the sense of "way, course" (in the physical sense), presumably because it was easy to tread and traverse it, with the result that normally it was trodden. It is for this reason that the derivatives of *SNN* were employed with reference to the course across which winds blew or along which water flowed [4].

---

1. I. Goldziher, *Muhammedanische Studien*, II edition, (Hildesheim, 1961); see vol. II, p. 3.
2. Aḥmad b. Fāris b. Zakariyyā, *Muʿǧam Maqāyīs al-Luġa*, ed. ʿAbd al-Salām Muḥammad Hārūn, 6 vols., (Cairo, 1368 A.H.), vol. III, pp. 60 f.
3. *Loc. cit.* See also Zamaḫšarī, *Asās al-Balāġa*, (Cairo, 1372 A.H.), p. 222.
4. See Ibn Fāris, *op. cit.*, p. 60. (The expression "*ǧā'at al-rīḥ sanā'in*" was used when winds came through the same course). See Zamaḫšarī, *op. cit.*, p. 222, especially the quotation of the couplet of ʿUmar b. Abī Rabīʿa: "*Qad ǧarrat al-rīḥ bihā ḏaylahā/wa-'ustanna fī aṭlālihā wābilu*".

The word had, therefore, the nuance of ease and facility in its original usage. It was this nuance which presumably paved the way for the use of *SNN* and its derivatives, particularly in ancient Arabic poetry, with reference to the admirable aspects of the face —its brightness and polish, its being smooth and well-shaped. This gave rise to the expression *masnūn al-wağh* meaning a person of comely shape, a person on whose face "flesh had been made even and smooth" [1], or even for its being "well-proportioned" (*muʿtadil*) [2]. The use with respect to the admirable features of the face became so common that *sunna* began to signify face itself [3].

The next stage in the evolution of the connotation of *sunna* seems to have been the extension of the signification of the term to human behaviour. "Way and course" began to be used in the sense of *sīra*. *Sunna* began to mean, therefore, "a way, course, rule, mode, or manner, of acting or conduct of life" [4], and became an equivalent

---

1. See Ibn Fāris, *op. cit.*, p. 60, and Zamaḫšarī, *op. cit.*, p. 222.

2. *Loc. cit.*

3. Lane, *Lexicon*, ed. Stanley Lane-Poole, Book I in 8 parts, (New York, 1893 A.D.), see part IV, p. 1438. (Cited hereafter as *Lexicon*). See also Ibn Manẓūr, *Lisān al-ʿArab*, 15 vols., (Beirut, 1374-76), vol. XIII, p. 224. (Cited hereafter as *Lisān*). See further for the use of *sunna* in this sense: *Dīwān Ḥassān b. Ṯābit*, ed. ʿAbd al-Raḥmān al-Barqūqī, (Cairo, 1929), p. 24, l. 3; Abū l-Farağ al-Iṣfahānī, *K. al-Aġānī*, 21 vols., (Beirut, 1956-57 A.D.), vol. V, p. 143, l. 3; vol. VI, p. 227, l. 7; vol. VII, p. 180, l. 3; vol. X, p. 241, l. 12. (Cited hereafter as *Aġānī*); *Tāğ al-ʿArūs*, vol. IX, p. 244, ll. 7 and 8; *Lisān*, vol. XVII, p. 88, ll. 9 and 11; *al-Mufaḍḍaliyyāt*, ed. Ch. Lyall, (Oxford, 1921 A.D.), p. 185, l. 15 (repeated p. 542, l. 12 and p. 791, l. 1); Farazdaq, *Dīwān*, ed. ʿAbd Allāh Ismāʿīl al-Ṣāwī, (Cairo, 1936 A.D.), p. 329, l. 4; Ḏū l-Rumma, *Dīwān Šiʿr Ḏī l-Rumma*, ed. C. H. H. Macartney, (Cambridge, 1919 A.D.), p. 4, l. 11; p. 266, l. 4; ʿUmar b. Abī Rabīʿa, *Dīwān*, ed. Muḥammad Muḥyi l-Dīn ʿAbd al-Ḥamīd, (Cairo, 1935 A.D.), p. 25, l. 14; p. 133, l. 7; al-Aḫṭal, *Šiʿr al-Aḫṭal*, (Beirut, 1891-92 A.D.), p. 278, l. 6; *Dīwān ʿUbayd al-Ăbraṣ al-Saʿadī al-Asadī*, ed. Charles Lyall (Leiden, 1913), p. 67 l. 13; Ṭabarī, *Taʾrīḫ*, 8 vols., (Cairo, 1358 A.H.), vol. V, p. 123, l. 5; vol. VII, p. 281, l. 1.

4. *Lexicon*, part IV, p. 1438. For instances of the use of the term *sunna* in this sense, see *Dīwān Ḥassān*, p. 24, l. 3; *Aġānī*, vol. VI, p. 128, l. 8; vol. VII, p. 179, l. 2; vol. IX, p. 139, l. 2; vol. XII, p. 379, l. 4; vol. XIII, p. 73, l. 13; Ğāḥiẓ, *K. al-Ḥayawān*, ed. ʿAbd al-Salām Muḥammad Hārūn, 7 vols. (Cairo, 1943 A.D.), vol. VII, p. 84, l. 2; *Tāğ al-ʿArūs*, vol. I, p. 256, l. 14 (*sunna* of al-Fārūq, i.e. ʿUmar, the second caliph); *Lisān*, vol. XIV, p. 291, l. 20, (a *sunna* and its leader, Labīd); *Mufaḍḍaliyyāt*, *op. cit.* p. 830, l. 1; *Dīwān Farazdaq*, p. 308, l. 3; *Dīwān Kuṯayyir b. ʿAbd al-Raḥmān al-Ḫuzāʿī*, (n.p., 1930 A.D.), p. 35, l. 7; ʿUbayd Allāh b. Qays, *al-Ruqayyāt*, ed. Muḥammad Yūsuf Nağm, (Beirut, 1378), p. 9, l. 12; al-Qālī, *Simṭ al-Laʾālī*, ed. ʿAbd al-ʿAzīz al-Maymanī, (Cairo, 1936 A.D.), p. 393, l. 18, (*qaḍāʾuhu sunna wa-qawluhu maṯal*); *Naqaʾiḍ bayn Ğarīr wa-Farazdaq*, ed. Anthony

of *sīra*. Apart from inheriting the meaning 'way and course' from the past, the root *SNN* also retained the sense of ease, smoothness, etc. *Sunna* therefore signified, *inter alia*, a mode of behaviour which a person could adopt without difficulty [1]. This seems to be the background in which the term *sunna* developed the nuance of moral appropriateness and normativeness [2]. Even if one might doubt that appropriateness and normativeness were essential ingredients of the meaning of the word *sunna*, there can be no doubt that it generally carried that nuance. Ḥassān (d. 54), the famous poet of the Prophet, mentions a group of people as having "explicated a *sunna* for the people which is followed" [3]. Another poet speaks of the *sunna* of al-Fārūq which contextually has a normative overtone [4]. The Umayyad poet Farazdaq (d. 110) refers to the *sunna* of the two ʿUmars which, in his words, is "a cure for the malady of the hearts" [5]. Another poet, exalting a person says that "his judgement is a *sunna*, and his saying, a *maṯal*" [6].

In the Qur'ān, the term *sunna* (including its plural, *sunan*) has been used sixteen times in all. The expression which occurs most often is that of the "*sunna* of Allāh", which seems to be a literary innovation of the Qur'ān. *Sunnat Allāh* refers to God's *modus operandi* in respect of those wayward peoples who had greeted God's message with contempt and hostility. This had led to their doom by virtue of the operation of God's law of retribution [7].

ASHLEY BIRAN, (Leiden, 1908-09 A.D.), vol. II, p. 1015, (the *sunna* of the two ʿUmars, i.e. of ʿUmar b. al-Ḫaṭṭāb and ʿUmar b. ʿAbd al-ʿAzīz); ṬABARĪ, *Ta'rīḫ*, vol. VII, p. 38, l. 1; BUḤTURĪ, *K. al-Ḥamāsa*, (Beirut, 1910 A.D.), p. 23, l. 10 (a couplet of Zuhayr). That *sunna* and *sīra* were interchangeable is proved, for instance, by the fact that the famous couplet of Ḫālid b. ʿUtba al-Huḏalī: *Fa-lā taǧziʿanna ʿan sunnatin anta sirtahā/Fa-awwalu rāḍin sunnatan man yasīruhā* (*Aġānī*, V, p. 128, l. 8), has been reported with slight variations which are significant. In one instance, *sirtahā* has been replaced by *sanantahā* (*ibid.*, vol. XIII, p. 73, l. 13) and in two other instances the word *sunna* in the first line of the couplet has been replaced by *sīra* (*Tāǧ al-ʿArūs*, vol. IX, p. 244, l. 7; *Lisān*, vol. I, p. 377, l. 12).

1. IBN FĀRIS, *op. cit.*, p. 61.
2. Cf. FAZLUR RAHMAN, *Islamic Methodology in History*, (Karachi, 1965), pp. 2 ff.
3. *Dīwān Ḥassān b. Ṯābit*, p. 248, l. 1.
4. *Tāǧ al-ʿArūs*, vol. I, p. 256, l. 14; *Lisān*, vol. I, p. 377, l. 12.
5. *Naqā'iḍ*, p. 1015, l. 15.
6. *Simṭ al-La'ālī*, *op. cit.*, p. 397, l. 18. For other instances showing the normative nuance of the word see *Dīwān Farazdaq*, p. 308, l. 3; *Mufaḍḍaliyyāt*, p. 830, l. 1; *Ruqayyāt*, p. 9, l. 12; *al-Muʿallaqāt al-ʿAšar*, ed. AL-ŠANQĪṬĪ, (Cairo, 1353 A.H.), p. 105, l. 6; *Tāǧ al-ʿArūs*, vol. IX, p. 173, l. 18.
7. *Qur'ān*, XL, 85; XLVIII, 23; XXXIII, 38; etc.

God's law of retribution, then, is the inalterable *sunna* of Allāh [1]. Another usage of the *sunna* of Allāh occurs in connection with God's mode of dealing with His prophets. The Qur'ān points out that when the bearers of God's message are received by a people with hostility, God supports His prophets and sustains their spirit, besides destroying those who oppose God's message. The other usual form in which the term *sunna* has been used is: *sunnat al-awwalīn* [2]. This refers, as Bayḍāwī has pointed out, to the "*sunna* of Allāh with regard to the ancients" [3]. For the verses in which *sunnat al-awwalīn* has been used, the reference is to God's scourge which overtook the nations that had spurned His message.

The concept which was to play an important part in moulding Muslim thought, however, was not that of the "*sunna* of Allāh", but of the "*sunna* of the Messenger of Allāh". In the Qur'ān itself this expression is conspicuous for its absence. This seems to support the view that the concept which this expression embodies must be a later invention. This, however, is altogether erroneous. It seems natural that the ramifications of this concept should have unfolded gradually, but the essence of the concept is very clearly and forcefully embodied in the Qur'ān itself which puts forth the conduct of the Prophet as conduct *par excellence*: "Certainly you have in the Messenger of Allāh a good example . . ." [4].

It was not surprising, therefore, that quite early in the history of Islām, the expression "*sunna* of the Prophet", began to be used,

1. XXXIII, 43; XLVIII, 23.
2. VII, 38; XV, 13; XVIII, 55; XXXV, 431. Cf. III, 137: "*Sunnas* have passed before you . . ." which, in this writer's view, refers to the same theme.
3. Bayḍāwī, *vide* his *Commentary*, verse VIII, 38. Cf. Hurgronje's remark: "*Sunna* . . . can be taken both in the active and the passive sense: a man's *sunna* is both the way in which he usually acts, and the way in which things happen to him. The manner in which Allah has usually treated, and still treats the generations who reject His Messengers, is repeated by Allah's *sunna* in the Koran, whereas the '*sunna* of the former generations' refers repeatedly to the manner in which, or the rule according to which, they had been treated. Thus the '*sunna* of the Prophet' is the way of acting, or, following an extension of the meaning which the later system applied to this term, the way of acting which he prescribed to others during his lifetime, or which he allowed to go on around him without reproof." H. C. Hurgronje, *Selected Works*, tr. and ed. J. Schacht and H. Bousquet, (Leiden, 1957), p. 268.
4. *Qur'ān*, XXXIII, 21. This is not an isolated remark about Muḥammad, but seems to be the consistent view of the Qur'ān with regard to the prophets as such. See, for instance, LX, 4.

despite its not having been used in the Qur'ān, and the Prophet himself is said to have used this expression a number of times [1]. There seems no reason why the Prophet should not have used this expression since it accurately embodies the above-mentioned Quranic concept of the model-behaviour of the Prophet.

Leaving that aside, one of the earliest uses of the expression is attributed to 'Umar who is reported to have explained the function of his officials as consisting of the instruction of people in their religion and in the *sunna* of their Prophet [2]. Another instance of the use of the expression "*sunna* of the Prophet" which has been reported, and which seems to be authentic—relates to the occasion of the choice of the caliph after the death of 'Umar in the year 23. Questions were put to both 'Uṯmān and 'Alī, the two candidates who stood the best chance of election, whether they were prepared to "work according to the *sunna* of the Prophet and the *sīra* of the two preceding caliphs" [3].

Another authentic writing of the first century wherein the expression "*sunna* of the Prophet" occurs is the letter of al-Ḥasan al-Baṣrī to the Umayyad caliph 'Abd al-Malik (65-86). Ḥasan defends his standpoint which is in opposition to *ǧabr*, claiming validity for his doctrine on the ground that it was the doctrine of the forbears (*salaf*). Ḥasan extols these forbears, pointing out that they "acted according to the ordinance of Allāh, narrated His Wisdom, and followed the *sunna* of the Messenger of Allāh . . ." [4].

1. See, for instance, MUSLIM, *Ṣaḥīḥ*, "*Masāǧid*", "*Īmān*"; TIRMIḎĪ, *Ṣaḥīḥ*, "*Ṣalāh*"; ABŪ DĀWŪD, *Sunan*, "*Ṭalāq*" and "*Sunna*"; IBN MĀǦAH, *Sunan*, "*Ṭalāq*", "*Nikāḥ*"; NASĀ'Ī, *Sunan*, "*Quḍāh*"; AḤMAD B. ḤANBAL, *Musnad*, 6 vols., (Cairo, 1315 A.H.), vol. II, p. 124.

2. *Ḫarāǧ*, pp. 14 and 115, Cf. FAZLUR RAHMAN, (*op. cit.*, pp. 8 f.) who argues on circumstantial grounds for the possible genuineness of this statement attributed to 'Umar.

3. ṬABARĪ, *Ta'rīḫ*, vol. III, p. 297. Schacht considers the connotation of the term *sunna* in this particular case to have been political and administrative rather than legal. J. SCHACHT, *Introduction to Islamic Law*, (London, 1964), p. 17. (Cited hereafter as *Introduction*). It is true that the occasion when this sentence was uttered the subject of the conversation was primarily administrative and political. This does not warrant, however, the conclusion that the expression itself signified this restricted scope of the *sunna*. Cf. Nabia ABBOTT, *Studies in Arabic Literary Papyri*, vol. II, (Chicago, 1967), p. 27

4. See al-Ḥasan al-Baṣri's "Treatise", ed. H. RITTER in *Der Islam*, vol. XXI, (1933), p. 68. (Emphasis is our own). This letter was written to 'Abd al-Malik and hence between the years 75 and 86 A.H. Cf. *Islamic Methodology*, p. 12 for the views of Fazlur Rahman as to the content of the concept

Again, in the letter of the founder of the Ibāḍiyyah sect, ʿAbd Allāh b. Ibāḍ (d. 86) to Caliph ʿAbd al-Malik, the expression "*sunna* of the Prophet" occurs several times. This letter is an apology of the Ibāḍī viewpoint in regard to ʿUṯmān. The main point that Ibn Ibāḍ makes is that ʿUṯmān introduced innovations and disregarded the Qurʾān, the *sunna* of the Prophet, and the *sunna* of the preceding caliphs—Abū Bakr and ʿUmar. He extols Abū Bakr for having followed the Book of Allāh and for having practised the *sunna* of the Prophet, and hence none blamed him [1]. Contrary to this was the attitude of ʿUṯmān who introduced innovations which were not in vogue in the time of his two predecessors [2]. Ibn Ibāḍ further accuses ʿUṯmān of persecuting those who admonished him by referring to the Book of Allāh, the *sunna* of the Prophet and traditions about the believers who had preceded him [3]. Ibn Ibāḍ also strongly denies that the accusation of religious extremism (*ġuluww fī l-dīn*) applied to him. This allegation, in his opinion, was applicable to those who attributed false things to God and were guided by things other than the Book of Allāh and the *sunna* set by the Prophet [4].

---

of the *sunna* of the Prophet as embodied in this letter. (It is incorrect, however, to state, which Rahman does, that "... Ḥasan tells ʿAbd al-Malik b. Marwān that although there is no *Ḥadīṯ* from the Prophet in favour of the freedom of the will and human responsibility, nevertheless this is the *Sunna* of the Prophet." (*Ibid.*, p. 12). Cf. also *Origins*, pp. 74 and 141. It needs to be pointed out here that the *sunna* of the Prophet has not been put forth by Ḥasan as the argument in support of his doctrine of *qadar*, which is the claim of Rahman and Schacht. What he is saying is that the doctrine of *ǧabr* did not constitute an item of belief to which the *salaf* subscribed. Hence the main argument of Ḥasan against the opponents is that the *salaf* did not subscribe to this doctrine and hence it is an innovation, a statement which he even explicitly makes. (See *ibid.*, p. 68). Here he is merely trying to fortify the authority of the *salaf* by stating their merits and one of those merits is that they followed the *sunna* of the Prophet.

1. See his letter in AL-BARRĀDĪ, *K. al-Ǧawāhir*, (Cairo, 1302 A.H.), p. 157.

2. *Ibid.*, 158. On p. 160 the same accusation is repeated in the following words: "*ḥakama bi-ġayr mā anzal Allāh wa-ḫālafa sabīl rasūl Allāh wa-sabīl ṣāḥibayh.*"

3. *Loc. cit.* For other examples of the expression "*sunna* of the Prophet", see *ibid.*, p. 165 (twice), and p. 166.

4. *Ibid.*, p. 164. He says that on the contrary those who are indignant at [the sight of] disobedience to God and who summon towards the "Book of Allāh and the *sunna* of His Messenger and the *sunna* of the believers ...." cannot be accused of extremism. (*Loc. cit.*). The expression *sunna* of the believers is significant. It seems to refer, broadly, to the way of life of the Muslims as a whole which was based on the Book of Allāh and the *sunna*

Considering the fact that only a few works of the first century have survived the ravages of time, not to mention the fact that not many works were composed during that century, the above-cited examples at least indicate that the expression "*sunna* of the Prophet" was well in use even during the first century.

Before proceeding to analyse the usages of the term *sunna* in the literature of the second century, it is worthwhile examining its use in a treatise which was composed *circa* 140 A.H. This is the treatise of Ibn al-Muqaffaʿ (d. *circa* 140), *al-Risāla fī l-Ṣaḥāba*. Since Ibn al-Muqaffaʿ was a government official and *littérateur*, rather than a jurist, his usages of the word *sunna* are of invaluable significance. For, the fact that he was not a jurist makes it unlikely that Ibn al-Muqaffaʿ would have used terms such as *sunna* in any other except the generally accepted sense.

Ibn al-Muqaffaʿ's interest lies in administrative matters, in matters which are the primary concern of the ruler: "the sending forth of military expedition and recalling it; the collection and distribution [of the revenue]; the appointment and dismissal of officials; passing judgements according to *ra'y* in matters regarding which there is no *aṯar*; the enforcement of *ḥudūd* and ordinances in accordance with the Book and the *sunna* . . ." [1]. Ibn al-Muqaffaʿ adds that even though man should obey none when obedience involves disobedience to God, yet administrative matters, and the matters with regard to which no *aṯar* exists, are questions of purely governmental discretion and disobedience to the ruler in such matters is tantamount to perdition [2]. Ibn al-Muqaffaʿ also urges the ruler to realize that the claim to which he is entitled against his subjects is not an absolute one. His right to claim obedience is conditioned with his enforcement of positive commandments and *sunan* [3].

Ibn al-Muqaffaʿ's view of the legal doctrines is tinged by his concern with administration. He desires to see the prevalence of a uniform code of laws everywhere. The spectacle which he observes

---

of the Prophet. Ibn Ibāḍ's reference to "*sunna* of the believers" is broadly the same as the concept of 'practice'. For 'practice', see this writer's doctoral dissertation, "The Early Development of Islamic *fiqh* in Kūfah", (typescript), McGill University, Montreal, 1966), pp. 209 ff. (Cited hereafter as "Early Development").

1. "*al-Risāla fī l-Ṣaḥāba*", in Muḥammad Kurd ʿAlī, ed., *Rasā'il al-Bulaġā'*, IV edition, (Cairo, 1954), p. 121.

2. *Loc. cit.*

3. *Ibid.*, p. 122.

around him, however, is one of shocking diversity: a diversity which is found between the doctrines of one town and the other, as well as within a particular town [1]. He is disconcerted at this diversity and tries to analyse its causes and hence denounces those who, in his view, are responsible for it. Says Ibn al-Muqaffaʿ:

> As for those who claim adherence to the *sunna*, among them are those who make into *sunna* something which is not a *sunna*. In this they go to such an extent as to shed blood without any *bayyina* (evidence) or *ḥuǧǧa* (proof) on the basis of something which they consider to be *sunna*. And if they were to be questioned about that, they would not be able to say that blood was shed in that case during the time of the Prophet or subsequently during the time of *aʾimmat al-hudā*.[2] And if it were said to them: "When was blood shed according to *sunnah* which you claim?", they would say: ʿAbd al-Malik b. Marwān or some other *amīr* from among the *umarāʾ* did that". [They believe in such a doctrine even while knowing that the innovator of a doctrine] merely follows *raʾy*. And they reach such a point of adamance with respect to their opinion (*raʾy*) as to subscribe to those doctrines concerning matters of momentous importance for Muslims with which not even a single Muslim agrees. Then they do not feel distressed at being isolated in this matter, and in enforcing judgements according to such doctrines, even though they acknowledge that they do not argue from a Book or a *sunna*.[3]

What is striking in the above passage is the basis of Ibn al-Muqaffaʿ's stringent criticism. Ibn al-Muqaffaʿ says that people made the claim of *sunna* even though they could not document that claim by establishing the existence of that practice during the lifetime of the Prophet or of the early Caliphs, and all that they could adduce as evidence was the practice of ʿAbd al-Malik or of some other rulers of a relatively late period, even though the practice concerned was based on their personal opinion, instead of being supported by arguments drawn from the Qurʾān and the *sunna* [4]. In other words, true *sunna* is that alone which can be traced back to the time of the Prophet and/or of the early Caliphs [5].

To revert to the expression "*sunna* of the Prophet": the meaning is clear enough in cases in which reference to the Prophet is explicit.

---

1. *Ibid.*, p. 126.
2. This meant the first four Caliphs. (See *Ḥuǧaǧ*, p. 32). Another expression for the same was "*al-ḫulafāʾ al-rāšidūn*" (the reference, in both the cases, being to the first four caliphs) and was used, for instance, by Layṯ in his letter to Mālik. (See Ibn al-Qayyim, *Iʿlām al-Muwaqqiʿīn*, 4 vols. Cairo, 1374 A.H., vol. III, p. 96).
3. *Ibid.*, p. 126.
4. This indictment is much the same as Abū Yūsuf's indictment of al-Awzāʿī and the Ḥiǧāzīs. (See *Tr.* IX, 1, p. 11, and 3, p. 21).
5. Cf. *Origins*, pp. 58 f, pp. 103 f. and 137.

Considerable difficulty arises, however, when one finds the term *sunna* being used without any genitive. It is also intriguing to find it being used occasionally with reference to others besides the Prophet. In fact the different uses of *sunna* lead one to the conclusion that it was used in a variety of meanings, and that though the term was in process of acquiring its technical connotation, so as to connote subsequently hardly anything else but "*sunna* of the Prophet", yet that process had not reached its culmination in the early part of the second half of the second century [1].

Thus, the examples of the use of the expression "*sunna* of the Prophet" [2] show the operation of a process similar to the one we have noted in regard to *ḥadīṯ* [3]. More important than these, however, are the few examples that we encounter of inadvertant substitution of the word "*sunna* for the expression "*sunna* of the Prophet", which show that the former term had begun to be regarded, in general, as an equivalent of the latter. One of these examples occurs in *Tr.* IX. Awzāʿī is mentioned as having said: "*Sunna* has come down from the Messenger of Allāh" (IX, 13). Abū Yūsuf refers to the same statement of Awzāʿī, but the expression "*sunna* . . . from the Messenger of Allāh", is replaced by the word "*sunna*" alone, which indicates that *sunna* in the sense of "*sunna* of the Prophet" was a well-established usage of the time [4].

Such a development could only have been the result of a fairly long period of the use of the term with reference to the Prophet. We have seen earlier the instances of its use during the first century as well as by Ibn al-Muqaffaʿ, which is an illustration of its use by a non-jurist. Some of the instances of the use of "*sunna* of the Prophet" by the specialists are extant in the *fiqh-aṯar* works of the second century. They show a consistent use of *sunna* with reference to the Prophet.

1. See pp. [4] ff. above.
2. See pp. [8] ff. above.
3. See above n. 1.
4. See *Tr.* IX, 25. For a similar example see the letter of Layṯ b. Saʿd (d. 165) the well-known Egyptian jurist in *Iʿlām al-Muwaqqiʿīn*, *op. cit.*, vol. III, p. 95. Speaking of the Companions who were sent to different places for *ǧihād*, Layṯ says: "And in each of their battalion there was a group who taught the Book of Allāh and the *sunna* of His Prophet and who exercised *iǧtihād* in matters which the Qurʾān and the *sunna* had not explained for them." It will be noted that in the last part of the sentence "*sunna* of the Prophet" was inadvertantly replaced by the term "*sunna*", which shows their equivalance.

In the Kūfian *fiqh-aṯar* works of the second century, for example, one of the earliest instances of the use of *sunna* of the Prophet occurs in traditions from Ibrāhīm al-Naḫaʿī (d. 95). Ibrāhīm al-Naḫaʿī relates that a certain person al-Ṣubayy b. Maʿbad replied accurately to questions regarding the rituals of pilgrimage at which ʿUmar said: "You have been guided to the *sunna* of the Prophet" [1].

Let us turn to Awzāʿī who represents a relatively earlier stage in the development of Islamic jurisprudence than Abū Ḥanīfa and Abū Yūsuf, in order to examine the connotation of the term *sunna*. The following examples are noteworthy:

(1) "*Sunna* has come down from the Prophet that . . . ." [2].
(2) Awzāʿī explicitly articulates the principle that the conduct of the Prophet is conduct *par excellence* (*aḥaqqu man uqtudiya bihi wa-tumussika bi-sunnatihi rasūl Allāh*) [3]. At another place, Awzāʿī cites the Quranic verse which embodies this concept: "Certainly you have in the Messenger of Allāh a good example" [4].

The use of the word *sunna*, however, is very infrequent in Awzāʿī. Is this scarcity of reference any index of the extent of its importance in the doctrine of Awzāʿī? The answer seems to be in the negative. For even though the term *sunna* has not been used very frequently by Awzāʿī with reference to the Prophet, reference to the precepts and practices of the Prophet with the implication that they are authoritative, is very frequent [5]. This only emphasises

---

1. Abū Yūsuf, *K. al-Āṯār*, ed. Abū l-Wafāʾ al-Afġānī, (Cairo, 1355 A.H.), 478. (The number cited here as well as elsewhere in connection with this book refers to the number of the tradition and not to the page). That authentic doctrines of Ibrāhīm al-Naḫaʿī have come down to us has been argued by this writer in "Early Development", pp. 92 f.

2. *Tr.* IX, 13.

3. *Ibid.*, 50.

4. *Qurʾān*, XXXIII, 21 cited by Awzāʿī in *Tr.* IX, 23. Only once does Awzāʿī use the term *sunna* without explicit reference to the Prophet. (See *ibid.*, 37).

5. For these references, see *Tr.* IX, 1, (a practice of the Prophet); 2 (a saying of the Prophet); 3 (a practice of the Prophet); 4 (the denial of the religious relevance of an institution because of its non-existence in the time of the Prophet); 5 (a practice of the Prophet continued by *aʾimmat al-hudā*. See, for the meaning of this expression above, p. [12], n. 2); 7 (a practice of the Prophet subsequently followed by the Muslims); 8 (a practice of the Prophet subsequently practised by Muslim rulers); 9 (the same as above); p. 46 (the same as above); 17 (a practice of the Prophet); 20 (a saying of the Prophet); 23 (a practice in the time of the Prophet); 26 (argues for the permissibility of a practice which was held as permissible in the time of the

the need of using the semantic evidence only tentatively and correlating it with other findings. For, the fact that Awzāʿī goes so far as to deny the religiously binding character of the institution of *dīwān* which had been introduced by ʿUmar on the ground that it was a post-Prophetic institution, only serves to show the intimate relationship between the practice to which Awzāʿī often refers as a legal argument and the assumption of its introduction by the Prophet [1]. It is also worth remembering that Awzāʿī's references to the practice of the Muslims, but for a few exceptions [2], are invariably preceded by reference to the Prophet as the initiator of these practices. Moreover, even when Awzāʿī refers merely to "practice", he seems to claim its authority on the ground that the practice concerned enjoyed the approval of all Muslims, particularly of the *ʿulamāʾ*. In fact when Awzāʿī cites a practice without claiming it to have been introduced by the Prophet, he seems to support it on the ground of *iǧmāʿ* [3].

In Mālik there is very frequent use of the term *sunna* as such, but the expression "*sunna* of the Prophet" occurs only rarely. As in the case of Awzāʿī, the scarcity of the use of this expression does not necessarily show that Mālik did not subscribe to, or that he did not have much use for, the concept of the "*sunna* of the Prophet". Such a view would be falsified even by a cursory reading of his *Muwaṭṭaʾ*, which contains no less than 822 traditions from the Prophet [4].

Mālik's reproduction of the following statement from the Prophet is highly significant: "I forget or I am made to forget so that I may

---

Prophet, supporting it by a saying of the Prophet); 31 (a saying of the Prophet); 34 (a practice of the Prophet); 48 (a practice of the Prophet (p. 129), and an analogy based on an event in the life of the Prophet (p. 130); 50 (a practice of the Prophet which, says Awzāʿī, has the greatest claim to be followed).

1. *Ibid.*, 4.

2. For instances of reference to practice without the mention of the Prophet, see *ibid.*, 3, 6, 9, 14, 19, 25, 32. As for references to practice as a supplementary evidence and claiming its introduction by the Prophet, see its instances in p. [14], n. 5 above.

3. See *ibid.*, 6, 9, 19, 25 and 32. In several of these, the reference is to the *aʾimma* and/or the *ʿulamāʾ* which shows the continuity of practice and thus reinforces the claim of *iǧmāʿ*. The reference to the *ʿulamāʾ* seems to serve the purpose of showing that the practice concerned was religiously unobjectionable.

4. *Origins*, p. 22, on the basis of Zurqānī.

establish a rule (*li-asunna*)" [1] and throws light on his view of the *sunna* of the Prophet [2].

In Abū Yūsuf, there are numerous instances of the use of the expression: "the *sunna* of the Prophet" as well as of *sunna* without any affix. Of these we shall consider presently only a few instances of the former category, leaving the instances of the latter category for a later discussion [3].

Ḫarāǧ, pp. 14 and 115. ʿUmar is reported as having stated that he had sent his officials to teach people their religion and the *sunna* of their Prophet.

Ibid., p. 76, Abū Yūsuf advises the Caliph that he should instruct the officials, *inter alia*, to administer according to the "*sunna* of the Messenger of Allāh".

Ibid., p. 164. "*Sunna* has come down from the Prophet and the two Caliphs . . ."

Tr. IX, 18 (p. 57). "No *sunna* has come down from the Prophet, nor from any of his Companions".

Ibid., 5, p. 24. In matters of *ḥalāl* and *ḥarām* one is not guided, says Abū Yūsuf, by the practice of people. In such matters one follows "the *sunna* of [literally, from] the Prophet, and of the forbears: the Companions and the *fuqahā*ʾ".

---

1. Mālik b. Anas, *Muwaṭṭa*ʾ, ed. Fuʾād ʿAbd al-Bāqī, (Cairo, 1370 A.H.), p. 100. (Cited hereafter as *Muw.*). The purpose of the tradition is that even what the Prophet forgot (or was caused by God to forget) had a normative significance. For another example of the use of the expression "*sunna* of the Prophet", see *Muw.* p. 513. For an instance where *sunna* has been used without any explicit reference to the Prophet, but contextually it could mean nothing else but *sunna* of the Prophet, see *ibid.*, p. 314 where Mālik states that in matters which are *farīḍa* or *nāfila* one may not innovate, and may only follow what the Muslims have followed. Mālik thereafter adds that the Messenger of Allāh performed *iʿtikāf* and the Muslims came to know thereby the *sunna* of *iʿtikāf*. For still another instance of the use of *sunna* meaning "*sunna* of the Prophet" see *ibid.*, p. 77 where Mālik quotes some scholars as holding the view that there had never been any call for prayer and *iqāma* in the two *ʿĪd*s "from the time of the Prophet till to-day". Thereafter Mālik adds: "And that is a *sunna* with regard to which there is no disagreement among us."

2. For this view that the *sunna* followed by the Medinese rested on the *sunna* of the Prophet, see "*Early Development*", pp. 209 f. and p. 503, n. 132.

3. Besides these, there are several uses of *sunna* without explicitly relating it to the Prophet or to the Companions. For a few instances, see *ibid.*, pp. 32 f. and nn. 4-6 below.

In Šaybānī too we come across numerous instances of the expression "*sunna* of the Prophet".

Muw. Š., p. 315. Šaybānī cites the following statement of Mālik: "There is nothing for you in the Book of God and we do not know that there is anything for you in the *sunna* of the Messenger of Allāh". (The remark is in regard to a question of inheritance).

Ibid., p. 389. Šaybānī mentions a tradition according to which ʿUmar b. ʿAbd al-ʿAzīz wrote to Abū Bakr b. Ḥazm, asking him to look up to whatever "*ḥadīṯ* or *sunna* of the Prophet" there might be and asked him to commit the same to writing [1].

Thus we find an unbroken continuity in the use of the expression "*sunna* of the Prophet" in poetry, literary prose as well as *fiqh* literature from a very early period. What does *sunna* mean, however, when it is used without any affix?

A scrutiny of the examples of the use of the word *sunna* during the second century reveals, as we have already noted, its use in a multiplicity of meanings [2]. We shall analyse below the main usages of the term, and note the light they throw on the legal theory of the period under study.

(1) One of the usages of the word *sunna* was in combination

---

1. Besides these there are numerous references in *Ḥuǧaǧ*. See for instance p. 137, l. 6 and l. 2 from below; see also pp. 141; 147; 169; 214; and often.

2. It should be emphasized that the term *sunna* has been used in the classical Islamic literature and continues to be used even to-day in a variety of meanings. S.v. "*Sunna*" in TAHĀNAWĪ, *Kaššāf Iṣṭilāḥāt al-Funūn*, (Calcutta, 1862 A.D.), pp. 703 ff., (cited hereafter as *Kaššāf*); ABŪ L-BAQĀʾ, *Kulliyyāt*, (Būlāq, 1253 A.H.), p. 203 (cited hereafter as *Kulliyyāt*). According to Abū l-Baqāʾ the term *sunna* is not restricted as such to the *sunna* of the Prophet; it means *ṭarīqat al-dīn* which is the model behaviour either of the Prophet (consisting of his sayings and deeds) or of his Companions. In Šāfiʿī, however, as Abū l-Baqāʾ points out, the use of the term *sunna* is restricted to the "*sunna* of the Prophet alone" (*ibid.*, p. 203). According to *Kaššāf* (p. 703) one of the meanings of the term is *šarīʿa*. It also means that which is proved by means of the *sunna* (i.e., one of the four *adilla*) is also called *sunna* (*loc. cit.*), and "established religious practice without its being made *farḍ* or *wāǧib* and by this established practice is meant that which the Prophet consistently practised such as the prayer of *tarāwīḥ*. And if deviation of any such *sunna* is considered blameworthy then it is termed *sunan al-hudā* or *sunna muʾakkada*" (*ibid.*, p. 704). Some of the examples mentioned by Abū l-Baqāʾ are noteworthy: "*Sunnat al-ʿibāda* or *sunnat al-ittibāʿ* such as pronouncing of *ṭalāq* during the *ṭuhr* in which a person has not had sexual intercourse; and the *sunna* of *mašāʾiḫ* such as brushing teeth nine times", etc., (*Kulliyyāt*, p. 203).

with the Qur'ān. In such cases the only satisfactory inference is that *sunna* meant "*sunna* of the Prophet". The following couplet of al-Kumayt, a poet of the first and early second century, serves a good instance in hand: *Bi-ayyi Kitābin aw bi-ayyati Sunnatin/ Tarā ḥubbuhum ʿārun ʿalayya wa-taḥsabu* [1]. The use of this juxtaposition of the Qur'ān and *Sunna* grew with the passage of time. Even at the time when this couplet was composed (*circa* 100 or even before), the manner in which the term occurs here assumes that the sense in which it is being used was well-established rather than an innovation.

In *fiqh* literature, in particular, this Qur'ān-*Sunna* combination has been used very frequently. In such combinations the term *sunna* could hardly signify anything else except the "*sunna* of the Prophet". For, it is hardly conceivable that anything else would have enjoyed sufficient prestige and authority so as to be mentioned side by side with the Qur'ān. The following are some of the examples of the Qur'ān-*Sunna* combination.

Muw., p. 513. Nothing is [laid down] for you in the Book of Allāh, and in the *sunna* of the Messenger of Allāh. (Regarding a question of inheritance) [2].

Tr. IX, 5, (p. 31). Abū Yūsuf warns against acceptance of *šāḏḏ* traditions and lays down the principle that the *ḥadīṯ*s which should be accepted should, *inter alia*, conform to the Qur'ān and the *Sunna*.

Ibid., 5, (p. 32). "Make the Qur'ān and the well-known *Sunna* your guide".

Loc. cit. ". . . whatever has not been explained in the Qur'ān and the *Sunna*".

Ḫarāǧ, p. 160. A man cuts another person's hand deliberately. The latter, on being given the right of retaliation (*qiṣāṣ*) cuts his hand as a result of which the former dies. One view was that the *ʿāqila* of the former was liable to pay *diya*. Abū Yūsuf, however, considered him blameless because it was not he, but "the Qur'ān and the *Sunna*" which had caused his death.

1. *Hāšimiyyāt al-Kumayt*, (Leiden, 1904 A.D.), p. 32, l. 4. See FAZLUR RAHMAN, *Islamic Methodology*, *op. cit.*, p. 8 for reasons why *sunna* here can possibly mean "*sunna* of the Prophet" only and nothing else. For another example of the use of *sunna* along with the Qur'ān, see the Treatise of Ibn al-Muqaffaʿ, *op. cit.*, p. 126.

2. Cf. *Muw. Š.*, p. 315.

Ḥuǧaǧ, p. 212. 'Umar instructs Abū Mūsā al-Aš'arī to have recourse to *qiyās* in matters which are not found in "the Book or the *Sunna*" [1].

(2) "*Sunna* and *sīra*" is another combination in which the reference to the Prophet is implied, even when he is not referred to explicitly.

Tr. IX, 21 (p. 67). "The *sunna* of the Prophet and his *sīra*". The reference to the Prophet here is explicit.

Ibid., 6, (pp. 36 f.). "I did not think that anyone who knows *sunna* and *sīra* would be ignorant of this". (*Sunna* here can only mean *sunna* of the Prophet, which is also proved by Abū Yūsuf's argument on p. 35).

(3) There is a number of instances which shows that "*sunna*" and "*ḥadīṯ*" were not used as equivalents in the early period, though they were quite often used as such later—though by no means invariably—by the scholars of the science of *ḥadīṯ* [2]. *Ḥadīṯ* generally referred, in the early period, to a communication from the authorities (narrowed down subsequently when the technical terms were fixed) i.e., from the Prophet as well as others, particularly the Companions [3]. As for *sunna*, it referred to an established religious norm. Thus, *ḥadīṯ* provided the documentation of the *sunna*, but was not *sunna* itself. For every *ḥadīṯ* is not necessarily authentic or *sunna*-yielding. As against a *ḥadīṯ*, therefore, *sunna* constitutes an established norm of practical life which has come down, presumably from the Prophet, and/or from the Companions, or, in some instances, has been inferentially derived from *sunna* proper and has been sanctified by consensus [4].

There are numerous instances which show that occasionally Abū Yūsuf made a sharp distinction between *ḥadīṯ* and *sunna*. In *Tr.* IX, 5 (p. 31) he warns against *šāḏḏ* (and he considered isolated

1. See also *Ḥuǧaǧ*, p. 225; *Muw. Š.*, p. 315, and often.
2. Even though this identity between the two was supported by a large number of scholars of *Ḥadīṯ*, this was not their unanimous view. See, for example, *Dustūr al-'Ulamā'*, vol. II, p. 15.
3. See above pp. [2] ff.
4. For, as Goldziher has pointed out, *sunna* referred to the substance of rules relating to practical life (*Muh. St.*, vol. II, p. 12). See also the examples through which Goldziher illustrates the difference between *sunna* and *ḥadīṯ* (*ibid.*, pp. 11 ff).

traditions to be *šāḏḏ* [1] traditions and urges that only the traditions which are, *inter alia*, in harmony with the Qur'ān and the *Sunna* should be accepted. In fact, in the light of the writings of Abū Yūsuf, it appears that by *sunna* he meant only those norms which were recognized as such by the Muslims in general, were accepted by the *fuqahā'*, and which had come down through reliable and learned people [2]. Hence, there are numerous instances of Abū Yūsuf's [3] emphasising the established character of *sunna* such as: "*sunna maḥfūẓa ma'rūfa*", "*sunna ma'rūfa*" [4], "*al-ḥadīṯ fī hāḏā kaṯīr, wa-l-sunna fī hāḏā ma'rūfa*" [5], and "*al-ḥadīṯ fī hāḏā ma'rūf mašhūr, wa-l-sunna fīh ma'rūfa*" [6].

(4) It is this aspect of *sunna*—its being a well-known and well-established norm which is emphasised when *sunna* is characterized with terms—either verbs or adjectives—derived from *maḍā*. Being well-established and coming down from the past—which is suggested by the term *maḍā*—*sunna* was regarded as reflecting the tendency which was diametrically opposed to innovation—*iḥdāṯ* or *bid'a* [7].

This brings us to the problem of the relationship between *sunna* and the actual customs or practices of the Muslim society in the opinion of the second century jurists, particularly the Kūfians. This relationship is an involved one. To some extent, the actual customs and practices were considered, or gratuitously assumed, to reflect the teachings of the Prophet. For, it was felt—and natu-

1. See *Tr.* IX, 9.
2. *Ibid.*, 1 (p. 5), 2 (pp. 15 f.), 5 (pp. 24 f. and 30 f.).
3. *Ibid.*, 14 (p. 49).
4. *Ibid.*, 5 (p. 32).
5. *Ibid.*, 7 (p. 38). The same seems to be the basis of distinction between *aṯar* and *sunna*. See, e.g., *Ḥuǧaǧ*, pp. 75, 77, and often.
6. *Tr.* IX, 8 (p. 40). See also *Ḫarāǧ*, pp. 95 and 96.
7. For this opposition of *sunna* to innovation, see *Muw.*, p. 314. Regarding matters which are religiously recommended or mandatory, says Mālik, "one acts according to the *sunna* which has come down from the past (*bi-mā maḍā min al-sunna*) and one is not entitled to innovate in opposition to what the Muslims have followed . . ." For the context of this passage see above, p. [16], n. 1. For usages of the word *sunna* with *maḍā*, see *ibid.*, pp. 290, 318, and often. In Abū Yūsuf, see *Ḫarāǧ*, p. 164; *Tr.* IX, 3, 13 (in a statement made by Awzā'ī), and 18 (in a statement made by Abū Yūsuf). See also *ibid.*, (p. 11) (*ǧarat al-sunna*); *Ḫarāǧ*, p. 59, (the same expression). For Šaybānī, see *Muw. Š.*, p. 290; *Ḥuǧaǧ*, p. 176 and often. See also the statement regarding Ša'bī that he was the most knowledgeable person in respect of *sunna māḍiya*. Wakī', *Aḫbār al-Quḍāh*, ed. 'Abd al- 'Azīz al-Marāġī, 3 vols., (Cairo, 1366 A.H.), vol. II, p. 427.

rally so—that those teachings were not restricted to verbal transmissions but had become incorporated into, and therefore, had become an integral part of, the way of life of Muslims. However, it was not practice or custom *per se* which was considered to be authoritative [1]. It is well-known that the concept of practice plays a particularly conspicuous part in the doctrines of Awzāʿī. It should be noted that the 'practice' to which even Awzāʿī refers is the one which has, *inter alia*, not been disapproved of by the *ʿulamāʾ* [2]. In Abū Yūsuf we find an illuminating passage which proves that the concept of *sunna* was not equivalent to 'actual practice', neither in the opinion of his own school, nor in the opinion of the Medinese or Syrian jurists. In the passage concerned, Abū Yūsuf taunts the Medinese for sanctifying their practices into *sunna* even though these practices might probably have been introduced merely by some market-inspector or administrative official [3].

Whether Abū Yūsuf's judgement about the activity of the Syrian and Ḥiǧāzī lawyers is factually correct or not, does not concern us here. What is of paramount importance is the biting indictment that his criticism contains. This bitter indictment makes it evident that there was no professed claim on anybody's part that practices were self-sanctifying, that they were synonymous with the *sunna*. This not applies to the Kūfian jurists, but to the Ḥiǧāzīs

---

1. Margoliouth has gone so far as to suggest that the acceptance of the Qurʾān and the *Sunna* as sources of law meant to the early generations that wherever the Qurʾān had no positive commands, the ancient Arabian custom should prevail. He seems to suggest that the attitude of Islām to "unobjectionable" customs was not just permissive, it was one of exalting them to the position of a full-fledged source of law. (See his *Early Development of Mohammedanism*, London, 1914, p. 68 and "Omar's Instruction to the Kādī", *JRAS*, (1910), p. 314). Such a view would have been tenable only if the *sunna* of what the Qurʾān terms as *ǧāhiliyya* had been extolled by the Qurʾān. The most that can be said about *ǧāhilī* practices is that the Qurʾān does not oppose them if they do not conflict with its teachings. This is quite different from putting the *ǧāhilī* practices and usages more or less on the same level as the Qurʾān.

2. *Tr.* IX, 6 (pp. 34 f.) and 8 (p. 42).

3. *Ibid.*, 1 (p. 11). In a parallel passage Abū Yūsuf says that to say that *ʿalā hāḏā kānat aʾimmat al-Muslimīn fīmā salaf* is like saying "*bi-hāḏā maḍat al-sunna*" even though this might be the personal opinion (*raʾy*) of some of the *mašāʾiḫ* of Syria who are neither well-versed in questions of *wuḍūʾ*, nor *tašahhud*, nor *uṣūl al-fiqh* (*ibid.*, 3, p. 21). Even Ibn al-Muqaffaʿ, who belonged to the class of secretaries of state, denounces the trend of considering administrative practices to be *sunna* even when there was no evidence of their having been in existence in the time of the Prophet or of the early Caliphs. See pp. [11] f. and [12] n. 2 above.

and the Syrians jurists as well. For, were it the case that the Ḥiǧāzīs and the Syrians had categorically proclaimed their practices *per se* to be synonymous with *sunna*, Abū Yūsuf's indictment would have been pointless. After making a strong attack on 'practice', Abū Yūsuf articulates his own view of *sunna* in the following words:

> In deciding questions of what is allowed and what is prohibited, one does not follow claims such as people have continually followed this doctrine. For, a majority of things that people have followed are not permissible and not proper. There are cases which I could mention where the great mass (*ʿāmma*) violates a prohibition of the Prophet. In these questions one has to follow the *sunna* from the Prophet and the forbears: his Companions and the *fuqahā'*.[1]

As against actual practice, therefore, Abū Yūsuf would have people derive their *sunna* from the Prophet and the Companions through the *fuqahā'* [2].

(5) On the basis of the above, it is not difficult to see that the word *sunna* came to signify "established religious practice" or "established religious doctrine", "*al-ṭarīqa al-maslūka fī l-dīn* [3]. In Mālik, the expression "*al-sunna ʿindanā*" seems to mean the same. Abū Yūsuf and Šaybānī also sometimes use *sunna* in this sense [4].

(6) Close to this is another expression which is peculiar to Mālik: *al-sunna allatī lā iḫtilāf fīhā ʿindanā*". This refers not merely to "established doctrine", but also points to the source wherefrom

1. *Ibid.*, 24 (p. 76).
2. For this inference of ours, see pp. [26] f. below.
3. *Kaššāf*, p. 703; *Kulliyyāt*, p. 203. See also *Muw.*, pp. 226, 268, 273, 568, and 843. Hence the expression: "To walk behind the funeral is a wrong *sunna*." It is in the same sense that Mālik quotes the tradition: "Treat them in the same manner as you should treat *ahl al-Kitāb*" (*Sunnū bi-him sunnat ahl al-Kitāb*"). (*Ibid.*, p. 278).
4. For Abū Yūsuf, see *Ḫarāǧ*, p. 90, p. 203 ("*aḫṭa'a l-ḥukm wa-l-sunna*"); *Tr.* IX, 15 (p. 53), and 41 (p. 116). For Šaybānī, see *Ḥuǧaǧ*, p. 77 (*sunnat al-ṣalāh*); *Muw. Š.*, p. 250, "*ṭalāq al-sunna*", see also *Ḥuǧaǧ*, pp. 40 and 79, "*al-sunna fī l-ǧamʿ bayn al-maġrib wa-l-ʿišā fī l-maṭar* . . ." This usage seems to have some relation to the following usage of the term in Arabic poetry by Dirham b. Yazīd; *Lā narfaʿ al-ʿabd fawqa sunnatihi/Ma dāma minna bi baṭnihā šarafu* (see *Šarḥ Dīwān Ḥassān*, p. 279, line 11). For another example of the use of the term *sunna* in the sense of authoritative religious doctrine, see the rescript of Umar II in IBN ʿABD AL-ḤAKAM, *Sīrat ʿUmar b. ʿAbd al-ʿAzīz*, (Cairo, 1927), pp. 93-100; see particularly Clause XII cited in H. A. R. GIBB, "*The Fiscal Rescript of Umar II*", *Arabica*, Tome II, fasc. 1, (1955), p. 6.

its authoritativeness was derived—the consensus of the Medinese [1]. In Mālik this is a very commonly used expression and seems to mean the same as or to approximate *al-amr al-muǧtamaʿ ʿalayh ʿindanā* [2].

(7) An aspect of *sunna*—and this follows from what we have said earlier regarding the connotation of *sunna*—is that it was of an authoritative nature. Hence it was opposed to *iǧtihād*. Says Mālik: "And in a matter with regard to which no fixed *talion* has come down from the Prophet, nor has any *sunna* come down, in such a case one resorts to *iǧtihād*" [3]. In the event of finding any *sunna*, i.e. authoritative rule, one may not use one's reasoning. Rabīʿa (d. 136) asked Saʿīd b. al-Musayyib (d. *circa* 93) the rationale of the apparently unjustifiable doctrine of 30 camels as *diya* for 3 fingers, and 20 camels for four, Saʿīd b. al-Musayyib's reply was: "This is *sunna* . . ." [4].

(8) It remains to be considered as to whose precept and practice constituted the *sunna* which the Muslims were required to follow. That the Prophet's conduct constituted *sunna* is obvious [5]. But side by side with the Prophet there was also the *sunna* of the Companions, as we shall see [6].

Both Abū Yūsuf and Šaybānī refer to the authority of the Companions, particularly to *a'immat al-hudā* (i.e. *al-ḫulafā' al-rāšidūn* [7], and even more particularly to the first two Caliphs [8]). In *Ḥuǧaǧ* in particular, Šaybānī confronts the Medinese again and again with the question whether their doctrines in question were supported by any traditions from the Prophet or from the Companions [9].

1. For this expression see *Muw. passim*. For Mālik's reasons for attaching so great an importance to "established practice supported by the consensus of the Medinese", see his letter to Layṯ in *al-Andalus*, vol. XV, pp. 416 f.
2. For this expression see *Muw. passim*.
3. *Ibid.*, p. 853.
4. *Ibid.*, p. 860.
5. It may be noted, however, that side by side with this there was the concept of the personal privileges of the Prophet so that a number of actions of his were considered to be uniquely peculiar to him and were not normative for others. See for instance, *Tr.* IX, 5 (pp. 24 and 34) and 39 (pp. 107 f.). For reference to it in Šaybānī, see *Muw. Š.*, pp. 178 and 180.
6. See, for instance, *Tr.* IX, 8, 24, and below, p. [12], n. 2.
7. For the connotation of this term, see above, p. [12], n. 9 below.
8. See below, p. [24], n. 3.
9. See *Ḥuǧaǧ, passim*.

This line of argument obviously shows the importance of the doctrines and practices of the Companions in the opinion of Abū Yūsuf and Šaybānī.

Abū Yūsuf, for instance, says that in matters of *ḥalāl* and *ḥarām*, practice as such is irrelevant. In such matters one follows "the *sunna* from the Prophet and from the forbears—his Companions and the *fuqahā'*" [1]. With regard to another problem he remarks: "As far as we know, no *sunna* has come down from the Messenger of Allāh, nor from any of his Companions . . . ." [2]. On another occasion, Abū Yūsuf mentions the *sunna* of the Prophet and of the two Caliphs who succeeded him [3]. Abū Yūsuf refers to the adherence, by ʿUmar b. ʿAbd al-ʿAzīz, of the policy of ʿUmar b. al-Ḫaṭṭāb, for which he uses the expression: "he followed the *sunna*", and makes an explicit statement about the authoritativeness of the decisions of *al-wulāt al-mahdiyyūn*", (which seems to mean the same as *a'immat al-hudā*) [4].

(9) Another usage of *sunna* refers to the degree of merit attached to a certain action. This usage too seems to have been well-established during the second century and has passed on to the classical Islamic *fiqh* and means "recommended but not obligatory". In this sense it was opposed, on the one hand, to *farīḍa* and *wāǧiba*, and to *nāfila* on the other. In this hierarchy its position was in between the two. To cite just a few examples [5]:

Muw., p. 487. "Sacrifice of animals is a *sunna* and not *wāǧib* but I do not like that anyone who can bear the expenses should abandon it".

Ibid., p. 824. ʿUmar is reported to have said: "*Sunna*s have been laid down for you and *farā'iḍ* have been made incumbent on you".

Āṯār A. Y., 404. *Sunna* is opposed to *nāfila* [6].

1. *Tr.* IX, 24 (p. 76).
2. *Ibid.*, 18 (p. 57).
3. *Ḫarāǧ*, p. 164. For the special position accorded to the first two Caliphs, see also the letter of Ibn Ibāḍ in *Ǧawāhir*, pp. 157 ff.
4. *Ibid.*, 58. For *a'immat al-hudā*, see above, p. [12], n. 2.
5. *Sunna* continued to be used in this sense even subsequently. See *Kaššāf*, p. 703; *Kulliyyāt*, p. 203; and NASAFĪ, *Kašf al-Asrār*, 2 vols., (Būlāq, 1316 A.H.) vol. II, p. 2; TAFTĀZĀNĪ, *al-Talwīḥ ʿalā l-Tawḍīḥ*, 2 vols., (Cairo, n.d.), vol. II, p. 124.
6. This seems to be peculiar to the Kūfian school and later became a part of the Ḥanafī scale of *Šarʿī* values. See *ibid.*, pp. 124 f.

Ḥuǧaǧ, p. 143. Abū Ḥanīfa and Šaybānī agree that *ʿumra* is *sunna*, but not *wāǧib*. Whoever performs it does a good thing, and earns extra merit [1].

Ibid., p. 45. There is disagreement as to whether *witr* is *sunna* or *wāǧib*.

The use of the term *sunna* in this sense seems to have begun as a result of realising difference in the degrees of importance between the injuctions derived from categorical verses of the Qur'ān, and those derived from other sources. This is evidenced by expressions such as Šaybānī's remarks: "The *masḥ* of the head is a *farīḍa* [derived] from the Book of Allāh" [2]. To some extent the Ḥanafī school retained this distinction, even subsequently [3].

(10) The following are some stray examples of the use of the term *sunna*:

If there is an ancient *ʿAǧamī sunna*, which Islām has not changed and has not declared as *bāṭil*, and some people complain about the harm caused by that *sunna* . . . [4].

A group of weavers came to Šurayḥ in connection with a dispute and said to him: "Our *sunna* is so and so". Šurayḥ said: "Your *sunna* is among yourselves" [5].

Abū Yūsuf extols the revival of *sunan*, but here he is referring not to the *sunan* of the Prophet, or of his Companions, but to the *sunan* set up by good people (*al-ṣāliḥūn*) [6]. These refer to "usages" or to "good usages" without necessarily referring to the Prophet or Companions.

To conclude from above, the following points emerge:

(i) The term had had an uninterrupted tradition of use with

1. Cf. *Muw.*, p. 347.
2. *Ḥuǧaǧ*, p. 5.
3. Āmidī, *al-Iḥkām fī Uṣūl al-Aḥkām*, 4 vols., (Cairo, 1332 A.H.), vol. I, p. 140; Taftāzānī, *op. cit.*, vol. II, p. 124.
4. Al-Balāḏurī, *Futūḥ al Buldān*, (Beirut, 1957), p. 629.
5. Wakīʿ, *op. cit.*, vol. II, p. 372.
6. *Ḫarāǧ*, p. 5. Another interesting example is that of the use of *sunna* in the sense of the creed of *ahl al-Sunna*. See in al-Ḥumaydī (d. 219), *Musnad*, ed. Ḥabīb al-Raḥmān al-Aʿẓamī, 2 vols., (Karachi, 1382 A.H.), his short treatise entitled: "*Uṣūl al-Sunna*", (vol. II, pp. 546-48). This meaning of the term *sunna* is confirmed if it is read in conjunction with Ibn Qutayba, *Taʾwīl Muḫtalif al-Ḥadīṯ*, (Cairo, 1326 A.H.), p. 59. See also *ibid.*, p. 98.

reference to the Prophet from the earliest period of Islām, a fact which is understandable in view of the Quranic doctrine that the conduct of the Prophet is exemplary. This is evidenced not only by the formulation of the expression "*sunna* of the Prophet" and its increasing use, but also by using the term *sunna* as such in the sense of the "*sunna* of the Prophet" [1].

(ii) The Muslims, however, regarded as authoritative not only the precepts and practices of the Prophet, but also those of his Companions. We have seen that the authority of the Companions was already well-established *circa* 75 [2]. It is noteworthy that the precepts and practices of the Prophet as well as of the Companions continued to be characterised as *sunna*. The only authentic example that we have of denying the religiously authoritative character of a *sunna* of a Companion is Awzāʿī's adverse remark about *dīwān* on the ground that it was a post-Prophetic institution [3]. This solitary example merely emphasises that practices generally derived their religiously binding character from their having some kind of association with the Prophet. This instance notwithstanding, the early Islamic literature, especially the Kūfian literature, frequently designated the practices of the Companions, especially of the first four Caliphs, as *sunna*, which was deemed to be part of what Šaybānī calls "binding information" [4].

(iii) Besides references to the *sunna* of the Prophet and of his Companions, there are also references to the *sunna* of the *fuqahā'* [5] and of the virtuous people [6]. So far as the latter use

1. See above, p. [13], n. 4.
2. *Vide.* "*Treatise of Baṣrī*", *op. cit.*, *passim*, and p. [9], n. 4 above.
3. *Tr.* IX, 4. Cf. *Āṯār A.Y.*, 339 f., which shows, however, that a Companion's practice was not invariably considered to be authoritative. In *Āṯār A.Y.*, 140, the basis of non-acceptance of a certain practice of Ibn ʿUmar is that it was based merely on his *ra'y* and that he had no *aṯar* in support of it. See also *Ḥuǧaǧ*, pp. 12 f., where the Medinese support their doctrine in regard to washing by referring to a practice of Ibn ʿUmar which the Kūfians reject on the ground that Ibn ʿUmar was too meticulous in the matter of washing.
4. *Tr.* VIII, 3, sc. ŠĀFIʿĪ, *K. al-Radd ʿala Muḥammad b. al-Ḥasan*, in *K. al-Umm*, 7 vols., (Būlāq, 1321-25 A.H.), in vol. VII. The number refers to sections of the treatise following Schacht's division of the text in *Origins*, p. 335.
5. *Tr.* IX, 24.
6. See p. [25] above. It is a non-technical usage and means "good example", or "good conduct".

is concerned, it seems to mean "good example" as such. It has been used in a broad moral sense. As for the *sunna* of the *fuqahā'* to which Abū Yūsuf refers side by side with the *sunna* of the Prophet and the Companions, the context elucidates the significance of its use. Abū Yūsuf mentions *fuqahā'* while stressing that in deciding what is allowed and what is prohibited it is not 'practice' to which one should turn for guidance; one should rather follow the *sunna* of the Prophet, the Companions, and the *fuqahā'*. The obvious question that arises is whether, in Abū Yūsuf's opinion, the *fuqahā'* were entitled to declare something to be allowed or prohibited on their own authority? The obvious answer, in the light of his own writings, is 'no'. So far as declaring things to be *ḥalāl* or *ḥarām* is concerned, Abū Yūsuf expresses the view that one should avoid making such statements except on the basis of a categorical Quranic verse, and should employ, instead, cautious expressions such as "This is *makrūh*", or "There is no objection to it", etc [1].

Hence, there can be no doubt that Abū Yūsuf's attitude to the Companions is quite different from his attitude to the *fuqahā'* and the two are not treated on par. So far as the Companions are concerned, he frequently refers to them as authorities, and characterises their practices as *sunna*. As for the *fuqahā*, their value is secondary, though important nevertheless. Firstly, it is they who can rightly interpret the traditions from the Prophet, etc., and derive *fiqhī* norms therefrom [2]. Moreover, it is the traditions attested by the learned specialists which are to be regarded as authentic—an idea which Abū Yūsuf repeatedly stressed [3]. In fact this appears to be one of the reasons for Abū Yūsuf's distinction between *ḥadīṯ* and *sunna* [4]. The expression *sunna* in relation to the *fuqahā'*, therefore, seems to mean substantially the same as the following statement of Abū Yūsuf: "*ḥadīṯ* transmitted by trustworthy people and supported by those noted for their *fiqh* (legal understanding)" [5].

(iv) *Sunna māḍīya.* As we have shown, this refers to normative

1. See *Tr.* IX, 23.
2. See, for example, *ibid.*, 2 and 20.
3. *Ibid.*, 2, 5 and 9.
4. See pp. [19] f. above.
5. *Tr.* IX, 2.

> rather than actual practice, and the assumption seems to be that the practice concerned originated in the time of the Prophet or of the Companions, and that it presumably embodied a religious norm. In Abū Yūsuf we find a protest against this attitude, and a demand for well-attested traditions [1] instead of vague references to practices coming down from the past. In this respect Abū Yūsuf anticipated Šāfiʿī.

In the light of the above, the conclusion that emerges is that the word *sunna* was used in a multiplicity of meanings, especially with reference to the Prophet and his Companions, but was increasingly tending towards its more restrictive connotation.

III. *Iǧmāʿ*

Consensus (*iǧmāʿ*), according to the classical Islamic theory, is one of the four 'roots' of Islamic law [2]. During the period under study, reference to consensus is quite frequent in all schools of Islamic law that we know of—the Kūfian, the Medinese and the Syrian.

During our discussion on *sunna* we have seen that the general acceptance of a practice by the community (or by its scholars in general) as normative was considered one of the essential characteristics of *sunna* [3]. If there had come down a certain practice from the past which had been generally considered by the Muslims to be meritorious or at least unobjectionable, this naturally strengthened the case for its being regarded as valid. It is not difficult to see the importance of consensus during the first and second centuries when the compendia of traditions were in process of coming into existence which later facilitated judgements by referring to a known body of authoritative traditions. During the period of our concern, not only was "agreed practice" put forward as a barrier against isolated traditions, but was also used quite frequently as an argument for further authentification of the traditions which supported a certain doctrine, or was sometimes adduced as an argument in favour of some doctrine without adducing any tradition in support of it.

1. See *ibid.*, 1, 2, etc.
2. See the standard works on *Uṣūl al-Fiqh*, for instance, TAFTĀZĀNĪ, *op. cit.*, vol. I., p. 26; ĀMIDĪ, *op. cit.*, vol. I, pp. 226 f., etc.
3. See Section II above, especially pp. [3] f.

A survey of the terms used for expressing the concept of consensus shows that the situation was approximately the same as in regard to *sunna*: *viz.*, that the technical terminology was in process of evolution but the process had not reached its final point, with the result that there was a lag between terminological and conceptual developments. No wonder then that the concept of consensus was expressed in a variety of forms. Nevertheless, the concept of consensus was close to acquiring a technical term—*iǧmāʿ*—for its expression, as we shall see.

Before studying the Kūfian case, let us cast a glance at "consensus" in Syria and Medina.

Awzāʿī, the only Syrian *faqīh* whose views are known in some detail, makes frequent reference to consensus. The following points are noteworthy about the forms employed by Awzāʿī to express the concept of consensus:

In a majority of cases Awzāʿī's reference to 'consensus' follows his prior mention of the practice or doctrine in question as going back to the Prophet. Thus, consensus generally constitutes a supplementary argument which seeks to reinforce the claim that the practice in question was *sunna*. Moreover, consensus perhaps also serves the purpose of reinforcing the evidence of the traditions [1] which, in the case of Awzāʿī, are devoid of *isnād*. However, aside from referring to consensus by way of a corroborative evidence in favour of practices or doctrines allegedly introduced by the Prophet, consensus has also been referred to in a manner which shows that it was also deemed to be an independent source of law. Even though such instances in Awzāʿī are not many, yet they are there [2].

The references to consensus in Awzāʿī are found in negative as well as positive forms. He supports a certain practice, for example, on the ground that "none has denounced this: neither any *wālī* of the *ǧamāʿa* (community) nor any *ʿālim*" [3]. Besides this, however,

1. For examples of Awzāʿī's reference to consensus as a supplement to the claim that the doctrine in question was based on the "*sunna* of the Prophet", see *Tr.* IX, 2 (an uninterrupted practice backed by a saying of the Prophet), 3,5, 13, 31. For a doctrine based on Abū Bakr's interpretation of the Qurʾan and followed by the Muslims subsequently, see *ibid.*, 29.

2. See *ibid.*, 5, 14, 15, 24 and 32. Awzāʿī's statement (*ibid.*, 9) apparently is a reference to consensus independent of traditions, etc., but Abū Yūsuf's observation (*loc. cit.*) seems to show that a tradition on that question did exist which seems to be pre-supposed in Awzāʿī's statement, but was not explicitly stated.

3. *Ibid.*, 6. For a similar expression, see *ibid.*, 14. In his reference to

there are instances of claims for positive consensus expressed by derivatives from "*aǧmaʿa*" [1].

The notion of consensus in Awzāʿī is essentially that of continued Muslim practice, continued not only actually, but also normatively, i.e., practice backed by the conviction of being appropriate on the part both of the rulers and the *ʿulamāʾ* [2]. The reference to *ʿulamāʾ* seems to guarantee that the practice in question was religiously unobjectionable. Besides the consensus of *aʾimmat al-hudā* [3] and *aʾimmat al-Muslimīn* and of *ʿulamāʾ*, Awzāʿī also makes use of the concept of the "consensus of all Muslims." This latter, however, is rather rare [4].

Coming to the Medinese school, reference to consensus generally takes the form of claiming the consensus of the Medinese. The doctrine seems to have been well-established from the first century [5]. In his letter to Layṯ, Mālik objects to his alleged deviation from the doctrines of the Medinese *ǧamāʿa* as a whole. He quotes two Quranic verses (IX, 100 and XXXIX, 18) and derives therefrom the doctrine that "people are bound to follow [the doctrines of] the Medinese." He further supports this contention by saying: "It is to Medina that migration took place; it is here that the Qur'ān was revealed, declaring what is permissible to be permissible, and what is prohibited to be prohibited. The Prophet was among them . . . who ordered them and they obeyed him; who set up examples (*sunan*) for them and they followed him . . . ." After the Prophet's death, says Mālik, people followed what they had come to know

---

consensus as a supplementary argument the usual form that Awzāʿī employs is to claim lack of disagreement, (see *passim*, e.g., 3), or to claim that the original practice introduced by the Prophet remained in operation until the assassination of al-Walīd (A.H. 126), see *ibid.*, 1 and 3.

1. See *ibid.*, 5 and 31. (On both the occasions *iǧmāʿ* has been claimed with regard to a practice or doctrine introduced by the Prophet).

2. See *ibid.*, 6, 9, and 14. In fact actual practice might have ceased to be in operation. See, for example, *ibid.*, 1 and 24.

3. For its meaning, see above, p. [12], n. 2.

4. See, for instance, *Tr.* IX, 3 (where reference has been made to uninterrupted adherence by the Muslims to a practice initiated by the Prophet without ever disagreeing about it, a statement which seems to be motivated by the purpose of reinforcing the claim that the practice in question was in fact a *sunna* of the Prophet), and 24 (where reference has been made to an uninterrupted and undisputed practice of the Muslims up to the assassination of Walīd (126 A.H.), but without any explicit reference to the Prophet).

5. For reference to the consensus of the Companions by Ibrāhīm, see "*Early Development*", p. 103 and n. 120. See also p. [31], n. 1.

and asked others about matters which they did not know, always accepting the best doctrines. The same was the practice of the succeeding generations. Hence, deviation from what they had agreed about was not permissible for outsiders (*ahl al-amṣār*) [1].

Mālik has numerous expressions for consensus. These expressions generally reflect the local character of his concept of consensus. Some of these are "*al-amr al-muğtamaʿ ʿalayh ʿindanā*"; or "*al-sunnat allatī lā iḫtilāf fīhā ʿindanā*" [2]; or "*al-amr allaḏī lam yazal ʿalayh al-nās ʿindanā*" [3]; or "*ʿalā ḏālika ahl al-ʿilm fī bilādinā*" [4]. This proves the lack of existence of a standard technical term. At times this consensus meant concurrence to consider a certain tradition, to the exclusion of others, to be authentic [5]; but it is not confined to that. In actual operation, consensus does not signify the complete uniformity of opinion among all Medinese scholars but merely the consensus of "approved scholars", in fact, only of their majority [6].

Coming to the Kūfians [7], as distinguished from the paraochial concept of consensus of the Medinese, and also perhaps of the Baṣrians [8], their concept of consensus seems to have a universal character. The Kufians refer to the "consensus of [all] people" [9], and to the "consensus of scholars in all countries" [10].

Šaybānī refers to "all Muslims without a dissenting voice", that is, all Ḥiğāzīs and Iraqians [11], and to the consensus of the Kūfians and the Medinese [12].

To come to the terms employed by the Kūfians in order to express

---

1. See Mālik's letter cited in the fragment of ʿIyāḍ's *al-Madārik* in *al-Andalus*, vol. XV, pp. 415 f.
2. See *Muw. passim*.
3. *Ibid.*, p. 502.
4. *Ibid.*, p. 522 and often.
5. See *Tr.* IV, *passim*; *Tr.* IV = Šāfiʿī, *K. Ğimāʿ al-ʿIlm* in *Umm*, vol. VII (cited by page numbers).
6. *Tr.* III, 148 (p. 248). *Tr.* III = Šāfiʿī, *K. Iḫtilāf Mālik wa-Šāfiʿī*, in *Umm*, vol. VII. (Citations are according to sections as divided by Schacht in *Origins*, p. 334). For the Medinese concept of consensus, see *Origins*, pp. 83 ff.
7. Cf. *Origins*, pp. 85 ff.
8. See the statement of the Baṣrian opponent of Šāfiʿī in *Tr.* III, 148 (p. 245).
9. Šāfiʿī, *K. Iḫtilāf al-Ḥadīṯ* (on the margin of *Umm* vol. VII), p. 71.
10. *Tr.* IV, p. 256.
11. *Tr.* VIII, 1.
12. *Ḥuğağ*, pp. 125 f.

consensus, they are quite numerous. Abū Yūsuf, like Awzā'ī, expresses this concept in negative as well as positive forms.

In the negative form, it assumes some such form as in his statement: "No disagreement on the question has come down from anybody" [1]. More frequent, however, is reference to positive agreement.

Tr. IX., 42, (p. 120). *'alā hāḏā ǧamā'at fuqahā'inā lā yaḫtalifūn* (a claim of *iǧmā'* backed by a tradition from the Prophet).

Ḫarāǧ, p. 174. On the question of stealing, 'Umar consulted people, and "they concurred (*aǧma'ū*) that . . . . ."

Ibid., p. 165. Abū Yūsuf reports that the drinking of intoxicants was punished by forty lashes during the time of the Prophet and Abū Bakr, but by eighty lashes during the time of 'Umar. This is followed by the statement: *wa-llaḏī aǧma'a 'alayh aṣḥābunā . . . . . ṯamānīn* [2].

Ibid., p. 166. The question whether the testimony of a convicted *qāḏif* was acceptable or not was a disputed issue in the early period, as we have seen [3]. Using the same expression, *aǧma'a aṣḥābunā*, Abū Yūsuf claims that the scholars of his school had arrived at consensus on the doctrine that the testimony of such a person should not be accepted.

Ibid., p. 167. "If a slave, whether male or female, commits illegitimate sexual intercourse", says Abū Yūsuf, "our *aṣḥāb* have concurred [Abū Yūsuf uses the same expression as above] that each of the two shall receive fifty stripes".

Ibid., p. 59. Abū Yūsuf refers to the consensus of the Companions of the Prophet. He blames the Ḫawāriǧ for not following a doctrine regarding which the Companions of the Prophet had concurred in the following words: "*Lam ya'ḫuḏū bi-mā iǧtama'a 'alayh aṣḥāb rasūl Allāh*".

Āṯār A. Y., 98 and 278. In a tradition from Ibrāhīm the consensus of the Companions is invoked in the following words: "*Lam yaǧtami' aṣḥāb Muḥammad kamā iǧtama'ū 'alā* . . ."

Šaybānī also argues from consensus quite often. To him it is

1. *Ḫarāǧ*, p. 48. For another instance see *Tr.* IX, 17 and 42 (a statement about consensus made in the positive form, supplemented by the claim of absence of disagreement).
2. See also *ibid.*, p. 129: *'alayh al-ǧamā'a wa-l-'amal.*
3. See "*Early Development*", p. 78.

authoritative and binding, and therefore, he opposes it to *ra'y* [1], which is not so. Indeed, in him we find a specific argument justifying *iǧmāʿ*—tradition from the Prophet: "Whatever the believers consider to be good is good in the sight of Allāh and whatever they consider bad [literally, ugly] is bad in the sight of Allāh" [2]. Šaybānī refers to the consensus of all Muslims [3] as well as to the consensus of the *fuqahā'* [4], particularly of the *fuqahā'* of his own school [5], and also to the *fuqahā'* of Kūfa and Medina [6].

He generally refers to consensus in the following ways:

(i) Šaybānī declares a certain doctrine to be preferable to its opposite and adds: *Wa-huwa l-qawl allaḏī aǧmaʿa ʿalayh ahl al-Kūfa*" [7].

(ii) Regarding a certain ritual prayer which was made congregational by ʿUmar, Šaybānī holds the view that that act on the part of ʿUmar was all right. Why? "*Li-anna l-Muslimīn qad aǧmaʿū ʿalā ḏālika wa-ra'awhu ḥasan*" [8].

(iii) On another occasion he remarks: "*Wa-hāḏā l-amr al-muǧtamaʿ ʿalayh lā iḫtilāf bayn al-fuqahā' fīh*" [9].

(iv) Šaybānī remarks in the vein of Awzāʿī: "[This is the] well-known *ḥadīṯ* from the Prophet which is not doubted and the affairs of the Muslims are run according to it everywhere" [10].

The above survey regarding consensus forces the conclusion that even though the concept of consensus of all Muslims as well as of the *fuqahā'* was quite well-known and frequently referred to, it had as yet not acquired a rigidly standardised form of expression. However, it was well on the way to acquiring a fixed technical term for its expression which is proved by the use of the derivatives of *aǧmaʿa* in a majority of cases in which consensus was claimed.

1. *Ḥuǧaǧ*, p. 161.
2. *Muw. Š.*, p. 140.
3. *Loc. cit.* Cf. above, p. [31] nn. 11 f.
4. *Ḥuǧaǧ*, p. 176.
5. See *Ḥuǧaǧ* and *Muw. Š.*, *passim*. Generally the expression is: "*ʿāmmatu fuqahā'inā*".
6. See p. [31], n. 12.
7. *Loc. cit.*
8. *Muw. Š.*, p. 140.
9. *Ḥuǧaǧ*, p. 161. This seems to have been derived from Mālik. Šaybānī also uses the expression: "*Hāḏā amr muǧmaʿ ʿalayh*" (*ibid.*, p. 184).
10. *Ḥuǧaǧ*, p. 236. See also *ibid.*, pp. 23 f.

IV. *Ra'y, qiyās, istiḥsān*

(A)

Ra'y is the genus of which *qiyās* and *istiḥsān* are species. As we have seen, *ra'y* signified the use of human reasoning, and it was for this reason that the school of law of Iraq, where the use of human reasoning was relatively more prominent, came to be known as the school of *ra'y* and *qiyās* [1].

In a society which was committed to the authority of revelation, the problem of the use of human reasoning in handling what were essentially religious laws, was understandably a delicate and involved one. Human reasoning, to say the least, could be used only to a certain extent—and the fixation of this extent naturally differed from one person to the other. It is also not difficult to imagine the constant danger of overstepping the proper limits within which human reasoning should operate. It was this danger which was articulated by the opponents of the so-called *ra'y*-tendency. However, even those who seem to have resorted to *ra'y* very frequently or were more or less consciously committed to the legitimacy of its use, opposed it to what they called "*aṯar*" or "*ḫabar lāzim*", implying a distinction between the two, and the relatively inferior position of *ra'y* [2]. A few instances would illustrate this.

In his letter to Ḥasan Baṣrī, ʿAbd al-Malik asks whether the doctrine of free will was based on the Qur'ān or any tradition from some Companion of the Prophet, or was it a *ra'y* (personal opinion) at which he had himself arrived [3]. This testifies to the consciousness that *ra'y* was different from other sources and also throws some light on the dichotomy between *ra'y* and what Šaybānī (and subsequently, Šāfiʿī) termed "binding information" [4]. In his reply Ḥasan claimed that his doctrine was the one upon which the forbears were agreed and that people had innovated a doctrine—the opposite of his doctrine—and in so doing they were driven by "their misguiding desires" (*al-ahwiya al-muḍilla*) [5].

---

1. See "*Early Development*", pp. 110 f.
2. For distinction between *aṯar* and *ra'y*, see *ibid.*, pp. 27 ff. and pp. 94 ff. and p. 111.
3. "*Treatise of Baṣrī*", *op. cit.*, p. 67.
4. *Tr.* VIII, 3.
5. "*Treatise of Baṣrī*", pp. 70 f. See also *ibid.*, p. 72 for the use of the same expression. To these "misguiding desires", Ḥasan opposed the Qur'ān which is "light and life" (*ibid.*, p. 70). The opponents of *ra'y* used the word

In Ibn al-Muqaffaʿ too we find this problem as well as the use of the term *ra'y*. According to Ibn al-Muqaffaʿ, God has ensured man's felicity by means of two things: (1) religion and (2) reason (*ʿaql*). Reason is a benediction of God, says Ibn al-Muqaffaʿ, and yet it is incapable of the cognition of true guidance unless this true guidance is revealed by God. Except for the things which have thus been authoritatively laid down, God has left the rest of the things to *ra'y* and has entrusted its administration to the rulers [1]. This is one form of the use of *ra'y*—which seems to mean deriving correct inferences from authoritative sources, and using ingenuity and discretion in enforcing them. This is the use of *ra'y* in a good sense. There is, at the same time, an instance of the use of *ra'y* in a bad sense. It is in the context of introducing objectionable practices merely on the basis of *ra'y* (personal opinion) without any reference to the "Book" or the "*Sunna*", and even though no Muslim subscribed to that doctrine. It is sheer vanity that a person should regard such a doctrine as enforceable particularly when enforcing it entailed violation of the sanctity of human lives [2]. In this context *ra'y* denotes arbitrary opinion.

In Abū Yūsuf and Šaybānī too we find the use of the term in both good and bad senses. It is used consistently in a good sense when it is used in the context of deriving a doctrine on some question on which there was no authoritative information. ʿUmar, according to a tradition cited by Abū Yūsuf, asked Ibn Masʿūd to make judgement according to his *ra'y* [3] on a question on which nothing authoritative was known.

The favourite Iraqian forms of the use of *ra'y* are the expression

in this sense when they denounced it. The motivation of the opposition was the fear that "misguiding desires" might distort religion. For an interesting discussion on *ra'y*, see Ibn al-Qayyim, *op. cit.*, vol. I, pp. 53 ff. Ibn al-Qayyim cites the use of the term *ra'y* with both good and bad shades of meaning.

1. Ibn al-Muqaffaʿ, *op. cit.*, p. 122.

2. *Ibid.*, p. 126. In the view of Ibn al-Muqaffaʿ *ra'y*, even in its logical and systematic form of *qiyās*, could lead to unhappy consequence (*ibid.*, p. 127). It is also interesting to note that this use of *ra'y* in a bad context is followed by its use in a good one. For instance, Ibn al-Muqaffaʿ advises the Caliph to codify legal doctrines in the light of "his *ra'y* inspired by God" (*ra'yuhu allaḏī yulhimuhu Allāh*) which should serve as the legal code of the caliphate. Ibn al-Muqaffaʿ hopes that the fixation of doctrines according to the *ra'y* of the Caliph (*bi-ra'y amīr al-mu'minīn*), would lead to the development of a uniform legal code.

3. *Āṯār A.Y.*, 607. See also *Muw. Š.*, p. 244.

a-lā tarā or *a-ra'ayta* [1]. It is only when one uses *ra'y* at the cost of something which is authoritative, e.g. *aṯar*, *sunna*, or consensus, that *ra'y* is considered to have overstepped its proper limits [2]. In his *Ḥuǧaǧ* Šaybānī criticizes the Medinese again and again for using *ra'y* in an arbitrary manner and for not basing their doctrines on *aṯar*. For this, he also uses the term *taḥakkum* [3].

(B)

The works of Abū Yūsuf and Šaybānī show an increasing use of *qiyās* and a clear formulation of its concept. When this is compared with the comparatively rare use of the term in the Medinese or Syrian writings, the obvious conclusion that follows is that it is the Iraqians who popularised the use of the term in legal discussions [4]. The references by Šāfi'ī to the Iraqians as the "adherents of *qiyās*" [5] or his statement that the "Iraqians allow none to diverge from *qiyās*" [6], also point to the leading role played by the Iraqians in making this term familiar.

The following are the main usages of *qiyās* in Abū Yūsuf and Šaybānī which will show not only that its use was quite standard, but also that the term itself had been precisely defined and its connotation fixed.

Tr. IX, (pp. 31 and 32). Abū Yūsuf stresses that everything ought to conform to the Qur'ān and the *Sunna* [in the latter instance, to *sunna ma'rūfa*]. Besides, Abū Yūsuf admonishes that the Qur'ān and the *Sunna* should be used for the purpose of "measuring" everything which has not been laid down in them. Abū Yūsuf claims that Abū Ḥanīfa derived the doctrine that the

---

1. *Tr.* I and *Tr.* IX, *passim*. See also *Ḫarāǧ*, p. 19. For *Tr.* I, see p. [44], n. 5.
2. *Ḥuǧaǧ*, p. 168. See also *ibid.*, p. 88, where Šaybānī finds it objectionable to use *qiyās* and *naẓar*—denoting thereby human reasoning—at the cost of *sunna* and *aṯar*. See also *Origins*, pp. 98 ff. and 103 ff.; and Goldziher, *Die Zahiriten*, (Leipzig, 1884), pp. 3 ff.
3. For *taḥakkum*, see *Ḥuǧaǧ*, pp. 224 and 234.
4. This conclusion is based on a broad comparative study of the contemporary writings of the Medinese and Syrians on the one hand, and the Kūfians on the other. The Medinese seem to have used the term *iǧtihād* either as an equivalent of, or in a sense close to, *qiyās*. See its use in *Muw.* p. 858, lines 1 and 4 (*laysa fī ḏālika illā iǧtihād*). See also *ibid.*, p. 859 where Mālik opposes it to *al-amr al-muǧtama' 'alayh*. Concerning the use of this term and the use of the method of *qiyās*, see *Origins*, pp. 116 f.
5. *Tr.* I, 137 (cited according to sections. See *Origins*, pp. 231f.).
6. *Ibid.*, 89.

pregnant Muslim woman who came from *dār al-ḥarb* might not be taken into marriage on the basis of *qiyās* from the saying of the Prophet which prohibited intercourse with a pregnant captive woman prior to child-birth.

Tr. I, 51. On the question of *muzāra'a*, Abū Yūsuf disagrees with the doctrine of Abū Ḥanīfa and in addition to citing traditions from the Prophet which testify to its legitimacy, he also asserts that *muzāra'a* is parallel to *muḍāraba* [and, therefore, permitted]. He claims: "This *qiyās* of ours is in addition to the *aṯar*" [1].

Ḫarāğ, p. 178. *Qiyās* is distinguished from *aṯar* on the one hand, and *istiḥsān* on the other [2].

In Šaybānī we find even a more precise and sharper formulation of the doctrine of *qiyās*.

Ḥuğağ, p. 6. "In respect of that for which there is no *aṯar*, what should be done is to resort to *qiyās* (analogy) on the basis of *aṯar* with regard to something which is parallel to it".

Ibid., p. 9. Repeats the same idea in almost the same words.

Ibid., p. 235. A similar expression.

Ibid., p. 234. Šaybānī points out that copper and lead do not resemble stones. They rather resemble gold and silver and hence the rule of *zakā* regarding gold and silver should be applied to copper and lead, rather than the rule with regard to stones. In view of the above Šaybānī criticizes the Medinese for having "erred in making *qiyās*" [3].

Ibid., p. 212. Šaybānī cites the instructions of 'Umar to Abū Musā al-Aš'arī urging him to find out parallel cases and to apply *qiyās*: "*wa-qis al-amr 'inda ḏālik*".

Ibid., p. 46. Opposes *qiyās* to *āṯār*, and points out that there can be no *qiyās* when there are *āṯār* i.e., on issues on which there are specific rulings in the authoritative sources. In such matters one should rather follow *āṯār*.

In Abū Yūsuf we have seen instances of opposing *qiyās* to *istiḥsān*,

---

1. See also *Ḫarāğ*, p. 160. It may also be pointed out that *bi-manzila* and *a-ra'ayta* and *a-lā tarā* were also frequently used to denote *qiyās*. See *Tr.* I and *Tr.* IX, and *Ḥuğağ*, *passim*.
2. See also *Ḫarāğ*, pp. 182 and 189, and *passim*.
3. For further examples, see *Ḥuğağ*, p. 66, lines 9 and 10, p. 153, p. 158 (*qiyās* as opposed to *aṯar*), p. 162, p. 174 and often.

a feature which is even more prominent in Šaybānī, as we shall see in our discussion on *istiḥsān* [1].

It may also be pointed out that even though the word *qiyās* seems to have already developed into a technical term by the time of Abū Ḥanīfa, yet the use of expressions such as *bi-manzila* [2], or that of *a-ra'ayta* and *a-lā tara* [3] shows that alternate expressions were still in use. Moreover, the actual application of analogy by the Kūfians evidences considerable technical skill as well as a fairly clear notion of *qiyās*. In applying *qiyās* the Kūfians seek the element which is common to both the original and the assimilated case, but they do not use the term *ʿilla*, which is the later term for it [4]. This is only one among several examples of the semantic lag and which only proves that semantic developments followed, rather than prededed, conceptual developments.

(C)

Coming to the usages of the term *istiḥsān* in Abū Yūsuf and Šaybānī one gets the impression that the term was formulated in opposition to *qiyās* and the purpose was not to deny the legitimacy of *qiyās* as such, but to restrict its scope so as to avoid the unhappy consequences that might follow from adhering to *qiyās* rigidly and to affirm the validity of the jurist's discretion to depart from strict analogy on the strength of some overridingly important considera-tion.

Ḫarāǧ, p. 178. A ruler or his judge sees a man commit theft or illegitimate sexual intercourse, etc. He should not enforce *ḥadd* merely on the basis of his own observation without any testimony. Abū Yūsuf designates this as *istiḥsān*, and the basis for this is an

1. See section below.
2. See above, p. [37], n. 1.
3. *Loc. cit.*
4. *Origins*, p. 110. For the actual use of *qiyās*, see below pp. 280 ff. It may be noted that often when *qiyās* was opposed to *istiḥsān*, the former generally signified a strict literalist or formalistic application of law in disregard of those considerations on which *istiḥsān* was based. For these examples, see below pp. 168 ff. and above pp. 300 ff. Noteworthy are also some of the conclusions of Schacht. According to him, a systematic conclusion from someone's doctrine was termed as *qiyās qawlih* (*Origins*, p. 110). Šāfiʿī often means by *qiyās* not strict analogy, but consistent systematic reasoning in a broader sense. (*Ibid.*, p. 126).

aṯar from Abū Bakr and ʿUmar, even though *qiyās* required that the *ḥadd* should be enforced [1].

Ibid., p. 189. Regarding a *ḥarbī* who enters *dār al-Islām*: if some Muslim steals his property, or deliberately amputates his hand, *qiyās* demands that the hand of the Muslim should be amputated. Abū Yūsuf is of the opinion, however, that this doctrine should not be followed, and he decides to give preference to a doctrine opposed to this doctrine in deference to the authority who followed the opposite doctrine [2].

Istiḥsān, in the view of Šaybānī, however, does not justify deviation from *aṯar*, but merely from *qiyās*. He accuses the Medinese of having resorted to *istiḥsān* as against "a *ḥadīṯ* from the Messenger of Allāh" [3].

As for opposing *istiḥsān* to *qiyās*, we have seen its examples in Abū Yūsuf. In Šaybānī this opposition is a regular feature [4]. In *Ǧāmiʿ Ṣaġīr*, for instance, *istiḥsān* occurs eighteen times, out of which it is only nine times that it has been used without reference to *qiyās* [5]. The following are a few examples of *istiḥsān* [6]:

Ǧāmiʿ Ṣaġīr, p. 21. A group of people prayed on horseback. According to *qiyās*, this is sufficient and acquits them of their duty; according to *istiḥsān*, it does not.

Ibid., p. 61. A person who confessed about another person that the latter was his son, and subsequently the latter died. That person and his mother would be entitled to inheritance according to *istiḥsān*, although, according to *qiyās*, the woman was not entitled to inheritance for the person might have had sexual intercourse with the woman in *šubha* (misunderstanding), not knowing that she was a free woman.

1. Thus *istiḥsān* sometimes also denoted avoidance of normal legal implications on account of *aṯar*.
2. For another instance, see *Ḫarāǧ*, p. 178, line 3 (in this case there is no pointed reference to *qiyās*).
3. *Ḥuǧaǧ*, p. 77. See for a similar accusation, *ibid.*, p. 59.
4. See Šaybānī, *Ǧāmiʿ Ṣaġīr*, (Lucknow, 1310 A.H.), (cited hereafter as *Ǧāmiʿ Ṣaġīr*). For reference to *istiḥsān* without specific reference to *qiyās*, see p. 32, l. 2; p. 6, l. 15; p. 107, l. 2; p. 118, l. 11; p. 120, l. 14; p. 136, l. 16; p. 137, l. 7; p. 144, l. 15; p. 156, l. 1. For further examples, see the other works of Šaybānī, *passim*, particularly *al-Ǧāmiʿ al-Kabīr*, ed. Abū l-Wafāʾ al-Afġānī, (Cairo, 1356 A.H.), *passim*. Cited hereafter as *Ǧāmiʿ Kabīr*.
5. For use with reference to *qiyās*, see *Ǧāmiʿ Ṣaġīr*, p. 21, l. 8; p. 61, l. 10; p. 69, l. 16; p. 83, l. 16; p. 84, l. 15; p. 113, l. 13; p. 124, l. 15; p. 160, l. 5 and 7. See for further examples the works of Šaybānī, *passim*.
6. For further examples of *istiḥsān*, see "*Early Development*", pp. 302 ff.

Ibid., p. 83. If some people commit theft and make one from among themselves carry the stolen goods: while *qiyās* demands that only the hand of the person who was carrying the stolen goods should be cut off, *istiḥsān* demands that punishment in respect of all the culprits.

Ibid., p. 69. A person says to his wife (who is already within the house): "If you enter into the house you are divorced". According to *qiyās*, this statement would be tantamount to *ṭalāq*, whereas according to *istiḥsān*, divorce becomes operative only if the woman re-enters the house.

Ibid., p. 107. A person usurped a slave, then he sold him to someone who, in turn, manumitted him. Subsequently the original owner allowed the sale of the slave. According to *istiḥsān* it is permitted [1]. Šaybānī, however, does not hold it to be permitted, probably owing to its irregularity from the technical legal point of view.

Schacht has disagreed with the conclusion of Goldziher that *istiḥsān* was introduced by Abū Ḥanīfa and has argued that *istiḥsān* existed even before Abū Ḥanīfa as a part of Iraqian legal reasoning, although the technical term for it appeared later, for the first time in Abū Yūsuf [2]. Whatever sources are available to us seem to confirm this, particularly the first part of the statement.

As for the connotation of the term, the above-cited examples lead to the conclusion that it signified departure from *qiyās*, sometimes on the ground that *aṯar* seemed to be opposed to the *qiyās* in question; or else it signified departure from *qiyās* in favour of considerations of equity and justice, or in favour of a doctrine which might have been formally less systematic, but more practicable and appealing to the commonsense [3].

V. Scales of religious and legal evaluation

The classical Islamic law, as is well-known, developed a scale for the evaluation of human acts in terms of their religious merit or demerit. This led to the formulation of the following five-fold scale:

---

1. In the two above-mentioned examples, *qiyās* denotes a literal and formalistic application of law, while *istiḥsān* signifies that over-ridingly important consideration which justifies departure from it.
2. *Origins*, p. 112.
3. For this see the examples cited above and those cited in "*Early Development*", pp. 302 ff.

(1) *Wāǧib, farḍ.*
(2) *Sunna, mandūb, mustaḥabb.*
(3) *Mubāḥ.*
(4) *Ḥarām.*
(5) *Makrūh.*

Besides this, it also developed a scale of legal validity [1] consisting of the following four categories:

(1) *Ṣaḥīḥ.*
(2) *Makrūh.*
(3) *Fāsid.*
(4) *Bāṭil.*

The *fiqhī* writings of the period under our study show that even though the concepts expressed by these terms were in use, yet the forms of expressing them had not been standardized. Hence, a wide range of alternative expressions was used. The use of long sentences for what was in later times expressed by a word or two, also shows that a number of technical terms had as yet not been definitively fixed.

We shall take up the scale of religious qualifications first and scrutinize the phraseology that was employed to express the concepts embodied by the terms of this scale.

(i) For the expression of the idea of religious obligatoriness, the terms which were generally used were derived from *waǧaba* and *faraḍa* [2].

(ii) The concept of *mandūb* [3] was expressed in numerous ways of which we shall list below only some important examples:

---

1. For these scales, see *Introduction*, pp. 120 f.
2. For its use in Abū Yūsuf, see *Āṯār A.Y.*, 56, 57 and 361. See also *Ḫarāǧ* and *Tr.* IX, *passim*. For its use by Šaybānī, see *Muw. Š.*, p. 48, p. 71, p. 75, p. 73 and p. 105. In this sense it is often opposed to what is recommended but not obligatory, for which the term was not yet rigidly fixed. All the above instances except that on p. 105, illustrate this. Šaybānī also defines *wāǧib*, though only by implication. This shows that by *wāǧib* he meant those acts the omission of which entailed sin (*iṯm*) (*Ibid.*, p. 48). For *farḍ* and *wāǧib*, see also *Ḥuǧaǧ*, p. 5 (*farīḍa fī Kitāb Allāh*), pp. 6 and 9 (used in opposition to *nāfila*), p. 17 and often. See also Šaybānī, *K. al-Āṯār* (Karachi, n.d. *circa* 1960), 94, 122 and often. (Cited hereafter as *Āṯār Š.*; numbers refer to traditions, not pages).
3. For the basis of this concept in the Qur'ān, see II, 78 and 237.

Muw. Š., p. 73. Ibrāhīm tries to justify his doctrine that taking bath on Friday and the two *ʿĪds* is religiously indifferent. In order to express this idea, Ibrāhīm points out that if one took bath on those occasions, it was good; but if one did not do so, it would not be reckoned against him. When asked how this doctrine could be justified in spite of the saying of the Prophet: "Whoever goes to [the] Friday [prayer], should take bath", Ibrāhīm replied: "This is all right, but it is not obligatory". This (i.e., the exhortation to take bath), argues Ibrāhīm, is similar to the ones contained in the Quranic verses II, 282 and LXII, 10. The last of these says that after the Friday prayers people should disperse. It was not blameworthy, says Ibrāhīm, if a person did not disperse after the Friday prayer [1]. This indicates the lack of standardisation of the term to convey the meaning which was later expressed by the term *mandūb*.

Loc. cit. Šaybānī himself expresses the same idea by using the term *afḍal*, which reflects some measure of both doctrinal and semantic development [2].

Ibid., p. 225. Some other forms of expressing this concept are to characterise something as *ḥasan*, with the clarification that it is not *wāǧib* [3] or by using the phrase: *aḥabbu ilayya* (or *ilaynā*), etc.

(iii) Again, instead of any precise word or expression for [4] the concept of *ibāḥa* (indifference) there were numerous expressions. The most common of these was *lā ba's* [5] or *mustaqīm ǧā'iz* [6] or *maʿrūf ḥasan ǧamīl* [7] or *ḥalāl* [8] or *fī saʿa* [9] or *ǧā'iz* [10].

(iv) The concept of *ḥarām* was expressed by various terms.

1. The pains that Ibrāhīm takes in order to make his concept clear and the lack of sharp distinction between indifference and recommended, constitutes a forceful argument in favour of the authenticity of this tradition. See the same doctrine of Ibrāhīm, without any explanation, in *Āṯār Š.*, 66, 67, 68.

2. *Muw. Š.*, p. 73 and *Āṯār Š.*, 67. This is a favourite word of Šaybānī. See for its use, *Muw. Š.*, p. 138, line 3.

3. For other instances, see *ibid.*, p. 75 and p. 150.

4. *Āṯār A.Y.*, 310, 811, 812; *Āṯār Š.*, 45, 48 and 50; *Muw. Š.*, p. 82; *Ḥuǧaǧ*, p. 1 and often. See also *Ḫarāǧ*, *Tr.* IX, *Tr.* I, *passim*.

5. See *Āṯār A.Y.*, *Muw. Š.*, *Ḥuǧaǧ*, etc., *passim*.

6. *Ḫarāǧ*, p. 68, *Tr.* IX, p. 13, 22, and other works, of Abū Yūsuf and Šaybānī, *passim*.

7. *Āṯār A.Y.*, 842, and often in the works of Abū Yūsuf and Šaybānī.

8. *Tr.* IX, p. 23, 26, and often.

9. *Ḫarāǧ*, p. 68; *Muw. Š.*, p. 184, and often.

10. *Tr.* I, p. 15, and often.

Sometimes the word *ḥarām* [1] itself was used, on other occasions, *kariha* or its derivatives, or *lā yaḥillu* [2].

(v) The concept of "disapproved but not sinful" was used, but not necessarily expressed by the term *makrūh* [3], which is the classical term for it. So far as the concept itself is concerned, we find it expressed in statements such as the following:

Āṯār Š., 57. Regarding the question whether the *mu'addin* might speak during the *adān*: Abū Ḥanīfa and Šaybānī were of the view that he should not do so; but if he does, that would not nullify (*intaqaḍa*) his *adān*.

Ḥuğağ, pp. 148 f. Šaybānī distinguishes between disapproval in the sense of *ḥarām*, and for the sake of *tanzīh*. (This distinction, as well as this terminology, became an integral part of classical Ḥanafī juristic tradition) [4].

Siyar Kabīr, p. 148 (in Saraḫsī, *Šarḥ al-Siyar al-Kabīr*, 3 vols., ed. al-Munağğid, Cairo, 1960). Šaybānī reports 'Alī's opinion that he considered marriage with Christian women in *dār al-ḥarb* to be *makrūh*. Šaybānī observes that this opinion resulted from the fear that the progeny would be left behind in *dār al-ḥarb*. He clarifies that 'Alī did not consider it to be *ḥarām*.

Tr. IX, 23, (p. 73). Abū Yūsuf reports that Ibrāhīm preferred to say: "This is *makrūh*" instead of saying: "This is *ḥarām*".

Thus, the concept of '*makrūh*' in its classical sense is well-known and used, but there was no uniform term for expressing that concept.

Coming to the scale of legal validity, the consideration of acts in terms of their legal as distinct, though not altogether divorced from, their religious value, constitutes an important aspect of the development of Islamic jurisprudence. This applied to rituals as well as to contracts. The basis of this line of development is the distinction between the religious-moral and legal quality of acts. A certain act might be *makrūh* in terms of its religious evaluation,

1. For *ḥarām*, see *Āṯār A.Y.*, 1003, 1007, 1009 and 1010; *Ḥuğağ*, p. 256 and often.

2. For the use of *makrūh* in the sense of *ḥarām*, see *Āṯār A.Y.*, 1012; *Muw. Š.*, pp. 28, 261 and 337; *Ḥuğağ*, p. 235. This was the sense in which *makrūh* was generally used. *Makrūh*, however, was also used in the more advanced sense, that is, "disapproved but not prohibited or sinful." See immediately below.

3. For its use in the sense of *ḥarām*, see note above. Schacht also tends to support this conclusion. (See *Origins*, p. 133).

4. See, for instance, TAFTĀZĀNĪ, *op. cit.*, vol. II, p. 125.

and yet acquit the person who performs it of his duty. A contract might have an element which, in religious terms, might not be laudable, and yet it is legally valid and therefore, enforceable. The idea that a man's act was disapproved, and yet valid is often expressed by Šaybānī in the following form: *"aǧza'ahu ḏālika wa-asā'a"* [1]. Šaybānī also gives expression to the view that an act might entail penalty, even though the person concerned might not have sinned. The problem on which he expresses this view is that of the woman who is in the state of consecration for pilgrimage, and is coerced by her husband into sexual intercourse: would she be liable to *kaffāra* (expiation) or not? The Medinese argued that since the act was not performed voluntarily it was not sinful and, therefore, did not necessitate expiation. Abū Ḥanīfa and Šaybānī, on the other hand, argued that at times one was obliged to make expiation [owing to a formal breach of some rule], even though one had not committed a sin. This is proved by the obligation to pay blood-money even for homicide without intent and to make expiatory sacrifice if one had unintentionally killed an animal in the state of consecration for pilgrimage [2]. Thus, there was a growing trend towards a purely legal evaluation of acts, the consideration of acts in terms of the legal effects which follow from them side by side with, and yet distinguished from, their religious or moral value. Subsequently, this distinction became increasingly vivid and led to the formulation of the four-fold scale of legal validity [3].

It will be noticed that the semantic development lagged behind the conceptual one in this case even as it generally lagged behind in other cases. The concept of *ṣaḥīḥ* was generally expressed by the term *aǧza'a, yuǧzi'u* [4]. As for *fāsid, bāṭil,* and *makrūh,* these were used quite frequently, but not necessarily in the sense in which they were used in the classical *fiqh* literature. Their connotations not having become precisely fixed, these terms seem to have been used interchangeably [5].

1. *Ḥuǧaǧ*, p. 188, and often.
2. *Ibid.*, p. 175.
3. It may be pointed out, however, that while the two scales were distinct, they were never quite unrelated to each other. What was *ḥarām*, for instance, was regarded as *bāṭil* (i.e. legally void) as well.
4. See, for example, *ibid.*, p. 188, *Āṯār Š.*, 3, and often.
5. See Abū Yūsuf, *Iḫtilāf Abī Ḥanīfa wa-Ibn Abī Laylā*, ed. Abū l-Wafā' al-Afġānī, (Cairo, 1357 A.H.), *Ḫarāǧ*, *Āṯār A.Y.*, and *Āṯār Š.*, *Ḥuǧaǧ*, etc., *passim*. *Iḫtilāf Abī Ḥanīfa* . . . = Tr.I.

VI. Conclusion

The above discussion leads to the following conclusions:

(1) That there was a marked lag between the conceptual and terminological aspects of the development of *fiqh*. A number of concepts remained in use for a long period of time before they could acquire standard, technical phraseology for their expression. This fact reinforces the testimony of other evidence that some of the fundamental concepts such as the *sunna* of the Prophet, consensus, etc., are anterior to the period when they acquired standard technical terms [1] for their expression. It follows from this that while the positive results of any survey of terms in use can be considered trustworthy, the same cannot be said about the negative results. In other words, if there is positive evidence about the existence of a concept as embodied by the term in use, we can confidently make an affirmative statement. But if, on the contrary, positive terminological evidence is lacking in regard to some concept, this does not necessarily signify the non-existence of that concept.

(2) The semantic evidence, despite being fragmentary, reflects the general direction in the development of *fiqh*. The increasingly elaborate terminology that was coming into use from around the middle of the second century of the *hiğra*, the neat distinctions which the technical terms were beginning to express, the trend towards an increasingly precise definition of terms that was taking place—all these reflect corresponding developments in *fiqh* itself: a more vivid *uṣūl*-consciousness reflected in the growing recognition of distinctions between the various sources of positive doctrines, and its corollary, an increasing formalism and finesse in technical legal thought.

(3) That even though there was a semantic lag, yet the formulation of technical terms with accurate connotations was well on its way and considerable progress seems to have been made in that respect. Some of these concepts had already acquired full-fledged technical terms for their expression such as *qiyās* and *istiḥsān*.

1. This conclusion is partial and should be combined with what follows, particularly the conclusion no. 3 to appreciate the findings of this writer. For even though the concepts were there even when technical terms were in the process of being formulated, they lacked rigidly standardised forms to express them.

There were others which seemed to be on the verge of that point—such as the concept of *sunna* (as a source of law) and *mandūb*, and *makrūh*, etc.

On the whole, the Kūfians seem to have prepared the ground not only for the conceptual contribution made by Šāfiʿī [1], but also for his semantic contribution which consisted of a more precise definition of terms such as *sunna*, *aṯar*, *qiyās*, etc.

---

1. For this, see the section on "*Sunna* and Traditions", in "*Early Development*", pp. 193 ff. Cf. *Origins*, *passim*., particularly part I.

10

WAS AL-SHAFI'I THE MASTER ARCHITECT OF ISLAMIC JURISPRUDENCE?

Wael Hallaq

I

During the last three or four decades, modern scholarship has increasingly come to recognize Muhammad Ibn Idris al-Shafiᶜi (d. 820) as having played a most central role in the early development of Islamic jurisprudence. It was Joseph Schacht who, more than anyone else, demonstrated Shafiᶜi's remarkable success in anchoring the entire edifice of the law not only in the Qurᵓan, which by his time was taken for granted, but mainly, and more importantly, in the traditions of the Prophet.[1] Shafiᶜi's prominent status has been further bolstered by the fact that he was the first Muslim jurist ever to articulate his legal theory in writing, in what has commonly become known as *al-Risāla*.[2]

Schacht's portentous findings, coupled with the high esteem in which Shafiᶜi is held in medieval and modern Islam, have led Islamicists to believe that Shafiᶜi was the "father of Muslim jurisprudence" and the founder of the science of legal theory, properly called *uṣūl al-fiqh*.[3] His *Risāla* is thought to have become "a model for both jurists and theologians who wrote on the subject."[4] And although it is acknowledged that later theory further elaborated the themes of Shafiᶜi's treatise and sometimes even modified them, the origination of legal theory nonetheless remains his achievement. The medieval dictum that "Shafiᶜi is to *uṣūl al-fiqh* what Aristotle was to logic" is still as valid as when it first appeared.[5]

This being the state of our knowledge, there appears to be little reason to question the purported fact that since its inception in the work of Shafiᶜi, *uṣūl al-fiqh*, as we now know it, became, in an unwavering continuity, the standard legal methodology of Sunni Islam. There is even less reason to question the 9th century, chronologically so close to Shafiᶜi, as an era that was dominated by the influential Shafiᶜites who were zealously safeguarding the teachings of their master. True, there were some tendencies in legal thought—such as the Zahiriyya—that diverged from the mainstream jurisprudence as expressed in the legacy of Shafiᶜi, but these soon dropped altogether out of the scene and, consequently, they are thought to be rather marginal. Thus, the continuity between Shafiᶜi's theory and classical *uṣūl al-fiqh* would seem to represent a natural development, especially in that it tallies with our perception of Shafi^ci, not only as the "master architect" of Islamic jurisprudence,[6] but as the jurist-victor who brought the 8th-century unbridled law down to the knees of revelation.

The assumption of this continuity, and of Shafi^ci as the master architect of legal theory, turns out, upon a close examination of the sources, to be seriously flawed. Historical evidence in the early and medieval sources is not only discordant with this assumption but, in its aggregate effect, also seems to contradict it. In the following pages I shall attempt to show that we have no good reason to believe that such a continuity ever existed; that Shafi^ci's *Risāla* and the theory that it embodied had very little, if any, effect during most of the 9th century; and that the image of Shafi^ci as the founder of *uṣūl al-fiqh* was a later creation.

II

The most striking fact about the 9th century is that it yields no single work on *uṣūl al-fiqh*. By that we mean a work whose primary task is to lay down a systematic, comprehensive, and organically structured legal methodology whose purpose in turn is to derive legal rulings from the material sources—as was clearly the case in the 10th century and thereafter.

That we possess no complete work on the subject from that century initially becomes clear from reading the later *uṣūl* authors who mention from this period no work that can be identified as a treatise on *uṣūl al-fiqh* proper. Nor do these authors mention any authority from this period with whom we can associate a complete exposition of legal theory. We do, however, notice occasional references to such thinkers as Nazzam (d. after 835), Dawud al-Zahiri (d. 884), ^cIsa ibn Aban (d. 835), and their like, but they, as we shall see, did not write works on *uṣūl al-fiqh*, and are nearly always cited as proponents of erroneous and even heretical doctrines that are to be refuted.

When biographical and bio-bibliographical dictionaries are consulted, the absence of such works from the 9th century becomes even more evident. But in searching for titles that refer to treatises on legal theory one must be cautious, for the term *uṣūl* had a wide range of applications. Ibn al-Nadim reports, for instance, that the Hanafite Abu Yusuf (d. 798) was the author of works on *uṣūl* (*lahu min al-kutub fī al-uṣūl* . . .). It immediately turns out that these books dealt with such subjects as prayer, fasting, sales, and so forth,[7] subjects clearly belonging to positive law (*furū^c*). Similarly, Abu Yusuf's younger contemporary, Shaybani (d. 805), is also reported as having written "books on *uṣūl*" regarding such subjects as prayer, alms tax, and so on.[8] Thus, when we read that Mu^calla ibn Mansur al-Razi (d. 826) and Ibn Sama^ca (d. 847) have transmitted the *uṣūl* of Abu Yusuf and Shaybani, respectively,[9] it is beyond doubt that what they have transmitted are positive-law works of the two Hanafite masters.

Ibn al-Nadim also informs us that al-Rabi^c ibn Sulayman al-Muradi (d. 884) has "transmitted Shafi^ci's works on *uṣūl*, and what he transmitted was entitled *al-Mabsūṭ*."[10] The latter, Taj al-Din al-Subki explicitly tells us, is a work on positive law, dealing with such issues as rituals, prayer, family law, and, we expect, the entire subject matter of *furū^c*.[11] It is significant that the application of the term *uṣūl* to a wide range of writings, not necessarily confined to *uṣūl al-fiqh*, was predominant not only during the lifetime of Ibn al-Nadim, but even as late as the time of Subki (d. 1370). Having read Ibn al-ᶜIfris's (d. ca. 1010) *Jamᶜ al-jawāmiᶜ fī nuṣūṣ al-Shāfiᶜī*—a work clearly treating positive law[12]—Subki, impressed with it, remarks that it is "one of the earliest *uṣūl* (*min al-uṣūl al-qadīma*) . . . and has become one of the *uṣūl* of the [Shafiᶜite] school of law."[13]

Although it is often possible to establish whether or not the term refers to works on legal theory, there are instances where the term could be misleading. An excellent example is Abu Yahya al-Saji's (d. 920) treatise entitled, interestingly enough, *Uṣūl al-fiqh*. This work, in fact, has nothing to do with legal theory. Its main subjects are positive law and *khilāfiyyāt*, disagreements on positive legal doctrine, particularly, in this treatise, among Abu Hanifa, his two students, Malik, Shafiᶜi, Ibn Abi Layla, Ibn Shubruma, Abu Thawr and others.[14] Likewise, one would have no reason whatsoever to doubt that Ibn Maryam al-Aswani's *Jumal al-uṣūl al-dālla ᶜalā al-furūᶜ fī al-fiqh*, written presumably in the very beginning of the 10th century, is a work that treats legal theory, but the fact is that it does not. Subki, to whom a copy of the work was available in the *waqfiyya* of Dar al-Hadith in Damascus, felt compelled to explain to us that "what is meant by *uṣūl* [in the title] are the doctrines (*nuṣūṣ*) of Shafiᶜi. . . . The author mentions that the work represents an abridgment of the doctrines. . . . In it, the author would occasionally object to these doctrines, *as he did in the chapter on bequests*" (italics mine).[15]

Now, if we take into account the ambiguities involved in the use of the term *uṣūl*, the 9th century produces no work whatsoever that has the complete characteristics of *uṣūl al-fiqh*.[16] In the hundreds of titles and bio-bibliographical notices belonging to the 9th century, there is no allusion to such works. And in his refutation of the *uṣūl* principles of Sunni juristic thought, al-Qadi al-Nuᶜman, writing around the middle of the 10th century, confirms the data provided by the bio-bibliographical sources.[17] All that is to be found in the sources are individual treatises, mainly polemical, bearing such titles as *Fī ithbāt al-qiyās*, *Naqḍ ithbāt al-qiyās*, *Ijtihād al-raʾy*, *Khabar al-wāḥid*, *al-Ijmāᶜ*, and *al-Khuṣūṣ wa-al-ᶜumūm*. ᶜIsa ibn Aban, for instance, wrote on qiyas and *ijtihād al-raʾy*.[18] Qasim ibn Sayyar (d. 889) also wrote two treatises, one on solitary traditions and the other in refutation of *muqallids*.[19] The authors associated with such specialized tracts are known to have been involved in the polemics that so much pervaded the 9th century. The purpose of these treatises, as attested in their titles, seems to have been the defense of one juridical—and perhaps theologically related—position or another, but not to lay down, consciously and deliberately, an organically structured legal methodology whose explicit raison d'être, as was declared later, is to discover God's law. In any case, it is significant that no jurist is reported to have written—whether in one or several treatises—on all of these issues, much less on all the issues subsumed under *uṣūl*. Dawud ibn Khalaf al-Zahiri, somewhat of an exception, composed a number of works in refutation of a variety of doctrines held by other jurists. But these works, as Goldziher rightly noted, are "pamphlets against Hanafite works . . . put into circulation in order to dismiss the theological scruples of the reaction inclined towards traditions."[20] Interestingly, among the works attributed to Dawud is a tract entitled *al-Uṣūl*. Ibn al-Nadim, however, lists the work in the midst of titles on positive law.[21] That the work did not treat *uṣūl al-fiqh* may also be gleaned from the fact that a student of Dawud, Abu Saᶜid al-Raqqi, wrote a work, also titled *al-Uṣūl*, "on the model of Dawud's work" that consists of a hundred chapters (*kutub*). Having already enumerated these *kutub*—clearly treating positive law—in the bio-bibliographical notice of the master, Ibn al-Nadim remarks that "we need not mention them here."[22]

The proposition that the 9th century was devoid of works on *uṣūl al-fiqh* finds further attestation in the manner in which the biographers cover this in comparison with their treatment of later centuries. The biographers never employ nomenclatures indicative of specialized knowledge of legal theory to characterize authors of the 9th century. Such descriptions as "*uṣūlī*," "he wrote on *uṣūl*," "he excelled in *uṣūl*," "he was most knowledgeable in *uṣūl*," were, with one partial exception,[23] absent from discourse on the 9th century. It is striking that once the biographers move to the 10th-century authors, such descriptions become not only frequent but indeed the norm. Moreover, on the pedagogical plane, while such statements as "he studied *uṣūl* under so and so" are countless in the biographies of the 10th century and onwards, they are markedly absent in those belonging to the 9th century.

To add to all this, the *Risāla* of Shafiᶜi is mentioned rarely in the context of the 9th century, and when it is alluded to, it is usually in passing. In the immense literature relative to the legal movement of the 9th century, there are three prominent references to the treatise in the sources, one of which is quoted frequently. The first appears in Ibn Hanbal's statement in which he allegedly recommends the *Risāla* to Ibn Rahawayh (d. 853).[24] But this recommendation is contradicted frequently by Ibn Hanbal's other statements where he reportedly shuns the work. Having been asked by his student Marwadhi whether the *Risāla* is worth studying, he is said to have replied in the negative, adding that it is religiously dubious.[25] The second instance concerns Abu ᶜAli al-Zaᶜfarani (d. 874), one of Shafiᶜi's most distinguished students, who is reported to have "read the *Risāla*" under his mentor. It is highly likely, however, that he read the old version of the treatise, since he is commonly associated with transmitting Shafiᶜi's old doctrines, doctrines the latter had presumably elaborated in Hijaz and Iraq, before he finally settled in Egypt where he is thought to have written the new *Risāla*.[26] The third, oft-quoted reference is to Muzani's statement, "I have been reading the *Risāla* for fifty years, and each time I read it I learn something that I have not known before."[27] We should, however, hasten to assert that such references to the treatise are relatively few and cannot be culled from the sources with ease.

It is curious, to say the least, that what is assumed to be the *uṣūl* equivalent of Aristotle's *Organon* should be thoroughly ignored in a century that is considered one of the most dynamic phases in Islam's intellectual history. One of the most significant pieces of evidence pointing to the marginal importance of the *Risāla* is the complete absence of any contemporary commentary on, or abridgement of, the treatise. This is at a time, we must emphasize, when commentaries and abridgments have already become commonplace. On the other hand, once the 10th century looms on the horizon, we are suddenly confronted with at least five commentaries on the *Risāla*. But more on this later.

The only so-called *uṣūl* commentary on Shafiᶜi known to us is Muzani's (d. 878) short work, *Kitāb al-amr wa-al-nahy ᶜalā maᶜnā al-Shāfiᶜī*.[28] Interestingly, it is a gloss not on any section of the *Risāla*, but rather on Shafiᶜi's *Kitāb ṣifat nahy Rasūl Allāh* which constitutes less than two pages of his multivolume *furūᶜ* work *al-Umm*.[29] The greater part of Muzani's work (consisting of a total of ten pages) turns out to be an exposition of his own views on the subject.[30] Fortunately, Muzani's treatise has survived the ravages of time, and we are able to confirm its elementary nature. That Muzani, the most prominent disciple of Shafiᶜi, should comment on a rather slim section of a work on positive law and ignore the *Risāla* altogether is a fact that speaks for itself.

Nor is there to be found a refutation of the *Risāla*—again in a century whose landmark was the intensity with which scholars refuted one another. There were several individuals and groups who must have disagreed with, and even resented, what Shafiᶜi had to say in his treatise. There were the rationalists and the extreme traditionalists,[31] for example, whose beliefs clearly ran counter to the ideas expressed therein. Yet there exists no trace of any attack directed explicitly against the treatise. Again we observe that in the 10th century we do come across such refutations, as shall be seen later.

The fact that the *Risāla* did not elicit any refutation in the first century of its life gains added significance in light of the critiques and refutations directed against Shafiᶜi's system of positive law. The Hanafite Bakkar ibn Qutayba (d. 884), for instance, wrote against Shafiᶜi's critique of Abu Hanifa.[32] And Muhammad ibn ᶜAbd al-Hakam al-Misri (d. 881), who abandoned Shafiᶜi in favor of the Malikite school, criticized his former mentor in a treatise he entitled *al-Radd ᶜalā al-Shāfiᶜī fīmā khālafa fīhi al-Kitāb wal-Sunna*.[33] Judging from the title, the work could be treating only some of Shafiᶜi's positive legal rulings that, Misri apparently thought, found no justification in the Qurᵓan and the Sunna. Since both Misri and Shafiᶜi obviously agree on the fundamental role of the two primary sources of the law and since the controversy about the textual authoritativeness (*ḥujjiyya*) of methodological principles is of a decidedly later origin, we must take it that the treatise dealt with issues of *furūᶜ*.[34] Thus, we need not stress the added significance of the fact that the *Risāla* attracted neither commentary nor criticism when Shafiᶜi's positive law was subject to both.

III

Thus, if we assume the *Risāla* to be the first treatise on legal theory and Shafiᶜi to be the father of the science of *uṣūl al-fiqh*,[35] our assumption would be challenged by evidence from the sources. It would then make perfect sense to question these assumptions, particularly our current perception of the nature of the *Risāla*. It would not be amiss at all to ask whether the treatise truly qualifies as a work of *uṣūl al-fiqh*.

We have earlier intimated that the *Risāla* we now know represents the new or last version of the work, which Shafiᶜi wrote after he settled in Egypt. Although virtually nothing is known about the old *Risāla*, it is thought that it "was written originally as an apologia for the supremacy of the traditions."[36] This is entirely in consonance with what we know of Shafiᶜi's scholarly achievement, namely, that his ultimate goal was to establish the Prophetic traditions, together with the Qurᵓan, as the exclusive material sources of the law. The characterization of the old *Risāla* quoted earlier is apt if we are to judge the old version by the new. The latter is predominantly a hadith work, in the sense that the emphasis on the role of Prophetic traditions in the law represents its overriding and recurrent theme. In the more recent Kilani edition of the work,[37] about 130 pages out of a total of 257 are entirely allotted to various issues of hadith. Significantly, a dozen pages, constituting an independent section, treat Qurᵓanic statements that, Shafiᶜi believes, make it incumbent upon Muslims to follow the Prophet and abide by his Sunna. Even when other issues are discussed, as in the case of *istiḥsān* and qiyas, the permeating theme remains the same: all law and legal reasoning must rest on the Sunna and the Qurᵓan. When issues of language—for example, the general and the particular (*khāṣṣ/ᶜāmm*)—are discussed, it is mainly for the purpose of demonstrating that the Sunna can, and should, particularize and explain the Qurᵓan. Other issues that receive treatment by Shafiᶜi are discussed not so much for their own sake as for the sake of defining their relationship with the Sunna. The exposition of the theory of abrogation, for instance, is intended to delineate the relationship between the Qurᵓan and the Sunna when there is a conflict between the two.

In the final analysis, the *Risāla* appears to offer a number of propositions: (1) law must derive from revealed scripture; (2) the Sunna of the Prophet constitutes a revelation binding in legal matters; (3) there is no contradiction between the Sunna and the Qurᵓan, or among verses or hadiths within each of the two sources; (4) the two sources complement each other hermeneutically; (5) a legal ruling derived from unambiguous and widely transmitted texts is certain and subject to no disagreement, whereas a ruling that is inferred by means of ijtihad and qiyas may be subject to disagreement; and finally, (6) the procedures of qiyas and ijtihad and the sanctioning instrument of consensus are prescribed by the revealed texts.

At best, Shafiᶜi's exposition of these propositions remains rudimentary as well as erratic. Substantively, the *Risāla* has little to offer in the way of systematic methodology. Even the section on legal reasoning (qiyas and ijtihad), which one may argue is the best the *Risāla* has to offer apart from the treatment of the Sunna, is superficial and hardly provides an adequate explanation of how Shafiᶜi arrived at his own legal rulings or, alternatively, how another jurist can learn from Shafiᶜi in reasoning about the law.[38] For after all, *uṣūl al-fiqh*'s whole purpose is universally acknowledged to be the prescription/description of a methodology by means of which legal rulings can be derived from the sources.

On the whole, the *Risāla* not only lacks depth and shirks from a satisfactory, let alone full, treatment of the issues it raises, but it also leaves out altogether a host of fundamental questions considered part of, and indeed indispensable for, *uṣūl al-fiqh*. Questions of legal language, which occupy on average one-fifth to one-fourth of later treatises, are virtually absent from this one. A legion of questions pertaining to consensus, abrogation, legal reasoning, causation, and so forth, receive little, if any, attention. In short, approaching the work without preconceptions and presuppositions, it would not be far off the mark if we characterize it as a work concerned mainly with the Sunna of the Prophet and the utilization of hadith in the elaboration of the law. Indeed, it is not without good reason that the Urdu translation of the treatise bears the title *Kitāb al-risāla yaᶜnī uṣūl-i fiqh va ḥadīṣ*.[39]

Once the *Risāla* is cut down to size, it is relatively easy to explain the lack of interest in it during the century that followed its author's death. There simply was very little—besides the affirmation that the Sunna and the Qurᵓan must constitute the exclusive foundations of the law—that Shafiᶜi offered in the way of founding principles of *uṣūl al-fiqh*. His achievement, as we now see it, and indeed as medieval Muslims seem to have viewed it, lies rather in his resilient affirmation that God and, more specifically, His Messenger are the ultimate sources of the law. If a similar thesis were advanced with any marked force before Shafiᶜi's time, we would not have thought Shafiᶜi's thesis an achievement. But we do consider it so precisely because, with the benefit of hindsight, we have come to realize that his was an unprecedented synthesis between the rationalists, who were reluctant to accept Prophetic traditions, and the traditionalists who spurned all human reasoning in religious matters. But if it is a synthesis, sensibly reconciling the two camps, why then was it met with such oblivion?

Among the aforestated propositions that Shafiᶜi advanced and brought together in the *Risāla*, propositions 1–4 were addressed to the rationalists and proposition 6 to the traditionalists. Neither side, except Shafiᶜi himself and perhaps a few others (such as Karabisi!),[40] subscribed to a synthesis of the entirety of these propositions. In other words, Shafiᶜi's theory appealed neither to the traditionalists nor to the rationalists, and Shafiᶜi himself does not seem to have allied himself unequivocally with either camp. A careful examination of the sources reveals that he was indeed difficult to classify. In later literature he is made the champion of both orthodoxy and the Sunna of the Prophet (*nāṣir al-Sunna*), which is intended to mean (when it rarely fails to be stated explicitly) that he was an antirationalist. But there are so many references to the contrary, in both early and later sources, that it would be imprudent to ignore them. Even if we set aside the allegation that he was a Shiᶜi,[41] Shafiᶜi was not entirely innocent of Muᶜtazilite association. Not only did he himself admit his intimate knowledge of rationalist kalam, but he studied under Muᶜtazili teachers, notably Ibrahim ibn Abi Yahya al-Madani and Muslim ibn Khalid al-Zanji.[42] Al-Fakhr al-Razi, himself a Shafiᶜite and an anti-Muᶜtazilite, reports that the scholars are unanimous on the fact that the latter had been Shafiᶜi's mentor.[43] Furthermore, the Shafiᶜite al-Abiri (d. 974), in a work entirely dedicated to the virtues and merits (*manāqib*) of Shafiᶜi, asserts that the staunch Muᶜtazilite Bishr al-Marisi was an associate (*ṣāḥib*) of the master.[44] Another of Shafiᶜi's Muᶜtazilite connections is associated with the name of Abu ᶜAbd al-Rahman al-Baghdadi.[45]

All these connections, however, do more to cast a shadow of doubt on Shafiᶜi as a traditionalist than to make him a Muᶜtazilite, which by the most intolerant traditionalist standards he clearly was not. If Shafiᶜi was decidedly a non-Muᶜtazilite and, strictly speaking, a nonrationalist, he certainly was no traditionalist. All indications in the sources point in one direction and one direction only: Shafiᶜi defended the traditions of the Prophet but he was neither a loyal traditionalist nor an outstanding traditionist. As a traditionalist he betrayed his comrades when he insisted on the essential role of qiyas in the law. And as a traditionist his knowledge was flawed. The list of 9th-century critics who disapproved of Shafiᶜi's qualifications as a traditionist includes Yahya ibn Muᶜin, Ishaq ibn Rahawayh, al-Qasim ibn Sallam, and, reportedly, even Ibn Hanbal.[46] In their standard collections, the prominent Bukhari (d. 870) and Muslim (d. 875) recorded not a single tradition from Shafiᶜi,[47] and they are widely reported to have considered him a weak traditionist (*kāna ḍaᶜīfan fī al-riwāya*).[48] And Ibn Hanbal is said to have told one of his students that the traditionist has no use for Shafiᶜi's books.[49]

Thus, while Shafiᶜi emerges as a non-Muᶜtazilite, he most certainly did not belong to the camp of the traditionalists[50] (it clearly being understood here that while the traditionists are not interchangeable with the traditionalists, those who criticized Shafiᶜi happened to belong to both groups). The most eloquent testimony for Shafiᶜi's uncertain status in the religious movement of the 9th century is the distinct absence of his name from Ibn Qutayba's (d. 889) two notorious lists of the traditionalists and the rationalists,[51] an absence that can be explained only when Shafiᶜi is situated properly in the ideological configuration prevailing during the century following his death.

It should not come as a surprise, therefore, that Shafiᶜi belonged neither to the camp of the rationalists nor to that of the traditionalists. Muzani, who is universally considered to have been Shafiᶜi's chief follower until the eighth decade of the 9th century, likewise belonged to neither camp. Muzani, true, was an outstanding faqih (*raᵓsan fī al-fiqh*) and dialectician, but as a *muḥaddith* he certainly was considered far from qualified.[52] In addition Muzani had strong leanings towards Iᶜtizal. Al-Fakhr al-Razi reports that he studied kalam under the distinguished Muᶜtazilite ᶜAmr ibn ᶜUbayd, and that all scholars agree that he had Muᶜtazilite tendencies.[53] Indeed, it is hard to imagine that the most prominent student of Shafiᶜi could have been as inclined to rationalism as the later enthusiastic Shafiᶜites reported him to be when his master is supposed to be a paragon of traditionalism. If Muzani could stand in the middle of the road between traditionalism and rationalism, it is because his illustrious mentor had stood there before him.

It is worth considering at this juncture the case of Karabisi, whom we have previously seen[54] to be the only early scholar explicitly associated with *uṣūl al-fiqh*, though no title on the subject has been associated with him. Karabisi has been revealed through the sources as a scholar with an experience similar to Shafiᶜi's: he first followed the doctrines of *ahl al-raᵓy* but was soon to find the *fiqhī* truth not only in the Qurᵓan but also in the Sunna of the Prophet.[55] Furthermore, he is known widely as a professor or an expert in speculative theology (*ustādhan fī ᶜilm al-kalām*),[56] and like Shafiᶜi and Muzani, his qualifications as a traditionist were considered suspect by some eminent hadith scholars.[57] That he may have studied or written on *uṣūl al-fiqh*, in the same sense Shafiᶜi and Muzani did, is quite possible. That his writings, if any, represented an advance over Shafiᶜi is improbable, and in any case they failed to make their way to later jurisprudence.

IV

It has already been noted that while the 9th century produced neither works on *uṣūl* nor commentaries on or refutations of the *Risāla*, the 10th century produced a proliferation of literature on the subject. Once the 10th century began, a stunning shift in bio-bibliographical discourse occurs. In what seems to be a rather rapid transformation, scholars are described in new terms quite particular to *uṣūl al-fiqh*; they now appear distinctly and technically as authors of *uṣūl al-fiqh*, as *uṣūlīs* proper, with titles that are indicative of an independent and even prominent science.[58] The following is a list of some of the first jurists who appear, from the sources, to have written or excelled in the field.

1. Abu Na^cim ibn ^cAdi al-Astarabadi (d. 935); no title is mentioned.[59]
2. Abu Bakr Ibn al-Ikhshid (d. 938), *al-Ma^cūna fī al-uṣūl.*[60]
3. Abu Bakr Muhammad ibn Ibrahim al-Sayrafi (d. 942), *al-Bayān fī dalā^ɔil al-a^clām ^calā uṣūl al-aḥkām.*[61]
4. ^cUmar Muhammad Abu Faraj al-Maliki (d. 943), *al-Luma^c fī uṣūl al-fiqh.*[62]
5. Abu Mansur al-Maturidi (d. 945), *Ma^ɔākhidh al-sharā^ɔi^c fī uṣūl al-fiqh* and *Kitāb al-jadal fī uṣūl al-fiqh.*[63]
6. Ahmad ibn Abi Muhammad al-Tabari known as Ibn al-Qass (d. 947); no title is mentioned.[64]
7. Abu Bakr Muhammad ibn Isma^cil al-Qaffal al-Shashi (d. 948); no title is mentioned.[65]
8. Abu Musa al-Darir (d. during the 940s) has a treatise on *uṣūl al-fiqh* "consisting of eight volumes."[66]
9. Abu Ishaq al-Marwazi (d. 951); title is not mentioned.[67]
10. Muhammad ibn Sa^cid ibn Abi al-Qadi (d. 951), *al-Hidāya.*[68]
11. Abu Bakr Muhammad ibn ^cAbd Allah al-Barda^ci (d. 951), *al-Jāmi^c fī uṣūl al-fiqh.*[69]
12. Abu Bakr al-Dab^ci (d. 953); "he was an outstanding scholar in *uṣūl.*"[70]
13. Abu ^cAli al-Shashi (d. 955), *al-Uṣūl.*[71]
14. Abu ^cAli al-Tabari (d. 961), *Uṣūl al-fiqh.*[72]
15. Abu Bakr al-Farisi (fl. ca. 960) wrote an extensive treatise on the subject.[73]
16. Abu al-Husayn al-Tawa^ɔifi al-Baghdadi (d. ca. 960); title is not mentioned.[74]

With the proliferation of *uṣūl* literature, we find a sudden interest in Shafi^ci's *Risāla* after long neglect. The treatise now succeeds in eliciting at least five commentaries, four of which belong to the 10th century. The commentators are Abu Bakr al-Sayrafi,[75] al-Qaffal al-Shashi,[76] Abu al-Walid al-Nisaburi (d. 960),[77] al-Jawzaqi (d. 989),[78] Abu Muhammad al-Juwayni (d. 1046),[79] and quite possibly ^cAbd al-Wahhab al-Baghdadi (d. 973).[80] The *Risāla* also manages to attract at least two refutations, one by the Shi^ci Abu Sahl al-Nawbakhti (d. 940s),[81] and the other by a certain ^cUbayd Allah ibn Talib al-Katib, who appears to have been a contemporary of Sayrafi.[82] Furthermore, the *Risāla* appears to have become a constitutive part of certain *uṣūl* education. It is reported, for instance, that around the middle of the 10th century Abu al-Fadl al-Nadrawi studied the work in Isfahan under Abu al-Walid ibn Mihran.[83]

The unprecedented and intense interest in the *Risāla* and in *uṣūl al-fiqh* during the first half of the 10th century seems to be associated with certain figures whose intellectual tendencies represent a new formation in the religious history of Islam. One of these figures was Abu al-^cAbbas Ibn Surayj (d. 918), without exaggeration the most significant jurist in the Shafi^cite school after Shafi^ci himself. Unfortunately, none of Ibn Surayj's works has survived, although if we go by the biographical and doctrinal data provided by early and later sources, he no doubt emerges as the most towering personality in the early history of Shafi^cism.

Unlike any other Shafi^c^ite after Shafi^c^i, Ibn Surayj is universally held to be the unrivaled leader of the school, far superior to all other contemporary and earlier Shafi^c^ites, including Muzani. Significantly, unlike Muzani, he is distinguished as Shafi^c^i's loyal and true disciple who single-handedly defended the *madhhab* and rendered it victorious. In his time, he was the most influential professor of Shafi^c^ite law, and his students were so numerous that he is credited with "spreading the *madhhab*" to unprecedented dimensions. He also is said to have been the first to teach juridical dialectic and to combine a superior knowledge of hadith and *fiqh*. And like Shafi^c^i, he combined all this with a knowledge of kalam. Small wonder then that he was known as the Little Shafi^c^i, and that he was thought by many as the *mujaddid* (reformer) of the fourth hijri century, Shafi^c^i having been assigned to the third.[84]

Although there is no evidence to indicate that Ibn Surayj wrote a complete work on *uṣūl al-fiqh*, he seems to have assimilated all teachings on the subject from within and without the Shafi^c^ite school. He fiercely debated with the Zahirites, both Dawud and his son Muhammad, on matters of legal methodology. He is reported to have written, while mortally ill, a fifteen-folio epistle, addressed to the jurists of Shash and Firghana, in which he expounded, in what must have been an outline, the *uṣūl* principles of the then prominent mujtahids, that is, Shafi^c^i, Malik, Sufyan al-Thawri, Abu Hanifa and his two disciples, and Dawud.[85] But it is indeed telling that even Ibn Surayj, with the intense detail of biographical notices he is accorded, is not reported to have written an *uṣūl* work proper.

Nonetheless, the first and foremost Shafi^c^ite authors who did write complete works on *uṣūl* were Ibn Surayj's students. Among these students, who are reported to have made up most of the prominent Shafi^c^ites during the first half of the 10th century,[86] are Ibn Haykuwayh (d. 930), Ibrahim al-Marwazi (d. 951), Abu Bakr al-Farisi, Ibn al-Qass, Abu Bakr al-Sayrafi, and al-Qaffal al-Shashi, to mention only a few.[87] Although all of them are associated with the first generation of scholars to have composed works on *uṣūl*, the latter two deserve special attention since in later biographical and *uṣūl* works they emerge as the most significant authors on the subject. Sayrafi, the first commentator on the *Risāla*, is reckoned not only the author of "an unprecedented treatise on *uṣūl*," but also "the most knowledgeable scholar on *uṣūl al-fiqh* after Shafi^c^i."[88] And, as we have seen, Qaffal was the author of both a commentary on the *Risāla* and a treatise on legal theory, as well as the first to have written on juridical dialectic.[89] That both were distinguished *uṣūlīs*, *muḥaddiths*, speculative theologians, and dialecticians betrays their debt to Ibn Surayj who mastered all these sciences and placed them in the service of the law.

The legacy of Ibn Surayj was passed by al-Qaffal to Abu Muhammad al-Juwayni, the last commentator on the *Risāla* we know. Abu Muhammad studied hadith and law under al-Qaffal and is said to have graduated only after he perfected the latter's *ṭarīqa*, the method and treatment of the law peculiar to a jurist.[90] It is therefore far from being a mere historical chance that the rise of *uṣūl al-fiqh*, and consequently the unprecedented interest in the *Risāla*, coincided with the emergence of a community of scholars, belonging to two consecutive generations, who had at their disposal a combination of traditionalist and rationalist sciences—a combination that had no antecedents and that proved to be so crucial.[91]

V

Turning back to the earlier centuries will shed further light on the question of why Shafi^c^i's theory, as innovative as it may have been, failed to arouse the interest of his followers for nearly a century and why the flourishing of *uṣūl al-fiqh* came only after a century after the demise of its supposed founder.

We begin with the 8th century, which saw the initial stages of the development of Islamic law and jurisprudence. The studies of Schacht, Goldziher, and others have shown that the 8th century started with an overwhelming movement towards human reasoning, commonly known as *ra^ɔ^y*. But by the middle of that century, another competing movement stressing the role of traditions was already on the rise. By the time Shafi^c^i, as an independent scholar, appeared on the scene, the movement of *ahl al-ra^ɔ^y* was beginning to decline, and this was due to the rapid increase in the volume of Prophetic traditions that have infiltrated legal doctrines. Shaybani's positive law exhibits, perhaps better than any other, this stage of development, where hadiths constitute an important, but by no means exclusive, element in the law. In Shafi^c^i, as we have seen, the ultimate sources of the law become the Qur^ɔ^an and the Sunna. *Ra^ɔ^y* as an expression of rationalist and utilitarian tendencies was to be wholly expunged, hence his vehement opposition to *istiḥsān*. This is precisely where Shafi^c^i was his own jurist. While he unconditionally rejected *ra^ɔ^y* and insisted on the overriding authority of the Qur^ɔ^an and Prophetic Sunna, he salvaged certain elements of *ra^ɔ^y* and molded them into arguments that may be used in the law only insofar as they derive their premises from revelation.

It has been little emphasized since Goldziher's death that the 9th century was as dynamic and as crucial as the 8th in the history of Islamic jurisprudence. And we tend to minimize, perhaps due to our preoccupation with Schacht's findings, the consequential role of the legal movements in the 9th century and their impact on Islamic legal theory and positive law in the centuries that followed. To be sure, Shafi^c^i in no way represented the culmination of Islamic law and jurisprudence. If anything, he stood somewhere in the middle of the formative period, half-way between the crude beginnings during the very first decades of the 8th century and the final formation of the legal schools at the beginning of the 10th. For Shafi^c^i succeeded neither in ejecting *ra^ɔ^y* from the domain of legal reasoning nor, in consequence, in rendering the Prophetic Sunna unconditionally admissible. During the decades after his death, most of the Hanafites and no doubt the Mu^c^tazilites continued to uphold, under different guises, the role of human reason in the law.

A more significant development after Shafi^c^i, and by far more influential, is the rise of the anti-*ra^ɔ^y* movement represented by Ibn Hanbal and Dawud ibn Khalaf al-Zahiri, among others. While both approved of Shafi^c^i, they went much further in their emphasis on the centrality of scripture and on the repugnant nature of reasoning. But their positions on reasoning, perhaps the best legal indicator to measure their tendencies, were by no means identical. Ibn Hanbal, as we can glean from his positive law, did not favor the practice of qiyas, unless it was absolutely necessary.[92] Dawud, on the other hand, rejected it categorically.[93]

There emerges here a clear pattern: Shafi^c^i's predecessors make recourse to their *ra^ɔ^y* with, more or less, little attention to the Sunna. Shafi^c^i regulates *ra^ɔ^y* in the form of qiyas and assigns it a role subsidiary to that of the revealed sources although it remains an essential part of his methodology. Ibn Hanbal seldom resorts to qiyas, and he would rather do without it. Dawud completely rejects it in favor of a literal reading of the Qur^ɔan and the Sunna. In both time and doctrine, then, Shafi^ci's position is located in the middle between the early *ra^ɔy* libertinism and the later Zahirite conservatism.

Contrary to the pattern according to which traditionalism had evolved in the 9th century, the rationalist movement began to experience a process of decline, particularly, as is well known, after the *miḥna*. From this point on, the rationalists were drawing closer to the traditionalists, but only in one sense: they could no longer afford to ignore the scripture as the exclusive foundation of the law, and they were compelled to submit to the divine decree as the first and last judge of human *shar^cī* affairs.

On the other side, the traditionalist camp also was compelled to make some concessions. Soon the Hanbalites, among others, were to ignore their eponym's dislike for qiyas, and their legal methodology was to become virtually interchangeable with that of the other schools' proponents. It is significant that those who did not make these concessions, such as the ultratraditionalist Hashwiyya and the Zahirites, were ultimately doomed to extinction.[94]

With the death of Shafi^ci and for long thereafter, Shafi^ci's middle-of-the-road thesis had relatively few supporters. If we go by Subki, the author of the most comprehensive biographical work on the Shafi^cites,[95] we find that the list of Shafi^ci's associates (*aṣḥāb*) did not exceed 41, including such jurists as Ibn Hanbal, Abu Thawr (d. 854), ^cAbd al-Hakam al-Misri, and Ibn Rahawayh, who did not follow his teachings and who had their own agendas.[96] Many others were merely associated with Shafi^ci, and we have no evidence that they studied under him more than some *fiqh* and hadith. His followers who had died by 912 but who did not know him in person, numbered only 31.[97] This is to be contrasted by the number of his followers who died in the fourth hijri century (A.D. 912–1009), which reached the astounding figure of 171.[98]

The rapid growth of the Shafi^cite school coincided with the emergence of the aforementioned compromise between the traditionalists and the rationalists, which resulted in *uṣūl al-fiqh*'s being finally defined, and that must have taken place sometime between the death of Dawud al-Zahiri and the generation of Abu Bakr al-Sayrafi. Being the ultimate synthesis of revelation and systematic human reasoning, *uṣūl al-fiqh* could not have become normative prior to the beginning of the 10th century. Shafi^ci's rudimentary thesis was not well supported and none of his students appears to have defended it. Muzani, who was most likely to have carried on Shafi^ci's mission, was, as we have seen, tending more to rationality than to hadith, and in any case he was deemed to have diverged from the path of Shafi^ci, both in positive law and legal theory.[99] The most important of Shafi^ci's immediate disciples turns out, after all, not to have been so faithful to the teachings of the master.[100]

It was not until Ibn Surayj and the generation of his younger contemporaries that the traditionalist–rationalist compromise manifested itself. He, and his disciples, were *muḥaddith*s, faqihs, and speculative theologians, without this entailing a contradiction in terms. And as such, they were to conceptualize legal theory as a synthesis between rationality and the textual tradition. Ibn Surayj's legal theory, we must stress, could have been only the child of its own environment. Aside from the proposition that embodied that synthesis, there is little in Shafi^c^i's theory that survived into the later works. But this synthesis was crucial, and Ibn Surayj as well as his followers accredited it to Shafi^c^i. This is why Ibn Surayj was considered the first true representative and the unequaled champion of the Shafi^c^ite school. And this is why he was, significantly, referred to as the middle-of-the-roader (*sālik sabīl al-inṣāf*).[101] Ibn Surayj, who was an excellent *muḥaddith* and a moderate mutakallim—and who battled the Zahirites to the end of his days—articulated the synthesis and paved the way for his students, the likes of Sayrafi and Qaffal, to discourse on it and elaborate it in greater detail.

When these students found their legal theory to coincide with Shafi^c^i's bare thesis that they began to glorify Shafi^c^i as an *uṣūlī* and as the founder of the discipline. This glorification became increasingly necessary as the other schools, especially the Hanafite, as is well known, to advertise their early masters as the founders of *uṣūl al-fiqh*.[102] But that Shafi^c^i's image as the founder of this discipline began to grow only from the beginning of the 10th century can be illustrated clearly in the development of the *manāqib* genre dedicated to him.

The first work of *manāqib* available to us belonged to Abu Hatim al-Razi (d. 938). In this work Razi allots a number of chapters to demonstrate Shafi^c^i's excellent knowledge of subjects upon which the construction of the law depended. In one chapter, which consists of about 51 lines, the author discusses Shafi^c^i's proficient knowledge of what he calls, significantly, *uṣūl al-^c^ilm*, by which he clearly means *uṣūl al-fiqh*.[103] In these lines, he mentions Shafi^c^i's doctrine of consensus (in one line), and he briefly speaks—in 15 lines—of his theory of qiyas. The rest of the lines deal with a miscellany of subjects including hadith. Nowhere in the entire treatise does Shafi^c^i appear as the founder of *uṣūl al-fiqh*. It is to be noted that Razi's work, in its published form, consists of about 300 pages, each containing an average of 8 lines. It is significant that out of an approximate 2,400 lines Razi should have devoted only 51 lines to Shafi^c^i's *uṣūl*. Moreover, in this chapter there is no reference whatsoever to the *Risāla*. In fact, in the entire work the *Risāla* is mentioned only twice, and then in passing. In both cases it is referred to, significantly, in the context not of law but rather of *ṭalab al-ḥadīth*.[104]

Over a century later, Bayhaqi (d. 1066) wrote another work on Shafi^c^i's *manāqib*. A comparison between his and Razi's work is most revealing. In Bayhaqi, Shafi^c^i is not only a genius of *uṣūl al-fiqh*, but the founder of the discipline,[105] and the *Risāla*, in its old and new versions, receives a comprehensive treatment, including the reasons for its composition.[106] The new *Risāla* is mentioned at least eighteen times, and the old three times. In addition to a chapter devoted to Shafi^c^i's *uṣūl al-fiqh*, which Bayhaqi uniquely characterizes as "portentous,"[107] there are other chapters describing the master's proficiency in the knowledge of hadith, Qur^ɔ^an, language, positive law, and other issues that are constitutive parts of, or relevant to, *uṣūl al-fiqh*. In contrast to Razi's 51 lines, Bayhaqi allocates a staggering 160 pages (out of a total of 918) to Shafi^c^i as an *uṣūlī*. The image of Shafi^c^i as the founder of the discipline is similarly drawn by al-Fakhr al-Razi (d. 1209) who devotes about 114 pages of his 525-page treatise to the same issues Bayhaqi had already raised.[108]

It would be safe to assume that sometime before Bayhaqi—but certainly after Abu Hatim al-Razi—Shafiᶜi's image as the founder of *uṣūl al-fiqh* had become firmly established. This intervening period between the two *manāqib* authors coincides, we must note, with the career of Abu Muhammad al-Juwayni, the last commentator on the *Risāla*.[109] That Shafiᶜi's treatise failed to attract further commentary in the decades and centuries that followed explains the role that Shafiᶜi, as the founder of the discipline, was required to play in his school. Once this image as the founder was irrevocably established, commentaries on his treatise ceased forever. In a field where commentaries were the norm, the discontinuity of interest in commenting on the *Risāla* also explains the irrelevance of the work's themes to the far more complex and different methodology of *uṣūl al-fiqh*. This irrelevance is attested to eloquently in the relatively infrequent citation of Shafiᶜi's views by later theoreticians.

VI

To conclude, the history of Shafiᶜi's *Risāla* is connected inextricably with the emergence of *uṣūl al-fiqh* as an organically structured and independent science. As a full-fledged methodology, *uṣūl al-fiqh* represents a synthesis of reason and revelation, the former being the means by which the latter is interpreted so that the divinely prescribed law can be known. The constitutive elements of *uṣūl al-fiqh*—epistemology, legal language, the theory of abrogation, transmission of the texts, consensus, qiyas, ijtihad, taqlid, and so forth—are organically interconnected and interdependent, and the absence of any such element would create an incorrigible imbalance in legal methodology. Therefore, *uṣūl al-fiqh* as a legal methodology is larger than the total sum of its constitutive parts. Our sources strongly indicate that this methodology, with all its constitutive parts, did not exist in the 9th century. This conclusion is further bolstered by additional evidence to the effect that in this century the *Risāla* was marginal, attracting neither commentaries nor refutations.

With the advent of the 10th century, *uṣūl al-fiqh* works begin to proliferate, and simultaneously the *Risāla* succeeds in attracting a number of commentaries and at least two refutative dissertations. This simultaneity should by no means be explained away as coincidental, for such an explanation would ignore blatantly the historical sequence of events that led up to the emergence, in the beginning of the 10th century, of *uṣūl al-fiqh* as an organically structured discipline.

Shafiᶜi's *Risāla* as the embodiment of his legal methodology has, in our view, gained the distinction of being the first attempt at synthesizing the disciplined exercise of human reasoning and the complete assimilation of revelation as the basis of the law. Because Islamic law and jurisprudence did finally come to accept this synthesis, we were led to believe that *uṣūl al-fiqh* as we know it began with Shafiᶜi. But Shafiᶜi's synthesis appeared at a time in which only a few were willing to embrace it. It would be rather simplistic to think that once Shafiᶜi laid down his synthesis, which attempted to reconcile the theses of the traditionalists and the rationalists, it was immediately adopted by the two camps. For Shafiᶜi's theory to prevail would have required that the two camps abandon their doctrines once and for all and join Shafiᶜi's ranks. But this did not happen, and evidence in fact points to the contrary: Shafiᶜi's synthesis was, and remained for a long time, a minority view. The traditionalists rejected his qiyas, and the rationalists were reluctant to accept his thesis that revelation is the first and last judge of human affairs. It was only towards the end of the 9th century that the two camps drew closer to each other, and a synthesis of traditionalism and rationalism was accomplished. With the emergence of this synthesis, whose causes and characteristics are yet to be studied, the way to *uṣūl al-fiqh* was finally paved. And once this science bloomed, at the hands of Sayrafi, Qaffal, and their like, the rudimentary synthesis created by Shafiᶜi a century earlier became relevant and thus was rejuvenated in the form of commentaries on the *Risāla* and by attributing the entire ramifications of the synthesis to Shafiᶜi himself. Shafiᶜi thus becomes the founder of *uṣūl al-fiqh*.

Our conclusion presents us with two significant implications. First, Shafiᶜi's achievement must not be carried too far. He advanced or, to put it more accurately, proposed an unprecedented synthesis of rationalism and traditionalism, but his proposal was not to become relevant until a century later, thanks not to him but to such jurists as Ibn Surayj, Sayrafi, and Qaffal whose achievement was the product of a combination of circumstances that arose at the end of the 9th century and the beginning of the 10th. In other words, Shafiᶜi's law and jurisprudence represented not the pivotal point of Islamic law, but rather a middle stage between the crude beginnings at the outset of the 8th century and the true culmination that took place nearly a century after his death. The second implication, which can hardly be overemphasized, is the central importance of the 9th century in the history of Islamic legal theory. This century, no less than the 8th, determined the direction that Islamic jurisprudence was to take in its future course.

NOTES

Author's note: This article represents an expanded version of two lectures delivered at the MESA annual meeting in New Orleans (19–22 November 1985) and at the University of Chicago (5 November 1987).

[1]See Joseph Schacht, *The Origins of Muhammadan Jurisprudence* (Oxford, 1975).

[2]Aḥmad Muḥammad Shākir, ed. (Cairo, 1892). For the original title of the work and the presumed reasons for its composition, see Majid Khadduri, trans., *Al-Imām Muḥammad ibn Idrīs al-Shāfiᶜī's al-Risāla fī Uṣūl al-Fiqh*, 2nd ed. (Cambridge, 1987), 19 ff.; Fakhr al-Dīn Muḥammad ibn ᶜUmar al-Rāzī, *Irshād al-ṭālibīn ilā al-minhāj al-qawīm fī bayān manāqib al-imām al-Shāfiᶜī*, ed. Aḥmad al-Saqqā (Cairo, 1986), 153; George Makdisi, "The Juridical Theology of Shāfiᶜī: Origins and Significance of *Uṣūl al-Fiqh*," *Studia Islamica* 59 (1984): 6, 9.

[3]See, for example, Ignaz Goldziher, *The Ẓāhirīs: Their Doctrine and Their History*, trans. W. Behn (Leiden, 1971), 20–21; N. J. Coulson, *A History of Islamic Law* (Edinburgh, 1964), 56; Joseph Schacht, *An Introduction to Islamic Law* (Oxford, 1979), 48.

[4]See Khadduri's introduction to his translation of the *Risāla*, 42.

[5]See, for example, Rāzī, *Irshād*, 156; Coulson, *History*, 61

[6]Coulson, *History*, 53.

[7]Ibn al-Nadīm, *Fihrist* (Beirut, 1978), 286.

[8]Ibid., 287.

[9]Ibid., 286, 289.

[10]Ibid., 297.

[11]Tāj al-Din al-Subkī, *Ṭabaqāt al-shāfiᶜiyya al-kubrā*, 6 vols., 2nd ed. (repr., Beirut, n.d.), 1:277.

[12]See n. 13 as well as Abū Bakr Hidāyat Allāh al-Ḥusaynī, *Ṭabaqāt al-shāfiᶜiyya*, ed. ᶜĀdil Nuwayhiḍ (Beirut, 1979), 90, where a reference is made to the chapter on ablution, a chapter that has no place in *uṣūl al-fiqh* works.

[13]Subkī, *Ṭabaqāt*, 2:227. The work clearly treats positive law because Subki remarks that he has in his possession an incomplete copy of the work "up to the chapter on bankruptcy (*taflīs*)."

[14]Subkī (ibid., 2:226) characterizes the work as one concerned with "*fiqh* and *khilāfiyyāt*"; see also ᶜAbd Allāh Muṣṭafā al-Marāghī, *al-Fatḥ al-mubīn fī ṭabaqāt al-uṣūliyyīn*, 3 vols. (Cairo, n.d.), 1:177.

[15]Subkī, *Ṭabaqāt*, 2:108. We ought to mention that the term *uṣūl* is at times used to mean "standard" or "classical" works; see Shams al-Dīn al-Dhahabī, *Siyar aᶜlām al-nubalāᵓ*, ed. Shuᶜayb al-Arnāᵓūṭ and Akram al-Būshī, 23 vols. (Beirut, 1986), 15:438, who speaks of a certain Abū al-ᶜAbbās al-Miṣrī as having usurped 500 *uṣūl* volumes from the library of a colleague.

[16]It is to be noted here that Shāfiᶜī does not know the designation *uṣūl al-fiqh*, and his use of the term *aṣl* or *uṣūl* does not carry the connotation attached to it later. He seems to have given his treatise the title *al-Kitāb*. Only later did it come to be known as *al-Risāla*, probably going through a period of transition in which it was known as *Kitāb al-risāla*. For evidence of the original title of the work, see Khadduri, trans., *Risāla*, pars, 96, 332, 573, passim.

[17]*Ikhtilāf uṣūl al-madhāhib*, ed. Muṣṭafā Ghālib (Beirut, 1973).

[18]Ibn al-Nadīm, *Fihrist*, 289.

[19]Subkī, *Ṭabaqāt*, 2:78.

[20]Goldziher, *Ẓāhirīs*, 34–35.

[21]Ibn al-Nadīm, *Fihrist*, 303.

[22]Ibid., 306; see also Subkī, *Ṭabaqāt*, 2:46.

[23]The exception is the case of Ḥusayn ibn ᶜAlī al-Karābīsī (d. 859 or 862) who is described by Abū ᶜĀṣim al-ᶜAbbādī in *Ṭabaqāt al-fuqahāᵓ al-shāfiᶜiyya* (ed. Gösta Vitestam [Leiden, 1964], 24–25) as "one of the early jurists who was knowledgeable in *uṣūl*" and by Abū Isḥāq al-Shīrāzī in *Ṭabaqāt al-fuqahāᵓ* (ed. Iḥsān ᶜAbbās [Beirut, 1970], 102) as having "written many works on *uṣūl al-fiqh* and *furūᶜ*"; see also Dhahabī, *Siyar*, 12:79–81. It is to be noted, however, that later sources report no work written by Karābīsī on the subject. In fact, the most detailed biographical account on Karābīsī provided by Subkī (*Ṭabaqāt*, 1:251–56) does not associate him with *uṣūl al-fiqh*, either as an author or as a scholar.

[24]Muḥammad ibn Abī Ḥātim al-Rāzī, *Ādāb al-Shāfiᶜī wa-manāqibuhu*, ed. ᶜAbd al-Ghanī ᶜAbd al-Khāliq (Cairo, 1953), 61–62.

[25]Muḥammad ibn Abī Yaᶜlā Ibn al-Farrāᵓ, *Ṭabaqāt al-ḥanābila*, ed. M. H. Fiqī, 2 vols. (Cairo, 1952), 1:57.

[26]Subkī, *Ṭabaqāt*, 1:250–1.

[27]See, for example, Aḥmad ibn al-Ḥusayn Abū Bakr al-Bayhaqī, *Manāqib al-Shāfiᶜī*, ed. Aḥmad Ṣaqr, 2 vols. (Cairo, 1971), 1:236; Subkī, *Ṭabaqāt*, 1:242.

[28]Muzanī's commentary is edited and translated by Robert Brunschvig in "Le livre de l'ordre et de la défense d'al-Muzani," *Bulletin d'études orientales* 11 (1945–46):145–94; Arabic text, 153–63.

[29]Muḥammad Zahrī Najjār, ed., 8 vols. (Cairo, 1961), 7:291–92.

[30]Only pp. 153–56 (line 4) of *Kitāb al-amr wa-al-nahy* treat the purported meaning (*ᶜalā maᶜnā*) of Shāfiᶜī's doctrine, although it is highly likely that even pp. 153 (line 20)–56 represent Muzanī's own views, not those of Shāfiᶜī.

[31]On the traditionalists (*ahl al-ḥadīth*) and the rationalists (*ahl al-raᵓy*), see Goldziher, *Ẓāhirīs*, 6–19; Schacht, *Origins*, 36–81, 253–57, passim.

[32]Zayn al-Dīn Qāsim ibn Quṭlūbughā, *Tāj al-tarājim fī ṭabaqāt al-ḥanafiyya* (Baghdad, 1962), 19–20.

[33]Dhahabī, *Siyar*, 12:500; Subkī, *Ṭabaqāt*, 1:224. Most biographical works attribute al-Miṣrī's critical attitude toward Shāfiᶜī to a personal conflict between the two.

[34]So must we take Abū Zakiriyyāᵓ al-Kinānī's (d. 902) *al-Ḥujja fī al-radd ᶜalā al-Shāfiᶜī*; see Fuat Sezgin, *Geschichte des arabischen Schrifttums*, 9 vols. (Leiden, 1967–), 1:475, 485.

[35]It is interesting to note the change in the title of Khadduri's translation of the *Risāla*. When it was first published in 1961, the title read *Islamic Jurisprudence: Shāfiᶜī's Risāla*. In the 1987 edition, however, it was entitled, significantly, *Al-Shāfiᶜī's Risāla fī Uṣūl al-Fiqh: Treatise on the Foundations of Islamic Jurisprudence*.

[36]Khadduri, *al-Risāla*, 41.

[37]Cairo, 1969.

[38]In his *Irshād*, 157, al-Fakhr al-Rāzī apologizes for the defects in Shāfiᶜī's *Risāla*, saying in effect that all pioneering works entail some shortcomings.

[39]Muḥammad Amjad ᶜAlī, trans. (Karachi, 1968).

[40]See n. 23.

[41]Ibn al-Nadīm, *Fihrist*, 295: "al-Shāfiᶜī was a staunch advocate of Shīᶜism" (*wa-kāna al-Shāfiᶜiyyu shadīdan fī al-tashayyuᶜ*).

[42]Rāzī, *Irshād*, 44, 104; on 66, Rāzī speaks of Shāfiᶜī's outstanding knowledge of dialectic, speculation and disputation—qualities that were entirely absent in the camp of the traditionalists. See also Aḥmad ibn Yaḥyā Ibn al-Murtaḍā, *Ṭabaqāt al-muᶜtazila*, ed. S. Diwald-Wilzer (Wiesbaden, 1961), 43.

[43]Rāzī, *Irshād*, 44.

[44]Cited in Subkī, *Ṭabaqāt*, 2:149.

[45]Ibid., 1:222.

[46]Rāzī, *Irshād*, 228–29.

[47]Subkī, *Ṭabaqāt*, 2:4; Rāzī, *Irshād*, 230.

[48]Rāzī, *Irshād*, 230.

[49]Ibn al-Farrā', *Ṭabaqāt*, 1:38.

[50]On Shāfiᶜī's opposition to the traditionalists, see Schacht, *Origins*, 128–29.

[51]ᶜAbd Allāh Ibn Qutayba, *al-Maᶜārif* (Karachi, 1976), 216–30.

[52]See n. 53.

[53]Rāzī, *Irshād*, 138. Also, Subkī alludes to Muzanī's Muᶜtazilite tendency (*Ṭabaqāt*, 1:241). On his skill as a dialectician and lack of qualifications as a traditionist, see Dhahabī, *Siyar*, 12:492–93; 14:371. That he was not, strictly speaking, a Muᶜtazilite is evidenced by the fact that he is not included in Muᶜtazilite biographical works. See, for example, Ibn al-Murtaḍā, *Ṭabaqāt al-muᶜtazila*.

[54]See n. 23.

[55]Subkī, *Ṭabaqāt*, 1:251–55.

[56]Shīrāzī, *Ṭabaqāt*, 102.

[57]Reported by Subkī on the authority of al-Khaṭīb al-Baghdādī (*Ṭabaqāt*, 1:252).

[58]It is significant that at this time titles carrying the term *furūᶜ* also begin to appear, *furūᶜ* and *uṣūl* being now dichotomous; see, for example, *Kitāb al-furūᶜ* by Ibn al-Ḥaddād al-Miṣrī, who died in 956; Dhahabī, *Siyar*, 15:446.

The evidence in our sources thus indicates that the appearance of the designation *uṣūl al-fiqh* as well as of complete works on the subject belongs to the beginning of the 10th century, not to the end of it, as Makdisi seems to suggest; see his "Juridical Theology of Shāfiᶜī," 5, 13–14.

[59]ᶜAbbādī, *Ṭabaqāt*, 55; Subkī, *Ṭabaqāt*, 2:242–43.

[60]Dhahabī, *Siyar*, 15:217–18; Ibn al-Nadīm (*Fihrist*, 245–46) states that the author did not complete the work.

[61]Ibn al-Nadīm, *Fihrist*, 300; ᶜAbd al-Ḥayy Ibn al-ᶜImād, *Shadharāt al-dhahab fī akhbār man dhahab*, 8 vols. (Cairo, 1931–32), 2:325; ᶜAbbādī, *Ṭabaqāt*, 69; Abū al-ᶜAbbās Aḥmad ibn Muḥammad Ibn Khallikān, *Wafayāt al-aᶜyān wa-anbā' abnā' al-zamān*, ed. Iḥsān ᶜAbbās, 8 vols. (Beirut, 1977), 4:199; Shīrāzī, *Ṭabaqāt*, 111.

[62]Ibn al-Nadīm, *Fihrist*, 283.

[63]Ibn Quṭlūbughā, *Tāj al-tarājim*, 59.

[64]Subkī, *Ṭabaqāt*, 2:103; Shīrāzī, *Ṭabaqāt*, 111.

[65]Shīrāzī, *Ṭabaqāt*, 112; Subkī, *Ṭabaqāt*, 2:176 ff.; Ibn Khallikān, *Wafayāt*, 4:200–201.

[66]Ibn Quṭlūbughā, *Tāj al-tarājim*, 86.

[67]Shīrāzī, *Ṭabaqāt*, 112.

[68]Subkī, *Ṭabaqāt*, 2:159.

[69]Ibn al-Nadīm, *Fihrist*, 330.

[70]Jamāl al-Dīn ᶜAbd al-Raḥīm al-Asnawī, *Ṭabaqāt al-shāfiᶜiyya*, ed. ᶜAbd Allāh al-Jubūrī, 2 vols. (Baghdad, 1970–71), 2:123; Subkī, *Ṭabaqāt*, 2:81–82.

[71]Beirut, 1982.

[72]Shīrāzī, *Ṭabaqāt*, 115; Subkī, *Ṭabaqāt*, 2:217.

[73]Ibn al-Murtaḍā, *Ṭabaqāt*, 102.

[74]Ibid., 109.

[75]ᶜAbbādī, *Ṭabaqāt*, 69.

[76]Shīrāzī, *Ṭabaqāt*, 112.

[77]Asnawī, *Ṭabaqāt*, 2:472; Ḥusaynī, *Ṭabaqāt*, 245–46.

[78]Khadduri, *al-Risāla*, 42.

[79]Subkī, *Ṭabaqāt*, 3:186, 208.

[80]Ibn Khallikān, *Wafayāt*, 3:219 ff.

[81]Dhahabī, *Siyar*, 15:328.

[82]Ṣayrafī not only commented on the *Risāla* but also wrote a rebuttal against al-Kātib's refutation of the work; see Ibn al-Nadīm, *Fihrist*, 300. It was not possible to establish al-Kātib's identity. We must note that the sources report at least three other critiques of Shāfiᶜī by two Mālikites and a Ḥanbalite. The two Mālikites are Bakr ibn Muḥammad al-Qushayrī (d. 955) and Abū Bakr al-Dīnawarī (d. after 940); see Dhahabī, *Siyar*, 4:427, 537. The Ḥanbalite is Ghulām al-Khallāl (d. 947); see Ibn al-Farrāᵓ, *Ṭabaqāt*, 2:119–20. However, it cannot be established whether the object of these critiques was Shāfiᶜī's positive law or legal theory.

[83]Subkī, *Ṭabaqāt*, 2:241.

[84]On Ibn Surayj, see ibid., 2:87–96; Dhahabī, *Siyar*, 14:201–4; Ibn Khallikān, *Wafayāt*, 1:66–67; ᶜAbbādī, *Ṭabaqāt*, 62–63; Ibn al-ᶜImād, *Shadharāt*, 2:247–48.

[85]Reported by Subkī (*Ṭabaqāt*, 2:307) on the authority of the historian ᶜAlī ibn Ḥusayn al-Masᶜūdī. Subkī had in his possession a copy of the epistle.

[86]Shīrāzī, *Ṭabaqāt*, 109.

[87]On Ibn Ḥaykuwayh, see Dhahabī, *Siyar*, 15:379. On al-Marwazī, Ibn al-Qāṣṣ, Ṣayrafī, and Shāshī, see Shīrāzī, *Ṭabaqāt*, 111–12; Ibn al-ᶜImād, *Shadharāt*, 2:339; Ibn Khallikān, *Wafayāt*, 4:199. On Abū Bakr al-Fārisī, see Ibn al-Murtaḍā, *Ṭabaqāt*, 102.

[88]Ibn Khallikān, *Wafayāt*, 4:199; Subkī, *Ṭabaqāt*, 2:170.

[89]Ibn Khallikān, *Wafayāt*, 4:200–201.

[90]Subkī, *Ṭabaqāt*, 3:208; Ibn al-ᶜImād, *Shadharāt*, 3:261–62.

[91]That a jurist of the 10th century combined a proficient knowledge of rationalist and traditionalist disciplines was still considered remarkable even in the 14th century. Subkī, for instance, clearly makes a point of mentioning such a combination; see his *Ṭabaqāt*, 2:79, 81.

[92]Susan Spectorsky, "Aḥmad Ibn Ḥanbal's *Fiqh*," *Journal of the American Oriental Society* 102 (1982): 461–65.

[93]For a brief account of Dawūd's teachings, see Goldziher, *Ẓāhirīs*, 27–39.

[94]See W. B. Hallaq, "Was the Gate of Ijtihad Closed?" *International Journal of Middle East Studies* 16 (1984): 7–10. On the Ḥashwiyya, see A. S. Halkin, "The Ḥashwiyya," *Journal of the American Oriental Society* 54 (1934):12.

[95]Subkī admits (*Ṭabaqāt*, 1:285, 2:18–20) that he includes the biographies of those who are worthy of mention because "there is no sense in mentioning the others, for it would be a waste of ink."

[96]Ibid., 1:186–285. On Ibn al-Ḥakam, Abū Thawr, and Ibn Rāhawayh, see ibid., 1:223–24, 227 ff., 232 ff. For more on Abū Thawr, see Ibn al-Nadīm, *Fihrist*, 297.

[97]Subkī, *Ṭabaqāt*, 1:285–301; 2:2–79.

[98]Ibid., 2:79–322. The rapid increase in the number of Shāfiᶜites during the 10th century must be in good part attributed to Ibn Surayj, under whom, as we have seen (section IV), the major figures of the Shāfiᶜite school have studied. Ibn Surayj's numerous students have in turn become influential and have attracted, in various parts of the Muslim world, a great number of disciples; see sources cited in nn. 86–89.

[99]Ibid., 1:244, 247; Asnawī, *Ṭabaqāt*, 1:34–35.

[100]Muzanī's position vis-à-vis Shāfiᶜī's doctrine is well illustrated in an anecdote that, even if not genuine, also portrays Ibn Surayj's attitude towards Muzanī as Shāfiᶜī's chief student. Ibn Surayj is reported to have said that "on the Day of Judgment Shāfiᶜī will appear [before God] and Muzanī will follow on his heel. Shāfiᶜī will say: O God, this man [Muzanī] has corrupted my sciences (*ᶜulūmī*). Thereupon, I (Ibn Surayj) shall say to him: Go easy on Abū Ibrāhīm [al-Muzanī] for I have mended what he had adulterated." If this anecdote truly illustrates Ibn Surayj's view of Muzanī, it must be taken to refer to Muzanī's rationalist inclination on certain matters of *uṣūl*, not *furūᶜ*, because we know that Ibn Surayj admired his works on positive law and, in fact, wrote in verse to extol them; see Subkī, *Ṭabaqāt*, 2:87, 92–93.

[101]ᶜAbbādī, *Ṭabaqāt*, 62.

[102]See Makdisi, "Juridicial Theology of Shāfiᶜī," 6–7.
[103]Rāzī, *Ādāb al-Shāfiᶜī*, 231–37.
[104]Ibid., 62, 63.
[105]Bayhaqī, *Manāqib*, 1:368–84.
[106]Ibid., 1:230–36.
[107]Ibid., 1:368.
[108]Rāzī, *Irshād*, 153–88, 189–268.
[109]See n. 79.

11

MUḤAMMAD B. DĀ'ŪD AL-ẒĀHIRĪ'S MANUAL OF JURISPRUDENCE, *AL-WUṢŪL ILĀ MA'RIFAT AL-UṢŪL*

Devin Stewart

Generic conventions, in legal literature as in court poetry and national epics, shape not only texts but also thought itself. Like language, they mould, while at the same time reflecting, institutional and ideological assumptions, boundaries, and commitments. The important role played by genre in the transmission of knowledge in the medieval Islamic world may be obvious enough from works in the various sciences themselves, but it is also apparent in medieval scholars' theoretical statements. Ibn Khaldūn, for example, clearly equates the genres of scientific works with the sciences or disciplines they describe. Sciences, like the works which detail them, are naturally divided into specific chapters or sections, and those chapters are divided into specific problems or questions. The chapters on ritual purity, prayer, alms, marriage, and manumission in compendia of law, or the chapters on the imamate and the attributes of God in theological works are not just convenient pegs on which to hang material relevant to the study of those fields; they represent the inherent structures of those sciences. To master these chapters and questions is to master the science. To produce a new genre, Ibn Khaldūn explains, is to invent a new science, even if its elements formerly existed scattered in works belonging to other genres. If learning is an acquired craft, it stands to reason that the genres through which learning is acquired shape categories and modes of thought.[1]

For the study of Islamic law, legal institutions, and intellectual history, one of the most important genres is arguably that of *uṣūl al-fiqh*, which, perhaps more than any other, seems to embody the community of interpretation of Muslim theoretical jurists. It was in *uṣūl al-fiqh* manuals devoted to legal theory and methodology that many of the great theoretical battles of Islamic legal history were fought. There, the sacred epistemology of Islam, or at least the jurists'

[1] Ibn Khaldun, *The Muqaddimah: An Introduction to History*, 2nd ed., 3 vols., trans. Franz Rosenthal (Princeton: Princeton University Press, 1967), 1:76–83; 3:284–87.

version thereof, was expressed, debated, and hammered out. Fakhr al-Dīn al-Rāzī (d. 606/1209) writes, "... the most important of sciences for the *mujtahid* is that of *uṣūl al-fiqh*; all other sciences are unimportant in this regard".[2] While one may imagine a cadre of jurists, a system of law, and a sophisticated community of legal interpretation existing without the particular genre of *uṣūl al-fiqh*—indeed, the Rabbinic legal tradition would seem to provide such a counterexample, having by and large produced no genre equivalent to *uṣūl al-fiqh*—an understanding of the tradition of *uṣūl al-fiqh* manuals is indispensable for an understanding of Islamic legal and intellectual history. Unfortunately, the early history of the genre is shrouded in mystery, primarily because so many works from its formative period, the eighth, ninth, and tenth centuries, have been lost. The present essay contributes .to the investigation of the *uṣūl al-fiqh* genre in this sparsely documented period, focusing on a work by Muḥammad b. Dā'ūd al-Ẓāhirī.

Abū Bakr Muḥammad b. Dā'ūd al-Ẓāhirī (255–97/868–909), litterateur, jurist, and son of the famous founder of the Ẓāhirī school of law, Dā'ūd b. Khalaf al-Iṣbahānī (d. 270/883), is reported to have authored a work entitled *al-Wuṣūl ilā ma'rifat al-uṣūl*. It is argued here that a number of passages preserved in the polemical text *Ikhtilāf uṣūl al-madhāhib* ("*The Divergence of the Juridical Principles of the Schools of Law*") by the Fatimid jurist al-Qāḍī al-Nu'mān (d. 363/974) derive from this text. Analysis of the passages in question, several of which are attributed explicitly to Muḥammad b. Dā'ūd, demonstrates that *al-Wuṣūl ilā ma'rifat al-uṣūl* ("*The Path to Knowledge of Jurisprudence*") was a manual of *uṣūl al-fiqh*, similar in conception, form, and content to extant manuals from later times. Furthermore, this work was not the first of its kind, but part of an existing genre with established conventions. The author was deeply engaged in legal theoretical polemics over the issues of consensus, legal analogy, *istiḥsān*, and *ijtihād*, drawing on other authors and responding to opponents, either past or contemporary, who had written independent and comprehensive works on *uṣūl al-fiqh*.

In a 1984 study, George Makdisi noted that one of the striking problems for the student of Islamic jurisprudence is the lapse in time,

---

[2] Fakhr al-Dīn al-Rāzī, *al-Maḥṣūl fī 'ilm uṣūl al-fiqh*, 2 vols. (Beirut: Dār al-kutub al-'ilmīyah, 1988), 2:499.

as much as two centuries, between the *Risālah* ("*The Epistle*") of al-Shāfi'ī (d. 204/820) and the first independent and comprehensive works on *uṣūl al-fiqh* that are extant.[3] This gap, narrowed to some extent by the recent publication of *al-Fuṣūl fī al-uṣūl* ("*The Chapters, On Jurisprudence*") by Abū Bakr al-Jaṣṣāṣ al-Rāzī (d. 370/980), *al-Muqaddimah* ("*The Introduction*") by Ibn al-Qaṣṣār (d. 398/1008), and *al-Taqrīb wa'l-irshād fī tartīb ṭuruq al-ijtihād* ("*The Assistance and Guide, Providing an Orderly Arrangement of the Methods of Legal Investigation*") by al-Bāqillānī (d. 403/1013),[4] remains an obstacle to scholarship, particularly since the ninth and tenth centuries, a period of tremendous intellectual ferment, witnessed many developments crucial for the subsequent history of Islamic law, legal theory, and the transmission of knowledge, not the least of which were the formation of the legal *madhhabs* and the collective professionalization of the jurists. To remedy this situation, Makdisi's study presents two medieval lists of independent *uṣūl al-fiqh* manuals and commentaries on al-Shāfi'ī's *Risālah*, one derived from al-Subkī's (d. 700/1371) commentary on the *Mukhtaṣar* ("*The Epitome*") of Ibn al-Ḥājib (d. 646/1249) and the other from Badr al-Dīn al-Zarkashī's (d. 794/1392) *uṣūl al-fiqh* work *al-Baḥr al-muḥīṭ* ("*The Surrounding Sea*"). Each reports four commentaries of the *Risālah*. Al-Subkī's list gives in addition 28 works on *uṣūl al-fiqh*, not counting the *Risālah* itself; al-Zarkashī's list gives 34.[5] These lists do not entirely demonstrate that the *uṣūl al-fiqh* genre reaches back in an unbroken tradition directly to al-Shāfi'ī's work. In each list, the first commentary on *al-Risālah* to appear is that of al-Ṣayrafī, who died in 330/942, well over a century after al-Shāfi'ī wrote the *Risālah*. The first *uṣūl al-fiqh* work mentioned by al-Subkī is *al-Taqrīb wa'l-irshād* by al-Bāqillānī (d. 403/10130). In al-Zarkashī's list, one may discount the work *Kitāb al-qiyās* ("*The Book on Legal Analogy*")

---

[3] George Makdisi, "The Juridical Theology of al-Shāfi'ī: Origins and Significance of Uṣūl al-Fiqh", *Studia Islamica* 59 (1984):5–47, here p. 13.

[4] See al-Jaṣṣāṣ, *al-Fuṣūl fī al-uṣūl*, 4 vols., ed. 'Ujayl Jāshim al-Nashmī (Kuwait: Wizārat al-awqāf wa'l-shu'ūn al-islāmīyah, 1994); Ibn al-Qaṣṣār, *al-Muqaddimah fī al-uṣūl*, ed. Muḥammad b. al-Ḥusayn al-Sulaymānī (Beirut: Dār al-gharb al-islāmī, 1996); al-Bāqillānī, *al-Taqrīb wa'l-irshād al-ṣaghīr*, 3 vols., ed. 'Abd al-Ḥamīd b. 'Alī Abū Zunayd (Beirut: Mu'assasat al-risālah, 1993). Also publised is an abridgement of the *Taqrīb*, Imām al-Ḥaramayn al-Juwaynī, *Kitāb al-Talkhīṣ fī uṣūl al-fiqh*, 3 vols., ed. 'Abd Allāh Jawlam al-Nibalī and Shubbayr Aḥmad al-'Amrī (Mecca: Maktabat dār al-bāz, 1996). The works of al-Jaṣṣāṣ and al-Bāqillānī are incomplete, lacking substantial sections, most regrettably the introductions.

[5] Maksidi, "Juridical Theology", 30–32.

attributed to al-Muzanī (d. 264/878) since its title suggests that it is devoted to only one constituent element of the science of *uṣūl al-fiqh.* The earliest comprehensive works included would then be *Kitāb al-iʿdhār wa'l-indhār* ("*The Book of Excuse and Warning*") by Ibn Surayj (d. 306/918) and *al-Dalā'il wa'l-aʿlām* ("*The Book of Indications and Signs*") by al-Ṣayrafī.[6] Even in combination, the two lists do not show the abundant production of *uṣūl al-fiqh* works in the ninth and tenth centuries.

Wael Hallaq has recently critiqued the received wisdom that al-Shāfiʿī founded the science of *uṣūl al-fiqh* with the *Risālah,* stressing the break between that work and the earliest known works of *uṣūl al-fiqh.* Drawing on biographical and bibliographical sources, Hallaq presents a list of *uṣūl al-fiqh* works demonstrating the proliferation of such works in the tenth century. The same, he claims, cannot be said for the ninth century. According to him, the earliest works in the genre were composed by Shāfiʿī students of Ibn Surayj, such as Ibn Ḥaykawayh (d. 318/930), al-Ṣayrafī (d. 330/942), Ibn al-Qāṣṣ (d. 335/946–47), al-Qaffāl al-Shāshī (d. 336/948), Abū Isḥāq Ibrāhīm al-Marwazī (d. 340/951), and Abū Bakr al-Fārisī (fl. ca. 350/960).[7] Reinhart also assigns Ibn Surayj a pivotal role in the development of *uṣūl al-fiqh,* reporting that he wrote a work on "Principles and Derivations" (*al-uṣūl wa'l-furūʿ*).[8] The present author compiled a list of *uṣūl al-fiqh* works up to and including those of al-Qāḍī ʿAbd al-Jabbār (d. 415/1025). This catalogue includes a number of early texts which Hallaq dismisses or overlooks, such as works attributed to al-Karābīsī (d. 848/962–63), al-Qāḍī Ismāʿīl b. Isḥāq b. Ḥammād al-Azdī (d. 282/895), and Ibn Surayj himself, but still does not show the extensive production of *uṣūl al-fiqh* manuals in the ninth century.[9]

Related to the question of the temporal gap between later works on jurisprudence and the *Risālah* is that of the relationship, in terms

[6] Ibn al-Nadīm gives this title as *al-Bayān fī dalā'il al-aʿlām ʿalā uṣūl al-aḥkām* ("*The Explanation, On the Signs' Indications of the Principles of Legal Rulings*"). Muḥammad b. Isḥāq al-Nadīm, *al-Fihrist,* ed. Riḍā Tajaddud (Tehran: Dār al-masīrah, 1988), 267.

[7] Wael B. Hallaq, "Was al-Shāfiʿī the Master Architect of Islamic Jurisprudence?", *IJMES* 25 (1993): 587–605; idem, *A History of Islamic Legal Theories: An Introduction to Sunnī uṣūl al-fiqh* (Cambridge: Cambridge University Press, 1997), 30–35.

[8] A. Kevin Reinhart, *Before Revelation: The Boundaries of Muslim Moral Thought* (Albany: State University of New York Press, 1995), 14–15.

[9] Devin J. Stewart, *Islamic Legal Orthodoxy: Twelver Shiite Responses to the Sunni Legal System* (Salt lake City: Utah University Press, 1998), 33–36.

of form, content, and intellectual pedigree, between them. Makdisi notes a significant shift in the content of jurisprudential works which he attributes to the introduction of theological topics on the part of Muʿtazilī theologians in the course of the ninth and tenth centuries. Questions such as the relationship of reason to revelation, the inherent permissibility or prohibition of acts, the legal status of acts before revelation became standard elements of the genre by the time al-Qāḍī ʿAbd al-Jabbār (d. 415/10250) composed his work *al-ʿUmad.*[10] Nevertheless, Makdisi views the *Risālah* as indeed an *uṣūl al-fiqh* work, the first of its kind. Hallaq holds, on the contrary, that the *Risālah* differs radically from later works of *uṣūl al-fiqh* in content. He sees that it focuses primarily on hadith and emphasizes the role of Prophetic traditions in the derivation of the law.[11] In a painstaking study, Lowry has shown that the *Risālah*'s organizing principle is quite different from that evident in later *uṣūl al-fiqh* works. It is essentially a discussion of hermeneutics describing various possible types of interaction between scriptural texts from the Koran and hadith. Furthermore, it does not uphold the theory of four sources—the idea that the law derives from or is based on the Koran, Sunnah of the Prophet, consensus, and legal analogy or *ijtihād*—that became widespread in later jurisprudence and which later scholarship, both in Islamic jurisprudence and in the Orientalist tradition, have attributed consistently to al-Shāfiʿī.[12]

Studies to date on the history of Islamic law thus leave two fundamental questions concerning *uṣūl al-fiqh* unanswered. It is still not clear when the genre began or how al-Shāfiʿī's work is related to subsequent treatments of Islamic jurisprudence. This being the case, modern scholars have some tools for the investigation of *uṣūl al-fiqh* in its early stages. Biographical and bibliographical sources are certainly useful, though they present a number of problems of interpretation. It is often difficult or impossible to tell from the title of a work whether it indeed belonged to the *uṣūl al-fiqh* genre. The term *uṣūl* does not always appear in the titles of such works, especially if the title cited is a truncated version of the original. Moreover,

---

[10] Makdisi, "Juridical Theology", 16.

[11] Hallaq, "Shafiʿi", 592.

[12] Joseph E. Lowry, *The Legal-Theoretical Content of the Risāla of Muḥammad B. Idrīs al-Shāfiʿī*, Ph.D. dissertation, University of Pennsylvanian, 1999; idem, "Does Shafiʿi Have a Theory of 'Four Sources' of Law?" in this volume.

the term *uṣūl* itself was used for a variety of meanings in a number of fields and does not necessarily indicate a work on jurisprudence. It may refer to questions of theological dogma, principal questions concerning the points of law,[13] principal questions in other sciences, or other dictated texts. Nevertheless, the continued and assiduous investigation of biographical and bibliographical sources such as the *Fihrist* of Ibn al-Nadīm (fl. 377/987) remains valuable. Another fruitful method of investigation involves culling citations from later works, primarily those in the *uṣūl al-fiqh* genre. This has served with relative success in one modern scholar's collection of the opinions on jurisprudence of Abū al-Ḥasan al-Karkhī (d. 340/952), the famous Ḥanafī professor.[14] Using these methods, this essay identifies several early manuals of jurisprudence and argues that the genre of *uṣūl al-fiqh* was well established already before the tenth century.

Before proceeding, it is necessary to define the genre under consideration. A bona fide *uṣūl al-fiqh* work is one that aims to present and explain a complete, finite, and ordered collection of "roots" or "sources" from which all legal assessments—an infinite number—may be derived. Most later *uṣūl al-fiqh* works, in their form and theoretical apparatus, owe a recognizable debt to this concept, which sets such works as the *Fuṣūl* of al-Jaṣṣāṣ or the *Taqrīb* of al-Bāqillānī apart from al-Shāfiʿī's *Risālah*. The *Risālah* may be seen as an *uṣūl al-fiqh* work in the sense that it aims to provide a comprehensive method for the derivation of rulings for all possible future cases. Nevertheless, it does not contain the features characteristic of later *uṣūl al-fiqh* works, nor can it likely have served as a model for them, since its organization is decidedly not based on an ordered list of *uṣūl*. The concept of a complete, finite, and ordered list of the roots of the law, however, existed already in the early ninth century, perhaps even during al-Shāfiʿī's day. Abū ʿUbayd al-Qāsim b. Sallām (d. 224/838–39), an early jurist who served as judge in Ṭarsūs, made the following statement concerning legal methodology:

> The sources of legal rulings (*uṣūl al-aḥkām*) which a judge cannot transgress to adopt others are: the Book, the Sunnah, and what the leading jurists and righteous ancestors have ruled on the basis of consensus

[13] Makdisi, "Juridical Theology", 7–9; Hallaq, "Shāfiʿī", 588–90.

[14] Abū al-Ḥasan al-Karkhī, *al-Aqwāl al-uṣūlīyah*, ed. Ḥusayn Khalaf al-Jubūrī (N.p.: Ḥ.Kh. al-Jubūrī, 1989).

> and *ijtihād*. There is no fourth category. *Ijtihād* in our view only refers to selection from these opinions if they differ or contradict one another by careful consideration and assiduous pursuit of what is closest to rectitude and correctness. . . .[15]

Abū 'Ubayd uses the term *uṣūl al-aḥkām* "the sources of legal rulings" here as an equivalent of *uṣūl al-fiqh*, in the same way it would be used in the later genre. He conceives of the *uṣūl* as a finite, countable collection of principles or sources from which all legal assessments may be derived. What is more, his remarks imply criticism of similar lists, proposed by other legal theorists, where *ijtihād* certainly, and possibly consensus as well, appeared as independent principles. This concept, absent in al-Shāfi'ī's *Risālah* and at the heart of the *uṣūl al-fiqh* genre, had become important by the early ninth century.

A second crucial feature of the *uṣūl al-fiqh* genre is the use of the term *uṣūl* itself, with the particular sense of basic sources or principles on which further elaboration of the law is based. Here again, al-Shāfi'ī's *Risālah* stands apart, for it neither bears the term in its title nor uses it as such in the text. Bibliographic information available shows that the term *uṣūl* "roots, principles" became popular in book titles in a number of fields in the ninth and tenth centuries. The terms *uṣūl al-fiqh* or *uṣūl al-aḥkām* belong to this general trend, as does the term *uṣūl al-dīn*, referring to theology. The term *uṣūl* here refers to principles on the basis of which the further conclusions of the science may be elaborated. A *Kitāb uṣūl al-dīn* is attributed to the Mu'tazilī Abū Mūsā 'Īsā b. Ṣubayḥ al-Mirdār (d. 226/840–41), reputed to have been the first to spread Mu'tazilī teachings in Baghdad.[16] Ibn Khallād al-Baṣrī (fl. 4th/10th c.) also wrote a work on dogmatic theology entitled *Kitāb al-uṣūl*.[17] Abū Marwān 'Abd al-Malik b. Ḥabīb al-Sulamī al-Mirdāsī al-Ilbīrī al-Qurṭubī (d. 238/853 or 239/854) supposedly wrote *Kitāb uṣūl al-farā'iḍ*, on inheritance law.[18] Another work with an analogous title is *Uṣūl al-naḥw* by Abū Bakr Muḥammad Ibn al-Sarrāj (d. 316/928).[19] These two fundamental

---

[15] Al-Qāḍī al-Nu'mān, *Ikhtilāf uṣūl al-madhāhib*, 212.

[16] Ibn al-Nadīm, *al-Fihrist*, ed. Tajaddud, 206–7.

[17] Ibn al-Nadīm, *al-Fihrist*, ed. Tajaddud, 222.

[18] Brockelmann, *GAL*, GI:156.

[19] The title is given thus in Abū Bakr Muḥammad b. al-Ḥasan al-Zabīdī al-Andalusī, *Ṭabaqāt al-naḥwīyīn wa'l-lughawīyīn*, ed. Muḥammad Abū al-Faḍl Ibrāhīm

conditions for the existence of the *uṣūl al-fiqh* genre, the concept of a finite, ordered set of sources of the law and the use of the term *uṣūl* to denote the fundamental principles of a science, had both been met by the early ninth century.

If the sources provide nothing more than a title, it is difficult to make a strong case for the existence of the *uṣūl al-fiqh* genre, but in some cases, they preserve more substantial hints of early works which have now been lost. These are sufficient to dispel any doubts that the works in question were manuals of *uṣūl al-fiqh* of the type familiar from later extant works. The earliest of these that has come to light so far is the description of a work on jurisprudence by ʿAmr b. Baḥr al-Jāḥiẓ (d. 255/869). The work is often referred to as *Kitāb al-futyā* ("*The Book of Legal Responsa*"), but citations in other sources give the title *Kitāb uṣūl al-futyā* ("*The Book of the Principles of Legal Responsa*").[20] Al-Jāḥiẓ himself describes the work in *Kitāb al-ḥayawān* as follows: *kitābī fī al-qawl fī uṣūl al-futyā wa'l-aḥkām* ("My book discussing the principles of legal responsa and legal rulings").[21] In an extant letter, he presents the work as a gift to the Muʿtazilī chief judge of Baghdad, Aḥmad b. Abī Du'ād al-Iyādī (d. 240/854).[22] It is clear from the letter that Ibn Abī Du'ād was serving as judge when al-Jāḥiẓ sent him the book, which must have been written before 233/848, because *Kitāb al-ḥayawān*, where he mentions the work, dates to that year.

Pellat discussed al-Jāḥiẓ' letter to Ibn Abī Du'ād in the Gibb Festschrift, expressing regret that so little is known about the legal scholarship of a thinker who wrote so brilliantly in other fields. He

(Cairo: Dār al-maʿārif, 1984), 112. Ibn al-Nadīm gives the work the title *Kitāb al-uṣūl al-kabīr* and reports another work entitled *Kitāb jumal al-uṣūl*. *al-Fihrist*, ed. Tajaddud, 68.

20 It is cited as such in Abū al-Ḥusayn al-Baṣrī, *Sharḥ al-ʿUmad*, 2 vols., ed. ʿAbd al-Ḥamīd b. ʿAlī Abū Zunayd (Medina: Maktabat al-ʿulūm wa'l-ḥikam, 1989), 2:6. I thank Aron Zysow for pointing out that the work published as *Sharḥ al-ʿUmad* is actually the *Mujzī* of the Zaydi Imam al-Nāṭiq bi'l-Ḥaqq (d. 424/1033), edited from MS Vat. arab. 1100. See Wilferd Madelung, *Der Imam al-Qāsim ibn Ibrāhīm und di Glaubenslehre der Zaiditen* (Berlin: Walter de Gruyter, 1965), 179–80.

21 ʿAmr b. Baḥr al-Jāḥiẓ, *Kitāb al-ḥayawān*, 7 vols. (Cairo: al-Maṭbaʿah al-ḥamīdīyah al-miṣrīyah, 1905–7), 1:9.

22 al-Jāḥiẓ, *al-Rasā'il*, 4 vols., ed. ʿAbd al-Salām Muḥammad Hārūn (Beirut: Dār al-jīl, 1991), 1:309–19. Ibn Abī Du'ād was appointed chief judge in Baghdad in 218/833 by the Abbasid Caliph al-Muʿtaṣim (218–27/833–42) and remained in this position, with his son Abū al-Walīd Muḥammad as deputy, until they were both dismissed by al-Mutawakkil (232–47/847–61) in 237/851–52. On Ibn Abī Du'ād, see K. V. Zettersteen and Ch. Pellat, "Aḥmad b. Abī Du'ād", *EI*², 1:271. On al-Jāḥiẓ, see Ch. Pellat, "al-Djāḥiẓ", *EI*², 2:385–87.

wrote, "Ce qui importe en effet c'est l'existence même de ce *Kitāb al-Futyā*, sorte d'avant-projet de codification de la *sharīʿa* et non simple traité d'*ikhtilāf* comme tant d'autres. Il est regrettable qu'on ne puisse en dire davantage sur les aptitudes juridiques d'un homme qui a brillé dans tant d'autres domaines et sur les résultats, sans doute éphémères, de ses efforts en vue de faire réduire par les 'autorités compétentes' des divergences qui heurtaient sa raison et son sens de la justice".[23] Pellat's description suggests to the reader that al-Jāḥiẓ' work is a compendium of *fiqh*, describing the points of law. Certainly that is what a codification of the *sharīʿah* would conjure up in the minds of most scholars. Pellat does not describe the work as treating *uṣūl al-fiqh* per se, and does not connect it with the tradition of *uṣūl al-fiqh* manuals.

Like Pellat's discussion, van Ess' study of al-Jāḥiẓ' *Kitāb al-futyā* does not identify it explicitly as a work on *uṣūl al-fiqh*. Van Ess, who collected and assembled passages quoted in later extant works, was particularly interested in the citations al-Jāḥiẓ' work preserved from al-Naẓẓām (d. 221/836) and notes that the medieval authors seem to have been interested the work mainly for that reason as well. Van Ess argues that the extant citations come from a work of al-Naẓẓām entitled *Kitāb al-nakth* ("*The Book of the Breach*") and that they provide, not a reconstruction of the work, but a basic idea of its structure and intent. *Kitāb al-nakth* apparently aimed to refute the validity of consensus as a legal argument. In the course of his presentation, al-Naẓẓām demonstrates the defects of the Prophet's Companions, and most of the extant citations have to do with these defects. It is not surprising, therefore, that Shiite authors such as al-Shaykh al-Mufīd (d. 413/1022) and al-Sharīf al-Murtaḍā (d. 436/1044) paid a great deal of attention to the work, or at least to the parts which al-Jāḥiẓ had transmitted.[24] They were of course concerned to impugn the character of Companions such as the first three Caliphs: Abū Bakr, ʿUmar, and ʿUthmān.

---

23 Charles Pellat, "À Propos du *Kitāb al-Futyā* de Jāḥiẓ", pp. 538–46 in *Arabic and Islamic Studies in Honor of Hamilton A. R. Gibb*, ed. George Makdisi (Leiden: Brill, 1965), 540–41.

24 Josef van Ess, *Das Kitāb al-nakṯ des Naẓẓām und seine Rezeption im Kitāb al-Futyā des Ǧāḥiẓ: Eine Sammlung der Fragmente mit Übersetzung und Kommentar* (Göttingen: Vandenhoeck & Reprecht, 1971). See also idem, pp. 170–201 in *Festschrift Spies: Der Orient in der Forschung* (Wiesbaden: Otto Harrassowitz, 1967).

Kitāb al-nakth apparently treated a single topic in jurisprudence, consensus, supporting the opinion that consensus is not in general a valid source of law. It was not, therefore, a discussion of jurisprudence as a whole, a comprehensive exposition of *uṣūl al-fiqh*. The work of al-Jāḥiẓ, however, may indeed have been a comprehensive work on jurisprudence that cited the material from *Kitāb al-nakth* under the heading of consensus, but presumably included as well the other topics dealt with in typical works of jurisprudence as we know them from the following centuries: the language of the Koran and the Sunnah, *qiyās*, *ijtihād*, and so forth. The picture we get of the original work has obviously been skewed by a number of factors which are difficult to gauge. Transmitters seem concerned with preserving the statements of al-Naẓẓām much more than those of his pupil, al-Jāḥiẓ. The fact that the main transmitters were Shiite theologians writing in particular polemical contexts also played a role in skewing the contents.

It is clear, though, that the work was not devoted to *fiqh*, the points of law. The fact that it is cited as *Kitāb al-futyā* in later works should not mislead us. This is merely an abbreviation of *Kitāb uṣūl al-futyā*, as is evident from al-Jāḥiẓ' own use of the title *Uṣūl al-futyā wa'l-aḥkām*. The larger topic dealt with in al-Naẓẓām's work, which was cited in extenso in *Kitāb uṣūl al-futyā*, is consensus, and not merely the defects of the Companions, which one might expect to find in a theological work on the Imamate. Consensus would not have been given such a prominent place, if any, in a work on the points of law. This is corroborated by al-Jāḥiẓ' description of the work in his letter. He refers to it as a comprehensive study of "the principles of issuing legal opinions" (*uṣūl al-futyā*) over which scholars have differed.[25] His statement clearly distinguishes *uṣūl* "roots, principles" from *furū'* "branches, particulars", placing the latter in parallel with *aḥkām* "rulings, assessments" and identifying the substance of the work as lying within the former category.

Citations preserved in later works on jurisprudence corroborate the assessment that al-Jāḥiẓ' work treats *uṣūl al-fiqh* in particular. The Zaydī jurist and Imam Abū Ṭālib Yaḥyā b. al-Ḥusayn, known as al-Nāṭiq bi'l-Ḥaqq (d. 424/1033) cites in *al-Mujzī* (published as Abū Ḥusayn al-Baṣrī's *Sharḥ al-'Umad*) the work of al-Jāḥiẓ. The passage

[25] Pellat, "À Propos du *Kitāb al-Futyā*", 542–44.

reads, "Among the rejectors of legal analogy who profess this opinion is al-Naẓẓām, because al-Jāḥiẓ related from him in *Uṣūl al-futyā* that he said, 'Legal rulings can only be established by a scriptural text or by causes which a scriptural text provides', and a group of Ẓāhirīs, such as al-Nahrabānī, al-Qāshānī, and al-Maghribī".[26] This text is significant because it treats neither the defects of the Companions, nor the general topic of the validity of consensus, but rather the validity of analogical reasoning as a source for the law. *Kitāb uṣūl al-futyā wa'l-aḥkām* thus included a significant discussion of *qiyās*, and al-Jāḥiẓ cited al-Naẓẓām in this discussion as well. *Al-Mujzī* also cites *Naqḍ al-futyā*, by the Muʿtazilī theologian and Ḥanafī jurist Abū 'Abd Allāh al-Baṣrī (d. 367/977–78), known as "al-Juʿl". While this title as well might imply that the work deals with the points of law, it is clearly an abbreviation of *Naqḍ uṣūl al-futyā*: the work is a refutation of al-Jāḥiẓ' *Kitāb uṣūl al-futyā wa'l-aḥkām*. The topics dealt with in these passages are *qiyās* and *ijtihād*.[27] Another anecdote reports that when the Ḥamdānid ruler Sayf al-Dawlah had sent a question on *ijtihād* to the famous Ḥanafī jurist Abū al-Ḥasan al-Karkhī, al-Karkhī had his student Abū 'Abd Allāh answer it. Abū 'Abd Allāh later incorporated the answer into both his manual of *uṣūl al-fiqh* and *Naqḍ al-futyā*.[28] In all likelihood, Abū 'Abd Allāh would have included a discussion of *ijtihād* in the refutation only if the original work had treated this topic. Al-Jāḥiẓ' *Kitāb uṣūl al-futyā wa'l-aḥkām* must therefore have treated *uṣūl al-fiqh*, including, at the very least, sections on consensus, legal analogy, and *ijtihād*.

Another ninth-century legal theorist, Dā'ūd b. 'Alī b. Khalaf al-Iṣbahānī (d. 270/884), the founder of the Ẓāhirī *madhhab*, probably wrote a comprehensive manual of *uṣūl al-fiqh*, despite the fact that his *Kitāb al-uṣūl* probably dealt with the principal questions of *fiqh* and not *uṣūl al-fiqh* per se.[29] In the *Fihrist*, Ibn al-Nadīm copied a catalogue of Dā'ūd's works from a fascicle written in an old hand by a certain Maḥmūd al-Marwazī, who, he guesses, was an earlier Ẓāhirī scholar, perhaps contemporary with Dā'ūd himself. This catalogue includes 146 titles, of which the first 118 appear to belong

---

[26] Al-Nāṭiq, *al-Mujzī*: al-Baṣrī, *Sharḥ al-ʿUmad*, 2:6.
[27] Al-Nāṭiq, *al-Mujzī*: al-Baṣrī, *Sharḥ al-ʿUmad*, 1:298–99, 2:6.
[28] Al-Qāḍī 'Abd al-Jabbār, *Faḍl al-iʿtizāl*, in collection *Faḍl al-iʿtizāl wa-ṭabaqāt al-Muʿtazilah*, ed. Fu'ād Sayyid (Tunis: al-Dār al-tūnisīyah li'l-nashr, 1974), 326.
[29] Ibn al-Nadīm, *al-Fihrist*, 271.

to a huge work on the points of law, following the standard chapter headings of *fiqh* compendia. That they refer to the chapters of one work is not surprising, for the term *kitāb* ("book") often refers to a chapter in a larger work, though it can also designate a substantial independent work, a short treatise, or a letter. Indeed, it was quite common to label the chapters of *fiqh* works "books", as evident from published *fiqh* works and from other entries in Ibn al-Nadīm's *Fihrist* where he lists as "books" the many individual chapters of larger works.[30] For example, referring to Muḥammad b. Ḥasan al-Shaybānī (d. 189/805), Ibn al-Nadīm remarks, "Muḥammad authored a book (*kitāb*) known as *The Book of Pilgrimage* (*Kitāb al-ḥajj*), which contains many chapters (*kutub*)".[31] To the Shāfiʿī jurist Muḥammad b. al-Ḥusayn al-Ājurrī (d. 360/970) he attributes *The Book of Advice* (*Kitāb al-naṣīḥah*), which contains a number of chapters (*kutub*) on the points of law".[32] He reports that al-Ṭaḥāwī's (d. 321/933) unfinished *Kitāb al-ikhtilāf bayn al-fuqahā'* ("*The Book of Disagreement among the Jurists*") contained eighty chapters (*kutub*).[33] Dā'ūd's *fiqh* work must have been very large indeed, for some of the individual chapters are reported as comprising 300, 400, 600, or 1,000 folios.[34] For this reason, apparently, al-Ṭabarī referred to Dā'ūd as *dhū al-asfār* "the man of many tomes" or "the bearer of books" in a treatise directed against him.[35] As Hallaq notes, Ibn al-Nadīm attributes another work to the later Ẓāhirī scholar Ibn Raqqī (fl. 4th/10th c.), stating that it contains one hundred chapters and follows the organization of *al-Uṣūl*, so that it is not necessary for him to list here all the chapter headings.[36] This suggests that the long list of "books" at the beginning of al-Marwazī's catalogue of Dā'ūd's works is indeed an index of the *Kitāb al-uṣūl* Ibn al-Nadīm had mentioned just above.[37]

---

[30] See, for example, the entries on Muḥammad b. Masʿūd al-ʿAyyāshī, Abū Yūsuf, and Muḥammad b. al-Ḥasan al-Shaybānī: Ibn al-Nadīm, *al-Fihrist*, 244–46, 256–57, 257–58.

[31] Ibid., 258.

[32] Ibid., 268.

[33] Ibid., 260.

[34] These indications of length might, however, be referring not simply to the immediately preceding titles but to the series of (chapter) titles preceding them. The phrase *dhū 'l-asfār* may be interpreted as a reference to Q 62:5, which compares Jewish scholars who transmit the Torah to a donkey bearing books (*ka-mithli 'l-ḥimāri yaḥmalu asfāran*). In other words, al-Ṭabarī is calling Dā'ūd a donkey, accusing him of transmitting loads of religious writings without understanding them.

[35] Yāqūt al-Ḥamawī, *Muʿjam al-buldān*, 18:78.

[36] Ibn al-Nadīm, *al-Fihrist*, 273.

[37] Hallaq, "Shafiʿi", 589–90.

This does not prove, however, that Dā'ūd did not write on *uṣūl al-fiqh*. Another series of "book" titles included in al-Marwazī's catalogue bears a strong resemblance to the chapter headings of a manual of *uṣūl al-fiqh*. It seems probable that here, as in the case of the *fiqh* titles, the catalogue is presenting the chapter titles of a comprehensive, systematic work on jurisprudence. The work seems to be organized in the following manner:

1. Chapter on Consensus.
2. Chapter Demonstrating the Invalidity of the Blind Adoption of Opinions (*taqlīd*).
3. Chapter Demonstrating the Invalidity of Legal Analogy.
4. Chapter on Unitary Traditions.
5. Chapter on Traditions which Provide Certainty.
6. Chapter on Incontrovertible Proof.
7. Chapter on Specific and General Scriptural Texts.
8. Chapter on Explained and Ambiguous Scriptural Texts.[38]

Taken as a whole, this list includes the main topics covered by extant *uṣūl al-fiqh* works from later centuries. This, together with the fact that the titles appear contiguously, suggests that they belong to a single work. The order may seem somewhat odd in comparison with that of later texts, which usually begin with the issues of legal language that appear at the end here. This might be the case since Dā'ūd had a particularly strong polemic concern with the issues of consensus, *taqlīd*, and legal analogy, and therefore placed them first in the book, while relegating other, less controversial topics to the end. The topics which appear to be missing, if one judges from the contents of later works in the genre, are abrogation and divine commands and prohibitions. The latter might be subsumed under the chapter entitled "Incontrovertible Proof", but it is difficult to tell what the intended meaning of "proof" (*ḥujjah*) is here. This chapter could be an epistemological discussion of the establishment of legal knowledge, in which case one would expect Dā'ūd to uphold the need for certainty in the law and to reject the proposition that speculation (*naẓar*) can lead to the truth. Perhaps most probable is that this chapter attempts to define and describe the limited set of hadith reports which can be taken as incontrovertible prooftexts. The well-known Muʿtazilī theologian Abū al-Hudhayl Muḥammad b. al-ʿAbdī (d. 235/849–50) wrote a work with the same title, *Kitāb al-ḥujjah*, in

[38] Ibn al-Nadīm, *al-Fihrist*, 272.

which he argued that only twenty hadiths could be considered incontrovertible proofs; other scholars, including Ibn Surayj, argued that the number of such hadiths was without limit.[39] Goldziher guessed that some of the titles attributed to Dā'ūd belonged to pamphlets written in response to specific Ḥanafī treatises such as *Kitāb ithbāt al-qiyās* and *Kitāb ijtihād al-ra'y* by the jurist 'Īsā b. Abān (d. 221/835–36).[40] While Dā'ūd's titles do imply a response to existing scholarship, it seems more likely that they represent chapters within a work on *uṣūl al-fiqh* which responds to other works with similar chapter headings. Further research may corroborate this tentative identification of an early manual of *uṣūl al-fiqh*.

The famous historian and jurist Abū Ja'far Muḥammad b. Jarīr al-Ṭabarī (d. 310/923) wrote four works which conceivably treated *uṣūl al-fiqh*. One of these, entitled *al-Ādar fī al-uṣūl*, al-Ṭabarī never completed, and the text reporting the title seems corrupt, the meaning of the word *ādar* not being at all clear.[41] Another work is entitled *al-Mūjaz fī al-uṣūl*, but the fact that it was prefaced by a discussion of ethics (*akhlāq*)[42] suggests that it might not have focused on jurisprudence. It is clear, though, that two works by al-Ṭabarī treated *uṣūl al-fiqh*. One of these was a treatise al-Ṭabarī prefaced to *Ikhtilāf al-'ulamā'* (also known as *Ikhtilāf al-fuqahā'*). A short passage describing its contents has been preserved in Yāqūt's *Irshād*: "He had made for the *Kitāb al-ikhtilāf* a treatise which he had prefaced to the book but then removed. In it, he discussed general consensus and traditions originating with single authorities of recognized probity, additions not in *Laṭīf*, as well as traditions whose chains of authority do not go all the way back to the Prophet (*marāsīl*) and abrogating and abrogated scriptural texts (*al-nāsikh wa'l-mansūkh*)".[43] Another was a

[39] Al-Qāḍī 'Abd al-Jabbār, *Faḍl al-i'tizāl*, 301.

[40] Ignaz Goldziher, *Die Ẓāhiriten, Ihr Lehrsystem und ihre Geshichte* (Hildesheim: Georg Olms, 1967), 35. Hallaq endorses this assessment in "Shāfi'ī", 589, though he acknowledges that Dā'ūd represents something of an exception to the statement that the ninth century produced no works on *uṣūl al-fiqh*.

[41] Franz Rosenthal, trans. and annot., *The History of al-Ṭabarī, vol. I: General Introduction and From the Creation to the Flood* (Albany: State University of New York Press, 1989), 85.

[42] Franz Rosenthal, *General Introduction*, 113–17.

[43] Yāqūt al-Ḥamawī, *Mu'jam al-udabā'*, 20 vols. (Beirut: Dār iḥyā' al-turāth al-'arabī, 1988), 18:73; Franz Rosenthal, *General Introduction*, 101–4, with slight modifications of the translation.

treatise prefaced to the legal work *Laṭīf al-qawl fī aḥkām sharā'iʿ al-islām* with the separate title *al-Bayān ʿan uṣūl al-aḥkām*. This treatise is cited in al-Ṭabarī's *Exegesis*, which shows that it treated general and particular scriptural texts, abrogating and abrogated scriptural texts, commands and prohibitions, and possibly consensus and legal analogy.[44] Another anecdote preserved in Yāqūt's *Irshād* shows that both works treated the topic of consensus.[45] Another passage gives a more detailed list of the topics included in the work:

1. Consensus
2. Traditions Transmitted by Single Authorities.
3. Traditions whose Chains of Authority do not Reach the Prophet.
4. Abrogating and Abrogated Texts on Legal Rulings.
5. Ambiguous and Clarified Traditions.
6. Commands and Prohibitions.
7. The Acts of the Messenger[46]
8. Particular and General Scriptural Texts.
9. *Ijtihād*.
10. The Invalidity of Juristic Preference (*Istiḥsān*).[47]

This work, *al-Bayān ʿan uṣūl al-aḥkām*, was a manual of *uṣūl al-fiqh* as sophisticated and comprehensive as many of the extant works from later centuries. Moreover, it was one of al-Ṭabarī's earlier works, written before his other work on *uṣūl al-fiqh*, the treatise prefaced to *Ikhtilāf al-ʿulamā'*. In addition, the fact that it is cited frequently in the *Tafsīr*, which he began ca. 270/883–84, suggests that al-Ṭabarī probably wrote it many years before the turn of the tenth century. Rosenthal's chronology dates it to between 255/869 and 270/883–84, before the composition of the *Tafsīr*, *Ikhtilāf*, and *Tahdhīb*.[48]

Further investigation draws attention to the existence of another early work on jurisprudence which scholarship to date has overlooked: *al-Wuṣūl ilā maʿrifat al-uṣūl* by Muḥammad b. Dā'ūd al-Ẓāhirī. Abū Bakr Muḥammad b. Dā'ūd b. ʿAlī was the son of the famous

---

44 Franz Rosenthal, *General Introduction*, 113–17.

45 Cited in Franz Rosenthal, *General Introduction*, 102–3.

46 The text has *afʿāl al-rusul* "acts of the Messengers", perhaps for an original *al-rasūl* "acts of the Messenger (Muḥammad)", the rubric which commonly appears in later works of jurisprudence.

47 Yāqūt, *Muʿjam al-udabā'*, 18:74.

48 Rosenthal, *General Introduction*, 153. As Rosenthal points out, this dating is only tentative, since al-Ṭabarī worked on many of his books for a number of years, so that one cannot fix their dates precisely.

jurist Dā'ūd b. 'Alī b. Khalaf, the founder of the Ẓāhirī *madhhab*. Dā'ūd, the father, was born in Kufa in 202/818 but settled as a young man in Baghdad, where he lived and taught until his death in 270/883–84. Ibn Dā'ūd was born in 255/868 in Baghdad.[49] There, under the grammarian Nifṭawayh (d. 323/935), he became accomplished in grammar, lexicography, and the literary arts. While still a youth, he wrote one of the first known Arabic works on the theory of love, *Kitāb al-zahrah*, which is extant though incomplete. His works on law, none of which has survived intact, date from later in his career. According to al-Mas'ūdī (d. ca. 345/956), he was an exceptional jurist. He took over teaching in his father's circle upon the latter's death in 270/884, despite his mere fifteen years of age. Like the famous minister and patron al-Ṣāḥib Ibn 'Abbād (d. 385/995) a century later, Ibn Dā'ūd was renowned for his infatuation with *saj'*, which he used in everyday speech. Anecdotes depict him delivering *fatwās*, utterly incomprehensible to his lay petitioners, in *saj'*. He is also famous for his lively and witty debates with Ibn Surayj, the great Shāfi'ī jurist. According to Massignon, both Ibn Dā'ūd and Ibn Surayj became assessors or advisors to the chief judge of the western section of Baghdad, the Mālikī Abū 'Umar al-Ḥammādī (d. 320/932), who had been appointed deputy to his father Yūsuf b. Ya'qūb al-Ḥammādī (d. 297/909–10). Ibn Dā'ūd is also famous for condemning al-Ḥallāj as a heretic in a *fatwā* delivered ca. 288/901. He died on 9 Ramaḍān 297/22 May 910, according to Ibn Khallikān, at the young age of 42.[50] According to one account, he explained

[49] In *Ṭabaqāt al-fuqahā'*, Abū Isḥāq al-Shīrāzī reports that Ibn Dā'ūd died at the age of 42 in 297/909–10. Al-Mas'ūdī gives the date 296/908–9. Ibn Khallikān gives 297, agreeing with al-Shīrāzī. Some MSS of *Ṭabaqāt al-fuqahā'* give the date 299 A.H. The statement by J. C. Vadet, "Ibn Dāwūd", *EI*[2] that Ibn Dā'ūd died in 294/909, repeated by Josef Van Ess, *Theologie und Gesellschaft im 2. und 3. Jh. H.*, 6 vols. (Berlin: Walter de Gruyter, 1991–97), 4:250, is an error since 294 A.H. corresponds to 906–7 A.D. See the sources given below.

[50] On Ibn Dā'ūd in general, see al-Mas'ūdī, *Murūj al-dhahab wa-ma'ādin al-jawhar*, 4 vols., ed. Qāsim al-Shammā'ī al-Rifā'ī (Beirut: Dār al-qalam, 1989), 4:271–72; Ibn al-Nadīm, *al-Fihrist*, 272; Abū Isḥāq al-Shīrāzī, *Ṭabaqāt al-fuqahā'*, ed. Iḥsān 'Abbās (Beirut: Dār al-rā'id al-'arabī, 1970), 175–76; al-Khaṭīb al-Baghdādī, *Tārīkh Baghdād* (Beirut: Dār al-kutub al-'ilmīyah, n.d.), 5:256–63; Ibn al-Jawzī, *al-Muntaẓam fī tārīkh al-mulūk wa'l-umam*, 18 vols., ed. Muḥammad 'Abd al-Qādir 'Aṭā and Muṣṭafā 'Abd al-Qādir 'Aṭā (Beirut: Dār al-kutub al-'ilmīyah, 1992), 6:93–95; Ibn Khallikān, *Wafayāt al-a'yān*, 8 vols., ed. Iḥsān 'Abbās (Beirut: Dār ṣādir, 1977), 4:259–61; al-Dhahabī, *Siyar a'lām al-nubalā'*, 23 vols., ed. Shu'ayb al-Arnā'ūṭ and Ḥusayn al-Asad (Beirut: Mu'assasat al-risālah, 1981–85), 9:23–25; idem, *Tadhkirat al-ḥuffāẓ*, 3d ed.,

to his teacher Nifṭawayh while on his deathbed that he was dying of an unconsummated love for another man. The object of his affections, one Muḥammad b. Jāmiʿ al-Ṣaydalānī, was the only beloved in history to support his admirer financially, the sources claim.

In his chronicle *Murūj al-dhahab*, al-Masʿūdī lists the following as legal works by Ibn Dā'ūd: *Kitāb al-indhār, Kitāb al-iʿdhār wa'l-ījāz, al-Intiṣār ʿalā Muḥammad b. Jarīr wa-ʿAbd Allāh b. Sharshīr wa-ʿĪsā b. Ibrāhīm al-Ḍarīr*, and *al-Wuṣūl ilā maʿrifat al-uṣūl*.[51] The title *al-Wuṣūl ilā maʿrifat al-uṣūl* begs attention. It uses the key term *uṣūl* which appears often in the titles of works treating *uṣūl al-fiqh*. It is designated here as a legal work and so cannot have focused on dogmatic theology (*uṣūl al-dīn*). The rhyming title matches quite closely the titles found in other works in the genre, such as al-Ṭabarī's *al-Bayān ʿan uṣūl al-aḥkām*,

---

rev., 2 vols. (Hyderabad: Dā'irat al-maʿārif al-ʿuthmānīyah, 1955–58), 2:209; idem, *Tārīkh al-islām*, ed. ʿUmar ʿAbd al-Salām Tadmurī (Beirut: Dār al-kitāb al-ʿarabī, 1991), 22:263–67; Ibn Kathīr ʿImād al-Dīn Ismāʿīl b. ʿUmar, *al-Bidāyah wa'l-nihāyah fī al-tārīkh*, 14 vols. (Cairo: Maṭbaʿat al-saʿādah, 1939), 11:110–11; al-Yāfiʿī, *Mir'āt al-janān wa-ʿibrat al-yaqẓān*, 4 vols. (Haydarabad: Dā'irat al-maʿārif al-niẓāmīyah, 1918–20), 2:228–30; Ṣalāḥ al-Dīn Khalīl b. Aybak al-Ṣafadī, *Kitāb al-wāfī bi'l-wafayāt* (Wiesbaden; Franz Stayner, 1962), 3:58–61; Ibn al-ʿImād al-Ḥanbalī, *Shadharāt al-shanab fī akhbār man dhahab*, 8 vols. (Cairo: Maktabat al-qudsī, 1932–33), 2:226; Louis Massignon, *la Passion de Husayn Ibn manṣūr Hallaj: martyr mystique de l'Islam, executé à Bagdad le 26 mars 922: étude d'histoire religieuse*, 4 vols. (Paris: Gallimard, 1975), 1:167–81; idem, *The Passion of al-Ḥallāj, Mystic and Martyr of Islam*, 4 vols., trans. Herbert Mason (Princeton: Princeton University Press, 1982), 1:338–61; Muḥammad b. Dā'ūd al-Ẓāhirī, *Kitāb al-zahrah* (first part), ed. A. R. Nykl (Beirut: Maṭbaʿat al-ābā' al-yasūʿīyīn, 1932); J. C. Vadet, "Ibn Dāwūd", *EI*², 3:744–45; Carl Brockelmann, *GAL*, 2nd ed., e vols., 3 supp. (Leiden: E. J. Brill, 1937–49), SI: 249–50 [Brockelmann's index also refers to GI: 520—this is apparently an error]; Fuat Sezgin, *GAS*, 9 vols. (Leiden: E. J. Brill, 1967–84), 1:521–22, 2:75; ʿUmar Riḍā Kaḥḥālah, *Muʿjam al-mu'allifīn*, 15 vols. (Cairo: Dār al-turāth al-ʿarabī, 1957–61), 9:296–97.

51 Al-Masʿūdī, *Murūj al-dhahab*, 4:272–72. In the *Fihrist*, 363, Ibn al-Nadīm lists his legal works as *Kitāb al-indhār, Kitāb al-iʿdhār, Kitāb al-wuṣūl ilā maʿrifat al-uṣūl, Kitāb al-radd ʿalā Ibn Sharshīr, Kitāb al-radd ʿalā Abī ʿĪsā al-Ḍarīr*, and *Kitāb al-intiṣār min Abī Jaʿfar al-Ṭabarī*. The three last titles appear to belong to one and the same book. Al-Masʿūdī evidently lists them as one work, and the *sajʿ* in the tile (. . . *Jarīr*, . . . *Sharshīr*, . . . *al-Ḍarīr*) suggests this as well. The Muḥammad b. Jarīr who appears in the title of *al-Intiṣār* is of course the famous jurist and historian al-Ṭabarī (d. 310/923). Yāqūt reports several anecdotes about this refutation, claiming that it was occasioned by al-Ṭabarī's work *Kitāb al-radd ʿalā dhī al-asfār*, written against Dā'ūd. These accounts report that the refutation focused on three questions and was quite insulting. Yāqūt al-Ḥamawī, *Muʿjam al-udabā'*, 18: 78–80. ʿAbd Allāh b. Sharshīr is probably the Muʿtazilī theologian and poet Abū al-ʿAbbās ʿAbd Allāh b. Muḥammad b. ʿAbd Allāh b. Mālik (d. 293/905–6), known as Ibn Sharshīr, al-Nāshī al-Akbar, or al-Nāshī al-Kabīr. I have not been able to identify ʿĪsā b. Ibrāhīm al-Ḍarīr. The statement that it focused on three questions is perhaps another indication that all three scholars were refuted in the same work, one question each.

Abū al-Isḥāq al-Marwazī's (d. 340/951) *Kitāb al-fuṣūl fī maʿrifat al-uṣūl*, al-Masʿūdī's *Kitāb naẓm al-adillah fī uṣūl al-millah* and *Kitāb naẓm al-aʿlām fī uṣūl al-aḥkām*, or al-Jaṣṣāṣ' *al-Fuṣūl fī al-uṣūl*.[52] It seems quite likely that this work was a manual of jurisprudence, a full-fledged member of the *uṣūl al-fiqh* genre. In *Irshād al-arīb*, Yāqūt mentions Ibn Dā'ūd's work in his notice on Abū Jaʿfar Muḥammad b. Jarīr al-Ṭabarī. The account gives the title of the book as *Kitāb al-wuṣūl ilā maʿrifat al-uṣūl* and refers to a passage in the chapter on consensus (*bāb al-ijmāʿ*) where Ibn Dā'ūd criticizes al-Ṭabarī's discussion of consensus, claiming that he contradicts himself.[53] This reference confirms that *al-Wuṣūl ilā maʿrifat al-uṣūl* is a work on jurisprudence rather than the points of law and shows that it included a chapter devoted to the topic of consensus in particular.

Considerable material from what appears to be *al-Wuṣūl ilā maʿrifat al-uṣūl* is preserved in a Fatimid Shiite work from the mid-tenth century. The Ismāʿīlī jurist al-Qāḍī al-Nuʿmān (d. 363/974), who served as chief judge and ideologue for the early Fatimid state, wrote a refutation of Sunni legal principles entitled *Ikhtilāf uṣūl al-madhāhib*. Composed between 343/954 and 359/969,[54] it is contemporary with the earliest extant works of *uṣūl al-fiqh*, such as the *Fuṣūl* of al-Jaṣṣāṣ (d. 370/980).[55] It may not have been the first Ismāʿīlī work to respond to Sunni *uṣūl al-fiqh*: the Central Asian *dāʿī* Muḥammad b. Aḥmad al-Nasafī, executed in 332/943 in Bukhārā by the Sāmānid ruler Nūḥ I (331–43/943–54), wrote a work whose title, *Kitāb uṣūl al-sharʿ*, suggests that it too refuted Sunni legal principles.[56] Despite the fact that

---

[52] See Stewart, *Islamic Legal Orthodoxy*, 34–35.

[53] Yāqūt al-Ḥamawī, *Muʿjam al-udabā'*, 18:72.

[54] There are two editions of the work: one by S. T. Lockandwalla, Simla, India: Indian Institute for Advanced Study, 1972 (henceforth designated L) and the other by Muṣṭafā Ghālib, Beirut: Dār al-andalus, 1973 [reprint, 1983] (henceforth designated Gh). Muṣṭafā Ghālib was apparently unaware of Lockandwalla's edition. Unless otherwise noted, all citations will be to the Lockandwalla edition

[55] The *Fuṣūl* probably dates to between the death of al-Jaṣṣāṣ' teacher Abū al-Ḥasan al-Karkhī in 340/952 and al-Jaṣṣāṣ' own death in 370/980. *Ikhtilāf uṣūl al-madhāhib* was composed after 28 Rabīʿ I 343/30 September 954, because it includes the letter of al-Muʿizz li-Dīn Allāh (341–65/953–75) appointing al-Nuʿmān chief judge on that date (p. 24). It must have been completed before al-Qāḍī al-Nuʿmān's death in 363/974, and it is improbable that the work was composed either after al-Qāḍī al-Nuʿmān moved from Tunisia to Egypt in 361/971 or after the Fatimid conquest of Egypt itself in 359/969, because there is no mention of that momentous event in the text. It seems most likely that the work was composed shortly after al-Qāḍī al-Nuʿmān's appointment as chief judge in 343/954.

[56] Ibn al-Nadīm, *al-Fihrist*, 240.

it argues regularly against Sunni positions on jurisprudence, *Ikhtilāf uṣūl al-madhāhib* adopts many of the formal features of Sunni texts in the genre of *uṣūl al-fiqh*. Al-Qāḍī al-Nuʿmān actually mentions very few works by title in the course of his refutation: the Koran (passim), the Torah (p. 13), the Gospels (p. 13), *Adab al-qāḍī* and *Ikhtilāf al-Shāfiʿī wa-Mālik* by al-Shāfiʿī (p. 214), and *al-Mujarrad* by al-Ḥasan b. Ziyād al-Luʾluʾī (d. 204/819–20), a student of Abū Ḥanīfah (p. 41), none of which is devoted to jurisprudence per se. Nevertheless, the material included in *Ikhtilāf uṣūl al-madhāhib* shows that the author was arguing against a sophisticated system of jurisprudence presented in a highly developed tradition of Sunni manuals. Careful examination of the work and comparison with other sources reveals a great deal about the Sunni genre which it addresses and the history of Sunni jurisprudence between the beginning of the ninth and the mid-tenth centuries.[57]

Al-Qāḍī al-Nuʿmān records that he wrote the *Ikhtilāf* in response to an opponent with whom he had debated the validity of *ijtihād*. He claims that he had soundly defeated his opponent but that the loser subsequently collected a treatise in one fascicle presenting the opinions of the champions of *ijtihād*, together with their arguments for its validity. Al-Qāḍī al-Nuʿmān reports that he first presented in his own book all of the arguments in favor of *ijtihād* that the opponent had included in his treatise, adding any other Sunni arguments that were available to him. Then, he decided to refute all the other principles to which the Sunnis resort in their jurisprudence, and not just *ijtihād*—i.e., *taqlīd*, *ijmāʿ*, *qiyās*, *istiḥsān*, *istidlāl*, as evident in the completed work.[58] The last two statements imply, of course, that he had access to many Sunni works of *uṣūl al-fiqh*. In the course of his discussion, al-Nuʿmān remarks several times that he is merely summarizing the Sunnis' arguments so as not to bore the reader, such as, for example, when he presents the arguments for the authority of consensus.[59] He says upon completing this section that if he had gone on at length on such topics, each chapter would require several

57 Hallaq dismisses *Ikhtilāf uṣūl al-madhāhib* rather quickly as a source for the history of Sunni jurisprudence, claiming that it tells us nothing additional to what is found in the biographical and bibliographic sources—i.e., that no works in the genre were produced before the tenth century. Hallaq, "Shāfiʿī", 589.

58 Al-Qāḍī al-Nuʿmān, *Ikhtilāf uṣūl al-madhāhib*, 232–33.

59 Al-Qāḍī al-Nuʿmān, *Ikhtilāf uṣūl al-madhāhib*, 93, 105–6, 193.

volumes.[60] This gives us some idea of the immense material on jurisprudence available to him. Writing in the mid-tenth century, he probably had at his disposal numerous works of Sunni jurisprudence written during that century and the previous century as well.

In the work, al-Qāḍī al-Nuʿmān often quotes or paraphrases directly from Sunni works on jurisprudence. Though he mentions no *uṣūl al-fiqh* title and rarely mentions a specific author, this does not obscure the fact that he is citing specific works. At one point, when discussing *ijtihād*, he cites what must be at least four separate sources (p. 207). One passage concerning definitions of consensus cites what appear to be six distinct sources (pp. 87–89). Al-Qāḍī al-Nuʿmān mentions al-Shāfiʿī a number of times and cites at least one passage from the *Risālah*, though without identifying the text by name (p. 162). Another author he quotes, giving his name as Aḥmad b. ʿAlī al-Ikhshādh al-Baghdādī (pp. 59–60), is the Muʿtazilī theologian and jurist Abū Bakr Aḥmad b. ʿAlī, known as Ibn al-Ikhshīd (d. 326/938). The topic discussed here is consensus; the work in questions is probably Ibn al-Ikhshīd's *Kitāb al-ijmāʿ*, or perhaps *Kitāb al-maʿūnah fī al-uṣūl*.[61] The author al-Qāḍī al-Nuʿmān cites most frequently is Abū Bakr Muḥammad b. Dā'ūd, the son of the famous founder of the Ẓāhirī *madhhab*. It is probable that al-Qāḍī al-Nuʿmān was citing passages of Ibn Dā'ūd's manual of *uṣūl al-fiqh, al-Wuṣūl ilā maʿrifat al-uṣūl*.

In the text of *Ikhtilāf uṣūl al-madhāhib*, al-Qāḍī al-Nuʿmān mentions Ibn Dā'ūd three times by name. He first mentions Ibn Dā'ūd with regard to an argument about consensus (p. 101). Later, he makes it clear that he has been citing from the work of Ibn Dā'ūd sections of a long argument concerning the rejection of legal analogy (pp. 153–61). At another point, he states that Ibn Dā'ūd was the author of an argument against *ijtihād* (pp. 199–202). Other passages which may be citing Ibn Dā'ūd concern the rejection of *ijtihād* again (pp. 205–6), the rejection of *istiḥsān* (pp. 183–86), and *istidlāl* "inference", the Ẓāhirīs' answer, in effect, to *qiyās* (pp. 186–87). All told, I have identified ten passages where I believe al-Qāḍī al-Nuʿmān is citing material by Ibn Dā'ūd.

---

[60] Al-Qāḍī al-Nuʿmān, *Ikhtilāf uṣūl al-madhāhib*, 105–6.
[61] Ibn al-Nadīm, *Kitāb al-fihrist*, 220–21.

I. pp. 100–101 on consensus
II. pp. 142–44 against legal analogy
III. pp. 151–52 against legal analogy
IV. pp. 153–54 against legal analogy
V. pp. 156–61 against legal analogy
VI. pp. 171–75 against legal analogy
VII. pp. 183–86 against *istiḥsān*
VIII. pp. 186–87 on *istidlāl*
IX. pp. 199–202 against *ijtihād*
X. pp. 205–6 against *ijtihād*

As just mentioned, Ibn Dāʾūd's name appears explicitly only three times, in connection with passages I, V, and IX. There are, however, indications that all of these passages are attributable to him. Passage II is introduced as the speech of a Sunni jurist who rejects legal analogy, and ends with a statement that this is the opinion of a jurist "who rejects legal analogy and upholds *istidlāl*" (pp. 142, 144). Passage III is introduced in the same manner as passage II (p. 151). Passage IV is introduced as the speech of a certain jurist who denies legal analogy and professes *istidlāl* (p. 153). Passage V begins with the statement, "The denier of legal analogy said, . . ." (p. 156). At the end of passage V appears a statement which makes it clear that the preceding four passages, II–V, all represent the work of Muḥammad b. Dāʾūd al-Ẓāhirī: "This speaker whose opinion we have quoted is one of the critics of legal analogy among the jurists of Baghdad among the Sunnis, the well-known Muḥammad b. Dāʾūd b. Alī. He and his father, Dāʾūd, were among those who used to deny legal analogy, respond to those who professed it, adopt opinions contrary to those of the jurists of Iraq and others who accepted it, express scorn for their opinions, and profess, as they claimed, *istidlāl*" (p. 161). Passage VI is attributed to a certain Sunni jurist who rejected legal analogy (p. 171). It ends with a statement that these have been some of the rebuttals of a Sunni opponent of legal analogy to those who champion it (p. 175). Passage VII is attributed to a Sunni opponent of *istiḥsān*: "There responded to those Sunnis who professed *istiḥsān* a certain Sunni who rejected it as we have, even though he professed something similar to it in meaning" (p. 183). This is clearly a reference to Muḥammad b. Dāʾūd; the method he adopted that al-Qāḍī al-Nuʿmān considers equivalent to *istiḥsān* is *istidlāl*. This is confirmed in the section on *istidlāl*, primarily, it seems, a commentary on a discussion of *istidlāl* by Ibn Dāʾūd. In the course of this discussion, al-Qāḍī al-Nuʿmān states, "with statements like this and similar things, you [i.e., the Ẓāhirīs] have produced proofs and argued against those who profess *ra'y, qiyās, istiḥsān*, and *ijtihād*, but then you have adopted the like of what you have denied" (p. 193). Ibn Dā'ūd and the Ẓāhirīs rejected *istiḥsān* while adopting *istidlāl*, and al-Qāḍī al-Nuʿmān considers the latter equivalent to the former. Passage VIII is attributed to those who uphold *istidlāl* (p. 186). Passage X presents the argument of a Sunni jurist against the reasoning of al-Shāfiʿī on a question of *ijtihād* (p. 205). The fact that the speaker rejects *ijtihād* and claims that one must seek evidence rather than resorting to arbitrary personal opinion makes it seem likely that the man in question is Muḥammad b. Dā'ūd.

In four other instances, al-Qāḍī al-Nuʿmān refers to "a certain Baghdadi" or "some Baghdadis" (*baʿḍ al-baghdādīyīn*) (pp. 87, 89). This might, on the face of it, include or designate Ibn Dā'ūd, but the opinions reported there seem to reflect positions Ibn Dā'ūd would not have held. These include the opinions that a consensus reached on the basis of a transmitted report is an incontrovertible proof; that all believers must agree in order for consensus to exist; and that a dissenting opinion on the part of one or a small group does not render consensus invalid. It seems most probable that al-Qāḍī al-Nuʿmān is citing other Sunni jurists from Baghdad here.

It is clear that al-Qāḍī al-Nuʿmān is citing an actual text and is not just presenting Ibn Dā'ūd's opinions reported in intermediate sources. He writes, "This is the verbatim text (*naṣṣ*) of the opinion of Muḥammad b. Dā'ūd" (p. 101). The passage in question cannot be a summary of his doctrine from a later source. The amount of material quoted also suggests that he was citing directly from a text at his disposal. The work cited was almost certainly a single book, for Ibn Dā'ūd refers to it as such three times in the excerpts quoted. In a passage treating consensus, he remarks, "One could go on at length about such things [obvious matters of consensus, such as the location of the Kaʿbah], but by listing them *this book* would grow too long" (p. 100). In a passage arguing against legal analogy, he writes, "(And he should be asked) about many similar cases, the exposition of which would render *the book* lengthy" (p. 159). In the discussion of *istiḥsān*, he warns, "There therefore applies to them what we presented above *in the introduction to this book* (*fī ṣadri hādhā 'l-kitāb*)" (p. 185). The fact that these remarks show up in sections treating different topics, consensus and legal analogy, suggest that the passages cited derive from one book and not several independent treatises. In addition, while the excerpts preserved here do not show an exaggerated penchant for *saj*ʿ, short passages of *saj*ʿ do appear in the text (e.g., pp. 158, 172, 173, 187, 202), and their occurrence in tightly argued forensic passages suggests that they conform to Muḥammad b. Dā'ūd's style.

Though the reconstruction of lost sources is fraught with difficulties,[62] one can argue that in this case the evidence justifies assigning the material included in *Ikhtilāf uṣūl al-madhāhib* to *al-Wuṣūl ilā maʿrifat al-uṣūl.* We know that Ibn Dā'ūd wrote a legal work entitled *al-Wuṣūl ilā maʿrifat al-uṣūl.* We know that this work included a chapter on consensus (*bāb al-ijmāʿ*), confirming that it was indeed a manual of *uṣūl al-fiqh.* It is clear that al-Qāḍī al-Nuʿmān is citing material authored by Ibn Dā'ūd which treats various topics normally included in *uṣūl al-fiqh.* Furthermore, the amount of material cited, together with the fact that the excerpts themselves refer to a book, suggests that al-Qāḍī al-Nuʿmān had a manual of *uṣūl al-fiqh* by Ibn Dā'ūd at his disposal. Since *al-Wuṣūl ilā maʿrifat al-uṣūl* is Ibn Dā'ūd's best known work on the topic—indeed, we know of no other work on jurisprudence by Ibn Dā'ūd—it seems reasonable to assign the excerpts to *al-Wuṣūl ilā maʿrifat al-uṣūl.* Doing so involves a number of assumptions, but none seems unwarranted given the context.[63]

Al-Qāḍī al-Nuʿmān apparently abridges many of the passages he cites. The occurrence of the phrases "then he said" or "then they said" a number of times in the middle of the passages cited indicates that they are composed of several non-contiguous sections of original text with intervening material omitted. Thus, passage II is composed of two sections, with the second introduced by "he said" (p. 143), passage V of two sections (pp. 156–61), passage VI of three

62 Ella Landau-Tasseron, "On the Reconstruction of Lost Sources", in *History and Historiography in Early Islamic Times: Studies and Perspectives*, ed. Lawrence I. Conrad (Princeton: Darwin Press, 1992); Lawrence I. Conrad, "Recovering Lost Texts: Some Methodological Issues", *JAOS* 113 (1993):258–63.

63 It is conceivable, for example, that al-Qāḍī al-Nuʿmān is quoting material from a manual of jurisprudence Ibn Dā'ūd wrote which does not otherwise appear in the sources. He could also be quoting from several manuals of jurisprudence by Ibn Dā'ūd, or from a manual of *uṣūl al-fiqh* together with one or more treatises on individual topics, or from other works which treat topics in jurisprudence within a larger framework but are not *uṣūl al-fiqh* manuals per se. It is simpler and more reasonable to conclude that al-Qāḍī al-Nuʿmān was quoting from a single major work in his possession, and that this work was probably *al-Wuṣūl ilā maʿrifat al-uṣūl.*

sections (pp. 172–73), passage VIII of five sections (pp. 186–87), and passage IX of six sections (pp. 200–2). These frequent breaks, indicating the omission of many intervening passages, suggest that the original was more lengthy and detailed than the text al-Qāḍī al-Nuʿmān actually quotes. In addition, at the end of passage VI al-Qāḍī al-Nuʿmān writes, "This is some of the argument of the one who rejected legal analogy among the Sunnis against those of them who considered it valid". (p. 175). The word "some" here suggests that this passage is merely part of a more detailed discussion.

The passages treating legal analogy (II–VI) appear to be presented by al-Qāḍī al-Nuʿmān in their original order and to be parts of a single comprehensive discussion. Passage II introduces the topic, providing a definition of legal analogy itself. Passage III restates part of passage II, focusing on the cause (*ʿillah*) of a legal ruling and holding that other causes could always be proposed such that there would be no way to prove the superiority of one over others. Passage IV changes tactics, arguing that the authority of the principle of legal analogy depends on a circular argument, an analogy based on the inductive observation that God grants similar cases similar rulings. Ibn Dā'ūd counters this view by observing that in many instances God assigns similar cases dissimilar rulings. Passage V refers explicitly to passage IV: "Now, then, we return to him asking, after having demonstrated to him that legal analogy is proved invalid by legal analogy itself, as he himself proved, . . ." (p. 156). Passage VI appears to wrap up the discussion, arguing against claims on the part of certain Sunni jurists, on the evidence of Q 30:28, that God Himself used legal analogy. This passage again defines *qiyās*, admitting that the word designates something which actually exists, that things actually may resemble each other, and that comparisons and analogies can be made, even by God in the Koran, while denying that analogy is a legitimate method for discovery of the law. This second definition seems to close the original discussion of legal analogy. In addition, passage VII, on *istiḥsān*, includes a remark referring to the discussion of the cause or occasioning factor (*ʿillah*) in passage IV (pp. 183, 153). This confirms that these discussions were part of a larger manual with distinct chapters and provides further evidence that al-Qāḍī al-Nuʿmān was including the excerpts from Ibn Dā'ūd's work in something like their original order.

From the material included in *Ikhtilāf uṣūl al-madhāhib*, one cannot actually reconstruct Muḥammad b. Dā'ūd's work, but one can gain some idea of its original plan and contents. The work included an introduction (*ṣadr*) to which Ibn Dā'ūd refers in the section on *istiḥsān*. His statement there implies that the introduction presented an over-arching argument against the Ẓāhirīs' opponents: "They make their preference (*istiḥsān*) capable of rendering licit what God made forbidden and their aversion capable of rendering forbidden what God declared licit in the text of His Book and the sanctioned practices of His prophets. There then applies to them what we have presented above in the introduction to this book, and they, God willing, will find no way to escape this (verdict). (p. 185)" This passage makes an explicit connection between the immediate argument, against *istiḥsān*, and a more general argument made in the introduction to the work. There Ibn Dā'ūd must have stated that by using unacceptable principles for the discovery of the law, his opponents were in effect declaring forbidden what God had declared licit and declaring licit what He had declared forbidden, arrogating to themselves a crucial function of the divinity. A similar passage, referring to the opponent who adopts personal opinion, *istiḥsān*, and legal analogy as legitimate methods of determining God's law, occurs not long after the first and seems logically connected with it: "He has claimed that he is a partner of God in His affairs and rulings, but Mighty and Glorious God did not grant this even to His prophets and messengers, as we have stated and explained". (p. 186) The phrase, "as we have stated and explained", probably refers to the introduction of the book as well. The introduction thus must have put forward an argument that served as a frame for the remainder of the work. Legal analogy, *istiḥsān*, and *ijtihād* were to be rejected because they ultimately led the jurists to set themselves up as partners to God, claiming for humans legislative powers that belonged exclusively to Him. *Al-Wuṣūl* was thus a systematic, integrated work, and not merely a collection of disparate critiques of individual legal methods.

The passages cited verbatim in *Ikhtilāf uṣūl al-madhāhib* derive from what appear to be five distinct chapters of *al-Wuṣūl*. The first of these, in the order of presentation in *Ikhtilāf*, is consensus. As mentioned above, an anecdote in Yāqūt's *Irshād al-arīb* shows that *al-Wuṣūl* contained a chapter devoted to consensus:

> When he authored his work known as *The Book of the Path to Knowledge of Jurisprudence*, Muḥammad b. Dā'ūd al-Iṣbahānī stated in the chapter on consensus, concerning Abū Ja'far al-Ṭabarī, that the (only valid) consensus, according to him, was the consensus of those eight individual

> authorities mentioned above and no others.[64] He based this claim on phrases of Abū Ja'far such as, "They agreed unanimously" and "Proof was unanimously established on such-and-such (a ruling)". (Ibn Dā'ūd wrote), "Then (al-Ṭabarī) said in the opening of the chapter on dissenting opinion (*khilāf*), 'Then they differed, and Mālik and al-Awzā'ī professed such and such opinion, and So-and-so professed such-and-such opinion,' so that those from whom (al-Ṭabarī) had reported[65] unanimous agreement were the same ones from whom he reported dissenting opinion". This is an error on the part of Ibn Dā'ūd. Had he consulted what (al-Ṭabarī) wrote[66] in the treatise appended to *al-Laṭīf* and the treatise appended to *al-Ikhtilāf*, and what he included in many of his books, to the effect that consensus is the transmission by many authorities of reports on which the Companions of the Messenger of God—may God bless him and grant him peace!—agreed unanimously, and not (agreement on) an opinion arrived at by way of legal analogy, then he would have realized that what he professed on this matter was a heinous mistake and manifest error.[67]

This anecdote is the only one found so far which refers to a specific chapter of *al-Wuṣūl* as such—the chapter on consensus. It is quite likely, though, that the excerpts in *Ikhtilāf uṣūl al-madhāhib* derive from distinct chapters treating consensus, the invalidity of legal analogy, the invalidity of *istiḥsān*, *istidlāl*, and the invalidity of *ijtihād*. These passages, particularly the five passages presenting arguments against legal analogy, represent a substantial portion of the text. They are not, however, limited to one topic within jurisprudence and so are unlikely to have come merely from a treatise refuting legal analogy, for example, which would not have included consensus, *ijtihād*, or *istidlāl*.

Other passages in *Ikhtilāf uṣūl al-madhāhib* may refer to the contents of *al-Wuṣūl* without quoting it verbatim. In the chapter on *ijtihād* al-Qāḍī al-Nu'mān at one point quotes a source in support of *ijtihād* which may be responding to Ibn al-Dā'ūd: "A certain jurist who professed *ijtihād* responded to one of those who had rejected it and argued for this rejection from the fact that *mujtahids* differ in opinion. If *ijtihād* were permissible, and if what it leads to were true, then it would be possible for the truth to lie in something and its opposite, when the *mujtahids* hold different opinions. The upholder

---

[64] The eight authorities are Mālik, Abū Ḥanīfah, al-Shāfi'ī, al-Awzā'ī, Sufyān al-Thawrī, Abū Yūsuf, Muḥammad b. al-Ḥasan al-Shaybānī, and Ibrāhīm b. Khālid al-Kalbī. Yāqūt, *Mu'jam al-udabā'*, 18:71.

[65] Reading *ḥakā* for *ḥukiya* in the text, twice in this sentence.

[66] Reading *kitābatihi* for *kitābihi* in the text.

[67] Yāqūt, *Mu'jam al-buldān*, 18:72.

of *ijtihād* responded . . ." (p. 215). Now it is not entirely certain that Ibn Dā'ūd is the scholar arguing against *ijtihād* here, but we would expect him to hold this opinion, and few other scholars whose work was available to al-Qāḍī al-Nuʿmān would have, except Dā'ūd himself. The chapter on the invalidity of *taqlīd* (pp. 29–43) also includes what are possibly additional references to the work of Ibn Dā'ūd. In this chapter, al-Qāḍī al-Nuʿmān argues against two types of *taqlīd*: first, the acceptance of the opinions of the Companions as true and correct in general, and second, the adoption of the opinions of the great jurists of the past, such as Abū Ḥanīfah, al-Shāfiʿī, and Mālik. Concerning the first type of *taqlīd*, he mentions that while many Sunnis adopt this doctrine, some have opposed it and met with vehement criticism from the majority.

> We have mentioned above (the Sunnis') doctrine concerning following the opinions of the Companions and avoiding deviation therefrom to other opinions, and some Sunnis' refutation of them in their blind adoption (of these opinions). This is something which Sunni commoners consider a very grave transgression and, in their ignorance, see as equivalent to apostasy. This has led a certain Sunni (scholar) who rejects *taqlīd* not to give an explicit refutation in his rejection of their *taqlīd* of the Companions, and only to indicate this with hints and allusions. If they were only aware, (they would see) that in their *taqlīd* of those whom Mighty and Glorious God did not command us to follow is the greatest denouncement against them, but they are senseless boors. That which came before them and has attained great status in their hearts has taken the place of the Truth for them. (pp. 32–33)

It is quite likely that al-Qāḍī al-Nuʿmān is referring here also to Ibn Dā'ūd. We know that Dā'ūd and Ibn Dā'ūd opposed the *taqlīd* of the Companions, the position evident here. It is also clear from the text that the thinker in question is a specific Sunni jurist who was opposed by the great majority of Sunnis. In another passage, al-Qāḍī al-Nuʿmān is probably referring yet again to the same author:

> Everyone among the Sunnis who holds the invalidity of *taqlīd* adopts this [the opinion that al-Qāḍī al-Nuʿmān has just explained], even though he did not voice it as explicitly, because of his fear of vituperation, directed at himself, of the ignorant masses, the common people, and the rabble. [Such authors avoid doing this] out of fear for themselves from the regimes we have mentioned above,[68] who, having sought out and attained the trappings of this world, relinquished the faith to

[68] This is a reference to the Umayyads and Abbasids.

> those who had relinquished mundane matters to them. They rejected faith and sought thereby to appease the common people. The faith became weak, legal rulings were changed, the ignorant mass multiplied, and the rabble became overbearing. (pp. 39–40)

Both these passages refer to a specific Sunni jurist or jurists who reject the acceptance of the uncorroborated opinions of the Companions as reliable indicators of God's law. The Sunni jurists in question adopt something akin to a Shiite position, critical of the Companions of the Prophet, but they refrain from voicing it in plain, explicit terms for fear of denunciation by the masses and despotic rulers. Rather, they resort to a type of *taqīyah*, using allusive terms to express their doctrine on this point. It seems quite likely that these passages refer to material included in Ibn Dā'ūd's work as well, material which would have appeared in a chapter devoted to the invalidity of *taqlīd*.

Citations in other works on jurisprudence may help provide a more complete picture of *al-Wuṣūl ilā maʿrifat al-uṣūl*, if we assume that most of the recorded opinions of Ibn Dā'ūd on the topics of jurisprudence derive, ultimately, from that work. In *al-Irshād al-ṣaghīr*, al-Bāqillānī reports as Ibn Dā'ūd's opinion the statement that it is impossible for the explanation of a general statement to be delayed if the general statement is intended to mean something particular.[69] Al-Bājī (d. 474/1071) writes, "Concerning a case where a Companion says, 'The Messenger of God commanded us to do such-and-such or prohibited us from doing such-and-such,' Abū Bakr b. Dā'ūd said: 'Whoever says that this should not be taken to indicate obligation until he transmits to us (the Prophet's) exact words (has voiced) a correct statement.'"[70] In another passage, he reports, "Dā'ūd and his son said, 'It is possible that worship may occur by it (legal analogy) according to reason, but the religious law did not permit it absolutely, and actually prohibits it.'"[71] These citations suggest that Ibn Dā'ūd's work included a discussion of Prophetic sunnah as opposed to the statements of Companions and a discussion of *ʿāmm* and *khāṣṣ*, that is, general and particular scriptural texts, or specifically *takhṣīṣ al-*

---

[69] al-Bāqillānī, *al-Irshād*, 3:387.

[70] Abū al-Walīd al-Bājī, *Iḥkām al-fuṣūl fī aḥkām al-uṣūl*, ed. Abdel-Magid Turki (Beirut: Dār al-kutub al-ʿilmīyah, 1980), 1:172.

[71] Al-Bājī, *Iḥkām al-fuṣūl*, 531.

'āmm, the particularization of an ostensibly general text, in addition to the topics cited by al-Qāḍī al-Nu'mān. It is not surprising that such topics fail to appear in *Ikhtilāf uṣūl al-madhāhib*, for al-Qāḍī al-Nu'mān is focusing on the individual "principles" adopted by Sunni jurists, and does not address the topics related to scriptural language normally discussed in *uṣūl al-fiqh* works, such as commands and prohibitions, general and particular texts, ambiguous and clarified texts, and abrogation. It seems safe to say that these topics failed to appear in al-Qāḍī al-Nu'mān's work simply because they were not subject to controversy between him and his Sunni opponents in Qayrawan. Further investigation will undoubtedly add to our knowledge of *al-Wuṣūl*; the evidence thus far provides the following sketch of the work's contents:

1. Introduction.
2. Consensus.
3. The Invalidity of *Taqlīd*.
4. The Invalidity of Legal Analogy.
5. The Invalidity of *Istiḥsān*.
6. *Istidlāl*.
7. The Invalidity of *Ijtihād*.
8. General and Particular Scriptural Texts.
9. Prophetic Sunnah.

This sketch, despite its limitations, suggests that *al-Wuṣūl* was a comprehensive manual of jurisprudence.

The material attributed to Ibn Dā'ūd gives some indication that he was responding to or drawing on earlier works of jurisprudence and provides a picture, albeit limited, of the state of the genre when he wrote. In two of the passages, al-Qāḍī al-Nu'mān reports that Ibn Dā'ūd is presenting the doctrine of his father Dā'ūd al-Ẓāhirī himself (pp. 101, 202). In addition, al-Qāḍī al-Nu'mān writes "others said" at the beginning of passage I and "they said" four times in passages VIII and five times in passage IX, all of which are clearly attributed to Ibn Dā'ūd. The use of the plural pronoun probably indicates that Ibn Dā'ūd was relating here the opinion of his father and of the Ẓāhirīs in general rather than merely his own. This is particularly the case with passage IX, which al-Qāḍī al-Nu'mān ends with the statement, "This is the speech of Muḥammad b. Dā'ūd al-Baghdādī, following the doctrine of his father and his (father's) disciples [i.e., the Ẓāhirīs] and their arguments against those who uphold *ijtihād*" (p. 202). At the end of passage VIII, al-Qāḍī al-Nu'mān sums up, "This and the like of it are inference. This is the fundamental principle on which they built their doctrine" (p. 187). Here, and throughout the chapter on *istidlāl*, "they" presumably refers to the Ẓāhirīs in general. As mentioned above, Dā'ūd, the founder of the Ẓāhirī school of law, may himself have written a work on *uṣūl al-fiqh*, now lost, and his son may have been citing or referring to it.

In another passage, Ibn Dā'ūd refutes an argument of al-Shāfiʿī concerning the use of *ijtihād* in determining the *qiblah*. This is certainly a reference to al-Shāfiʿī's *Risālah*, for in the *Risālah*, al-Shāfiʿī uses this example as one of his main arguments for the permissibility of *ijtihād*. With Q 2:150, "From wherever you head out, turn your face toward the sacred mosque" as a basis, al-Shāfiʿī argues that when one cannot see the Kaʿbah, one must estimate its direction. For al-Shāfiʿī, this process of estimation is not only a legitimate means of determining the *qiblah* in that situation but also a legitimate model for the practice of *ijtihād* in all other circumstances where estimation is required.[72] Ibn Dā'ūd argues against this position that al-Shāfiʿī expounded in the *Risālah*. In addition, his remarks on consensus in passage I, referring to obvious matters of general consensus, may be seen as well as a response to a passage in the *Risālah*. Al-Shāfiʿī distinguishes between two types of knowledge, one of which is plain and apparent to all, both laymen and scholars, and the other of which is only understood by scholars.[73] This seems to be the text behind later distinctions between two types of consensus, the consensus of scholars and laymen alike, and the consensus of scholars alone.[74] In these instances, Ibn Dā'ūd's text responds to specific passages in *al-Risālah*.

A passage cited by the famous Shāfiʿī jurist al-Juwaynī shows that Ibn Dā'ūd dealt quite directly with a key feature of al-Shāfiʿī's *Risālah*, probably also in *al-Wuṣūl ilā maʿrifat al-uṣūl*. Al-Juwaynī's work *al-Burhān fī uṣūl al-fiqh* is, to the best of my knowledge, the only extant manual of jurisprudence that attempts to reconcile the organization of al-Shāfiʿī's *Risālah* with that of the standard *uṣūl al-fiqh* genre. That he does this is not surprising, since he also wrote a commentary on

---

[72] Hallaq, *Islamic Legal Theories*, 22–23; Lowry, *The Legal-Theoretical Content of the Risāla*, 206–7; Muḥammad b. Idrīs al-Shāfiʿī, *al-Risālah*, ed. Aḥmad Muḥammad Shākir (Cairo: Dār al-turāth, 1979), 487–90.

[73] al-Shāfiʿī, *al-Risālah*, 357–60.

[74] al-Khaṭīb al-Baghdādī, *Kitāb al-faqīh wa'l-mutafaqqih*, 2 vols., ed. Ismāʿīl al-Anṣārī (Beirut: Dār al-kutub al-ʿilmīyah, 1980), 1:172.

the *Risālah* itself. The contents of the *Burhān* are divided into five large chapters or sections:

1. Discussion of *al-bayān.*
2. Section on Consensus.
3. Section on Legal Analogy.
4. Section on the Marshalling of Evidence (*kitāb al-istidlāl*).
5. Section on the Weighing of Conflicting Evidence (*kitāb al-tarjīḥ*).

The striking element in this scheme is the first chapter, which adopts a key term from al-Shāfiʿī's *Risālah, al-bayān.* At the beginning of this section, al-Juwaynī presents al-Shāfiʿī's main statement on *al-bayān,* which provided the basis for the organization of the *Risālah.* Here he describes five levels (*martabah*) of *bayān,* which we may understand to mean, roughly, "how the text indicates legal rulings". This term is used to set out a five-part hermeneutic scheme showing how the law derives from the Koran and hadith and how conflicting injunctions in those texts may be reconciled. This use of the term *bayān* seems odd from the perspective of later jurisprudence, where *bayān* and *mubayyan* refer to a priori ambiguous texts which have been explained or clarified. Al-Juwaynī, however, uses *bayān* as a rubric for his first chapter, which deals with the interpretation of scriptural language. He thus subsumes under one chapter the framework of al-Shāfiʿī's *Risālah,* equating the material it covers with the discussions of scriptural language, such as abrogation, general and particular texts, commands and prohibitions, clarified and ambiguous texts, that had become standard divisions within the *uṣūl al-fiqh* genre.

After presenting al-Shāfiʿī's scheme, al-Juwaynī then quotes a comment by Ibn Dā'ūd:

> Abū Bakr b. Dā'ūd al-Iṣfahānī said, "Al-Shāfiʿī—may God have mercy on him!—ignored, among these levels, consensus, which is one of the principle indicators of the Law. If someone were to justify this, stretching the argument, by claiming that consensus indicates (the Law) when it is based on a report, so that (al-Shāfiʿī) made do with mentioning hadith reports, then (one would counter): Should he not have mentioned consensus first, and thereby obviated the need to mention legal analogy, because legal analogy depends on consensus? Wouldn't it have been more fitting to mention consensus, since it is higher than [i.e., logically prior to] legal analogy? Then legal analogy would fall under the contents of consensus. This objection could not be refuted."[75]

[75] Imām al-Ḥaramayn al-Juwaynī, *al-Burhān fī uṣūl al-fiqh,* 2 vols., ed. Ṣalāḥ b. Muḥammad b. ʿUwayḍah (Beirut: Dār al-kutub al-ʿilmīyah, 1997), 1:40–41.

Ibn Dā'ūd criticizes al-Shāfi'ī here for not following what had become by his own time the standard method of presenting *uṣūl al-fiqh*. He expects al-Shāfi'ī's statement to present a list of the *uṣūl* or *adillah*, the indicators of the law. When consensus does not appear in what Ibn Dā'ūd assumes to be a list of the indicators of the law, he interprets this as an error or failing. Ibn Dā'ūd's comment shows that al-Shāfi'ī's work became part of the *uṣūl al-fiqh* tradition before the tenth century, earlier than Hallaq supposes. Of the ninth century, Hallaq writes "It is curious, to say the least, that what is assumed to be the *uṣūl* equivalent of Aristotle's *Organon* should be thoroughly ignored in a century that is considered one of the most dynamic phases in Islam's intellectual history".[76] There are a number of indications that this may not have been the case. It is worth remarking that al-Ṣayrafī not only wrote his own commentary on the *Risālah* but also countered an earlier refutation of the *Risālah* by a certain secretary, 'Ubayd Allāh b. Ṭālib.[77] In addition, the Imāmī Shiite and Mu'tazilī theologian Abū Sahl al-Nawbakhtī (d. 311/924) wrote a refutation of the *Risālah*.[78] In light of Ibn Dā'ūd's discussion, the claims that al-Shāfi'ī's *Risālah* was totally ignored and met with "oblivion" during this period seem unwarranted. In addition, by Ibn Dā'ūd's time, the conception of *uṣūl al-fiqh* as an ordered list of indicators of the law was already so ingrained that any departure from this organizing principle met with great resistance. Furthermore, Ibn Dā'ūd and, no doubt, his contemporaries conceived already of al-Shāfi'ī's *Risālah* as a work of *uṣūl al-fiqh*, though they at the same time fundamentally misunderstood, or at least rejected, its organizing principles.

Al-Qāḍī al-Nu'mān is, on the whole, impressed with Ibn Dā'ūd's reasoning, and seems gratified to find a Sunni text that refutes a number of the Sunnis' fundamental arguments about principles of jurisprudence. He writes, approvingly, "This speaker spoke the truth

---

[76] Hallaq, "Shāfi'ī", 590.

[77] Ibn al-Nadīm, *Kitāb al-fihrist*, 267. The fact that no secretary by this name appears in the sources raises at least the possiblity that a copyist's error has occurred in the text. One is tempted to identify the author mentioned with a famous namesake from the period in question, 'Ubayd Allāh b. 'Abd Allāh b. Ṭāhir (d. 300/913), scion of the influential Ṭāhirid family who served as the governor of Baghdad and was known for his wide learning. See C. E. Bosworth, "The Ṭāhirids and Arabic Culture", *Journal of Semitic Studies* 14 (1969): 45–79, esp. pp. 71–77.

[78] Ibn al-Nadīm, *Kitāb al-fihrist*, 225; Wilferd Madelung, "Abū Sahl Nawbakhtī", *Encyclopaedia Iranica*.

and hit the mark in his statement and in presenting convincing proof against his opponent". (p. 152). Another laudatory comment reads, "We say to this speaker, 'You have debated your opponent excellently in what you have pointed out and indicated to him, regarding (the necessity of) abandoning legal analogy in God's Faith . . .'" (p. 154). At the end of a section arguing against legal analogy, he remarks, "This is some of the argument presented by a certain Sunni jurist who rejected legal analogy against those Sunnis who consider it valid. It contains excellent adduction of proof (*iḥtijāj ḥasan*)" (p. 175). Ibn Dā'ūd's dialectic skill in refuting his opponents' arguments, outstanding in this work, thus earns praise from al-Qāḍī al-Nuʿmān on several occasions. This corroborates what we are told in the biographical sources of Ibn Dā'ūd's impressive skill in disputation. The style of Ibn Dā'ūd's work differs radically from that found in al-Shāfiʿī's work and reflects the extensive incorporation of formal dialectic into the genre.

We are indebted to al-Qāḍī al-Nuʿmān for preserving so much of Ibn Dā'ūd's work primarily because their works shared so much in intent and conception. Both aimed to disprove or invalidate many of the methodological principles that the Sunni jurists had adopted as fundamental elements of their theories of legal interpretation. Because so much material related in *Ikhtilāf uṣūl al-madhāhib* derives from Ibn Dā'ūd's work, we may hazard a guess that the overall organization of the former owes a great deal to that of the latter. For this reason especially, it seems abundantly clear that Ibn Dā'ūd's work, like *Ikhtilāf uṣūl al-madhāhib*, presupposes an existing genre of *uṣūl al-fiqh*. That this is so has to do with the conservative nature of generic conventions in legal literature as in many other fields. We have already mentioned how the work of al-Qāḍī al-Nuʿmān, though critical of and written against the Sunni science of *uṣūl al-fiqh*, nevertheless reflects the structure of that science as formulated by Sunni jurists. It is only natural that refutations end up reflecting the structures of the works they criticize. Ibn Dā'ūd was arguing against works which upheld *qiyās, istiḥsān*, and *ijtihād* and contained separate chapters on *ijmāʿ, qiyās, istiḥsān*, and *ijtihād*, at the very least. If he were merely presenting his own legal methodology, there would be no need for chapters on legal analogy and *ijtihād*, but only consensus and *istidlāl*, in addition, one presumes, to chapters on various aspects of the language of the Koran and Sunnah. The same may be said for his father Dā'ūd's work on jurisprudence. Already when Dā'ūd, al-Ṭabarī, and Ibn Dā'ūd wrote, *uṣūl al-fiqh* was a sophisticated science presented in comprehensive manuals. Who wrote these manuals and how far back the tradition goes is still unclear, though one may state with confidence that they originated before the late ninth century, probably even before 233/848, by which time al-Jāḥiẓ had completed *Kitāb uṣūl al-futyā wa'l-aḥkām.*

Extrapolation from the contents of these works will provide an idea of the structure of the genre to which our ninth-century authors were responding.

Contents of Dā'ūd's Putative Manual of Jurisprudence:

1. Consensus.
2. Invalidity of *Taqlīd.*
3. Invalidity of Legal Analogy.
4. Traditions Transmitted by Single Authorities.
5. Traditions which Provide Certainty.
6. Incontrovertible Proof.
7. Particular and General Scriptural Texts.
8. Clarified and Ambiguous Scriptural Texts.

Chapters of al-Ṭabarī's *al-Bayān ʿan uṣūl al-aḥkām*:

1. Consensus.
2. Traditions Transmitted by Single Authorities.
3. Traditions whose Chains of Authority do not Reach the Prophet.
4. Abrogating and Abrogated Texts on Legal Rulings.
5. Ambiguous and Clarified Traditions.
6. Commands and Prohibitions.
7. The Acts of the Messenger.
8. Particular and General Scriptural Texts.
9. *Ijtihād.*
10. The Invalidity of Juristic Preference (*istiḥsān*).[79]

Chapters of Ibn Dā'ūd's *al-Wuṣūl ilā maʿrifat al-uṣūl*:

1. Introduction.
2. Consensus.
3. Invalidity of *Taqlīd.*
4. Invalidity of Legal Analogy.
5. Invalidity of Juristic Preference.
6. Inference (*Istidlāl*).
7. Invalidity of *Ijtihād.*
8. Prophetic Sunnah.
9. General and Particular Scriptural Texts.

[79] Yāqūt, *Muʿjam al-udabā'*, 18:74.

Using these three reconstructed tables of contents as a guide and eliminating the chapters on *istidlāl* on the grounds that they are a well-known Ẓāhirī innovation, the approximate contents of the pre-existing *uṣūl al-fiqh* genre are as follows:

1. Consensus.
2. Legal Analogy.
3. Juristic Preference.
4. *Ijtihād.*
5. Prophetic Sunnah.
6. *Taqlīd* or Opinions of the Companions.
7. Abrogating and Abrogated Scriptural Texts.
8. General and Particular Scriptural Texts.
9. Ambiguous and Clarified Scriptural Texts.

The excerpts of *al-Wuṣūl ilā maʿrifat al-uṣūl* leave no doubt as to the original author's polemic concern with *qiyās, ijtihād,* and *istiḥsān* and the energy he expended in refuting the methods of his opponents. It was above all this aspect of his work that attracted al-Qāḍī al-Nuʿmān, who appreciated being able to cite clever Sunni arguments against the methods of the Sunnis themselves. While Ibn Dā'ūd was arguing against a developed science of jurisprudence, al-Qāḍī al-Nuʿmān's excerpts unfortunately do not preserve references to his opponents by name except, perhaps, in the case of al-Shāfiʿī. Yāqūt's citation shows that Ibn Dā'ūd criticized Muḥammad b. Jarīr al-Ṭabarī in particular. Another possible opponent behind the diatribe against legal analogy is the famous Ibn Surayj. We know that Ibn Dā'ūd debated Ibn Surayj on numerous occasions. Ibn Surayj wrote a treatise arguing against Ibn Dā'ūd on legal analogy, *Kitāb fī al-radd ʿalā Ibn Dā'ūd fī al-qiyās*, and another refutation dealing with points where Ibn Dā'ūd disagreed with al-Shāfiʿī. Al-Subkī apparently had access to both of these works in the fourteenth century and describes the latter as copious and valuable (*ḥāfil nafīs*).[80]

In Hallaq's view, *uṣūl al-fiqh* came into existence after a "genuine synthesis . . . between rationalism and traditionalism" owed primarily to the influence of Ibn Surayj and his students. *Uṣūl al-fiqh*, one gathers from his presentation, did not and could not exist without the acceptance of the validity of *qiyās*.[81] Therefore, the works of the

[80] Tāj al-Dīn al-Subkī, *Ṭabaqāt al-shāfiʿīyah al-kubrā*, 10 vols., ed. ʿAbd al-Fattāḥ al-Ḥilw and Maḥmūd Muḥammad al-Ṭanāḥī (Cairo: Hajr, 1992), 3:23.
[81] Hallaq, *Islamic Legal Theories*, 32–35.

Ẓāhirīs Dā'ūd and Ibn Dā'ūd, who rejected *qiyās*, could not have been comprehensive presentations of *uṣūl al-fiqh*. On the contrary, however, the general acceptance of legal analogy as one of the key sources of Islamic jurisprudence was the result of an historical debate which took place within the genre of *uṣūl al-fiqh*. The tradition of manuals on the subject most likely predated the compromise or synthesis of which Hallaq speaks. Al-Jaṣṣāṣ, for example, omits the opinions of Ibn Dā'ūd on purpose on the grounds that he was incapable of performing *qiyās*,[82] but this had not always been the case. Even in the eleventh century, the opponents of legal analogy were not entirely marginalized. Shiite jurists such as al-Qāḍī al-Nu'mān and the Twelvers al-Shaykh al-Mufīd (d. 413/1022), al-Sharīf al-Murtaḍā (d. 436/1044), and al-Shaykh al-Ṭūsī (d. 460/1067) wrote against legal analogy in their manuals of *uṣūl al-fiqh*, but Sunni jurists as well, such as Ibn Ḥazm (d. 456/1064) and al-Khaṭīb al-Baghdādī (d. 463/1071), also wrote *uṣūl al-fiqh* works which severely restricted legal analogy as a valid method of discovering the law. As Bernard Weiss sums up, "It was not a foregone conclusion among medieval Muslim jurisprudents that analogy was to be counted among the indicators of the divine law, the instruments whereby the law became manifest".[83]

It is unlikely that Ibn Surayj was the only or even the principal innovator in the field of *uṣūl al-fiqh* against whom Dā'ūd, al-Ṭabarī, and Ibn Dā'ūd were arguing. This is particularly clear from the refutations of *istiḥsān* included in the works of al-Ṭabarī and Ibn Dā'ūd. *Istiḥsān* was generally rejected by the Shāfi'īs. Al-Shāfi'ī himself wrote a work entitled *Ibṭāl al-istiḥsān*, and to him is attributed the statement *man istaḥsana fa-qad sharra'a* ("He who adopts *istiḥsān* has legislated"), equating *istiḥsān* with a heretical usurpation of God's role as the sole determiner of the law.[84] From early on, *istiḥsān* was most strongly associated with jurists of the Ḥanafī tradition. Muḥammad b. al-Ḥasan al-Shaybānī (d. 189/804), Abū Ḥanīfah's disciple, wrote a work entitled *Kitāb al-istiḥsān*.[85] Later Ḥanafī jurists such as Abū

---

[82] Al-Jaṣṣāṣ, *al-Fuṣūl fī al-uṣūl*, 3:296.
[83] Bernard G. Weiss, *The Search for God's Law: Islamic Jurisprudence in the Writings of Sayf al-Dīn al-Āmidī* (Salt Lake City: Utah University Press, 1992), 633.
[84] al-Shāfi'ī, *al-Umm*, 8 vols. (Cairo: Dār al-fikr, 1990), 7:309–20; idem, *al-Risālah*, 503–8. Weiss, *The Search for God's Law*, 672.
[85] Ibn al-Nadīm, *al-Fihrist*, 257.

al-Ḥasan al-Karkhī upheld *istiḥsān*, and it became widely accepted in the Ḥanafī *madhhab*.[86] The fact that both al-Ṭabarī and Ibn Dā'ūd included a refutation of *istiḥsān* in their manuals of *uṣūl al-fiqh* suggests that they were not writing primarily or exclusively against Shāfiʿī opponents like Ibn Surayj. Rather, they must have been writing, at least in part, against earlier or contemporary jurists in the Ḥanafī tradition who upheld *istiḥsān*. This, coupled with the evidence presented above that al-Jāḥiẓ wrote a work on *uṣūl al-fiqh*, suggests that Ibn Surayj could not have founded the genre of *uṣūl al-fiqh*. Jurists associated with the Ḥanafī tradition must have played an important role in shaping the genre during the ninth century, though later biographical and legal sources, skewed quite heavily toward the Shāfiʿīs, have obscured this.

The Fatimid jurist al-Qāḍī al-Nuʿmān preserves in *Ikhtilāf uṣūl al-madhāhib* substantial portions of a manual on *uṣūl al-fiqh* by the renowned Ẓāhirī jurist Abū Bakr Muḥammad b. Dā'ūd. In all likelihood, these passages derive from the work *al-Wuṣūl ilā maʿrifat al-uṣūl*, which presented a comprehensive and sophisticated legal methodology, covering the topics of consensus, *taqlīd*, *istiḥsān*, *istidlāl*, and *ijtihād* in distinct chapters within a unified framework. The work probably dates to the late ninth century, some years after the death of Ibn Dā'ūd's father in 270/884. The evidence concerning this work, as well as works by al-Jāḥiẓ, Dā'ūd al-Ẓāhirī, and al-Ṭabarī, allows a revision of the view that Ibn Surayj's students were the first authors of *uṣūl al-fiqh* manuals. The two Ẓāhirīs and Muḥammad b. Jarīr al-Ṭabarī were not the creators of the genre either. All three were writing against others who had upheld *istiḥsān*, *ijtihād*, and legal analogy, and the most likely authors to have done so consistently were jurists in the Ḥanafī tradition.

Hallaq has argued that the science of jurisprudence, as formulated in a genre of works termed *uṣūl al-fiqh*, did not arise until the tenth

[86] On *istiḥsān* in general, see George Makdisi, "Ibn Taimīya's Autograph Manuscript on *Istiḥsān*: Materials for the Study of Islamic Legal Thought", in George Makdisi, ed., *Arabic and Islamic Studies in Honor of Hamilton A. R. Gibb* (Leiden: E. J. Brill, 1965), 446–79; John Makdisi, "Legal Logic and Equity in Islamic Law", *American Journal of Comparative Law* 33 (1985):63–92; Weiss, *The Search for God's Law*, 672–76; Hallaq, *Islamic Legal Theories*, 107–13; al-Jaṣṣāṣ, *al-Fuṣūl*, 4:223–52; Abū al-Ḥusayn al-Baṣrī, *al-Muʿtamad*, 2 vols. (Beirut: Dār al-kutub al-ʿilmīyah, 1983), 2:295–97; Ibn Ḥazm, *al-Iḥkām fī uṣūl al-aḥkām*, 2 vols. (Cairo: Dār al-ḥadīth, 1984), 2:192–226; al-Āmidī, *al-Iḥkām fī uṣūl al-aḥkām*, 4 vols. (Cairo, n.d.), 4:136–39.

century. He goes so far as to claim that the lack of literature on jurisprudence in the ninth century is "causally connected with the very development of legal theory, which was to emerge only as late as a century after al-Shāfiʿī's death".[87] On the contrary, it is more likely that the lack of literature on jurisprudence from this century is due particularly to the ravages of history. In jurisprudence, as in many other fields such as law, theology, and philosophy, very few works have survived intact from this period. It is reported that when al-Ṭabarī decided to write a comprehensive work on legal analogy, his bookseller, Abū al-Qāsim al-Ḥusayn b. Ḥubaysh, gathered over thirty titles devoted to the topic.[88] This anecdote gives some idea of the sheer number of legal works, the vast majority of which are now lost, that were produced before 310/923, al-Ṭabarī's death date. Similarly, of the over four hundred works attributed to Ibn Surayj, only a tiny fraction survives. Assiduously combing extant sources demonstrates the existence of a number of early works on *uṣūl al-fiqh*; we must assume that these represent only a handful among many lost works which have escaped mention.

Works on jurisprudence from later times preserve indications that the ninth century was a period of dynamic intellectual production in the field of legal theory, and it seems reasonable to see these indications as traces of sophisticated debates on legal theory originally presented in works now lost. One cannot take the fact the manuals themselves have not been preserved and have not been mentioned specifically in biographical dictionaries as proof that they did not exist. The opinions of such major ninth-century figures as ʿĪsā b. Abān (d. 221/835–36), al-Naẓẓām (d. 220–30/835–45), al-Karābīsī (d. 248/862–63), al-Jāḥiẓ (d. 255/869), Dā'ūd b. Khalaf al-Iṣfahānī (d. 270/883), and Abū ʿAlī al-Jubbā'ī (d. 303/915–16) are cited prominently in later works on *uṣūl al-fiqh*, a fact which suggests that they at one time made major contributions to the development of legal theory. Dialectic is one of *uṣūl al-fiqh*'s central features, and extant works in the genre, like an archive, preserve, sometimes in vestigial form, the historical debates which played a role in its com-

[87] Hallaq, *Islamic Legal Theories*, 36.

[88] As it turns out, al-Ṭabarī never actually completed the work, and the books were returned. Yāqūt, *Muʿjam al-buldān*, 18:81.

position. The opinions of earlier authorities such as al-Jāḥiẓ, Dā'ūd, al-Karābīsī, and others are not included simply as straw men representing heretical theories or positions which should be rejected,[89] but rather as a record of the debates which shaped the science and gave it its present form. After having passed through the wringer of the tradition for two or more centuries, their contributions have dwindled radically to a few odd statements. Nevertheless, the fact that they continue to be cited in the tradition suggests the possibility that they derive from works in the *uṣūl al-fiqh* genre and have been preserved in part for that reason.

The structure of *al-Wuṣūl ilā maʿrifat al-uṣūl* shows a close affinity with the later genre of *uṣūl al-fiqh* and is at the same time quite distant from that of al-Shāfiʿī's *Risālah*. Despite the place of honor assigned to it by the later tradition, al-Shāfiʿī's work could not have begun the *uṣūl al-fiqh* genre as evident in *al-Wuṣūl* and later extant works, and indeed seems outside the main lines of development of the genre. This is particularly so if one looks at its organization, which does not present a list of *uṣūl*. The genre of *uṣūl al-fiqh* did not arise, though, only after the turn of the tenth century, its first authors were not students of Ibn Surayj, and the genre as a whole did not result from a compromise between rationalism and traditionalism engineered primarily by Ibn Surayj himself. *Al-Wuṣūl ilā maʿrifat al-uṣūl* was one of many *uṣūl al-fiqh* works authored in the ninth century. Its contents, as well as those of al-Ṭabarī's *al-Bayān ʿan uṣūl al-aḥkām*, suggest that numbers of works were written before them by jurists outside the circle of Ibn Surayj. *Uṣūl al-fiqh* was created and developed during the ninth century, and its roots may indeed go back to al-Shāfiʿī's time. Only further investigation of such early works will allow us to understand the rise of the *uṣūl al-fiqh* genre and the development of Islamic jurisprudence in this crucial, formative period.

---

89 Hallaq, "Shafiʿi", 588.

12

EARLY *IJTIHĀD* AND THE LATER CONSTRUCTION OF AUTHORITY

Wael Hallaq

I

The creation of an archetype, i.e., an ideal authoritative model or standard to which all other types must conform or emulate, is undeniably a prime concern of juristic typologies. In the case of Islamic law, this archetype is the absolute *mujtahid* whose legal knowledge, presumed to be all-encompassing and wholly creative, is causally connected with the founding of a school. The school is not only named after him, but he is purported to have been its originator. The comprehensive and wide-ranging knowledge attributed to the absolute *mujtahid* is matched only by his assumed in-depth knowledge of, among other things, legal methodology or *uṣūl al-fiqh* (which is by necessity of his own creation), Quranic exegesis, *ḥadīth* criticism, the theory of abrogation, legal language, positive and substantive law, arithmetic, and the science of juristic disagreement.

The salient feature of the founders' *ijtihād*ic activity is no doubt the direct confrontation with the revealed texts, for it is only this deified involvement with the divine word that requires and presupposes thorough familiarity with so many important fields of knowledge. Even when certain cases require reasoning on the basis of established legal rules and derivative principles, the founding jurist's hermeneutic is held to be, in the final analysis, thoroughly grounded in the revealed texts. The founder's doctrine constitutes therefore the only purely juristic manifestation of the legal potentiality of revealed language. Without it, in other words, revelation would remain just that, revelation, lacking any articulation in it of the legal element. His doctrine lays claim to originality not only because it derives directly from the texts, but also because it is gleaned systematically, by means of clearly identifiable principles, from these sources. Its systematic character is seen as a product of a unified and cohesive methodology which only the founder could have forged; but a methodology, it must be asserted, that is itself inspired and dictated by revelation.

Now, what is striking about this typological conception of the founder *mujtahid* is its absoluteness not only in terms of credentials or epistemic, and indeed moral, authority,[1] but also in terms of chronological rupture with antecedents. At the juncture of this rupture, the precise point at which the most accomplished type of *mujtahid* is formed, the typology suffers from a memory loss, overlooking in the process the existence in reality of the founder's predecessors and his own immediate intellectual history. For it was with the latter that the *mujtahid*–imams formed a continuity, and of the former that they were necessarily a product. In the constructed typology, as perceived by the later legal profession, the founders became disconnected from previous generations of jurists as well as from a variety of historical processes that indeed culminated in the very achievements of the imams.[2]

II

The following pages argue that this rupture did in fact take place and that it was certainly strategic and by no means fortuitous. As jurists, the founding fathers were highly accomplished, but not as absolutely and as categorically as they were made out to be. Dissociating them from the achievements of their past was only one of many ways to increase their prestige and augment the resumé of their accomplishments. But

[1] That the founders' authority also contained a strong moral element is abundantly attested by the *manāqib* literature. See, for instance, Aḥmad b. Ḥusayn Abū Bakr al-Bayhaqī, *Manāqib al-Shāfiʿī*, ed. Aḥmad Ṣaqr, 2 vols. (Cairo: Maktabat Dār al-Turāth, 1971), I, 260–385, 486–550, and passim; Shams al-Dīn Muḥammad b. Muḥammad al-Rāʿī, *Intiṣār al-Faqīr al-Sālik li-Tarjīḥ Madhhab al-Imām Mālik*, ed. Muḥammad Abū al-Ajfān (Beirut: Dār al-Gharb al-Islāmī, 1981), 139 ff., 167 ff., 173 ff.; Muḥammad b. Yūsuf al-Ṣāliḥī, *ʿUqūd al-Jummān fī Manāqib al-Imām al-Aʿẓam Abī Ḥanīfa al-Nuʿmān* (Hyderabad: Maṭbaʿat al-Maʿārif, 1394/1974), 211–31, 239–96. On epistemic and moral authority, see sources cited in the preface, n. 1.

[2] Shams al-Dīn b. Shihāb al-Dīn al-Ramlī, *Nihāyat al-Muḥtāj ilā Sharḥ al-Minhāj*, 8 vols. (Cairo: Muṣṭafā Bābī al-Ḥalabī, 1357/1938; repr. Beirut: Dār Iḥyā' al-Turāth al-ʿArabī, 1939), I, 41, reports, on the authority of Ibn al-Ṣalāḥ, that none other than the four imams may be followed, either in the issuing of *fatwās* or in courtroom litigation. Representing the authority of school affiliation, this opinion of Ibn al-Ṣalāḥ became widely accepted by many later jurists of all four schools. Ḥaṭṭāb, *Mawāhib al-Jalīl*, I, 30, quotes Ibn al-Ṣalāḥ's statement and enhances it with another by Ghazālī (p. 31) who declares the founders' and schools' legal doctrines superior to those of earlier jurists. See also ʿAbd al-Raḥmān b. Muḥammad Bāʿalawī, *Bughyat al-Mustarshidīn fī Talkhīṣ Fatāwā baʿḍ al-A'imma min al-ʿUlamā' al-Muta'akhkhirīn* (Cairo: Muṣṭafā Bābī al-Ḥalabī, 1952), 274.

it was perhaps the only way to construct their supreme authority. True, they were *mujtahids* – or some of them were, at any rate – but not without qualification and certainly not absolutely. We shall try to show that none of them exercised *ijtihād* across the board, in each and every case they addressed or opinion they held. Indeed, we shall attempt to demonstrate that many of the opinions they held were inherited from other authorities.

Let us begin with Ḥanafism. In this school, and wholly in line with Ibn Kamāl's typology as we earlier outlined it,[3] the limits of hermeneutical activity were set by the imposition of a hierarchical taxonomy of legal authority,[4] at the top of which stood the doctrines of Abū Ḥanīfa (d. 150/767) and, immediately following, those of Abū Yūsuf (d. 182/798) and Shaybānī (d. 189/804).[5] Embodied in written narratives, these doctrines, known as *ẓāhir al-riwāya*, were transmitted through several channels by trustworthy and highly qualified jurists. A marginal number of cases (*masā'il*) belonging to the category of *ẓāhir al-riwāya* were also attributed to Zufar and al-Ḥasan b. Ziyād, two of Abū Ḥanīfa's foremost students.[6] Now, these doctrines were deemed binding, and no later *mujtahid*, however qualified he may have been, was permitted to reinterpret or diverge from them. For the Ḥanafites, they represented not only the highest authority in the school, but were chronologically the earliest. Some doctrines belonging to the later *mujtahids* were also deemed authoritative, but, in theory at least, they were second in prestige and were interpreted in light of the principles that Abū Ḥanīfa and his two distinguished students elaborated.[7]

Despite the authority which Abū Ḥanīfa carried as the eponym and ultimate founder of the school, its jurists could not wholly deny the

[3] Chapter 1, section IV, above.

[4] Fakhr al-Dīn Ḥasan b. Manṣūr al-Ūzajandī Qāḍīkhān, *Fatāwā Qāḍīkhān*, printed on the margins of *al-Fatāwā al-Hindiyya*, ed. and comp. al-Shaykh al-Niẓām et al., 6 vols., as vols. I–III (repr.; Beirut: Dār Iḥyā' al-Turāth al-ʿArabī, 1400/1980), I, 3; Wael B. Hallaq, "From *Fatwās* to *Furūʿ*: Growth and Change in Islamic Substantive Law," *Islamic Law and Society*, 1 (February 1994): 39.

[5] The fact that in terms of hierarchical authority Abū Ḥanīfa stood first did not mean that his opinion had precedence in all cases. When, for example, the two disciples held the same view, and the master held another, the jurist was allowed to adopt the opinion of the disciples. See ʿUmar b. ʿAbd al-ʿAzīz al-Ḥusām al-Shahīd Ibn Māza, *Sharḥ Adab al-Qāḍī*, ed. Abū al-Wafā al-Afghānī and Muḥammad Hāshimī (Beirut: Dār al-Kutub al-ʿIlmiyya, 1414/1994), 20. For various Ḥanafite opinions on the matter, see Ibn ʿĀbidīn, *Sharḥ al-Manẓūma*, 14 ff.

[6] On ranking the five Ḥanafite masters in terms of hierarchical doctrinal authority, see ʿAlā' al-Dīn Muḥammad ʿAlī al-Ḥaṣkafī (al-ʿAlā'ī), *al-Durr al-Mukhtār*, printed with Ibn ʿĀbidīn's *Ḥāshiya*, I, 70–71.

[7] Ibn ʿĀbidīn, *Ḥāshiya*, I, 70 ff.

obvious fact that Ḥanafite law, as it originated with Abū Ḥanīfa, owes a certain debt to his predecessors.[8] But this debt and the legal doctrine that it represented carried no real authority. In fact, the authorities from whom Abū Ḥanīfa appropriated his doctrine never formally entered into the orbit of authoritative doctrine, as schematized in the hierarchy of Ḥanafite law. As we have seen, the highest authoritative form of this law *begins* with Abū Ḥanīfa, not with anyone earlier. Furthermore, it is to be stressed that this recognition of indebtedness to the past was highly nominal, originating as it did in the desire to increase the founder's prestige and authority by the construction and articulation of a pedigree extending back, through the Followers and Companions, to the Prophet. Nevertheless, there is much historical truth to this construction. The Ḥanafite jurists articulated a genealogy, elegantly stated in both prose and verse, indicating the extent of Abū Ḥanīfa's debt: *Fiqh*, they said, "was planted by ᶜAbd Allāh Ibn Masᶜūd, irrigated by ᶜAlqama, harvested by Ibrāhīm al-Nakhaᶜī, threshed by Ḥammād, milled by Abū Ḥanīfa, kneaded by Abū Yūsuf, and baked by Shaybānī. The Muslims are nourished by his bread."[9]

The real debt owed to pre-Ḥanafite sources, on the one hand, and the construction of Abū Ḥanīfa's authority, on the other, created in Ḥanafism a serious doctrinal conflict. This conflict manifested itself in the emergence of a duality of doctrinal orientation. In a report classified as having the highest authority in the school, Abū Ḥanīfa is said to have remarked: "I refuse to follow (*uqallidu*) the Followers because they were men who practiced *ijtihād* and I am a man who practices *ijtihād*" (the Followers in this case being his immediate predecessors). Yet in another report which was relegated, in terms of authority, to a secondary status, Abū Ḥanīfa is said to have maintained the opposite view, accepting in particular the doctrines of the senior authorities among the Followers.[10]

These two contradictory reports raise a couple of important issues. The first is what their ranking was in terms of school authority. The anti-*taqlīd* position of the Followers emerged as superior to the other, a fact which attests to the dominance of the authority-construction process

[8] See, for instance, Abū Muḥammad Maḥmūd b. Aḥmad al-ᶜAynī, *al-Bināya fī Sharḥ al-Hidāya*, 12 vols. (Beirut: Dār al-Fikr, 1980), I, 52, who argues that the later commentators understood Marghīnānī's phrase "early reasoners" (*awā'il al-mustanbiṭīn*) to refer to Abū Ḥanīfa and his two students. He argues that the phrase was meant in a general way so as to include jurists earlier than Abū Ḥanīfa.

[9] Ibn ᶜAbidīn, *Ḥāshiya*, I, 49–50. The verse runs as follows: "*al-fiqhu zarᶜu bni Masᶜūdi wa-ᶜAlqamatu / ḥaṣṣāduhu thumma Ibrāhīmu dawwāsu; Nuᶜmānu ṭāḥinuhu Yaᶜqūbu ᶜājinuhu / Muḥammadun khābizu wal-ākilu al-nāsu.*"

[10] Ibn Māza, *Sharḥ Adab al-Qāḍī*, 19.

over acknowledgment of the debt to predecessors. The second is the relationship between these positions, on the one hand, and Abū Ḥanīfa's substantive law, on the other. The later Ḥanafites argued that the second position justified Abū Ḥanīfa's debt to the generation that immediately preceded him; whereas the first showed that when his opinions were identical to those held by the predecessors, it was because his otherwise independent *ijtihād* corresponded with theirs. It was further argued that this correspondence enhanced Abū Ḥanīfa's opinions and lent them added support and authority.[11] The focus, therefore, is Abū Ḥanīfa: authority resided in him however things might turn out, and whether or not he owed his predecessors any debt. If he adopted none of their opinions, then his authority as an independent *mujtahid* and a founder was categorically confirmed, and if he did in fact adopt them, then due to the authority bestowed upon him by Followers such as Nakhaʿī (d. 96/714) and Ḥammād (d. 120/737), his authority as a *mujtahid* who reached conclusions identical to his predecessors was also confirmed.

As Abū Ḥanīfa's teacher, Ḥammād figures prominently in the former's doctrine. He, and to a lesser extent several others, appear either as links to earlier authorities, or as the ultimate reference. In a certain case pertaining to prayer, for instance, Abū Ḥanīfa explicitly adopts Ḥammād's opinion as his own.[12] The list of his indebtedness to Ḥammād can run long.[13] In another case involving prayer under threat (*ṣalāt al-khawf*), he espouses Nakhaʿī's opinion, which the latter seems to have inherited in his turn from ʿAbd Allāh Ibn ʿAbbās (d. 68/687).[14] As a matter of interest, we should also note that Ibn Abī Laylā (d. 148/765), another presumably absolute *mujtahid* and an Iraqian authority, disagrees with Abū Ḥanīfa and upholds ʿAṭā' b. Rabāḥ's opinion.[15] Here, both *mujtahids* defer to earlier authorities. In addition to Ḥammād and Ibrāhīm al-Nakhaʿī, ʿAbd Allāh b. Jaʿfar appears, to a lesser extent, as one of Abū Ḥanīfa's authorities.[16] Likewise, Ibn Abī Laylā's *ijtihād*ic authorities include al-Ḥakam, the Medinese jurists, and even Abū Ḥanīfa himself.[17] In a case involving preemption, for instance, he first adopted Abū Ḥanīfa's view then renounced it in favor of another opinion held by the Hijazi

[11] Ibid.
[12] Muḥammad b. Idrīs al-Shāfiʿī, *Kitāb Ikhtilāf al-ʿIrāqiyyīn*, in his *al-Umm*, ed. Maḥmūd Maṭarjī, 9 vols. (Beirut: Dār al-Kutub al-ʿIlmiyya, 1413/1993), VII, 211.
[13] See, for instance, ibid., VII, 184–85 (a case of *wadīʿa*), 218, 219 (cases of prayer), 223 (ritual purity), 230 (blood-money), and passim.
[14] Ibid., VII, 214.
[15] Ibid. ʿAṭā' b. Rabāḥ (d. 114 or 115/732 or 733) was a Meccan jurist.
[16] See, e.g., ibid., VII, 237. [17] Ibid., VII, 176, 218, 227, 233.

jurists.[18] Abū Yūsuf, a companion of Abū Ḥanīfa and a student of his, also espoused certain of Ibn Abī Laylā's opinions.[19] In two penal cases, Shaybānī espouses opinions originally held by Nakhaʿī and Ḥammād, but apparently passed on to him by Abū Ḥanīfa.[20]

Abū Yūsuf's and Shaybānī's doctrines can thus be attributed to three distinctly different sources: Abū Ḥanīfa's *ijtihād*ic teachings, the inherited tradition of other, mainly earlier, jurists, and their own *ijtihād*. Since both authorities were considered by the Ḥanafite school as carrying nearly equal weight to that of Abū Ḥanīfa himself, it becomes obvious that the latter cannot, in reality, be considered the school's actual founder. He owed as much, or nearly as much, to his predecessors as his two distinguished students owed to him. He was no more a founder or even an absolute *mujtahid* than were his immediate predecessors and younger contemporaries, such as Abū Yūsuf, Shaybānī, and al-Ḥasan b. Ziyād.

The evolution of Abū Ḥanīfa's authority as the most important figure in the school is best exemplified in the transformation that took place in the case of the tithe levied on cultivated land. Abū Yūsuf reports on the authority of Ibrāhīm al-Nakhaʿī, through Ḥammād, that whatever grows on land, however small or large, is subject to a tithe. Abū Yūsuf then adds that Abū Ḥanīfa adopted this opinion (*kāna Abū Ḥanīfa ya'khudh bi-hādhā al-qawl*).[21] The later jurist Sarakhsī presents the matter as follows:

> The basis of the duty to pay tithe is God's statement [2:267]: "Spend of the good things which ye have earned, and of that which we bring forth from the earth for you." The meaning of "earned" is material wealth on which the alms-tax is paid. The meaning of the statement "that which we bring forth from the earth for you" is tithe. God also said [6:142]: "And pay the due thereof upon the harvest day." Likewise, the Prophet said: "Whatever land produces is subject to tithe."

[18] Ibid., VII, 176.

[19] Ibid., VII, 230. Abū Yūsuf's authority was likewise constructed by means of making him the only teacher of al-Ḥusayn b. Ḥafṣ who is reported to have introduced Ḥanafism to Iṣfahān, when in fact the latter studied under twenty-three scholars. Abū Yūsuf thus becomes the sole authority from which Iṣfahānī Ḥanafism was derived. Moreover, al-Ḥusayn studied only *ḥadīth* with Abū Yūsuf, but later sources claim the latter to have been his teacher of law. See N. Tsafrir, "The Beginnings of the Ḥanafī School in Iṣfahān," *Islamic Law and Society*, 5, 1 (1998): 2–3.

[20] Muḥammad b. al-Ḥasan al-Shaybānī, *Kitāb al-Aṣl al-Maʿrūf bil-Mabsūṭ*, ed. Abū al-Wafā al-Afghānī, 5 vols. (Beirut: ʿĀlam al-Kutub, 1990), IV, 439, 477. For other cases where Abū Yūsuf and Shaybānī followed the opinions of the Medinese and other jurists, see Ibn ʿĀbidīn, *Sharḥ al-Manẓūma*, 1–53, at 31; Ibn ʿĀbidīn, *Ḥāshiya*, I, 75.

[21] Yaʿqūb b. Ibrāhīm Abū Yūsuf, *Kitāb al-Kharāj* (Beirut and Cairo: Dār al-Sharq, 1405/1985), 158.

> Abū Ḥanīfa's principle is that whatever grows in gardens and is meant to be cultivated of the land is subject to tithe, be it cereals, legumes, dates, herbs, chlorophyta (*wasma*), saffron, roses or dyeing plants (*wars*).[22] This is also the opinion of Ibn ʿAbbās. It is reported that when he was governor of Baṣra, he imposed the tithe on legumes, levying one measuring unit out of ten. Abū Ḥanīfa rationalized this opinion by the general Prophetic tradition "Whatever the heavens water and whatever the land produces is subject to tithe." He held the opinion that tithe, like *kharāj*, is an encumbrance on cultivable land. Just as the development of the land gives rise to the levy of *kharāj*, so does it give rise to tithe.[23]

Note here that Nakhaʿī, who appears in Abū Yūsuf as the original, authoritative source of the doctrine, has been entirely removed from Sarakhsī's reconstruction, and instead replaced by a cluster of revealed statements supplemented by the authority of Ibn ʿAbbās, a Companion. The function of inserting this authority subsequent to the Quranic and Apostolic citations is to give the otherwise unspecific and highly general stipulations of the Quran a clearly defined and precise meaning, a meaning that is determined by Ibn ʿAbbās's concrete practice. Thus, the latter's supplementary report is an exegetical exercise which permits the clarification and delimitation of the legal significance of the two Quranic verses.

In this passage, two more points are to be noted: on the one hand, there is a presentation of the revealed subject matter together with Sarakhsī's annotation; on the other, there is Abū Ḥanīfa and his opinion. The logical sequence of how authority proceeds directly from revelation to Abū Ḥanīfa's reasoning (partly manifested in the analogy with *kharāj*) becomes crystal clear. In this exercise of authority reconstruction, Sarakhsī erases the debt to Nakhaʿī, thereby dissipating the latter's authority altogether. Abū Ḥanīfa, on the other hand, emerges as the first and direct interpreter of revelation par excellence, a necessary condition of an absolute *mujtahid* and founder of a school.

At this juncture, a natural question poses itself perforce: Why did Abū Ḥanīfa – not Nakhaʿī, Ḥammād, or, for that matter, Abū Yūsuf or Shaybānī – become credited with founding the school, and henceforth achieve the status of an absolute *mujtahid*? A comprehensive answer cannot be offered at this point in time, especially as to the choice of Abū Ḥanīfa as putative founder of his school (or the choice of any of the other

[22] The *wasma* and *wars* are south Arabian plants whose leaves are used as dyes, the former imparting a green pigment and the latter a yellow one. See Jamāl al-Dīn Ibn Manẓūr, *Lisān al-ʿArab*, 15 vols. (repr.; Beirut: Dār Ṣādir, 1972), VI, 254, XII, 637.

[23] Muḥammad b. Aḥmad Abū Sahl al-Sarakhsī, *al-Mabsūṭ*, 30 vols. (Cairo: Maṭbaʿat al-Saʿāda, 1324–31/1906–12), III, 2.

presumed founders), given the state of our present knowledge. But it is fairly clear that Abū Ḥanīfa's rise to a status of founder had to do with the emergence of the concept of authority in law. In view of the near total aloofness of the state and of any of its organs from the domain of law, legal authority had to be anchored in a source, and this source was the arch-jurist as an individual legal personality. In other words, we cannot at this juncture explain why Abū Ḥanīfa specifically and the other eponyms were chosen to play the role of founder, but we do know that they fulfilled the requirements that were imposed by the idea of legal authority. In the case of Abū Ḥanīfa, he certainly emerged as an authority *ex post facto*; this is attested in a revealing remark made by Jāḥiẓ to the effect that Abū Ḥanīfa rose to importance after having virtually been a *persona non grata* (*ʿaẓuma sha'nuhu baʿda khumūlihi*).[24] It is significant that Jāḥiẓ, who died in 255/868, was, in terms of chronology, sufficiently close to the realities of Abū Ḥanīfa's immediate successors to be considered by us a reliable observer, and too early to have succumbed to the ideological biases of authority construction that developed in the period after him. Jāḥiẓ's evidence is bolstered by the credible testimony of ʿAbd al-Raḥmān b. Mahdī who, around the very end of the second century A.H. (800–820 A.D.), observed that the most distinguished jurists of his time were Sufyān al-Thawrī, Mālik, Ḥammād b. Zayd, and ʿAbd Allāh Ibn al-Mubārak.[25] Abū Ḥanīfa is conspicuously absent from this list.

The lack of any work by Abū Ḥanīfa himself, and the improvements and virtually indistinguishable contributions made by his two students on his behalf, makes Abū Ḥanīfa a difficult case study. In this respect, Mālik b. Anas (d. 179/795), the eponym of the Mālikite school, provides a better illustration of the process by which an early jurist was subsequently made an absolute *mujtahid* and a founder.

In the *Muwaṭṭa'*, Mālik himself is primarily a transmitter of earlier or contemporary doctrine, particularly the consensus of the Medinese jurists.[26] In certain instances though he maintains his own opinion, especially, one gathers, when the Quran or Prophetic Sunna elaborates

[24] Abū ʿUthmān ʿAmr b. Baḥr al-Jāḥiẓ, *Rasā'il*, ed. ʿAbd al-Salām Hārūn, 2 vols. (Cairo: Maktabat al-Khānjī, 1964), II, 272.

[25] Abū Isḥāq Ibrāhīm b. ʿAlī al-Shīrāzī, *Ṭabaqāt al-Fuqahā'*, ed. Iḥsān ʿAbbās (Beirut: Dār al-Rā'id al-ʿArabī, 1970), 94.

[26] Mālik was under the influence of several leading jurists, including Ibn Shihāb al-Zuhrī, Ibn Hurmuz, Zayd b. Aslam, Abū al-Zinād, Abū al-Aswad Yatīm ʿUrwa, Ayyūb al-Sikhtyānī, Rabīʿa b. Abī ʿAbd al-Raḥmān, Yaḥyā b. Saʿīd al-Anṣārī, Mūsā b. ʿUqba, and Muḥammad b. ʿAjlān. Shams al-Dīn Muḥammad Ibn Farḥūn, *al-Dībāj al-Mudhahhab fī Maʿrifat Aʿyān ʿUlamā' al-Madhhab* (Beirut: Dār al-Kutub al-ʿIlmiyya, 1417/1996), 79–80.

certain legal themes. An example in point is the issue of a woman's right to inheritance within the family. Here Mālik renders his own opinion while relying on the Quran and Prophetic Sunna.[27] Less frequently do we find him formulating legal norms on the basis of Prophetic Sunna alone.[28] In still other instances, Mālik can be found to espouse an opinion with neither the textual evidence nor legal reasoning in justification of the opinion.[29] Even if we assume that such opinions were his own, that is, that they were reached by him through *ijtihād* – an assumption, we shall see, that is largely unwarranted – it remains the case that the totality of these opinions is comparatively marginal in the *Muwaṭṭa'*.

It is often clear that not all opinions stated by Mālik in the *Muwaṭṭa'* are his own,[30] although it is also often the case that the picture is not very clear. In certain instances, Mālik is made to state opinions that initially seem to be his, when it later transpires that they are not. In a case pertaining to alms-tax, for instance, Mālik states an opinion which he later qualifies with the formula "This is the best I have heard."[31] Were it not the best he had heard, it is highly probable that he would have avoided making any remark. Similarly, in a case involving preemption, an opinion is introduced by the oft-used formula "Mālik said" (*qāla Mālik*). Having stated the opinion, Mālik falls silent, and Yaḥyā, the most renowned transmitter and narrator of the *Muwaṭṭa'*,[32] interjects himself with another *qāla Mālik* formula that is followed by yet another of Mālik's common formulas, namely, "This is the opinion which we hold" (*wa-hādhā al-amr ʿindanā*).[33] Of special importance in this phrase is the last word, *ʿindanā*, which is in the plural and which refers to the Hijazi jurists in general and the Medinese in particular. It turns out here too that the opinion is not Mālik's. The expression of a collective opinion varies in detail and

27 Mālik b. Anas, *al-Muwaṭṭa'* (Beirut: Dār al-Jīl, 1414/1993), 462.

28 Ibid., 467. For a detailed study of the *Muwaṭṭa'*'s hierarchy of doctrine, see Yasin Dutton, *The Origins of Islamic Law: The Qur'an, the Muwaṭṭa' and Medinan ʿAmal* (Richmond: Curzon, 1999).

29 E.g. ibid., 452, 461, 464, 756, and passim.

30 This is consistent with the well-known and oft-quoted report that Mālik refrained from giving, or at least was reluctant to offer, his own opinions on all questions addressed to him: Ibn Farḥūn, *Dībāj*, 69–70. This reluctance is said to have been motivated by piety, but it is just as likely that it was due to the fact that Mālik did not always have an answer to give, much less his *own* answer. In this context, it is perhaps fruitful to compare this account with Mālik's own student, Ḥārith b. Asad, who did not issue *fatwās* because he, by his own admission, often did not know the answers: ibid., 176. What could be acknowledged in the case of Ḥārith, however, would have been unthinkable in that of Mālik, since an admission of ignorance would have flagrantly contradicted the epistemic authority so carefully built around him by his school.

31 Mālik, *Muwaṭṭa'*, 251, 267, 282, 771, and passim.

32 Ḥaṭṭāb, *Mawāhib al-Jalīl*, I, 6 (l. 14). 33 Mālik, *Muwaṭṭa'*, 624, also at 584.

emphasis, and the significance of these variations is not always clear.[34] The following statements illustrate its various uses:

1. "I have long observed jurists in our region follow this opinion."[35]
2. "This is what I heard from the jurists, and have long observed Muslims practice the matter in this manner in our midst."[36]
3. "This is the opinion which the jurists have been adopting in our midst."[37]
4. "The opinion on which we reached consensus, and which is not subject to disagreement, and which I have long observed the jurists follow in our region is . . ."[38]
5. "The opinion on which we have reached a consensus, and the *sunna* on which there is no disagreement, and what I have long observed the jurists follow in our region is . . ."[39]

Such statements refer to anonymous practice and agreement, without attaching to them the name of any particular jurist. They accompany no less than one-eighth (13 percent) of the opinions in *al-Muwaṭṭa'*, judging by an inventory of the chapter on sales, a rather important part of the work.[40] Our count furthermore shows that 27 percent of the opinions are attributed to earlier jurists, notably Saʿīd Ibn al-Musayyib, Yaḥyā b. Saʿīd, Ibn Shihāb, and Salmān b. Yasār.[41] Some 21 percent of the opinions are based on revealed texts, mostly Prophetic Sunna. The remainder, 39 percent, are opinions voiced by Mālik without authority, be it textual or personal. As we have seen earlier, we can in no way be sure that the source of such opinions is Mālik himself. This means that the corpus of Mālik's own opinions must be much smaller than 39 percent, and that both the *ḥadīth* and juristic material which he transmitted constitute far more than 61 percent of the *Muwaṭṭa*''s contents – that is, if we go by our statistical count in the chapter on sales. A random investigation of the rest of the *Muwaṭṭa'*, though admittedly impressionistic, tends to confirm this

34 Ibid., 245, 452, 453, 454, 455, 456, 458, 459, 460, 461, 463, 755, 756, 757, 759, 761, 763, 768, 769, and passim.

35 Ibid., 464: "*wa-ʿalā dhālika adraktu ahl al-ʿilm bi-baladinā.*"

36 Ibid., 688: "*fa-hādhā al-ladhī samiʿtu min ahl al-ʿilm wa-adraktu ʿamal al-nās ʿalā dhālika ʿindanā.*"

37 Ibid., 583: "*wa-hādhā al-amr al-ladhī lam yazal ʿalayhi al-nās ʿindanā.*"

38 Ibid., 459: "*al-amr al-mujtamaʿ ʿalayh ʿindanā al-ladhī lā ikhtilāfa fī-hi wal-ladhī adraktu ʿalayhi ahl al-ʿilm bi-baladinā . . .*"

39 Ibid., 463: "*al-amr al-mujtamaʿ ʿalayh ʿindanā wal-sunna al-latī lā ikhtilāfa fī-hā wal-ladhī adraktu ʿalayhi ahl al-ʿilm bi-baladinā . . .*"

40 Ibid., 539–93.

41 Ibid., 682, 684, 745, 747, 748, 750, 751, 752, 753, 758 (and passim, for Ibn al-Musayyib); 456, 676, 669, 680, 681, 743, 775 (and passim, for Ibn Saʿīd); 676, 743, 744, 746, 755 (and passim, for Ibn Shihāb); 456, 687, 744, 749, 753 (and passim, for Salmān b. Yasār).

estimate, which may in fact be overgenerous in its appraisal of Mālik's own contributions.

These results are substantially corroborated by Ibn Uways's report of Mālik's own, revealing explanation of what he attempted to do in the *Muwaṭṭa'*, a report that is in all likelihood authentic though seldom encountered in Mālikite works:

> Indeed, most of the contents of the book are not my opinions but rather those which I heard (*samāʿī*) from many leading scholars. Their opinions were so many that they overcame me (*ghalabū ʿalayya*). But their opinions are the ones which they took from the Companions, and I in turn took these opinions from these leading scholars. They are a legacy which devolved from one age to another till these times of ours. When I say "My opinion," so it is. [When I say] "The matter subject to agreement," it means that matter on which they [the scholars] reached a consensus. When I say "The matter as we have it," (*al-amr ʿindanā*) it means the matter which constitutes the practice in our midst and region, which jurists apply, and with which both laymen and scholars are familiar. When I say "Some scholars [held]," then it is an opinion that some scholars espoused and to which I am inclined. If I have not heard (*lam asmaʿ*) an opinion [on a matter] from them, then I exercise my *ijtihād* according to the doctrine of someone I have met, so that [my *ijtihād*] does not swerve from the ways (*madhhab*) of the Medinese. If [on a given matter] there is no opinion to be heard [at all], then I will formulate an opinion by conducting *ijtihād* on the basis of the Sunna and in accordance with the jurists' doctrines, as well as with the practices of our region since the time of the Prophet.[42]

These pronouncements cannot be unauthentic, not only because of the unlikely possibility that they would have been put with flagrant impunity in the mouth of Mālik by later jurists of the school, but also because they quite simply undermine the very authority giving structure to the school itself, which furthermore explains why these declarations did not gain much notoriety in Mālikite literature. Mālik himself admits his vast debt to the authority and legacy of the Medinese and his own predecessors, and this he does readily. It was his followers, especially during the period of the school's formation, who sought, consciously or not, to minimize this debt.

Now, in the space of slightly over half a century after Mālik's death, the Mālikite jurists succeeded in promoting Mālik to a status of a chief authority, a status that put him well on his way to being made the founder of the school. This process of what we term authority construc-

[42] Aḥmad Bābā al-Tinbaktī, *Nayl al-Ibtihāj bi-Taṭrīz al-Dībāj*, ed. ʿAbd al-Ḥamīd al-Harāma (Ṭarāblus, Libya: Kulliyyat al-Daʿwa al-Islāmiyya, 1989), 295–96; Ibn Farḥūn, *Dībāj*, 72–73.

tion manifests itself in the *Mudawwana*, a work associated with the name of ʿAbd al-Salām b. Saʿīd al-Tanūkhī, known as Saḥnūn (d. 240/854). In this work, Mālik appears as one of the foremost authorities on law. He is held up as the author of juristic doctrines and opinions, whether or not he truly formulated them himself. Surprisingly, many of the opinions in the *Muwaṭṭa'* which Mālik merely transmitted on the authority of his predecessors or anonymous contemporaries appear in the *Mudawwana* as his own. Consider the following examples:

1. "Yaḥyā told me that Mālik heard (*samiʿa*) that blood-money should be paid within the span of three or four years. Mālik said: Three years is the best I have heard concerning this matter."[43] It is obvious here that this is not Mālik's own opinion, though he quotes it quite approvingly. In the *Mudawwana*, the opinion becomes Mālik's: "Saḥnūn was asked: 'Over how many years should the blood-money be paid according to Mālik's opinion?' Saḥnūn said: 'In three years.'"[44]
2. "Yaḥyā told me that Mālik heard (*balaghahu*) that if the faculty of hearing in both ears is completely lost [due to injury], then the full blood-money is due." This opinion from the *Muwaṭṭa'*[45] is, again, clearly not formulated by Mālik himself. But in the *Mudawwana* it is transformed into Mālik's own opinion. Interestingly, it is introduced thus: "Mālik said: If hearing in both ears is completely lost [due to injury], then the full blood-money is due."[46]
3. "Yaḥyā told me that Mālik said: The opinion on which we have reached a consensus (*al-amr al-mujtamaʿ ʿalayhi ʿindanā*) is that if a man buys linen in one town, then carries it into another and sells it for a profit, the price of the linen should not include the costs of commissions, or of packaging, loading, or storage. The transportation fees, however, should be considered an integral part of the linen's price (*yuḥsab fī aṣl al-thaman*) and do not constitute a profit. If the seller informs the buyer of these [additional] costs, and he bargains with him as to obtain compensation, and if the buyer accepts [to make payment], then all is well (*fa-lā ba'sa bi-hi*)."[47] This, obviously, is not Mālik's own opinion but one which emerged out of a consensus reached by the Medinese jurists. Again, in the *Mudawwana*, the opinion is attributed to Mālik himself. It is restated in a nearly identical form, but the opening line is different and, for that matter, revealing: "Mālik said concerning linen bought in one town and transported into another: *I opine* (*arā*) that . . ."[48] The exclusive attribution to Mālik is emphatically manifest.

[43] Mālik, *Muwaṭṭa'*, 743.
[44] Mālik b. Anas, *al-Mudawwana al-Kubrā*, ed. Aḥmad ʿAbd al-Salām, 5 vols. (Beirut: Dār al-Kutub al-ʿIlmiyya, 1415/1994), IV, 567.
[45] Mālik, *Muwaṭṭa'*, 748. [46] Mālik, *Mudawwana*, IV, 563.
[47] Mālik, *Muwaṭṭa'*, 581.
[48] Mālik, *Mudawwana*, III, 238 (italics mine). The original phrasing is even more revealing: "*qāla Mālik fī al-bazz yushtarā fī balad fa-yuḥmal ilā baladin ākhar, qāla arā an lā . . .*"

It is obvious, beyond a shadow of doubt, that Mālik, here and elsewhere, is made responsible not only for unattributed opinions (which, as we have seen, do not necessarily belong to him) but also for opinions that clearly originate with other, identifiable authorities, be they individual or collective (i.e., Medinese consensus). Mālik's role is thus transformed by the later Mālikites from being a transmitter in the *Muwaṭṭa'* into that of the foremost authority for what was then emerging as the Mālikite school.[49]

The change in Mālik's role and image is by no means identical to that which occurred in the case of Abū Ḥanīfa, for the Mālik of the *Muwaṭṭa'* functioned also in the role of a traditionist, unlike Abū Ḥanīfa. But it is well-nigh certain that great many of the opinions which the latter transmitted from Ḥammād, Nakhaʿī, and others were later attributed to him. All the schools, not only the Mālikites, contributed to this process of authority construction. In the later sections of this chapter we shall see that this process was further enhanced by attributions to the founder of opinions garnered not only from their predecessors but also from their successors. The construction of the founders' authority *qua* founders and imams drew on sources both prior and subsequent to them.

Like Abū Ḥanīfa and Mālik, the figure of Muḥammad b. Idrīs al-Shāfiʿī (d. 204/820) was subjected to the same process. But unlike Mālik, Shāfiʿī appears much less as a transmitter of *ḥadīth* and legal opinion and more as a jurist holding opinions of his own. This is the impression left upon a casual reader of his *magnum opus*, *al-Umm*, which consists substantially of unattributed opinions, statements of legal norms formulated without textual support or legal reasoning. However, a careful study of this work reveals that Shāfiʿī was no less indebted to his predecessors than

[49] It is quite significant that Mohammad Fadel, who has studied the Mālikite school closely but who has not addressed the issue of what I have called authority construction, makes the following remark with regard to Ibn al-Qāsim (d. 191/866) who was considered, together with Saḥnūn, the most reliable transmitter of Mālik's doctrine:

> It was impossible to rely solely on Ibn al-Qāsim's teachings, for there were many issues of law for which Ibn al-Qāsim could not *attribute* an opinion to Mālik. This obliged later jurists to use the opinions of Mālik's other disciples, who often *attributed* positions to Mālik on precisely those cases for which Ibn al-Qāsim had not been able to provide a solution. More importantly, however, Ibn al-Qāsim's privileged position as the authoritative transmitter of Mālik's doctrine seems to have been developed at a later date. Presumably, for the first centuries of Mālikite jurisprudence, opinions had been evaluated on the basis of their individual worth and not on the *authority* of the transmitter of that opinion.

See his "The Social Logic of *Taqlīd* and the Rise of the *Mukhtaṣar*," *Islamic Law and Society*, 4 (1996), 218 (italics mine). Note here that Fadel senses, but does not articulate, the process of authority construction in the Mālikite school.

were Mālik and Abū Ḥanīfa. It is often the case that when the doctrine or opinion is standard and shared by the community of jurists, Shāfiʿī relates it without attributing it to any particular authority. A typical example of this can be seen in the case of hiring beasts for the purpose of transporting goods:

> Shāfiʿī said: If a man hires a beast [to use for transportation] from Mecca to Marw,[50] but he travels with it [only] to Medina, then he must pay the hiring fees agreed upon for traveling to Marw . . . If the beast perishes, he must pay the hiring fees to Marw plus the value of the beast. If it came to suffer from a defect while he is traveling with it – such as a wound in the rear, blindness, etc. – and this defect has affected its performance, he may return it [to its owner from whom] he is entitled to receive the equivalent value of the defective part.[51]

This opinion certainly circulated prior to Shāfiʿī, as attested by the early authorities cited in the *Mudawwana*.[52] The same type of evidence may be found in two opinions concerning collective homicide of the kind initially caused by bodily injury, such as severing of a limb. Shāfiʿī presents the opinions without textual support or legal reasoning, and gives no juristic authority for them. Yet the same opinions had already surfaced, with some variation, in the *Muwaṭṭa'*.[53] Similarly, Shāfiʿī acknowledges no authority or textual evidence in favor of the opinion that the full amount of blood-money becomes due when the sense of hearing is completely impaired as a result of bodily injury.[54] Yet it turns out that this opinion is stated in the *Muwaṭṭa'* as having been heard by Mālik from another authority.[55]

Much of *al-Umm* is made up of such opinions.[56] At times, however, the opinions are clearly defended in terms of consensus or, alternatively, in terms of the absence of disagreement. Concerning the law of rent and hire, Shāfiʿī, like most later *muqallids*, argues that it is justified by the Sunna, the practice of a number of Companions, and the "absence, as far as I know, of disagreement on it among the jurists of all regions

[50] In the text the city is called Marr, a place name which I could not locate in the standard geographical dictionaries. The context suggests that it is a distortion of Marw, a city in Khurasan.

[51] Shāfiʿī, *Umm*, IV, 29. [52] Mālik, *Mudawwana*, III, 486–87.

[53] Shāfiʿī, *Umm*, VI, 42, 59; Mālik, *Muwaṭṭa'*, 760, 762, 743, respectively.

[54] Shāfiʿī, *Umm*, VI, 89. [55] Mālik, *Muwaṭṭa'*, 748.

[56] This perhaps explains Shāfiʿī's requirement that for a jurist to qualify as a *muftī*, he must master, among other things, the legal doctrines of his predecessors and contemporaries (*aqāwīl ahl al-ʿilm qadīman wa-ḥadīthan*). See his *Kitāb Ibṭāl al-Istiḥsān* in *Umm*, VII, 497.

including ours."[57] In many instances, Shāfiʿī's sole defense or justification is the absence of disagreement, which implies, or is made to imply, the existence of consensus.[58] Less often, he explicitly states that two or more opinions exist concerning a particular case. In the matter of death resulting from bodily injury, Shāfiʿī introduces two opinions after the formula "*qīla*" (it was held).[59] It is clear that he had formulated neither of the two opinions himself. Here Shāfiʿī is practicing *taqlīd*, in precisely the same manner as his followers have practiced it for centuries since his death.

Shāfiʿī practiced another form of *taqlīd* frequently resorted to by later jurists belonging to all the four schools, namely, the reenactment of *ijtihād* which later came to be known as *ittibāʿ*.[60] By Shāfiʿī's time, it had become a firmly established doctrine that if a man wished to marry a fifth wife, he had to divorce one of the first four, in accordance with the Quranic verse 4:25. The interlocutor asks Shāfiʿī if other jurists have held this opinion, whereupon Shāfiʿī replies that the Quranic evidence is sufficient. But he then admits that others did hold this opinion, and proceeds to give two chains of authority, one consisting of ʿAbd al-Majīd → Ibn Jurayj → Abū al-Zubayr → Jābir, and the other including the first two of these names followed by Ṭāwūs who transmitted it on the authority of his father.[61]

The reluctance of Shāfiʿī to admit his propensity to *taqlīd* may be observed sporadically throughout *al-Umm*. With regard to the question of a gift made under coercion by a wife to her husband, he criticizes Abū Ḥanīfa's opinion and offers instead that of Ibn Abī Laylā. Having done so, he states his own opinion, which is identical to that of the latter.[62] That he states his opinion without providing its textual basis, and without explaining his own legal reasoning in justification of it, suggests that Shāfiʿī either adopted Ibn Abī Laylā's opinion as it is, or, what is more likely, accepted it in the way of *ittibāʿ*. In either case, he is not the originator of the opinion, even though he lets us assume that it is his own, independent doctrine.

Nonetheless, Shāfiʿī does at times acknowledge his debt to other jurists. With regard to the question of dedicating alms-giving as a charitable trust, Shāfiʿī again attacks Abū Ḥanīfa's opinion, and introduces, this time, the argument propounded by Abū Yūsuf and Shaybānī who disagreed with their mentor – a phenomenon of frequent occurrence among the three Ḥanafite authorities. Shāfiʿī admits – this time not so reluctantly – that Abū Yūsuf's reasoning in favor of an alternative opinion is exquisite

[57] Shāfiʿī, *Umm*, IV, 30.
[58] Ibid., IV, 30, 33, 109, 143; V, 6, 10–11, 16, 313, and passim. [59] Ibid., VI, 43.
[60] See chapter 4, section I, below. [61] Shāfiʿī, *Umm*, V, 15. [62] Ibid., IV, 73.

and that it proved superior to his own. At the end of the statement, Shāfiʿī intimates that he sides with, or adopts, Abū Yūsuf's opinion.[63] This example can be found repeated on a number of occasions,[64] but the following is representative:

> Shāfiʿī said: Some jurists maintained that if a man left [an inheritance of] 300 dinars, then his two sons would divide it between themselves, each receiving 150 dinars. One of the two then acknowledges that a [third] man is his brother, but the other denies this claim. What I recall of the early Medinese opinion (*qawl al-Madaniyyīn al-mutaqaddim*) is that the [third] man's filiation is not acknowledged and that he receives no amount whatsoever [of the inheritance]. This is so because the brother [who made the claim] did not acknowledge a debt to him, nor did he leave him a bequest. Rather, he merely claimed that he is entitled to inherit. If he could prove that he has a right to the inheritance, then he should inherit and he will also be liable to the payment of blood-money.[65] But since this relationship cannot be established, he cannot inherit. This, in my view, is the soundest opinion.[66]

In order to become the final authority in his school, Shāfiʿī was required to shed the image of a *muqallid*,[67] a process of authority construction to which both Abū Ḥanīfa and Mālik were subjected. One example should suffice to make our point. With regard to land rent, Shāfiʿī holds an opinion that he explicitly attributes to the chain of authority: Mālik → Ibn Shihāb → Saʿīd Ibn al-Musayyib. It was not long after Shāfiʿī's death that he was made responsible for this opinion.[68] In his *Mukhtaṣar*, Ibrāhīm al-Muzanī (d. 264/877) states the same opinion, but there attributes it, without the slightest ambiguity, to Shāfiʿī.[69]

As obvious as is the *ex post eventum* construction of the authority of these three imams, it appears to have been even more flagrant in the case of Aḥmad Ibn Ḥanbal (d. 241/855). Abū Ḥanīfa and Shāfiʿī were admittedly jurists of the first caliber (although one might incidentally

63 Ibid., IV, 69–70.

64 Ibid., V, 3; VI, 45 (a verbatim restatement of *Muwaṭṭa'*, 645–46); VII, 7, and passim.

65 Being the closest agnate, he is liable to the payment of blood-money should one of his brothers commit murder. The right to inheritance and the obligation to pay blood-money are defined, by the operation of the law, as the functions of agnatic relationships.

66 Shāfiʿī, *Umm*, VI, 276–77.

67 This image is borne out by the *manāqib* literature which assigned to Shāfiʿī, in a gradual fashion, the role of the master architect of legal theory. On these developments in the *manāqib* genre, see Hallaq, "Was al-Shafiʿi the Master Architect?" 599–600.

68 Shāfiʿī, *Umm*, IV, 30.

69 Ibrāhīm al-Muzanī, *Mukhtaṣar*, published as vol. IX of Shāfiʿī's *Umm*, IX, 139.

remark that the eighth-century Taqī al-Dīn al-Subkī, among others, possessed a far more acute legal mind). Mālik does not appear to have stood on par with them as a legal reasoner or as a seasoned jurist. But he was jurist of a sort, nonetheless. Ibn Ḥanbal was none of these things. He was in the first place a traditionist and theologian, and his involvement with law as a technical discipline was rather minimal. This much of his background is acknowledged by followers and foes alike. Among the latter, the well-known Ṭabarī refused to acknowledge him as a jurist apparently because "he never taught law, and never had law students."[70] Even as late as the fifth/eleventh century, this perception persisted in some circles, probably among certain of the Ḥanbalites themselves.[71] In their various works on the legal and learned professions, Ibn Qutayba, Maqdisī, Ṭaḥāwī, al-Qāḍī al-Nuʿmān, Dabbūsī, and al-ʿAlāʾ al-Samarqandī neglected even to include him, although Maqdisī listed him among the traditionists.[72] Ibn ʿAbd al-Barr wrote a whole treatise on the virtues of the schools' founders – at least those schools that had survived by his time – but Ibn Ḥanbal was not one of them.[73] Abū Bakr Ibn al-Athram, a Ḥanbalite, is reported to have said that he used to study law and the science of legal disagreement (*khilāf*) until he came to sit in the circle of Ibn Ḥanbal, at which time he categorically abandoned this course of learning in favor of *ḥadīth*.[74] The later Ḥanbalite jurist Ṭūfī openly acknowledged that Ibn Ḥanbal "did not transmit legal doctrine, for his entire concern was with *ḥadīth* and its collection."[75] This image of Ibn Ḥanbal was so pervasive that it never faded away for many centuries to come.[76]

70 See the introduction to Abū Jarīr Jaʿfar al-Ṭabarī's *Ikhtilāf al-Fuqahāʾ* (Beirut: Dar al-Kutub al-ʿIlmiyya, 1980), 10.

71 ʿAbd al-Raḥmān Shihāb al-Dīn Ibn Rajab, *Kitāb al-Dhayl ʿalā Ṭabaqāt al-Ḥanābila*, 2 vols. (Cairo: Maṭbaʿat al-Sunna al-Muḥammadiyya, 1952–53), I, 156–57, quoting Ibn ʿAqīl's observation that some of the younger legal scholars, most probably law students, thought Ibn Ḥanbal lacking in juristic skills. He argues to the contrary, however, which is to be expected from a later Ḥanbalite who is, by definition, a loyalist.

72 Ṭabarī, *Ikhtilāf*, 15–16. For al-Qāḍī al-Nuʿmān b. Muḥammad (d. 351/962), see his *Kitāb Ikhtilāf Uṣūl al-Madhāhib*, ed. Muṣṭafā Ghālib (Beirut: Dār al-Andalus, 1973), 66. Speaking of the Sunnī community of jurists, Nuʿmān (ibid., 127) reports that they claimed consensus to be limited to Mālik, Abū Ḥanīfa, Shāfiʿī, Awzāʿī, and their fellow jurists.

73 Ibid., 16.

74 Muḥammad b. Abī Yaʿlā al-Baghdādī Ibn al-Farrāʾ, *Ṭabaqāt al-Ḥanābila*, ed. M. H. al-Fiqī, 2 vols. (Cairo: Maṭbaʿat al-Sunna al-Muḥammadiyya, 1952), I, 72, 296.

75 Najm al-Dīn al-Ṭūfī, *Sharḥ Mukhtaṣar al-Rawḍa*, ed. ʿAbd Allāh al-Turkī, 3 vols. (Beirut: Muʾassasat al-Risāla, 1407/1987), III, 626–27: "*fa-innahu kāna lā yarwī tadwīn al-raʾy bal hammuhu al-ḥadīth wa-jamʿuhu.*"

76 Manṣūr b. Yūnus Ibn Idrīs al-Bahūtī (d. after 1046/1636), *Kashshāf al-Qināʿ ʿan Matn al-Iqnāʿ*, 6 vols. (Beirut: ʿĀlam al-Kutub, 1983), VI, 21.

Ibn Ḥanbal thus emerges as less of a founder than any of the other three eponyms. A traditionist par excellence, he was by definition preoccupied with *ḥadīth*, not law. We may suppose, only because of the later developments which made of Ḥanbalism a legal school, that he did address some legal problems and that he rendered legal opinions mostly in terms of *ḥadīth*. This is probably the nucleus with which his followers worked, and which they later elaborated and expanded.[77] It is therefore not an exaggeration to assert that the bare beginnings of legal Ḥanbalism are to be located in the juristic activities of the generation that followed Ibn Ḥanbal, associated as it is with the names of Abū Bakr al-Athram (d. 261/874), ʿAbd Allāh al-Maymūnī (d. 274/887), Abū Bakr al-Marrūdhī (d. 275/888), Ḥarb al-Kirmānī (d. 280/893), Ibrāhīm b. Isḥāq al-Ḥarbī (d. 285/898), and Ibn Ḥanbal's two sons Ṣāliḥ (d. 266/880 ?) and ʿAbd Allāh (d. 290/903).[78] (It is curious that Ibn al-Athram is said to have been a central figure in the early development of legal Ḥanbalism when his study of law came to a halt once he entered Ibn Ḥanbal's circle.) But these scholars, among other less major figures, are said to have been no more than bearers of Ibn Ḥanbal's opinions and doctrines. None of them, for instance, constructed a complete, or even near complete, system of the eponym's legal subject matter. It was left to Aḥmad b. Muḥammad Abū Bakr al-Khallāl (d. 311/923) to bring what was seen as the master's dispersed doctrines together. Khallāl was reported to have traveled widely in search of Ibn Ḥanbal's students who heard him speak of matters legal, and he was in touch with a great number of them, including Ibn Ḥanbal's two sons and Ibrāhīm al-Ḥarbī.[79] Ibn al-Farrā', a major biographer and a jurist of the Ḥanbalite school, remarks that Khallāl's collection of the eponym's opinions was never matched, either before or after.[80]

It would not be then an exaggeration to argue that, had it not been for Khallāl's enterprise and ambition, the Ḥanbalite school would never have emerged as a legal entity. For to do so, Ibn Ḥanbal would have

[77] Ibn Ḥanbal's marked lack of interest in law and legal questions does not tally with the fact that later Ḥanbalite works routinely report two or three opinions (usually known as *riwāyāt*) which Ibn Ḥanbal is said to have held with regard to a single case. The only conceivable explanation, as far as I can see, is that these *riwāyāt* were later attributions by his followers, but attributions made by means other than *takhrīj* (which we shall discuss shortly in this chapter).

[78] Muwaffaq al-Dīn Ibn Qudāma, *al-Kāfī fī Fiqh al-Imām Aḥmad b. Ḥanbal*, ed. Ṣidqī Jamīl and Yūsuf Salīm, 4 vols. (Beirut: Dār al-Fikr, 1992–94), I, 10; Ibn al-Farrā', *Ṭabaqāt*, II, 12. The fact that Subkī (*Ṭabaqāt*, II, 26) gives al-Ḥarbī a biographical notice suggests that Ibn Ḥanbal's students were not trained exclusively – nor even principally – under him, as is also evidenced in the case of Ibn al-Athram.

[79] Ibn al-Farrā', *Ṭabaqāt*, II, 12–13. [80] Ibid., II, 113.

had to furnish a wide range of legal doctrine and opinion, and in this task he certainly needed help. This help came from his followers and particularly the generation that succeeded them. They, like the Ḥanafites, Mālikites, and Shāfiʿites before them, attributed to their eponym opinions that he held or was thought to have held, whether or not these opinions originated with him as a *mujtahid*. In the case of Ibn Ḥanbal, a charismatic theologian and traditionist and the hero of the *Miḥna*, the clothing of his personality with legal authority was a much less difficult task both to undertake and accomplish, and this despite his notoriously imperfect record as a jurist.

The construction of authority around the figures of the presumed founders must also be viewed in the larger context of the development of Islamic law. Multifarious in nature and evolving from the outset as a jurists' law, legal authority during the first two centuries of Islam was dispersed and diluted. There were many jurists who advocated doctrines that were made up of various elements, some belonging to their predecessors and older contemporaries, and some of their own making. It is important to realize, as we have shown in some detail above, that none of these jurist-founders constructed his own doctrine singlehandedly, as the later typologies – and tradition at large – would have us believe. In fact, Ibn Ḥanbal's case is in itself an argument precisely to the contrary. But the argument can be taken still further: If Ibn Ḥanbal was transformed, despite all the odds, into a school founder, then it is no surprise that any one of the major *mujtahids* during this early period could have become a founder too.

Throughout the second/eighth and third/ninth centuries, juristic authority was so widely dispersed that it was unable to fulfill the requirements and demands of legal evolution. Authority, by definition, must have a clearly defined locus, and to be effective, it must be perceived to be such. Both these conditions were fulfilled in the person of the jurist–scholar who was made, through a process of authority attributions, the founder of a school. Even in later centuries, with the stupendous doctrinal accretions of later followers, the founder's authority remained the most significant, although the entirety of his doctrine, both attributed and original, was insufficient to meet the exigencies of later judicial application and unable to sustain singlehandedly the entire school. Although in later centuries the founder remained the most sanctified legal figure in the school, he remained little more than *primus inter pares*. The authoritative school doctrine, the *madhhab*, consisted of opinions originating with various jurists. But all these jurists and the opinions they held were enlisted under the nominal tutelage of the founder. The creation of authority in the figure of the founder was part of the wider effort to construct the school's authority, one of the greatest achievements of Islamic law.

III

We have already intimated that the process of authority construction did not only involve the dissociation of the eponyms from the contributions of their predecessors, to whom they were indebted. The process also entailed augmenting the authority of the supposed founders by attributing doctrines to them which they may never have held. It is the juristic constitution of these doctrinal contributions and the manner in which they underwent the process of attribution that will occupy us in the following pages.

It may at first glance seem a contradiction to speak of *ijtihād* as part of the *muqallid*'s activity, but this is by no means the case. We have seen in chapter 1 that the typologies acknowledge a group of jurists who stood below the rank of the absolute *mujtahids*, a group that was distinguished by the dual attribute of being *muqallids* to the founding imam and, simultaneously, *mujtahids* able to derive legal norms through the process of *takhrīj*.[81] Virtually overlooked by modern scholarship,[82] this important activity was largely responsible for the early doctrinal development of the personal schools, its zenith being located between the very beginning of the fourth/tenth century and the end of the fifth/eleventh, although strong traces of it could still be observed throughout the following centuries.[83]

[81] The origins of this term's technical meaning are by no means easy to reconstruct. None of the second/eighth-century jurists, including Shāfiʿī, uses the term in any obvious technical sense. To the best of my knowledge, the first semi-technical occurrence of it is found in Muzanī's *Kitāb al-Amr wal-Nahy*, where the author uses the term *makhraj* (lit. an outlet) to mean something like a solution to a problem, a way, that is, to get out of a problem through legal reasoning. It is quite noticeable, however, that Muzanī employs the term while taking Shāfiʿī's doctrine into account, which in this treatise is nearly always the case. See his *Kitāb al-Amr wal-Nahy*, in Robert Brunschvig, "Le livre de l'ordre et de la défense d'al-Muzani," *Bulletin d'études orientales*, 11 (1945–46): 145–94, at 153, 156, 158, 161, 162, and passim. Incidentally, it is noteworthy that *takhrīj* as a way of reasoning is not expounded, as a rule, in works of legal theory. As a technical term, it appears in none of the major technical dictionaries, e.g. Tahānawī's *Kashshāf Iṣṭilāḥāt al-Funūn* and Jurjānī's *Taʿrīfāt*.

[82] The only work that allocates some discussion to the later, not early, activity of *takhrīj* is, to the best of my knowledge, Sherman Jackson, *Islamic Law and the State: The Constitutional Jurisprudence of Shihāb al-Dīn al-Qarāfī* (Leiden: E. J. Brill, 1996), 91–96. Jackson deals with this issue from the limited perspective of Qarāfī and, at any rate, addresses neither the structure of reasoning involved in this activity nor its role in early legal evolution.

[83] See nn. 130–32, below.

According to Ibn al-Ṣalāḥ, the limited *mujtahid* exercises *takhrīj* on either of two bases: a particular text of his imam where a specific opinion is stated or, in the absence of such a text, he confronts revelation and derives from it a legal norm according to the principles and methodology established by his imam. This he does while heeding the type and quality of reasoning that is habitually employed by the imam,[84] and in this sense *takhrīj* exhibits the same features as the reasoning which constitutes the conventional, full-fledged *ijtihād* of the arch-jurist. In both types of *takhrīj*, however, conformity with the imam's legal theory and the general and particular principles of the law is said to be the prime concern.

The first type became known as *al-takhrīj wal-naql*, while the second, being a relatively more independent activity, was given the unqualified designation *takhrīj*. This latter involves reasoning, among many things, on the basis of general principles, such as the principle that necessity renders lawful what is otherwise illicit, or that no legal obligation shall be imposed beyond the limit of endurance or optimal capability. In this type of activity, the limited *mujtahid* takes these principles as his rule of thumb and solves problems accordingly.

The following example, from Ḥanbalite law, illustrates the activity of *al-takhrīj wal-naql*: If someone intends to perform prayer while wearing ritually impure clothes – the assumption being that ritually pure clothes are not available at the time – he or she must still pray but must also repeat the prayer when the proper apparel can be had. This is said to have been Ibn Ḥanbal's opinion. Another reported opinion of his concerns prayer in a ritually impure place. He held, contrary to the first case, that if someone prays in such a place, he need not pray again in compensation. In the later Ḥanbalite school, the principle emerged that both the ritual purity of the location of the prayer and the clothes worn while performing this duty constitute a condition for the validity of prayer. This being so, the two issues become cognate and, therefore, subject to mutual consideration. In other words, the legal norms attached to the two cases become interchangeable, thus creating two contradictory legal norms for each. Najm al-Dīn al-Ṭūfī explains how this comes about:

> The stipulation that wearing ritually impure clothes requires repetition of the prayer is a legal norm that is transferred (*yunqal*) to the [issue of] place. So a new legal norm emerges in the case of place (*yatakharraj fī-hi*). The stipulation that praying in a ritually impure place does not require repetition of the prayer is a legal norm that is transferred to [the issue of]

[84] Ibn al-Ṣalāḥ, *Adab al-Muftī*, 97.

clothes. Accordingly, a new legal norm emerges in the case of clothes. This is why each of the two cases will have two legal opinions, one held by the founder, the other reached by *al-naql* (*wal-takhrīj*).[85]

On the authority of Majd al-Dīn Ibn Taymiyya (d. 652/1254), the grandfather of Taqī al-Dīn, Ṭūfī reports another case of *takhrīj wal-naql*: A bequest given in handwriting is considered valid in the opinion of the imam. But the attestation of a bequest in handwriting is considered null and void if the witnesses are left ignorant of its particulars. The invalidity of the testimony thus renders the bequest itself void. The reasoning we have observed in the case of prayer prevails here too, since the common denominator is the handwritten bequest. The outcome of this reasoning is that each case will acquire two contradictory legal norms, one of validity, the other of nullity.[86]

During the post-formative period of the schools, when the authority of the founder imam was at last considered undisputed, the activity of *al-takhrīj wal-naql* came to be restricted, in terms of source material, to the imam's or his followers' opinions. In actual fact, however, and before the formation of the schools as guilds, this was by no means the case. The early Shāfiᶜite jurist Ibn al-Qāṣṣ (d. 335/946) reports dozens, perhaps hundreds, of cases in which *takhrīj* was practiced both within and without the boundaries of the imam's legal principles and *corpus juris*. (In fact he acknowledges, despite his Shāfiᶜite affiliation, that his work *Adab al-Qāḍī* is based on both Shāfiᶜī's and Abū Ḥanīfa's doctrines.)[87] In the case of a person whose speaking faculty is impaired (*akhras*), Shāfiᶜī and Abū Ḥanīfa apparently disagreed over whether or not his testimony

[85] Ṭūfī, *Sharḥ Mukhtaṣar al-Rawḍa*, III, 641: "*wa-man lam yajid illā thawban najisan ṣallā fī-hi wa-aᶜāda, naṣṣa ᶜalayhi. Wa-naṣṣa fī-man ḥubisa fī mawḍiᶜ najis fa-ṣallā, annahu lā yuᶜīd. Fa-yatakharraj fī-himā riwāyatān wa-dhālika li'anna ṭahārat al-thawb wal-makān kilāhumā sharṭ fī al-ṣalāt. Wa-hādhā wajh al-shabah bayna al-mas'alatayn. Wa-qad naṣṣa fī al-thawb al-najis annahu yuᶜīd, fa-yanqul ḥukmahu ilā al-makān, wa-yatakharraj fī-hi mithluhu, wa-naṣṣa fī al-mawḍiᶜ al-najis ᶜalā annahu lā yuᶜīd, fa-yanqul ḥukmahu ilā al-thawb al-najis, fa-yatakharraj fī-hi mithluhu, fa-lā jarama ṣāra fī kulli wāḥidatin min al-mas'alatayn riwāyatān, iḥdāhumā bil-naṣṣ wal-ukhrā bil-naql.*"

[86] Ibid., III, 642.

[87] Abū al-ᶜAbbās Aḥmad b. Abī Aḥmad al-Ṭabarī Ibn al-Qāṣṣ, *Adab al-Qāḍī*, ed. Ḥusayn Jabbūrī, 2 vols. (Ṭā'if: Maktabat al-Ṣiddīq, 1409/1989), I, 68. The absence of schools, and therefore of school loyalty, during the second/eighth and third/ninth centuries also explains the cross-influences between and among the schools' founders. Thus we should not consider unlikely the report that when Abū Yūsuf and Shaybānī met Mālik, they abandoned nearly one-third of the doctrine which they had elaborated in Kūfa in favor of Mālik's doctrine: Rāᶜī, *Intiṣār al-Faqīr*, 204. Despite the propagandist uses that were made of this report, it can still be considered authentic in light of what we know about interdoctrinal influences.

might be accepted if he knows sign language (*yaʿqil al-ishāra*). Ibn Surayj (d. 306/918), a distinguished Shāfiʿite and Ibn al-Qāṣṣ's professor, conducted *takhrīj* on the basis of these two doctrines, with the result that two contradictory opinions were accepted for this case: one that the testimony is valid, the other that it is void.[88] What is most interesting about Ibn al-Qāṣṣ's report is that Ibn Surayj's activity was deemed to fall within the hermeneutical contours of the Shāfiʿite school. He reports Ibn Surayj to have reached these two solutions "according to Shāfiʿī's way" (*fa-kharrajahā Abū al-ʿAbbās Ibn Surayj ʿalā madhhab al-Shāfiʿī ʿalā qawlayn*).[89] A similar attribution may be found in the case of the *qāḍī*'s (un)equal treatment of the plaintiff and defendant in his courtroom. Ibn al-Qāṣṣ reports that "the opinion of Shāfiʿī is that the *qāḍī* should not allow one of the two parties to state his arguments before the court without the other being present. Ibn Surayj produced this opinion by way of *takhrīj*" (*qālahu Ibn Surayj takhrījan*).[90] Ibn Surayj's *takhrīj* becomes Shāfiʿī's authoritative opinion.

Drawing on Abū Ḥanīfa's doctrine appears to have been a frequent practice of Ibn Surayj.[91] The former held, for instance, that if four witnesses testify that an act of adultery took place, but all disagree as to the precise location in the house in which the act took place, then the *ḥadd* punishment should be inflicted nonetheless. Admittedly, Abū Ḥanīfa's reasoning is dictated by *istiḥsān*,[92] since *qiyās* does not allow for the penalty of *ḥadd* when doubt exists; rather it demands that the penalty only be meted out when all witnesses agree on the specific location in which the act was said to have taken place. Now, in another case of adultery, the authoritative doctrine of the Shāfiʿite school held that if two witnesses testify that a man had sexual intercourse with a consenting woman, and

[88] Ibn al-Qāṣṣ, *Adab al-Qāḍī*, I, 306. [89] Ibid.

[90] Ibid., I, 214. See also Subkī, *Ṭabaqāt*, II, 94–95.

[91] And on Shaybānī's doctrine as well. It should not come as a surprise then that Ibn Surayj, the most illustrious figure of the Shāfiʿite school after Shāfiʿi himself, and the one held responsible for the phenomenal success of Shāfiʿism, should be remembered in Shāfiʿite biographical literature as having elaborated his legal doctrine on the basis of Shaybānī's law and legal principles. In the very words of Shīrāzī, Ibn Surayj "*farraʿa ʿala kutub Muḥammad ibn al-Ḥasan*," i.e., he derived positive legal rulings on the basis of Shaybānī's doctrine. It is perhaps because of this that the later Shāfiʿites expressed some reservations about the nature of Ibn Surayj's doctrines. One of the oft-quoted utterances is that made by Abū Ḥāmid al-Isfarāʾīnī who said that "we go along with Abū al-ʿAbbās [Ibn Surayj] on doctrine generally, but not on matters of specifics" (*naḥnu najrī maʿ Abī al-ʿAbbās fī ẓawāhir al-fiqh dūna al-daqāʾiq*). See Shīrāzī, *Ṭabaqāt*, 109; Ibn Qāḍī Shuhba, *Ṭabaqāt*, I, 49.

[92] On *istiḥsān*, see Wael B. Hallaq, *A History of Islamic Legal Theories* (Cambridge: Cambridge University Press, 1997), 107–11, and passim.

two other witnesses attest that he raped her, then he would not be deemed liable to the death penalty dictated by *ḥudūd*. Following the principles of *takhrīj* as outlined above, Ibn Surayj transferred the legal norm in the Ḥanafite case to the Shāfiᶜite one, the result being that if doubt exists as to whether sexual intercourse occurred as rape or by mutual consent, the man should suffer capital punishment regardless.[93]

Ibn al-Qāṣṣ too exercised *takhrīj*, harvesting for his school the fruits cultivated by the Ḥanafites and other jurists, including Shaybānī and Mālik.[94] His *takhrīj* is more often than not based on Shāfiᶜī's doctrine along with Ḥanafite opinion, but he frequently relies on Abū Ḥanīfa's opinions exclusively[95] and comes up with derivative opinions that he and his successors considered to be of Shāfiᶜite pedigree. This practice of borrowing from the doctrinal tradition of another school and attributing the confiscated opinion to one's own school and its founder was by no means limited to the Shāfiᶜites. It is not uncommon, for instance, to find Ḥanbalite opinions that have been derived through *takhrīj* from exclusively Ḥanafite, Mālikite, and/or other sources.[96] But if the activity of *takhrīj* routinely involved dipping into the doctrinal reservoir of other schools, the Shāfiᶜites could be considered the prime innovators, for, as Ṭūfī testifies, they were particularly given to this activity.[97]

But the Ḥanafites were not far behind. Earlier in this chapter, we discussed in passing the first level of the hierarchical taxonomy of Ḥanafite legal doctrine. In this taxonomy, there exist three levels of doctrine, each level consisting of one or more categories. The highest level of authoritative doctrine, known as *ẓāhir al-riwāya* or *masā'il al-uṣūl*, is found in the works of the three early masters, Abū Ḥanīfa, Abū Yūsuf,

[93] Sayf al-Dīn Abū Bakr Muḥammad al-Qaffāl al-Shāshī, *Ḥulyat al-ᶜUlamā' fī Maᶜrifat Madhāhib al-Fuqahā'*, ed. Yāsīn Darārka, 8 vols. (Amman: Dār al-Bāzz, 1988), VIII, 306.

[94] Ibn al-Qāṣṣ, *Adab al-Qāḍī*, I, 105, 106, 109–10, 112, 114, 136, 146, 195, 198, 213, 251, 253–54, 255; II, 359, 423, and passim. See also nn. 84–87, above.

[95] Ibid., I, 112, 213; II, 359, 420, 447, and passim. See, for instance, ibid., I, 251; II, 417, for exclusive reliance on Abū Ḥanīfa and his two students.

[96] ᶜAlā' al-Dīn ᶜAlī b. Muḥammad b. ᶜAbbās al-Baᶜlī, *al-Ikhtiyārāt al-Fiqhiyya min Fatāwā Shaykh al-Islām Ibn Taymiyya* (Beirut: Dār al-Fikr, 1369/1949), 15. Ibn al-Mundhir (d. 318/930) is frequently cited in Ḥanbalite works as an authority, although he was not a Ḥanbalite. In fact, he was said by biographers to have been an independent *mujtahid*, although he is also said to have been a distinguished member of the Shāfiᶜite school and heavily involved in *takhrīj* according to Shāfiᶜism. On Ibn al-Mundhir, see Nawawī, *al-Majmūᶜ*, I, 72; Subkī, *Ṭabaqāt*, II, 126–29.

[97] Ṭūfī, *Sharḥ Mukhtaṣar al-Rawḍa*, III, 642. Ṭūfī's explanation is that Shāfiᶜī's doctrine, having often included more than one opinion for each case, gave rise to a rich activity of *takhrīj*.

and Shaybānī.[98] What gives these works the authority they enjoy is the perception that they were transmitted through a large number of channels by trustworthy and highly qualified jurists. A marginal number of cases belonging to this category of doctrine are attributed to Zufar and al-Ḥasan b. Ziyād. The second level is termed *masā'il al-nawādir*, a body of doctrine also attributed to the three masters but without the sanctioning authority either of highly qualified transmitters or a large number of channels of transmission.[99] The third level consists of what is termed *wāqiʿāt* or *nawāzil*, cases that were not addressed by the early masters and that were solved by later jurists. These cases were new and the jurists who were "asked about them" and who provided solutions for them "were many."[100] Of particular significance here is the fact that the great majority of these cases were solved by means of *takhrīj*.[101] Among the names associated with this category of Ḥanafite doctrine are ʿIṣām b. Yūsuf (d. 210/825), Ibrāhīm Ibn Rustam (d. 211/826), Muḥammad b. Samāʿa (d. 233/848), Abū Sulaymān al-Jūzajānī (d. after 200/815), Aḥmad Abū Ḥafṣ al-Bukhārī (d. 217/832), Muḥammad b. Salama (d. 278/891), Muḥammad b. Muqātil (d. 248/862 ?), Naṣīr b. Yaḥyā (d. 268/881), and al-Qāsim b. Sallām (d. 223/837).[102]

That *takhrīj* was extensively practiced over the course of several centuries is a fact confirmed by the activities and writings of jurists who flourished as late as the seventh/thirteenth century.[103] Although the

[98] The works embodying the doctrines of the three masters are six, all compiled by Shaybānī. They are *al-Mabsūṭ*, *al-Ziyādāt*, *al-Jāmiʿ al-Kabīr*, *al-Jāmiʿ al-Ṣaghīr*, *al-Siyar al-Kabīr*, and *al-Siyar al-Ṣaghīr*. See Ibn ʿĀbidīn, *Ḥāshiya*, I, 69. However, in his *Sharḥ al-Manẓūma*, 17–18, Ibn ʿĀbidīn introduces Ibn Kamāl's distinction between *ẓāhir al-riwāya* and *masā'il al-uṣūl*, a distinction which he draws in turn on Sarakhsī's differentiation. The former, according to Ibn Kamāl, is limited to the six works enumerated. The latter, on the other hand, may include cases belonging to *nawādir*, which constitutes the second category of doctrine.

[99] These works include Shaybānī's *Kīsāniyyāt*, *Hārūniyyāt*, and *Jurjāniyyāt*; Ibn Ziyād's *Muḥarrar*; and Abū Yūsuf's *Kitāb al-Amālī*.

[100] Ibn ʿĀbidīn, *Ḥāshiya*, I, 69. See also Ḥājjī Khalīfa, *Kashf al-Ẓunūn ʿan Asāmī al-Kutub wal-Funūn*, 2 vols. (Istanbul: Maṭbaʿat Wakālat al-Maʿārif al-Jalīla, 1941–43), II, 1281.

[101] Ibn ʿĀbidīn, *Ḥāshiya*, I, 50; Ibn ʿĀbidīn, *Sharḥ al-Manẓūma*, 25; Shāh Walī Allāh, *ʿIqd al-Jīd*, 19.

[102] Ibn ʿĀbidīn, *Ḥāshiya*, I, 69.

[103] Ibn Abī al-ʿIzz al-Ḥanafī, *al-Ittibāʿ*, ed. Muḥammad ʿAṭā' Allāh Ḥanīf and ʿĀṣim al-Qaryūṭī (Amman: n.p., 1405/1984), 62. For a general history of *takhrīj* – to be used with caution – see Yaʿqūb b. ʿAbd al-Wahhāb Bāḥusayn, *al-Takhrīj ʿInda al-Fuqahā' wal-Uṣūliyyīn* (Riyadh: Maktabat al-Rushd, 1414/1993). Ibn al-Ṣalāḥ, who died in 643/1245, asserts that the practice of *takhrīj*, when an already established opinion is nowhere to be found, "has been prevalent for ages" (*yajūzu lil-muftī al-muntasib an yuftī fī-mā lā yajiduhu min aḥkāmī al-waqā'iʿi manṣūṣan ʿalayhi li-Imāmihi bi-mā yukharrijuhu ʿalā madhhabihi, wa-hādhā huwa al-ṣaḥīḥ al-ladhī ʿalayhi al-ʿamal wa-ilayhi mafzaʿ al-muftīn min mudadin madīda.*" See his *Adab al-Muftī*, 96.

activity itself was known as *takhrīj*, its practitioners in the Shāfiᶜite school became known as *aṣḥāb al-wujūh*.[104] In the Ḥanafite, Mālikite, and Ḥanbalite schools, however, the designation *aṣḥāb al-takhrīj* persisted, as attested in the terminological usages of biographical dictionaries and law manuals. In addition to the names we have already discussed, the following is a list of jurists who are described in these dictionaries as having seriously engaged in *takhrīj*:

1. The Shāfiᶜite Ibrāhīm al-Muzanī, whose *takhrīj* was so extensive that the later Shāfiᶜite jurists distinguished between those of his opinions that conformed to the school's hermeneutic (and were thus accepted as an important part of the school's doctrine), and those that did not.[105] These latter, however, were still significant enough to be considered by some jurists sufficient, on their own, to form the basis of an independent *madhhab*.[106]
2. ᶜAlī Ibn al-Ḥusayn Ibn Ḥarbawayh (d. 319/931), claimed by the Shāfiᶜites, but a student of Abū Thawr and Dāwūd Ibn Khalaf al-Ẓāhirī.[107]
3. Muḥammad b. al-Mufaḍḍal Abū al-Ṭayyib al-Ḍabbī (d. 308/920), a student of Ibn Surayj and a distinguished Shāfiᶜite.[108]
4. Abū Saᶜīd al-Iṣṭakhrī (d. 328/939), a major jurist of *aṣḥāb al-wujūh*.[109]
5. Zakariyyā b. Aḥmad Abū Yaḥyā al-Balkhī (d. 330/941), "one of the distinguished Shāfiᶜites and of the *aṣḥāb al-wujūh*."[110]
6. The Ḥanbalite ᶜUmar b. al-Ḥusayn al-Khiraqī (d. 334/945), who engaged extensively in *takhrīj* but whose writings containing his most creative reasoning were destroyed when his house was reportedly consumed by fire.[111] His *Mukhtaṣar*, however, which survived him long enough to have an influence, contained many cases of his *takhrīj* which he nonetheless attributed to Ibn Ḥanbal.[112]
7. The Shāfiᶜite ᶜAlī b. Ḥusayn Abū al-Ḥasan al-Jūrī (d. ca. 330/941), considered one of the *aṣḥāb al-wujūh*.[113]
8. Ẓāhir al-Sarakhsī (d. 389/998), a major Shāfiᶜite jurist. Yet, despite being one of the *aṣḥāb wujūh*, little of his doctrine, according to Nawawī, was transmitted.[114]

[104] Ibn al-Ṣalāḥ, *Adab al-Muftī*, 97.

[105] Muḥyī al-Dīn Sharaf al-Dīn b. Yaḥyā al-Nawawī, *Tahdhīb al-Asmā' wal-Lughāt*, 3 vols. (Cairo: Idārat al-Tibāᶜa al-Munīriyya, 1927), I, 285; Ibn Qāḍī Shuhba, *Ṭabaqāt*, I, 8; Subkī, *Ṭabaqāt*, I, 243–44.

[106] Nawawī, *Tahdhīb*, I, 285; Ibn Qāḍī Shuhba, *Ṭabaqāt*, I, 8.

[107] Subkī, *Ṭabaqāt*, II, 301–02. [108] Ibn Qāḍī Shuhba, *Ṭabaqāt*, I, 66.

[109] Ibid., I, 75. [110] Ibid., I, 76.

[111] Ismāᶜīl b. ᶜUmar Ibn Kathīr, *al-Bidāya wal-Nihāya*, 14 vols. (Beirut: Dār al-Kutub al-ᶜIlmiyya, 1985–88), XI, 228.

[112] See the editor's introduction to Shams al-Dīn Muḥammad b. ᶜAbd Allāh al-Miṣrī al-Zarkashī, *Sharḥ al-Zarkashī ᶜalā Mukhtaṣar al-Khiraqī*, ed. ᶜAbd Allāh b. ᶜAbd al-Raḥmān al-Jabrīn, 7 vols. (Riyadh: Maktabat al-ᶜUbaykān, 1413/1993), I, 47–48.

[113] Subkī, *Ṭabaqāt*, II, 307. [114] Nawawī, *Tahdhīb*, I, 192.

9. The Ḥanafite Abū ʿAbd Allāh Muḥammad b. Yaḥyā b. Mahdī al-Jurjānī (d. 398/1007), the teacher of Qudūrī and Nāṭifī, who was deemed one of the *aṣḥāb al-takhrīj*.[115]
10. ʿAbd Allāh b. Muḥammad al-Khawārizmī (d. 398/1007), one of the *aṣḥāb al-wujūh* and considered a leading jurist of the Shāfiʿite school.[116]
11. Yūsuf b. Aḥmad Ibn Kajj (d. 405/1014), a prominent Shāfiʿite jurist who is considered one of the most exacting of the *aṣḥāb al-wujūh* (*min aṣḥāb al-wujūh al-mutqinīn*).[117]
12. ʿAbd al-Raḥmān Muḥammad al-Fūrānī Abū al-Qāsim al-Marwazī (d. 461/1068), who is described as having articulated "good *wujūh*" in the Shāfiʿite *madhhab* (*wa-lahu wujūh jayyida fī al-madhhab*).[118]
13. Al-Qāḍī Ḥusayn b. Muḥammad al-Marwazī (d. 462/1069), a major figure in the Shāfiʿite school and one of the *aṣḥāb al-wujūh*.[119]
14. ʿAbd al-Raḥmān Ibn Baṭṭa al-Fayrazān (d. 470/1077), a Ḥanbalite jurist who is described as having engaged in *takhrīj* in a variety of ways (*kharraja al-takhārīj*).[120]
15. Abū Naṣr Muḥammad Ibn al-Ṣabbāgh (d. 477/1084), considered by some as an absolute *mujtahid* and a towering figure of the *aṣḥāb al-wujūh* in the Shāfiʿite school.[121]
16. The Mālikite Abū Ṭāhir b. Bashīr al-Tanūkhī (d. after 526/1131), whose *takhrīj* was said by Ibn Daqīq al-ʿĪd to be methodologically deficient.[122]
17. The famous Ḥanafite jurist and author Burhān al-Dīn al-Marghīnānī (d. 593/1196), the author of the famous *al-Hidāya* and one of the *aṣḥāb al-takhrīj*.[123]

The biographical works took special notice not only of those who engaged in *takhrīj*, but also of those who specialized in or made it their concern to study and transmit the doctrines and legal opinions derived through this particular juristic activity. We thus find that Aḥmad b. ʿAlī al-Arānī (d. 643/1245), a distinguished Shāfiʿite, excelled in the transmission of the *wujūh* that had been elaborated in his school.[124] Similarly, the biographers describe the Shāfiʿite ʿUthmān b. ʿAbd al-Raḥmān al-Naṣrī (d. 643/1245) as having had penetrating knowledge (*baṣīran*) of the doctrines elaborated through *takhrīj*.[125]

Ṭūfī's remark that the Shāfiʿites engaged in *takhrīj* more than did the other schools is confirmed by our general survey of biographical works. In Ibn Qāḍī Shuhba's *Ṭabaqāt*, for instance, there appear some two dozen major jurists who engaged in this activity, only a few of whom we have

[115] Laknawī, *al-Fawāʾid al-Bahiyya*, 202.
[116] Ibn Qāḍī Shuhba, *Ṭabaqāt*, I, 144. [117] Ibid., I, 197. [118] Ibid., I, 266–67.
[119] Nawawī, *Tahdhīb*, I, 164–65. [120] Ibn Rajab, *Dhayl*, I, 26–27.
[121] Ibn Qāḍī Shuhba, *Ṭabaqāt*, I, 269–70. [122] Ibn Farḥūn, *Dībāj*, 87.
[123] Ibn ʿĀbidīn, *Sharḥ al-Manẓūma*, 49; Qurashī, *al-Jawāhir al-Muḍīʾa*, II, 559.
[124] Ibn Qāḍī Shuhba, *Ṭabaqāt*, II, 125. [125] Ibid., II, 145.

listed above.[126] Our survey of the biographical dictionaries of the four schools also shows that the Shāfiᶜites and Ḥanbalites could each boast a larger number of jurists who engaged in this activity than the other two schools combined.[127] On the other hand, of all four schools, the Mālikites are said to have engaged in this activity the least.[128]

The Shāfiᶜite involvement in *takhrīj* seems to have reached its zenith in the fourth/tenth and fifth/eleventh centuries, the last jurists associated with it, according to Ibn Abī al-Damm, having been Maḥāmilī (d. 415/1024), Māwardī (d. 450/1058), and Abū al-Ṭayyib al-Ṭabarī (d. 450/1058).[129] But Ibn Abī al-Damm's claim cannot be fully or even substantially confirmed by data from either biographical dictionaries or works of positive law. During the later centuries – especially after the fourth/tenth – the activity in the Shāfiᶜite school continued, albeit with somewhat diminished vigor.[130] In the other schools, it also found expression in later doctrines, as attested in the juristic production of two towering Ḥanbalite figures, Ibn Qudāma (d. 620/1223) and Taqī al-Dīn Ibn Taymiyya (d. 728/1327),[131] as well as in the writings of a number of Ḥanafite and Mālikite jurists.[132]

[126] Ibid., I, 99–100 (Ibn Abī Hurayra), 149 (Muḥammad b. al-Ḥasan al-Astrabādhī), 152 (Muḥammad Abū Bakr al-Ūdanī), 154 (Muḥammad b. ᶜAlī al-Māsarujsī), 177 (Abū al-Qāsim al-Ṣaymarī), 207 (al-Ḥasan Abū ᶜAlī al-Bandanījī), 221 (Muḥammad b. ᶜAbd al-Malik al-Marwazī), 233 (al-Ḥusayn b. Muḥammad al-Qaṭṭān), 241 (Abū al-Ḥasan al-Māwardī), 262 (Abū al-Rabīᶜ Ṭāhir b. ᶜAbd Allāh al-Turkī), 264–65 (Abū Saᶜd al-Nīsābūrī), 266–67 (ᶜAbd al-Raḥmān al-Fūrānī al-Marwazī).

[127] In addition to those listed by Ibn Qāḍī Shuhba (previous note), see Nawawī, *Tahdhīb*, I, 92–94, 113, 164, 238. For the Ḥanbalites, see Zarkashī, *Sharḥ*, I, 28 ff.

[128] This is the claim of Qarāfī. See Rāᶜī, *Intiṣār al-Faqīr*, 169. Qarāfī's claim, it must be noted, does find initial support in the sources, notably in Ibn Farḥūn's *Dībāj*.

[129] Ibrāhīm b. ᶜAbd Allāh Ibn Abī al-Damm, *Adab al-Qaḍā' aw al-Durar al-Manẓūmāt fī al-Aqḍiya wal-Ḥukūmāt*, ed. Muḥammad ᶜAṭā' (Beirut: Dār al-Kutub al-ᶜIlmiyya, 1987), 40.

[130] See, for example, Taqī al-Dīn ᶜAlī al-Subkī, *Fatāwā al-Subkī*, 2 vols. (Cairo: Maktabat al-Qudsī, 1937), I, 324; II, 468, 525; Subkī, *Ṭabaqāt*, VI, 186 ff., 193. Sharaf al-Dīn al-Nawawī, who died in 676/1277, is still speaking of *takhrīj*. See his *al-Majmūᶜ*, I, 68.

[131] See Nawawī, *al-Majmūᶜ*, I, 68; Bāḥusayn, *Takhrīj*, 266 (quoted from Muwaffaq al-Dīn Ibn Qudāma, *al-Mughnī*, 12 vols. (Beirut: Dār al-Kitāb al-ᶜArabī, 1983), IX, 131); Ṭūfī, *Sharḥ Mukhtaṣar al-Rawḍa*, III, 628; Ibn al-Ṣalāḥ, *Adab al-Muftī*, 126, is still speaking of *takhrīj*. So is ᶜAlī b. Sulaymān b. Muḥammad al-Mirdāwī, *Taṣḥīḥ al-Furūᶜ*, printed with Shams al-Dīn Muḥammad Ibn Mufliḥ, *Kitāb al-Furūᶜ*, ed. ᶜAbd al-Sattār Farrāj, 6 vols. (Beirut: ᶜĀlam al-Kutub, 1405/1985), I, 51.

[132] ᶜAlā' al-Dīn Abū Bakr Ibn Masᶜūd al-Kāsānī, *Badā'iᶜ al-Ṣanā'iᶜ fī Tartīb al-Sharā'iᶜ*, 7 vols. (Beirut: Dār al-Kitāb al-ᶜArabī, 1982), I, 2, where he makes a preliminary remark to the effect that his book examines legal cases and the modes of their *takhrīj* according to the principles and general precepts laid down presumably by the founding fathers (*yataṣaffaḥ . . . aqsām al-masā'il wa-fuṣūlahā wa-takhrījahā ᶜalā qawāᶜidihā wa-uṣūlihā*); W. B. Hallaq, "A Prelude to Ottoman Reform: Ibn ᶜĀbidīn on Custom

IV

Be that as it may, there is no doubt that *takhrīj* constituted, in the authoritative doctrinal structure of the four schools, the second most important body of legal subject matter – second, that is, to the actual doctrines of the eponyms, and second only when disentangled from the eponym's *corpus juris*. For it was often the case that attributions to the imam became indistinguishably blended with their own doctrine or at least with what was thought to be their own doctrine (a qualification that has been established in the previous section). We have thus far seen a number of examples which make it demonstrably clear that the *takhrīj* of later authorities becomes the property of the eponyms. This process of attribution, it is important to stress, did not go unnoticed by the jurists themselves. They were acutely aware of it not only as a matter of practice, but also as a matter of theory. Abū Isḥāq al-Shīrāzī, a Shāfiʿite jurist and legal theoretician, devotes to this issue what is for us a significant chapter in his monumental *uṣūl* work *Sharḥ al-Lumaʿ*. The chapter's title leaves us in no doubt as to the facts: "Concerning the Matter that it is not Permissible to Attribute to Shāfiʿī what his Followers have Established through *takhrīj*."[133]

Shīrāzī observes that some of the Shāfiʿites did allow such attributions, a significant admission which goes to show that this process was recognized as a conscious act,[134] unlike that of attributing to the eponyms the opinions of their predecessors. Shīrāzī reports furthermore that proponents of the doctrine defended their position by adducing the following argument: The conclusions of *qiyās* are considered part of the Sharīʿa, and they are thus attributed to God and the Prophet. Just as this is true, it is also true that the conclusions of *qiyās* drawn by other jurists on the basis of Shāfiʿī's opinions may and should be attributed to Shāfiʿī himself. Shīrāzī rejects this argument though, saying that the conclusions of *qiyās* are never considered statements by God or the Prophet himself. Rather, they are considered part of the religion of God and the Prophet (*dīnu*

and Legal Change," proceedings of a conference held in Istanbul, May 25–30, 1999 (New York: Columbia University Press, forthcoming). See also the Mālikite Ḥaṭṭāb, *Mawāhib al-Jalīl*, I, 41. On the discourse of the Mālikite Qarāfī concerning the theory of *takhrīj*, see Jackson, *Islamic Law and the State*, 91–96. Jackson remarks that "Qarāfī himself engages in this practice on occasion" (p. 96).

133 Abū Isḥāq Ibrāhīm b. ʿAlī al-Shīrāzī, *Sharḥ al-Lumaʿ*, ed. ʿAbd al-Majīd Turkī, 2 vols. (Beirut: Dār al-Gharb al-Islāmī, 1988), II, 1084–85: "*Fī annahu lā yajūz an yunsab ilā al-Shāfiʿī mā kharrajahu aḥad aṣḥābihi ʿalā qawlihi.*"

134 The controversy and its relevance are still obvious at least two centuries after Shīrāzī wrote. See Ibn al-Ṣalāḥ, *Adab al-Muftī*, 96–97.

Allāh wa-dīnu Rasūlihi).[135] Besides, Shīrāzī continues, even this attribution in terms of religion is inadmissible, for neither Shāfiʿī nor any of the other founding *mujtahids* have their own religion.

Shīrāzī then cites another argument advanced by his interlocutor: If the eponym holds a certain opinion with regard to one case, say, the proprietorship of a garden, then his opinion about another case, such as the proprietorship of land surrounding a house, would be analogous. The implication here, in line with the first argument, is that an analogous opinion not necessarily derived by the eponym belongs nonetheless to him, since the principles of reasoning involved in the case dictate identical conclusions. Shīrāzī counters by arguing that there is in effect a qualitative difference between the interlocutor's example, which is analogical, and *takhrīj*, which always involves two different, not similar, cases. Analogical cases, Shīrāzī argues, may be attributed to the eponym despite the fact that one of them was not solved by him. But when the two cases are different, and when one of them was solved by another jurist, no attribution of the latter to the eponym should be considered permissible.[136]

Ṭūfī provides further clarification of Shīrāzī's argument. If the eponym established a certain legal norm for a particular case, and also explicated the rationale (*ʿilla*) which led him to that norm, then all other cases possessing this identifiable *ʿilla* should have the same norm. In this sense, the eponym's doctrine, used to solve the first case, can be said to have provided the solution of the latter ones, even though the eponym may not have even known of their existence. In other words, the latter cases can be attributed to him.[137] On the other hand, should he solve a case without articulating the *ʿilla* behind it, and should he not predicate the same legal norm he derived for this case upon what appears to be an analogous case, then his doctrines (*madhhab*) in both cases must be seen as unrelated. The disparity is assumed because of the distinct possibility that he would have *articulated* a different *ʿilla* for each case or set of cases. But, Ṭūfī adds, many jurists (*al-kathīr min al-fuqahā'*) disregarded such distinctions and permitted the activity of *takhrīj* nonetheless.[138]

Ṭūfī's testimony, coupled with that of Shīrāzī, is revealing. It not only tells of the presence of a significant juristic–interpretive activity that dominated legal history for a considerable period, but also discloses the

[135] Shīrāzī, *Sharḥ al-Lumaʿ*, II, 1084. [136] Ibid., II, 1085.

[137] Ṭūfī, *Sharḥ Mukhtaṣar al-Rawḍa*, III, 638: "*idhā naṣṣa al-mujtahid ʿalā ḥukm fī mas'ala li-ʿilla bayyanahā fa-madhhabuhu fī kulli mas'ala wujidat fī-hā tilka al-ʿilla ka-madhhabihi fī hādhihi al-mas'ala.*" See also the introduction to Zarkashī, *Sharḥ*, I, 28 ff.

[138] Ṭūfī, *Sharḥ Mukhtaṣar al-Rawḍa*, III, 639.

methodological issues that such activity involved. The penchant to attribute doctrines to the eponym constituted ultimately the crux of the controversy between the two sides. Curiously, the theoretical exposition of *takhrīj* did not account for the contributions of authorities external to the school of the founder. The recruitment of Ḥanafite doctrine and its assimilation into the Shāfiʿite school was not, for instance, given any due notice. In fact, because the theoretical elaboration of *takhrīj* appeared at a time when the schools had already reached their full development, it must not have been in the best interest of the affiliated jurists to expose their debt to other schools. We might conjecture that the debt was to a large extent reciprocal among all the schools, which explains why no jurist found it opportune or wise to expose the other schools' debt to his own. His own school, one suspects, would have been equally vulnerable to the same charge.

V

It is therefore clear that *ijtihād* through *takhrīj* was a dominant interpretive activity for several centuries and that at least a fair number of jurists were in the habit of attributing the results of their juristic endeavors to the founders.[139] This process of attribution, which is one of back-projection, both complemented and enhanced the other process of attribution by which the founder imams were themselves credited with a body of doctrines that their predecessors had elaborated. This is not to say, however, that both processes were of the same nature, for one was a self-conscious act while the other was not. The process of crediting the presumed founders with doctrines which had been constructed by their predecessors was never acknowledged, whether by legal practitioners or theoreticians. Islamic legal discourse is simply silent on this point. Attributions through *takhrīj*, on the other hand, were widely acknowledged.

The explanation for this phenomenon is not difficult: The attribution of later opinions to a founder can be and indeed was justified by the

[139] See the statement of the Ḥanbalite Ibn Qāsim in this regard, quoted in Zarkashī, *Sharḥ*, I, 31–32. This process of attribution gave rise to an operative terminology which required distinctions to be made between the actual opinions of the imams and those that were placed in their mouths. Ibn ʿĀbidīn, for instance, argues that it is improper to use the formula "Abū Ḥanīfa said" (*qāla Abū Ḥanīfa*) if Abū Ḥanīfa himself had not held the opinion. The *takhrījāt* (pl. of *takhrīj*) of the major jurists, he asserts, must be stated with the formula "Abū Ḥanīfa's *madhhab* dictates that . . ." (*muqtaḍā madhhab Abī Ḥanīfa kadhā*). See his *Sharḥ al-Manẓūma*, 25.

supposed fact that these opinions were reached on the basis of a methodology of legal reasoning constructed in its entirety by the presumed founder. The assumption underlying this justification is that the founder would have himself reached these same opinions had he addressed the cases which his later followers encountered. But he did not, for the cases (*nawāzil*) befalling Muslims were deemed to be infinite. Here there are two distinct elements which further enhance the authority of the presumed founder at the expense of his followers. First, it makes their interpretive activity, or *ijtihād*, seem derivative but above all mechanical: all they need to do is to follow the methodological blueprint of the imam. This conception of methodological subservience permeates not only the juristic typologies but also all structures of positive law and biographical narrative; that is, the doctrinal, interpretive, and sociological make-up of the law. As we shall see in chapter 4, positive law depended on the identification of the imam's principles that underlie individual legal norms just as much as it depended on a variety of other considerations emanating from, and imposed upon them by, their own social exigencies. Similarly, the biographical narrative, a central feature of Islamic law, was thoroughly driven by hierarchical structures which would have no meaning without the juristic foundations laid down by the arch-figure of the imam. The second element is the wholesale attribution to the founder imam of creating an entire system of legal methodology that constitutes in effect the juridical basis of the school. I have shown elsewhere that legal theory and the methodology of the law emerged as an organic and systematic entity nearly one century after the death of Shāfiʿī and a good half-century after the death of the last of the eponyms whose school has survived, namely, Ahmad Ibn Ḥanbal.[140] The fact of the matter is that both legal theory (*uṣūl al-fiqh*) and the principles of positive law (also known as *uṣūl*)[141] were gradual developments that began before the presumed imams lived and came to full maturity long after they perished.

Given the prestige and authority attached to the figure of the founder imams, it was self-defeating to acknowledge their debt to their immediate predecessors who were jurists like themselves.[142] That link had to be suppressed and severed at any expense. It had to be replaced by another link in which the imams confronted the revealed texts directly, as we have seen

[140] Hallaq, "Was al-Shafiʿi the Master Architect?" 587 ff. [141] See chapter 4, below.

[142] We have already seen that Abū Ḥanīfa was associated with the highly authorized statement that "I refuse to follow (*uqallidu*) the Followers because they were men who practiced *ijtihād* and I am a man who practices *ijtihād*." This statement, especially in light of the authoritative status it acquired in the school, must have been intended to defy any admission of debt. See n. 10, above.

in the instructive example provided by Sarakhsī concerning the levy of the tithe.[143] Obviously, the link with the immediately preceding jurists could not have been dwelt upon, much less articulated as a theoretical issue. *Takhrīj*, on the other hand, was articulated in this manner, and therein lies the difference.[144]

143 See section II, above. One implication of our finding in this chapter pertains to the controversy among modern scholars over the issue of the gate of *ijtihād*. Against the age-long notion that the gate of *ijtihād* was closed – a notion advocated and indeed articulated by Schacht – it has been argued that this creative activity continued at least until late medieval times. See Wael B. Hallaq, "Was the Gate of Ijtihād Closed?" *International Journal of Middle East Studies*, 16 (1984): 3–41. Norman Calder has argued that "Schacht will be correct in asserting that the gate of *ijtihād* closed about 900 [A.D.] if he means that about then the Muslim community embraced the principle of *intisāb* or school affiliation. Hallaq will be correct in asserting that the gate of *ijtihād* did not close, if he distinguishes clearly the two types of *ijtihād* – independent and affiliated." See Calder, "al-Nawawī's Typology," 157. Now, if our findings are accepted, then Calder's distinction – previously suggested by others – becomes entirely meaningless, for it never existed in the first place. If there was ever a claim in favor of closing the gate of *ijtihād*, it could have meant one thing and one thing only, i.e. precluding the possibility of a new school, headed, of course, by an imam who would have to offer a legal methodology and a set of positive legal principles qualitatively different from those advocated by the established schools.

144 The findings of this chapter find corroboration in several quarters, each approaching the same general theme from a completely different angle. See Hallaq, "Was al-Shāfiʿī the Master Architect?" reprinted in Wael B. Hallaq, *Law and Legal Theory in Classical and Medieval Islam* (Variorum: Aldershot, 1995), article VII, including the addenda; Melchert, *Formation of the Sunni Schools*; and Jonathan E. Brockopp, "Early Islamic Jurisprudence in Egypt: Two Scholars and their *Mukhtaṣars*," *International Journal of Middle East Studies*, 30 (1998): 167 ff. To these writings one may cautiously add Norman Calder, *Studies in Early Muslim Jurisprudence* (Oxford: Clarendon Press, 1993); cautiously, because Calder makes too much of the evidence available to him. For critiques of this work, see the sources cited in Harald Motzki, "The Prophet and the Cat: On Dating Mālik's *Muwaṭṭa'* and Legal Traditions," *Jerusalem Studies in Arabic and Islam*, 22 (1998): 18–83, at 19, n. 3.

13

THE FORMATION OF THE SUNNĪ SCHOOLS OF LAW

Christopher Melchert

EVERY SUNNĪ JURISPRUDENT is affiliated with one or another of four schools of law, the Shāfiʿī, Ḥanafī, Mālikī, or Ḥanbalī (to list them by approximate order of size today). They are named for famous jurisprudents of the eighth and ninth centuries CE (now in chronological order): Abū Ḥanīfa (d. Baghdad, 150/767), Mālik ibn Anas (d. Medina, 179/795), al-Shāfiʿī (d. al-Fusṭāṭ, 204/820), and Aḥmad ibn Ḥanbal (d. Baghdad, 241/855). It has long been a scholarly commonplace, though, that none of these eponyms founded a school.[1] One naturally asks, then, when the schools did first appear. This is the question to which I addressed my doctoral dissertation, which appeared with some changes as a book in 1997.[2] The present essay summarizes that study, then sketches the state of the question five years later. Given the space available, I refer readers to the book for documentation from the primary sources, restricting references here mainly to the work of modern scholars. In brief, it seems certain that the schools as we know them go back to the early tenth century; however, the nature and organization of jurisprudence before then is more difficult to characterize and remains controversial.

---

[1] E.g. Ignaz Goldziher, *Introduction to Islamic Theology and Law*, trans. Andras and Ruth Hamori (Princeton, 1981), 49; Duncan Black Macdonald, *Development of Muslim Theology, Jurisprudence, and Constitutional Theory* (New York, 1903), 94, 96–97; N.J. Coulson, *A History of Islamic Law* (Edinburgh, 1964), 48–49, 70–71; Marshall G.S. Hodgson, *The Venture of Islam* (Chicago, 1974), I, bk. 2, chap. 3, esp. 335; Andrew Rippin, *Muslims: Their Religious Beliefs and Practices*, I: *The Formative Period* (London, 1990), 76. Several recent textbooks use the passive voice to gloss over historical doubts. See David Waines, *An Introduction to Islam* (Cambridge, 1995), 65 ("four scholar-jurists who were recognized as the founders of the Sunnī legal schools"); Sachiko Murata and William C. Chittick, *The Vision of Islam* (London, 1996), 31 ("The four *madhhabs* of Sunnī Islam are named after those who are looked back upon as their founders"); Abdulkader Tayob, *Islam: a Short Introduction* (Oxford, 1999), 38 ("Abū Ḥanīfa became the reputed founder of the Kūfan legal school").

[2] Christopher Melchert, "The Formation of the Sunnī Schools of Law, Ninth–Tenth Centuries C.E.", Ph.D. dissertation, Univ. of Pennsylvania, 1992; *idem*, *The Formation of the Sunnī Schools of Law, 9th–10th Centuries C.E.* (Leiden, 1997).

Locating the Pivot

The obvious research strategy is to define the school, then go back in time through the sources to discover where it first appears. *Madhhab*, the Arabic word conventionally translated as "school", most often refers in the sources to doctrine. At its simplest, this means a particular tenet, possibly having to do with theology or piety rather than law. In the field of law, *madhhab* most often refers to a jurisprudent's opinion concerning a particular case or to the opinion of a whole school; say, of practically all the Shāfiʿīya, to which a deviant opinion may be contrasted. From *madhhab* as the doctrine of a school, it is only a short step to *madhhab* as the school itself, a body of jurisprudents loyal to their school's eponym.

Joseph Schacht, whose sketch of the evolution of Islamic law remains the standard, was chiefly concerned with doctrine. The stages that most interested him were defined by doctrine: first, when the law was derived mainly from Umayyad practice and the opinions of local wise men (earlier eighth century); second, when increasing amounts of *ḥadīth* came into circulation and it gradually became necessary to justify one's doctrine by appeal to the documented opinions of much earlier figures, ultimately the Prophet himself (later eighth century); and finally, when al-Shāfiʿī expressly laid out the theory of inference from Qur'ān and *ḥadīth* that would broadly govern Islamic jurisprudence until the twentieth century. Schacht located the formation of schools at around the middle of the third century AH (860s CE). This is when, he thought, the old Iraqi school became completely Ḥanafī, when Mālikī and Shāfiʿī doctrines were crystallized in the respective handbooks of Abū Muṣʿab al-Zuhrī (d. Medina, 242/857) and al-Muzanī (d. al-Fusṭāṭ, 264/877?), and the opinions of Aḥmad ibn Ḥanbal were collected by his disciples.[3]

It certainly is a crucial sign of school formation that jurisprudents should collect the doctrine of one jurisprudent of the past, as opposed to collecting the doctrine of many past figures (e.g. the *Muṣannaf*s of ʿAbd al-Razzāq [d. 211/827] and Ibn Abī Shayba [d. al-Kūfa, 235/849]) or setting out their own doctrine in their own names. It is presumably the characteristic literary activity of the personal school of law. Recent scholarship has added detail to Schacht's sketch. Jonathan Brockopp has observed that Ibn ʿAbd al-

[3] Joseph Schacht, *The Origins of Muhammadan Jurisprudence* (Oxford, 1950); *idem*, "The Schools of Law and Later Developments of Jurisprudence", in Majid Khadduri and Herbert J. Liebesny, eds., *Law in the Middle East*, I: *Origin and Development of Islamic Law* (Washington, D.C., 1955), 57–84, esp. 63, 67; *idem*, "Sur quelques manuscrits de la bibliothèque de la mosquée d'al-Qarawiyyīn à Fès", *Etudes d'orientalisme dédiées à la mémoire de Lévi-Provençal* (Paris, 1962), I, 271–84, esp. 274.

Ḥakam (d. al-Fusṭāṭ, 214/829) wrote a *Mukhtaṣar* ("epitome") fixing Mālikī doctrine a generation before Abū Muṣʿab.[4] On the other hand, Miklos Muranyi has shown that the *Mudawwana* and *Mukhtaliṭa* of Saḥnūn (d. al-Qayrawān, 240/854), the leading Mālikī teacher of Ifrīqiya ("Africa", i.e. modern Tunisia), were not distinguished from each other until the later ninth century.[5] In al-Andalus, some of Mālik's disciples, especially Ibn al-Qāsim (d. al-Fusṭāṭ, 191/806), seem to have been superior authorities to Mālik himself until late in the century.[6] As for the collection of Aḥmad's doctrine, numerous small collections of his opinions (concerning models of piety and *ḥadīth* criticism as well as law) were assembled in the mid-ninth century, but they were not synthesized until the end of the century. In short, the authoritative collection of the eponym's opinions might take as long as a century.

A controversial question is the extent to which ninth-century jurisprudents built up the eponyms' doctrine by pseudonymous attribution. Norman Calder has proposed that the very doctrines of Mālik, Abū Ḥanīfa, and al-Shāfiʿī were still being worked up by disciples writing in their names in the later ninth century.[7] The most effective refutations of Calder have all concerned Mālikī texts.[8] Although his chapter on early Ḥanafī texts does not go into sufficient detail, I predict that future research will largely confirm Calder's assertion that the works ascribed to al-Shaybānī (d. 189/804–805) did not achieve their present form until well into the ninth century. His perception of widespread posthumous attribution to al-Shāfiʿī in the later ninth century has been broadly confirmed by some of my own researches.[9] A

[4]Jonathan E. Brockopp, *Early Mālikī Law: Ibn 'Abd al-Ḥakam and His Major Compendium of Jurisprudence* (Leiden, 2000), based on *idem*, "Slavery in Islamic Law: an Examination of Early Mālikī Jurisprudence", Ph.D. dissertation, Yale University, 1995; *idem*, "Early Islamic Jurisprudence in Egypt: Two Scholars and Their *Mukhtaṣars*", *IJMES* 30 (1998), 167–82.

[5]Miklos Muranyi, *Die Rechtsbücher des Qairawāners Saḥnūn b. Saʿīd* (Stuttgart, 1999), esp. 122.

[6]See Isabel Fierro, "The Introduction of *Ḥadīth* in al-Andalus", *Der Islam* 66 (1989), 68–93, esp. 74, 82, 84.

[7]Norman Calder, *Studies in Early Muslim Jurisprudence* (Oxford, 1993).

[8]Yasin Dutton, "*'Amal* v. *Ḥadīth* in Islamic Law: the Case of *sadl al-yadayn* (Holding One's Hands by One's Sides) When Doing the Prayer", *Islamic Law and Society* 3 (1996), 13–40, esp. 28–33; Miklos Muranyi, "Die frühe Rechtsliteratur zwischen Quellenanalyse und Fiktion", *Islamic Law and Society* 4 (1997), 224–41; Harald Motzki, "The Prophet and the Cat: On Dating Mālik's *Muwaṭṭa'* and Legal Traditions", *JSAI* 22 (1998), 18–83; Wael B. Hallaq, "On Dating Malik's *Muwatta*", *UCLA Journal of Islamic and Near Eastern Law* 1 (2001–2002), 47–65.

[9]See Christopher Melchert, "Qur'ānic Abrogation Across the Ninth Century", in Bernard Weiss, ed., *Studies in Islamic Legal Theory* (Leiden, 2002), 75–98; *idem*, "The

second stage in the formation of self-conscious schools is the point when we begin to see not only works under the names of their eponyms, but express commentaries on those works. The commentary literature turns out to go back to about the turn of the tenth century CE, with series of commentaries on the two *Jāmi*'s of al-Shaybānī (d. Ranbūyah, near Rayy, 189/804–805) among the Ḥanafīya and on al-Muzanī's *Mukhtaṣar* (which already adds express commentary to quotation) among the Shāfi'īya.

There is more to the school, though, than doctrine. George Makdisi was the pioneer in describing the school of law as a teaching institution.[10] Where Schacht made out two stages, the regional school and the personal, Makdisi has proposed a third, mainly the guild (what I have usually called the "classical school"), which actively certified qualified jurisprudents.[11] The crucial importance of certification alongside doctrine comes out in a remark by the famous Shāfi'ī al-Māwardī (d. Baghdad, 450/1058) with reference to another Shāfi'ī who had held that a *qāḍī* known for adhering to one school might no longer rule according to the doctrine of any other, "since the settling of the schools and the distinction of those qualified in them (*ba'da istiqrār al-madhāhib wa-tamayyuz ahlihā*)".[12] There were no fully formed schools until there were clear means to distinguish the qualified from the unqualified; that is, qualified first to give authoritative opinions (*fatāwā*, sing. *fatwā*), then to teach jurisprudence (*tadrīs*). A regular course of study with clearly identified teachers and students, in law (*fiqh*) as distinct from *ḥadīth*, turns out to go back to the early tenth century. Here, I say, is the pivot: before this point, we do not see schools like what we are familiar with from our standard eleventh-century and later sources; after this point, we do.

The clearest case is the Shāfi'ī school as it formed around Abū l-'Abbās Ibn Surayj (d. Baghdad, 306/918). Before his time, the learning of Shāfi'ī

Meaning of *qāla al-Shāfi'ī* in Ninth-Century Sources", forthcoming in *Proceedings of the School of Abbasid Studies* (2003).

[10] George Makdisi, *The Rise of Colleges: Institutions of Learning in Islam and the West* (Edinburgh, 1981); see also *idem*, *The Rise of Humanism in Classical Islam and the Christian West* (Edinburgh, 1990).

[11] George Makdisi, "La Corporation à l'époque classique de l'Islam", *Présence de Louis Massignon: hommages et témoignages* (Paris, 1987), 35–49; almost identical in C.E. Bosworth *et al.*, eds., *Essays in Honor of Bernard Lewis* (Princeton, 1989), 193–209, justifying the term "guild"; above all, *idem*, "*Ṭabaqāt*-Biography: Law and Orthodoxy in Classical Islam", *Islamic Studies* (Islamabad) 32 (1993), 371–96, for the three historical stages.

[12] Al-Māwardī, *Adab al-qāḍī*, ed. Muḥyī Hilāl al-Sirḥān (Baghdad, 1972), I, 185 = *Al-Ḥāwī al-kabīr*, ed. Maḥmūd Maṭarjī *et al.* (Beirut, 1414/1994), XX, 75.

jurisprudence was more like the gathering of *ḥadīth* reports from a number of teachers, the more the better. From his time forward, by contrast, Shāfi'ī jurisprudents have normally had an identifiable teacher and identifiable students. No particular literary production characterized the study of law before Ibn Surayj, unless it was to compose a *Mukhtaṣar*, which Ibn Surayj did after his teacher al-Mundhirī (*fl.* later ninth cent.) and others. From his time forward, however, there was a normal course of advanced study leading to the production of a *ta'līqa*, virtually a doctoral dissertation, defending the juridical opinions chosen by the Shāfi'ī school. With Ibn Surayj's students and their students in turn, the *ta'līqa* was normally a commentary on al-Muzanī's *Mukhtaṣar*. It was a mark of the classical school of law that it had a local chief (*ra'īs*), and Ibn Surayj seems to have been the first jurisprudent described as having the chieftaincy of the Shāfi'īya. No one before him is said to have been recognized as chief of the school, but from his time forward, the chieftaincy was usually said to have ended up with someone.

Only two marks of the classical school of law did not appear first in the lifetime of Ibn Surayj. First was the explicit distinction between graduate students (*aṣḥāb*), seeking a licence from their master to teach, and undergraduates (*talāmīdh*), seeking a licence to give opinions. The distinction was important to the school as an institution for forming jurisprudents, and first appeared with a student of Ibn Surayj's and the students under him. The second mark was the biographical dictionary of adherents of the school. The first freestanding biographical dictionary of the Shāfi'ī school appears to have been that of the Nīshāpūran al-Muṭṭawwi'ī, *Al-Mudhhab fī shuyūkh al-madhhab*, from about a century after Ibn Surayj's death.[13] There was a forerunner of the biographical dictionary in the generation before Ibn Surayj though, for the *Manāqib al-Shāfi'ī* of Dāwūd al-Ẓāhirī (d. Baghdad, 270/884) certainly included a section on al-Shāfi'ī's students, as indicated by extant quotations.[14]

[13]Kātib Çelebī, *Kashf al-ẓunūn*, ed. Şerefettin Yaltkaya and Rifat Bilge (Istanbul, 1941–43), 1645, where it is alternatively attributed to Abū l-Ṭayyib al-Ṣu'lūkī (d. Nīshāpūr, 404/1014). Al-Subkī often quotes from al-Muṭṭawwi'ī concerning figures of the tenth century, for which see *Ṭabaqāt al-shāfi'īya al-kubrā*, ed. Maḥmūd Muḥammad al-Ṭanāḥī and 'Abd al-Fattāḥ al-Ḥulw (Cairo, 1964–76), III, index, *s.n.* 'Umar ibn 'Alī. *Al-Mudhhab* in the title looks odd, but *adhhaba* may mean to gild, so that the meaning would be "the gilt book concerning the shaykhs of the school"; alternatively, it might be taken as a noun of place, hence "where one is led concerning the shaykhs of the school".

[14]Al-Khaṭīb al-Baghdādī, *Ta'rīkh Baghdād* (Cairo, 1349/1931, repr. Cairo and Beirut, n.d.), X, 449; Abū Isḥāq al-Shīrāzī, *Ṭabaqāt al-fuqahā'*, ed. Iḥsān 'Abbās (Beirut, repr. 1401/1981), 103.

The classical Ḥanafī school formed at about the same time. The teacher who corresponds most closely to Ibn Surayj is Abū al-Ḥasan al-Karkhī (d. Baghdad, 340/952). Like Ibn Surayj among the Shāfiʿīya, he had many more identifiable students than any Ḥanafī before him. Like Ibn Surayj with the *Mukhtaṣar* of al-Muzanī, he wrote a commentary on *Al-Jāmiʿ al-ṣaghīr* of al-Shaybānī, as well as a *Mukhtaṣar* of his own, epitomizing Ḥanafī jurisprudence. Students of his produced commentaries on both the *Jāmiʿ*s and his own *Mukhtaṣar*. He seems to have been the first recognized chief of the Ḥanafī school. And just as one traces the intellectual lineages of the great Shāfiʿī jurisprudents of the eleventh century back through Ibn Surayj, so the lineages of most of the great eleventh-century Ḥanafī jurisprudents go back to al-Karkhī. There had already been biographical treatments of the Ḥanafī school in the generation before him, notably at the end of the *Manāqib Abī Ḥanīfa* of al-Ṭaḥāwī (d. al-Fusṭāṭ, 321/933).[15]

The strongest candidate for the pivotal figure of the Ḥanbalī school, comparable to Ibn Surayj and al-Karkhī, is Abū Bakr al-Khallāl (d. Baghdad, 311/923). Before him, various individuals collected what they had heard from Aḥmad, but he seems to have made the first great synthetic collection of Aḥmad's opinions, a work of twenty volumes, now mostly lost.[16] F.E. Peters actually credits him with forming a Ḥanbalī school by writing

[15]Kātib Çelebī, *Kashf*, 1836–37. Many quotations in the biographical literature. On the Ḥanafī biographical tradition, see further Nurit Tsafrir, "Semi-Ḥanafīs and Ḥanafī Biographical Sources", *Studia Islamica* 84 (1996), 67–85, and Eerik Dickinson, "Aḥmad b. al-Ṣalt and His Biography of Abū Ḥanīfa", *JAOS* 116 (1996), 406–15. Admittedly, Tsafrir supposes that the source of later quotations from al-Ṭaḥāwī is normally *Al-Taʾrīkh al-kabīr*, which must have comprehended more than just Ḥanafīya ("Semi-Ḥanafīs", 74). Certainly, al-Ṭaḥāwī is often quoted in non-Ḥanafī sources concerning non-Ḥanafīya; e.g. for the year when the Shāfiʿīya al-Rabīʿ ibn Sulaymān, al-Muzanī, and Muḥammad ibn Naṣr were born: Ibn Ḥajar, *Tahdhīb al-tahdhīb* (Hyderabad, AH 1325–27, repr. Beirut, n.d.), III, 246. Presumably, the *Taʾrīkh* was the source of these quotations. It seems to me likely that *Manāqīb Abī Ḥanīfa* was more important for the Ḥanafī biographical tradition than the *Taʾrīkh* because it is the work analogous to Dāwūd's *Manāqib al-Shāfiʿī*, important for the Shāfiʿī biographical tradition. The analogy is reinforced by comparison with two other *manāqib* works that are extant: *Manāqib Abī Ḥanīfa* of al-Ṣaymarī (d. Baghdad, 436/1045), which includes a long biographical section concerning Abū Ḥanīfa's followers at the end much used by Tsafrir herself, and Ibn ʿAbd al-Barr (d. Jativa, 463/1071), *Al-Intiqāʾ fī faḍāʾil al-thalātha al-aʾimma al-fuqahāʾ Mālik wa-al-Shāfiʿī wa-Abī Ḥanīfa* (Cairo, AH 1350), which includes a biographical section of followers after the entry for each eponym. The origin of the specifically Ḥanafī biographical tradition I have identified as Ibn Shujāʿ al-Thaljī (d. 266/880?): Christopher Melchert, "How Ḥanafism Came to Originate in Kufa and Traditionalism in Medina", *Islamic Law and Society* 6 (1999), 318–47, at 342–43.

[16]See Fuat Sezgin, *Geschichte des arabischen Schrifttums* (Leiden, 1967–proceeding), I, 507.

a biographical dictionary of it.[17] On the other hand, one can draw up no long list of his students in law, comparable to lists for Ibn Surayj and al-Karkhī. There were important Ḥanbalī jurisprudents of the century after him, even in Baghdad, who studied primarily under others. This is probably because the Ḥanābila, as the fiercest upholders of traditionalism, were still unwilling to recognize the authority of recent teachers, even so august as Aḥmad ibn Ḥanbal, as opposed to the Prophet and his Companions; therefore, they would not form a school of law comparable to the Shāfiʿī and Ḥanafī. Anyway, al-Khallāl himself may have aimed not so much at establishing a Ḥanbalī school comparable to Ibn Surayj's Shāfiʿī guild as at establishing a guild that comprised all traditionalists in law and theology.[18] This often seems to be the sense of al-Maqdisī's references to Ḥanbalism in Iranian cities.[19]

There was a Mālikī school in Iraq alongside the nascent Shāfiʿī and others. In the later ninth century and through most of the tenth, for example, the *qāḍīs* of Baghdad were normally either Ḥanafī or Mālikī.[20] The *qāḍī* Ismāʿīl ibn Isḥāq (d. Baghdad, 282/896) appears to have been the most important figure of the ninth century, forming clearly identified students in Islamic law and strenuously promoting the Mālikī school (especially against the Ḥanafī). A Mālikī school similar to Ibn Surayj's Shāfiʿī school and al-Karkhī's Ḥanafī then appears to have developed with the teaching of al-Abharī (d. 375/986). The line of his students and theirs in turn continued until the later eleventh century, when the Mālikī school of Iraq appears to have become extinct. The last Baghdadī Mālikī mentioned by Abū Isḥāq al-Shīrāzī is an Ibn ʿAmrūs (d. 452/1060), while al-Qāḍī ʿIyāḍ mentions somewhat later Mālikī scholars in al-Baṣra (d. 487/1095–96) and Wāsiṭ (d. after 480/1087–88).[21]

One reason for the decline of the Iraqī Mālikī school was probably political, mainly dependence on ʿAbbāsid patronage in the form of appointments

[17] F.E. Peters, *Allah's Commonwealth* (New York, 1973), 467. An extract of al-Khallāl's biographical dictionary is extant, for which see Sezgin, *GAS*, I, 512 no. 2. It was plainly a major source for Ibn Abī Yaʿlā, *Ṭabaqāt al-ḥanābila*, ed. Muḥammad Ḥāmid al-Fiqī (Cairo, 1371/1952).

[18] Makdisi, "*Ṭabaqāt*–Biography", 379.

[19] Al-Maqdisī (Muqaddasī), *Descriptio imperii moslemici*, ed. M.J. de Goeje (Leiden, 1906), 365 (Qūmis, Ṭabaristān), 395 (Rayy), 415 (Khūzistān).

[20] See Ṣāliḥ Aḥmad al-ʿAlī, "Quḍāt Baghdād fī l-ʿaṣr al-ʿabbāsī: dirāsa fī l-idāra al-islāmīya", *Majallat al-majmaʿ al-ʿilmī al-ʿirāqī* 18 (1969), 145–208.

[21] Abū Isḥāq al-Shīrāzī, *Ṭabaqāt*, 169; al-Qāḍī ʿIyāḍ, *Tartīb al-madārik*, ed. Aḥmad Bakīr Maḥmūd (Beirut, 1967, 1968?), IV, 791–92 = ed. Muḥammad ibn Tāwīt al-Ṭanjī *et al.* (al-Muḥammadīya, 1966–83), VIII, 99–100. On Ibn ʿAmrūs, see also al-Dhahabī, *Taʾrīkh al-islām*, ed. ʿUmar ʿAbd al-Salām Tadmurī (Beirut, 1407–21/1987–2000), XXX (AH 441–60), 333–34, with further references.

to judgeships: this lost most of its value with the advent of the Būyids, who occupied Baghdad in 334/945. The *coup de grâce* may have been Mālikī refusal to allow the endower of a *madrasa*, a mosque devoted exclusively to the teaching of law and ancillary sciences, to appoint and dismiss its personnel: unlike the other schools, the Mālikī reserved this right for the caliph, just as in ordinary mosques. In consequence, there was little attraction to founding a Mālikī *madrasa*. George Makdisī discovered this distinction and so explained the paucity of *madāris* in North Africa.[22] I have suggested that the Mālikī school died out in Iraq just when *madāris* were being founded there partly because prospective students could see that stipends were available only for the study of Shāfi'ī and Ḥanafī law, not Mālikī.[23]

Meanwhile, the Mālikī school survived in North Africa even without *madāris*, as also without yet any clearly identifiable teaching tradition comparable to that of Ibn Surayj. A political reason can be found for this, too, mainly the advent of the Fāṭimids (conquered Ifrīqiya 296/909, Egypt 358/969). First, the Fāṭimids kept out the competition, mainly the efficient new Shāfi'ī and Ḥanafī guild schools. Without the Fāṭimid occupation, Shāfi'ī jurisprudents in the Surayjī line and Ḥanafī in the Karkhī might have moved in from Iraq and supplanted the Mālikī school, as they did absorb local traditions in Khurāsān to the east. Second, it appears that the Ḥanafīya tended to collaborate with the new dynasty, even convert to Ismā'īlism, discrediting them when the Fāṭimids were overthrown (lost Ifrīqiya 443/1051).[24] In al-Andalus, of course, the Mālikī school was established by the Umayyad dynasty.[25]

The Iraqī Ẓāhirī school faded away even sooner than the Mālikī. It went back to Dāwūd ibn 'Alī ibn Khalaf al-Iṣbahānī (d. Baghdad, 270/884), an adherent of the ninth-century Shāfi'ī school of law and theology (on which more below). He was succeeded by his son, Abū Bakr Muḥammad (d. Baghdad, 297/910), who was succeeded in turn by his student Ibn al-Mughallis (d. 324/936). This looks like the start of a succession of chiefs not

---

[22] Makdisi, *Rise of Colleges*, 37–38.

[23] The classic study of the *madrasa* in Baghdad is George Makdisi, "Muslim Institutions of Learning in Eleventh-Century Baghdad", *BSOAS* 24 (1961), 1–56. For its earlier history, see Heinz Halm, "Die Anfänge der Madrasa", *ZDMG Supplement* III.1: *XIX. deutscher Orientalistentag*, ed. Wolfgang Voigt (Wiesbaden, 1977), 438–48.

[24] On the Ḥanafīya and Mālikīya under the Fāṭimids, see further now Wilferd Madelung, "The Religious Policy of the Fatimids toward their Sunni Subjects in the Maghrib", *L'Égypte fatimide* (Paris, 1999), 97–104.

[25] Famous medieval testimony from al-Maqdisī, *Descriptio*, 237, and Ibn Ḥazm, *Al-Iḥkām fī uṣūl al-aḥkām*, ed. Aḥmad Muḥammad Shākir (Cairo, AH 1345), IV, 230 = (Beirut, n.d.), I, 625.

unlike what starts for the Shāfiʿī school with Ibn Surayj. Other figures are said to have introduced Ẓāhirism to regions outside Iraq. The geographer al-Maqdisī, writing in 375/985, noted the school's presence in Fars and Sind, confirmed in the next century by Abū Isḥāq al-Shīrāzī.[26] But Abū Isḥāq also remarks that the last Ẓāhirī jurisprudent of Baghdad was Ibn al-Akhḍar (d. 429/1038), composer of a biographical dictionary of the Ẓāhirī school.[27] It seems to be an example of a personal school (until the eleventh century, it was usually known as the Dāwūdī) that never made the transition to a guild. Additional reasons for its extinction were probably its association with the Būyids, good for judicial appointments for a time but a definite liability when the dynasty fell; the association of too many Ẓāhirī jurisprudents with Muʿtazilism, a doomed theological school; too emphatic a position against *taqlīd* (accepting the superior authority of a past jurisprudent), which must have inhibited the operation of a school; and, finally, too emphatic a position against *qiyās* (analogy), which became by consensus a main source of Islamic law.[28]

Another unsuccessful school was the Jarīrī, loyal to Muḥammad ibn Jarīr al-Ṭabarī (d. Baghdad, 310/923). Al-Ṭabarī was a polymath famous especially for his work in history, Qur'ān commentary, and law (in descending order for the twentieth century but ascending for the tenth). There survive only fragments of some of his legal work, but that work was sufficiently impressive that numbers of tenth-century jurisprudents were identified as his followers. Like the Ẓāhirī school, it appears never to have made the transition to the guild stage, developing no regular means of forming new adherents. Unlike the Ẓāhirī school, it never depended on patronage and endorsed no outré theory such as the rejection of *qiyās*; however, a number of its leading adherents were Muʿtazila, and it may have had altogether too élite and literary a character to survive in the long term, as the caliphs reasserted themselves on a new, traditionalist basis. (Another unsuccessful school to which one sees references was the Awzāʿī. Gerhard Conrad has gone over the extant biographical record to reconstruct the earliest forms of the tradition and found that its eponym, al-Awzāʿī [d. Beirut, 157/773–74?], did not emerge as the foremost representative of Syrian jurisprudence until the later ninth century, while references to his school are back-projections from later still.[29])

---

[26] Al-Maqdisī, *Descriptio*, 439, 481; Abū Isḥāq al-Shīrāzī, *Ṭabaqāt*, 178–79.

[27] Abū Isḥāq al-Shīrāzī, *Ṭabaqāt*, 178; al-Khaṭīb al-Baghdādī, *Ta'rīkh Baghdād*, III, 38.

[28] *EI*², *s.v.* "Ẓāhiriyya", by Abdel-Magid Turki, discusses only the Andalusian school in the eleventh century and after.

[29] Gerhard Conrad, *Die Quḍāt Dimašq und der Maḏhab al-Auzāʿī* (Beirut, 1994).

This much of *The Formation of the Sunnī Schools of Law* seems well established. It has attracted few substantial corrections beyond Devin Stewart's observation that there must have been an Imāmī guild school from the time of al-Shaykh al-Mufīd (d. Baghdad, 413/1022?), recognized as the head of his school and author of an epitome, *Al-Muqni'a*, that became the regular basis of Imāmī teaching.[30] Parallel studies by Wael B. Hallaq and A. Kevin Reinhart have confirmed Ibn Surayj's importance for the developing Shāfi'ī school and the science of *uṣūl al-fiqh* (jurisprudence proper).[31] Hallaq's book-length study of school loyalty suggests many new lines of research.[32]

Before the Classical Schools

The question of schools before the tenth century is much less settled. The argument of *The Formation of the Sunnī Schools of Law* was twofold: first, that the regional and personal schools had no regular means of forming and certifying jurisprudents such as we find at the guild stage with the work of Ibn Surayj and his contemporaries; second, that the ideological challenge of traditionalism is what unhinged the old regional system, provoked the formation of personal schools, and eventually forced virtually all jurisprudents to adopt the combination of inspired texts and rational manipulation of them that has characterized Islamic law throughout the guild period. As for the first point, it is fairly easy to show that there was scant distinction in the ninth century and before between the study of law and of *ḥadīth*. We do have lists of teachers and students, especially for the personal Ḥanafī school, that anticipate the intellectual lineages of the classical period; however, there are also numerous signs in these lists of back-projection, such as contradictory reports of who learnt from whom or was loyal to whom and a suspicious contrast between fullness of information about the eponyms and their circles (Abū Ḥanīfa in al-Kūfa, Mālik in Medina) and scantiness of information about the next two or three generations.[33]

---

[30]Devin J. Stewart, review of Melchert, *Formation*, in *Islamic Law and Society* 6 (1999), 275–81.

[31]Wael B. Hallaq, "Was al-Shafi'i the Master Architect of Islamic Jurisprudence?", *IJMES* 25 (1993), 587–605; A. Kevin Reinhart, *Before Revelation: the Boundaries of Muslim Moral Thought* (Albany, 1995), Chap. 2. Ibn Surayj's importance in Shāfi'ī intellectual lineages was earliest pointed out by Heinz Halm, *Die Ausbreitung der šāfi'itischen Rechtsschule* (Wiesbaden, 1974), 22, 28.

[32]Wael B. Hallaq, *Authority, Continuity, and Change in Islamic Law* (Cambridge, 2001).

[33]Nurit Tsafrir is presently the leading student of the early Ḥanafī school: see "The Spread of the Ḥanafī School in the Western Regions of the 'Abbāsid Caliphate", Ph.D. dissertation, Princeton, 1993; *idem*, "Semi-Ḥanafīs"; *idem*, "The Beginnings of the Ḥanafī

The second point is more difficult to establish: that the greatest division of Muslim jurisprudents before the tenth century was not among adherents of different schools, whether regional or personal, but between *aṣḥāb al-ra'y*, the rationalistic jurisprudents, and *aṣḥāb al-ḥadīth*, their adversaries the traditionalists.[34] (As established by George Makdisi, "traditionist" indicates a *muḥaddith*, someone who studies and transmits *ḥadīth*, whatever his theological inclination, whereas "traditionalist" indicates someone who systematically prefers to base his law and theology on textual sources as opposed to speculative reasoning.[35] Writing before Makdisi, Schacht referred only to "traditionists", and for the early period that concerned him, reputable traditionists normally were traditionalists. In the later ninth century, however, there emerged outstanding traditionists whose orthodoxy traditionalists did not recognize; e.g., al-Bukhārī and al-Ṭabarī.) According to ninth-century and later traditionalist histories, of course, most Muslim men of religion from the Companions forward had been traditionalists. But examination of the earliest sources shows that practically all the major figures engaged in jurisprudence by *ra'y*. Moreover, the leading (and arguably most extreme) traditionalist of the ninth century, Aḥmad ibn Ḥanbal, studied for some time under Abū Yūsuf (d. Baghdad, 182/798), leader of the earliest, nascent Ḥanafī school. Traditionalists and rationalists could hardly have existed as distinct, hostile parties before then. My tentative suggestion is that the thesis of a created Qur'ān, evidently a Ḥanafī doctrine, was what precipitated the break between *aṣḥāb al-ra'y* and *aṣḥāb al-ḥadīth* at about the early 180s/late 790s.[36]

Apart from some specific theological principles, what the traditionalists had against rationalist jurisprudence was largely moralistic disquiet with its flexibility. That is, traditionalists thought that the rationalists continually evaded the demands of the law through *ḥiyal* (legal devices honouring the

School in Iṣfahān", *Islamic Law and Society* 5 (1998), 1–34. She is readier than I to accept the claims of Ḥanafī biographical literature and to reject contrary claims from non-Ḥanafī. Cf. Melchert, "How Ḥanafism Came to Originate in Kufa", 342–43, 346 n. It was a manifest error on my part to assert there that al-Ṭaḥāwī died in Baghdad; however, it is plain from later quotations that biographical data were transmitted from al-Ṭaḥāwī by Abū Bakr al-Dāmaghānī (on whom see al-Dhahabī, *Ta'rīkh*, XXVI [AH 351–80], 225, with further references), who certainly transferred from Egypt to Baghdad.

[34] Esp. for the ninth century, see Christopher Melchert, "Traditionist-Jurisprudents and the Framing of Islamic Law", *Islamic Law and Society* 8 (2001), 383–406.

[35] George Makdisi, "Ash'arî and the Ash'arites in Islamic Religious History", *Studia Islamica* 17 (1962), 37–80, at 49.

[36] On the created Qur'ān and the Ḥanafī school, see *EI*², *s.v.* "Miḥna", by Martin Hinds, with references to the pioneering work of Josef van Ess.

letter of the law; sing. *ḥīla*), preferred their own sophisticated reasoning to venerable *ḥadīth*, and allowed continual change, even in what one jurisprudent said concerning one problem. What the traditionalists offered instead was not their own opinions that would not change, but rather *ḥadīth* reports of what the Prophet and (to the mid-ninth century) outstanding experts of his Companions and their Followers had said. Where the rationalists were devoted to *munāẓara*, debate about points of law (as if superior casuistry were the way to God's will), the traditionalists favoured *mudhākara*, a contest to recall variant chains of transmission for important *ḥadīth* reports.[37]

As for the ninth century, some jurisprudents naturally tried to bridge the gap between rationalism and traditionalism, especially the followers of al-Shāfiʿī. In theology, bridging the two approaches meant defending traditionalist tenets by means of rational argument, also sometimes qualifying traditionalist tenets so as to make them more defensible; for example, conceding that one's pronuncitation of the Qur'ān was created, although not the Qur'ān itself. In law, it meant reliance on inspired texts, as opposed to rationalist reliance on experience and common sense, yet combining them by rational means, as opposed to the traditionalist preference for simply repeating the inspired texts, even if some apparently contradicted others.[38] Al-Shāfiʿī himself was known as a compromiser between rationalism and traditionalism (not, as Schacht tended to suppose, a simple advocate of traditionalism).[39] Many of the leading advocates of this compromise theological tendency were followers of al-Shāfiʿī in Baghdad: Abū Thawr, Dāwūd al-Ẓāhirī, and al-Muḥāsibī, among others.[40] Almost none of their legal writings survive, but we have a great deal from the Shāfiʿī school in Egypt, which certainly exemplifies the compromise approach. By the end of the ninth century, jurisprudents of all schools were won over to such an approach.[41]

---

[37] Melchert, *Formation*, 9–22. For instances of *mudhākara*, see Munir-ul-Din Ahmed, "The Institution of al-Mudhākara", *ZDMG* Suppl. 1, Teil 2 (1969), *17. Deutscher Orientalistentag Wurzburg 1968* (Wiesbaden, 1983), 595–603.

[38] Traditionalist practice is described by Susan A. Spectorsky, "Aḥmad Ibn Ḥanbal's *Fiqh*", *JAOS* 102 (1982), 461–65. Christopher Melchert, "The Adversaries of Aḥmad Ibn Ḥanbal", *Arabica* 44 (1997), 234–53, based on a paper presented to the American Oriental Society, Madison, March 1994. There has also now appeared a masterful analysis of al-Shāfiʿī's *Risāla*, stressing the rational combination of inspired texts to derive the law: Joseph Edmund Lowry, "The Legal-Theoretical Content of the *Risāla* of Muḥammad b. Idrīs al-Shāfiʿī", Ph.D. dissertation, Univ. of Pennsylvania, 1999.

[39] Similarly, Hallaq, "Was al-Shafi'i the Master Architect?", 591–94.

[40] See Melchert, "Adversaries", 234–53. The tendency was first noticed by Josef van Ess, "Ibn Kullāb und die Miḥna", *Oriens* 18–19 (1965–66), 92–141, trans. with additional notes by Claude Gilliot, "Ibn Kullāb et la *Miḥna*", *Arabica* 37 (1990), 173–233.

[41] See Melchert, "Traditionist-Jurisprudents", 383–406.

Working mainly from al-Shāfiʿī's polemics against the Iraqis and Medinans, Schacht documented a shift from regional tradition to *ḥadīth* as the formal basis of legal doctrine. The rules themselves evidently did not change significantly; therefore, either the rules were based on *ḥadīth* all along, just not explicitly, or *ḥadīth* reports were generated to support the rules that the jurisprudents believed anyway. Confirming the second possibility, certain jurisprudents of the mid-ninth century are accused in the biographical literature of fitting out Ḥanafī doctrine with supporting *ḥadīth*, as one would expect to find, along with the retrojection of acceptable theological doctrines (for example, the created Qur'ān did not remain a characteristic Ḥanafī doctrine).[42]

If there was a transition from regional schools to personal, one should be able to supplement Schacht's account of al-Shāfiʿī's polemics against the Medinans with other examples of collision between old and new. Indeed, in both al-Baṣra and al-Fusṭāṭ there were indignant protests at the intrusion of Ḥanafī *qāḍīs*, who were expected not to respect local traditions of *waqf* (a foundation reserving designated property from some of the normal operations of Islamic law, such as division among heirs).[43] It seemed to me that it must have been traditionalism that unhinged the old regional schools; that their rationalistic jurisprudents must have felt more comfortable relying on the doctrine of one venerable teacher than on a more diffuse and less uniform regional tradition. Other scholars and some of my own subsequent research have raised difficulties.

First, whereas I had assumed from Schacht that the Ḥanafī school spread from al-Kūfa, I later noticed that those identified as the followers of Abū Ḥanīfa by Ibn Saʿd (d. Baghdad, 230/845) were nearly all Baghdadi, while none was Kūfan, tending to confirm that the Ḥanafism of many outstanding eighth-century Kūfans must have been retrojected by the later Ḥanafī biographical tradition, akin to the retrospective fitting out of Ḥanafī jurisprudence with *ḥadīth*.[44] But of what, then, was the personal Ḥanafī school a transformation? Second, Eric Chaumont has sensibly questioned

[42]Brought out by Eerik Dickinson, "Aḥmad b. al-Ṣalt", as well as by me. My only major quarrel with Dickinson's account is his apparent assertion that collections of *ḥadīth* used by Abū Ḥanīfa were usually the work of the Ḥanafī school. Actually, most of the known collections were by traditionists not claimed by the Ḥanafī school. See Melchert, "Traditionist-Jurisprudents", 396.

[43]See also Tsafrir, "Spread", Chaps. 2, 3, 9; additionally, on Egyptian juridical independence, Baber Johansen, "Wahrheit und Geltungsanspruch: zur Begründung und Begrenzung der Autorität des Qadi-Urteils im islamischen Recht", *La Giustiza nell'Alto Medioevo* (Spoleto, 1997), 975–1074, esp. 998–1015.

[44]Melchert, "How Ḥanafism Became Kufan".

whether anyone troubled by traditionalist arguments would have chosen Abū Ḥanīfa as a personal authority.[45] (On the other hand, Maribel Fierro accepts just this mechanism, the superior comfort of a personal authority in the face of the traditionalist challenge, to explain the adoption of Mālik in al-Andalus.[46]) Third, Hallaq has questioned Schacht's whole scheme of a regional stage preceding the personal, pointing out that our earliest books of law (with the partial exception of Mālik's *Muwaṭṭa'*) normally cite individual authorities, not anonymous local tradition.[47] Although Hallaq has left me unconvinced, I would say that he has shifted the burden of proof onto anyone who would still refer to regional schools, which need sharper definition and more documentation than what Schacht offered (naturally enough, 50 years on).[48]

Further Lines of Research

More will surely be done with the organization of teaching in the eighth and ninth centuries. From Gregor Schoeler and Michael Cook, we have excellent studies of the technology of transmission, mainly by word of mouth as opposed to writing.[49] An important finding of Schoeler's is that we should

[45] Eric Chaumont, review of Melchert, *Formation*, in *Bulletin critique des Annales islamologiques* 16 (2000), 71f. His further argument that there was no traditionalization of Ḥanafī doctrine, since al-Shaybānī had already relied on *ḥadīth*, rests on the assumption that the works attributed to al-Shaybānī actually go back, as we have them, to the eighth century, which needs to be demonstrated in the face of Calder, *Studies*, Chap. 3 (as apparently conceded by Chaumont himself in EI^2, *s.v.* "Shaybānī").

[46] Maribel Fierro, "Proto-Mālikīs, Mālikīs and Reformed Mālikīs in al-Andalus", unpublished MS, citing A. Fernández Félix, "Al-'Utbī (m. 255/869) y su compilacíon jurídica al-'Utbiyya", Ph.D. dissertation, Madrid, 1999. Fierro is responsible for a superior account of the introduction of traditionalist jurisprudence to al-Andalus: "The Introduction of *Ḥadīth* in al-Andalus". Cf. *Formation*, 156–64. Fierro's MS, "Proto-Mālikīs", promises a superior history of the Andalusian Mālikī school as a whole in *Political Legitimacy, Knowledge and Heresy in al-Andalus*, forthcoming.

[47] Wael B. Hallaq, "From Regional to Personal Schools of Law? A Reevaluation", *Islamic Law and Society* 8 (2001), 1–26.

[48] Note, however, Patricia Crone's identification of several major doctrines distinguishing rival Kūfan and Medinan blocs, with the Kūfan preserved in Ḥanafī and Shī'ī law, Medinan in Mālikī, Shāfi'ī, and Ḥanbalī: Patricia Crone, *Roman, Provincial, and Islamic Law* (Cambridge, 1987), 23.

[49] See Gregor Schoeler, "Die Frage der schriftlichen oder mündlichen Überlieferung der Wissenschaften im frühen Islam", *Der Islam* 62 (1985), 201–30; *idem*, "Mündliche Thora und Ḥadīṯ", *Der Islam* 66 (1989), 213–51; *idem*, "Writing and Publishing on the Use and Function of Writing in the First Centuries of Islam", *Arabica* 44 (1997), 423–34, trans. Peter Butler, abbr. from "Schreiben und Veröffentlichen", *Der Islam* 69 (1992), 1–43; Michael Cook, "The Opponents of the Writing of Tradition in Early Islam", *Arabica* 44 (1997), 437–530.

normally not expect fixed texts before the mid-ninth century. Before then, texts were more in the nature of lectures, expected to vary from one occasion to another and from one students' notebooks to another's. Miklos Muranyi has scrutinized tenth- and eleventh-century manuscript fragments from al-Qayrawān for signs of how books were transmitted in the ninth century.[50] One looks forward eagerly to the appearance in book form of Nurit Tsafrir's work on the early Ḥanafī school. Meanwhile, Nimrod Hurvitz has begun to publish concerning the early Ḥanbalī school.[51]

Still, as for the period of the classical schools, the bulk of important new work will probably come from the study of actual books of law, not ancillary works like biographical dictionaries. I was certainly conscious when working on my dissertation that its biographical evidence about schools needed confirmation from law books, although also that no one was about to support me financially if I put off submitting it in favour of reading law books for another ten years. Norman Calder's argument for redating the best-known law books of the eighth and ninth centuries has been mentioned already. Its stress on the fluidity of texts throughout the ninth century is complementary with Schoeler's work but apparently independent of it and probably somewhat overdrawn: the tendency of critical scholarship has not been to dismiss the idea of fluid texts, but it has been to push the dates of our familiar texts back in time from where Calder put them.[52] Calder's proposed dates fit quite well with some of my own findings in *Formation*; for example, the start of the commentary literature at about the turn of the tenth century, which suggests that the works being commented upon (particularly by al-Shaybānī and al-Shāfi'ī) were still being formed in the ninth century. The fluidity of texts and uncertainty of attributions become more severe difficulties the further back in time one goes. Therefore, characterizations of Islamic law in the eighth century will always have to be more tentative

---

[50]Muranyi, *Rechtsbücher*, with references to earlier studies in the bibliography.

[51]Nimrod Hurvitz, "Schools of Law and Historical Context: Re-examining the Formation of the Ḥanbalī *Madhhab*", *Islamic Law and Society* 7 (2000), 37–64, stressing the piety that held together Aḥmad's disciples and successors. See also *idem*, "Aḥmad ibn Ḥanbal and the Formation of Islamic Orthodoxy", Ph.D. dissertation, Princeton University, 1994, also now the basis of a book to appear shortly from Curzon.

[52]E.g. Miklos Muranyi has both published a fiercely critical review of Calder and described AH 200 (AD 815–16) as the "magic boundary" on the further side of which one cannot rely on the verbatim transmission of texts: Miklos Muranyi, "Die frühe Rechtsliteratur zwischen Quellenanalyse und Fiktion", *Islamic Law and Society* 4 (1997), 224–41; *idem*, *Rechtsbücher*, esp. 78. Yasin Dutton offers some effective criticism of Calder but seems dogmatical, doubtfully capable of being convinced by any evidence that any early text was significantly fluid: see Yasin Dutton, "*'Amal* v. *Ḥadīth* in Islamic Law", esp. 28–33; *idem*, *The Origins of Islamic Law* (Richmond, Surrey, 1999), esp. Chap. 2.

than characterizations of Islamic law in the ninth. But scholarship is always probabilistic, anyway, and considerable progress from where we now stand looks very possible.

14

THE CALIPHS, THE 'ULAMĀ', AND THE LAW: DEFINING THE ROLE AND FUNCTION OF THE CALIPH IN THE EARLY 'ABBĀSID PERIOD*

Muhammad Qasim Zaman

Abstract

The early 'Abbāsid period is usually thought of as a time when a definitive and enduring separation between religion and politics took place. On this view, expressed most notably by Lapidus and Crone and Hinds, the failure of the *Miḥna* instituted by the caliph al-Ma'mūn, a major showdown with prominent 'ulamā', is taken as the critical moment which marked the end of any involvement of the caliphs in matters of law. Arguing against any such separation between the religious or legal and the political realms, this essay analyses various indications in juristic and historical sources from the early 'Abbāsid period to show that the caliph continued to be recognized as a participant in the function of commenting on or resolving obscure matters of a legal import. There is, moreover, considerable evidence to show caliphal participation in religious life in general, before as well as after the *Miḥna*, and no evidence to indicate a separation between religion and politics.

Introduction

The question of the caliph's position in relation to the law in the first centuries of Islam is a subject of considerable significance for the social and political history of Islam, as it also is for the history of Islamic law. The terms of any inquiry into what role (if any) the caliph had in resolving legal problems or, generally, in religious life must be defined, of course, according to the peculiarities of the specific period about which this question is posed. In this essay, I shall address this question with reference to the early 'Abbāsid era—understood here as the period from the establishment of the 'Abbāsid dynasty in 132/750 to the death of al-Mutawakkil in 247/861.

The early 'Abbāsid period saw the emergence of the religious scholars, the *'ulamā'*, as a visible and increasingly influential religious elite, the beginnings of schools of law, major developments in the study

---

* I should like to thank Professors Donald P. Little, Wael B. Hallaq, and Patricia Crone for comments on earlier incarnations of this article. I am also grateful to Professor David Powers and the outside readers for *ILS* for their helpful suggestions.

of *ḥadīth* and towards the formalization of the concept of the Prophet's *sunna*, and other developments which eventually led to the crystallization of Sunnī and Shīʿī Islam. This period also witnessed some remarkable initiatives, which we shall briefly review in this essay, towards defining and regulating the relationship between the caliphs and the ʿulamāʾ. Considering the significance of this period in Islamic intellectual and social history, it is not surprising that much of the debate on questions of religious authority has tended to be focused on the early ʿAbbāsid era; this essay will not be a *bidʿa* so far as this tradition is concerned. It is striking, however, that despite varied approaches to questions of religious authority and to early ʿAbbāsid history in general there is remarkable agreement among modern scholars on the "classical model", so to speak, of the relations between the caliphs and the ʿulamāʾ and of the caliph's place and function (or rather, the lack of any) in the sphere of the law. This model, which postulates a comprehensive separation between religion and the state, may be paraphrased thus: the caliphs and the ʿulamāʾ were in sharp conflict over matters of religious authority; the caliphs lost the contest and came effectively to be excluded from all say in matters of the law and in whatever else the ʿulamāʾ defined as their exclusive preserve; and, once in place, this model of separation essentially persisted for much of medieval Islamic history.

In an influential article on the "Separation of State and Religion in the Development of Early Islamic Society", Ira Lapidus has argued, for instance, that the function of *al-amr biʾl-maʿrūf* came to be effectively taken over from the caliph by religious leaders and vigilante groups in the wake of the civil war between al-Amin (r. 193-98/809-13) and al-Maʾmūn (r. 198-218/813-33), and that the loss of this function in turn signifies the end of the caliph's role in the religious sphere of the community's life. The failure of the *Miḥna*, the "Inquisition" instituted by al-Maʾmūn to have the *fuqahāʾ* and *qāḍī*s conform to the doctrine of the "createdness" of the Qurʾān, only confirmed this separation between religion and state, a separation which also entailed one between society and state.[1] Tilman Nagel sees the ideological initiatives of the early ʿAbbāsid caliphs as ultimately unsuccessful efforts to build their authority on the idea of the *sunna* or of the *imāma* (or both), with the

[1] Ira M. Lapidus, "The Separation of State and Religion in the Development of Early Islamic Society", *International Journal of Middle East Studies*, VI (1975), 363-85. Also see id., "The Evolution of Muslim Urban Society", *Comparative Studies in Society and History*, XV (1973), 21-50, esp. 28ff.; id., *A History of Islamic Societies* (Cambridge: Cambridge University Press, 1988), 120ff.

result that Sunnī Islam developed not just in separation from, but in opposition to, the ʿAbbāsids.[2] While Nagel considers devotion to the *sunna* and the idea of the *imāma* as "*Ersatzinstitutionen*" intended to substitute for the Prophet's inimitable authority, Patricia Crone and Martin Hinds argue that religious authority did not die with the Prophet but rather continued in the person of "God's caliph".[3] On their showing, the Umayyad caliphs enjoyed religious authority, as also did the early ʿAbbāsids. However, it is argued that by the time the ʿAbbāsids came to power, the ʿulamā', armed with the concept of an immutable *sunna* of the Prophet of which they alone claimed to be the sole interpreters, were already well-advanced on the way to terminating the caliph's religious authority. The showdown did come with al-Ma'mūn, but "the fact that the ʿulamā' had managed to produce even al-Shāfiʿī before the collision came evidently meant that al-Ma'mūn's chances of winning were slim";[4] it was not long before "the vulgar masses [acting] ... under the leadership of Ibn Ḥanbal ... rejected caliphal guidance in religious matters once and for all."[5]

This essay seeks to reexamine some of the key assumptions of views such as the foregoing. It will be argued here that except for the period of the *Miḥna*, there is little evidence to suggest that the early ʿAbbāsid caliphs were competing with the ʿulamā' or challenging the latter on the prerogative to define and interpret matters of law and dogma. Rather, caliphs prior to al-Ma'mūn seem essentially to have subscribed to the emerging Sunnī ʿulamā's views of what the caliph's role and function ought to be. The scholars, inasmuch as it is possible to generalize about their views, did not seek to separate or divorce religion from the state, or to divest the caliph of any role in matters of

[2] Tilman Nagel, *Rechtleitung und Kalifat: Versuch über eine Grundfrage der islamischen Geschichte* (Bonn: Bonner orientalische Studien [Neue Serie, Bd. 27], 1975).

[3] P. Crone and M. Hinds, *God's Caliph: Religious authority in the first centuries of Islam* (Cambridge: Cambridge University Press, 1986).

[4] Ibid., 93. That it took at least a century after al-Shāfiʿī's death (204/820) for his influence to be felt should caution us against the authors' appraisal that "al-Shāfiʿī's views were simply nails in the caliphal coffin." On the slow growth of al-Shāfiʿī's influence, see Wael B. Hallaq, "Was al-Shafiʿi the Master Architect of Sunni Jurisprudence?", *International Journal of Middle East Studies*, XXV (1993), 587-605; cf. Norman Calder, *Studies in Early Muslim Jurisprudence* (Oxford: Clarendon Press, 1993), 67-68.

[5] Ibid., 96. Also see *Encyclopaedia of Islam*, new edition (Leiden: E. J. Brill, 1960-. [hereafter *EI(2)*]), s.v. "Miḥna" (M. Hinds). In an earlier work, *Slaves on Horses: The evolution of the Islamic polity* (Cambridge: Cambridge University Press, 1980), Patricia Crone had come to a similar conclusion regarding the separation of religion and the state, though as part of a more ambitious argument. See, for instance, *Slaves on Horses*, 85.

law. The caliph's participation in religious life was not in competition with, or over and above that of, the emergent Sunnī ʿulamāʾ, but in conjunction with them; and both the caliphs before and after the *Miḥna and* the Sunnī ʿulamāʾ all along seem to have recognized this.

In what follows, I shall first review three treatises, all purporting to be from the early ʿAbbāsid period, which address questions of the caliph's role and function as well as his position vis-à-vis the law. Some of what is known about the participation of the caliphs in matters of law in the early ʿAbbāsid period will be discussed next, followed by a brief analysis of how the *Miḥna* of al-Maʾmūn tried, but failed, to alter the pattern and principles on which the relations of the caliphs and the ʿulamāʾ had come to be based in early ʿAbbāsid times.

Defining the Caliph's Function: Three Second/Eighth Century Views

Of the texts to be analyzed here, the earliest is the *Risāla fiʾl ṣaḥāba* by Ibn al-Muqaffaʿ (d. ca. 139/756), a secretarial official of the caliph al-Manṣūr (r. 136-58/753-75). While the *Risāla* analyzes the problem of the caliph's function and role from the "secular" side, so to speak, the other two works come from the *fuqahāʾ*. One purports to be a detailed letter from a Basran *qāḍī*, ʿUbaydallāh b. al-Ḥasan al-ʿAnbarī (d. 168/785), to the caliph al-Mahdī (r. 158-69/775-85), and is a document of quite considerable interest. The other work, of far wider scope and greater interest, is the treatise on taxation which the celebrated chief *qāḍī* Abū Yūsuf (d. 182/798) is reported to have addressed to the caliph Hārūn al-Rashīd (r. 170-93/786-809). The attribution of this treatise to Abū Yūsuf has recently been questioned by Norman Calder, though, as will be briefly argued in due course, Calder's reasoning is far from being conclusive or convincing. The attribution of this work to Abū Yūsuf will, therefore, be accepted here, and the work will be analyzed as a product of, and as reflecting, early ʿAbbāsid times.

A. *Ibn al-Muqaffaʿ's* Risāla

Of the wide-ranging concerns of Ibn al-Muqaffaʿ in his *Risāla fiʾl-ṣaḥāba*, we need note here only what he has to say as regards the caliph's religious and, specifically, legal authority.[6] The caliph, he

[6] On Ibn al-Muqaffaʿ, see *EI(2)*, s.v. (F. Gabrieli); D. Sourdel, "La biographie d'Ibn al-Muqaffaʿ d'après les sources anciennes", *Arabica*, 1 (1954), 307-23; J. D. Latham, "Ibn al-Muqaffaʿ and early ʿAbbāsid Prose", in J. Ashtiany et al., eds., *The Cambridge History of Arabic Literature: ʿAbbāsid Belle-lettres* (Cambridge: Cambridge University Press, 1990), 48-77; G. E. Lampe, Jr., "Ibn al-Muqaffaʿ:

suggests, ought to write an "*amān*" containing principles which must be faithfully adhered to by the Khurāsānī troops, so that their wayward religious beliefs will be reformed.[7] To the caliph also belongs the sole prerogative, he says, to enact and promulgate legal decisions and doctrines in the form of a uniform code (*kitāb jāmiʿ*); and it is for him rather than anyone else to define what normative *sunna* would consist of at any given time.[8] No judicial decisions are thereafter to be allowed to contravene what is thus formalized in terms of the caliph's binding *ra'y*.[9]

If Ibn al-Muqaffaʿ's advice tends rather blatantly in the direction of making the caliph the source of religious authority, what function or role does he envisage for the ʿulamā'? In so far as his "*ahl al-fiqh wa'l-sunna wa'l-siyar wa'l-naṣīḥa*"[10] are to be taken as religious scholars (or at least as a people including religious scholars) Ibn al-Muqaffaʿ makes it clear that he conceives of their role essentially as functionaries of the caliph and part of the state apparatus. Serving as the caliph's "companions" (*ṣaḥāba*) is one of the functions he has in mind for them.[11] More striking perhaps is his suggestion that they should act as moral administrators of the communities they live in, serving to discipline and reform the people, restrain them from innovations (*bidaʿ*) as well as civil strife (*fitan*), supervise their affairs, and report to higher authorities on matters they cannot themselves handle.[12]

Ibn al-Muqaffaʿ's suggestions are of considerable interest for articulating the possibilities that may have existed, or been considered, at the outset of the ʿAbbāsid rule. That this advice comes from a Persian

---

political and legal theorist and reformer", unpublished Ph.D. diss., Johns Hopkins Univ , 1987.

The text of the *Risāla* used here is that published by C. Pellat, *Ibn al-Muqaffaʿ: "conseilleur" du calife* (Paris: G.-P. Maisonneuve et Larose, 1976). For an analysis of the contents of the *Risāla*, see S. D. Goitein, "A Turning Point in the History of the Islamic State", in his *Studies on Islamic History and Institutions* (Leiden: E. J. Brill, 1966), 149-67. Also see Joseph Schacht, *The Origins of Muhammadan Jurisprudence* (Oxford: Clarendon Press, 1950), 58-59, 95, 102-03, 137.

7 *Risāla*, §11. Latham ("Ibn al-Muqaffaʿ", 67) translates *amān* as a "religious code". Goitein (*Studies*, 167) uses the term "catechism" for it, and Pellat (*Ibn al-Muqaffaʿ*, p. 24, §11) "règlement". Lampe ("Ibn al-Muqaffaʿ", 91) simply renders it as manual. On this term, also cf. S. Shaked, "From Iran to Islam: notes on some themes in transmission", *Jerusalem Studies in Arabic and Islam*, V (1984), 34. That Ibn al-Muqaffaʿ conceived of this "*amān*" as a document of some religious significance is clear from the context.

8 *Risāla*, §36; and cf. generally §§34-37.

9 Ibid., §36.

10 Ibid., §55.

11 Ibid., §49.

12 Ibid., §55-56; cf. ibid., §49. Also cf. Schacht, *Origins*, 137.

bureaucrat is not fortuitous, for it suggests the vision of a determinate religious establishment working as part of the administrative bureaucracy, somewhat in the ancient Persian tradition. Ibn al-Muqaffaʿ's advice can also be interpreted as a plea to the caliph to check the autonomy of the religious scholars and to make them dependent on himself. The suggestion concerning the caliph's enactment of legal doctrine says as much with reference to the need for uniformity of legal practice in the empire, and the advice to co-opt the ʿulamāʾ into the service of the state can also be construed to have similar implications.

If Ibn al-Muqaffaʿ's suggestions ever reached al-Manṣūr, we know nothing about how the caliph reacted to them. There are some reports, however, according to which the caliph intended to promulgate the *Muwaṭṭāʾ* of the Medinese jurist Mālik b. Anas (d. 179/795) as the single and uniform basis of legal decisions in the empire, certain accounts even asserting that it was al-Manṣūr himself who commissioned the *Muwaṭṭāʾ*. Mālik, for his part, remained unimpressed with what the caliph supposedly intended, dissuading him by pointing out precisely what Ibn al-Muqaffaʿ had also noted, but to opposite effect.[13] While Ibn al-Muqaffaʿ had called for the caliph's promulgating a code because legal diversity was too inconvenient, Mālik reportedly argued that such regional diversity in legal matters was too developed to be harmonized or regulated.[14]

It is impossible to be certain about the authenticity of the aforementioned reports concerning Mālik. There is the possibility that they may have come about as an effort to extol Mālik by suggesting, for example, that he was considered the most authoritative of the *fuqahāʾ*

[13] Probably the earliest available source on al-Manṣūr's asking Mālik to compile the *Muwaṭṭāʾ* is ʿAbd al-Malik b. Ḥabīb (d. 238/852), *Kitāb al-taʾrīkh*, ed. J. Aguadé (Madrid: Instituto de Cooperacion con el Mundo Arabe, 1991), 160 (nr. 489); cf. Crone and Hinds, *God's Caliph*, 86 n. 184. U. F. Abd Allah, "Mālik's Concept of *ʿAmal* in the light of Mālikī Theory", unpublished Ph.D. dissertation., Univ. of Chicago, 1978, I, 100ff., notes that several works similar to Mālik's *Muwaṭṭāʾ* were written at this time; he suggests that the possibility of one of these being officially promulgated may have played a part in encouraging their composition. Other sources for the exchange between al-Manṣūr and Mālik include: Ibn Abī Ḥātim, *Kitāb al-jarḥ waʾl-taʿdīl* (Beirut: Dār al-kutub al-ʿilmiyya, 1952), 29, cited in G. H. A. Juynboll, *Muslim Tradition* (Cambridge: Cambridge University Press, 1983), 62-63; al-Ṭabarī, *al-Muntakhab min kitāb dhayl al-mudhayyal min taʾrīkh al-ṣaḥāba waʾl-tābiʿīn*, published in his *Taʾrīkh al-rusul waʾl-mulūk* (ed. M. J. De Goeje [Leiden: E. J. Brill, 1879-1901], III, 2295-2561), 2519-20, cited in Crone and Hinds, *God's Caliph*, 86 n. 185.

[14] Later al-Shāfiʿī was to expend much effort in his *Risāla* justifying such diversity, in the form of *ikhtilāf*, among the scholars. See Norman Calder, "Ikhtilāf and Ijmāʿ in Shāfiʿī's *Risāla*", *Studia Islamica*, LVIII (1983), 55-81. (I owe this reference to Professor W. B. Hallaq.)

by the caliph; or that as a paragon of the (later) Sunnī orthodox spirit, he respected and was prepared to work with the fact that there existed a diversity of approaches to matters of law. Whatever their provenance, however, these reports reveal a quite different understanding of the caliph's function than what Ibn al-Muqaffaʿ prescribes, and they may even be thought of as a comment on ideas such as Ibn al-Muqaffaʿ's: it is an *ʿālim* the caliph invites to draw up a legal code, proposing to make it the law of the land; the *ʿālim* refuses to oblige, and the caliph apparently leaves it at that. The moral of the story, if indeed it is no more than a story, is that *no one*, not even a prominent *ʿālim*, has the authority to draw up a code which might be given the sanction of law. The story is not about the separation of religion and politics, as one might be tempted to suppose, but only about the way legal understanding (*fiqh*) properly evolves in an Islamic society.

B. *al-ʿAnbarī's Letter to al-Mahdī*

Like Ibn al-Muqaffaʿ's *Risāla*, the letter of the Basran *qāḍī* ʿUbayd Allāh b. al-Ḥasan al-ʿAnbarī is primarily a treatise on administration.[15] Its basic concern is to draw the attention of the caliph, al-Mahdī, to four administrative matters which, according to the author, require the caliph's concern more than anything else does. These include: (1) the

[15] On al-ʿAnbarī, see Muḥammad b. Khalaf Wakīʿ, *Akhbār al-quḍāt*, ed. ʿAbd al-ʿAzīz Muṣṭafā al-Marāghī (Cairo: Maṭbaʿat al-istiqāma, 1947-1950), II, 88-123 (the most detailed treatment by far); Khalīfa b. Khayyāṭ, *Taʾrīkh*, ed. Akram Ḍiyāʾ al-ʿUmarī (Najaf: Maṭbaʿat al-Adab, 1967), 457, 462, 470, 472, 473; Ibn Ḥajar, *Tahdhīb al-Tahdhīb* (Haydarabad: Maṭbaʿat majlis dāʾirat al-maʿārif al-niẓāmiyya, 1325-27 A.H.), VII, 7ff. For further references to the sources on him, cf. the editor's footnote in al-Dhahabī, *Taʾrīkh al-Islām*, ed. ʿAbd al-Salām Tadmurī (Beirut: Dār al-kitāb al-ʿArabī, 1987), X, 344, n. 1. For a brief study of al-ʿAnbarī, see J. van Ess, "La liberté du juge dans le milieu basrien du VIIIe siècle (IIe siècle de l'hégire)", in G. Makdisi et al., eds., *La notion de liberté au moyen âge: Islam, Byzance, Occident* (Paris: Société d'Édition les Belles Lettres, 1985), 25-35; id., *Theologie und Gesellschaft im 2. und 3. Jahrhundert Hidschra: Eine Geschichte des religiösen Denken im frühen Islam* (Berlin and New York: Walter de Gruyter, 1991-), II, 155-64.

Wakīʿ, *Akhbār*, II, 97-107, is apparently the only available source for al-ʿAnbarī's letter. For brief references to this letter, cf. Crone and Hinds, *God's Caliph*, 93, 98, 103; I. Blay-Abramski, "From Damascus to Baghdad: the ʿAbbāsid administrative system as a product of the Umayyad heritage (41/661-320/932)", Ph.D. diss., Princeton, 1987, 163; id., "The Judiciary (*Qāḍīs*) as a Governmental-Administrative Tool in Early Islam", *Journal of the Economic and Social History of the Orient*, XXXV (1992), 51, 66ff., 70; van Ess, "La liberté", 28; id., *Theologie und Gesellschaft*, II, 167; Iḥsān ʿAbbās's introduction to his edition of the *Kitāb al-kharāj* by Abū Yūsuf (Beirut and London: Dār al-Shurūq, 1985), 46-48. It should be noted that none of these scholars call into question the authenticity of al-ʿAnbarī's letter.

frontiers of the state (*thughūr*) whose defences have to be constantly guarded; (2) attention to the laws which are in force and to the affairs of those who administer them; (3) the collection of *fay'*, the administration of the lands and the people liable for its payment, and the proper distribution of the proceeds of *fay'* among those entitled to it; and, finally (4), the levy and administration of the *ṣadaqāt* taxes.

There is, however, more to this short treatise than advice on administrative matters (which need not detain us here) or of the use of religious formulae to buttress it. A notable feature of this work is the author's consistent reference to the practice of the pious. The identity of these pious men is not quite clear. One passage suggests that they include prophets (*anbiyā', rusul*), rightly-guided caliphs (*al-khulafā' al-rāshidīn*), and leading scholars (*al-a'imma al-fuqahā' al-ṣiddīqīn*).[16] Further on in the same passage, a more picturesque characterization is offered:

> They are rightly-guided guides (*al-hudāt al-muhtadūn*) and compassionate imāms (*al-a'imma al-'ā'idūn*),...[17] men of knowledge (*'ulamā'*) [and?] deputies [of God?] (*al-khulafā'*),[18] in whom refuge is sought and who are unblemished (*al-mu'taṣam bihim wa'l-ma'ṣūmūn*). They [include] the prophets, the veracious ones (*al-ṣiddīqūn*), the martyrs (*al-shuhadā'*), and the upright people (*al-ṣāliḥūn*)....Through them has God strengthened this religion ... charted its path and established His ordinances among the people: thereby the [share of the] weak was taken [back for them] from the strong, that of the wronged from the oppressor ... and that of the pious from the vile; [through them] were the ways of the people straightened ... the land became peaceful and the people upright.[19]

---

[16] Wakī', *Akhbār*, II, 97.

[17] The signification of the term *al-a'imma* is uncertain here. It could refer to caliphs or to scholars or to both. Note, however, that on several occasions al-'Anbarī uses the term "*imām*" to refer unequivocally to the caliph: Wakī', *Akhbār*, II, 99 (l. 18), 100 (l. 15), 101 (l. 18), 103 (l. 14), 104 (l. 14), 105 (l. 5). On the variety of ways in which the term "imām" is used in early juristic literature, see Norman Calder, "The Significance of the Term *Imām* in Early Islamic Jurisprudence", *Zeitschrift für Geschichte der arabisch-islamischen Wissenschaften*, ed. F. Sezgin, I (Frankfurt, 1984), 253-64.

The sense of "*al-'ā'idūn*" too is rather uncertain. According to the *Lisān al-'Arab*, someone characterized as "*dhū safḥ wa 'ā'ida*" is one who is "kind and compassionate" ("*dhū 'afw wa ta'aṭṭuf*"). Ibn Manẓūr, *Lisān al-'Arab* (Beirut: Dār Ṣādir, 1955-56), III, 316. Note too that a "*mu'īd min al-rijāl*" is one "who knows things, one who is not inexperienced" ("*al-'ālim bi'l-umūr alladhī laysa bi-ghumr*"). Ibid., 315.

[18] The term "khulafā'" as used here need not exclusively refer to caliphs, though it is very likely that they are among those the author has in mind.

[19] Wakī', *Akhbār*, II, 98.

For all its rhetorical effect, al-ʿAnbarī's text is vague on who exactly comprises this body of the elect. There is little doubt, however, that it is not only the prophets, nor only the religious scholars who do so, though both are of course very prominent. Some of the caliphs are certainly there, though they are left anonymous.[20] The elect need not all belong to a bygone age, though the sense is that most do. In any case, a sketch of the piety and practice of the elect forms the context in which the caliph al-Mahdī is called upon to follow them in their rectitude. One of the points the author wishes rather obliquely to bring home is that in the case of the rulers among these pious forbears, piety also entailed worldly success;[21] further, that the ruler's obedience to God's commands increased the subjects' obedience to the ruler as well.[22]

Perhaps the most interesting, if somewhat problematic feature of the letter attributed to al-ʿAnbarī is, however, the delineation, in one of its passages, of the bases of authority to which administrative and legal decisions (*al-aḥkām*) should conform. First of all comes the Qur'ān; then it is the *sunna* of the Prophet which has to be consulted for such *aḥkām*; and in case the *sunna* too has nothing to offer on the matter at hand, the decision is to be made in accordance with what the leading scholars have agreed upon (*mā ajmaʿa ʿalayhi al-aʾimma al-fuqahāʾ*).[23] If none of these three sources of authority give any guidance, however, the governor (*al-ḥākim*) is to have recourse to his *ijtihād*, in consultation with the scholars (*ahl al-ʿilm*), provided the caliph (*al-imām*) has permitted him this function (sc. *ijtihād*).[24] Elsewhere in the letter, the

---

20 al-ʿAnbarī also refers to *al-khulafāʾ al-rāshidūn*, though the reference does not necessarily mean that he has the Rāshidūn caliphs of the Sunnī tradition in mind here, or all four of them, or only them. Note that the only caliphs who are actually named in this group of the elect are ʿUmar I, and ʿUmar II. See Wakīʿ, *Akhbār*, II, 103. al-Manṣūr is also mentioned in the letter in a certain context (ibid., 102), but hardly as a member of the elite group in question.

21 Ibid., 98.

22 Ibid., 98; also cf. ibid., 100, where the same point is made with specific reference to the caliph al-Mahdī himself.

23 For the use of this, and similar, expressions, which were used before the technical term "*ijmāʿ*" (=consensus) came into vogue, see Z. I. Ansari, "Islamic Juristic Terminology before al-Shāfiʿī: A semantic analysis with special reference to Kufa", *Arabica*, XIX (1972), 282ff.

24 Wakīʿ, *Akhbār*, II, 101. Cf. Abū ʿUbayd al-Qāsim b. Sallām, *Kitāb al-amwāl*, ed. M. H. al-Fiqī (Cairo: Maṭbaʿat al-ʿĀmira, 1353 A.H.), 171-71 (paras 467-74), where an ʿAbbāsid governor of Hārūn's time, ʿAbd al-Malik b. Ṣāliḥ, is reported to have written to prominent *fuqahāʾ* on how he should respond to an act of aggression/treaty violation (*ḥadath*) by the Cypriots. "The *fuqahāʾ* at that time were numerous", Abū ʿUbayd notes (p. 171), and reproduces (from the governor's *dīwān*, as he tells us) the responsa of the following eight: al-Layth b. Saʿd, Mālik b. Anas, Sufyān b. ʿUyayna, Mūsā b. Aʿyan, Ismāʿīl b. ʿAyyāsh, Yaḥyā b. Ḥamza, Abū Isḥāq al-Fazārī and Makhlad b. Ḥusayn. Abū ʿUbayd informs us that these

author briefly returns to the same question, but with a rather different emphasis:

> In such matters confronting the people about which the *a'imma* are perturbed, and which are not regulated by the Qur'ān or the *sunna* of the Prophet, no one is to have precedence over the *walī amr al-muslimīn* and the *imām jamā'atihim*. Such matters are not to be decided without him; rather it is incumbent on those who are subordinate to him to refer these matters to him and to accept his ruling on them.[25]

The second passage quoted here seems to refer to a concrete historical situation, as does much else in the treatise. It is apparently directed against the tendency of provincial governors to take the initiative in deciding the matters at hand without deferring them to the caliph. Instances of such initiative being assumed by provincial governors are well-attested for our period.[26] Taking both the aforementioned passages (which refer to the sources of authority) together, the author's point seems to be that if any initiative belongs to the caliph's subordinate officials, it is only in so far as the caliph has specifically delegated it to them. For it is ultimately the *caliph's* prerogative to decide matters on which other sources of law are silent. Even as he calls for the

fuqahā' differed in their opinions and advice, but that those who counselled leniency outnumbered those who stood for severe retribution (ibid., 171). In making up his mind on what advice to follow, the governor would probably have exercised his own *ijtihād*. It is quite remarkable that the whole episode, as reported here, does not appear to have involved the caliph at all. But then this governor was known for his independent ways, and was subsequently to fall a victim to the caliph's suspicions, possibly on this account. On 'Abd al-Malik b. Ṣāliḥ see *EI(2)*, s.v. (K. V. Zettersteen); H. Kennedy, *The Early Abbasid Caliphate* (London: Croom Helm, 1981), 74-75 and index s.v.

25 Wakī', *Akhbār*, II, 105. The letter's original text reads, in part: "... *fa-inna walī amr al-muslimīn wa imām jamā'atihim lā yuqaddam fīhā bayna yadayhi, wa lā yuqḍā' dūnahu bal 'alā' man dūnahu raf'u dhālik ilayhi wa'l taslīm li-mā qaḍā.*" The "*walī amr al-muslimīn*" and "*imām jamā'atihim*" here is to be understood as a reference to the caliph and not to the provincial governor. Compare Abū Yūsuf's "*wulāt al-amr*" whom Allāh has made "*khulafā' fī arḍihi*": *Kharāj*, 71. The reference here is evidently to the caliphs; but see ibid., 262, l. 7, and 266, l. 4, where 'Umar I is quoted as referring to his governors as "*wulāt bi'l-ḥaqq*" and "*a'immat al-hudā*". On the term "imam", cf. Calder, "Significance", 253-264. *Pace* Calder, there is little justification "to see caliphal use of the term *imām* as an attempt to steal the jurists' clothes" (ibid., 264). Early juristic texts do not restrict the term *imām* to the caliph, but nowhere is there any hint that its use for the caliph signifies a competition with the jurists, or that it was used for leading jurists (and traditionists) before being used for caliphs. In numerous instances, of course, jurists themselves used the term unequivocally for the caliph. See al-Shāfi'ī, *al-Umm* (Būlāq, 1321-25 A.H.; reprinted Cairo: al-Dār al-Miṣriyya li'l-ta'līf wa'l-tarjama, 1407 A.H.), IV, 118-22.

26 Cf. Jacob Lassner, *The Shaping of 'Abbāsid Rule* (Princeton: Princeton University Press, 1980), 3-90 passim.

conformity of administrative practice with what the sources of religious authority prescribe, al-ʿAnbarī makes the caliph himself an auxiliary of that chain of religious authority. The caliph too has a say in resolving legal problems which confront the people. His is a residual authority, which comes into play when all the other sources of religious authority are silent (and "the scholars are perturbed"), but it is no less real for being such.

Though the two passages discussed above seem, in several of their implications, to conform to the conditions of the early ʿAbbāsid period, they also raise some suspicion regarding authenticity. The reference to a hierarchy of the bases or sources of religious authority, to which the ruler's *aḥkām* should conform, may seem to presume too developed a juristic theory for a *qāḍī* to espouse a generation before al-Shāfiʿī (d. 204/820).[27] But al-Shāfiʿī did not invent the four-fold schema comprising the Qur'ān, *sunna*, consensus and *ra'y*. A somewhat similar schema (with the absence of consensus, however) occurs in the longer of the two versions of a letter the caliph ʿUmar I is supposed to have written to Abū Mūsā al-Ashʿarī. Serjeant has argued that this version of the letter in fact originated in the early second century A.H., which means that we must also "date [the] existence of the theory on Qur'ān —*sunna*—*qiyas*—*ra'y* to early in the second century A.H."[28] To Wāṣil b. ʿAṭā', the putative "founder" of the Muʿtazila, is also attributed a four-fold schema of "*kitāb nāṭiq wa khabar mujtamaʿ ʿalayh wa ḥujjat ʿaql wa ijmāʿ*; these, to him, were the criteria for the discernment of truth (*al-ḥaqq*), and he is said to have originated the schema.[29] al-ʿAnbarī's plea for conformity of the ruler's decisions to the Qur'ān, the Prophet's *sunna*, and the scholars' agreed opinion is thus hardly exceptional, for it had already surfaced in the thinking of the scholars of the age and

27 On al-Shāfiʿī's hierarchy of the sources of law, cf. Schacht, *Origins*, 134ff.; N. Calder, "Ikhtilāf and Ijmāʿ", 77-78. That it was al-Shāfiʿī who shaped once and for all the future course of Islamic jurisprudence no longer carries the conviction it did for Schacht: see Hallaq, "Was al-Shafiʿi the Master Architect of Islamic Jurisprudence?"

28 R. B. Serjeant, "The Caliph ʿUmar's Letters to Abū Mūsā al-Ashʿarī and Muʿāwiya", *Journal of Semitic Studies*, XXIX (1984), 65-79; the quotation is from p. 78.

29 Abū Hilāl al-ʿAskarī, *al-Awā'il*, ed. Muḥammad al-Miṣrī and Walīd al-Qaṣṣāb (Damascus: Wizārat al-thaqāfa wa'l-irshād al-qawmī, 1975), II, 135, cited in J. van Ess, "L'autorité de la tradition prophetique dans la theologie muʿtazilite", in G. Makdisi et al., eds., *La notion d'autorité au moyen âge: Islam, Byzance, Occident* (Paris: Presses Universitaires de France, 1982), 213-14; and ibid.: "Le contexte ne laisse pas douter que Wāṣil pense au *ḥadīth*.... L'enumeration correspond au scheme quadripartite des *uṣūl al-fiqh* classiques, la preuve rationelle tenant la place du futur *qiyās*."

milieu to which he belonged. On the other hand, al-ʿAnbarī's point about the caliph's *ijtihād* can also be related to some contemporary concerns of theʿAbbāsid caliphs (vis-à-vis their governors, for instance, in which case it would have been in line with the centralizing tendencies of the early ʿAbbāsid period).

To al-ʿAnbarī is also attributed the view that "every *mujtahid* is correct [in his judgment]" ("*kull mujtahid muṣīb*"), and that the Qurʾān, and *sunna*, allow the validity of opinions which may be mutually contradictory.[30] If this view is indeed al-ʿAnbarī's, we might ask what implications it has for the bases of religious authority discussed in the aforementioned passages of his letter to the caliph. In asserting the rectitude of every *mujtahid*'s judgment, al-ʿAnbarī is *not* severing judgments from (a basis in) the traditional sources of religious authority but only pointing out that diversity in judgment is itself attested and thus accepted in these sources. Such a view strengthens the case for *ijtihād*, which is put forth in the letter with reference to the caliph and his governor. But, *pace* van Ess, the rectitude of every *mujtahid*'s judgment —leading to differences among scholars—does not contradict the authority of the scholars' agreement,[31] which al-ʿAnbarī's letter upholds. Not only has consensus always coexisted with the doctrine of the *mujtahid*'s rectitude,[32] al-Shāfiʿī's arguments, a generation after al-ʿAnbarī, for the admissibility of *ikhtilāf* may have been intended precisely to undergird the ʿulamāʾs collective authority.[33] A recognition of their mutual differences was, for al-Shāfiʿī, the basis on which to bring them together; and, as for their mutual differences, they were to be thought of as the result of valid disagreement but not of error on anyone's part.[34]

If a ring of authenticity is to be heard in the overall tone and tenor of al-ʿAnbarī's letter—and in its echoing many of the concerns of the time

---

[30] Ibn Qutayba, *Taʾwīl mukhtalif al-ḥadīth* (Cairo: Maṭbaʿat Kurdistān al-ʿilmiyya, 1326 A.H.), 55-57. Also cf. Ibn Ḥajar, *Tahdhīb*, VII, 8. For a pioneering discussion of this dictum, see van Ess, "La liberté", 25-35; id., *Theologie und Gesellschaft*, II, 155-64. al-Shāfiʿī's justification, in his *Risāla*, of the *ikhtilāf* of scholars and the latter's rectitude even as they disagree among themselves bears fundamental similarity to the position enshrined in this dictum, though he does not quote it. See Calder, "Ikhtilāf and Ijmāʿ", 55-81, esp. 67. Calder's certitude that this dictum "obviously had not emerged while Shāfiʿī was writing, but ... clearly derives from his thinking" (ibid., 67) may, however, be a bit too dogmatic in both of its affirmations. Cf. van Ess, *Theologie und Gesellschaft*, II, 164 n. 93.

[31] Cf. van Ess, *Theologie und Gesellschaft*, II, 162.

[32] I owe this point to Prof. W. B. Hallaq.

[33] Calder, "Ikhtilāf and Ijmāʿ", 55-81, esp. 64ff., 71-72.

[34] Ibid.

to which it purports to belong—then we must also ask what this scholar's vision amounts to in so far as the caliph's function and relationship with the 'ulamā' are concerned. al-'Anbarī posits conformity with the tradition and practice of the elect as the essential basis of the caliph's conduct; and it is noteworthy that the 'ulamā' figure prominently in this body of the elect. He is to be seen here as taking a position drastically opposed to that of Ibn al-Muqaffa': it is not the caliph who can determine what the normative *sunna* is; rather, it is for the *sunna* of the pious forbears (as carried on by the 'ulamā') to define how the caliph is to conduct himself. But even as he derives his legitimacy from adherence to this normative tradition, the caliph, for al-'Anbarī, is also integral to its perseverance and continued vigour.

Finally, as a *qāḍī* working in the 'Abbāsid administration, it is not surprising to see al-'Anbarī visualize the caliph and the 'ulamā' as working in close association with each other. In concluding his letter, al-'Anbarī advises the caliph "to have with him a select group of people who are truthful, have knowledge of the *sunna*, and are men of worldly experience (*ḥunka*), intellect, and piety, to help him deal with and decide on such public matters as are brought to him.... For though God has bestowed on the Commander of the Faithful knowledge of His book and *sunna* (sc. God's *sunna*?) the affairs of the people of this *umma* keep pouring in[35] so that attending to some of them causes him to neglect others; ... [having an advisory council] will, God willing, be a real help in these circumstances."[36]

Before returning to the question of the caliph's advisory council, let us first examine some of Abū Yūsuf's ideas, as set out in his *Kitāb al-kharāj*, on the caliph's function and relationship with the 'ulamā'.

C. *Abū Yūsuf's Kitāb al-kharāj*

As already noted, the attribution to Abū Yūsuf of the *Kitāb al-kharāj* which conventionally bears his name[37] has recently been questioned by

35 Reading *yaridu 'alayhi* instead of *radda 'alayhi*.

36 Wakī', *Akhbār*, II, 107.

37 On Abū Yūsuf, see: Wakī', *Akhbār*, III, 254-64, and index, s.v.; *Ta'rīkh Baghdād*, XIV, 242-62; al-Dhahabī, *Manāqib al-imām Abī Ḥanīfa wa ṣāḥibayhi Abī Yūsuf wa Muḥammad b. al-Ḥasan*, ed. Muḥammad Zāhid al-Kawtharī and Abu'l-Wafā al-Afghānī (Haydarabad: Lajnat iḥyā' al-ma'ārif al-Nu'māniyya, 1947); id., *Ta'rīkh Islām*, XII, 496-503. For further references to the sources, see the editor's note in ibid., 496f. n. 6; also see F. Sezgin, *Geschichte des arabischen Schrifttums* (hereafter *GAS*), I (Leiden: E. J. Brill, 1967), 419-21. For a modern evaluation of Abū Yūsuf's contribution to Islamic law, see, in particular, Schacht, *Origins*, passim.; id., *An Introduction to Islamic Law* (Oxford: Clarendon Press,

Norman Calder. If Calder is right, there is not much point in studying this work in the context of early ʿAbbāsid history. It becomes necessary then to begin by briefly reviewing some of Calder's arguments.

Calder argues that the present text of the *Kitāb al-kharāj* is "the product of a single redactional effort" which must be dated to the middle of the third century A.H.[38] This view is part of a more elaborate argument which seeks to show, *inter alia*, that "[t]here are no secure examples of any works of Islamic fiqh redacted before the third or fourth decades of the third century."[39] While essentially an exercise in literary analysis, Calder's treatment of the *Kitāb al-kharāj* also offers a historical reconstruction of the circumstances in which the redaction of this work is likely to have occurred. He suggests that this treatise is to be identified with the *Kitāb al-kharāj* attributed to the Ḥanafī al-Khaṣṣāf (d. 261/874), which the ʿAbbāsid caliph al-Muhtadī (r. 255-56/869-70) had commissioned him to write.[40] The conditions of al-Muhtadī's time, it is argued, are in accord with the concerns the *Kitāb al-kharāj* shows: al-Muhtadī was very pious and sought to reform everything from morals to finances; the caliphate faced acute political and economic crises; and there is "evidence of wholesale restructuring of the financial system".[41] The *Kitāb al-kharāj* seeks to affirm "absolute caliphal authority",[42] especially the caliph's discretionary powers in taxation. Nothing thus was better suited to the needs of those chaotic times.

The merits of Calder's literary analysis, or the validity of his conclusions on that basis, will not be examined here. It should be pointed out, however, that his hypothesis about the *historical* origins of the *Kitāb al-kharāj* is rather dubious—unless, of course, one is already convinced that the work in question *could not* have originated before the mid-third century. Calder is right in arguing that the treatise seeks to promote the caliph's administrative authority, but there is no reason why the historical Abū Yūsuf could not himself have been engaged in such an effort in favour of the caliph Hārūn. Whether or not the historical Abū Yūsuf could have had a similar agenda is a question he does not raise: since, to him, this *Kitāb al-kharāj* could not have

1964), index, s.v.

38 Calder, *Studies*, 105-60, esp. 145ff.; the quotation is from p. 145.

39 Ibid., 146.

40 Ibid., 147, and n. 22 for Calder's bibliographic references to al-Khaṣṣāf and his *Kitāb al-kharāj*.

41 Calder, *Studies*, 147ff.; the quotation is from 149-50.

42 Ibid., 160 and 105-60, passim.

originated before the time to which he dates it, any effort to see how this treatise might fit the age of Hārūn al-Rashīd and Abū Yūsuf, rather than that of al-Muhtadī and al-Khaṣṣāf, would seem to be pointless. Calder correctly points out that a *Kitāb al-kharāj* is attributed to al-Khaṣṣāf; but, oddly enough, he fails to note that bio-bibliographical sources also attest to the production of earlier treatises on the same subject and often bearing the same title. "Now", Calder writes, "if Abū Yūsuf had produced prior to 182 the book that we now know as the *Kitāb al-kharāj* in the form we now have it and with the subtlety that we have recognized in it, there would have been little need for another call from the Caliph to a *faqīh* to produce another such work."[43]

The implications of the foregoing statement are worth spelling out here. If Abū Yūsuf's work were correctly attributed to him, then, by Calder's reasoning, *no* further works on *kharāj* ought to have been written; nor, by the same token, should any have been written *after* that of al-Khaṣṣāf if he is the author of what is usually attributed to Abū Yūsuf. This is clearly an extreme position. What about reports then that Abū Yūsuf's *Kitāb al-kharāj* was not the first work on the subject (any more than al-Khaṣṣāf's was the last)?[44] In fact, one of the three works on *kharāj* which are extant is attributed to Yaḥyā b, Ādam (d. 203/818), also a contemporary of the caliph Hārūn.[45] Calder would probably reply that the reports about earlier works of this genre are tendentious or their attributions inadmissible, again a rather high-handed way of dealing with the bio-bibliographical literature (though it must be conceded that Calder's position on this point is consistent with his over all thesis). There would still be no compelling, even plausible, reason to think, however, that al-Khaṣṣāf was the author of *this* particular, rather than just another, *Kitāb al-kharāj*. Qudāma b. Ja'far (d. ca. 320/932), for one, apparently quotes *both* Abū Yūsuf and al-Khaṣṣāf in his own *Kitāb al-kharāj*,[46] thus raising the distinct

43 Ibid., 147. "On the other hand", Calder continues, "if the Caliph al-Muhtadī summoned al-Khaṣṣāf to produce such a work, then he might well have produced a work which called upon the authority of Abū Yūsuf. There was an obvious felicity in ascribing to him systematic opinions on taxation." Ibid., 147.

44 Of the twenty-one works on *kharāj* that Ben Shemesh lists in a roughly chronological order, al-Khaṣṣāf's is the *seventh*. For this list, largely based on Ibn al-Nadīm's *Kitāb al-fihrist*, see A. Ben Shemesh, *Taxation in Islam*, I (Leiden: E. J. Brill, 1958), 3-6.

45 On Yaḥyā b. Ādam see Sezgin, *GAS*, I, 520; Ben Shemesh, *Taxation in Islam*, I: *Yaḥyā b. Ādam's Kitāb al-Kharāj*. Yaḥyā is reported to have visited Hārūn al-Rashīd in Ḥīra (Ben Shemesh, *Taxation in Islam*, I, 1), though there is no indication that he wrote this treatise for the caliph.

46 The name al-Khaṣṣāf does not figure in Qudāma's *Kitāb al-kharāj*, but one

possibility that he may have had access to the work of both. If both works were indeed available to him, then we would have little reason to think that both Abū Yūsuf and al-Khaṣṣāf could not each have written on *kharāj*, or that the latter necessarily attributed his own work to the former.

That the pious al-Muhtadī, much concerned with efficient government, should have commissioned al-Khaṣṣāf to write a treatise on taxation certainly merits attention, for it tells us something about this caliph's concerns. The case of Abū Yūsuf's *Kitāb al-kharāj* shows that such works may not necessarily have been limited to administrative advice,[47] but might also help further the cause of caliphal authority and legitimacy, and perhaps also assist in creating a pious image for the caliph. It is easy to see, then, why al-Muhtadī should have found it useful to have such a work addressed to him. But, by the same token, it is not difficult to imagine that an earlier caliph—Hārūn al-Rashīd—would have liked a similar work produced for himself.[48] In the absence of conclusive evidence to the contrary, therefore, the *Kitāb al-kharāj* of Abū Yūsuf must be treated as a work *by* Abū Yūsuf himself and

"Aḥmad b. Yaḥyā al-Shaybānī" does (once: 168). Ben Shemesh is probably right in emending the name to Aḥmad b. *'Umar* al-Shaybānī (A. Ben Shemesh, *Taxation in Islam*, II [Leiden: E. J. Brill, 1965], 8, 31), which is how al-Khaṣṣāf's name is recorded in Ibn al-Nadīm's *Kitāb al-fihrist*, ed. R. Tajaddud, 3rd edn. (Beirut: Dār al-Masīra, 1988), 259. Abū Yūsuf, on the other hand, is quoted several times (see Qudāma b. Ja'far, *Kitāb al-kharāj*, Köprülü Library MS. 1076, published in facsimile by F. Sezgin [Frankfurt: Institute for the History of Arabic-Islamic Science, 1986], index, s.v. Ya'qūb b. Ibrāhīm Abū Yūsuf).

47 Note that the *Kitāb al-kharāj* of Qudāma b. Ja'far, the third of the three extant works in this genre, also contains a chapter which Rosenthal considers to have the elements of a Fürstenspiegel (F. Rosenthal, *History of Muslim Historiography* [Leiden: E. J. Brill, 1968], 117). S. A. Bonebakker, however, has expressed doubts whether this chapter was originally part of Qudāma's *Kitāb al-kharāj* (see *EI(2)*, s.v. "Ḳudāma b. Dja'far" (S. A. Bonebakker). Whether Qudāma, a *kātib*, was commissioned by anyone to write his *Kitāb al-kharāj* is not known, though it is reported that he showed it to 'Alī b. 'Īsa, a famous vizier of the middle 'Abbāsid period (ibid.).

48 Abū 'Ubayd Allāh Mu'āwiya b. 'Abdallāh is said already to have written for the caliph al-Mahdī what Qudāma b. Ja'far alternately characterizes as a "*risāla*" and "*kitāb*", and which he quotes from: see Qudāma b. Ja'far, *Kitāb al-kharāj*, 178 and 200-01. Very much later, the caliph al-Muttaqī (r. 330-33/940-43) had a vizier, 'Abd al-Raḥmān b. 'Īsā, who too wrote an incomplete *Kitāb al-kharāj*, though it is not known whether the request for the work had come from the caliph. See Ibn al-Nadīm, *Kitāb al-fihrist*, 143. Many others to whom works of this genre are attributed were *kuttāb*, and thus in caliphal service; whether or not such works were commissioned by the caliphs or were written for them, they could hardly have failed to help promote the interests of the state, perhaps specifically those of the caliph. (The aforementioned 'Abd al-Raḥmān b. 'Īsā had himself been a *kātib*, as was Qudāma b. Ja'far; for other examples, see Ibn al-Nadīm, *Kitāb al-fihrist*, 145, 151.)

written *for* Hārūn, as the sources say; in what follows, it is analyzed accordingly.

As the title of his work suggests, Abū Yūsuf seeks to offer to the caliph such advice as would help regulate the system of taxation in the 'Abbāsid state. The concern, however, is not just with a well-regulated system; it is also (and perhaps primarily) with bringing this system into conformity with the opinions and principles enunciated by religious authorities such as the Prophet, his Companions (above all, 'Umar I), the Successors, and leading jurists. These two concerns are of course complementary: to organize affairs according to the given traditions and opinions is, for the author, to ensure the justice and efficiency of the system. While the bulk of the treatise addresses itself to intricate matters of financial administration, Abū Yūsuf's introduction to this work has a much wider scope and significance. The main body of the work is not without interest for our purposes, though we shall primarily focus on the introduction.

A salient characteristic of the work under discussion is Abū Yūsuf's exhortation to the caliph, in explicit terms in the introduction and implicitly throughout the treatise, to conform to and revive the *sunna* of *al-qawm al-ṣāliḥūn*.[49] The *sunna* which the caliph is being referred to is apparently similar to, though far more concretely perceived and known than, what al-'Anbarī had in mind; for both, however, it is conformity to this *sunna* which ought to define the caliph's conduct and the character of his polity. Abū Yūsuf gives generous examples to illustrate where such normative traditions come from and what they consist in. Several of such traditions—for instance, in the form of statements ascribed to Abū Bakr, 'Umar I, 'Alī, etc. on how they conceived of their functions as caliphs—also serve to conjure up the image of a "golden age" in the past,[50] an image clearly intended to serve the practical purpose of providing guidance to rulers and administrators in the present. Inasmuch as the *sunna* that the caliph is called upon to revive and conform to is a precisely known entity, it is the 'ulamā' who are its living legatees.[51] Abū Yūsuf seems to visualize the latter not only as the bearers of the sacred tradition but, *ipso facto*, also as the locus of religious authority. Admittedly, the latter point is not explicitly stated; that much of the book is concerned with what the *fuqahā'* think about

49 *Kharāj*, 71; also cf. Abū Yūsuf's reference to those he calls "*al-wulāt al-mahdiyyūn*", though without further identification, ibid., 171, 174.

50 Cf. *Kharāj*, 84ff.

51 Cf. Crone and Hinds, *God's Caliph*, 88-89, 91-92.

various administrative and legal matters, and how *they* understand the bearing of the *sunna* of *al-salaf al-ṣāliḥ*—of which, again, it is the scholars who are the repositories—may, however, be legitimately taken to argue for the scholars' religious authority.

Abū Yūsuf does not forthrightly address the question of the caliph's authority in religious matters, though some of his statements do shed some light on his views in that regard. The caliphs are "deputies on [God's] earth", and they are endowed with a "light" whereby they clarify and resolve matters which are obscure to their subjects.[52] Being divinely endowed with the "light" does not, however, have any of those connotations which a similar endowment would manifestly have in case of a Shīʿī imām.[53] For Abū Yūsuf's caliphs, the "light" essentially signifies the duty to enforce law, safeguard the rights of people, revive the *sunna* of *al-qawm al-ṣāliḥūn*, promote justice and, of course, explain obscure matters.[54] These are the kinds of obligations which the caliph owes to the people and to God, and for which he is responsible to God. Neglect of such obligations, Abū Yūsuf emphatically warns the caliph, can lead not only to the ruin of the community but also to his own perdition.

Abū Yūsuf's reference to the caliph's function of clarifying matters obscure to his subjects is of especial interest here. Such a function had already been noted by al-ʿAnbarī, if rather obliquely, and, as we shall observe, occurs frequently in official documents of the ʿAbbāsid period. The appearance of this motif in Abū Yūsuf's *Kitāb al-kharāj* is of interest not only because it suggests the caliph's participation in the community's religious life, and (implicitly) in matters having a legal import, but also because this suggestion comes, in the instance under review, from one of the leading jurists of the time. Inasmuch as it occurs both in juristic treatises such as al-ʿAnbarī's and Abū Yūsuf's *and* in ʿAbbāsid documents, there seems to have been a shared perception between caliphs and many a scholar on this function; and since it occurs in ʿAbbāsid documents from both before *and after* the *Miḥna*, as we shall see, this motif may be taken to indicate a certain continuity

---

[52] *Kharāj*, 71: "*inna'llāha ... jaʿala wulāt al-amr khulafā' fī arḍihi wa jaʿala lahum nūran yuḍī'u li'l-raʿīya mā uẓlima ʿalayhim min al-umūr fīmā baynahum wa yubayyin mā ishtabaha min al-ḥuqūq ʿalayhim...*" The "*wulāt al-amr*" seems to refer here to the caliphs.

[53] On the notion of divine light in Imāmī Shīʿism, see U. Rubin, "Prophets and Progenitors in early Shīʿa Tradition", *Jerusalem Studies in Arabic and Islam*, I (1979), 41-65. Also see M. A. Amir-Moezzi, *The Divine Guide in Early Shīʿism* (Albany: State University of New York Press, 1994).

[54] *Kharāj*, 71.

in the caliph's religious functions, a continuity all too often obscured in thinking of the *Miḥna* as a watershed in 'Abbāsid, and Islamic, history.

In concluding our discussion of the *Kitāb al-kharāj*, Abū Yūsuf's concern to provide for a close relationship of the 'ulamā' with the state should finally be noted. His insistence that the administrative cadres be staffed by trusted, pious, and God-fearing men is interpretable as an advice to recruit more people from the religious circles.[55] The 'ulamā's participation in the administration is, for Abū Yūsuf, the way to reform administrative abuses and a means too through which the "revival" of the *sunna* of old ought to be accomplished.[56] What seems equally important, though he does not say so, is that the involvement of the piety-minded would also give them a direct stake in the 'Abbāsid state, and that would not only help the 'Abbāsids with their religious prestige and legitimacy, but perhaps also moderate somewhat that autonomous position of the 'ulamā' in society about which the early 'Abbāsids had some misgivings.

The Caliphs and Questions of Law

So far as the 'Abbāsid caliphs prior to al-Ma'mūn are concerned, the lines on which al-'Anbarī and Abū Yūsuf were thinking seem to have suited their interests well. Caliphal religious policies generally tended towards courting the 'ulamā's favour and playing up the caliph's role of defending the interests of Islam and the Muslims; the advice of these authors affirms both concerns, not to mention the advocacy, by Abū Yūsuf particularly, of 'Abbāsid legitimism. Thus far, it is as if the caliph concerned is being addressed with an exhortation he would have liked, and expected, to hear—an exhortation to which the caliph's conspicuous submission would enhance his religious image. That both al-'Anbarī and Abū Yūsuf appear, despite their differences, to affirm the primacy of the 'ulamā's religious authority may seem rather more

---

55 *Kharāj*, 204 (section 129), 247 (sec. 188, 189), 252 (sec. 198), 253 (sec. 200), 288 (sec. 220), etc. Perhaps even more specifically, the advice could have referred to the Ḥanafīs. For it is scarcely unwarranted to suppose that Abū Yūsuf should have wanted to promote the influence of his own *madhhab*. How successful he actually was in doing so is another question, and one it is impossible to answer with any certitude: cf. Nurit Tsafrir, "The Spread of the Ḥanafī School in the Western Regions of the 'Abbāsid Caliphate up to the End of the Third Century A.H.", Ph.D. dissertation, Princeton University, 1993, 69ff.

56 Compare Abū Isḥāq al-Fazārī, *Kitāb al-siyar*, ed. Fārūq Ḥammāda (Beirut: Mu'assasat al-risāla, 1987), for a thoroughgoing concern to see the conduct of the holy war and matters of military administration on the frontiers evaluated, and regulated, by the opinions of the scholars. The opinions quoted in this case are primarily those of the Syrian jurist al-Awzā'ī (d. 157/774).

problematic from the ʿAbbāsid viewpoint. But this would seem problematic only if it is already taken for granted, as Crone and Hinds do, that the early ʿAbbāsids laid claims to religious authority for themselves and were actively, if against increasing odds, competing with the scholars in that regard.[57] Before al-Maʾmūn took the initiative, the caliphs do not seem, however, to have challenged the ʿulamāʾs authority. It is, after all, Mālik whom the caliph is supposed to have asked to codify law rather than taking the initiative himself; and Abū Yūsuf was, of course, a member of the official establishment, was writing under royal patronage, and was not likely to antagonize the caliph in either his affirmation of the scholars' authority or his delineation of the caliph's functions.

Far from being antagonized, in fact, the caliph subscribed to a view of his function that had a striking affinity to what Abū Yūsuf prescribed for him. The following passage from Hārūn al-Rashīd's letter to Harthama b. Aʿyan, appointed governor of Khurasan, offers an illustration:

> The caliph commands Harthamah to keep in mind the fear of God, to obey Him and to show concern for and watch over God's interests. He should make the Book of God a guiding example in all he undertakes and, accordingly, make licit what is legally allowable according to it and prohibit what is not allowable. When he is faced with anything doubtful and uncertain in it (*mutashābihihi*), he should pause and consult those with a systematic training and acquaintanceship with God's religion and those knowledgeable about the Book of God (*uliʾl-fiqh fī dīn Allāh wa uliʾl-ʿilm bi-kitāb Allāh*), or alternatively, he should refer it to his Imām, so that God, may He be magnified and exalted, may make manifest to him His judgment in the matter and so that he may execute it according to his right guidance.[58]

At issue in this passage is not simply a matter of scriptural exegesis, but of determining how local problems are to be resolved in accordance with the Book of God. For inasmuch as the document is addressed to a governor, the context suggests that it is not just (or not primarily) the difficulties of understanding the *kitāb Allāh* itself, but the problems which might arise in its application—that is, legal problems—that require resolution. The caliph affirms the authority of the *kitāb Allāh*, but also his own authority to elucidate that which is doubtful in (or with

[57] Crone and Hinds, *God's Caliph*, 80-96.

[58] Ṭabarī, III, 717; translation as in *The History of al-Ṭabarī*, XXX, tr. C. E. Bosworth (Albany: State University of New York Press, 1989), 274 (with minor modification); also cf. Crone and Hinds, *God's Caliph*, 89.

reference to) it. Tellingly, however, his authority is described in conjunction (not in competition) with that of the local religious scholars. Abū Yūsuf could have had little to disagree with on the advice to consult such scholars; as noted, he was in fact much concerned to see a closer relationship between them and the 'Abbāsid administration. Hārūn's advice to Harthama about the option of referring the problems in question to the imām, i.e. to the caliph himself, likewise figures in Abū Yūsuf's advice to Hārūn. The recognition that the 'ulamā' and the caliph are *both* fit to rule on obscure matters (*mā uẓlima 'alayhim*, *mā ishtabaha*, in Abū Yūsuf's formulation)[59] is thus independently attested from both a scholar and a caliph. The caliph's authority to clarify obscure matters may perhaps be taken as comparable with the authority of the 'ulamā' to do so, which suggests at once a recognition that the latter are the locus of religious authority *and* an effort to make the caliph a part of such authority. Nor is the recognition of the caliph's religious competence peculiar to Abū Yūsuf among the 'ulamā'. Mālik, for instance, recognised the caliph's *ijtihād*[60] as did al-Shāfi'ī[61] and Aḥmad b. Ḥanbal (d. 241/855);[62] later al-Māwardī (d. 450/1058) was to speak of "the knowledge which conduces to *ijtihād* in problems that occur (*nawāzil*) and in legal decisions (*aḥkām*)" as one of the seven preconditions for *imāma*.[63] That Harthama, the governor-designate, should have been advised to refer problematic issues to local scholars *or to the caliph* does not suggest two competing sources of authority here. Not only might the caliph and the 'ulamā' try to resolve obscure matters together, but the caliph's ability to do so is based on the *same* sources—the Book of God, the *Sunna* of the Prophet, and, of course, *ijtihād*—from which the 'ulamā' themselves draw their expertise and authority.

The following report, which relates to a Basran *qāḍī* of Hārūn, may throw further light on the caliph's aforementioned advice to his

---

59 *Kharāj*, 71.

60 Schacht, *Origins*, 116.

61 al-Shāfi'ī, *al-Umm*, IV, 138, 167.

62 See the "Qiṭ'a min muqaddimat al-shaykh al-imām Abī Muḥammad b. Tamīm al-Ḥanbalī fī 'aqīdat al-imām al-mubajjal Aḥmad b. Ḥanbal...", appended to Ibn Abī Ya'lā, *Ṭabaqāt al-Ḥanābila*, ed. Muḥammad Ḥāmid al-Fiqī (Cairo: Maktabat al-sunna al-Muḥammadiyya, 1952), II, 280.

63 al-Māwardī, *al-Aḥkām al-Sulṭāniyya*, ed. M. Enger (Bonn: Adolphum Marcum, 1853), 5. On al-Māwardī and the "classical" view on the caliph's position and functions, see A. K. S. Lambton, *State and Government in Medieval Islam* (Oxford: Oxford University Press, 1981), esp. chs. 5 and 6; also cf. N. Calder, "Friday Prayer and the Juristic Theory of Government: Sarakhsī, Shīrāzī, Māwardī", *Bulletin of the School of Oriental and African Studies*, XLIX (1986), 35-47.

governor, Harthama. A woman brought a case to the *qāḍī*, ʿAbd al-Rahmān b. Muḥammad al-Makhzūmī, but seems to have grown impatient with the *qāḍī*'s slow handling of it. "So [the *qāḍī*] said [to her]: 'Your case is difficult; you will have to wait ... if I am to understand it properly. But if you want me to refer the case to the *amīr*, who can gather the Basran *fuqahāʾ* for you, I will do so; or if you wish I can write to the Commander of the Faithful so that he might ask the *fuqahāʾ* who are with him.'[64] That the caliph had *fuqahāʾ* with him is no surprise. More instructive is the information that the *qāḍī* could, and no doubt did, write for decision or advice on difficult matters to the caliph (or the governor). Letters of appointment to *qāḍīs* stipulated, in fact, that they write to *the caliph* when faced with difficult problems. A standard example of such a letter, preserved in Qudāma b. Jaʿfar's *Kitāb al-kharāj* reads, in part, as follows:

> [The commander of the Faithful] has ordered him [sc. the *qāḍī*] that if something is difficult to decide, he should resort to consultation and discussion with people of [sound] opinion and insight in judicial matters (*qaḍāʾ*) so that the matter can be resolved.[65] If [the matter at hand] remains obscure to the *qāḍī*, let him write to the Commander of the Faithful [and] explain the matter fully and truthfully ... so that [the latter] can give an answer according to which ... [the *qāḍī*] may [then] act.[66]

Resolving legal problems was thus not exclusively the ʿulamāʾs business but was a calling that involved the caliph too. Occasions on which early ʿAbbāsid caliphs are reported to to have instructed their *qāḍīs* on matters of legal import are not lacking in our sources. Abū Yūsuf's *Ikhtilāf Abī Ḥanīfa wa Ibn Abī Laylā* records an instance when the first ʿAbbāsid caliph, Abū'l-ʿAbbās al-Saffāḥ (r. 132-36/750-54), wrote to his Kūfan *qāḍī*, Ibn Abī Laylā, on a matter relating to pre-emption (*shufʿa*); the *qāḍī*, who had hitherto agreed with Abū Ḥanīfa's view on the matter, now acted according to the caliphal directive, which also accorded with the position of the scholars of the Ḥijāz.[67] al-

---

64 Wakīʿ, *Akhbār*, II, 142.

65 On the *qāḍī*'s "*consilium*", as Emile Tyan characterizes it, see Tyan, *Histoire de l'organisation judiciaire en pays d'Islam*, 2nd edn. (Leiden: E. J. Brill, 1960), 214ff. Tyan does not, however, discuss the *fuqaha*ʾ's assisting the caliph in his decisions.

66 Qudāma b. Jaʿfar, *Kitāb al-kharāj*, 23.

67 Abū Yūsuf, *Ikhtilāf Abī Ḥanīfa wa Ibn Abī Laylā*, ed. Abu'l-Wafāʾ al-Afghānī (Haydarabad, 1357 A.H.), 37-38 (= al-Shāfiʿī, *al-Umm*, VII, 99-100). Ibn Abī Laylā is also said to have written to al-Manṣūr on a theological matter, viz., Abū Ḥanīfa's espousal of the doctrine of *khalq al-Qurʾān*: see Wakīʿ, *Akhbār*, III, 141-42.

Manṣūr is reported to have written to ʿAbdallāh b. Lahīʿa, his *qāḍī* in Egypt, on a matter of inheritance.[68] The same caliph instructed Sharīk b. ʿAbdallāh al-Nakhaʿī, who was supposedly reluctant to be appointed the *qāḍī* of Kūfa, to "implement what you are able to, and write to me regarding what you are unable to [decide]".[69] In appointing the Kūfan scholar ʿAlī b. Mushir as his *qāḍī* of Mawṣil, al-Mahdī is reported to have questioned him about false testimony (*shahādat al-zūr*). "There are various views regarding it, O Commander of the Faithful", the *qāḍī* said. "[There is] the opinion (*qawl*) of Shurayḥ [according to which the person guilty of false testimony] is brought to his tribal community and they are told that he has lied in his testimony, so beware of him; and [there is] the opinion of ʿUmar b. al-Khaṭṭāb [according to which] he is to be flogged forty times, his head shaved, his face blackened, he is to be shown around [in that condition], and then imprisoned for a long time. al-Mahdī said: 'Follow ʿUmar's opinion, for God has made the truth reside in ʿUmar's words."[70] The same caliph, al-Mahdī, wrote in 159/775-76 to his governor of Baṣra invoking a *ḥadīth* embodying the well-known legal dictum that "the child belongs to the marriage bed...", and instructing him to annul a decision the first Umayyad caliph had taken in contravening that principle.[71] It is worth noting too that in his discussion of the *dīwān* instituted by ʿUmar I, al-Shāfiʿī makes it a point also to record some changes that were introduced as late as al-Mahdī's time in the shares which had been determined by ʿUmar.[72]

Many of the scholars would undoubtedly have had reservations about the ruling elite's legal (and other) decisions. At least some of those decisions were later evaluated by jurists and agreement or disagreement with them was recorded. A Mālikī work on *jihād* notes, for instance, the impropriety of accepting *jizya* from anyone who is not subject to the Muslim dominion (*lā tuqbal al-jizya illā mimman yajrī ʿalayhi ḥukmunā wa sulṭānunā*), and therefore expresses disagreement with al-Mahdī's decision to accept *jizya* from the Byzantines.[73] The

---

68 al-Kindī, *Kitāb al-wulāt wa kitāb al-quḍāt*, ed. R. Guest (Leiden: E. J. Brill, 1912), 370: "'*an ibn Lahīʿa qāla: kataba ilayya Abū Jaʿfar amīr al-mu'minīn annahu lā yajūzu li'l-ḥāmil ṣadaqa ʿalā wārith* [sic]". Also cited in Crone and Hinds, *God's Caliph*, 91 n. 211.

69 Wakīʿ, *Akhbār*, III, 150: "*idhhab fa-anfidh mā aḥsanta wa taktub ilayya fīmā lā tuḥsin*".

70 Wakīʿ, *Akhbār*, III, 219-20; cf. ibid., 316.

71 al-Ṭabarī, III, 480. For a study of the said *ḥadīth*, see U. Rubin, "'al-Walad li'l-firāsh': On the Islamic campaign against 'zinā'", *Studia Islamica*, LXXVIII (1993), 5-26.

72 al-Shāfiʿī, *Umm*, IV, 82.

73 Mathias von Bredow, *al-Jihād ḥasab al-madhhab al-Mālikī maʿa taḥqīq*

same source reports that al-Ma'mūn, when confronted with a similar situation, consulted the *fuqahā'*, who advised him against accepting *jizya* from the enemy, whereupon "he deemed their opinion correct and came back to it [sic]".[74] It is noteworthy, however, that even in the (retrospective) Mālikī disagreement with al-Mahdī's decision, there is no indication that the latter was (or was seen as) a challenge to the authority of the scholars, or that their disagreement represented an effort to divest the caliph of a say in matters of religion and the law. The Mālikī source merely says that "our 'ulamā' disliked [the decision]",[75] a formulation which leaves open the possibility that other 'ulamā' might have supported it.

As the foregoing instances indicate, whether the caliph himself decided, or participated in the *fuqahā'*s deliberations, or had the latter alone give their verdict, or chose from their conflicting advice, he was a part of the process whereby such problems were resolved and answered.[76] Why else should the governor and the *qāḍī* be instructed to have recourse to the caliph in difficult problems? Not that every caliph necessarily exercised this function; but given his inclination and ability,

---

kitāb al-jihād min kitāb al-nawādir wa'l-ziyādāt li-Abī Muḥammad 'Abdallāh ibn Abī Zayd al-Qayrawānī al-Nafzī (Beirut: Franz Steiner Verlag, 1994), 430. For another instance, see Wakī', *Akhbār*, II, 96-97, where al-Mahdī is reported to have written to his Baṣran *qāḍī* al-'Anbarī "to see what canals have existed since the days of 'Umar and 'Uthmān and impose *ṣadaqa* on them, and to impose *kharāj* on those which have come about since [their time]." The *qāḍī* proved to be non-compliant, however, gathering the local legal experts (*ahl al-'ilm bi'l-qaḍā'*) to have them witness that he had imposed the *ṣadaqa* (rather than *kharāj*) on *all* the canals which exist in the Arabian peninsula, thus contravening the caliph's directives.

74 Von Bredow, *al-Jihād ḥasab al-madhhab al-Mālikī*, 430.

75 Ibid., 430.

76 See Wakī', *Akhbār*, II, 92-95, for an instance where al-Mahdī forces his Baṣran *qāḍī*, 'Ubayd Allāh al-'Anbarī, to publicly annul a decision of his. For other instances, see al-Kindī, *Quḍāt*, 413 (cited in E. Tyan, *Histoire de l'organisation judiciare en pays d'Islam*, 1st. edn. [Leiden: E. J. Brill, 1938-43], I, 180), on the caliph al-Amīn's instructing his Egyptian *qāḍī* to annul a decision of the latter's predecessor; al-Kindī, *Quḍāt*, 474-75 (cf. Tyan, *L'organisation judiciare*, I, 180) for al-Mutawakkil's bringing together Kufan *fuqahā'* to examine an Egyptian *qāḍī*'s decision. That decision was overturned and the *qāḍī*, who was *'alā madhhab al-Madaniyyīn*, resigned. Note that it is, appropriately enough, *the caliph* who then instructs the new *qāḍī* to annul the decision of his predecessor, for all that the caliph himself is explicitly stated to have been guided by the council of the *fuqahā'*. Compare Wakī', *Akhbār*, II, 96, for a report which has al-Mahdī order his governor of Baṣra to gather the town's *fuqahā'* in order to examine a decision by the Basran *qāḍī*, and to implement that decision if those *fuqahā'* uphold it. Finally, for an example of a caliph (al-Mu'tamid) choosing between the scholars' conflicting advice, see D. Sourdel, *Le vizirat abbaside de 749 à 936* (Damascus: Institut Francais de Damas, 1959-60), I, 342-43; id., "L'Autorité califienne dans le monde sunnite", in *La notion d'autorité au moyen âge*, 110.

he might; and it is not only documents from the ʿAbbāsid chancery but also writings by *fuqahāʾ* that say so.

The caliph's participation in resolving legal questions gives him a religious function akin to that of the scholars, not one over and above, still less against, theirs. What emerges from a careful study of the pre-*Miḥna* ʿAbbāsid period is not a struggle over religious authority, with the caliphs and the scholars as antagonists, but rather the effort, on the part of the ʿAbbāsid caliphs, to lay claim to the sort of competence the ʿulamāʾ were known to possess. This effort was not meant as a challenge to the ʿulamāʾ. It signified rather a recognition of their religious authority, an expression of the caliphal intent to act as patrons of those scholars, and, what is more, the assertion of a public commitment to those fundamental sources of authority on which the ʿulamāʾs expertise, and a slowly evolving Sunnism, were based.

The Miḥna and its Aftermath

The *Miḥna* instituted by al-Maʾmūn in 218/833 to test the belief of *qāḍīs*, *fuqahāʾ* and *muḥaddithūn* on the "createdness" of the Qurʾān was the most dramatic form in which the scholars' religious authority and the emerging pattern of their relationship with the caliphs was challenged.[77] But the *Miḥna* was not an isolated event. It was preceded by other, implicit, challenges to the nascent Sunnī religious elite, such as the caliph's proclamations that the first Umayyad caliph, Muʿāwiya, was not to be favourably mentioned,[78] that ʿAlī was to be ranked above all other Companions of the Prophet,[79] and, of course, that the Qurʾān was the "created" word of God.[80] It was this last mentioned doctrine that the caliph made, six years after he had first proclaimed it in 212/827, the basis of the *Miḥna*. Rather than act in religious matters in

[77] Modern studies on the *Miḥna* include: W. M. Patton, *Aḥmad ibn Ḥanbal and the Miḥna* (Leiden, 1897); W. Madelung, "The Origins of the Controversy concerning the Creation of the Koran", in *Orientalia hispanica sive studia F. M. Pareja octogenario dicata*, ed. J. M. Barral, I (Leiden: E. J. Brill, 1974), 504-25; J. van Ess, "Ibn Kullāb et la *Miḥna*", *Arabica*, XXXVII (1990), 173-233; id., *Theologie und Gesellschaft*, III, 446-80; J. A. Nawas, "A Reexamination of three current explanations for al-Maʾmūn's introduction of the *Miḥna*", *International Journal of Middle East Studies*, XXVI (1994), 615-29; *EI(2)*, s.v. "Miḥna" (M. Hinds), and the sources cited there. Also see Michael Cooperson, "The Heirs of the Prophets in Classical Arabic Biography" (unpublished Ph.D. dissertation, Harvard University, 1994), 329-506, for an analysis of the treatment of Ibn Ḥanbal and the *Miḥna* in medieval biographical dictionaries.

[78] al-Ṭabarī, III, 1098.

[79] Ibid., III, 1099.

[80] Ibid., III, 1099.

conjunction with the emergent (or "proto"-) Sunnī ʿulamāʾ, or conform to *their* view of what constituted "orthodox" conduct, al-Maʾmūn tried, through the *Miḥna*, to bring their own "orthodoxy" into question. The implication of imposing a criterion whereby to measure their "orthodoxy" not only was that the authority of the caliph to institute such a procedure was being asserted, but also that the caliph would come across as more "orthodox" than anyone else, and more worthy of being the guardian and defender of that "orthodoxy".[81] In his communications to the governor of Baghdad, the caliph made it plain that a refusal to accept the doctrine being officially sponsored would strip the ʿulamāʾ in question of recognition *as* ʿulamāʾ by the state[82]—the implication being that it was from the state that such a recognition was to be had.[83] Conversely, only those who subscribed to it could serve as *qāḍīs*, and they would also have to function as agents of the state in imposing and upholding this doctrine.[84] But the Inquisition was not confined only to *qāḍīs*. The probity (*ʿadāla*) of all those who failed to testify to the Qurʾān's createdness was to be nullified and their legal testimony (*shahāda*) invalidated, and they were to be disallowed from narrating *ḥadīth* or giving *fatwās*.[85]

In addition to demanding that the scholars conform to a criterion of right belief which *the caliph* had set for them, al-Maʾmūn also launched into savage and highly personal attacks on the reputation of many of them.[86] In his long catalogue of invectives, the criticism which is perhaps most suggestive of the caliph's concerns seems to be that the *fuqahāʾ* and traditionists being examined aspired, in deluding the ignorant populace with their erroneous beliefs, to positions of leadership in society.[87] This is an allegation which tells us something not only about

---

[81] In his communications to the governor of Baghdad, al-Maʾmūn presents himself as *upholding* an "orthodoxy" rather than *instituting* it. He implicitly claims, in fact, that the doctrine he is enforcing is *not* an innovation (cf., for instance, al-Ṭabarī, III, 1130)—which is what his critics said it was. Contrast Ibn Ḥanbal's refrain during his interrogation in al-Muʿtaṣim's court: "Give me something from the Qurʾān or sunna of the Prophet [as proof of the Qurʾān's createdness]". See Ṣāliḥ b. Aḥmad, *Sīrat al-imām Aḥmad ibn Ḥanbal*, ed. Fuʾād ʿAbd al-Munʿim Aḥmad (Alexandria: Muʾassasat shabāb al-jāmiʿa, 1981), 56, 59, 63.

[82] al-Ṭabarī, III, 1120.

[83] Ibid., III, 1116.

[84] Ibid., III, 1116.

[85] Ibid., III, 1115, 1120; al-Kindī, *Quḍāt*, 445-47.

[86] al-Ṭabarī, III, 1127ff; Van Ess, "Ibn Kullāb", 179.

[87] al-Ṭabarī, III, 1114. Later, al-Muʿtaṣim too is reported to have accused Ibn Ḥanbal of "coveting leadership" (*qad balaghanī annaka tuḥibb al-riyāsa*): Ḥanbal b. Isḥāq, *Dhikr miḥnat al-imām Aḥmad ibn Ḥanbal*, ed. Muḥammad Naghash (Cairo, 1977), 56.

the caliph's suspicions of the scholars, but also, perhaps, about the latter's growing social influence. Conversely, given the stigma which often attaches in the Islamic tradition to promoting oneself for positions of leadership, this charge indicts the scholars in insinuating that if they really were scholars they would not be seeking to promote their influence in society.

The *Miḥna* may be seen, in short, as a challenge calculated to undermine the authority as well as the social standing of the ʿulamā'. Whether al-Ma'mūn's conflict with the ʿulamā' was provoked by his assertion of religious authority, to which he saw them as a threat, or his claims to religious authority were themselves called forth by the need to make his challenge effective, need not be decided here. For either way, his claim to define right belief signified an attack on the authority and, in general, the position and influence of the ʿulamā'.[88]

Who were the scholars at whom the *Miḥna* was directed? A number of *fuqahā'*, judges, and *muḥaddithūn*, both from Baghdad and the provinces, are mentioned in our sources. The latter include such prominent figures as Muḥammad b. Saʿd, Yaḥyā b. Maʿīn, Abū Khaythama Zuhayr b. Ḥarb, Aḥmad b. Ismāʿīl al-Dawraqī, Abū Muslim the *mustamlī* of the Wāsiṭī traditionist Yazīd b. Hārūn,[89] ʿAlī b. al-Jaʿd al-Jawharī,[90] ʿAlī b. ʿAbdallāh b. Jaʿfar al-Madīnī,[91] Abū Mushir ʿAbd al-Aʿlā b. Mushir al-Ghassānī,[92] Nuʿaym b. Ḥammād,[93] and, of course, Aḥmad b. Ḥanbal.[94] With some notable exceptions, of whom Ibn Ḥanbal is the most prominent, most scholars who were questioned in the course of the *Miḥna* assented to the official position, and not all seem to have done so under duress. Even Ibn Ḥanbal himself is alleged by some hostile reports to have given in,[95] though in view both of the subsequent favour he enjoyed with al-Mutawakkil (r. 232-47/847-61) and his harsh attitude towards those traditionists who had easily

88 Cf. Nawas, "Reexamination", 615-29.

89 These five, as well as Ismāʿīl b. Dāwūd and Ismāʿīl b. Abī Masʿūd are the seven scholars who were the first to be summoned to Raqqa for questioning by the caliph about *khalq al-Qur'ān*. All of them testified to the doctrine, both in Raqqa and later, publicly, in Baghdād. al-Ṭabarī, III, 1116-17; also cf. Ḥanbal b. Isḥāq, *Dhikr miḥna*, 34-36. On Ibn Saʿd, see Sezgin, *GAS*, I, 300-01; on Yaḥyā b. Maʿīn, ibid., I, 106-07; on Abū Khaythama, ibid., I, p. 107; on al-Dawraqī, ibid., I, 112.

90 al-Ṭabarī, III, 1121; on him, cf. Sezgin, *GAS*, 105.

91 al-Khaṭīb al-Baghdādī, *Ta'rīkh Baghdād* (Cairo: Maktabat al-khānjī, 1931), XI, 466-67 (nr. 6349); on him, cf. Sezgin, *GAS*, I, 108.

92 al-Ṭabarī, III, 1130. On him, cf. Sezgin, *GAS*, I, 100-01.

93 al-Kindī, *Quḍāt*, 447; *EI(2)*, s.v. "Nuʿaym b. Ḥammād" (C. Pellat); Sezgin, *GAS*, I, 104-05.

94 Sezgin, *GAS*, I, 502-09.

95 See *EI(2)*, s.v. "*Miḥna*"; Cooperson, "Heirs of the Prophets", 340ff.

consented to al-Ma'mūn's doctrine, that seems rather unlikely.[96] But for our purposes at least, who consented and under what sort of pressures is less important than whose consent *mattered* to the ruling elite carrying on this persecution.

The lists of names our sources preserve—of which the foregoing is a small sample from among the *muḥaddithūn*—are untidy. Among them, there are prominent scholars and obscure ones, reliable (for Sunnī *rijāl*-critics at least) and unreliable ones. Those interrogated and persecuted also included many jurists,[97] which means that the Inquisition cannot be said to have been directed only against the *aṣḥāb al-ḥadīth*. There were *fuqahā'* on the side of the persecuters too, and doubtless traditionists as well.[98] The identity of the schools of law was still in the process of articulation at the time of the *Miḥna*,[99] but insofar as individual scholars are recognizable as Ḥanafīs, there were adherents of this school on both sides.[100] To a certain extent, then, the *Miḥna* can also be seen as a conflict *between* the scholars themselves.[101] Yet, the prominence of the *aṣḥāb al-ḥadīth* among those interrogated, the identification of the doctrine in question with the Mu'tazila, and the virtual absence of any prominent Shī'a in the ranks of those who were questioned[102]

---

[96] Among the scholars who were interrogated by the governor of Baghdād, only two men, Ibn Ḥanbal and Muḥammad b. Nūḥ, are said to have remained defiant: al-Ṭabarī, III, 1131. Many of those who assented to the official dogma could hardly have done so out of conviction, however, as the caliph himself was apparently aware (cf. ibid., 1132). For Ibn Ḥanbal's refusal to narrate *ḥadīth* from those *muḥaddithūn* who had given in to government pressures during the Inquisition, see Ṣāliḥ b. Aḥmad, *Sīra*, 80; Ibn Ḥajar, *Tahdhīb*, I, 273-74; ibid., XI, 287.

[97] For general references to the "*fuqahā'*" interrogated during the *Miḥna*, see al-Kindī, *Quḍāt*, 447; al-Ṭabarī, III, 1121.

[98] Cf. Ḥanbal b. Isḥāq, *Dhikr miḥna*, 43, where Isḥāq b. Ḥanbal, Ibn Ḥanbal's uncle, is said to have asked the governor of Baghdad, Isḥāq b. Ibrāhīm, to "gather the *fuqahā'* and 'ulamā'" to engage in disputation with the imprisoned Ibn Ḥanbal, and to release the latter should he win the argument. "But I did not mention the *ahl al-ḥadīth wa'l-āthār* to him", Isḥaq b. Ḥanbal is said to have reminisced. The implication of the latter statement is not clear, though it can perhaps be taken to mean that Ibn Ḥanbal would not have wanted to debate with some of his erstwhile colleagues (the *muḥaddithūn*) who had been won over by the government. In any case, *fuqahā'* and judges are mentioned as attending the questioning of Ibn Ḥanbal in al-Mu'taṣim's court. Ibid., 49.

[99] As Tsafrir has argued: "Ḥanafī School", 1ff. and passim.

[100] Tsafrir, "Ḥanafī School", 107ff.; *EI(2)*, s.v. "al-Miḥna"; W. M. Watt, *The Formative Period of Islamic Thought* (Edinburgh: University of Edinburgh Press, 1973), 284-85.

[101] H. F. I. Kasassebeh, "The Office of Qāḍī in the Early 'Abbāsid Caliphate, 132-247/750-861", unpublished Ph.D. diss., University of London, 1990, 131-32.

[102] Note, however, that Ibn Ḥanbal is reported to have cited the Imāmī Shī'ī imām Ja'far al-Ṣādiq as one of those who did not adhere to the doctrine of *khalq al-Qur'ān*: Ṣāliḥ b. Aḥmad, *Sīra*, 91. To Ja'far is attributed the position that the

suggests that the Inquisition was directed not at scholars in general but against scholars associated with a certain trend. I do not wish to draw sharper lines than a messy body of evidence permits, but it does seem, at least from the names in the foregoing list, that the *Miḥna* is best characterized as an assault on the proto-Sunnī religious scholars. It was these scholars whose religious authority—most notably, perhaps, in the form of a growing specialization in *ḥadīth*, with all the prestige this vocation conferred—and influence among the people were disquieting to al-Ma'mūn, and it was they in particular he tried to rein in through the *Miḥna*.

The nature and implications of the religious authority that al-Ma'mūn appears to have claimed for himself merits a brief excursus here. It is tempting but erroneous, I think, to view this caliph as "assuming for himself the prerogatives of [the Shī'ī] imām, displaying the religious authority which he had won thereby in the institution of the *Miḥna*."[103] The claims of the imām, at least as depicted in the early Imāmī Shī'ite tradition, are far more extensive than what al-Ma'mūn appears to have coveted for himself. This caliph saw it as the caliphs' function

> to guide back to Him [*scil*. God] the one who has turned aside from Him...; trace out for ... [his] subjects the way of salvation for them; draw their attention to the limits of their faith and the way to their heavenly success and protection from sin; and reveal to them those of their affairs which are hidden from them and those which are dubious and obscure by means of what will remove doubt from them and bring back illumination and clear knowledge to them all.[104]

The sort of knowledge al-Ma'mūn claims for himself here would enable him to guide his subjects to the right path and ultimately to salvation; such knowledge is evidently not given to his subjects, which is why they need someone like him. But this knowledge is quite different, it seems, from the esoteric knowledge of everything past, present and future, to which the Shī'ī imām lays claim, and which is

---

Qur'ān is *laysa bi-khāliq wa lā makhlūq*: ibid.; also see Madelung, "The Origins of the Controversy", 508.

103 Crone and Hinds, *God's Caliph*, 94. Also cf. D. Sourdel, "La politique religieuse du calife 'abbaside al-Ma'mun", *Revue des Etudes Islamiques*, XXX (1962), 27-48; A. Arazi and A. Elad, "L'épître à l'armée: al-Ma'mūn et la seconde da'wa", *Studia Islamica*, LXVI (1987), 44ff.

104 al-Ṭabari, III, 1117. The Arabic text reads, in part: "*wa yakshifū lahum 'an mughaṭṭayāt umūrihim wa mushtabahātihā 'alayhim bi-mā yadfa'ūn al-rayb 'anhum wa ya'ūd bi'l-ḍiyā' wa'l-bayyina 'alā kāffatihim*". (Note that al-Ma'mūn speaks of the caliphs in the plural here, thus rhetorically claiming that his vision is—or ought to be—shared by other caliphs as well.

among the fundamental bases of his claim to be the imām.[105] The notion of clarifying obscure matters for his subjects recalls statements by Abū Yūsuf and Hārūn. As we have seen, al-Ma'mūn goes further and claims a religious authority which would not only be uniquely his, but which would also enable him to define the criteria of right belief rather than merely deciding and enforcing matters according to such criteria. Yet it does not follow that he thereby becomes, or seeks to become, a Shīʿī imām, say, in the tradition of the early Imāmiyya. The sort of knowledge al-Ma'mūn claims for himself is ultimately more akin to that of the emerging Sunnī ʿulamā's than it is to the Shīʿī imām's. True, the latter too is an *ʿālim*—indeed, the *ʿālim* par excellence—but, unlike al-Ma'mūn, the sort of *ʿilm* he claims is in large part, at least in the early stages of the development of Imāmī doctrine, supernatural and esoteric. The analogy of al-Ma'mūn's claims with those attributed to the Shīʿī imām is thus not just superficial but also misleading.

After the death of al-Ma'mūn (d. 218/833), the *Miḥna* continued in operation under his two immediate successors. Rather curiously, though, his claims to religious authority were neglected, and in this sense there already was a reversion to the pre-Ma'mūnid tradition. The *Miḥna* was now prosecuted more as a matter of commitment to the *sunna* of their predecessor, and, as our sources insist, due to the influence of Muʿtazilī scholars, of whom the chief *qāḍī* Ibn Abī Du'ād (d. 240/854) was the most influential, than for any apparent interest the caliphs may have had in asserting their own religious authority.[106] Or so it seems. It is important to bear in mind that most of our sources represent the viewpoint not of the prosecutors of the *Miḥna* but of the persecuted. Ibn Ḥanbal may have come out of the Inquisition as a hero,

---

[105] Amir-Moezzi, *Divine Guide*, 69ff. Contrast Hossein Modarressi, *Crisis and Consolidation in the Formative Period of Shīʿite Islam* (Princeton: The Darwin Press, 1993), 3-105 passim, for the view that the "moderate" or "mainstream" Imāmiyya of the second-third/eighth-ninth centuries considered the imām essentially as the most learned of scholars. Yet he recognizes that the imām's "knowledge was qualitatively different from that of other learned men for it was the knowledge of the House of the Prophet, which derived ultimately from the Prophet himself. It was, therefore, unquestionable truth and indisputable authority, representing in effect a part of the revelation that the Prophet had received from God." (Modarressi, ibid., 9). In general, Modarressi probably draws too sharp a line between his "moderates" and "extremists"; and though his work demonstrates the differences in early Shīʿī conceptions of the imām's authority, the "moderate" views need not have been quite so uniform as he suggests. Could one not believe in the imām's esoteric knowledge and yet distance oneself from other "extremist" positions?

[106] For a sympathetic biography of Ibn Abī Du'ād, see van Ess, *Theologie und Gesellschaft*, III, 481-502.

but the Sunnī sources also have a definite interest in representing him as such. By the same token, it is possible that presenting the caliphs al-Muʿtaṣim and al-Wāthiq as only half-heartedly continuing the policy of their predecessor may have been a way of demonstrating the moral bankruptcy of the whole affair and, perhaps also, of mitigating their culpability for it.[107] Yet, even as tendentious representation, early accounts of the *Miḥna* reveal much about the 'ulamā''s religious authority, especially in relation to the caliphs. I shall base some brief remarks in this regard on two of the earliest treatments of the *Miḥna*, one of which comes to us from Ṣāliḥ b. Aḥmad, a son of Ibn Ḥanbal, and the other from his nephew, Ḥanbal b. Isḥāq.

That these sources purport to be almost contemporary with Ibn Ḥanbal does not, of course, vouch for their truth-claims, but it does mean that they can give us a fair idea of how the position of the caliphs vis-à-vis the 'ulamā' was visualized in the milieu in which these texts originated. In this regard, it is striking that the influence which Ibn Abī Du'ād is shown to wield over the caliphs here makes the same general point as does al-Muʿtaṣim's ironic admiration and solicitude for Ibn Ḥanbal: this caliph comes across as utterly convinced of the scholars' authority, and the only question is whose authority, among the scholars, he would defer to. It is the Muʿtazilī chief *qāḍī*, of course, who eventually has his way, but the celebrated flogging of Ibn Ḥanbal does not take place before the caliph has exhausted his patience and energy trying to persuade the latter to give in. The image of al-Muʿtaṣim these sources conjure is that of a caliph who seeks collaboration, not confrontation, with the scholars: as this caliph is supposed to have said, Ibn Ḥanbal is the kind of scholar he would like by his side "to stave off the heretics (*ahl al-milal*) from me";[108] and he vows to break Ibn Ḥanbal's fetters with his own hands if only the latter should relent.[109]

If the purpose of the *Miḥna* was to curb the scholars' religious authority, then, on the above view at least, it had failed long before al-Mutawakkil officially terminated it. The accounts of Ibn Ḥanbal's son and nephew may represent al-Mutawakkil's ostentatious deference to the 'ulamā''s authority rather more than they do the attitudes of al-

---

[107] For the treatment of the *Miḥna* in biographical literature, see Cooperson, "Heirs of the Prophets", 340-400. My analysis, though indebted to Cooperson's, differs from his in being concerned not with how later biographers may have dealt with the uncomfortable suggestion (which Cooperson is inclined to accept) that Ibn Ḥanbal may have capitulated during the *Miḥna*, but rather with the representation of the 'ulamā''s authority in some of the earliest accounts of the Inquisition.

[108] Ṣāliḥ b. Aḥmad, *Sīra*, 59; cf. Ḥanbal b. Isḥāq, *Dhikr miḥna*, 52.

[109] Ṣāliḥ b. Aḥmad, *Sīra*, 59, 60; Ḥanbal b. Isḥāq, *Dhikr miḥna*, 52.

Muʿtaṣim and al-Wāthiq. Yet they do indicate how the authority of scholars—even of vicious scholars—was seen by those who were intimate members of Ibn Ḥanbal's circle. In general, this view is in remarkable accord with the pattern we have observed as emerging in the caliph's relations with the ʿulamāʾ before the *Miḥna*: nowhere in these accounts of Ibn Ḥanbal's Inquisition is the propriety of the ʿulamāʾs acting in concert with the caliphs questioned. What is deplorable here is only that the caliph was influenced by the wrong scholars,[110] not that scholars associated themselves with him; indeed, as noted, one is made to believe that al-Muʿtaṣim already wanted to utilize the services of Ibn Ḥanbal, just as al-Mutawakkil tried to after the Inquisition. Nor, in these accounts, is there any hint that the caliph's participation in religious life ought to cease. If anything, these accounts seem concerned to exonerate a caliph like al-Muʿtaṣim for the role he almost inadvertently found himself playing;[111] but there is no denial that, under the right circumstances and for the right cause, the caliph's role is desirable.

The *Miḥna* was a severe shock for the emergent Sunnī ʿulamāʾ, and it is not unlikely that the gravity of the Inquisition's challenge to their autonomy contributed towards what Norman Calder, in another context, characterizes as the "developing professionalization of the juristic classes".[112] Yet, despite its significance as an unprecedented challenge to their authority and social influence, the *Miḥna* was hardly a watershed in the religious policies of the early ʿAbbāsid caliphs. The failure of the Inquisition did not alter but only confirmed the trends and tendencies which were emerging before it was instituted. Contrary to what is sometimes suggested,[113] its failure did not result in a usurpation by the ʿulamāʾ of the caliph's role as the guardian of the community's religious life. The ʿulamāʾ, of course, shared this function with the

---

110 Or rather, by people who were not scholars at all. Ibn Ḥanbal is quoted as saying, for instance, that Ibn Abī Duʾād "was the most ignorant of people in *ʿilm* and *kalām* ....; he had no knowledge of anything" (*mā kāna lahu maʿrifa bi-shayʾ*): Ḥanbal b. Isḥāq, *Dhikr miḥna*, 51.

111 Cf. Ḥanbal b. Isḥāq, *Dhikr miḥna*, 51.

112 Calder, *Studies*, 185.

113 For example, by Lapidus, "Separation of State and Religion"; cf. Crone and Hinds, *God's Caliph*, 93-97. Crone and Hinds concede, however, that "the desanctification of the institution [of the caliphate] was never complete.... There is no point in Islamic history at which the caliphate can be said to have been entirely devoid of religious meaning." Ibid., 97. This "religious meaning" was, however, essentially symbolic, so that "the caliph had to satisfy himself with political power." Ibid., 97.

caliph, but they never denied it to him, nor do the caliphs ever seem to have relinquished it. We have noted, with Calder, al-Muhtadī's commitment to reform—not just of the finances but also of public morality. al-Mas'ūdī speaks explicitly of this caliph's "ordering the good and forbidding evil", and gives many examples of that activity on his part.[114] He wanted, as he is represented as saying to those who eventually murdered him, "to have [the people] follow the *sīra* of the Prophet, of his household, and of the *khulafā' al-rāshidūn*".[115] This did not appeal much to his detractors, and there is the suggestion that he may have carried his religious zeal to what many thought were inordinate lengths.[116] Yet the role of *al-amr bi'l-ma'rūf*, and the caliph's general guardianship of religious life, continued. One telling instance of the caliph's engagement with religious trends and attitudes in the (post-*Miḥna*) society over which he presided is worth considering here.

In 284/897, the caliph al-Mu'taḍid intended to have a document cursing Mu'āwiya, the first Umayyad caliph, read to the populace, but it is said that his advisers eventually dissuaded him from putting this intention into effect. al-Ma'mūn had had a similar intention, and al-Ṭabarī notes that the document al-Mu'taḍid wanted to have read out may, in fact, have been based on the one which had been prepared at al-Ma'mūn's behest.[117] The following passages are among some of its more remarkable:

> Praised be God Who made the Commander of the Faithful and his rightly guided and directed forbears the heirs of the Seal of the prophets and Lord of the messengers! He has put them in charge of the religion of Islam, charged them with setting straight God's believing servants, and entrusted them with the preservation of the pledges of wisdom and the heritage of prophethood.... The Commander of the Faithful has learned that a number of ordinary people have been beset by doubt (*shubha*) in their religious beliefs and have been affected by corruption in their faith.... [He] takes a very serious view [of this, and] ... considers a failure to express his disapproval as harmful to himself regarding the religion of Islam, as detrimental to the Muslims whose affairs God has entrusted to him, and as a neglect of the duty imposed upon

114 al-Mas'ūdī, *Murūj al-dhahab*, ed. M. Muḥyī al-dīn 'Abd al-Ḥamīd (Cairo: Maktabat al-tijāriyya al-kubrā, 1958), IV, 183, and 183-94, passim.

115 Ibid., IV, 186. al-Muhtadī's piety served his later image well. According to a report transmitted by the historian Muḥammad b. Yaḥyā al-Ṣūlī, many a *faqīh* and *muḥaddith* agreed that al-Muhtadī ought to be counted among a select group of caliphs comprising the four *khulafā' al-rāshidūn* and 'Umar b. 'Abd al-'Azīz. See al-Lālakā'ī, *Sharḥ uṣūl i'tiqād ahl al-sunna wa'l-jamā'a*, ed. Aḥmad b. Sa'd al-Ghāmidī (Riyaḍ: Dār ṭiba li'l-nashr wa'l-tawzī', 1994), VIII, 1473.

116 Cf. al-Mas'ūdī, *Murūj*, IV, 183, 186.

117 al-Ṭabarī, III, 2165-66.

> him by God to set straight opponents, inform the ignorant, establish proofs against doubters, and control the obstinate.... Good people! Get away from what makes God angry at you and turn to what makes Him pleased with you!.... Follow the straight path, the manifest road, and the people of the house of mercy, through whom God guided you in the beginning and saved you from injustice and hostility in the end.... O people! It is through us that God has guided you aright. We are the ones appointed to preserve God's concerns among you. We are the heirs of the Messenger of God (*warathat rasūl Allāh*) and the ones who are in charge of the religion of God. Thus stay where we put you, and execute what we command you to do! For as long as you obey the vicegerents of God and leaders toward right guidance (*a'immat al-hudā*) along the path of faith and the fear of God, you will be all right...[118]

Whether this document is in fact based on an earlier version ordered by al-Ma'mūn, and if so to what extent, it is impossible to say. There is no characteristically "Ma'mūnid" assertion of religious authority here which would necessitate that it be placed in his time, and the documents that have come down to us from his reign, e.g. his letters on the createdness of the Qur'ān,[119] are markedly different: to take only the most striking example, they show none of the reliance on the authority of *ḥadīth* that al-Muʿtaḍid's document so amply exhibits. Note should also be taken of the fact that al-Ṭabarī reproduces this document in his account of the reign of al-Muʿtaḍid, not of al-Ma'mūn. But even if it is granted that the document originated in al-Ma'mūn's reign, the fact that al-Muʿtaḍid could seriously think of having it proclaimed suggests that he subscribed not only to what is said in it about Muʿāwiya but also to what it asserts about the caliph's functions. But then, as I have argued, there is as little reason to suppose that after the *Miḥna* the caliphs came to lose their religious functions to the ʿulamā' as there is to view the caliphs and the ʿulamā' as engaged in a bitterly unrelenting struggle for religious authority before the *Miḥna*. As for the *Miḥna* itself, it was precisely this role of being the defender of the faith that al-Mutawakkil was asserting in terminating it, and Ibn Ḥanbal is on record as having acknowledged it for the caliph.[120]

"According to Aḥmad b. Ḥanbal," Lapidus writes, "it was the duty of the ʿulamā' to revive and preserve the law, and the duty of all Muslims to 'Command the good and forbid the evil', that is, to uphold

118 For the full text of the document, see al-Ṭabarī, III, 2166-77; translation as in *The History of al-Ṭabarī*, vol. XXXVIII, tr. F. Rosenthal (Albany: State University of New York Press, 1985), 48-63 (with some modifications).

119 al-Ṭabarī, III, 1112ff., 1117ff., 1125ff., 1131-32.

120 al-Khallāl, *Masā'il*, fols. 5a, 176b-179a.

the law, whether or not the Caliphate would properly do so.... The implication of Aḥmad's view is to circumscribe the authority of the Caliphs in religious matters and, though Aḥmad did not have a language to express it, to recognize a practical distinction between secular and religious authority."[121] Ibn Ḥanbal certainly did not have to be convinced of the 'ulamā's religious authority, nor was he unique in that position. But an assertion of such authority does not necessarily signify that the caliph is being stripped of all religious functions, and that he is no longer relevant to the community's religious life. The following paraphrase of what purports to be Ibn Ḥanbal's views in this regard comes from a later Ḥanbalī, Abū Muḥammad Rizq Allāh b. 'Abd al-Wahhāb al-Tamīmī (d. 488/1095):

> [Ibn Ḥanbal] used to command that the true faith should be brought forth whenever corrupt doctrines made their appearance. The purpose, he said, is to establish the proofs of [the religion of] God; but doing so should not lead to hardship.... If it is possible to take [the matter] to the authorities (*al-sulṭān*), so that the latter can put an end to that [particular threat to the true faith], then one should not become involved with it [lit.: not stretch the hand towards it]. The authorities are better suited to dealing with it (*bihi awlā*). However, if one fears that the opportunity to act would be lost before the matter is brought to the authorities, then he must hasten [to act] provided that [in so acting] he does not endanger his life, or stir turmoil (*fitna*), or expose religion to disgrace and thereby weaken it. It is incumbent (*yajibu*) on all to assist the authorities when the latter seek assistance in putting an end to what is reprehensible. It is incumbent upon the 'ulamā' to contest whatever innovations (*bida'*) and false beliefs arise, by establishing proofs which would eliminate doubts and end the darkness of error. On the Imām and his deputy [for their part], it is incumbent to enforce [what the 'ulamā' have established as proofs] and to oblige the deviant (*ahl al-zaygh*) to abandon their ways after the proofs have been made clear to them. If they refuse, the Imām, following the dictates of his *ijtihād*, should punish them to the extent he deems necessary to ensure their return [to right belief].... Likewise, in case of rebels (*al-bughāt*), he should call upon them to return to the truth, should dispel their doubts, and [try to] bring them back [to the community's fold?] in the most lenient way possible. He should then deal with them according as his *ijtihād* guides him, resorting to force if he despairs of them, and if they refuse his call and war breaks out.[122]

---

[121] Lapidus, "Separation of State and Religion", 383.

[122] "Qiṭ'a min muqaddimat al-shaykh al-imām Abī Muḥammad...", in Ibn Abī Ya'lā, *Ṭabaqāt*, II, 280. On Abū Muḥammad, the source of this *'aqīda*, see Ibn Rajab al-Baghdādī, *Kitāb al-dhayl 'alā ṭabaqāt al-Ḥanābila*, ed. H. Laoust and S. Dahan (Damascus: al-Ma'had al-Faransī li'l-dirāsāt al-'Arabiyya, 1951), 96-106. There is no compelling reason to suppose that the views attributed to Ibn Ḥanbal

The significance of the foregoing statement is two-fold. It recognizes, firstly, that the caliph has an essential role to play in religious life, and it is only when such role is lacking that others may step in and even then not unconditionally. Secondly, the statement emphasizes the functional interdependence and intimate collaboration of the caliphs and the ʿulamāʾ. They do have different functions—which is what makes it a collaboration—but there is no sense here that caliphs are any less integral to the preservation of religious life, or any less involved in it, than are the ʿulamāʾ. Crone and Hinds have concluded their study of "religious authority in the first centuries of Islam" by arguing that *because* "all aspects of life are covered by a single sacred law ... collaboration between [God's] rival representatives [*scil.* His caliphs and the ʿulamāʾ] was ruled out until one or the other side had won.... As it was the ʿulamāʾ won."[123] But except for the interregnum of the *Miḥna*, there is little to suggest that there was even a contest between the caliphs and the ʿulamāʾ, much less that the failure of the Inquisition permanently altered either the character of caliphal authority or the caliph's relations with the ʿulamāʾ. A difference of function between the caliphs and the ʿulamāʾ in and by itself does not necessarily signify a *separation* of state and religion; nor even are the functions all too rigidly separated. The caliph too exercises his *ijtihād* after all, and with the ʿulamāʾ establishing the proofs of religion, as the foregoing statement has it, he too dispels the rebels' doubts to bring them back to the community's fold. Some of the other juristic texts we have analyzed earlier make clear that it is not only the doubts of the rebels but also legal and administrative matters obscure to his governor and *qāḍī* that are to be referred to him. The caliph does not define the law; but, even after the *Miḥna*, he remains part of the religious circles in which it is interpreted.

---

here were not espoused by him, but even if that turns out to be the case, they would still reflect the thinking of Ḥanbalī circles and be significant for that reason.

[123] *God's Caliph*, 109-110.

GENERAL INDEX

In this index, the Arabic definite article (*al-*) at the beginning of an entry, the transliteration symbols for the Arabic letters *hamza* and *'ayn*, and the distinction between different letters transliterated by the same Latin character (e.g. *d* and *ḍ*) are ignored for purposes of alphabetization. Inconsistencies in spelling and transliteration in the text reflect the varying conventions of the publications in which the articles originally appeared.